Attachment and the Perils of Parenting

Helen Barrett

The National Family and Parenting Institute is the UK's leading centre of expertise in families and parenting. We carry out research, listen to what parents want and deliver messages from research to people working with families. We advocate policy changes to help parents address challenges successfully as they raise children. Visit our website at www.nfpi.org for more information.

Helen Barrett has researched on and worked with children, their families and their carers in a wide range of family and community settings. Formerly a senior lecturer in developmental psychology, she joined the National Family and Parenting Institute as Research Fellow in July 2002. She is particularly interested in close attachments and the influence of non-traditional care settings and separation experiences on children's and parents' emotional development and relationships.

She is currently Chair of the International Attachment Network, an educational charity promoting wider understanding of Attachment Theory. More information can be found at www.attachmentnetwork.org

Series Editor: Clem Henricson, Director of Research & Policy at the National family and Parenting Institute. She was formerly a social policy consultant with a variety of family policy organisations and has published widely in the field of family research.

© NFPI 2006

Published by
National Family and Parenting Institute
430 Highgate Studios
53–79 Highgate Road
London NW5 1TL

Tel: 020 7424 3460
Fax: 020 7485 3590
Email: info@nfpi.org
www.nfpi.org

Design and print: www.intertype.com
Reprinted: May 2011, by the Lavenham Press
ISBN 1 903615 42 9
Registered charity no. 1077444

Contents

Part One **Theory and assessment**

Introduction — 9

1 The emergence of Bowlby's Attachment Theory — 17
  Bowlby's social background — 17
    School — 18
    Higher education — 19
    Early work experience and interest in children's
    emotional development — 20
    Medical and psychoanalytic training — 22
    Clinical experience and completion of psychoanalytic training — 22
    Work on delinquency — 23
    Early research papers: the theme of maternal deprivation — 24
    The war years: fears for the welfare of evacuated children — 25
  Work on separation — 26
    Campaign work with James and Joyce Robertson — 26
    The Protest-Despair-Detachment story — 27
    World Health Organization report and growing
    concern about maternal deprivation — 29
  Work with Mary Ainsworth — 30
    Ainsworth's previous research — 30
    England and Uganda — 31
    Baltimore — 33
  Seeking a broader understanding of early
  infant-mother relationships — 34
  A very white and upper middle-class man's theory? — 34

2 Attachment Theory: Basic tenets and major claims — 36
  Bowlby's theory of attachment — 36
  The influence of ethology on the development
  of Bowlby's theory of attachment — 37
    Niko Tinbergen — 39
    Konrad Lorenz — 41
    Studies of effects of separation/social isolation in other animals — 43
  The emergence of attachment behaviour in early childhood — 47
    Phase I: Pre-attachment — 47
    Phase II: Attachment-in-the-making — 48
    Phase III: Clear-cut attachment — 49
    Phase IV: Goal-corrected partnership — 50
  Internal working models — 51
  Major tenets of Attachment Theory — 53

3	**Assessing attachment security**	**55**
	Background	55
	But what is attachment security?	55
	Developing tools to assess attachment relationships	56
	How to prove that a psychological test measures what it aims to measure	58
	Creating an operational definition of the construct to be measured	58
	Testing and making sure that the tool is reliable	59
	Testing whether the tool produces valid results	60
	Concurrent validity	60
	Discriminant validity	60
	Predictive validity	61
	Does it matter that no operational definition of attachment behaviour across the lifespan exists?	61
	The Strange Situation Procedure	62
	The Strange Situation classificatory system	66
	The interpretation and description of patterns of attachment	68
	Problems with the Strange Situation classificatory system	71
	Identification of the 'disorganised' pattern	71
	Refinement of the classificatory system	72
	Categories or continua?	73
	The need for assessment in addition to the Strange Situation procedure	74
	The Adult Attachment Interview (AAI)	75
	Interview format	75
	Analysis of the interview material	76
	AAI classifications	77
	Interpretation of adult attachment classifications	80
	Self-reports of adult attachment	81
	Summing up	85

Part two **Evidence**

4	**Exploring the validity of attachment assessments**	**91**
	Overview	91
	The argument: Attachment security across the lifespan	92
	The evidence	96
	Infants, pre-schoolers and attachment	100
	Representations of family	100
	Problem-solving and compliance with mother	101
	Social interactions	102
	Exploration, play and aggression	103

    Self-control and sense of self   104
    Behaviour problems   104
  Middle childhood   106
    Family interactions   106
    Social interactions   107
    Exploration, play and aggression   108
    Cognitive skills   108
    Self-control and sense of self   109
    Coping   111
    Behaviour problems   111
  Adolescence   113
    Relationships with parents   113
    Relationships with peers   114
    Emotional self-regulation   114
    Psychosocial adjustment and risk-taking   117
  Adulthood   119
    Young adulthood/late adolescence: Studies of students   119
    Other adults   123
    Couple relationships: Satisfaction and stability   121
    Older people   123
    Summary   125
    Mental health   125
    What attachment security is not related to: the question of discriminant validity   126
    Attachment, intelligence and perceptual ability   126
    Attachment and biological sex   126
    Attachment and temperament   127
  Concluding comments   134

5 Links between quality of parental care and attachment security   **137**
  The importance of quality of care   137
  Maternal sensitivity: Ainsworth's measure   138
  Antecedents to attachment   141
    Intersubjective synchrony   142
    Interactional synchrony   144
    Affective attunement   146
    Helpfulness   147
    Psychobiological regulation   147
    Schore and the development of the 'social brain'   151
  Antecedents to poor social relationships: Autism   160
    Similarities between patterns of autism and attachment   160
    Baron-Cohen and Theory of Mind   162
    Reflective functioning and Maternal Mind-mindedness   164
  Growing up in a stressful family environment   167
  Links between attachment insecurity and environmental stress   173
    Resource-rich and resource-poor environments   173
    Attachment disorganisation   175

	The effect of parents' own histories on patterns of attachment in children	179
	Other caregivers besides mother	188
	Fathers as attachment figures	189
	Other relatives and day care	190
	Cultural considerations	193
6	**Early experience, infant determinism, social brain development: What do we really know?**	**197**
	The importance of the earliest years	197
	Hard and soft models of development: Determinists and Constructivists	198
	Four recurrent controversial themes and their more recent reincarnations	199
	Early separation experiences and later development	199
	Institutional care	201
	Orphan studies	203
	Romanian orphans: early reports and the UK study	204
	Later reports from Canada	209
	Stress responses in Romanian adoptees	211
	"Virtual black holes where their brains should be"	212
	Further studies of Romanian orphans in Bucharest	214
	Day care	216
	Is there a critical period for the development of attachments in humans?	222
	The distinction between critical and sensitive periods	225
	Experience-expectant versus experience-dependent development	226
	Postnatal depression	228
	Skin-to-skin contact and baby-carrying	238
	Skin-to-skin contact	239
	Skin-to-skin contact for full-term babies	241
	Kangaroo care for preterm infants	243
	The role of oxytocin	245
	The effect of the caregiving environment on personality development	249
	Prenatal stress and depression	250
	Patterns of attachment across the lifespan	255
	Six longitudinal studies (from infancy to adulthood)	256
	Concluding comments	264

Part three Applications/Implications

7	**Attachment difficulties and therapy**	**267**
	Links between patterns of attachment and mental health problems	267
	Attachment disorders – definitions and debates	271
	Are parents to blame for attachment difficulties?	285
	Therapy and right-hemisphere processes	278
	Effectiveness of therapy	279

Meta-analyses of therapy interventions	279
Therapeutic approaches	284
Therapy with irritable babies	284
Bowlbian principles and therapy	287
The Circle of Security project	289
UK-based interventions influenced by or based on Attachment Theory	293
PIPPIN (Parents in Partnership – Parent Infant Network)	293
NEWPIN	294
The SUNDERLAND INFANT PROGRAMME (SIP)	295
OXFORD PARENT INFANT PROGRAMME (OXPIP)	295
Attachment-oriented family therapy	297
Attachment Therapy	302
Controversial practices	303
Re-birthing	303
Holding therapy	304
Therapeutic foster care	306
Children in care	306
Concluding remarks	311

8 Summing up: How secure are the foundations of Attachment Theory? — 313

The conceptual status of Attachment Theory	313
Characteristics of human behaviour systems	313
Human behaviour systems have evolved for the benefit of the species	315
Human behaviour systems operate in certain lawful ways	318
Human behaviour systems can respond to the external environment	320
The development and organisation of behaviour systems changes across the lifespan	320
There is a dynamic pattern of relationships between different behaviour systems	321
Summary: general characteristics of behaviour systems	326
What is a good theory?	327
Testability	327
Testability:How Attachment Theory weighs up	328
Fertility	329
Fertility:How Attachment Theory weighs up	329
Generalisability	329
Generalisability:How Attachment Theory weighs up	332
Explanatory power	333
Explanatory power:How Attachment Theory weighs up	334
– coherency and comprehensibility	334
– usefulness	334
– parsimony	335
– explanation of past and prediction of future behaviour	335
– account of interacting variables	335

Summing up: how secure are the foundations of
Attachment Theory? 336

9 Attachment, attachment myths and the perils of parenting: Summary and conclusions 340
Distinguishing features of Bowlby's approach 340
The Bowlby/Ainsworth theory of attachment 341
The 'working model' of an Attachment theory 341
The first part of the book 342
The second part of the book 343
The third part of the book 343
Attachment theory post-Bowlby 344
The development of attachment measures
beyond infancy 344
The identification of 'disorganised' attachment 346
Disagreements over classification of infant attachment 348
Results of long-term follow-up studies 348
Larger-scale studies incorporating attachment measures 349
Meta-analyses of attachment studies 350
'New' data from Romanian (and other) orphans 351
Attachment mythology and 'the new brain science' 351
Video-based observational research 353
Video-based attachment-oriented therapy approaches 354
Attachment-oriented family therapy 354
The emergence of 'Attachment Therapy' and
'Attachment Parenting' 355
Messages from Attachment Theory for parents
and work with parents 357

Bibliography 360

References 365

Appendices
Appendix 3.1 Measures related to Attachment:
An indicative selection 396
Appendix 3.2 The original Strange Situation classifications 412
The Adult Attachment Interview
Information about training
Appendix 5.1 Ainsworth's (1969) Maternal sensitivity scales 421
Appendix 5.2 The CARE-Index (Crittenden) 429
The Empathic Understanding (Insightfulness) Procedure
(Oppenheim)
Emotional Availability Scales (Biringen)
Appendix 7.1 Diagnostic criteria for Reactive Attachment Disorder 432
Appendix 7.2 Attachment Disorder Checklist 434

Author index 436

Subject index 445

Introduction

Bowlby: About 60 per cent of mothers do a very good job, so the majority of women have a good model to follow, and there's an awful lot to be said for that.

Interviewer: So are you saying that 40 per cent of mothers don't do a good job?

Bowlby: I am.

Interviewer: (pause) What does that mean?

Bowlby: Well. It means a lot of mental ill health and disturbance and delinquency and ... what have you.

Out of the Doll's House, BBC TV, October 9th 1988

Being a parent is a tremendous responsibility and a hugely complex task. It can call upon an almost infinite range of skills that parents may need to develop, test, add in, try out, or discover within their existing repertoires. These skills involve more than giving birth and keeping a child alive, which in themselves are no small achievement. They also involve more than maintaining relationships between parents, between parents and children, between family members, or between the family and the outside world. They involve more than creating a safe physical environment, and more than teaching children how to behave. They include all of the above, and more besides.

Many parents, reflecting on the way that they were parented, hope that they can relate to their children in ways that their parents failed to relate to them. Some, striving to emulate parents or other role models, feel that their way of running a family does not always quite match up with their good intentions. Altogether, commonplace though the condition of being a parent is, it is pretty rare for parents, either looking ahead or back, to feel supremely confident about their ability to fulfil their role. Because of this, the information that four out of ten do not do a good job seems unlikely to reassure even the six who do, and certainly will not comfort the four who do not. The assertion that mental health, psychological disturbance and delinquency result directly from lack of good role models is even less likely to be received with neutrality. Did Bowlby mean to imply that all parents of wayward teenagers or with psychiatrically disturbed children have only themselves to blame? Is this what his theory of child development really states? And, anyway, where did the idea that 40 per cent of parents are so damaging come from? These are some of the questions that this book aims to address.

During the course of his professional career, Bowlby's works were published widely and his theory about the association between the quality of intimate relationships and emotional wellbeing, in childhood and throughout the lifespan, developed into what has become known as Attachment Theory (AT). In this book we aim to present an overview of this theory, to discover what it really claims in respect of the relationship between quality of parenting and outcomes for children, and to assess the evidence base for these claims. Finally, we consider which, if any, of its key messages might provide the most useful insights into the nature of parent-child relationships and what lessons might have been learned from the enormous body of research now associated with Attachment Theory.

Before going further, we should point out that although, throughout this book, we will refer to Attachment Theory (AT) as though John Bowlby was its main proponent, we are aware that it is not a theory 'set in stone' by a single author. First, as we shall show, it might be better viewed as a set of 'working models' or as a conceptual framework than as a theory and, second, it is actually more correctly named 'the Bowlby-Ainsworth-and-others Ethological Theory of Attachment'. For Attachment Theory is actually the intellectual property of Mary Ainsworth as well as of John Bowlby and, as it has evolved, substantial contributions to its development have come from other workers too. Even so, largely for pragmatic reasons, we will continue to refer to it as though Bowlby was its main proponent. This is not because we are dismissive of the contribution of Mary Ainsworth and other workers. On the contrary, we recognise that it is very largely due to Mary Ainsworth that AT has achieved its standing as a testable theory. But it seems true to say that, whereas Mary Ainsworth contributed much to the understanding and interpretation of observations of infant-mother interactions, many of the key theoretical propositions were initially put forward with Bowlby as sole author. Although we have no good reason for believing that Mary Ainsworth would have disputed any particular aspects of Bowlby's theory, neither do we have sufficient written proof to assume that she concurred with all the views published under his name. For this reason, we have chosen to refer to Attachment Theory as though it were Bowlby's theory but recognise nevertheless the very considerable and vital role of Mary Ainsworth both in facilitating the development of Bowlby's ideas and in enabling many aspects of Attachment Theory to be established so that others can continue to test and develop it.

We will also take this opportunity to comment on the curious fact that, although a large number of theories have been put forward to account for the very special quality of relationships between infants and their carers[1] and although various theories of attachment are currently discernible within almost all academic disciplines (including the multiple branches of psychology, sociology, biological sciences, health sciences, neuroscience, political sciences, economics, anthropology, religious studies, the arts, philosophy as well as more esoteric studies), the term Attachment Theory seems to have come to be used as though Bowlby's theory were either the only or the most popular one in existence. This fact not only attests to its extensive influence but also affords a glimpse of the degree of confusion surrounding it. This confusion in turn combines rather too readily with the habitual tendency of research findings either to bury themselves deeply within academic mists and mystification, or to emerge in more popular arenas as pale and distant relatives of their original selves. As though these sources of obfuscation were not enough, long after his death, not only has Bowlby's theory continued to evolve and mutate as more evidence for or against various aspects has been amassed but different accounts of the theory have also arisen. Some of these interpretations are far more deterministic and prescriptive than others, for example, they reflect the views of those who hold that particular kinds of experience during pregnancy and the early years are critical determinants of all later development. In this book, we refer to such views as 'hard forms' of AT and, in our assessment of the evidence for and against AT, we will attempt to take account of both hard and 'softer' versions of the theory.

---

1   Rajecki et al's 1978 article remains an informative and concise discussion of a number of these views while Fonagy 1999 provides an excellent comparative review of psychoanalytic theories.

From the time that Bowlby first began to propound his theories about the importance of childhood experiences for later development (e.g. Bowlby 1944, 1951, 1953/65, 1958a, 1969/1982, 1973a, 1980a) even until his death in 1990, by which time many of his works had been reprinted several times and translated into numerous languages, Bowlby's views received a mixed and often distinctly hostile reception. In spite of this, much that is central to Bowlby's thesis, namely, an appreciation of young children's vulnerability to stressful experiences and a conviction of the extreme importance of close emotional ties, has in fact percolated into popular lore and thinking. Nowadays, for example, it is relatively common to come across people who are convinced that babies and very young children are better off if they are well, or even not so well, looked after by their own biological mothers rather than cared for by people who have no special relationship with them. It is also widely accepted that it is normal for children of all ages (though particularly when they are young) to crave the support of their parents when they are upset or frightened, and it is commonly understood that being brought up without a family or with chaotic, haphazard parents puts children's well-being at serious risk and is likely to lead to problem behaviours. Interestingly, most people who hold these views are unlikely ever to have heard of Bowlby let alone to have read his work.

On the other hand, of those people who have heard of Bowlby, a number will remember him as *"that* man!" – the man who said that children need their mothers 24 hours a day until the age of three at least, that only mother will do, that separation of any sort from mother causes serious, long-term mental and emotional damage to children, that delinquency is a direct outcome of poor parenting, that blood ties are essential for adequate childcare, that hard-line strategies are needed to deal with problem parents and to teach parents the right way to bring up children, etc.[2] For some of these people, it was Bowlby the Arch-Misogynist who was at the spearhead of the movement to keep women penniless and shackled to the kitchen sink. But how accurate is this picture?

Surprisingly few writers have seriously addressed the task of teasing out the truth from the fiction that surrounds Bowlby and his theory of attachment. Most of the extant literature on attachment has been published in a growing number of academic journals, which in turn have produced an increasing number of articles each year. Anyone hoping to find specific information about any particular aspect of AT is likely to find themselves sifting through thousands of potentially relevant papers but very few that undertake to dispute the fundamental tenets of the theory. Numerous books are currently available and these tend to collate research findings for the use of students or attachment theory specialists (e.g. Belsky and Nezworski 1988, Greenberg et al. 1990, Holmes 1993, Karen 1994, Colin 1996, Fonagy 1999, Solomon and George 1999, Cassidy and Shaver 1999, Crittenden and Claussen 2000, Goldberg 2000) although some also address parents and professionals (e.g. Schore 1994, Heard and Lake 1996, Howe et al. 1999, Knox 2003, Gerhardt 2004, Biringen 2004, Rolfe 2004). Among these texts, there is a tendency for those directed at less specialist audiences (i.e. those which do not assume a basic understanding of the theory) to over-simplify or, at times, to misrepresent theoretical arguments and research findings, to lack any substantial critique of the ideas they present and to present rather one-sided views which, though engaging, may be of dubious evidential status. This description can also be said to apply to much information available on the worldwide web.

---

2   As we discuss elsewhere, these views tend to be associated with what we identify as the 'hard form' of AT.

Taken together, all these considerations have prompted us on our quest to discover exactly what the current status of Bowlby's Attachment Theory really is. We hope that this information may be of use to people working with parents in all settings, policy-makers, students, parents and, indeed, anyone interested in making sense of this vast and controversial literature. In the hope of avoiding the pitfalls that some others may have encountered, we have adopted several strategies: first, we have stayed as close as possible to the text of Bowlby's words; second, we have tried to show how key workers in the AT field have developed Bowlby's ideas; third, we have provided clear indications of our sources of evidence by including names and dates, even though this may have made for less easy reading, so that readers can have quick access to further information; finally, fourth, we have tried to consider as many sides of the various arguments as possible. In this way, we have aimed to present as fair and balanced a perspective as possible whilst flagging up questions or directions for future inquiry.

Often, opinions offered on the subject of infant-adult attachment are emotional and reflect the particular agenda of speakers. We recognise this difficulty and admit to having our own agenda, which is very much premised on a belief that, despite the fact that parents have probably (though even this is not absolutely certain) been caring for their own biological offspring for as long as the human race has existed, perhaps the only thing that they share in common is an inability to predict exactly how their children will develop or what kinds of events they may have to deal with in making provisions for their children's future, that is, an inability to control absolutely every aspect of their children's environment. The variety of circumstances and, consequently, the range of strategies and attitudes that parents develop to cope with their own unique situations is enormous. While some strategies may be more or less effective than others in dealing with specific problems, we believe that there is a clear need to keep as many strategies in play as possible (with the exception, of course, of abusive practices though, arguably, even some of these may be to some extent culturally defined or situationally determined[3]). In other words, we start from the premise that it is unlikely that any one strategy or set of strategies will suit all parents or all situations.

Having said this, as we have already acknowledged, it is difficult in this emotive field to present a pure, unbiased opinion. Bowlby was keenly aware of this, as is evident in the following quote: "In a field in which strong feelings are aroused and almost everyone has some sort of vested interest, clear unbiased thinking is not always easy" (Bowlby 1988b, p.24). Perhaps the best we can hope for is that, rather than provoking strong disagreements, criticism or, worse still, disinterest, we will encourage more people to take a fresh look at the important issues raised by Bowlby's theories. In doing this, we hope to sow its seeds more widely and to facilitate valuable discussions which could possibly enable a degree of re-thinking and re-energising of some of the debates which continue to characterise this field.

In the first part of the book, we describe Attachment Theory and the tools that have been developed to assess attachment relationships and behaviour across the lifespan. In Chapter One, we portray the emergence of Attachment Theory, its roots in psychoanalysis, medicine, cognitive psychology and ethology, and the concerns from which it emanated. In the second chapter, we identify three key tenets of Bowlby's theory (Table 1). In doing this, we attempt to show how the work of ethologists influenced Bowlby's early thinking. In Chapter Three, we consider the problem of assessment of attachment behaviours and attachment relation-

---

3 For example, a parent who grabs a child by the hair to rescue them as they fall out of a window is unlikely to be defined as abusive; parents who regularly threaten to pull their children's hair, even if they do not do it, are likely to be defined as abusive.

ships across the lifespan and show how some of the most widely used assessment tools have been developed and trialled.

Table 1: Major claims of Attachment Theory

I	Attachment relationships are important across the lifespan. Attachment security is associated with positive social and emotional development.
II	Attachment security is associated with particular qualities in caregivers. These qualities may be discernible across generations of carers.
III	Early social experiences lay the foundations for later development

In the second part of the book, we consider the evidence for and against the three major claims outlined in Table 1. A number of arguments and predictions have been associated with each claim, some overtly stated by Bowlby, some implied, and some overtly stated by other people working in the field. Many of these hypotheses have now been repeatedly tested and, in Chapters Four to Six, we explore and discuss the evidence for and against them.

In the third part of the book, we consider some of the applications and implications of Attachment Theory. Chapter Seven describes attachment-related problems and briefly outlines some interventions and therapies based on Attachment Theory as well as some approaches which purport to be based on Attachment Theory but which, we argue, are not. Chapter Eight draws together the theoretical arguments presented throughout the book and attempts to weigh up the current status of Attachment Theory. In Chapter Nine, we discuss some of the implications of Attachment Theory and research, for parents, for work with parents and for policies relating to parenting and parent support.

Part One

Theory and assessment

1 | The emergence of Bowlby's Attachment Theory

In this chapter, we explore the background against which Bowlby's theory of attachment emerged and try to ascertain whether and how this background might have given the theory its particular shape and character. First, we look at Bowlby's early life, his social background and his schooling. Then we go on to consider his work experience, training and the development of his interest in mother-child relationships. Part of this story also includes the arrival of Mary Ainsworth in the UK. We discuss the influence of her work on Bowlby's thinking. In a final section, we ask how or whether Attachment Theory might have been constrained by this background.

Bowlby's social background

Edward John Mostyn Bowlby was born on 26 February 1907 into a London-based, upper-middle class family. The six Bowlby children (Winnie, Marion, Tony, John, Jim and Evelyn) were born (in that order) to a mother, Mary Bridget Mostyn (known as May) who had married at the age of 31, had her first child one year after her marriage, gave birth to John at age 40 and, it has been suggested, may have felt that six children were at least two too many (Van Dijken 1998). John's father, Anthony Alfred Bowlby, a highly reputed surgeon knighted for his services to the royal family and further honoured for services to his country, was 43 when he married and already well established in his profession. Shortly after the marriage, at the outbreak of the Boer War in 1899, Anthony went to work in South Africa where, for six months after the birth of Winnie, his wife joined him, leaving Winnie in the care of a nursemaid and family nanny who had been appointed when Winnie was one month old. On the outbreak of the 1st World War, when John was seven, Bowlby's father was again posted abroad for the duration of the war.

The Bowlby children, like many children of that class and era, were cared for by a nanny and her staff in a nursery room located out of earshot of the rest of the house. Mother visited the nursery in the mornings to receive a report from nanny. For one hour each weekday (5-6 p.m.), the children, dressed specially for the occasion, were taken to see their mother. Anecdotal evidence suggests that while during these times May might often read to the children, she may also have left them to choose for themselves how to spend the time (Van Dijken 1998). On Sundays, the family spent more time together.

Regular spring and summer visits to the countryside broke this London routine. While these visits seem to have involved more time with mother, this was not always the case as some of the children appear to have been sent elsewhere during the holidays. However, according to Holmes (1993), it may have been these country visits that first encouraged John's interest in nature. Both his mother and father shared an interest in nature and his maternal grandfather, known as 'Grampy', was particularly well informed.

There is some indication that the relationship between the girls and their mother may have been more strained than that between mother and the boys, although it has also been suggested that mother may have favoured Tony as the eldest son (Byng-Hall 1987) and that both parents were very reluctant to accept that Jim, towards whom John is thought to have been protective (Holmes 1993), had learning difficulties (which were due to late diagnosis of a thyroid deficiency).

According to Holmes (1993), the children's nanny, Nanna Friend, was an intelligent, well-read disciplinarian from a working-class background. She stayed in the service of the family until her death at 97. John, known as Jack as a child and sometimes affectionately called the 'jackal' by his father, was also known in the nursery as 'Admiral Sir Nosey Know-All' and 'Bogey' (a name that Tony continued to use even as an adult). He appears to have been much less close to Nanna Friend than to his own nursemaid, Minnie, who left the household when John was about four.[1] Later, Bowlby recalled the departure of Minnie as a significant loss to him (Richard Bowlby, personal communication).

School

Most accounts describe the relationship between John and his older brother, Tony, as very close but also rivalrous. According to Van Dijken (1998), Bowlby's parents were not in favour of boarding schools for young children: until he was five, John was taught at home by a governess, then, at about seven, he went to a day school in London. Despite the 13-month gap between them, Tony and John were in the same junior school class and went to boarding school in the same year.

There is some debate about the age at which John went to boarding school. Van Dijken (1998) states that London had become too dangerous by 1918 so that in this year, at age 10, John was sent to Lindisfarne preparatory boarding school in Worcester. A slightly different account is given by Holmes (1993) who claims that it was the outbreak of war in 1914 that necessitated evacuation when John was seven.[2] However, Van Dijken's examination of school records produced no evidence of John's attendance before 1918 and also revealed that the school was still located in London until 1916. Nevertheless, the idea that it wasn't until the beginning of 1918 that London was considered too dangerous, particularly since the other four children may have stayed in London, seems to suggest that there might be more to the story than either Van Dijken's or Holmes' accounts can explain.

There is more agreement about the fact that John was unhappy at his first boarding school, although the reasons for his unhappiness are not clear. Certainly, it seems that this may have been his first time away from home, and the first time that he was in a class with boys of his own age rather than with his brother, Tony. A distressing event occurred during school holidays when John was 12. While John watched him playing football, his godfather suffered a heart attack and died. How John may have coped with this bereavement, or been helped to coped with it, is unknown, though it seems that the event may not have

---

1 It is possible that Bowlby may have been older than four at the time of Minnie's departure.
2 Juliet Hopkins, John Bowlby's niece, explains the discrepancy between Holmes' and Van Dijken's accounts as possibly due to Bowlby's having misrecalled events at the time of his interview by Holmes (Hopkins 2005, personal communication).

been talked about openly in the family (Van Dijken 1998). There are questions, then, about whether it may have been at this time that John experienced something of the sadness and loss that later became so central to his theories of attachment. Much later, he expressed the opinion that children younger than 13 should not be sent to boarding school (Hunter 1990) and, indeed, that he would not make a dog suffer that experience (Van Dijken 1998). Even so, given the context of his wartime childhood, his father's absences and other family circumstances, it is perhaps unwise to attempt to pinpoint exactly where Bowlby's insights may have had their origin.

John appears to have been much happier at the public school, Dartmouth Royal Naval College, that he attended from 14 to 17. Both Tony and John attended public schools associated with the services and, at this point, there seems to have been some intention of preparing each son for a career in the army and navy, respectively. John is said to have achieved top marks in all subjects, to have been an excellent all-rounder, skilled at sports and practical subjects (including engineering) as well as at more academic subjects. He also enjoyed hobbies, such as bird-watching, photography, drama and music.

Subsequently, Bowlby did join the navy but, feeling that peacetime naval life afforded him little opportunity to make any real contribution to society, succeeded in persuading his father to buy him out. His father did so on the understanding that John was to pursue a career in medicine like himself. That Bowlby was able to appeal to his father for help at this point seems to suggest that he did not consider his father unapproachable in spite of the degree to which the latter had been away from home. However, while many letters from John to his mother give a modicum of insight into his relationship with her, far less is known about his relationship with his father, other than that John may have resembled his father in some respects (Van Dijken 1998).

It is tempting to speculate that it may have been the lack of his own father's physical presence that contributed towards Bowlby's heavy emphasis on the importance of mother-child relationships and his relative lack of attention to the role of fathers. But such an interpretation seems somewhat tenuous. Perhaps equally plausible is the possibility that Bowlby needed to devote so much energy in order to convince a resistant audience of the importance of the child's tie to the mother that this left little scope for him to elaborate on other aspects of parent-child relationships. Whatever the truth may be in this matter, there is no getting away from the fact that Bowlby was a man of his times and social class. Like the majority of his contemporaries, he believed that the roles of male and female parents were distinct and that this inevitably led to imbalances in responsibilities for childcare and material provision (Bowlby 1951, 1953/1965).

Bowlby's beliefs are likely to have deep roots in the bedrock of sexual and gender relationships prevalent in UK society in the twentieth century. Van Dijken (1998) suggests that his mother, like other women of her time, may have accorded her sons, particularly the eldest, a different quality of respect than her daughters, of whom only one (the youngest) was prepared to talk about her childhood, saying that it was "horrible". John, on the other hand, described himself, somewhat equivocally, as "sufficiently hurt but not sufficiently damaged" (cited in Holmes 1993, no derivation stated).

Higher education

After a year at University College, London, studying to qualify for entrance to medical school, Bowlby gained a place at Cambridge where he took the first part of a Natural Sciences Tripos. This not only covered a wide range of subjects including, for example, zoology, botany, anatomy and mineralogy, but also introduced Bowlby to the, then, relatively new field of psychoanalysis and psychology. As, at this time, Cambridge was developing a reputation for being at the forefront of work in the psychological sciences, on gaining first class honours in the first part of his degree, Bowlby seized the opportunity to study psychology further and so switched to Moral Sciences (psychology and philosophy), temporarily putting the medical training which his father had financed on a back burner.

At that time, psychology was still a 'young' discipline, seeking to establish itself as a respectable branch of science and to loosen ties with its roots in more speculative philosophy. It was then, and to a large extent still is, dominated by empiricist and behaviourist traditions characterised by the notion that understanding can only be arrived at through 'hard' data. In this school of thought, intangible processes, like thinking and feeling, and intangible constructs, like self-esteem, love or nurturance, must be understood by first transforming them, using well-established scientific methods, into measurable units. To establish the worth of a theory the only recognised way is then thought to be through the use of quantitative research methods which involve experimentation and hypothesis-testing.

Against this background, though, there was also a lot of excitement about theories of development which had been derived from observations made outside the laboratory, for example, observations by ethologists and naturalists studying animals in their own habitats, observations by anthropologists exploring societies far removed from middle-class London, and observations made by clinicians working with psychologically disturbed people. Bowlby's early training therefore not only acquainted him with the ideas of people working outside the discipline of mainstream behaviourist psychology, for example, Sigmund Freud, Charles Darwin and Margaret Mead, it also brought him into direct contact with experimental psychologists at the cutting edge of research on mental processes, for example, Frederick Bartlett who demonstrated how memory for stories changes systematically over time with features being lost, substituted, rationalised, and re-created (Bartlett 1932) and others who were interested in discovering, for example, the relationship between brain damage and cognitive ability.

These must have been heady days in the field of psychology, with considerable optimism about the possibility that, despite difficulties, it would eventually be possible to reduce all psychological processes to observable phenomena and so, through rigorous scientific testing, to reach the only real understanding of psychological states. That Bowlby was influenced by this optimism is apparent throughout his writings, but it was not a view that was universally held and, certainly, in psychoanalytic circles, there was very considerable resistance to the notion that all important psychological processes might be measured in this way. These differences of opinion were to play an important role in the development of Bowlby's theory of attachment.

Early work experience and interest in children's emotional development

On graduating from Cambridge in summer 1928, Bowlby took the rather unconventional decision not to go on to complete his medical training immediately but to work as a teacher with emotionally disturbed children. Not much is known about what it was that encouraged him to defer his medical training, for example, whether at this point he may have been having doubts about pursuing his father's profession. Parkes (1995) suggests that it may have been his father's death that freed Bowlby to make this choice and Holmes (1993) claims that, had Bowlby's father been alive, he would have opposed the move. However, the fact that his father died in 1929, at least four months after Bowlby had started teaching, seems to indicate that Bowlby's deferral of medical training by one year bore little relation to his father's wishes (whatever these may or may not have been).

In September 1928, Bowlby spent a few months teaching in a progressive co-educational school, Bedales. During this time, he visited Priory Gate school in Norfolk, a residential school for 'maladjusted' children as they were then termed[3] and, after meeting another teacher there, John Alford, decided "...he knew more about what was of interest to me than anyone I had met so far" (Smuts 1977, p.2). As a result, Bowlby spent the next six months working at Priory Gate and later asserted that, "...when I was there, I learned everything that I have known: it was the most valuable six months of my life, really" (Senn 1977, p. 2). This rather extreme and somewhat challenging pronouncement seems in many ways characteristic of Bowlby's style. Logically, the assertion that he learned nothing from his formal medical and psychoanalytic training has to be seen to be preposterously inaccurate. On a more emotional level, though, we can perhaps understand that what Bowlby may have been trying to convey was the immense importance of this front-line, first-hand experience for him, at this point in his professional and intellectual development. Paradoxically, far from being forceful or pugnacious, he seems, in his inimical way, to have been stating with a certain degree of humility that he felt the experience had made a stronger impression on him than any other experience before or after.

So what was it that Bowlby found so valuable about Priory Gate? The school catered for 22 children, and its ethos was founded upon an understanding that children learn through experience and that therefore each individual child's point of view is valid. This approach was new and afforded the possibility of unusually rich and mutually respectful relationships between staff and children. Staff were acquainted with psychoanalytic and other psychological ideas, opposed to harsh discipline and appreciative of the fact that the key to children's future psychological adjustment would lie in the nature of their experiences at the school.

Bowlby was given sole responsibility for teaching 10 children and a free hand in determining how he should work with them. This meant that he was able to engage fully with the children and get to know them much better than he might have done in most other educational or therapeutic settings, even though he was relatively, if not completely, untrained. At the same time, he was able to discuss his work in depth with his colleagues, particularly with John Alford whose opinion he clearly respected.

Although Bowlby did not discuss his work very much with his family, it would appear from letters to his mother as well as from his brother's observations, that his relationships with some of the most difficult children at the school made a deep impression on him. It seems highly possible that it was here that he first began to develop his conviction of the potency of positive interactive experience, and its role in children's emotional development.

One child is thought to have particularly influenced Bowlby's understanding of child development (Bowlby 1981b, Van Dijken 1998, Holmes 1993). This boy, the illegitimate son of well-to-do parents, had a history of disrupted early care relationships and had subsequently been expelled from Eton for repeated stealing. At 16, though socially conforming, this boy had no friends and seemed very isolated. Bowlby speculated about the connection

---

3   Nowadays it is often thought preferable to use terminology that acknowledges the possibility that the disturbed behaviour of troubled children may constitute an adaptive response to very challenging circumstances rather than to further compound their difficulties by dubbing them dysfunctional or 'maladjusted'.

between the boy's compulsion to steal and his inability to form meaningful relationships with people: "Those in charge attributed his condition to his having never been cared for during his early years by any one motherly person, a result of his illegitimate birth. Thus, I was alerted to a possible connection between prolonged deprivation of maternal care during early childhood and the development of a personality apparently incapable of making affectional bonds and, because immune to praise and blame, prone to repeated delinquencies" (Bowlby 1981b, p.2).

Medical and psychoanalytic training

The next year saw Bowlby, apparently on Alford's advice, returning somewhat reluctantly to complete his medical training at University College, London. By now, he had set his heart on training to be a psychoanalyst and understood that, to do this, he would have to finish his medical training. However, as soon as he could, he applied to the Institute of Psychoanalysis and, by the age of 22, had been assigned to Joan Riviere for a training analysis related to psychoanalytic work with children.

Child psychoanalysis had not become established in Britain at this time and, interested though he was in psychoanalytic ideas, Bowlby found much to quarrel with in psychoanalytic accounts of child development. From its inception, too, the psychoanalytic scene in Britain has been so riven by factions that it has often borne more resemblance to a battleground for rival religious cults than to an open forum for serious scientific debate (Gellner 1985). Bowlby had little patience with this, explaining later that: "As a somewhat arrogant young man with a number of academic friends...I was in no mood to accept dogmatic teaching" (Bowlby 1991a, p.11). He further found great difficulty in working with Joan Riviere, who could not accept his need for evidence: "My analyst was not altogether happy with my critical attitude and complained on one occasion that I would take nothing on trust and was trying to think everything out from scratch, which I was certainly committed to doing" (Bowlby 1991a, p.11). Even at the end of this seven-year analysis, it seems, neither Bowlby nor Riviere was satisfied.

Whether, as some analysts would aver, Bowlby's need for intellectual understanding (which, one suspects, must already have been a trait apparent in "Admiral Sir Nosey Know-it-All") stemmed from a deep, pathological insecurity or from an unusually healthy persistence in the face of opposition, we will perhaps never know. What seems clear is that Bowlby was energetic, humorous, creative and often rather rebellious in his approach to life. Holmes (1993) describes how, to relieve the tedium of his medical studies, Bowlby set up a sandwich bar at University College called 'Bogey's Bar'. Van Dijken (1998), contradicting Holmes' account, explains that the bar was set up to help a former colleague from Priory Gate who was looking for catering experience. The bar seems to have been a success financially and socially. It is tempting to wonder what significance might accrue to his identification with his rather ignominious nickname. Might this contain a clue to the nature of his sympathetic interest in anti-social children?

Clinical experience and completion of psychoanalytic training

On qualifying as a doctor in 1933, Bowlby reluctantly remained in analysis with Joan Riviere, mainly for pragmatic reasons as he was advised that changing analysts might jeopardise his chances of being accepted for psychoanalytic training. In the same year, hoping to qualify for a commonwealth fellowship in child psychiatry which necessitated experience of work with adults, Bowlby found a job as clinical assistant at the Maudsley Hospital in London, which was then considered to be at the forefront of research in adult psychiatry. He also registered as a PhD student at University College (though this PhD was never completed) and began, under supervision of Nina Searle and Ella Sharpe, to work with two patients as a trainee psychoanalyst.

The following year, 1934, Bowlby took on additional work, as a clinical assistant at University College, with children with learning difficulties and, later that year, also became honorary research fellow at the Institute for the Scientific Treatment of Delinquency.

As several colleagues in these posts were extremely sceptical about psychoanalysis, Bowlby's own questioning attitude was possibly nurtured during this time. Indeed, he appears to have flouted the Institute of Psychoanalysis rules since, in 1935, the Training Committee led by Edward Glover strongly objected to the fact that, before having qualified as an analyst, Bowlby was not only working unsupervised with a private patient but was also treating patients at the Maudsley with an unconventional form of psychoanalytic treatment (seeing them for three rather than the recommended five times per week). How this situation was resolved is unclear but it did not prevent Bowlby from completing his psychoanalytic training in 1937. Whether nowadays a candidate with Bowlby's qualities would experience more or less difficulty in negotiating the training is a moot point. Given his tendency not to follow a party line, it almost seems surprising that he was allowed to qualify at all.

Work on delinquency

On completion of his psychoanalytic training, Bowlby took up work as a child psychiatrist in the London Child Guidance Clinic and remained there until the outbreak of the war in 1939. Here, working alongside psychiatric social workers, his conviction of the importance of actual childhood experiences deepened. He became aware that, while training as an analyst, despite his critical attitude, he had in fact been more influenced by the views of analysts like Melanie Klein than he later considered useful (Bowlby 1991a) but also that his views had probably been more at variance with those of the other analysts than he had realised at the time (Grosskurth 1986).

The essential point of divergence concerned the influence of actual life circumstances and experiences and how these realities should be managed in the therapeutic setting. Bowlby increasingly believed that an understanding of life events was essential for progress to be made in understanding and helping patients. Other analysts were more concerned to focus on what they saw to be more fundamental, underlying processes, related to patients' phantasies.

When working with children who steal, for example, the two approaches are likely to produce quite different relationships between patients and therapists. Bowlby, in his interest to discover what family circumstances and experiences might have led to a child's compulsion to steal, would be more likely to encourage his patients to engage in an exploration of thoughts, feelings and memories for real social experiences. Kleinian analysts, making the assumption that the meaning of the stolen objects is associated with the continuation of early internal world conflicts (infantile phantasies), would be more likely to interpret patients' behaviour in terms of their supposed phantasies relating to the symbolic meaning of stealing. While Bowlby became more and more convinced of the importance of understanding the impact of past and ongoing experiences, for most Kleinians, at that time at least, real life circumstances were of no great interest. In Bowlby's lifetime, this rift, complicated by resentment and stubbornness on both sides, was later to lead to what ostensibly amounted to Bowlby's ostracism from the most powerful psychoanalytic circles.

Early research papers: the theme of maternal deprivation

During the Thirties and Forties, Bowlby produced several papers which expounded his view that many of the psychological disorders seen in children could be explained by difficult childhood experiences. Among these he included death of close family members, violence and unsatisfactory mother-child relationships but increasingly drew attention to the effects of prolonged early child-mother separations.

As early as 1939, writing about substitute homes, he argued that "the emotional bond between child and mother is the basis for all further social development" (Bowlby 1939b, p.3), that institutionalised children showing deviant behaviour had often never had a lasting emotional relationship with a mother or substitute mother figure, that lack of opportunity to form "solid emotional ties ... more than any other single thing... accounts, I believe, for the withdrawn impersonality of the institutional child" (Bowlby 1939b, p.6) and that even those adopted children who appear to be well-adjusted "for all their apparent gayness suffer from a sense of inner emptiness and gloom" (Bowlby 1939b, p.7). In this paper, already, he argued that a bad home is better than a good institution. This notion, much later, was to become a cornerstone of childcare policies (e.g. Goldstein et al. 1973, 1979, 1986).

Bowlby continued to explore the notion that a history of disrupted care and, most specifically, prolonged separation from mother, is implicated in the development of anti-social behaviour. He examined 44 consecutive case records kept from the years 1936 to 1939 on children referred to the London Child Guidance Clinic for whom stealing was "either a serious or a transitory symptom" (Bowlby 1944, p.21) and compared these children with 44 children of similar age and intelligence who were also referred to the clinic and did not steal. He classified the characters of the 44 thieves as 'normal' (appearing fairly normal and stable; two children), 'depressed' (formerly unstable and now in a more or less depressed state of mind; nine children), 'circular' (showing alternate depression and over-activity; two children), 'hyperthymic'[4] (tending to constant over-activity; 13 children), 'affectionless' (lacking normal affection, shame or sense of responsibility; 14 children) and 'schizoid' (showing marked schizoid or schizophrenic symptoms; four children). He particularly drew attention to the affectionless children and suggested that these children might be viewed as prototypical delinquents: "I am doubtful...whether the law-abiding Affectionless Character exists...they have a remarkably distinctive early history – prolonged separations from their mothers or foster-mothers ... we have here... an unusually clear example of the distorting influence of a bad early environment upon the development of personality" (Bowlby 1944, p.39).

In this seminal paper, Bowlby further expanded upon his thesis that early separation impacts on ability to form and maintain loving relationships "owing to absence of opportunity at a critical period and the inhibition of love by rage and the phantasies resulting from rage...(*which gives rise to*) the determination at all costs not to risk again the disappointment and the resulting rages and longings which wanting someone very much and not getting them involves" (Bowlby 1944, pp. 123-124). He concluded with strong recommendations that all possible steps be taken to avoid prolonged early separations and argued that "if all those who had to advise on the upbringing of small children...were aware of the appalling damage which separations of this kind have on the development of a child's character, many could be avoided and many of the most distressing cases of chronic delinquency prevented" (Bowlby 1944, p.126).

---

4 More commonly known as hyperactivity nowadays and linked with difficulties in paying sustained attention.

The war years: fears for the welfare of evacuated children

Although Bowlby volunteered for war service in 1940, he was not called up to fight but to work in the Emergency Medical Service. He also joined an army officer selection team, which had the task of carrying out personality tests. For some time, too, he continued to work in the Child Guidance Clinic when it was evacuated in 1940 to Cambridge. These posts both afforded him the opportunity to extend his experience of research methods and statistical analysis and gave him a good vantage point from which to develop his understanding of personality development.

Bowlby's conviction that prolonged separations were potentially damaging now led him, along with colleagues such as Donald Winnicott (then working as consultant psychiatrist for the Government Evacuation Scheme in Oxfordshire), to be concerned about the possible negative effects of mass evacuation. In a letter to the *British Medical Journal*, Bowlby and colleagues advised against evacuation of very young children, arguing that a likely long-term consequence may be "a big increase in juvenile delinquency in the next decade" (Bowlby, Miller and Winnicott 1939, p.1203) and that the danger for children under five is far greater than mere sadness: "such an experience in the case of a little child can mean far more than the actual experience of sadness. It can in fact amount to an emotional "black-out", and can easily lead to a severe disturbance of the personality which may persist throughout life" (Bowlby et al. 1939, p.1202). He wrote other letters, too, which were not published and seems to have felt that his concerns were not being taken seriously or, worse still, were being deliberately suppressed (Van Dijken 1998). A chapter on evacuation illustrates Bowlby's belief that the negative effects of separation for very young children chiefly lay in their inability to make sense of why their parents had sent them away (Bowlby 1940e). Although recognising that older children may also find separations difficult, he stressed that they, unlike younger children, would be more able to understand, first, that their parents had not sent them away because they did not want them or were cross with them and, second, that they would see their parents again some time in the future. He concluded that children under two should not be evacuated at all (or should be sent to people they know) while children between two and five should, wherever possible, be evacuated with their mothers. Later, he asserted that, "Evacuation was a bad mistake and it was the child guidance people who had to pick up the pieces" (Inglis 1990, p.154).

It is worth remarking at this point that, although Bowlby did take considerable interest in case records of evacuees (e.g. Burlingham and Freud 1942) and advised on the Cambridge Evacuation Survey, which largely consisted of case studies (Isaacs 1941), he did not personally carry out any systematic study of the experiences of evacuated children. His views on this matter, therefore, have to be seen to be based on speculation and inductive reasoning rather than on direct, more substantial or systematic evidence. This seems a pity. The experience of evacuation impinged on the lives of huge numbers of children of all ages in the UK yet very few systematic records of its impact are available. Bowlby's hypothesis that children under five would be more negatively affected by evacuation than older children has, unfortunately, never been tested. However, this belief that relationship experiences in the first few years of life carry more weight than those in later years was to become central to Bowlby's later formulation of Attachment Theory.

Even more immediate experiences may have influenced the development of Bowlby's views at this time, for the war and his work often necessitated his own absence from home. He had married in 1938 and, although three of his four children were born during the war years, for much of the time between 1939 and 1945, he was billeted away from home and, even when he was in London, did not always coincide with his wife and children who stayed with relatives to avoid the dangers of London. Holmes describes Bowlby as somewhat challenged by his fatherhood role and away so often that his eldest son is purported to have asked, at about age seven (c1946), "Is Daddy a burglar? He always comes home after dark and never talks about his work!" (Holmes 1993, p.25). It seems plausible that Bowlby's own family circumstances, both as a child and as an adult, contributed considerably to his assumptions about the importance of mothers and of the relatively less direct role of fathers in the lives of young children. However, this cannot be taken as hard evidence that he considered fathers any less important than mothers in the overall picture of family life (Bowlby 1984a/1988b).

Work on separation

Campaign work with James and Joyce Robertson

After the war, Bowlby returned to London and took up a post as deputy director in the newly developing Department for Children at the Tavistock Clinic. A substantial part of this job required him to undertake research and he used this as an opportunity to study early mother-child separation more systematically. As he was unable to use clinical cases for the kind of research he wished to undertake, he decided to raise funds to set up a separate research unit and to focus on effects of separation "because separation was an event on record, unlike disturbed family interaction, of which, in those days, there were no adequate records" (Ainsworth and Bowlby 1991, p.2).

One project involved a retrospective study of the experiences of 66 school-children who had spent time away from their families in TB sanitoria, between the ages of one and four. Another longitudinal study was carried out by James Robertson who observed children separated from their mothers and placed in different institutional settings, either due to their own or to their mother's hospitalisation.

This work produced two sets of outputs: a series of films which subsequently became extremely influential in drawing attention to the extreme difficulty that young children experience when separated from their mothers, even for a matter of days, and a series of papers documenting children's responses to separation.

The films[5] showed, first, two-year-old Laura hospitalised for eight days for repair of an umbilical hernia with daily visits by parents (Robertson 1952) and, second, a hospital where mothers were able to stay with their sick children (Robertson 1958). The films illustrate graphically the stressfulness of Laura's experience and the contrasting supportiveness of a situation where mothers can be available to look after their own children and can interact with other mothers, their children and hospital staff.

A further five films document young children (aged 17 months to two years and five months) in care while mother goes to hospital for the birth of a second child (Robertson and Robertson 1967, 1968, 1969, 1971, 1973). One film shows a child in a residential nursery while the others document the progress of four children individually cared for in the home of James and Joyce Robertson. The children were selected as being of "good previous experience"

---

5   Very possibly inspired by a powerful American film produced by Rene Spitz in 1947, entitled *Grief: A peril in infancy*.

(Robertson and Robertson 1976), i.e. having not previously been separated from the mother and having two parents living together.

The films themselves are edited versions of observations made throughout the children's stay and, with the exception of one (Robertson and Robertson 1971), which does include some of the child's speech, are silent with a voiced-over commentary. Each film shows children struggling with varying degrees of distress to overcome the insurmountable task of coping with separation from their own family setting. Robertson and Robertson (1976 p.6) describe the four fostered children as being maintained in "a state of 'manageable anxiety'", unlike 17-month-old John who stayed in a residential nursery for nine days and who was badly affected by his experience: "No normal family child could stand up to this kind of experience... When John returned home he was extremely anxious and insecure... John's trust in his mother had been badly shaken" (Robertson and Robertson 1976, p.27).

Robertson and Robertson stressed the risks attached to separations for very young children and pointed to the need for children to be carefully prepared, by getting to know their substitute carers as well as possible, by being afforded opportunities for contact with parents, through the use of photographs and transitional objects (favourite teddies, blankets, etc.) and by assigning key workers in group care situations (Robertson and Robertson 1976, 1989; Robertson 1962). Above all, they stressed the need for separations to be avoided if at all possible.

The films probably did more than research papers or talks to impress upon professionals, policy-makers and the public the risks associated with separation for young children. They were adopted by campaigners and so, directly and indirectly, influenced moves to alter hospital visiting practices and lengths of hospital stays, as well as many other aspects of childcare practices, including the phasing out of residential nurseries, the introduction of key worker schemes and decisions about fostering and adoption.

The Protest-Despair-Detachment story

In a number papers ensuing from this and related research, Bowlby and Robertson elaborated on the theme that pathological processes are set in motion by early child-mother separation (Bowlby 1953/1965, 1958a, 1961b, 1963, 1968a, 19691982, 1973a; Robertson and Bowlby 1952a). Drawing attention to resemblances between children's responses to separation and adults' responses to bereavement, they described three stages: "When a child of 18-24 months of age, who has previously had a normal relationship with his mother and has not been separated from her for more than a few hours, is parted from her and cared for in an impersonal environment (that is, an environment which does not provide substitute mothering) he commonly progresses through three phases of emotional response which we describe as the phases of *protest, despair,* and *denial*" (Robertson 1953, p.383).

In developing his theory of separation anxiety, Bowlby reiterated this description but later re-named the final phase *detachment*, in keeping with his theory that the whole sequence of responses constitutes a reaction to disruption of attachment bonds or loss of a primary attachment figure (Bowlby 1960a, 1960b). In this paper, Bowlby argued that the protest-despair-detachment pattern directly reflected Freud's three-stage account of response to loss as shown in Table 1.1.

Table 1.1: Links between separation and mourning

PSYCHOLOGICAL STATE	FREUDIAN ACCOUNT	SEPARATION RESPONSE
THREAT OF LOSS	Anxiety/Anger about potential loss	PROTEST
MOURNING	Pain associated with retreat from lost object	DESPAIR
DEFENCE	Strategy of managing anxiety and pain	DETACHMENT

The Protest phase is therefore characterised by a reaction to the danger of losing contact with mother, the Despair phase by the child's realisation that he or she is helpless to restore contact, and the Detachment phase by defensive behaviour designed to prevent the re-emergence of painful feelings. Bowlby considered that the protest-despair-detachment pattern could arise in response to all types of separation in infants and young children more than about six months of age:[6] "When they for any reason lose their loved object the three phases of mourning described are experienced. At all ages, we now see, the first phase of mourning is one of Protest, the second one of Despair, and the third one of Detachment" (Bowlby 1961a, p.338); "The initial phase, that of protest, may begin immediately or may be delayed" (Bowlby 1969/1982, p.49). Bowlby argued that enforced detachment at this early age almost inevitably led to later difficulties in establishing close relationships.

Subsequent research has given rise to serious doubts about the universality of the Protest-Despair-Detachment pattern which, arguably, is rather too heavily informed by theory and insufficiently supported by evidence. Barrett (1997) has posited both that there may be an early stage equivalent to that noted in respect of bereavement (Table 1.2) and that there may be considerably more individual variation than stage models imply. In some ways, it is rather curious that, in revising his stage model of grieving and extending it from a three- to a four-stage model, Bowlby did not think to re-visit his conceptualisation of separation responses. As he pointed out, "always in the history of medicine it is the end result of a pathological sequence which is first to be noted. Only gradually are the earlier phases identified, and it may be years before the exact sequence is understood" (Bowlby 1960b, p.91). Given more time and more data, perhaps, he might have revised the original account.

Table 1.2: Stages of mourning and the missing first stage of separation responses

PSYCHOLOGICAL STATE	RESPONSES TO BEREAVEMENT	SEPARATION RESPONSE
THREAT OF LOSS	Numbness/Disbelief/Denial	DENIAL/HYPOMANIA
LOSS (REALISATION)	Searching/Pining	PROTEST
MOURNING	Disorganisation/Despair	DESPAIR
DEFENCE	Reorganisation/Recovery	DETACHMENT

---

6   During the first four to six months of life, infants were thought by Bowlby possibly to be insufficiently attached to react in a focused way to separation, though he recognised the need for more research on this matter.

World Health Organization report and growing concern about maternal deprivation

In 1949, Bowlby was asked to undertake a study of the needs of homeless children under the auspices of the Social Commission of the United Nations. This work involved surveys of relevant literature (including studies of deprived animals) and interviews with professionals working with homeless children throughout the UK, the Netherlands, France, Sweden, Switzerland and the USA. The report produced at the end of 1950 (published in 1951) was later revised for more general readership in 1953 and this latter volume was reprinted in 1965, with two chapters added by Mary Ainsworth.

In the original report, Bowlby expressed the now famous sentiment: "...maternal care in infancy and early childhood is essential for mental health. This is a discovery comparable to that of the role of vitamins in physical health" (Bowlby 1951, p.59). Continuing the medical analogy, he further argued that deprived children "whether in their own homes or out of them, are a source of social infection as real and serious as are carriers of diphtheria and typhoid" (Bowlby 1951, p.157).

The report enabled Bowlby to develop and widely publicise his views about the serious effects of maternal deprivation. He summarised his conclusions as follows:

a) In general, brief experiences of deprivation and/or separation do not produce later difficulties for children or their parents. Although the child might show signs of increased anxiety as a result of separation, if s/he has not reached the stage of detachment, this anxiety usually dissipates within weeks. But the child will be more vulnerable to negative effects if separations are repeated. Therefore, recovery is not as complete as it appears due to "the presence of this hidden impairment" (Bowlby 1953/1965, p.224).

b) Although children may appear to have recovered after months of deprivation in early infancy, there may still be hidden long-term effects on intellectual and personality development. Speech is particularly likely to be affected, but other social abilities too, especially if the deprivation continues beyond 11 or 12 months of age.

c) Prolonged and severe deprivation, beginning early in the first year and continuing for three years, usually leads to non-remediable problems relating to the development of children's intellect and personality.

d) If prolonged and severe deprivation begins in the second year of life, the negative effect on intellectual ability can usually be reversed but "an impaired ability to form and maintain close and mutually satisfying affectional ties" (Bowlby 1953/1965, p.225) tends to persist.

e) Although more research is needed before it is possible to be sure whether there are ages at which children are particularly vulnerable to negative effects of deprivation, "there is evidence, nevertheless, that the period from seven months of age to perhaps ten or eleven months is one during which the infant is especially vulnerable to the disruption of ties newly formed" (Bowlby 1953/1965, p.225). This may be a sensitive period of development.

f) Infants are at their most vulnerable to effects of deprivation in the first year of life. The longer the deprivation at this age, the worse the consequences for later development. Effects of deprivation beginning after the first year are easier to remedy, depending on their duration.

g) Once deprivation has affected speech, thinking or ability to form close relationships, it is almost always difficult to remedy these problems.

h) Nothing less than intensive early therapeutic intervention will effectively alleviate the negative effects of deprivation.

i) Early experiences of deprivation sensitise children to later milder stresses. This, too, can lead to further difficulties and lower chances of recovery.

Bowlby also acknowledged many gaps in understanding the relationship between delinquency and disrupted child-mother relationships and pointed to the need for new studies of possible links. However, although he did recognise a need for further research, his interim conclusions were quite alarming: "Nothing encourages a sanguine view of the reversibility of impairment caused by early and severe maternal deprivation... Evidence of covert and subtle effects persisting after even a relatively mild separation raises a doubt, moreover, whether, in cases where deprivation has been early and severe, complete reversibility is possible. Perhaps 'complete reversibility' is an illusory product of crude methods of appraisal" (Bowlby 1953/1965, p.227). This perspective formed the basis of his early theory of attachment, much of which, by the late Fifties, was already well in place and can be seen to reflect what, in this book, we describe as the 'hard form' of Attachment Theory. In light of later research, Bowlby was to modify some aspects of this early formulation.

Work with Mary Ainsworth

Ainsworth's previous research

As mentioned earlier, Mary Ainsworth played a key role in enabling the development of Bowlby's theory of attachment. In 1940, supervised by William Blatz, she had completed a PhD at the University of Toronto, entitled *An evaluation of the concept of security* (Salter 1940). Blatz (e.g. Blatz 1966) argued that young children need initially to be free of anxiety (the etymological derivation of the term security is from the Latin *'sine cura'*, which literally means 'without care/anxiety') if they are to be able to explore the world around them and to become self-sufficient. He proposed that the role of parents in early childhood is to provide a secure base (a family environment without anxiety) so that children can progress from 'immature dependent security' to 'independent security'. During this process, children need gradually to gain enough knowledge and skills to be able to take more and more responsibility for themselves. By adulthood, they no longer have the need for parents to provide a secure base but may nevertheless draw selectively upon other people's skills and knowledge if necessary. Blatz labelled this the stage of 'mature dependent security'.

During her dissertation, Ainsworth had devised a system for classifying differences in levels of individual interdependency relationships, with the aim of assessing "the degree to which a person was secure rather than insecure" (Ainsworth and Bowlby 1991, p.3). Had the war not broken out, she may have continued this work. However, in the event, she was diverted into the field of army personnel selection and, on de-mobilisation, pursued her newly developed interest in personality testing, though still in connection with the work of Blatz.

England and Uganda

In 1950, for reasons of her husband's work, Ainsworth travelled to England and, while here, fortuitously, obtained work as research assistant to Bowlby. In this post, she examined the literature gathered on the World Health Organization project, and also worked as data analyst on the other two separation projects. She, like Bowlby, was impressed with the complexity of the data and convinced of the value of more extensive research (Ainsworth and Bowlby 1953). Perusing the social worker interview data in Robertson's sanatorium follow-up study, she was particularly intrigued to note that, on being restored to the family home, although few children remained in a state of 'affectionless detachment', equally few appeared to have established secure relationships with their mothers (Bowlby, Ainsworth, Boston and Rosenbluth 1956).

In 1954, Ainsworth's husband's work took him to Uganda. Whilst with him there, Ainsworth continued her studies of infant-mother relationships. Inspired by the observations made by James Robertson (Ainsworth and Marvin 1995) and by Bowlby's interest in cultural differences in infant-mother relationships, Ainsworth was keen to acquire as detailed a picture as possible of infants and mothers in the Ganda tribe. With the help of an interpreter-assistant, she made fortnightly visits to 28 mothers and their infants, 15 boys and 13 girls, over a period of nine months. At the start of the study, the infants ranged in age from newborn (one girl) to 19 months; 11 were first-born. Mothers' marital status was varied: seven were in polygamous relationships, about 14 monogamous and the remainder had either never married, were separated, or father had deserted.

On each visit, Ainsworth asked mothers questions about babies' development and about how they were managing their babies. She also observed how infants and mothers interacted with each other and was especially interested to discover evidence of the development of any 'special relationship' between them. She identified a number of infant behaviours that she considered to be signs of a special attachment having been formed. These behaviours occurred at different ages in different children and also varied in frequency and intensity. Table 1.3 illustrates these infant behaviours and the ages at which Ainsworth first observed them. Ages must be seen as purely indicative, as it must be remembered that observations did not start from birth, were based on relatively small samples of time and specific behaviours were not systematically sought for.

On the basis of these observed behaviours, Ainsworth subsequently classified infants as securely attached, insecurely attached and non-attached. However, she later considered the criteria used for classification unsatisfactory and concluded that the five children identified as 'non-attached' may have simply been too young or delayed as opposed to having failed to make a good relationship with their mothers. Even so, she did consider one mother (of ailing twins) to be rather rejecting.

The 16 infants labelled 'secure' cried very little unless demanding food or ill and "when they were with their mothers they seemed especially content and secure" (Ainsworth 1963, p.84). The seven labelled 'insecure' cried much more, demanded more attention and rarely explored even when mother was nearby.

Table 1.3: Attachment behaviours identified in Ganda infants (Ainsworth, 1967)

BEHAVIOUR	COMMENT	Age (weeks)
Differential crying	*Crying only stopped by mother*	8-15
Differential smiling	*Baby smiles more to mother than others*	10-26
Differential vocalisation	*More babbling, etc. to mother than others*	20
Crying when mother leaves	*Includes not being able to see mother*	15-29
Following mother	*Crawling after mother*	24-51
Visual motor orientation	*Keeping an eye on mother's whereabouts*	18-31
Greeting	*Signs of excitement in response to mother*	21-22
Lifting arms in greeting	*Rarer in Ganda than US infants*	
Clapping hands in greeting	*Occurs frequently in Ganda, not US infants*	28-48
Scrambling over the mother	*E.g. playing with mother's hair, etc.*	22-41
Burying face in mother's lap		28-53
Approach through locomotion		33-52
Exploration, mother present	*Use of mother as secure base*	30-42
Flight to mother	*Use of mother as safe haven*	28-56
Clinging	*Often in response to insecurity*	40-59

Further, Ainsworth (1963) found that security of attachment appeared to be associated with:
- degree of mother's involvement in childcare[7]
- mother's excellence as an informant
- mothers' enjoyment of breastfeeding

It did not appear to be associated with:
- total amount of care[8]
- maternal warmth
- multiple caretakers
- whether babies were schedule vs self-demand fed (though there was a statistically non-significant tendency for secure babies to be given the breast more often as a comforter)

When Ainsworth first presented these findings at the second Tavistock seminar in 1961, there was considerable discussion about the advisability of using a value-laden term like

---

[7] This measure was a composite of the extent to which mothers left the care of babies to others, were available to care and spent time with the child.
[8] Scores on this variable may have reflected a definition which was insensitive to variations and created 'ceiling effects'.

'security' and about what attachment and security of attachment might mean in terms of psychological health. Bowlby emphatically asserted that the significance of different types of attachment for later development were not known at all (Ainsworth 1963, p.111).

Baltimore

In 1963, Ainsworth continued her study of infant-mother relationships in Baltimore. From 1963-1964, she and Barbara Wittig made home visits to 15 infants and their mothers. Visits lasted four hours and were carried out every three weeks starting when the baby was three weeks old. Another 11 infants and mothers were later added to the sample when Marvin and Allyn joined the research team in 1966-1967. The final sample of 26 babies and their mothers, originally contacted through paediatricians in private practice, were from white, middle-class families.

Home visits were similar to those carried out in Uganda but information from the Ugandan study was used to create more systematic records which focused more deliberately on the attachment behaviours previously identified. Home observations were also complemented by observations of mother-infant interaction in the more controlled setting of a university laboratory playroom. These laboratory observations, known as the Strange Situation procedure, and the classificatory system that Ainsworth developed on the basis of them, were to form the key research tool used by workers in the field of attachment. In the next chapter, this procedure and the classifications produced will be described in more detail.

Despite the relatively small sample, the data produced by Ainsworth's observations were extensive and took many years to analyse fully.[9] Key findings included the following points:
- clear-cut attachment behaviours first emerge around the middle of the first year
- separation anxiety, which also emerges at this time, indicates the establishment of preferential ties (attachment)
- attachment relationships, which are to be distinguished from attachment behaviours, develop subsequently
- mothers who respond sensitively (contingently) to infants are most likely to have securely attached infants
- more physical contact, when appropriate and timely, does not 'spoil' babies
- securely attached infants respond positively to being picked up and to being put down by their attachment figures
- insecure behaviours in the home are magnified by the increased stress of the unfamiliar laboratory

---

9 Mary Main, a student of Ainsworth's, explains that Mary Ainsworth discouraged her from including large numbers of participants in the later Berkeley longitudinal study because of the length of time required for thorough analysis (Main et al. 2005).

Seeking a broader understanding of early infant-mother relationships

Bowlby, meanwhile, had become increasingly sure that a full understanding of the significance of mother-child relationships was not going to come from psychoanalytic tracts alone. At the time, the main thrust of psychoanalytic accounts tended to suggest that attachment relationships only existed because of their association with feeding (e.g. Freud 1946) and Bowlby felt that no psychoanalytic account could adequately account for separation anxiety. Although some psychoanalytic accounts may have been more compatible with the theory that Bowlby was developing (Fonagy 1999), it seems that, at this point, he felt there was much more to be gained from perusal of theories drawn from other perspectives. Already, his work on homeless children had drawn him into an international and interdisciplinary network of people interested in the psychobiology of the child. In the next years, Bowlby extended and facilitated stronger links among workers in these related fields through, among other things, biennial London-based seminars. The series of books that document these discussions (four volumes edited by Foss, 1961, 1963, 1965, 1969) still provide a fascinating insight into how lively, thought-provoking and fruitful these exchanges must have been.

Highly impressed by the work of Charles Darwin on the theory of evolution and by Darwin as an individual, Bowlby delved further into the fields of ethology, evolutionary and systems theories. Nor did he discount ideas from mainstream academic and clinical psychology, for example, work on information-processing, social cognition, remembering, understanding, as well as studies of grief and mourning both in children and in adults. He had become very interested in studies of effects of social deprivation and maltreatment in animals (e.g. non-human primates and dogs), and was particularly struck by work on imprinting behaviours in birds and other species. As we show in the next chapter, evolutionary theory came to play a fundamental role in the theory of attachment that Bowlby and Ainsworth jointly developed.

A very white and upper middle-class man's theory?

From the description that we have given so far, the reader may have gathered that John Bowlby's childhood was not typical of the majority of children of his time, though it was possibly not that unusual for children growing up in upper middle-class families at that time. In these families, relationships between children and their parents might typically be more distant and formal, and family organisation, aspirations and emotional stresses may be of quite a different order to those of the wider population. This raises questions about how much understanding or insight Bowlby might actually have had into the everyday lives of families where children were not raised by nannies and nursemaids and where parents were much more closely connected with the daily grind of raising small children in far less affluent circumstances. Combine this with the gender discrimination that was so prevalent throughout Bowlby's lifetime and we might justifiably ask whether any theory that Bowlby produced would inevitably be limited by a world view in which sympathetic insight into the nature of mothering and the needs of ordinary mothers would be lacking.

As already mentioned, Bowlby's writings, like those of Sigmund Freud, reflected the belief that the roles of mothers and fathers are, necessarily, qualitatively different: "We've got good evidence that both in the Western world and also in Mexico, they are different – mothers treat children differently from the way fathers do; they are complementary. There's a big overlap but there's a good deal of difference. The differences make perfectly good biological sense and to suppose that they are interchangeable is probably just wrong" (Bowlby et al. 1986, p.52). In the World Health Organization report he asserted that the needs of single-parent mothers and fathers differed too: while fathers should be supplied with domestic help in the home to free them to go out to work, mothers should be given financial incentives to stay at home (Bowlby 1951, 1953/1965). For every hundred mothers in work, he argued, a further 50 people are needed to look after their children, while absenteeism makes mothers unsatisfactory employees. In fact, immediately after the war, nursery provision had been cut and unequal pay for men and women performing the same jobs was the norm. Within this context, arguments against the need for mothers to work may have seemed eminently sensible to Bowlby.

However, such views, at various times, brought Bowlby into conflict with "extreme feminists who take the line, 'I can have my children, I needn't look after them, I'm going to go ahead with my career and I'm damned if I'm going to be handicapped by having to look after children'" (Bowlby et al. 1986, p.51). He often expressed his belief in the importance of parents with passion: "To be a successful parent means a lot of very hard work. Looking after a baby or a toddler is a twenty-four-hour-a-day job seven days a week, and often a very worrying one at that. And even if the job lightens a little as children get older, if they are to flourish they still require a lot of time and attention. For many people today, these are unpalatable truths. Giving time and attention to children means sacrificing other interests and activities. Yet I believe the evidence for what I am saying is unimpeachable" (Bowlby 1984a/1988b, p.2).

By the time Bowlby died, aged 82, in 1990, he had tempered some of his earlier views considerably. By then, though there may have been the beginnings of a shift, of kinds,[10] in his favour on the part of the psychoanalytic community. However, as he developed his theory of attachment, Bowlby often felt distinctly unsupported if not shunned and, it has to be said, at times he may also have spurned them. To the end, he remained a somewhat controversial figure who was highly articulate and often impassioned in his assertions about the importance of the role of mothers in the early lives of their children. In the next chapter, we look more closely at the arguments that he put forward in support of these strong feelings.

---

10 To this day, arguably, Bowlby's Attachment Theory, though dubbed a psychoanalytic theory, sits uneasily in the arms of its conflict-ridden psychoanalytic 'parents'.

2 | Attachment Theory: Basic tenets and major claims

Bowlby's theory of Attachment

As discussed in Chapter One, long before Mary Ainsworth had left for Uganda, and then returned from there to the US, Bowlby had become convinced that the relationship that emerges between infants and their principal carers is important not just for survival but also for later emotional health and wellbeing. He had already begun to feel that the strength of this link and the fundamental significance of the relationship was not well accounted for by any currently available explanations and so had begun to look more widely as he developed his own understanding. While trying to formulate his theory, he drew upon observations and ideas from a wide range of sources, including his knowledge of engineering, psychological models of cognitive processes, learning and of social learning, psychoanalysis, observations of young children and their parents, and findings from evolutionary theory and ethology.

In several papers, Bowlby described how his report on the effects of separation in early childhood had left him dissatisfied with available explanations of the nature of the bond between children and parents. He argued that learning theory could not account for the emotional significance of bonds: ".. the learning theorist seems always to be struggling to cram a gallon of obstreperous human nature into a pint pot of prim theory" (Bowlby 1957a, p.230); "If we adopt the whole-hogging learning theory point of view we shall conceive of Man as an animal with no built-in social responses" (Bowlby 1957a, p.238). In spite of his emphasis on the importance of experience, therefore, Bowlby did not consider that behaviourism or the learning theories which emanated from it, could adequately account for the formation of social bonds. In this sense, he was not a pure environmentalist but believed that a significant part of social bonding in humans must be due to other, possibly biologically pre-programmed, processes (Bowlby 1969/1982).

He also rejected psychoanalytic accounts: "At that time the only theory of the child's tie to his mother was the notion that he learned to become interested in her because she fed him: as Anna Freud put it, a cupboard love theory of love, of human relationships. Well, I didn't go along with that." (Bowlby et al. 1986, p.41). In fact, as Fonagy (1999) points out, other psychoanalytic accounts were available: theorists such as Fairbairn and Suttie had suggested that close attachments may be formed by a primary need for self affirmation which is independent of physical needs. However, Bowlby's search for a more empirically based explanation appears to have discouraged any very serious interest in such views. He rejected the 'cupboard love theory' of attachment formation because he had become increasingly convinced that close observation of human infants showed that they, like other animals, displayed innate biases for social interaction which were independent of the need for food: "There is now abundant evidence that not only in birds but in mammals also young become attached to mother-objects despite not being fed from that source... What is now known of the ontogeny of affectional bonds suggests that they develop because a young creature is born with a strong bias to approach certain classes of stimuli and to avoid other classes" (Bowlby 1969/1982, p.84).

It seems highly likely that this view was influenced by Bowlby's reading within the field of ethology (the study of animals mainly in their natural habitats and also under experimental conditions). Arguably, it was this work that had the most substantial influence on his thinking and so it seems important to spend a little more time considering why it was that Bowlby may have found ethology so interesting.

The influence of ethology on the development of Bowlby's theory of attachment

Already as a student in Cambridge, Bowlby had been very interested in evolutionary biology (Bowlby et al. 1986) and certainly, throughout his life, he was an admirer of the work of Charles Darwin. But it was not until the early fifties that, encouraged by friends such as Julian Huxley and Robert Hinde, Bowlby set himself the task of finding out more about ethology (Bowlby 1960c, Bowlby 1991b). He described his response to this work as follows, "I was at once excited. Here were a body of biologists studying the behaviour of wild animals who were not only using the concepts, such as instinct, conflict and defence mechanism, extraordinarily like those which are used in one's day to day clinical work, but who made beautifully detailed descriptions of behaviour and had devised an experimental technique to subject their hypotheses to test" (Bowlby 1957a, p.231). Elsewhere he wrote, "A main reason I value ethology is that it gives us a wide range of new concepts to try out in our theorizing. Many of them are concerned with the formation of intimate social bonds – such as those tying offspring to parents, parents to offspring, and members of the two sexes (and sometimes of the same sex) to each other... Ethological data and concepts are therefore concerned with phenomena at least comparable to those we as analysts try to understand in man" (Bowlby 1960c, p.313).

What were these concepts? As Bowlby suggested, they were of direct relevance to the question that he was struggling to resolve, the question of what it is that motivates individuals to form social bonds early in life and why these early-formed bonds should be important for later development. To Bowlby, it must have seemed as though ethologists were grappling in a much more concrete and testable way with problems that were at the heart of social interaction. In its classical form, ethology explained behaviour in terms of innate patterns of response (stereotyped behaviours, reflex chains or 'fixed action patterns') to specific environmental stimuli (releasers, or innate releasing mechanisms/IRMs). Ethologists had studied animal behaviours in a huge variety of species and were showing that the behaviours most essential to survival appeared to be characterisable in terms of these reflexive patterns of response to distinctive stimulus configurations.

Aggressive behaviours, for example, stinging in worker honey-bees, had been shown to be triggered by specific attributes such as the smell of human sweat, particular patterns of movement, dark colours and the smell of sting venom; prey-catching in the praying mantis had been found to be associated with how the prey moved at particular distances from the mantis, while chemical and tactile attributes of victims triggered prey-catching in water-beetles. Caregiving behaviour in adults had also been linked with specific attributes of the young in different species, for example, distress calls from conspecific young were found to trigger protective responses from mother hens while female white mice would automatically respond to distress calls in unrelated young mice. Sexual mating behaviours had also been observed to be triggered by distinctive stimulus configurations in different species, for example, male silkworms were more likely to approach a female if their smell was of a particular kind while sexual pursuit of females by male butterflies depended on particular species-specific configurations of components such as wing patterning, colour, size, shape, movement (e.g. speed of wing flicker, forward propulsion, dipping, etc.) and distance; male mounting of females in a variety of species had also been found to depend, for example, on the posture of the female. And feeding behaviours had also received considerable attention, particularly in birds, where specific stimuli (e.g. the red mark on the parent herring-gulls beak) had been shown to elicit beak-opening and food-begging in nestlings.

Ethological investigators did not stop at observation. Using experimental methods that were capable of relatively objective verification and replication, they tested many of the hypotheses formed on the basis of their direct observations. Their perspective therefore afforded a distance from data that Bowlby craved and that most clinicians did not have. To Bowlby (see Figures 2.1a and 2.1b), this must have felt like a breath of fresh air!

Figure 2.1a View from the non-ethologist's perspective

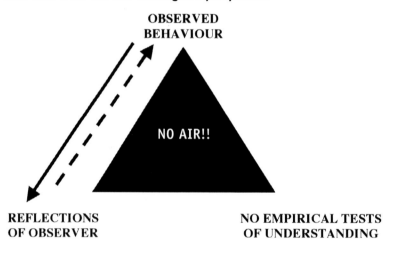

Figure 2.1b View from the ethologist's perspective

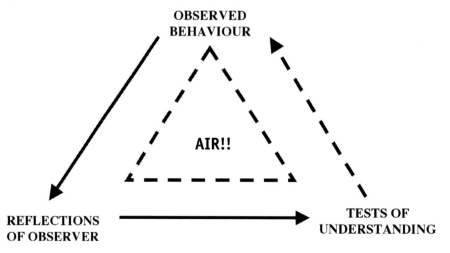

Bowlby's friend and fellow explorer, Robert Hinde (Hinde 1972), further described four separate aspects of animal studies which made them valuable as a means for increasing understanding human behaviour:
1) Practical advantages: They develop potentially relevant methods of observation, recording and analysis.
2) Ethical advantages: Since they may use methods that are not permissible in studies of humans, animal studies can call attention to processes that cannot be studied in humans.
3) Advancing theory: They develop concepts and perspectives that may later be found to be relevant to humans.
4) Cross-species comparisons: Although direct extrapolation from animal to human or from human to animals is not sensible, findings from animal studies can call into question conclusions based only on humans and can provide clues for further investigation.

Bowlby (1976) added two further benefits:
5) Highlighting typical behaviours: Identification of salient patterns in other species can raise the question of whether these patterns are also typical of humans.
6) Experimental demonstration of uncomfortable ideas: If controversial hypotheses are put to the test and results confirm otherwise rejected possibilities, more intelligent debate about these unwelcome ideas is encouraged.

That Bowlby felt the need to add these two further advantages almost certainly reflected his own rather painful intellectual experience. When he first presented his views on the importance of early mother-child relationships for later development, he was quite surprised at how poorly they were received. Animal studies of the effects of early social deprivation and of the nature of imprinting, for example, could enable his opinions to be tested. It also created a dialogue between him and a respected scientific community, in a way that did not happen within psychoanalytic circles. Although his ideas were not necessarily supported, his hypotheses were entertained and this must have decreased his sense of isolation.

In many ways however, the community towards which Bowlby was drawn was no nearer to agreeing upon solutions to any of the fundamental problems being addressed. Numerous and wide-ranging though studies of behaviours in different species were, by the beginning of the fifties, for example, within the entire field of ethology, no consensus had been reached on basic concepts such as the nature of instinct or the relationship between learned and innate behaviours. Indeed, there was still considerable debate about the significance of observed behaviours and how to organise or make sense of all the information being yielded from often very diverse studies. In some senses, then, far from swimming towards calmer waters, the torrent that Bowlby had begun to dabble in was distinctly turbulent. Yet many of the voices calling out across these waters were powerful and resonated much more deeply with Bowlby's own concerns. The work of two men in particular captured his attention, namely, Niko Tinbergen and Konrad Lorenz.

Niko Tinbergen

Niko Tinbergen has perhaps become best known for his description of 'fixed action patterns' in the herring gulls that he observed in Holland, though his studies also encompassed other species, including wasps, fishes and, later in life, humans. By the early 50s, several of his works had become available in English (e.g. Tinbergen 1942, 1950, 1952) while the publication of two books *The Study of Instinct* (Tinbergen 1951) and *Social Behaviour in Animals* (Tinbergen 1953) would also have brought him to Bowlby's attention.

Tinbergen set out to investigate variations in gulls' behaviour both across and within species with the aim of understanding what might explain differences. As a believer in evolutionary theory, he entertained a basic assumption that all behaviour has an adaptive function (a view later questioned by other ethologists) and that its emergence can therefore be explained in four different ways each corresponding to a discrete level of explanation. These levels have come to be known as the "four whys" of ethology (Table 2.1).

Table 2.1: The four whys of ethology

LEVEL OF EXPLANATION	PARAMETER	EXAMPLE Question: What is a butterfly wing?
CAUSAL	PROXIMATE (within individual)	Physiological description: appearance, structure, what it does, how it works
ONTOGENY	PROXIMATE (within individual)	How it changes across the lifespan; what makes it more or less efficient
FUNCTION	ULTIMATE (history of species)	Its contribution to species survival: role in sexual reproduction, promotion of fitness
EVOLUTION	ULTIMATE (history of species)	How and why it evolved: why in this form, how it has adapted to particular environments

Tinbergen suggested that the function of any specific behaviour would only be fully understood if careful attention were paid to questions at all four levels. In his work on feeding behaviour in herring gulls, he demonstrated the value of this perspicacious approach. He observed several ways in which adult gull behaviours enhanced the chances of survival of fledgling gulls, including turning eggs during incubation to ensure that the embryos developed evenly, removing broken eggshells after hatching to reduce the risk of attack from predators, regurgitating food in response to chicks pecking on their bill, quickly learning to identify their own chicks by distinctive markings, responding to particular postures and calls made by fledglings and so being able to be very effective in driving non-related gulls out of the chicks' feeding area, etc. Pecking behaviour in young gulls was observed to coincide with their sight of the red spot on a parent gull's bill. Experimentation using models of varying shapes of adult head, bills of different lengths and with different types of red spot (varying in hue, intensity, size, etc.) showed the difficulty of eliciting responses from stimuli that were insufficiently similar, yet also demonstrated that more vigorous responses could be elicited if key characteristics were exaggerated in ways that would not be naturally encountered.

These observations led Tinbergen to formulate his theory of 'fixed action patterns', stereotyped sequences of behaviour that had a distinct adaptive purpose and which, when interrupted or frustrated, could lead to non-consummatory or 'displacement' activities. Both he and Lorenz suggested that these stereotyped patterns, once elicited, would continue regardless of changes in the triggering stimulus. For this (and other) reasons, Tinbergen considered the possibility that these patterns might be associated with particular neural configurations which had evolved to maximise the chance of species survival and which were instinctive and unalterable. He defined instincts as behaviours that conformed to three criteria (Tinbergen 1951), that is, they:

- are not changed by learning
- are genetically determined
- are subject to evolution (i.e. they must have an adaptive function).

Subsequent work has challenged this view (Hinde 1982a 1982b, Archer 1992), suggesting a far more complex relationship between learning and reflexive behaviours. While the value of describing species-typical behaviours is still recognised, the term 'fixed action pattern' has been brought into question and has sometimes been modified in an attempt to acknowledge the fact that the most commonly occurring species-typical behaviours are not usually as fixed and invariable as either Tinbergen or Lorenz believed. This point is further addressed in our discussion of Lorenz' work on imprinting.

Another aspect of Tinbergen's work reflected in Bowlby's theory of attachment is the concept of behavioural control systems. Both Tinbergen and his colleague, Baerends, attempted to describe the nature of complex patterns of gull behaviour. Tinbergen had noted that although potentially competing sets of behaviours might be expected to be elicited by the presence of multiple triggers, this rarely appeared to result in a conflict between the different motivations. To account for this outcome, he postulated the existence of a hierarchy among the various behaviour systems, so that activation of a more dominant system would inhibit the less dominant systems. Behaviours related to feeding or preening, for example, would be inhibited if distress signals from chicks or other adult birds elicited protective or escape responses or if other danger signals indicated the presence of an intruder. The systems highest in the hierarchy, in other words, are those that ensure basic physical safety. Once this is assured, other systems such as those concerned with increased physical wellbeing, extending territory, increasing resources, and so on, can come into play.

Baerends produced highly complicated models of sequences of behaviour, identifying first low-level simple behaviours such as snapping, shaking, stroking, pecking, quivering, ruffling, waggling, each of which served slightly higher-level sub-systems such as trimming, nest-building, locomotion, which, in turn, contributed to higher-level systems such as incubation of eggs, preening or escape. At the highest level were systems relevant to sexual reproduction and physical maintenance. Behavioural systems were divided into those which were goal-directed and those without goals (which would include fixed action patterns that, once triggered, would only terminate once the full sequence had run). Goal-directed systems would each have their own 'set goal' and would be activated by comparison processes the outcome of which indicated a discrepancy between current state and goal. As we discuss in Chapter Three, Bowlby incorporated this kind of control systems theory into his theory of attachment.

Konrad Lorenz

The work of Konrad Lorenz on filial imprinting is well known, not least because of the availability of stunning pictures showing the welly-booted Lorenz trailed by a long string of goslings or swimming in a pond with the gaggle of goslings in pursuit. These pictures powerfully portray the effect of interference in natural social bonding processes. By presenting himself to a brood of newly hatched goslings, who were biologically pre-programmed to follow the first figure that loomed before them, Lorenz had tricked the unsuspecting birds into becoming imprinted on him. They subsequently followed him about and treated him as they would have treated their natural mother (who, of course, in more natural conditions, would normally have been the first social being they would have encountered). Once imprinted on Lorenz, however, nothing altered the goslings' preference for him.

Such a demonstration of the gullibility (excuse the pun) of precocial birds drew attention to the delicate nature of imprinting. What was the significance of the fact that young birds could be seduced into becoming attached to a man who was neither one of their species nor even a phylogenetically close relative? Just how easy was it to re-direct pre-programmed proclivities so that later development would be completely thrown off course? If, by altering events in the 'average expected environment' of young hatchlings within this very narrow time window, such startling outcomes could be achieved, surely this indicated that what happens in early development is of crucial importance? The obvious resonance between these findings and Bowlby's own views is difficult to miss.

Lorenz' first reports on imprinting appeared in the 1930s though it was not until much later that English translations became more easily available (Lorenz 1951). In a seminal work, Lorenz (1937) had described imprinting processes in several species of birds. For example, by experimenting with different kinds of object presented to newly hatched birds at different times after hatching, Lorenz had established that certain parameters constrained their capacity to imprint. Ducklings, for example, could be induced to imprint on a wooden decoy duck emitting recorded duck-like sounds but only if the decoy was presented within a time window of nine to seventeen hours after birth. They had also been observed to become imprinted on a moving cardboard box. Ducklings reared in social isolation for longer than a day no longer appeared to respond in the same way. Since attaching to a protective adult bird was thought to be important for survival, socially deprived ducklings were inevitably at much greater risk from predators.

While Lorenz' work described subtle variations in imprinting processes in birds of different types and in different natural habitats, it clearly indicated the existence of instinctive social bonding processes across all species observed. In other words, his data appeared to support explanations at several levels of how and why social bonds were formed in birds: he explained how and when imprinting occurred (the causal and ontogenetic explanations); he suggested that its function was to decrease the likelihood of predation and so to increase the chances of survival for the individual bird and, ultimately, by preserving a socially engaged and competent individual, increasing the likelihood of fitness[1] and sexual reproductivity in the species (the third level of explanation); in addition, his observations of variations between species gave some indication of the way that imprinting processes might have evolved as adaptations to different habitats.

Lorenz (1937) described five defining characteristics of the imprinting process:
- it occurs only during a limited or *critical* time period
- it is irreversible
- it occurs automatically and spontaneously (instantaneously)
- it is generally species-specific and facilitates protection of the young
- it is established before other signs of bonding preferences are observed.

The first two of these criteria re-surface from time to time in some 'hard' forms of attachment theory. For example, it has been claimed that early skin-to-skin contact is essential if mothers and infants are to be able bond with each other well, that lack of sensitively responsive care in the first two years can prevent optimal development of the part of the infant brain responsible for social interaction and that poor social skills might be traced back to birth-related trauma. We examine the evidence for these claims in Chapter Six but,

---

1 Fitness in ethological terms relates to the capacity of one individual to contribute to the next generation.

for the present, confine our comments to noting that, in the early days of the development of his theory, Bowlby seriously considered the possibility that imprinting processes might form a template for human attachment relationships.

Even by the time he wrote the first book of his trilogy, Bowlby (1969/1982) was aware that at least the first three of the characteristics specified by Lorenz as defining the imprinting process had been challenged and that Lorenz' hydraulic model of imprinting was no longer tenable (Bowlby 1957a, p.234). Even so, he still considered that certain aspects of imprinting were valuable in explaining how social bonds develop in all species: "Once Lorenz's experiments were repeated and his findings verified, it was natural to consider whether attachment behaviour in mammals and in man himself develops in a comparable manner. There is now substantial evidence that it does so" (Bowlby 1969/1982, p.260). Bowlby referred here to the propensity that human infants have from very early on to produce behaviours such as clinging, crying, calling and smiling that are very similar to those seen in other species. He believed that babies instinctively produce these behaviours in response to people even before they have any real understanding that other people exist. He also took the view from ethology that attachment relationships between infants and their main carers must serve an evolutionary purpose, that is, that they must have some kind of value in terms of species survival.

Studies of effects of separation/social isolation in other animals

When Bowlby became interested in ethology, some studies were already being carried out to investigate the impact of early experiences on later development, for example, Harry and Margaret Harlow at the University of Wisconsin were studying non-human primates. Workers besides Lorenz and Tinbergen were also interested in different bird species, and other ethologists were studying other mammals both large and small, such as sheep, goats, cats, dogs, rats, voles, mice, etc. Inspired by Bowlby, Robert Hinde was later also to carry out laboratory-based studies of non-human primates at the University of Cambridge while, in turn, Hinde encouraged Jan Van Lawick-Goodall to study wild chimpanzees in the Gombe.

Researchers who were studying animals in the wild were almost exclusively carrying out observational studies aimed at finding out how animals behave in their natural habitats. Laboratory-based researchers were more likely to be carrying out experiments from a behaviourist perspective, aiming to discover how different animals respond to varied reinforcement schedules or to more or less complex problem-solving tasks. The kinds of questions being asked might be how quickly can a cat reach a food reward if first they have to negotiate a maze, whether an animal can learn to operate a door or which animals can learn to avoid stepping in areas associated with electric shocks. Others investigated effects of drugs or brain lesions on behaviour.

Some experiments were showing how different reward schedules could re-shape animals' natural responses, for example, rats or chicks given consistent, predictable food rewards for bar-pressing or pecking emitted less frenetic activity than the same animals given less predictable rewards (i.e. rewarding animals for bar-pressing or pecking every third press or peck encouraged faster responding than rewards for every press or peck). Introducing slight changes in reward schedules at strategic points could also increase the rate of responding, for example, not rewarding quite as the animal expected but rewarding at a time which was very close, or giving slightly more food than expected every so often. Even reward schedules that included long periods of no reward at all would not necessarily result in extinction of the once-rewarded response: if responses did eventually become more rare, giving up on responding usually only occurred after a long period at the beginning of which many animals may have frantically increased their rates of responding.[2] Perhaps even more pertinent was the finding that half-starved, underfed puppies became more rather than less prepared to seek social contact with handlers who consistently ignored them than better fed puppies with normally responsive handlers (Stanley and Elliot 1962). In other words, once a connection had been made between reward and behaviour, it was clear that it would take a lot to stop the behaviour altogether. In addition, the relationship between reward and behaviour clearly involved more complex principles than a simple formula such as 'bigger rewards yield more positive responses'. These principles were found to apply across many species and to many kinds of sociable behaviour, including, as we shall discuss next, abusive relationships.

Linking established responses to aversive experiences produced some rather disturbing results. Some of the experiments carried out on imprinting in the mid-twentieth century showed that linking imprinted objects with painful experiences could actually increase contact-seeking! For example, if an object to be imprinted on was uncomfortably cold, far from deterring chicks from following it, it actually encouraged them to follow more, even when contact with the cold object made the chicks so stiff-legged that they could barely move! The same effect was obtained with both chicks and ducklings when imprinted objects were associated with painful electric shocks. Once chicks had started following the imprinted object, even extremely painful shocks introduced within the sensitive period for imprinting did not deter following. Older birds, too, showed preferences for imprinted objects over novel objects, even when the imprinted object was associated with pain. In fact, experiments on chicks were showing that chicks would seek contact even with attachment figures who subjected them to severe abuse. In one experiment, Rajecki et al. (1978) compared the behaviour of chicks who were given pleasant treatment to that of chicks who were pummelled every ten seconds for two and a half minutes by a glove worn by the experimenter. The abused chicks were hit hard enough to be knocked off their feet and against the walls of the cage and showed clear signs of distress. Even so, curiously, in the presence of the offending glove, abused chicks emitted three times as many contentment calls as non-abused chicks! The researchers concluded that "no procedure involving pain has reliably prevented the formation (or greatly altered the existence) of some degree of attachment in precocial birds" (Rajecki et al. 1978, p.424).

In another experiment designed to test the effects of negative social experience in dogs, Fisher (1955) compared four groups of young dogs. Over a three month period (when pups were three weeks old until they were sixteen weeks), the experimenter gave one group of 'indulged' dogs a daily thirty minute session of kind, permissive treatment. A second group of 'indulged-punished' also received this treatment but in addition were given another thirty minutes of contact with the experimenter during which they were mistreated (beaten or given electric shocks). A third group of 'punished' dogs only received the abusive treatment while a fourth group was raised with no human contact at all. Figure 2.2 shows that, when dogs were tested for social orientation (measured as the amount of time spent alongside or in contact with the experimenter), the group of dogs treated both kindly and unkindly showed more contact-seeking than those treated only kindly. Also, even though dogs in the punished group were the least likely to seek contact, they still appeared willing to spend a substantial amount of time close to their abuser. Like the experiments with birds, this seemed to suggest that young dogs, too, could become attached to abusing attachment figures and that the motivation to interact socially was difficult to quash. It also showed that the relationship

---

2   Somewhat like the over-exaggerated sociability observed by the Robertsons in the initial stages of separation in small children.

between amount of contact-seeking and amount of pleasurable interaction was not linear. Contrary to what might be expected, the most pleasurable interactions did not result in the highest amounts of close contact, rather, animals who had experienced an equal mixture of pleasant and unpleasant interaction were the most highly motivated to seek contact. Findings such as these alerted attachment researchers to the need for multiple measures of attachment. Measures of contact-seeking alone could not reflect the full picture. If amount of contact was to be seen as an indicator of the strength or goodness of an attachment, then the message for parents might be to temper kindness with cruelty!

Figure 2.2: Effect of different kinds of treatment on the amount of time dogs spend with their handlers

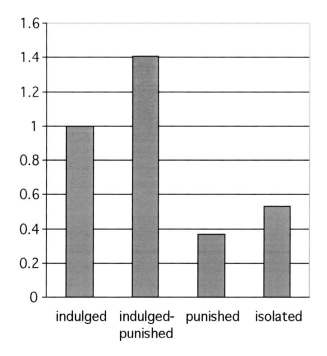

Studies of animals in the wild had already convinced Bowlby that young chimpanzees separated from parents showed extreme distress, very much like children (Bowlby 1969/1982). But experiments which included the study of effects of social isolation were also of particular interest to him because they investigated, in a more controlled way than is usually possible under natural conditions in humans, the effects of particularly severe types of separation of varying lengths, at different points in early development.

During the fifties and later, many experiments of this sort were carried out in the University of Wisconsin by Harry Harlow and his associates, as well as by Hinde here in the UK. Both sets of workers studied the effects of relatively short periods of separation of infant rhesus macaque monkeys from their mothers. The Wisconsin research team also observed other species such as pintail and bonnet macaques, and separated infant rhesus monkeys from their mothers for periods as long as the first 18 months of life. Subsequently, they tracked the effects of this early social deprivation on monkeys' later ability to form relationships, to reproduce and to rear children. They reported severe difficulties. The deprived female monkeys showed high levels of aggression and poor parenting skills that included abuse and a greater propensity to reject offspring (Seay et al. 1964, Harlow et al. 1966).

Such experimentation is not now considered ethical but demonstrated clear negative effects even of relatively short periods of social isolation in early life for monkeys. Baby monkeys isolated from mothers showed signs similar to those observed by the Robertsons in young children. They initially protested, then gradually sank into apathy, became less and less inclined to play and more and more inclined to huddle motionless, even in the presence of peers (some of whom, by adopting the role of 'therapists' and refusing to leave the mourning monkeys in peace, did sometimes manage to re-invigorate them). Reunion with mothers rarely produced instant relief, happiness or contentment. Instead, the infant monkeys regressed, showing more immature behaviours, clinging more than they had before separation, and manifesting other signs of disturbed relationships with their mothers, such as periods of over- or under-activity, tantrums, anger towards the mother and anti-social behaviour to peers. This kind of behaviour was present in all monkeys but more pronounced in some than others. Monkeys whose mothers had been more rejecting of physical contact prior to separations tended to show the highest levels of disturbance both during separation and after reunion.

In several now classic experiments, Harlow and his colleagues had also observed contact-seeking behaviour in young monkeys reared not by live monkey mothers but by inanimate models acting as 'surrogates'. In one well-known experiment (Harlow and Zimmerman 1959), young rhesus macaque monkeys were reared in cages that contained two 'surrogate mothers', one made of wire mesh and the other covered in soft terry cloth. For four of the monkeys, only the cold wire mesh model included a feeding bottle; for the other four, only the warmer cloth model had a feeding bottle attached. If feeding was the key attraction, then all the infant monkeys could be expected to spend most time on the model with the bottle, regardless of how the model was constructed. In fact, this did not happen. Instead, infant monkeys spent very little time on the wire mesh model, whether or not it had the bottle. Rather, they spent most time clinging to the cloth model and did this almost as much when that model did not provide food as when it did. When alarmed, they never went to the wire mesh model but clung to the softer cloth one. They even continued to cling to the cloth model if it delivered aversive blasts of air (which would have been experienced as highly unpleasant). Only if the cloth model was as cold as ice did they reject it.

Findings from this study therefore confirmed Bowlby in his opinion that the need for contact comfort has a significance independent of the feeding situation. It also furnished him with more evidence against the 'cupboard love' theory of attachment proposed by Anna Freud. Feeding alone was clearly not enough to explain the need for baby monkeys to be in contact with mothers. Far from being a secondary reward system dependent upon the primary reward of food, contact-seeking behaviours had been shown to be important in their own right. The way was now clear for Bowlby to develop an alternative account of attachment which provided a more convincing role for contact-seeking and contact-maintaining behaviours. This theory was to expand and build upon his earlier formulations that emphasised the importance of the mother-child tie for later physical and mental health.

In the work of ethologists, Bowlby had found evidence to bolster his deep conviction that children have a primary need for continuous, stable and responsive care. In developing this thesis, he was to argue that, far from being a superfluous by-product of social organisation, the young child's preference for a few rather than many carers was a biological imperative. It simplifies and facilitates a process that involves the passing on of vital information needed by children if they are to be effective as social beings capable both of surviving and of contributing towards the maintenance and continuation of the human species. Bowlby argued that the Attachment Behaviour System is formed in the way that it is because it is a system, much like any other physical system, that is vital both for individual well-being and, ultimately, for the survival of humans as a species. And he stressed that it is important not just in childhood but right through the lifespan.

Central to Bowlby's thesis is the notion that the need for security which humans share with animals has a crucial biological function, "All of us find security in being with people we know well and are apt to feel anxious and insecure in a crowd of strangers. Particularly in times of crisis or distress do we seek our closest friends and relatives. The need for companionship and the comfort it brings is a very deep need in human nature – and one we share with many of the higher animals" (Bowlby 1958b, p.3).

Inability to form or to maintain close and meaningful relationships, Bowlby was to argue, not only puts very young infants at greater risk of physical danger, it also disconnects individuals of any age from society and, by cutting off vital psychological supplies, reduces the likelihood that they will be able to negotiate their social experience or contribute very meaningfully to society. The role of attachment figures and close attachment relationships, throughout the lifespan, is therefore not just to protect the young but to enable the young to learn social skills that will equip them to raise their own young successfully. Throughout the entire lifespan, the attachment behaviour system is therefore a key survival mechanism. In the next section, we outline Bowlby's account of how attachment behaviours develop.

The emergence of attachment behaviour in early childhood

Bowlby had noted that, in human infants, organised attachment behaviour appears to emerge gradually, beginning with random reflexive acts associated with social orientation and, usually, developing over the first few years into more effective, organised patterns (Table 2.2).

Table 2.2: Phases in the development of the attachment behaviour system

	PHASE	AGE AT ONSET
I	PRE-ATTACHMENT	0 (or in pregnancy?)
II	ATTACHMENT-IN-THE-MAKING	c6-12 weeks onwards
III	CLEAR-CUT ATTACHMENT	c7 months onwards
IV	GOAL-CORRECTED PARTNERSHIP	c4 years

Phase I: Pre-attachment

In the first phase, according to Bowlby (1969/1982), infants do not demonstrate any obvious preference for particular carers but instead orient indiscriminately toward sounds, smell, touch and visual stimuli that are presented within their perceptual range. Even at this stage, infants show a propensity for social interaction, although most of their actions are reflexive and accidental rather than intentional. Reflex actions include rooting, sucking, grasping and swallowing and the baby is also equipped with signalling behaviours such as crying, smiling and other non-verbal noises. It is noticeable, too, that newborn babies look very different from older children, being smaller, having a different head-to-body ratio and generally having softer, stubbier features. This point must seem rather obvious but this, too, is thought to attract positive attention from older con-specifics (as others of the same species are called in the jargon of ethology) and so to improve the chances that infants will survive.[3]

All these signs indicate that newborns are pre-disposed to orient socially while carers are pre-disposed to respond to their babies' in a protective and nurturing manner. This suggests that, as they are not 'blank slates' waiting for life to write on them (as some 'environmentalists' or 'empiricists' believed) and that, as most babies from the start are biased toward social engagement, it will take particular conditions to extinguish this bias. This is an important point which we discuss further in later chapters (especially Chapters Five and Six).

Over the last few decades, research has been showing that infants respond preferentially, even within hours of birth, to the sound of their mothers' voices, rather than to the voice of a female stranger (DeCasper and Fifer 1980, Field 1985, Mehler et al. 1978), and that they prefer to listen to a story previously read to them in utero by their mother than to another story (DeCasper and Spence 1986). There is also some evidence that newborns can imitate tongue-poking within hours of birth (Meltzoff and Moore 1977, 1993), a fact that has been taken by some to indicate self-other representational capacities even at this early age. This view is held by several groups of researchers investigating the nature of early interactive experiences, including Colwyn Trevarthen and Elizabeth Fivaz-Depeursinge whose work is further discussed in Chapter Five. However, there are several alternative interpretations of these data and the fact that infants will also tongue-poke in response to an inanimate configuration, for example, a pencil being poked towards them through a ring (Jacobson and Kagan 1979) might suggest that their responses are reflexive rather than mediated by higher cognitive functions requiring concepts of self and other.

In sum, there does seem to be some support for Bowlby's view that preferential orientation governed by the capacity to hold an image of a caregiver in mind even in their absence may not be associated with the first months of life and that it may only emerge when infants have reached Piaget's stage of object permanence, that is, when more advanced memory and cognitive skills have appeared. But this view has been challenged and there continues to be considerable debate about when attachments to specific people are first encoded, what these representations might comprise and what impact the disruption of early attachment relationships might have on the developing sense of self.

Phase II: Attachment-in-the-making

In the second phase, the quality of the relationship between the baby and key attachment figures changes. Rather paradoxically, human infants seem to become more not less dependent on particular adults so that, by the end of their first year, most infants will have begun to form a very close relationship with one person or a few chosen people. As Bowlby remarked, "What puzzles so many human parents is that, instead of becoming more independent during their first two years or so, their infants become more and more attached as they get older" (Bowlby 1958b, p.4). Not only does the baby begin to direct attachment behaviours more consistently towards specific people but those people tend also to be better at calming the

---

[3] The possibility that attachment relationships between parents and offspring may alter as the baby's shape and size becomes less cute has not been the subject of extensive research but is worth noting (Prevatt-Goldstein 2004).

baby if s/he is upset. In fact, a rudimentary hierarchy of preferred figures might begin to emerge at this stage, with some people being turned to more readily than others.

Bowlby, slipping rather unfortunately into the dubious habit of his fellow men in white coats of speaking in the language of sandal-wearing men in togas or tunics, called this tendency to have a hierarchy of preferences for people 'monotropy' (meaning literally, 'turning towards one'). By this, apparently, he never intended to suggest, as many people have subsequently assumed, that babies only become attached to one person.[4] Nor did he ever stipulate that that person must be the infant's biological mother (e.g. Bowlby 1958a, 1958b). Perhaps, had he spoken English rather than Greek, this mistake might never have arisen. He did acknowledge, though, that the person to whom most infants direct most of their attachment behaviours during their first few years is usually their mother because, in the society with which he was most familiar, mothers did tend to be the principal caregivers (as already remarked, in his own experience, fathers very often took a back seat when it came to one-on-one caregiving).

Phase III: Clear-cut attachment

At any time from six or seven months, though sometimes not until the beginning of the next year, most infants begin to organise their attachment behaviours to achieve a 'set goal' of proximity, that is, they will begin to show uneasiness if, for any reason, they sense that key people are not available. Although some infants take longer than others to establish clear patterns, during this third phase, most babies begin to show consistent preferences about how much distance they will tolerate between themselves and their attachment figures. Some babies will not venture far away and become easily alarmed whereas others are more confident. Some babies in an unfamiliar social setting will not be comfortable unless the key figure is physically close or even holding them. Others seem happy enough so long as the key figure is around somewhere. And other patterns also exist. These differences, though to some extent influenced by the babies' and the carers' temperaments, were thought by Bowlby and Ainsworth to be more closely linked to the quality of the relationships between infants and their key attachment figures.

During this stage, babies begin to be more active about making contact with and keeping close to key attachment figures. They monitor the whereabouts of key people, follow if they leave the room and greet them on their return. When they are tired, stressed, unwell or in any other form of danger or need, infants at this age will usually seek attention from particular people and will not be comforted by any but the chosen few. They often now also begin to use the key figures more as a secure base from which to explore, checking back with them for guidance or reassurance, wanting to show things that they have found and sharing new experiences. In this way the key figure, or figures, are recruited by infants at this stage to help with making sense of new experiences. Again, individual differences can be observed in ways that infants make use of their chosen attachment figures.

In this third phase, infants are thought to be able to discriminate between people to be trusted and those to be feared. When an unfamiliar person appears, they often become anxious and may retreat to the attachment figure, seeking reassurance. This does not mean

---

4   Bowlby (1969, p.362 footnote) wrote: "…it has sometimes been alleged that I have expressed the view that mothering should always be provided by a child's natural mother, and also that mothering "cannot be safely distributed among several figures" (Mead, 1962). No such views have been expressed by me."

that, if their principal attachment figure is temporarily unavailable, infants at this stage will not be able to bear separation since other figures in the hierarchy of attachment relationships that has begun to form may be able to substitute: "Certain other people (*i.e. other than the mother*) are selected to become subsidiary attachment figures; others are not so selected" (Bowlby 1969/1982, p.321). Even so, lengthy separations from key attachment figures at this age were thought by Bowlby to cause most infants considerable distress and to lead to the kind of separation responses outlined in Chapter One. Bowlby attributed this to limited cognitive ability and explained that it is not usually until the age of about three or even four that children begin to tolerate separation better. By this time, he considered, young children generally become more able to keep alive a sense that key figures, though absent, are still available.

Nevertheless, already in this phase, Bowlby postulated the existence of rudimentary mental representations of close social interactions, that is, what he came to refer to as 'internal working models'. Though not yet well integrated, due both to the baby's openness to new experiences (i.e. not yet having enough experience to be sure of what to expect) and to their relatively immature ability to order memories sequentially, infants are now usually beginning to build up a store of memories of intense social interactive experiences and to have some more consistent sense of themselves in relation to others.

In the second volume of his trilogy, Bowlby (1973a) put forward three propositions in relation to the nature of mental representations of interactions with key attachment figures:
1) Children who are confident that attachment figures will be available when needed will be much less prone to either intense or chronic fear; conversely children lacking this confidence will be far more prone to intense or chronic fear
2) Confidence in the availability and responsiveness of attachment figures is only acquired gradually during infancy, childhood and adolescence (a 'sensitive period') but these expectations tend to persist, often at an unconscious level, throughout life
3) These expectations about the availability and responsiveness of attachment figures are "tolerably accurate reflections of the experiences those individuals have actually had" (Bowlby 1973a, p.235).

Bowlby was careful to emphasise that this account lay somewhere between the view that expectations are formed early and never change and the alternative view that expectations are always completely independent of real experience. He stated that, "the period during which attachment behaviour is most readily activated, namely from about six months to about five years, is also the most sensitive in regard to the development of expectations of the availability of attachment figures; but that nevertheless sensitivity in this regard persists during the decade after the fifth birthday, albeit in steadily diminishing degree as the years of childhood pass" (Bowlby 1973a, p.236).

Phase IV: Goal-corrected partnership

Bowlby identified the fourth phase as possibly beginning not much before age three or four, when memory and thinking skills have developed enough for children to begin to be able to take into account reflections on their own experiences and feelings, and when they have more understanding of the plans and intentions of other people. Goal-corrected behaviour will already have begun to develop throughout Phase Three to some extent but it now becomes more highly informed by expectations based on previous patterns of social experience. Earlier memories of intense experiences with key figures have now begun to become more organised into what workers in the field of social cognition (understanding and interpretation of social interactions) have referred to as schema, scripts or generalised event representations (Nelson and Gruendel 1981, Schank and Abelson 1977), what Stern later described as 'Representations of Interactions that have been Generalised' or RIGS (Stern 1985) and what Bowlby referred to as 'internal working models' or mental representations of self in interaction with others. These early schema or scripts are usually far less complex than the internal narratives that develop later in childhood but they will already be beginning to form the basis for children's appraisal of social situations. Not only do they increase most children's ability to keep alive a sense of their attachment figures' availability when those people are no longer physically present, but they can also increase their ability to negotiate with others effectively.

In developing his notion of 'internal working models', Bretherton (1995) explains that Bowlby (1969/1982) drew upon an idea he had come across while reading the work of a neurobiologist called Young. This work had introduced him to Craik's concept of 'internal working models' which were essentially concerned to explain decision-making rather than emotional processes. Craik (1943) suggested that the way we make sense of our perceptions and experience is by constructing rough, relatively undetailed mental models of the dynamic relationships between actions and their consequences. These 'mental experiments' are used to inform our understanding and to guide our actions and consist of prototypes or adjustable sketches rather than fully worked-out 'set in stone' accounts of any possible scenario. The more flexible the model, the more likely it is to be capable of adapting appropriately to ongoing experience. As Bretherton points out, Bowlby's notion of internal working models elaborated on Craik's emotion-free model but retained the basic principle of being a mental experiment: "Bowlby's characterization of representation as 'internal working models' calls for a representational system that is able to simulate experience of self-with-other. Such a representational system must operate with meaningful event structures (intentional and unintentional actions carried out by agents on objects or vis-a-vis other agents) rather than lists of cognitive categories" (Bretherton 1995, p.237).

Internal working models

Some people have considered Bowlby's concept of the 'internal working model' (IWM) as overly cognitive and as not having sufficient regard for emotional aspects of children's development. It is difficult to fathom quite what the source of this criticism might be. While the notion of a working model might conjure up computer models based on binary or linear processing, this does not seem to be what Bowlby had in mind, at all. Rather, he suggested that, from a very early age, children begin to use their memories and experiences of themselves in interaction with significant others to make sense of new experiences. In doing this, they form 'internal working models' which are built up from their impressions of what happens to them when they encounter other people. These IWMs are therefore made up of salient experiences which almost always carry a strong affective element which is often only partially processed consciously and, so, possibly only partially accessible to conscious inspection. To think of them just as a set of abstract and neutral thoughts is therefore a mistake.

As mentioned earlier, Bowlby considered the basic structure of 'internal working models' as being formed by result of actual experiences. Once formed, internal working models operate as a set of working hypotheses governing the way children expect others to behave towards them and, consequently, how children behave in relation to others. The argument is that children whose real-life experiences of close social interactions have been rewarding will feel valued themselves and will value other people. For these children, the key attachment figures will function as a secure base from which they can explore and to whom they can return when in need of comfort, reassurance or guidance. As a result, they will generally anticipate continued positive experiences and will approach new social situations prepared to expect the best.

For children who have been rejected, abused, humiliated or treated in ways that have left them feeling confused about what to expect from other people, the converse will be the case. Such children will not feel able to use their attachment figures as a secure base and will be more likely to be pessimistic both about the chances of people liking them and about the way people will treat them. However, as suggested by animal studies, due to the intrinsic need to attach, even in these children pessimism is likely to be tempered by a certain motivation towards relating (or 'aggression' which, literally translated, means 'movement towards').

Bowlby described two sets of influences on children's social development. One set concerns actual experiences, including the nature of the relationship between children and their key attachment figures. The second set concerns the sense that children make of their experiences and how this influences future experiences. He wrote: "Throughout life, the two sets of influences interact in complex and circular ways. In one direction the kinds of experience a person has, especially during childhood, greatly affect both whether he expects later to find a secure personal base, or not, and also the degree of competence he has to initiate and maintain a mutually rewarding relationship when opportunity offers. In the reverse direction the nature of the expectations a person has, and the degree of competence he brings, play a large part in determining both the kinds of person with whom he associates and how they then treat him" (Bowlby 1973b/1979c, p.104).

At the outset, then, small children are seen as being open to experience. Gradually, these experiences lead to the formation of internal working models that enable them to make sense of social situations and that inform how they understand and interact with other people. At first, the models are tentative and, since they may or may not be congruent with new experiences, are open to revision. Bowlby believed that this openness to revision, or permeability as he called it, is retained throughout the lifespan to greater or lesser degrees although, overall, there is a gradual trend towards greater rigidity. As children get older, parts of their sets of working hypotheses will usually receive confirmation through experience with the result that these working hypotheses come more and more to resemble beliefs that form the basis for expectations about and interpretations of other people's social behaviour. In consequence, they may or may not enable a child to make the most of new social encounters, by encouraging pre-judgements that are more or less accurate.

Soon, internal working models (IWMs) come to be used almost prescriptively in response to social cues. Instead of treating each situation as if it were a completely new event needing lengthy analysis, IWMs enable swift appraisals derived from many social situations with more or less similar characteristics. However, Bowlby asserted that, "whatever pattern is first established tends to persist. This is the main reason why the pattern of family relationships a person experiences during childhood is of such crucial importance for the development of his personality" (Bowlby 1973b/1979c, p.104). This primacy of early experience is a key tenet of Attachment Theory but, as we have hinted earlier, it was not Bowlby who insisted that only the first years of life matter. This issue is discussed more fully in Chapter Six. Here, we simply note a key tenet of Attachment Theory, namely, that early experiences can be crucially important for later development.

With regard to the accuracy of predictions from internal working models, Bowlby explained that models that have been built up on the basis of painful experiences are likely to give rise to defensive processes that can limit children's ability both to engage positively with others and to understand or acknowledge their own and other people's feelings. On the other hand, Bowlby stated that working models that have been built on the basis of positive interactions between children and their attachment figures can be expected to be freer from defensive distortions. Therefore, they are more likely to contain hypotheses that are better informed by deeper reflection upon experiences and so will be a much better basis for accurate judgements.

Bowlby also described how, due to the fact that children usually have powerful emotional experiences with more than one key figure, it is perfectly plausible for them to have more than one working model of self-in-interaction with others. He suggested that the holding of multiple working models might be associated with psychological disturbance: "A particular clinical and research problem is that disturbed individuals seem often to maintain within themselves more than one working model both of the world and of the self in it. Such multiple models, moreover, are frequently incompatible with each other and can be more or less unconscious" (Bowlby 1973b/1979c, p.118). However, Bowlby also suggested the possibility that, in less disturbed personalities, multiple models may complement each other. In these cases, he postulated that the multiple models could become organised hierarchically so that the most salient models are uppermost and exert the most influence on the individual's understanding of social situations.

Internal working models can therefore be seen to operate in a number of ways in relation to reality. They can:
- be more or less congruent with the child's actual personality
- be more or less affirmed by real life experiences
- represent more or less defensive distortion of real life experiences
- be held more or less consciously
- operate in agreement with each other or not
- be held singly or multiply
- be simple or complex
- distinguish more or less clearly between the roles of self and other.

Bowlby (1988b, p.132) further explained that, "because a child's self-model is profoundly influenced by how his mother sees and treats him, whatever she fails to recognise in him he is likely to fail to recognise in himself. In this way, it is postulated, major parts of a child's developing personality can become split off from, that is, out of communication with, those parts of his personality that his mother recognises and responds to, which in some cases include features of personality that she is attributing to him wrongly." He went on to explain that mothers' failures to recognise parts of their children's personalities can often be traced back to their own childhood experiences, that is, to their own parents' failures to respond to those parts of their children's personalities. We identify this idea as another key tenet of Attachment Theory, namely, that how parents care for their children and for each other is influenced by the care they received themselves from their own parents.

Major tenets of Attachment Theory

Summing up, in this chapter, we have presented an overview of the Bowlby-Ainsworth Attachment Theory and have identified several key tenets which can be listed as follows:
1) Internal Working Models constructed on the basis of secure attachment relationships provide children with social and interpersonal skills and understanding, specifically,

children whose IWMs have emerged from positive relationships will have greater capacity for accurate introspection and so will have superior self and other understanding. This understanding, in turn, will promote success in forming and maintaining social relationships, and in dealing with stressful social encounters.
2) Attachment security is directly linked to children's experience of being parented: greater security is associated with stable, consistent and responsive care. How parents care for their own children and for each other will be influenced by the care they received from their own parents.
3) Early experiences lay the foundations for later development.

Although these tenets underlie most of the proposals that have emanated from Attachment Theory, they are not intended to be inclusive of all of its claims. Rather, they have been selected on the grounds that they can perhaps be seen to represent the claims most closely connected to parenting. Essentially, Attachment Theory proposes that it is within the nature of the relationship between parents and children, and between parents and their own parents, their own parents and their own parents, ad infinitum, that the vital ingredients necessary for the health of future generations lie. It also proposes that the most life-enhancing ingredients will be those associated with secure attachments. And, because of its own 'internal working model' of inter-generational relationships as conduits, it proposes that it is at the earliest time in life, when the hand-over from one generation to another first begins, that it is most important to ensure that undesirable ingredients are syphoned off and desirable ones added in. The hidden message seems to be something along the lines of "Plug that gap! Mend that kink... Catch that parent before it's too late!"

In the next chapters, we attempt to discover the extent to which this rather uni-linear conceptualisation of individual and family development holds water by examining the evidence that has been amassed both for and against it. We will also investigate each of the three key tenets outlined above, the first in Chapter Four, the second in Chapter Five and the third in Chapter Six. In each of these chapters, we will present evidence from research on attachment, evaluate what empirical support there might be for each of the key tenets and try to discover what messages, if any, emerge with respect to requirements for successful parenting.

Before doing this, though, in Chapter Three, we outline and briefly discuss some of the most widely used assessment instruments in research on attachment and the classificatory systems associated with them. In doing this, we draw attention to the way in which the instruments were developed, their scope and some of their limitations. We hope that readers not familiar with attachment research will find this description helpful as they read further and attempt to draw their own conclusions from the evidence that we present in part two of this book. Readers already familiar with the tools used in attachment research may prefer to skip to Chapter Four.

3 Assessing attachment security

Background

When John Bowlby asserted that 40 per cent of mothers do not do a good job, he was basing his assertion on findings from attachment research. This research suggested that, in most non-clinical samples, around 60 to 65 per cent of children are assessed as securely attached to their mothers. The remainder (around 35 to 40 per cent) are not securely attached. In samples where parents or children have psychological or social problems, this proportion can rise as high as, or higher than, 80 per cent. To Bowlby, this provided evidence that the parents of insecurely attached children must be failing them in some way. Whether he would have intended blame to fall quite so heavily is perhaps questionable, but that he felt confident about the veracity of the data that was emerging seems undeniable.

The view that attachment security is linked to good care experiences and insecure attachment to poor parenting has now become widely accepted, among professionals and practitioners, as well as more generally. The message for parents is that their children are testimonies to their own success or failure as parents: "When parents express genuine interest, involvement, and a positive attitude, their children develop more secure relationships within the family group. Children with emotionally connected parents are more attentive and concentrate better. When parents are emotionally reachable and are able to 'read' the emotional signals of their kids, the children will perform better in a wide variety of situations" (Biringen 2004, p.7). This message applies not only to biological parents but to other caregivers too: "*secure* attachment relationships in early childhood setting *promote* the psychological wellbeing of the child; and *insecure* attachment relationships in early childhood settings will have a *negative impact* on the child's wellbeing" (Rolfe 2004, p.219).

But what is attachment security?

In this chapter we consider how such conclusions may have been arrived at and how sound they might be. First, we look at the tools that have been developed to assess quality of attachment and what quality of attachment actually is. We focus particularly on how reliable and valid the instruments are, that is, how confident we can be that they really reflect attachment relationships and attachment behaviours across the lifespan.[1] In doing this,

---

1   It is important to distinguish between tools which assess the quality of attachment relationships and those that focus more on individual attachment behaviours. The former try to capture both (a) the individual's behaviour when the Attachment Behaviour System (ABS) is not highly activated (when the individual might feel relaxed enough to use the attachment figure as a secure base for exploring) as well as when the ABS is highly activated (leading the individual to seek reassurance or a safe haven) and (b) the attachment figure's response to the individual's bids for attention. The latter tend to focus more on the individual's behaviour when the ABS is activated.

because the number of available instruments is now so large, we have chosen to take as examples for our discussion only those that have been most widely used and most extensively tested. A brief description of some of the other assessments that are available can be found in Appendix 3.1 along with, where possible, details of how to obtain these instruments, their scope and their psychometric properties.

The main focus of discussion in this chapter is the Strange Situation procedure (Ainsworth and Wittig 1969, Ainsworth et al. 1978) and two instruments that have been designed to assess attachment in adult relationships, the Adult Attachment Interview (George, Kaplan and Main 1984/1985/1996) and the Relationships Questionnaire (Bartholomew and Horowitz 1991). Fuller details of these instruments and information about how to become trained as a reliable assessor is provided in Appendix 3.2.

As detailed in Appendix 3.2, training in the use of the two best-established attachment assessments (the Strange Situation and the Adult Attachment Interview) is costly and takes some time to achieve. Today in the UK, there are no training centres and no qualified people offering training in either method. In addition, the Strange Situation (SS) requires special facilities and equipment and is only reliable when used with infants aged 12-18 months. Further, both the SS and the Adult Attachment Interview (AAI) are very labour intensive, both in the data-gathering and the data-coding stages. These problems have encouraged the development of alternative, more easily administered measures. These, in turn, have produced a proliferation of papers, mainly associated with attachment in adulthood, based on measures whose validity as assessments of attachment is not always obvious. Against this background, the Strange Situation has often been seen as the 'gold standard'. Throughout this book, we will return to the question of whether we know what it actually assesses and whether it deserves to retain this status.

In the following section, we consider what needs to be done in order to develop a reliable and valid instrument for assessing a psychological construct such as attachment security. We then describe the SS and the AAI and consider how they match up to these requirements.

Developing tools to assess attachment relationships

One of the most convincing ways to test hypotheses is to subject them to experimental test. The objective of this kind of approach is to isolate a particular behaviour of interest, for example, jumping, from all other influences. The experimenter then deliberately attempts to observe how this behaviour changes when different conditions obtain, for example, when ambient temperature is either very high or very low. The chief advantage of this kind of experimentation is that it is accepted as being the most effective way to measure, in a controlled and systematic way, relationships between causes and effects. This was the approach adopted by the Harlows when they investigated effects of rearing rhesus macaque monkeys on inanimate 'mother' models and when they systematically deprived very young animals of normal contact with their natural mothers. However, for ethical reasons, it is not possible to test humans in this way. Indeed, many would argue that such tests on animals are unethical and that, since findings from animal research cannot generalise across species, they do not add much to an understanding of humans anyway.

Whether or not we agree with this view on animal research, it is undeniably true that, although Bowlby was drawn to the work of ethologists largely because they were putting to the test hypotheses that were remarkably similar to his own, direct experimental testing of his theories about the effects of poor maternal care, separation or social deprivation on the later development of children was not an ethical option.

Under these circumstances, there were several alternative possibilities:
1) researchers could carry on regardless of ethical issues
2) they could wait for naturally occurring experimental situations to arise
3) they could carry out 'quasi-experiments' where they have limited control over at least some of the behaviours of interest
4) they could use observational approaches (such as those favoured by ethologists)
5) they could use interview or survey methods, which may or may not include 'projective' tests.

Attachment researchers have tended to opt for the latter four approaches. First, they have, as James Robertson did and others before and after him, observed children separated from biological parents under a variety of circumstances, in hospitals, orphanages or other types of non-parental care (e.g. day care or school). Second, they have used quasi-experimental interventions designed to improve the quality of the relationship between parents (usually mothers referred for professional help) and children. Third, they have used a variety of observational approaches both in natural settings and in the more artificial setting of research laboratories. Fourth, particularly with older children and adults, they have used a proliferation of interview and questionnaire approaches, some of which have included the use of projective tests.

These methods have produced a huge mass of data relevant to attachment relationships across the lifespan. But such non-experimental methods have clear limitations. They can show associations between behaviours but they cannot establish or test causes and their effects. Nor can they specify exactly how behaviours might be associated with each other.[2] It is extremely rare, for example, for a naturally occurring experiment to control all influences sufficiently for confident conclusions to be drawn about the precise relationships between outcomes, preceding events or circumstances that continue to influence outcomes.

The biggest question, therefore, that non-experimental approaches leave is that of which of the many preceding *and* concurrent events are really implicated in outcomes. As an example, we can consider the rare cases of children brought up in complete isolation from human contact, for example, 'wolf children' or children like Genie (Newton 2003). Because we do not know what these children were like before their social isolation began (for example, whether they were born with congenital abnormalities or whether there were birth or pregnancy complications), it is not possible to be sure whether later observed behaviours are due to children's experiences of extreme deprivation or to additional influences no longer available for measurement. The same can be said of many studies of children in day care and children reared in institutions. Some of these studies may also contain children whose circumstances are so unusual and idiosyncratic that, even if sample sizes were large (which they tend not to be), there would be risks in assuming that findings in relation to them could generalise across other samples of children.

---

2   This is the old storks and babies problem: it has been suggested that the origin of the myth that storks bring babies lies in the tendency for birth rates and numbers of storks to rise in the spring. Putting two and two together and making five, as they say, produced the belief that one caused the other. Though we may laugh at such a naive belief, or even disbelieve the tale of its origin(!), scientists (e.g. Wason 1960, Tversky and Kahneman 1974, Ross 1977) have demonstrated that similar errors of judgement are widespread among both adults and children.

The third approach (observational studies) was adopted by Mary Ainsworth, while the fourth approach (interview and questionnaire approaches) have tended to be the main strategy employed by researchers interested in assessing attachment in adolescents and older people. Mary Ainsworth observed mothers and infants both in the familiar environment of their home and in an unfamiliar playroom. In the playroom, Ainsworth systematically manipulated the physical (and psychological) availability of the baby's carer and also introduced an unfamiliar figure. These alterations, which became known as the Strange Situation, were designed to subject the baby to mild but cumulative stress. Under such circumstances, most babies would be expected to seek comfort from their attachment figures so the procedure was designed to elicit attachment behaviours from them. In this way, Ainsworth and her colleagues were able to observe individual differences in patterns of relating. By comparing observational and interview data gathered from both familiar and unfamiliar settings, they began to build up a picture of the nature of attachment relationships (Ainsworth et al. 1978).

For many years, the Strange Situation procedure (Ainsworth and Wittig 1969) was considered the only reliable means of classifying different attachment patterns. Related measures did exist but these often tended to measure constructs attributable more directly to the infant than to the relationship between the infant and his or her carer (e.g. Separation Anxiety tests and Attachment Q-Sorts, described in Appendix 3.1). But what was it, exactly, that the Strange Situation assessed?

How to prove that a psychological test measures what it aims to measure

Psychologists and other social scientists usually adopt tried and tested methods in order to establish that research instruments measure what they are intended to measure. These usually involve several steps:
1) Creating an operational definition of the construct to be measured
2) Testing and making sure that the tool is reliable
3) Testing whether the tool produces valid results.

These steps may sound rather dreary and technical but, as understanding these matters is fundamental to making sense of psychological research, it seems important to consider what the above steps might involve in terms of Attachment Theory and what the consequences might be of devising an assessment tool without having carried them out.

1) Creating an operational definition of the construct to be measured

This involves specifying exactly what is to be measured, a simple enough matter when measuring overt behaviours such as ability to jump, where we can specify, for example, height of jump, speed, number, etc., but much more tricky when it comes to non-overt constructs such as 'thoughtfulness', 'jealousy' or 'attachment security'. To specify or to create an operational definition of an abstract construct like attachment security, it is necessary first to identify all the relevant behaviours to be observed in relation to it so that they can be observed and recorded.

Readers may remember that Ainsworth and Bowlby had already identified a series of attachment behaviours that emerged in infants during the first years of life. These included behaviours such as smiling, looking, calling, crying/protesting, reaching towards, approaching, following and clinging. Ainsworth further identified social interactive behaviours related to activation of the Attachment Behaviour system in one-year-olds. These included proximity- and contact-seeking, contact-maintaining, resistant/angry behaviour, avoidance and distance interaction.

Because Ainsworth regarded the observational technique that she had developed as an exploratory tool for investigating the nature of attachment relationships and did not appear to have expected it to become used as a 'benchmark' assessment instrument in the way that it did, neither she nor Bowlby attempted to create any operational definitions of attachment security on the basis of the attachment behaviours that they had identified. In a 1979 presidential address to the Society for Research in Child Development, Ainsworth explained how, once the exploratory stage was past, she hoped to be able to dispense with the Strange Situation procedure, "the more we use... [the Strange Situation], the sooner we can be finished with it" (Waters and Beauchaine 2003, p.3).

The Strange Situation procedure, therefore, produced a classificatory system which still functions as a set of 'working definitions' of different patterns of attachment in one-year-olds. The classification of attachment relationships developed by Ainsworth et al. (1978), however, being more concerned with observation and description of individual variations in response, did not produce any formal operational definition either of attachment security or of attachment behaviour system activation. For this reason, identification of observable attachment-related behaviours throughout the lifespan, equivalent to those observed in one-year-olds, has also proved difficult. Two fundamental problems confront attachment researchers:
a) how to assess attachment behaviour at later stages given that attachment needs are often expressed and met less overtly at later ages
b) how to be sure that tools devised for assessment at later stages really measure the same construct.

2) Testing and making sure that the tool is reliable

Once an instrument has been devised, its properties need to be clearly specified so that it can be used reliably. This process is called standardisation and ensures that, each time the assessment is carried out, measurement errors do not creep in due to different ways of measuring. Standardisation is needed both in data gathering and data analysis if researchers are to be able to compare results across studies.

Ainsworth et. al (1978) provided a comprehensive account of most aspects of the Strange Situation procedure but some aspects of the procedure were not standardised. Although to some extent these problems can be contained if researchers are trained rigorously, this tends to be a less efficient way of protecting against unwanted variability. With regard to the data-analysis stage, as mentioned earlier, Ainsworth had not anticipated that the classification system she had evolved would be the definitive method for classifying patterns of attachment. Rather, it was a work in progress and, though her classification system was on the whole based on very clear criteria, it did not classify all the children even in the small sample that she initially observed. This left room for further development and exploration which has had the advantage of enabling new categories to be identified. But it also had the disadvantage of introducing some inconsistency as well as a potential for disagreement where different groups of researchers have been engaged on developing different systems of classification (e.g. the divergence between the group led by Mary Main and that led by Patricia Crittenden, discussed later in this chapter).

3) Testing whether the tool produces valid results

As well as ensuring the instrument's *reliability*, it is necessary to make sure that it is *valid*, i.e. that it measures what was intended or performs as expected. To examine this, its performance is tested to see if it produces:
a) the same results as other instruments measuring the same construct *(concurrent validity)*
b) results that are not the same as instruments measuring different constructs *(discriminant validity)*
c) results that predict future performance in line with expectations *(predictive validity)*.

Concurrent validity

Since there were no other tools available, Ainsworth was not able to demonstrate the validity of her assessment directly. Until additional tools became available, therefore, the concurrent validity of the Strange Situation procedure could not be tested. This is not unusual when an instrument is being developed to pioneer a new field of investigation for which no ready-made assessment tools are available.

However, because of the problem of not having an operational definition of the construct, even after other tools had been developed to assess attachment relationships, in infancy and at other ages, it has proved difficult to be confident that the different instruments do assess exactly the same thing as each other.

One strategy that is often adopted when an instrument is unique in measuring a construct, as the Strange Situation procedure was, is to rely, in the first instance, on comparisons with measures of related constructs, such as Separation Anxiety. Some of these are listed in Appendix 3.1. This kind of comparison can gradually build up a picture of how the 'mystery' new construct relates to other constructs. Much early work on attachment involved this kind of descriptive, comparative study.

Discriminant validity

Tests of discriminant validity show whether the assessment tool *does* measure construct A, as intended, and not constructs B to Z. This means that the tool produces a different pattern of scores to those produced by tools designed to measure other constructs.

When construct A is not clearly defined, i.e. when there is no clear operational definition of construct A, a potentially serious threat is posed: instead of measuring the ill-defined construct A, the tool may, inadvertently, capture effects of other related constructs.

The way that the procedure for assessment of attachment relationships developed seems to have risked this potential difficulty. Because Ainsworth was keen to observe as wide as possible a spectrum of patterns of attachment and degrees of attachment security and so refrained from premature creation of an operational definition of secure attachment behaviour, she laid herself open to the possibility that her assessment procedure would pick up on variations in behaviour that were due to many other influences besides the one she sought to investigate. Potential influences include individual attributes (e.g. intelligence, temperament), attributes more or less closely related to social class, cultural or educational experience (e.g. parents' education, socio-economic status, articulacy or language ability, performance on tests of cognitive ability, etc.) and influences related to social interactive experience (such as capacity for empathy, emotional self-regulation; social conformity, conservatism, moral integrity, etc.). While the latter group of influences, related to social interactive experience, can be expected to vary as a function of attachment status, those related to individual attributes or social contextual characteristics are not.

This means that if, for example, it were to be found that all the differences between securely and insecurely attached individuals could be explained in terms of differences on another attribute, such as IQ or emotional self-regulation, we would need to question whether attachment security exists at all. To prove that attachment security is a valid construct, it is necessary to demonstrate that it varies independently of other factors to which it is theoretically unrelated. In the next chapter, we look at how well the construct of attachment security fares in respect of discriminant validity.

Predictive validity

Tests of predictive validity are used to find out whether the assessment tool can reliably predict future performance. For example, it might be expected that securely attached infants will score higher than insecurely attached infants on measures of positive interaction in play with their mothers. If evidence fails to support this prediction, the validity of the assessment would come into question.

Mary Ainsworth claimed that the Strange Situation procedure identified different patterns in attachment relationships and, later, that it discriminated between groups of children, some of whom could be described as securely attached and some insecurely attached. Since both Bowlby and Ainsworth believed that children who are securely attached differ from those who are insecurely attached in major ways, such as being less likely to have behaviour problems or to be anti-social, more likely to have carers who are kind and caring, etc., they could predict that children classified as secure in the Strange Situation test would score higher on measures of social skills, psychological adjustment, etc. than children classified as insecure, and that the behaviour of the attachment figures of securely attached children would differ in predictable ways from that of insecurely attached children. In the next chapter, we also look at how well the construct of attachment security fares in respect of predictive validity.

Does it matter that no operational definition of attachment behaviour across the lifespan exists?

Lack of an operational definition of attachment security across the lifespan has certainly not deterred researchers from exploring the nature of attachment behaviour and nor does it appear to have prevented Attachment Theory from stimulating much lively debate or from being influential in many spheres of public life. In some form or other, the theme of attachment crops up in an enormous number of discourses, among parents and professionals, across a wide number of disciplines and orientations, from social care and policy, through education to more abstract studies such as literary criticism, art history, etc. There is no denying that Attachment Theory is an extremely fertile theory.

In practice, lack of an operational definition seems to have acted as a spur rather than as a brake. It has produced and seems set to continue to produce more efforts to define and measure attachment security (e.g. Cummings 2003). But this also seems to have resulted in a certain degree of confusion. It is not really clear exactly what quality or construct assessments of attachment tap, nor how the constructs that they tap relate to each other, if at all.

In some ways, perhaps, this does not matter. If different tools converge towards similar conclusions, then the chances that they all tap near enough the same construct, it could be argued, are likely to be very high. On the other hand there remains a logical possibility that, if this fundamental lack of a clear definition is overlooked or unsatisfactorily resolved, erroneous conclusions may be drawn. The various tools could be converging towards the same conclusions only because the central construct they all tap is so vague and amorphous.

Waters and Beauchaine (2003, p.418) urge that true taxonomies "should be considered suspect because we so readily see patterns and types when there are none. And because we find the simplification afforded by typological thinking and description so agreeable... We are simply too good at abstracting categories and types to believe our own eyes". They argue the need for caution on the grounds that categories can lead to misconceived social policies based on unfortunate stereotypes and prejudices.

Ainsworth's classification system, and many others since, cannot definitively answer the question of what variations in attachment behaviour signify in the absence of an operational definition of attachment security across the lifespan. This fundamental question seems to have become more and more deeply buried under the welter of research findings that have so rapidly amassed. At the risk of appearing to take the role of the Bad Fairy (or the much-maligned fairy, depending on one's perspective), we have decided to try to exhume it and see whether we can find out exactly what it is that assessments of attachment relationships really measure. In doing this, one concern that is uppermost throughout this book is the possibility that assessments may be the product of a value system based on stereotypes and prejudices against less frequently occurring patterns rather than a more objective assessment based on an acceptance of diversity.

In the next part of this chapter, we consider the Strange Situation procedure, the classificatory systems that have developed from it and their implications for children. Next, we discuss other two Adult Attachment assessment tools and the classificatory system that emerge from them.

The Strange Situation Procedure

The Strange Situation procedure was devised with the aim of eliciting attachment behaviour so that the nature of the relationship between infants and their attachment figures could be observed and assessed. Both Bowlby and Ainsworth were careful to distinguish between attachment behaviours and organised attachment patterns associated with attachment relationships. As explained in Chapter Two, Bowlby considered that attachment behaviours emerge early in the first year of life but do not start becoming organised within attachment relationships until the second half of the first year of life. Around this time, infants begin to show anxiety about separation from key attachment figures and, by the beginning of the second year (12 months and upwards), clearer patterns of organised attachment behaviour have begun to be established.

Mary Ainsworth, following Bowlby's lead in focusing clearly upon separation experiences, devised the Strange Situation procedure to observe more closely the behaviour of infants at a developmental stage during which separation anxiety responses are normally intense and when infants have usually begun to develop individual strategies to cope with their anxiety. She recommended that her procedure should only be carried out with infants aged between 12 and 18 months and suggested (Ainsworth et al. 1978) that towards the older end of this age range, the procedure becomes less reliable. She stressed the need to ensure that at the start of the Strange Situation procedure, infants are not ill, tired, hungry or in pain. As a psycho-diagnostician, she also saw the importance of supplementing information gathered from the artificial setting of the Strange Situation test with contextual information about the infants' behaviour in other, more natural, settings.

In the Strange Situation procedure, infant-carer dyads are observed as they interact in a playroom that is equipped with video-cameras. When Ainsworth first developed the procedure, researchers observed through a two-way mirror and took narrative records. This method was soon replaced by video recordings which are more satisfactory, providing that the quality of recording is good enough, because they enable replays of sequences and can be judged by people who do not have direct contact with or information about the people being assessed (being 'blind' in this way increases the likelihood that judgements will be objective).

At the start of the procedure, after introducing the carer[3] to the playroom, the researcher explains to the mother what will happen (see Table 3.1). The mother is instructed to respond to any bids from her baby as she normally would but only to initiate play if the child has not started playing after two minutes. She is also told how she will be signalled so that she knows when she needs to leave the room.

---

3   For ease, we will refer to the carer as the mother, although the Strange Situation procedure has been used with fathers, mothers, nursery nurses, Israeli metapelet and other attachment figures.

Table 3.1: Episodes in the strange situation procedure

EPISODE	DESCRIPTION	PEOPLE PRESENT	TIME (minutes)	
1	Mother and baby introduced to room	Mother Baby Researcher	30 secs	
2	Mother reads while baby explores; mother only encourages infant to play if necessary	Mother Baby	3	
3	Stranger enters, sits quietly opposite mother Stranger talks to mother about baby Stranger approaches baby, mother slips out	Mother Baby Stranger	1 1 1	3 in total
4	Stranger with baby (First separation)	Baby Stranger	3 or less*	
5	Mother calls from outside room then enters Stranger leaves; Mother settles baby back to play (First reunion)	Baby Mother	3 or more*	
6	Mother leaves again, saying goodbye Baby alone (Second separation)	Baby	3 or less*	
7	Stranger enters room and interacts with baby as necessary	Baby Stranger	3 or less*	
8	Mother returns, stranger leaves (Second reunion)	Baby Mother	3	
* Episode can be curtailed by mother if baby becomes too distressed, or can be prolonged if baby takes longer to settle back to play		Total	21.5 (+/-)	

In the original Ainsworth et al. (1978) sequence, the room was equipped with three chairs as shown in Figure 3.1. The chair placed between squares two and three was surrounded by toys which were described by Ainsworth et al. in the initial studies, although number or type of toys is one aspect of the SS that has not been standardised. The mother was instructed to sit in the chair on square 16 and, on entry to the room in episode three, the stranger sat in the chair in square 13 opposite the mother. Reading material was usually available for both the mother and the stranger to look at during the procedure. To begin, the mother was asked to place the baby on the floor between squares 14 and 15.[4] This means that, to explore the toys, the baby would need to travel a fair distance away from the mother.

---

4 The set-up of the room as described by Ainsworth et al. 1978 is not strictly adhered to by researchers using the Strange Situation procedure. The addition of wall-mounted video cameras reduces the necessity for two-way mirrors while door location and thus relationship of chairs to door is, within reason, free to vary. Room shape also differs between studies as do furnishings: some rooms will be softly furnished (e.g. carpeted), others are colder and more clinical. While the effect of these variations is unlikely to be large, it seems important to recognise that these aspects of the Strange Situation procedure have not been fully standardised.

ASSESSING ATTACHMENT SECURITY

Figure 3.1: Lay-out of the Strange Situation playroom

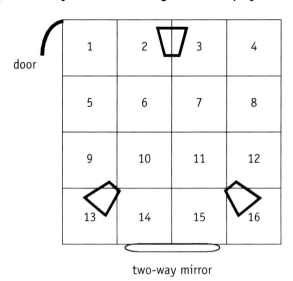

two-way mirror

The stranger who comes into the room for episodes three, four and seven is, to our knowledge, always female, her ethnicity and class is rarely if ever recorded in publications. Although instructed to follow the protocol outlined in Table 3.1, the stranger is not given standardised instructions on how to interact with the infant, that is, how to approach the baby or what to say to calm the baby if s/he is distressed. In other words, the Strange Situation stranger is likely to be stranger for some infants than for others, both within the same study and across studies. The procedure is considered sufficiently robust to tolerate variability from this source.

After the first introductory episode, seven three-minute episodes follow. During separation episodes, the mother, who observes from outside the room during the separation episodes, is free to return before the three minutes are over if she feels that the baby is becoming too distressed (or if she is becoming too distressed whilst watching).[5] The procedure subjects the infant to gradually increasing stress but, because the mother is available to intervene if necessary, this stress is considered to be within ethical limits. The first stressor is the unfamiliar room. To this is added an unfamiliar person (the Stranger), then two separations from the carer, the second potentially more alarming than the first since the baby is then left completely alone. By the time of the second reunion, most infants seek some kind of comfort from their carers and most carers respond more or less effectively to their babies' distress. The way infants and carers interact in this second reunion provides a substantial proportion of the information necessary to classify the attachment relationship.

Throughout, observers note how the infant responds to the unfamiliar room and toys, to the unknown female, and to the carer's departure and return. Although the whole procedure

---

5   To our knowledge, few if any studies have systematically reported the nature or effect of mothers' decisions about when to return to a distressed infant so we have no way of knowing whether any sample differences are associated with this aspect. There is some anecdotal evidence that late return may be associated with some clinical conditions, e.g. postnatal depression, and that early return or even inability to leave may have been associated with some Japanese samples, but it is not clear whether such findings are of any significance.

normally takes only about 20 to 25 minutes (depending on how long it takes for the baby to settle back down to play in episode five as well as on the degree to which separation episodes are curtailed), it provides an extremely rich source of information as it includes so many different levels and types of 'strangeness'. Coding and classification of observational material is influenced by a wide range of dimensions infant and infant-mother interactive behaviour, some of which are indicated in Table 3.2.

Table 3.2: Some dimensions observed in the strange situation

ONE EXTREME	OTHER EXTREME
high activity	low activity/passivity
focused attention	unfocused attention
high level exploration	low level exploration
reaction to familiar person	reaction to non-familiar person
organised behaviour	disorganised behaviour
positive emotionality	negative emotionality
high expressivity	low expressivity
contact maintaining	contact resisting
contact seeking	contact avoiding
high soothability	low soothability
proximal interaction preference	distal interaction preference

Despite the way Table 3.2. is arranged, none of these dimensions is naturally dichotomous. Rather, the dimensions represent continua along which behaviours can vary: not only can infants be high or low on each dimension, hypothetically they can be anywhere in between, and some infants' behaviour will vary considerably more than others. The fact that the SS procedure involves eight differently toned episodes complicates the picture even further, for example, while some children may be high on contact-resisting in the first reunion episode and low in the second, others may show the opposite pattern. Calculating averages across episodes is therefore likely to lose sight of very different patterns. With potential variations involving so much variability along so many dimensions, there are clear challenges for researchers keen to observe patterns of behaviour. In the next section, we describe the strategies that Mary Ainsworth and her colleagues developed to deal with this highly complex data.

The Strange Situation classificatory system

As mentioned in Chapter One, Ainsworth was not comfortable with the initial classificatory system by which she had identified infants in the Ganda study as secure or insecure. This was possibly due less to reservations expressed by some of the audience during the 1961 Tavistock seminar (with regard to the use of value-laden terms) but perhaps more to her own awareness of not having collected information systematically enough in respect of key attachment behaviours and of not having developed a sufficiently reliable or comprehensive classificatory system.

Developing a reliable classificatory system for behaviours which vary along so many dimensions is no easy task, particularly at a time when adequate computer technology was not widely available. Further delays also arose due to more pressing personal and professional commitments (including a divorce). However, by 1978, Ainsworth and her colleagues were ready to publish details of the first full analysis of the more substantial Baltimore sample of 106 one-year-olds, drawn from white, middle-class families.

This larger sample included data gathered from four separate studies: 23 children from Ainsworth's original longitudinal study (nine girls, 14 boys), Bell's 1970 study of 33 children (12 girls, 21 boys), 23 children in Ainsworth's test-retest study (11 girls, 12 boys) and 27 children in a sample studied by Mary Main (14 girls, 13 boys).

Attachment behaviours elicited from these infants in the Strange Situation were analysed by breaking down the behaviours into incidence and number of specific behaviours (including movements, affective signals, type of contact and vocalisation) during each episode, and ratings of interactive behaviour (i.e. proximity- and contact-seeking, contact-maintaining, resistant/angry behaviour, avoidance and distance interaction). This data was subsequently examined for similarities (Ainsworth et al. 1978).

Three major clusters of behaviours were identified and these three major clusters, labelled A, B, C, were further sub-divided into eight sub-groups: two A sub-groups; four B sub-groups; two C sub-groups (see Appendix 3.2). No descriptive labels were applied at first as the primary intention was to classify as objectively as possible and not to make interpretative or value judgements. At either end of the four B sub-groups (numbered one to four), there was a degree of similarity with the adjacent sub-group in the A and C categories. Patterns of attachment of children in the A2 sub-group resembled those of children in the B1 sub-group in that both sub-groups tended to show a preference for distal interaction particularly on reunion and did not appear to need to seek contact in order to resume play. Patterns of behaviour among the B4 sub-group of children resembled those of the C1 sub-group in showing a preference for proximal interaction: these children tended to seek and maintain contact more than other children in B sub-groups and their interactions also tended to have a more immature, angry quality than children in the other B sub-groups. In other words, the behaviours of children in the B group were not as sharply distinguished from those of A or C group children as many people have subsequently come to believe.

Figure 3.2 illustrates some of these differences in children's behaviours during selected pre-separation (Episodes two and three) and reunion (Episodes five and eight) episodes of the Strange Situation procedure (based on data placed on the website of Stony Brook Attachment Lab by Everett Waters, 2005).

Figure 3.2: Differences in behaviour during the Strange Situation

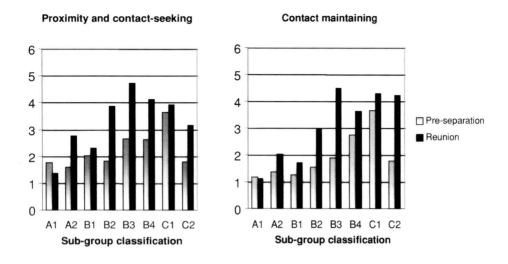

As already mentioned, Ainsworth regarded her initial A/B/C classificatory system, like Attachment Theory itself, as still at an exploratory stage and remained open to the possibility that additional patterns of attachment behaviour organisation might be discovered (Ainsworth et al. 1978). She also thought that the discovery of new patterns might alter both cut-off points between major clusters and within-cluster groupings. It is important to note that her interest in the sub-group classifications and the differences between them was limited more by sample size than by a belief that sub-group differences were insignificant. Indeed, Ainsworth asserted that distinctions between the childcare experiences of children in sub-groups may eventually prove to be as important as major group differences (Ainsworth et al. 1978, p.234).

The interpretation and description of patterns of attachment

Although Ainsworth resisted the use of descriptive labels for attachment patterns in the first instance, the notion that the attachment figure might be defined by their function as a 'secure base' from which to explore was never far from her thoughts. It clearly influenced the decision-making process which resulted in three major groups rather than eight separate ones. It was also clearly reflected in the labels which were later assigned to the three groups.

Patterns classified as 'B' were considered to show the effective use of the attachment figure as a secure base (described both as a person sought when in need of comfort or reassurance as well as one who functions as a base from which to explore). Subsequently, infants classified within the B group were described as 'securely attached'. Infants in the other two groups were considered to be insecurely attached, that is, they did not appear to use the attachment figure as a secure base from which to explore and, if they did turn to the attachment figure for comfort when they were distressed (which many did not), the attachment figure did not appear capable of giving them the comfort they sought. Infants in the latter two groups were therefore considered to be anxiously or 'insecurely attached' to their caregivers. Figure 3.3 illustrates this pattern.

Figure 3.3: Patterns of response in Strange Situation

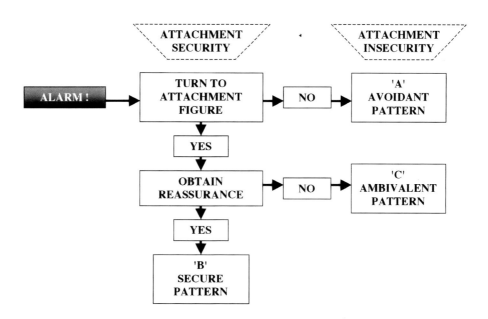

Although infants' behaviour during the second reunion episode (Episode 8) tended to show differences in attachment patterns most markedly, some differences are also apparent even during earlier pre-separation episodes. Whereas B group children generally begin to explore the unfamiliar playroom and most reference back to their carer from time to time, showing toys and sharing their new experiences, the behaviour of children subsequently labelled A or C has a different tone. A-group children tend not to reference back to the carer but do engage with play and give the impression, superficially at least, of being rather self-contained. C-group children, on the contrary, are the least likely to play contentedly and might already begin to fuss, show distress or anxiety, and to seek their carer's attention even before the arrival of the stranger.

Perhaps in response to an idea elaborated by Sroufe and Waters (1977), Bowlby (1980a) suggested that the underlying differences in patterns of attachment reflected different levels of activation of the Attachment Behaviour System (ABS). The avoidant pattern, Bowlby suggested, may be associated with under-activation or even de-activation of the ABS, and the ambivalent/resistant pattern with over-activation: "One of the commonest forms of disturbance is the over-ready elicitation of attachment behaviour, resulting in anxious attachment. Another... is a partial or complete deactivation of attachment behaviour" (Bowlby 1980a, p.41). Taking up this idea, Goldberg (2000) described C-group children as having the lowest and A-group children as having the highest threshold for activation of the Attachment Behaviour System. In other words, C-group children are the most likely to show comfort-seeking behaviour throughout the Strange Situation while A-group children are the least likely to do so. In addition, the play of A-group children is least likely to vary in response to the stressfulness of the Strange Situation procedure. Figure 3.4 illustrates a hypothetical continuum of activation across all three major categories and all eight sub-groups.

Figure 3.4: Levels of ABS activation underlying different patterns of attachment

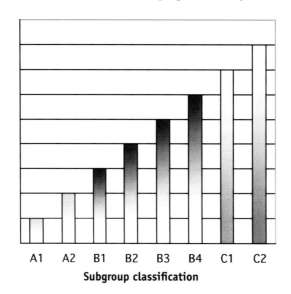

Whether Goldberg and others would hypothesise quite such a linear relationship between ABS activation and sub-group classification as Figure 3.4 suggests is debateable. But such an account raises the possibility that differences between sub-groups within the B-group (e.g. B1 versus B4 classifications) might be expected to be as great as differences between major groups. In other words, on logical grounds, grouping by major category could systematically decrease the likelihood of finding overall differences between categories. Unequal sub-group cell sizes could further compound this problem.

Certainly, in the Baltimore sample, sub-group sizes were very unevenly distributed, with well over a third of children being classified as B3 (45/106 or 42 per cent). Only the A1 sub-group contained more than 10 per cent (12/106; 11 per cent). Overall, 20 per cent of children were assigned A group classifications (21/106), 66 per cent to the B group (70/106) and 12 per cent to the C group (13/106).

If other samples contain similar distributions of sub-group cell sizes and if ABS activation occurs along a continuum from A1 to C2, then we might expect to find greater or more consistent differences between B-group behaviours and A-group patterns (since the majority emanate from the B3 sub-group, which is, respectively, four and five intervals away from A2 and A1 sub-groups) than between B-group behaviours and C-group patterns (since the B3 sub-group is only two or three intervals away from C1 and C2 sub-groups, respectively).

In most studies, as in the Baltimore study, sample sizes have continued to yield very unevenly distributed cell sizes which have precluded reliable analysis of differences by sub-group and, as explained above, may also have obscured, distorted or exaggerated major category differences. It is not known whether all samples include a 'B3 bulge' since so few researchers report sub-group distributions. Certainly, in the largest dataset to be reported to date, the National Institute of Child Health and Development (NICHD) Early Child Care Study, a slightly different distribution obtained among 15 month SS sub-group distributions (Spieker, personal communication, 2005; Figure 3.5).

Figure 3.5: 15-month SS sub-group distribution in NICHD sample (n = 1191)

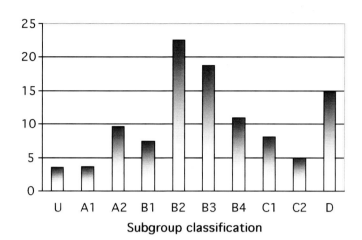

Problems with the Strange Situation classificatory system

The Strange Situation classificatory system requires coders to assign children to a category using a 'forced-classification' procedure, that is, children are assigned to the closest fitting category. In the earliest reported studies, although there were some difficulties with this forced-classification procedure, difficulties with classification were not treated as of very considerable scientific interest. Gradually, classification difficulties, which were reported to be as high as ten per cent in some white, middle-class samples (e.g. Sroufe and Waters 1977), began to be more routinely reported (either as 'not-to-be-classified' or as 'Unclassifiable' with a forced classification subscript, e.g. U_A, U_B, U_C) and gradually received more attention. As more clinical samples were analysed, including children with experiences of having been abused or at high risk of maltreatment, alternative codings also began to appear in the literature. For example, A/C began to be used to indicate a combination of avoidant and ambivalent behaviours (Spieker and Booth 1988, Radke-Yarrow et al. 1985, Crittenden 1987). This A/C pattern tended to be associated with mothers who had histories of depression but was not, at this stage, applied systematically across the various studies from which it had been reported.

Identification of the 'disorganised' pattern

Awareness of these problems led Mary Main to re-visit the tapes of infants whose behaviours in the Strange Situation were difficult or impossible to classify, in the hope of identifying new attachment patterns. In the first published review of this work, Main and Weston (1981) described 152 Strange Situation classifications of which 19 (12.5 per cent) had been judged to be unclassifiable. They reported that 13 of these children would have been assigned to the B group if the Ainsworth et al. (1978) forced-classification procedure had been strictly adhered to, yet these infants appeared in various ways to be conflicted throughout the Strange Situation, and seemed very unsure of their mothers' emotional availability. Expanding the data-base to 268 Strange Situation tapes (including both father- and mother-infant dyads),

Main and Solomon (1986, 1990) reported that even this inspection of a larger number of profiles of unclassifiable infants (36 dyads, of which only two appeared in any way organised) had failed to identify any new patterns of organised attachment behaviour. Rather, the most striking characteristic of the highly diverse behaviour of these infants was their lack of organisation. Some appeared distinctly disoriented and gave the impression of being a bit 'out of it', unable to make sense of where they were, others looked at times dazed or frozen. These behaviours (Table 3.3) were observed both in the presence of the parent and alone. They were considered particularly significant if they occurred in the parent's presence as this was thought likely to indicate a seriously disturbed parent-child relationship.

Table 3.3: Indices of disorganisation and disorientation

1	Sequential displays of contradictory behaviours
2	Simultaneous display of contradictory behaviour patterns
3	Undirected, misdirected, incomplete, and interrupted movements and expressions
4	Stereotypes, asymmetrical movements, mis-timed movements, and anomalous postures
5	Freezing, stilling, and slowed movements and expressions
6	Direct indices of apprehension regarding the parent
7	Direct indices of disorganisation or disorientation

Main and Solomon (1990) recommended procedures for assigning unclassifiable cases to a new category labelled D, to denote disorganised or disoriented. They recognised though that, even using this new category, a few infants would remain unclassifiable and that there remained a need to assign secondary best-fit A/B/C classifications to both D and U (unclassifiable) classifications.

As Figure 3.5 illustrated, in the more recent large-scale study of day care (NICHD Early Child Care Research Network (ECCRN) 1997), out of the 1,191 infants classified at 15 months using Main's system, 42 infants were not classifiable (3.5 per cent) while 177 (14.9 per cent) were classified as 'D', disorganised (Spieker, personal communication, 2005).

Refinement of the classificatory system

These changes in methods of classification appear in some ways to have improved the quality of data analysis and to have reduced the number of unclassifiable cases. However, the introduction of a new category combined with the blurred categories already associated with forced-choice categorisation can make it more difficult to make straightforward comparisons between samples classified using different methods. Fortunately, a fair proportion of studies have now been re-classified using both methods but, unfortunately, this has not prevented further disagreements which have arisen as a result of differences in approach between Mary Main's research group and other workers who had already begun to develop alternative taxonomies.

When Mary Main identified the 'disorganised' pattern of attachment, other workers had already been finding difficulties in classifying a rather substantial proportion, particularly, of clinical cases. As a result, researchers such as Crittenden (1985, 1988, 2002) and Radke-Yarrow (Radke-Yarrow et al. 1985, Radke-Yarrow 1991) had begun to extend the Strange Situation system of classification. This process eventually resulted in the creation of an A/C category in Radke-Yarrow's system and of two additional A and C sub-groups, and other non-A/B/C sub-groups in Crittenden's system (Table 3.4). In Crittenden's system, a number of the patterns labelled by Main as 'disorganised', for example, role reversal, are labelled insecure but organised. Although there appears to be substantial overlap between the two systems, to our knowledge no published paper has yet provided sufficient detail of results using both methods to enable findings to be sensibly compared.

Table 3.4: Patricia Crittenden's classification system codes

CODE	DESCRIPTION
A1-A2	Avoidant behaviour *(cf Ainsworth?*)*
A3	Compulsive compliance
A4	Compulsive caregiving
B1-B4	*Secure behaviour (cf Ainsworth?*)*
C1-C2	Ambivalent/Resistant behaviour *(cf Ainsworth?*)*
C3-C4	'Flip-flopping' between aggression and feigned helplessness
Dp	Depressed marker/modifier *(coded in addition to sub-group classification)*
Dx	Disorganising affect marker/modifier *(coded in addition to sub-group classification)*
IO	Insecure other

* Although it seems possible that these sub-groups do map onto the original Ainsworth descriptions, it also seems likely that they will reflect the necessary revisions which were made once the 'disorganised' group was identified. To our knowledge, no published account provides, in as much detail as was provided by Mary Ainsworth (Ainsworth et al. 1978), a description of the impact of these changes on Strange Situation classifications. As a result, since the publication of Ainsworth's now classic text, knowledge appears to have taken, in some ways, a slightly retrograde step, although, in other ways, there have been clear advances.

Categories or continua?

Because of these difficulties, questions remain about what exactly it is that the classifications might capture and whether they represent naturally occurring, real categories at all. Recently, Fraley and Spieker (2003a, 2003b) applied newly developed statistical procedures which examine data to determine whether the relationships between scores are best understood as discrete categories or as continuous scales. They used data from the NICHD study mentioned above and specifically investigated ratings of interactive behaviours across all eight episodes (proximity- and contact-seeking, contact maintenance, avoidance and resistance). They concluded that "the data are most consistent with a dimensional view of individual differences " (Fraley and Spieker 2003a, p.399) and, proposing a two-dimensional model of individual differences of attachment with Proximity-seeking versus Avoidance as one dimension and Angry and Resistant behaviour as the other dimension, stated, "we believe that it is difficult to justify the sole use of categorical models in attachment research" (Fraley and Spieker 2003a, p.402). Fraley and Spieker did acknowledge that there were limitations to their analysis and that other dimensions, such as disorganisation, might be important to include. However, their work calls clearly for caution about the dangers of over-reliance upon categories which might be both imprecise and artificial.

Fraley and Spieker's analyses provoked comments from a number of attachment researchers, some of whom (e.g. Cassidy 2003, Waters and Beauchaine 2003) took the approach that the analyses, though interesting, were limited in the proportion of data that they included (since coding of SS behaviours usually takes into account more than just the interactive behaviour ratings), in having averaged behaviours across all episodes (which is likely to have lost important information) and in their over-reliance on Strange Situation behaviours as opposed to attachment behaviours that occur in natural settings. Others (e.g. Cummings 2003, Sroufe 2003) applauded the search for a measure of attachment security as a continuous dimension but pointed out, first, that Fraley and Spieker's findings had not achieved this as it was still not clear how their two-dimensional model might relate to one scale measuring attachment security and, second, that the difficulties involved in creating dimensional measures of attachment (which many researchers had been trying for many years to do) would possibly result in continued reliance upon Mary Ainsworth's system for some time to come. None of these commentators was averse to the continued search for more precise ways of assessing attachment behaviour.

The need for assessment in addition to the Strange Situation procedure

Although Mary Ainsworth's Strange Situation procedure (Ainsworth and Wittig 1969; Ainsworth et al. 1978) proved very successful at discriminating different patterns of attachment relationship, it does have distinct limitations. First, it is only reliable when used with infants aged between 12 and 18 months and, even within this age span, its reliability tends to diminish toward the 18-month end of the time window (Ainsworth et al. 1978). Second, repeating the measure carries risks since, as Ainsworth et al. (1978) pointed out after having re-tested infants two weeks later, infants appear to become sensitised to the stress involved in the procedure. As it is rare for an infant not to find the procedure stressful and some infants find the procedure more stressful than others, Ainsworth et al. advised that re-testing was problematic. Infants initially assessed as coping relatively well with the stress on the first occasion become less able to organise their defensive strategies on a second test. For infants who did not appear to cope well on the first occasion, the procedure was likely to have to be aborted on second testing. On the other hand, older infants, perhaps now with slightly more experience of separations and reunions or with generally more advanced coping strategies, might (or might not) find a second Strange Situation test less stressful. In sum, infants who had found the procedure mildly, moderately or highly stressful on the first occasion, far from becoming familiarised and less stressed on second occasion, appeared to associate the procedure with unpleasant experiences to be avoided.

These difficulties have generated interest, therefore, in finding supplementary and alternative methods for assessing the relationship between infants and their key attachment figures. Particular difficulties were associated with assessment of attachment relationships in situations where infants had, as most did, more than one attachment figure, for example, mother, father and day caregiver (sometimes grandmother or other relative) or metaplot, if the infant was being reared in the group care setting of an Israeli kibbutzim.

Although the problems associated with repeated testing did not deter a number of researchers from repeating the procedure within the space of three months in order to compare, for example, attachment to father with attachment to mother,[6] at the same time, the need to develop alternative and comparable methods for assessing quality of attachment at later ages became very apparent. To our knowledge, only one researcher (Kotelchuck 1976) has attempted to observe infants in the Strange Situation in the company of both parents (though the work being carried out by Fivaz-Depeursinge and colleagues, described in Chapter Five, may now also be addressing this) and this researcher appeared not to have managed to devise a classificatory system that satisfactorily identified triadic relationship patterns.

Another problem also emerged for, without additional measures, there was no way of knowing whether quality of attachment relationships might normally stay the same or change within the six-month time period between 12 and 18 months, or later. For this reason, in the decades following Mary Ainsworth's original report, numerous researchers set about devising new measures for assessing patterns of attachment in later life.

As there is not space here to consider all of these various measures in detail, we have chosen to describe the two most widely used procedures and the classificatory systems associated with these, that is, the Adult Attachment Interview (George et al. 1984/1985/1996) and the Relationships Questionnaire (Bartholomew and Horowitz 1991). More information about related scales can be found in Appendix 3.1.

The Adult Attachment Interview (AAI)

Interview format

The Adult Attachment Interview (AAI) is a structured semi-clinical interview that was developed by Mary Main, Nancy Kaplan and Carol George (George et al. 1984/1985/1996). It is premised on the notion that individuals with different experiences of attachment relationships will, as Bowlby suggested, have different Internal Working Models of close attachments which, in adulthood, will have resulted in different ways of conceptualising or thinking about attachment relationships reflected in different ways of talking about them.

The interview focuses on early attachment experiences and their effects and the questions and prompts aim to elicit memories of childhood experiences with key attachment figures (including parents and/or surrogate parents). The interviewer explores who the interviewee felt closest to, why, whether s/he ever felt rejected or threatened in any way, what understanding they have of their parents' behaviour and how s/he feels their childhood experiences might have affected their personality development. Interviewees are also asked about experiences of any major separation or loss during childhood.

---

6   The rationale for this particular practice does not appear anywhere in the literature to have been firmly established: since no study appears to have examined the effect of repetition with different people in comparison with repetition with the same person, there would appear to be few grounds for confidence in studies incorporating a three-month re-test design. Sensitisation, maturation or intervening experience effects seem more than likely to obtain. While counter-balancing the order of testing (i.e. testing half the babies with person A first and person B second but testing the other half with person B first and person A second) might in theory appear to reduce the likelihood that negative effects of re-testing will become disproportionately associated with either person, this strategy seems unlikely to eliminate those effects entirely.

At the start of the AAI, the interviewer briefly explains what the interview is about. This part of the interview is not fully standardised and researchers usually follow the ethical codes of their individual organisation when they decide what information to give about the nature of the questions to be asked and the reasons for asking them. Usually, research participants will already have had an explanation of the nature of the study and will have given their informed, written consent for participation at an earlier point. Importantly, interviewees should come fresh to interviews, that is, they have not been asked to carry out other taxing tasks beforehand (as part of the study they have agreed to take part in, for example) and they should not be in crisis due to a major loss of any sort. The interview lasts about an hour, questions are asked in a set order and the respondent's account is audio-taped (not videotaped as the richness of material gathered in this way is extensive and it is not thought that additional visual information would add appreciably to the picture already obtained). Fuller details of questions and probes can be found in Appendix 3.2.

The technique of the AAI is thought to 'surprise the unconscious' (George et al. 1984/1985/1996) since the 20 questions (fewer in some versions) and their prompts allow opportunities for interviewees to contradict themselves and also to make statements that they may then either support or fail to support with evidence. It also gives interviewees scope to structure their own accounts to some extent, in more or less orderly ways. Classifications of attachment style are made on the basis of the quality of narrative.

Approaches to information-gathering that rely solely on interviews can be prone to 'interviewer bias', that is, the quality of the relationship between the interviewer and the interviewee can impinge on the extent to which interviewees feel able to divulge personal material. Other social contextual constraints may also influence the quality of information given. For these reasons, training of interviewers includes preparation for managing their own feelings about the sometimes difficult material that emerges, for example, interviewers may need to be careful about letting their own response to interviewees' distress or embarrassment influence interviewees' accounts, wary of being coerced into straying from the topic, or aware that they may find themselves feeling intimidated or frustrated by interviewees who handle questions in certain ways, e.g. interviewees who give particularly clipped or succinct answers, those who give the impression of finding the questions extremely tedious, those who are very slow or confused, etc. Learning to conduct Adult Attachment interviews and to carry out analyses normally requires at least two full weeks' intensive training, during which trainees aim to reach certain standards of reliability in interview-coding.

Analysis of the interview material

Coders analyse a full transcript of the interview, including non-verbal sounds and gaps in speech, using scales that measure whether, in the coder's opinion, attachment figures were experienced as loving, rejecting, neglecting, involving or pressurising.

Scoring of the interview is based, first, on:
- the nature of childhood experiences described
- the language used to describe past experiences
- the ability to give an integrated, coherent, believable account of experiences and their meaning.

A second set of scales is used to assess the interviewee's state of mind and discourse style. This includes the overall coherence of transcript and of thought, idealisation, insistence on lack of recall, active anger, derogation, fear of loss, metacognitive monitoring and passivity of speech.

This discourse analytic approach to coding is based on Grice's four maxims for effective conversational exchange (Table 3.5; Grice 1975). They are premised on the notion that effective communication requires adherence to principles of cooperation that are governed by rational processes.

Table 3.5: Grice's conversational maxims

Quality	Be truthful, and have evidence for what you say
Quantity	Be succinct, and yet complete
Relation	Be relevant to the topic as presented
Manner	Be clear and orderly

Violations of Grice's maxims are operationally defined as follows:
- 'Quality' is violated when speakers make statements but provide evidence that contradicts the statement, for example, they may state that they had a kind, loving mother but proceed to describe incidents where she treated them very badly, ignored them, etc.
- 'Quantity' is violated when speakers curtail their answers in some way, for example, refusing to answer the question; it is also violated by speakers who evince 'verbal diarrhoea', rambling, being highly repetitive, long-winded or hogging the conversation, going on and on, never getting to the end of their explanation …
- 'Relation' is violated when speakers stray in response to questions, onto unrelated topics, for example, giving information about their own children in response to questions about their parents, or giving information about current relationships when asked about relationships during their childhood.
- 'Manner' is violated when speakers over-use jargon, fail to complete sentences, speak confusedly or cannot be understood for any reason other than mis-articulation.

AAI classifications

The scale scores are used to assign the adult to one of three major attachment classifications: dismissing (D), preoccupied (E), autonomous (F) (which, like the SS, contain sub-groups: four D, five F and three E sub-groups). These major categories map directly onto the three major categories identified by Ainsworth et al. (1978) in infancy (see Table 3.6). Rather confusingly, the letters allocated to the adult categories are in a different alphabetical order which seems to suggest a move away from the initial relationships between major categories implied by Ainsworth's ordering, though the actual reasoning behind this system of lettering has not, to our knowledge, been explained in any published work.

Fortunately in some respects, most reports of AAI classifications use category names rather than letters and this has reduced the potential for confusion. Simultaneously and less fortunately, because the names are value-laden to the point of being pejorative, the literature on adult attachment has tended to encourage considerably more negative stereotyping than Bowlby may have wished.

Table 3.6: Relationship between AAI and SS categories

SS CATEGORY	INFANT DESCRIPTION	ADULT DESCRIPTION	AAI CATEGORY
A	Avoidant	Dismissing	D
B	Secure	Autonomous	F
C	Ambivalent/Resistant	Preoccupied	E
D	Disorganised/Disoriented	Unresolved/Disorganised	U/d

Table 3.7 illustrates the general patterning of interview narratives in relation to Grice's conversation maxims among AAI classifications. Few actual interview transcripts will fit neatly into this overall pattern, for example, parts of transcripts where individuals have been classified as autonomous may violate one or other maxim even though the overall transcript may be considered to be coherent and well substantiated.

Table 3.7: Relationship between AAI categories and Grice's maxims

	DISMISSING	AUTONOMOUS	PREOCCUPIED	UNRESOLVED/ DISORGANISED
Quality	Poor	Adequate	Adequate	Inconsistent
Quantity	Poor	Adequate	Adequate	Inconsistent
Relation	Adequate	Adequate	Poor	Inconsistent
Manner	Adequate	Adequate	Poor	Inconsistent

The 'Autonomous' (F) classification

Interview transcripts of respondents labelled 'autonomous' are **coherent** and convey that interviewees:
- value attachment relationships
- regard attachment-related experiences as having influenced their personality development
- are more or less freely able to explore their thoughts and feelings
- are relatively objective in giving accounts of particular experiences or relationships (both negative and positive)
- engage cooperatively with the interviewer
- consistently substantiate their assertions
- seem relatively at ease with themselves and with the interviewer.

As mentioned above, although all interviewees categorised as autonomous with regard to attachment share the ability to talk openly about their experiences, the quality of interviews varies. These variations will determine sub-group allocation which, to some extent, reflects the kind of self-reflective processes involved. For example, F1 transcripts may contain evidence of active and deliberate 'moving on' from the past; F2 transcripts contain elements of defensiveness but also 'warm up' and breakthrough of these defences; F3 transcripts are the least likely to contain traces of defensive mechanisms; F4 transcripts evince mild tendencies towards sentimentality or preoccupation with the past; F5 transcripts contain evidence of some ambivalence or anger towards parents but accounts will nevertheless give the impression that criticisms have been contained and can be expressed with humour and acceptance.

Although these variations may appear to reflect habitual ways of thinking, they nevertheless are thought not to have resulted from adoption of a rigid perspective which limits the interviewees' ability to reflect on past or current experiences. Some individuals labelled 'autonomous' will have had extremely difficult upbringings but, unlike non-autonomous respondents, they will have managed to stay in touch with their feelings so that they are not overwhelmed by them any more.

The 'Dismissing' (D) classification

Interview transcripts of respondents labelled 'dismissing' are considered **incoherent** and convey a sense of interviewees who:
- do not place a high value on attachment relationships
- do not regard attachment-related experiences as important influences currently or in the past
- avoid exploration of their thoughts and feelings
- tend to use defensive strategies such as idealisation or minimisation
- generally portray themselves as in control or of having feelings which are under control
- contradict themselves or make assertions but fail to provide supporting evidence
- can come across as haughty, critical or contemptuous
- can make the interviewer feel silly.

Again, although interviewees assigned to this category are all thought to have a current state of mind which is more or less dismissive of attachment relationships and their importance, sub-group categories reflect qualitatively different defensive strategies. Transcripts of interviewees allocated to the D1-D3 sub-groups, but less so the D4 group, implicitly reflect interviewees' self-image as strong, normal and self-reliant.

Strategies employed to bolster self-image include over-idealisation of parents (despite contradictory evidence or lack of supporting evidence), minimisation or dismissal of potential effects of poor parenting or of negative close interpersonal experiences on self development, over-reliance on self with concomitant illusions of extreme autonomy, and derogation or dismissal of the influence of attachment figures or attachment-related phenomena.

The 'Preoccupied' (E) classification

Interview transcripts of respondents labelled 'preoccupied' are considered **incoherent** and convey a sense of interviewees who:
- appear preoccupied with past attachment relationships
- regard attachment-related experiences as overwhelmingly important influences currently or in the past
- have great difficulty exploring their thoughts and feelings objectively
- appear angry, conflicted, overwhelmed, confused, inarticulate
- generally portray themselves as neither in control and able to control themselves
- may be passive, vague or fearful
- come across as needy, immature, or overly dependent on others for approval or reassurance
- their sentence structure is often convoluted, entangled
- their language is often punctuated by meaningless or vague noises (e.g. 'and that', 'whatever').

Individuals classified as preoccupied may appear either to accept this state passively (E1) or to struggle against it without success (E2). Although, unlike dismissing individuals, preoccupied individuals will talk openly about and appear to value attachment-related experiences, they seem unable to achieve any sense of themselves as of value in these relationships and give the impression of being constantly in search of an elusive goal.

The 'Unresolved/disorganised' (U/d) classification

Interview transcripts of respondents labelled 'unresolved/disorganised' are considered **incoherent** and reflect interviewees who:
- appear disconnected from their experiences in some way, particularly during discussions of loss or abuse
- may seem to 'switch off' at different points throughout the interview
- may lose track of questions entirely
- may talk about someone who is dead as though they believed they were still physically present
- may evince 'magical thinking', for example, that a childhood thought was responsible for a feared person's death
- may lapse into eulogistic speech.

Besides these apparent lacuna in conversations, many interviewees in this category may come across as fitting quite well into one of the other three categories.

Interpretation of adult attachment classifications

Discourse analytic techniques almost by definition involve interpretation of material which, in turn, involves value judgements. With regard to analysis of AAI transcripts, a number of judgements are made both about the speaker's ability to engage cooperatively in conversation with another person and about what their style of public self-disclosure might indicate in terms of their attitude toward close personal relationships. As indicated above, only the transcripts of 'autonomous' individuals are considered coherent basically because violations of Grice's conversation maxims are equated with lack of coherency. It seems important to note that this definition of coherency is therefore associated as much with judgements about semantic (meaning) considerations and narrative truth as with syntactic (structural) considerations. This can be seen from the fact that narratives can be highly coherent and succinctly articulated, but if they omit information to substantiate assertions made about experiences of close relationships, they will be consigned to the 'incoherent' bin and the narrator will be considered as dismissing or devaluing attachment relationships. We are deliberately using emotive terminology here to draw attention to potential stereotyping processes inherent within a system of classification of this kind.

As discussed previously, after an initial period in which infant attachment patterns were not labelled descriptively, they eventually came to be associated with imputed attachment security. By contrast, the labels given to adult patterns reflected value judgements from the outset. Superficially only the labels relate to degrees of dependency versus independency. In practice, although there are patterns to be discerned in relation to dependency, the term 'autonomous' is not synonymous with 'independent' but rather refers to the interviewer's ability to freely value attachment relationships.

Autonomous individuals will seek help from others when they are in trouble though the way they do this is qualitatively different to non-autonomous individuals. Support networks available to autonomous individuals are likely to reflect their valuing of attachment relationships and their enjoyment of positive emotional connections with others. Within their social circles, therefore, they are likely to give as much as to receive support, unlike less autonomous individuals. This reflects Bowlby's view that, "Paradoxically, the truly self-reliant person ... proves to be by no means as independent as cultural stereotypes suppose. An essential ingredient is the capacity to rely trustingly on others when occasion demands and to know on whom it is appropriate to rely. A healthily self-reliant person is thus capable of exchanging roles when the situation changes: at one time he is providing a secure base from which his companion(s) can operate; at another he is glad to rely on one or another of his companions to provide him with just such a secure base" (Bowlby 1973a, p.407).

Dismissing individuals are more likely to choose to rely on themselves and to be extremely selective about who they will seek help from and on which issues. Preoccupied individuals tend to be far less selective, more likely to present as 'needy' and less protective of their private, personal space. It is almost as though preoccupied individuals are in some way addicted to the journey towards independence but repelled by the concept of arrival whereas, conversely, dismissing individuals are repelled by the thought of the journey but addicted to a belief in arrival (even if it is something of an illusion). Autonomous individuals, by contrast, are more able to fluctuate between journeying and arriving and, depending upon the demands being placed upon them, will be more or less prepared to rely on others. This flexibility or freedom to fluctuate opens up more opportunities for choice of strategy and so more variety in the range of relationships available to them.

Parallels between infant attachment classifications and classifications emerging from analyses of AAI transcripts seemed apparent even from initial reports. To some more sceptical onlookers, this convergence of taxonomic categories may have seemed almost too good to be true. Did the correspondence between adult and infant patterns provide the evidence needed to support claims that patterns of attachment established in infancy persist into adulthood and that the assessment of adult attachment was really tapping the same construct as the Strange Situation? Although it is generally assumed that this is the case, in fact, there remains to this day no easy way of being sure about this.

Self-reports of adult attachment

As we have already stipulated, due to the huge number of instruments at large, we have limited this discussion of self-reports of adult attachment to those most prominent in the literature. A brief explanation of the way these instruments were developed may help readers to understand what these instruments actually measure.

As Shaver and Fraley (2005) explain, self-report measures of romantic attachment were primarily developed with the aim of understanding adults' (including adolescents') feelings and behaviours in relation to romantic relationships rather than tapping into feelings and attitudes associated with models of close relationships in childhood.

In a now well-known early study, Hazan and Shaver (1987) placed a two-page 'love quiz' in a local newspaper. Questions were asked about experiences in and expectations of love experiences. Among these questions was an item designed to translate Ainsworth et al.'s (1978) descriptions of infants into terms appropriate to adult love (Table 3.8). The aim was to identify attachment style differences in adults equivalent to those identified earlier by Ainsworth.

Secure adults were considered likely to endorse a description of themselves as not being preoccupied with fears of abandonment, as being comfortable about being close to others, depending on others and being depended upon. Adults describing themselves as uncomfortable with close relationships were thought likely to be either avoidant or ambivalent.

It is worth noting the extent to which this classification of adult attachment patterns diverges from the system devised by Ainsworth et al. (1978). In Ainsworth's system, ambivalent/resistant behaviour in infants involved both clinginess *and* concomitant pushing away. Hazan and Shaver's description, like the notion of preoccupied entanglement that emerged from AAI classifications, on the contrary, seems to have lost sight of the element of angry ambivalence and of approach/escape conflict that was the defining dynamic characteristic of infant-carer relationships in Ainsworth's C group. Instead, the 'preoccupied' group of adults is conceptualised as being desirous of a state of one-ness only obstructed by the other person's non-collaboration. Clearly, this relationship is not that originally conceptualised by Ainsworth and is likely to be underpinned both by distinctly different internal models of close relationships as well as by different experiences of close relationships. Possibly, this divergence between adult and infant classifications is associated with identification of the 'disorganised' infant category. Certainly, since the introduction of this new category, C group classification in non-clinical samples of infants has become noticeably more rare (Main et al. 2005). That ambivalence in the original sense may have dropped out of the picture of 'preoccupied' adults seems also to raise questions about its presence in more recent infant classification systems.

Table 3.8: Descriptions of adult attachment (Hazan and Shaver 1987, p.515)

Question: Which of the following best describes your feelings?	
Secure	I find it relatively easy to get close to others and am comfortable depending on them and having them depend on me. I don't often worry about being abandoned or about someone getting too close to me.
Avoidant	I am somewhat uncomfortable being too close to others; I find it difficult to trust them completely, difficult to allow myself to depend on them. I am nervous when anyone gets too close, and often, love partners want me to be more intimate than I feel comfortable being.
Anxious/Ambivalent	I find that others are reluctant to get as close as I would like. I often worry that my partner doesn't really love me or won't want to stay with me. I want to merge completely with another person, and this desire sometimes scares people away.

Interestingly, Hazan and Shaver (1987) reported that of their sample of 620 men and women (415 women, 205 men), 56 per cent described themselves as secure, 25 per cent avoidant and 19 per cent ambivalent (21 did not answer the question and 25 ticked more than one description). Treating the 46 who did not endorse questions as requested as equivalent to 'unclassifiable' in other classification systems within attachment research, these proportions became 51 per cent secure, 23 per cent avoidant and 17 per cent ambivalent which, though ordinally similar in size to distributions in most non-clinical samples, indicate lower endorsement of the secure attachment style than might have been expected.

Given the usual tendency for quizzes of this nature to contain social desirability response biases (that is, people choose the most flattering rather than the most accurate self-description), it is notable that only just over half the respondents described themselves as secure.

ASSESSING ATTACHMENT SECURITY

This could suggest either that self-report methods produce rather different information to observational approaches (as would be expected) or that they do not capture the same information about attachment patterns, or both (other explanations could, of course, also account for differences).

In 1990, Kim Bartholomew put forward an alternative conceptualisation of adult attachment styles and suggested a link between different styles of attachment and how one views oneself and others as either generally positive, generally negative or neutral (Bartholomew 1990, 1991). Despite the potential nine-category classification that this conceptualisation suggested, a four-category model emerged which did not reflect the element of neutrality (Table 3.9).

Table 3.9: Model of adult attachment (Bartholomew 1990)

		MODEL OF SELF (DEPENDENCE)	
		POSITIVE (low dependence)	NEGATIVE (high dependence)
MODEL OF OTHER (AVOIDANCE)	POSITIVE (low avoidance)	**SECURE** Comfortable with intimacy and autonomy	**PREOCCUPIED** Preoccupied with relationships
	NEGATIVE (high avoidance)	**DISMISSING** Dismissing of intimacy Counter-dependent	**FEARFUL** Fearful of intimacy Socially avoidant

Bartholomew and Horowitz (1991, p.227) refined this model along these lines, "If a person's abstract image of the self is dichotomized as positive or negative (the self as worthy of love and support or not) and if the person's abstracted image of the other is also dichotomized as positive or negative (other people are seen as trustworthy and available vs. unreliable and rejecting), then four combinations can be conceptualized" (Bartholomew and Horowitz 1991, p.227). This re-conceptualisation led to four descriptions which they referred to as 'attachment style prototypes' (Table 3.10).

Table 3.10: Self-report adult attachment style prototypes
Bartholomew and Horowitz (1991, p.244)

Secure	It is relatively easy for me to become emotionally close to others. I am comfortable depending on others and having others depend on me. I don't worry about being alone or having others not accept me.
Preoccupied	I want to be completely emotionally intimate with others, but I often find that others are reluctant to get as close as I would like. I am uncomfortable being without close relationships, but I sometimes worry that others don't value me as much as I value them.
Dismissing	I am somewhat uncomfortable being too close to others; I find it difficult to trust them completely, difficult to allow myself to depend on them. I am nervous when anyone gets too close, and often, love partners want me to be more intimate than I feel comfortable being.
Fearful	I am somewhat uncomfortable getting close to others. I want emotionally close relationships, but I find it difficult to trust others completely, or to depend on them. I sometimes worry that I will be hurt if I allow myself to become too close to others.

As can be seen from Table 3.10, the labels applied to Hazan and Shaver's three initial prototypical styles had been altered by Bartholomew and Horowitz so that they resembled the AAI categories more closely. Avoidantly attached individuals were now divided into those who avoid because they are dismissive of the value of attachment relationships (labelled dismissing) and those who, although appreciative of the value of attachment relationships, avoid them because they are fearful of rejection and/or hurt. This notion that similar behavioural outcomes might be associated with different attributional processes, though apparently implicit within sub-categories of the AAI, until then (and, arguably, since) had not received very much attention from attachment researchers.[7] Bartholomew and Horowitz (1991) also arranged the elements within their four-category description to form separate items to be rated in a self-report scale. In this way, they converted their categorical measure into a continuous scale.

Subsequently, researchers have attempted to design self-report measures capable of identifying possible additional adult attachment styles that map onto other aspects of mother-child relationships described by Bowlby (Bowlby 1980a). For example, Feeney and Noller (1996) explored whether 'compulsive caregiving', hypothetically mapping onto a pattern of child-mother role reversal described both by Bowlby (1980a) and associated with disorganised attachment in infancy by Mary Main (e.g. Main et al. 1985, Main 2000), might characterise some forms of adult attachment.

In a similar vein to conclusions from infant attachment data, Fraley and Waller (1998) put forward an argument that adult attachment behaviour is not well described in terms of qualitatively different types or styles. Rather, it is better measured as varying along two continuous dimensions, anxiety and avoidance, with attachment security being associated with both low anxiety and low avoidance (see Figure 3.6). This conclusion was borne out

---

7   During the 1980s and 1990s, links between workers in the field of social cognition and those in the field of attachment, despite obvious overlaps between domains, were tenuous, to say the least. Despite what was hailed as the "move to the level of representation" among attachment workers, cross-fertilisation seemed to be more a matter of chance than of more informed choice.

by Brennan et al. (1998) who combined all 323 statements from all 14 currently available multi-item attachment scales into one questionnaire. Respondents were asked to rate on a seven-point scale the extent to which each statement was like them.

Subsequent factor analyses, confirming Fraley and Waller's findings, indicated that responses clustered around two global dimensions, anxiety and avoidance. This formed the basis for the first Experiences in Close Relationships Questionnaire (Brennan et al. 1998; Appendix 3.1).

Figure 3.6: Two-dimensional model of adult attachment

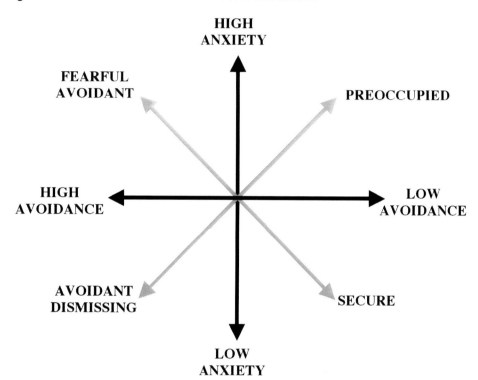

Summing up

This brief account of the development of adult and infant assessments of attachment highlights the complexity of measurement issues and gives some indication of the confusion that can ensue when lifespan attachment security as a construct has never been fully specified. It particularly draws attention to the potential mismatch between self-report, interview and observational approaches. Even more importantly, it indicates that, although adult and infant attachment researchers may seem to be using similar labels to describe individual differences, subtle differences seem to have crept in and these differences, which involve value judgements and extrapolations from data and potential for unjustified negative stereotyping, still need attention.

The two-dimensional model of adult attachment, beguilingly simple, appears to provide an elegant solution to the problem of understanding differences in patterns of attachment. Attachment security is associated with feeling positive both about yourself and about others. Attachment insecurity is associated with feeling negative about either yourself, or others, or both. From this picture, some adult attachment researchers have argued that secure adults report positive experiences of close relationships both in childhood and in adulthood. However, we know that this is not always the case. Sroufe and Waters (1977) pointed out many years ago that, for some children, attachment security is 'given' but, for others, it is 'earned'. How likely is it that internal working models in these two cases are identical? In addition, we must bear in mind the possibility of multiple sources of developing Internal Working Models. Despite the principle of monotropy, the main caregiver is not the only source of important or memorable information about self in interaction with others. While the relationship between the child and his or her main caregiver is likely to be highly influential, other relationships also contribute to the development of Internal Working Models: relationships with supplementary caregivers, for example, which fathers often are, or with others, such as teachers, grandparents, or other relatives and key figures, who can also be influential. This is not to ignore the distinction that Bowlby made between attachment relationships and relationships more concerned with affiliative needs (which friendships with peers and siblings tend to be). Nor is it to suggest that mental representations of self-other interactions in less intimate settings are as formative as those with key attachment figures. But it is to emphasise the complexity and the multiplicity of available developmental pathways.

There is no denying that the study of relationships is complicated, even when only two people are considered. As the development of the SS procedure has demonstrated and continues to demonstrate, it can take decades to arrive at a valid or reliable system. The system appears now to be up and running. But, even so, these are not grounds for complacency. There are still some big questions to be answered.

As an adult, being in a satisfying long-term relationship may be an indication of attachment security, but it is not proof of this. Conversely, not having the good fortune to have achieved or sustained a satisfying long-term relationship and so being increasingly, necessarily, self-reliant may, or may not, be an indication of attachment insecurity but is it really proof of an underlying negativist attitude that de-values and derogates close relationships? Does the avoidant infant really have no concept of how satisfying it can be to snuggle up close to another human and to feel accepted? Has the older avoidant child really come to the conclusion that close, loving relationships are not for them? Come to that, if secure adults are so globally positive about their fellow humans, is it not possible that these tendencies will expose them to greater danger when conditions become less benign and they have no concept or experience of people who are not to be trusted. Rather than protecting them and increasing their chances of survival, might they not be more susceptible to unforeseen dangers? These questions are slightly 'tongue-in-cheek' but have the more serious intention of drawing attention to the potential dangers of over-simplification and to the potential superficiality of conceptualisations of attachment patterns that are too dependent on theory and not sufficiently rooted in careful, systematic observation.

Evolutionary theory does not predict that only one style of adaptation to environmental conditions will promote survival of the species. Rather, diversity is an essential feature of successful adaptation. We are not all right-handed even though the majority of us are and our social environment is constructed as though we all were. This clearly disadvantages the substantial minority who are left-handed. In the not-so-distant past in Britain, children who used their left hand to write were punished. It was relatively common for a left-handed child to be hit for using their dominant hand (wrapped on the knuckles or hit with a ruler), or to have it tied behind their back to prevent the temptation to use it. Not only were they disadvantaged because the majority hand preference was unfairly promoted as the only acceptable modus operandi, they were additionally oppressed by negative stereotyping.[8] But being left-handed is not a perverse choice, any more than being ambidextrous is. It is a simple biological fact.

Individual differences in attachment seem likely to reflect similar diversity of distribution within the human species and it may well turn out that the minority group patterns are as important for the continuation of the whole species as the majority patterns. As Crittenden (2000, p.10) comments, "I fear we have taken a deficit approach to thinking about 'anxious' attachment… Recognizing the accomplishment and adaptation implied in the non-B patterns and placing them in the ecological context of family, culture and history can help us understand human relationships better and change the negative value placed on Type A and C patterns." Might there not be an evolutionary role for the avoidant, or to avoid negative terminology, the more distal attachment style? In other words, is it possible that the more distal attachment style might be adaptive in terms of the long-term interests of homo sapiens? We return to this question again and again throughout this book.

In this chapter, we have attempted to describe some of the processes whereby tools were developed to assess attachment relationships. We have drawn attention to the lack of an operational definition of attachment security across the lifespan and have indicated some of the difficulties involved in proving that assessment tools are all measuring similar constructs. Further discussions of these issues can be found in numerous publications (e.g. Crowell and Treboux 1995, Stein et al., 1998, Crowell et al. 1999, Fraley et al. 2000, Shaver et al. 2000). Finally, we have raised the possibility that the terminology used by attachment researchers might encourage undesirable negative stereotyping.

In the next chapter, we explore these issues further. As explained earlier in this chapter, one way of establishing whether instruments measure what they claim to measure is to examine their validity and reliability. In the next chapter, we consider the extent to which different measures of attachment security predict, as Bowlby hypothesised, better psychological adjustment and ask whether there really are firm grounds for viewing 'secure' attachment as the ideal to be aimed for or whether it might simply be one of several adaptive modes.

---

8   The term 'left', even now, in many languages and countries has negative connotations, e.g. 'sinister', 'gauche' while 'right' is still right!

Part Two

Evidence

4 | Exploring the validity of attachment assessments

"... human beings of all ages are found to be at their happiest and to be able to deploy their talents to best advantage when they are confident that, standing behind them, there are one or more trusted persons who will come to their aid should difficulties arise."

(Bowlby 1973a, p.359)

"... an unwanted child is likely not only to feel unwanted by his parents but to believe that he is essentially unwantable, namely unwanted by anyone. Conversely, a much-loved child may grow up to be not only confident of his parents' affection but confident that everyone else will find him lovable too."

(Bowlby 1973a, pp. 204-5)

Overview

In this chapter, we explore the first of the major tenets of Attachment Theory that we identified in Chapter Two: that Internal Working Models constructed on the basis of secure attachment relationships will provide children with better social and interpersonal skills and understanding and that this, in turn, will promote success in forming and maintaining social relationships, and in dealing with stress. In doing this, we will focus mainly on studies that have used the Strange Situation to assess attachment security and so will also be trying to evaluate the predictive and discriminant validity of the Strange Situation test.

The chapter is organised into three sections as follows:
- First, we present arguments from Attachment Theory that give rise to the claim under consideration.
- Next, we consider the question of *predictive* validity. Here we investigate what evidence there might be that secure attachment during childhood, adolescence, adulthood and across generations is associated with benefits that are not associated with insecure patterns of attachment.
- In the third section, we go on to discuss the question of the *discriminant* validity. Here we consider the extent to which empirical evidence supports the notion that attachment behaviour is a real, independent phenomenon and not a side effect of some other theoretically unrelated influence.

The argument: Attachment security across the lifespan

Central to Attachment Theory is the notion that there will be clear differences in behavioural outcomes for children who have learned to expect that key people will be emotionally available for them when needed and those whose experiences have not facilitated this basic sense of trust.

Some children come to expect that key people in their lives will be able to protect them, and will care about them, understand and value them. Others feel more or less sure about these things. Children who learn to trust that key figures will be available when needed also tend to refer back to those figures when they are unsure about how to deal with events or circumstances. In this way, they use their attachment figures to help them to make sense of experiences. Their attachment figures, in turn, to make sure that their children are as safe as possible, equip their children not just with food but with information about how to conduct themselves most efficiently (how to behave and how to keep fit and well) and how to make sense of their experiences.

On this basis, Attachment Theory predicts that children who have had more positive experiences from the outset will hold the view that others, like the most important people closest to them, will be rewarding and will potentially prove to be valuable both as sources of comfort and information. Their experiences will have led them to a view of themselves as worthy of love and protection. As a result, they develop mental representations (Internal Working Models) of themselves in relation to others which are positive and which positively value close relationships with others.

On the other hand, children with less positive experiences will develop qualitatively different self-other representations. They will expect less from interactions with others, will have less confidence that others will respect or value them and will have less feedback from attachment figures to guide them in how best to handle their emotional responses to social experiences.

As the sense of being valued is tied in with a higher-level long-term objective of ensuring survival (or the capacity for genetic reproduction), this does not mean that children with predominantly positive experiences of self-other interactions will feel so self-assured that they will charge out into the world recklessly. On the contrary, they will continue to check back constantly with key figures and will seek ongoing reassurance. However, as they get older, the 'checking back' will consist less and less of overt help-seeking and will become more internalised. Gradually, instead of calling out for help in times of minor difficulty, children will begin to rely more and more on memories of how they were helped to negotiate similar situations. They will begin to be able to apply the same principles to new situations. However, they will also continue for a long time to enjoy relating their experiences to their key attachment figures and to learn from and to gain reassurance from the feedback they get. As they get older, they will begin to transfer these learning and sense-making experiences to wider social contexts as well as to other social relationships.

Such securely attached children are thought to have a secure base from which they can, with a reasonable amount of confidence, go out into the social world beyond the family. They will be equipped with sound social skills, a positive attitude to relationships and a sense that, should things get difficult, there will be people to turn to for help. There is, in other words, a good balance between their need for security and their desire to explore. This balanced outlook affords them freedom to operate effectively in the wider social context (Figure 4.1).

Figure 4.1: Secure attachment

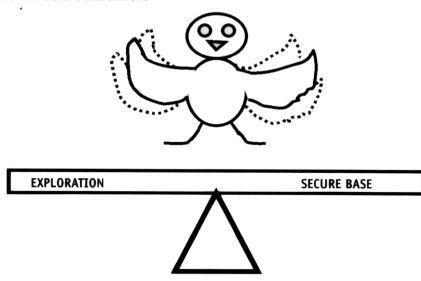

Conversely, children who set off without this secure base lack the experience of co-constructing an understanding of themselves in interaction with others and so are at a distinct disadvantage. Not only are they more vulnerable to negative outside influences (both in the sense of being less able to recognise danger and of being less able to seek assistance when in difficulty) but they are also likely to have less well developed social skills (both through not having had so much experience of appraising or evaluating social events and because they are less likely to conceptualise the behaviour of themselves and others as well-intentioned or understandable). In both a real and a metaphorical sense, it is as if securely attached children are equipped with an emotional tool box that insecurely attached children either do not have, have only in bits or don't know how to use.

The most disadvantaged group of children are likely to be those who have not developed any organised strategy, that is, the children who, in the Strange Situation, are classified, according to Mary Main's system, as 'disorganised' (Figure 4.2). These children, (and possibly also the children who cannot be classified, about whom even less is known) are neither able to gain comfort from their attachment figure nor to explore effectively outside the home. Some may have developed a role reversal strategy in which they, prematurely and therefore rather in a rather haphazard manner, have taken over a quasi-parental role. Others are literally 'all-over-the-place'. Watching such children in the Strange Situation can be harrowing. The baby might, for example, run one way, stop, lie down, bang his or her head on the floor, hide under a chair, or huddle up as if confused or 'frozen' with fear. The impression given by some is that they have no idea how to comfort themselves.

Figure 4.2: Disorganised attachment

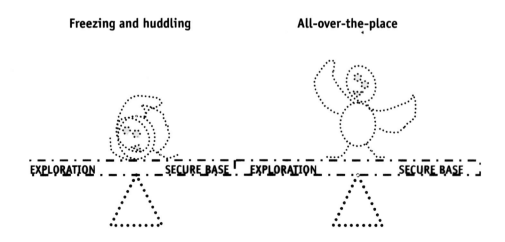

Other insecurely attached children have more organised patterns (Figure 4.3). The avoidantly attached infant has already learned, even by the age of 12 months, that showing him/herself as needing reassurance is likely to cause problems so, pushing those needs aside, has become prematurely self-reliant and precociously interested in the world beyond the most immediately available close attachment figure. These children, when challenged, tend to focus more than others on exploration, as though they have learned to seek reassurance from this sphere rather than from the attachment figure. However, home observations tend to indicate that they are not particularly independent but are quite demanding of their carers' attention.

Ambivalently attached infants are perhaps the most demanding and seem unable to obtain the reassurance they seek from their caregivers. The balance between exploration and secure base seeking, for them, is tipped toward a continuous, rather desperate and frustrated search for love and reassurance, with little expectation of success and rather more expectation of failure, and a failure to move on. As a result, they tend to be the least well motivated explorers of the world beyond, the worst equipped to make sense of their social experiences and emotionally the least well regulated (though perhaps not quite as poorly regulated as children with disorganised attachment patterns[1]).

---

1   This point is somewhat contentious: according to Patricia Crittenden, who considers some of the disorganised patterns to be organised responses to chaotic situations, some children considered 'disorganised' by Mary Main (e.g. 'controlling' or 'parentified' children who have adopted the parental role) may be as well regulated emotionally as children with organised insecure patterns.

Figure 4.3: Organised insecure patterns

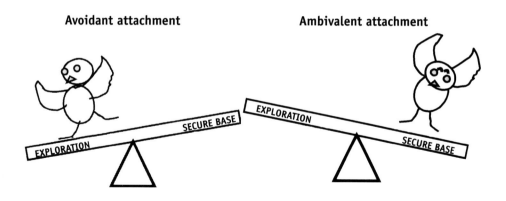

In essence, then, the argument from Attachment Theory is that Internal Working Models constructed on the basis of secure attachment relationships entail reliable, predictable and loving experiences of intimate relationships. As a result, they provide children not only with a more positive sense of self and others but also with greater understanding and stronger motivation to accept and understand self and others. This, in turn, leads to better social and interpersonal skills, superior self and other care, better strategies for dealing with stress, and greater success in forming and maintaining social relationships.

Attachment security is therefore predicted to manifest as:
- better psychosocial adjustment, i.e. fewer behavioural difficulties, less anxiety, depression, etc.
- better social skills
- better emotional self-regulation, more effective coping skills
- higher motivation to achieve
- better self and other understanding
- greater motivation to cooperate, i.e. more openness, honesty, personal integrity
- better self-care leading to healthier lifestyles
- a higher propensity for making and sustaining enduring relationships
- greater reproductive potential and capacity
- and, ultimately, better parenting skills.

Predictions from Attachment Theory are slightly less clear with respect to attributes (for example, problem-solving and language ability) that could be said to depend on intrinsic (from within) as well as on extrinsic (emanating from the social context) rewards. However, it is likely that, at least by the time the child is school age, if not considerably earlier, relationship experience may also have begun to impact on motivation to achieve in these areas too so that performance may vary as a function of attachment security and not just as a function of intrinsic motivational properties. So Attachment Theory also predicts an interaction between attachment security and motivation to achieve in respect of:
- language ability
- communicative skills
- problem-solving skills
- performance on cognitive tests.

However, since attachment security is conceptualised as constructed in consequence of having had particular social interactive experiences, it is not expected to bear any relationship to individual traits such as intelligence or temperament, or to attributes such as perceptual ability, physique or biological sex; nor is it expected to vary as a function of parental attributes that are not directly associated with social interactive experience (we discuss parental influences in the next chapter).

Attachment Theory therefore also predicts that attachment security will *not* be closely associated with a number of child traits or attributes including:
- IQ
- perceptual ability
- biological sex
- temperament.

The evidence

In fact, as we shall show, there is still plenty of room for debate about exactly how attachment security might influence different behavioural outcomes. These debates arise in part from the way in which environmental influences impact on genetic endowment and environment but also from the difficulties, mentioned in the previous chapter, concerning assessment of attachment across the lifespan. As a result, many of the findings relating to children are based on studies in which assessment of individual attachment status has been derived principally from one Strange Situation test with mother at age one. Assessments of social and emotional behaviour have then been made either using concurrent measures or subsequent measures in a short-term longitudinal design. Figure 4.4 illustrates a typical design.

Designs of this sort provide no grounds for assuming that attachment security in infancy is *causally* related to later behaviour outcomes. Indeed, because most aspects of human social behaviour are multiply determined, it is almost impossible to be sure which social experiences might have contributed to particular behavioural outcomes. For example, parents who consistently provide high-quality care from infancy into childhood may tend to have happier, better adjusted children than parents who, for whatever reason, are unable to provide the same quality of care. It also happens that infants with high-quality carers tend to be assessed as securely attached while infants with poorer quality care tend to be assessed as insecurely attached. Even so, we cannot conclude from this that it was the attachment security rather than the quality of parental care (or both or neither) that produced the good outcomes for children. All we can be sure of is that there appears to be an association between positive outcomes, security of attachment and high-quality care.

Figure 4.4: Typical design for study of correlates and sequelae of attachment

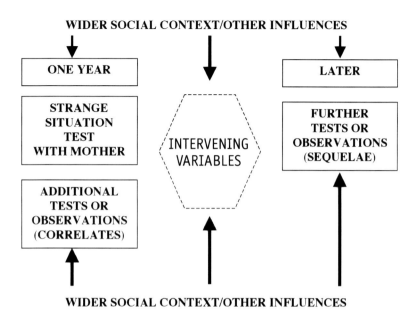

Nor does this kind of problem fade into the background as children grow older. Rather, it grows, exponentially! Let us suppose that, having followed a sample of infants into childhood or adolescence, we find that securely attached individuals continue to perform better on indices of social and emotional development than insecurely attached individuals. We still have no firm grounds for attributing these differences in later behaviour to security of attachment in infancy. Why? Because we still have no way of isolating the effects of attachment security from other influences. For all we know, the children's behaviour could be due to any of a number of other factors, for example, to the continued high quality of parental care and factors associated with this, to some positive attribute inherent within the child, or to a combination of these factors, or even to extraneous, unmeasured influences (for example, the quality of the parental relationship, the relationship of the child to the father, extrafamilial support, etc.). Nevertheless, the possibility that good outcomes for children do depend on mother-infant attachment security remains. But, without very complex and rigorous research designs, it is not possible to determine exactly which factors are most influential nor what kind of role each factor has. We return to this issue in Chapter Six.

Conundrums of this kind have led to considerable debate, both within the field of attachment research and outside it, about how early attachment patterns influence later outcomes. Jerome Kagan, who has spent years conducting painstaking research into the question of temperamental differences in infants and children, takes issue with attachment researchers, accusing them, amongst other sins, of wavering in their opinions about the significance of early attachment relationships. He attacks Sroufe, for example, for putting forward contradictory views and claims that "these inconsistencies are common in scientific fields, like psychology, that rest on weak evidence" (Kagan 1998, p.105). Sroufe (1988), on the other hand, has protested that he never asserted either that all behaviour is fixed from the early years nor stated that it would be infinitely malleable. He did postulate though (Sroufe 1983) that, since development is hierarchical, it can be expected to be coherent to some extent and that vestiges of earlier adaptation are bound to remain. Later, however, describing attachment theory as "a sophisticated sensitive period hypothesis", Sroufe (1988, p.22) emphasised that "The idea of *working* models means both that such models are active constructions forged over time and they are subject to change. The inner aspect is meant to imply that the model is not simply formed and reshaped from the outside; rather, new experiences are engaged from within the framework of the models already constructed, and change is an active rather than a passive process."

Kagan, nevertheless, berates Sroufe and claims that, in a later paper (Carlson and Sroufe 1995), he offers a far more deterministic account of the role of early attachment experiences. It is true that, in this paper, Carlson and Sroufe (1995, pp. 609-610) write, "From early relationships emerges the inner organization of attitudes, feelings, expectations, meanings, and behavior that is the self. Just as regularities in early dyadic interaction become regularities in individual organization, early relationship difficulties may result in distortions in individual functioning." However, the main thrust of this paper is to emphasise the need for more multidisciplinary research into the question of continuity and change in relation to relationship history.

Kagan's work has been of immense importance in increasing understanding of the complexity of the construct of temperament. In some respects, in fact, his work has been more focused, detailed and rigorous than many studies in the field of attachment. But, even so, the work of researchers like Sroufe and others too countless to name has also been gradually adding to our understanding of attachment behaviour. Yet, as Kagan is correct to remark, there is still considerable work to be done. In the remainder of this chapter, we review some of the enormous body of evidence so far amassed.

First, we consider the pre-school years; second, early and middle childhood; third, adolescence; and fourth, adulthood. In carrying out this task, we have to acknowledge that our account of findings is by no means exhaustive. To collate and evaluate all the research findings that are now available in this area would be a task of gargantuan proportions. Because of this, we have found it necessary to draw a rather arbitrary line in our consideration of the evidence. As a result, our account may be seen to over-represent somewhat studies from the 1970s and 1980s, before the time when the 'disorganised' attachment style had been identified and before alternative assessments to the Strange Situation (SS) procedure had emerged. At that time, considerable research effort was still being devoted to understanding what the correlates and sequelae of Strange Situation attachment classification might be. Many of the more widely cited findings emerged from the studies listed in Table 4.1, the majority of which were carried out in the US.

Table 4.1: Main studies from which findings are drawn for this chapter

PLACE	SAMPLE	KEY REPORTERS
Germany, Bielefeld	49 infants (range of family incomes) observed from two months to 22 years	Grossmanns, Lutkenhaus, Schwan, Spangler, Suess, Unzner, Wartner, Zimmermann
Germany, Regensburg	51 non-risk infants, observed from birth to 22 years	
Israel	Observed samples of infants with metaplot in kibbutzim (n=86) or with parents in city (n=36); 59 from kibbutzim followed up @ 4 years	Oppenheim, Sagi, Lamb, Estes, Gardner, Lewkowicz, Shoham, Dvir
Japan, Sapporo	Several samples varying in size (usually less than 40)	Miyake, Chen, Ujiie, Tajima, Satoh, Takahashi, Chen, Campos
Japan, Tokyo	36 infants	Durrett, Okaki, Richards
Netherlands	Original sample contained 136 mother-infant pairs	Van IJzendoorn, Goossens, Swaan, Kroonenberg, Tavecchio, Vergeer
Sweden	Observed 51 infants at home during first year of life and in SS at 11/13 months with mother/father	Lamb, Hwang, Frodi, Frodi
US: Ann Arbor	75 infants (mean age 20 months) of middle- and upper-middle class mothers; SS with mother/father at two times, with one month in between	Easterbrooks, Goldberg, Lamb, Perotta, Minde
US: SF, California: Berkeley, Social Development Project	36 infants initially, white middle-class mothers, SS + follow-up at 21 months and 6 years, sample added to over time	Main, Weston, Londerville, Kaplan, Stadtman, Tomasini, Tolan, Cassidy
US: Charlottesville	52 six-year-olds, white middle class,	Cassidy
US: Bloomington, Indiana	168 babies of mainly middle-class families, observed from 6-13 months; follow-up at 24 months, 3, 5 and 6 years; high attrition rate	Bates, Bayles, Maslin, Frankel
US: Harvard Child Maltreatment Project	71 maltreated infants (17 at 12 months; 26 at 18 months; 28 at 24 months) from low-income families cf control groups	Cicchetti, Carlson, Brunwald, Schneider-Rosen

Table 4.1 continued

PLACE	SAMPLE	KEY REPORTERS
US: Massachusetts	76 high-risk cf matched controls in Family Support Project	Lyons-Ruth, Connell, Grunebaum, Botein, Zoll, Stahl, Repacholi, Alpern
US: Miami	46 adolescent, low-income or high-risk mothers with 11-24 month infants; 98 maltreating and 29 'adequate' families; additional more recent work	Crittenden
US: Michigan	43 middle class mother-infant dyads	Thompson, Lamb, Estes, Gardner
US: Minneapolis, Minnesota Parent-Child Project	267 firstborns from disadvantaged families, observed from 3-18 months, at home and SS; 212 in SS at 12 months; 189 at 18 months; further follow-up of 62 at 18-24 months; further follow-ups through to 22 years	Brunnquell, Carlson, Dodds, Egeland, Erickson, Farber, Fox, Gove, Joffe, Shulman, Sroufe, Urban, Vaughn, Waters, Weinfield
US: Minnesota longitud-inal study	48 infants from middle-class families, SS at 18 months, IQ test at 23, play obs at 24 months	Matas, Arend, Sroufe, Gove, Pancake, Pastor, Rosenberg
US: Pennsylvania Infant and Family Project	200+ mainly middle-class families, recruited in three cohorts of c50-70 and observed from birth to just over one year	Belsky, Rovine, Taylor, Isabella, Von Eye, Garduque, Most, Hrncir

Due to the now massive and constantly burgeoning database of studies of adult attachment, our treatment of these findings too is necessarily somewhat cursory. We nevertheless hope that this partial overview will afford readers a glimpse of the much larger picture that has been and still is emerging.

Infants, pre-schoolers and attachment

Representations of family

It is not a very straightforward task to assess very young children's internal models of their family because of the difficulty of ensuring, first, that children have understood what they are being asked to do and, second, that they have the skills to execute what is being asked of them. Nevertheless, researchers have used a variety of methods to investigate how securely and insecurely attached children might represent their families.

Lay et al. (1995) showed three-and-a-half year-olds vignettes, either positive or negative, and either relating or not relating to mothers. The aim was to induce particular moods and feelings about close relationships. Though the researchers found little difference in respect of the positive stimuli, they found large differences in the ways that securely and insecurely attached children responded to the negative vignettes. Securely attached children appeared to experience more difficulty than insecurely attached children when they were confronted with situations where mothers were portrayed as not being available. Conversely, insecurely attached children produced less coherent and more defensive responses than securely attached children when confronted with situations where mothers were available. These results seem to confirm the prediction that, in situations of stress when attachment behaviours are evoked, securely and insecurely attached children will draw upon very different 'working models' of family relationships and that these leave them with qualitatively different perspectives on how to make sense of and negotiate social relationships.

As further confirmation of such differences, Kaplan and Main (1985) also reported that avoidantly attached children tend to draw rather stylised pictures of members of their families. The characters portrayed have fewer distinctively individual characteristics, appear less well connected to each other emotionally and more stereotyped. The implication is that avoidantly attached children are in some way disconnected from their emotional experiences and unable to appreciate fully the emotional life of other family members. However, there is also the possibility that it is their expression of their understanding that is curtailed rather than their actual understanding.

Problem-solving and compliance with mother

Similar findings emerged from observations of two-year-old children engaged with their mothers in problem-solving and clean-up tasks (Matas et al. 1978). Four progressively difficult tasks were involved (e.g. pushing a toy out of a slot with a stick, weighting a board with a block in order to get candy up through a hole in a large box), at the end of which parents were instructed to interrupt their child to clean up. Distinctly different qualities of mother-toddler interaction were found to be linked to different attachment histories (as assessed by the Strange Situation at 18 months).

Securely attached children tended to show greater enthusiasm, and more persistence, flexibility and positive affect. They were also better at enlisting their mothers' help when they needed assistance, listened to their mothers more carefully, ignored them less and were generally more cooperative. Avoidant infants, by contrast, tended not to seek help even when they were clearly unable to solve problems. They were much less likely to show positive affection or to seek physical contact when aroused and, instead, either directed their anger towards objects or became angry and non-compliant. Ambivalent/resistant toddlers were the most affectively negative, fussy and irritable, gave up easily and got cross quickly. They engaged in very little symbolic play and tended to divert their energies into getting into tussles with their mothers.

These findings by Matas et al. (1978), which were carried out with a middle-income sample, have been replicated with other middle-class samples and in high-risk samples (e.g. Erickson et al. 1985). In addition, 62 children from the same sample of children were re-tested by Pastor (1981) when they were aged between 20 and 23 months. On many dimensions, Pastor found fewer differences between children but he did find significant differences between securely and non-securely attached children on levels of compliance with mothers' directives (securely attached children complied more) and on the number of times mothers rejected infants' bids for attention (insecurely attached children were rejected more). Pastor also found that securely attached children were better than avoidantly attached children at restoring harmony after conflict, generally because they were more skilful at re-directing attention onto other activities.

Further support for predicted differences in respect of attachment security came from a study by Londerville and Main (1981) of thirty-six 21-month-old infants who had previously been assessed in the Strange Situation at 12 months. The 22 infants who were securely attached were more cooperative with the person who carried out an IQ test on them, more likely to rescue a doll from danger (in the form of an advancing peer and a toy dog) in a play session, more compliant with their mothers and more likely to evidence control over their own impulses. By contrast, both the seven avoidant and the three ambivalent/resistant children (four in this sample were unclassifiable) more often actively and angrily disobeyed their mothers, while their mothers more frequently described them as troublesome.

Erickson and Farber (1983), following up the Minnesota sample of disadvantaged families at 42 months, partially confirmed some of the earlier findings by Matas and colleagues but found fewer differences between avoidantly and securely attached children than between ambivalently and securely attached children. Three-year-olds with histories of either avoidant or secure attachment were significantly more persistent, enthusiastic and compliant, and relied less on their mothers' support than did children with a history of ambivalent attachment. Erickson and Farber (1983) also failed to find differences between attachment groups on negativism, expression of affection or avoidance of mother.

Arend et al. (1979) also re-contacted 26 of the sample studied by Matas et al. (1978) when children were aged between 54 and 70 months. They obtained reports from nursery teachers and administered a battery of tests to the children. Securely attached children got higher scores on measures of ego resiliency and were also higher on ego control. Grossmann and Grossmann (1991) in Germany found similar advantages for securely attached children, but others (e.g. Easterbrooks and Goldberg 1990, Howes et al. 1994) have not replicated these results.

Some explanation for the slightly different results produced by different studies possibly comes from work by Main and Weston. In one study, Main and Weston (1981) reported that securely attached pre-schoolers were more friendly and responsive to an adult clown and also that children who were insecure with mother but secure with father also tended to be more relaxed in approaching the clown than children who were insecure with both parents. Examining the data more closely and returning to Ainsworth's finding that children re-tested two weeks after the initial Strange Situation behaved differently the second time round, Main and Weston raised the possibility that the forced-classification system then in use may be causing some children to be mis-assigned to the secure group. They suggested that the inclusion of these 'false-secure' children may have introduced an element of error. It was partly in consequence of these observations that they set about the task of refining the Strange Situation classification procedures.

Social interactions

Nevertheless, many studies continued to provide evidence of predicted associations between attachment security and outcomes for children, especially those that investigated children's interactions with other children. On the basis of these, many researchers have arrived at the view that children's internalised expectations from early parent-child relationships do inform how they interact with peers and others outside the family (e.g. Youngblade and Belsky 1992, Belsky and Cassidy 1994).

Several studies have shown that securely attached pre-schoolers are more socially competent, less impulsive, more popular and higher on self-esteem than insecurely attached children (Sroufe 1983, Vandell et al. 1988, Booth et al. 1991, Howes et al. 1994, Olson et al. 1990, Rose-Krasnor et al. 1996). Securely attached children have also been perceived to be more compliant, higher on ego-resilience and empathy, higher on positive, lower on negative affect and lower on dependency than insecurely attached children (Sroufe 1983, Sroufe et al. 1983).

After observing 40 four-to-five year olds in interaction with peers and having collected reports from teachers of children's social competence as well as from peers of sociometric status (popularity), LaFreniere and Sroufe (1985) concluded that securely attached children were the most positive, confident and effective in their interactions with peers: they were active explorers and they were also very competent in the way they manipulated and played with objects.

A number of studies indicate that avoidantly attached pre-schoolers initiate fewer positive interactions with other children (e.g. Jacobson and Wille 1986), show less empathy towards pre-school peers (Kestenbaum et al. 1989) and tend to be perceived by teachers to be more hostile and antisocial (Sroufe 1983). LaFreniere and Sroufe (1985) further observed that avoidantly attached children displayed greater negative affect and hostility in interaction with their peers and were both more hostile and more distant towards their caregivers (they neither sought interaction nor attention as much as other children). Avoidantly and securely attached pre-schoolers tended not to differ, though, in respect of quality of exploration, skills in object manipulation or level of self-assertiveness.

Ambivalent/resistant pre-schoolers, on the other hand, appear to be the least competent in their interactions both with other children and with objects (LaFreniere and Sroufe 1985) and have been found to be the least self-assertive, the most hesitant and the least socially dominant in interaction with peers (Pastor 1981, Erickson et al. 1985, LaFreniere and Sroufe 1985). In the study by LaFreniere and Sroufe (1985), they were also judged as not exploring either very much or very effectively, as lacking skills in object manipulation, and as low on sense of self-efficacy. Under stress, they tended to resort either to extreme passivity or to become disorganized. Some of these differences between children appear to be associated more with girls than with boys but most samples have been too small for this to be explored fully.

Exploration, play and aggression

Similar patterns of difference have been found in studies of exploration, play and aggression in pre-school children. Examining differences in the play of four-and-a-half year-old children in the Minnesota longitudinal study, Rosenberg (cited in Carlson and Sroufe 1995) reported that children who had been assessed as securely attached in infancy engaged well with fantasy play and often included situations that involved imagined social skills. They were also able to confront frightening situations or to describe conflict resolution. Avoidantly attached children, by contrast, did not engage so well in fantasy play, portrayed people or social situations less often and frequently conveyed aggressive thoughts. The themes present in the fantasy play of ambivalent/resistant children reflected unresolved interpersonal conflicts, danger, fear and aggression.

Wartner et al. (1994) also reported that securely attached pre-schoolers were more competent in play and conflict resolution while others have also reported on the tendency of avoidant children to engage in more struggles over objects (e.g. Pastor 1981, McElwain et al. 2003). Ambivalently attached pre-schoolers tend to play with and manipulate toys less frequently and less competently (Miyake et al. 1985) and have been found to be less self-controlled and less assertive (McElwain et al. 2003). They are also more restricted in their exploration of physical space (Hazen and Durrett 1982) and have been thought to have lower executive capacity, or cognitive mastery (Belsky et al. 1984a). This view concurs with that of Sroufe (1983) who observed that securely attached children appeared better able to think about, control and organise their behaviour.

Differences in handling feelings have also been observed by Lutkenhaus et al. (1985) who found that, on losing during competitive tower-building, avoidantly attached children tended to appear sad while playing but did not show this sadness when they interacted with others shortly after. Securely attached children, on the other hand, showed sadness after the game too. The possibility that these differences might be linked to affective states was tested by Belsky et al. (1996b) in a study of the ability of three-year-olds to remember positive and negative events. Results confirmed their prediction that, on a delayed recognition task, securely attached children would recall more positive than negative events while insecurely attached would recall more negative than positive events.

Self-control and sense of self

Such observations have led researchers to postulate that different attachment histories in young babies and pre-school children have already begun to influence how they manage their feelings. Sroufe (1983) suggests that avoidantly attached children may have bottled up and suppressed negative or angry feelings, because they have learned that it is not safe to express these feelings in relationship to their key caregivers. As a result, he argues, they behave in a hostile and aggressive way that causes them to become socially isolated. Often they are disconnected from their own feelings and so are unaware of the angry element in their behaviour. Ambivalently attached children, too, have not learned to cope effectively with arousal but, rather than detaching from uncomfortable states and distancing their feelings as avoidantly attached children do, they remain snarled up in a state of tension, permanently close to distress and unable to trust themselves to manage challenging situations. This leads them either to be very clingy and demanding or very dependent, passive or helpless.

Behaviour problems

Of course, it was of great interest to Bowlby, as he was developing this theory of attachment, to be able to explain the nature of the relationship between attachment patterns and pathological outcomes. Accepting that development was complexly determined because subject to interactive effects of within-individual and environmental influences, Bowlby (1973a), influenced by Waddington's model of development, likened development to a network of branching pathways (Figure 4.5).

Figure 4.5: Routes to healthy and poor outcomes

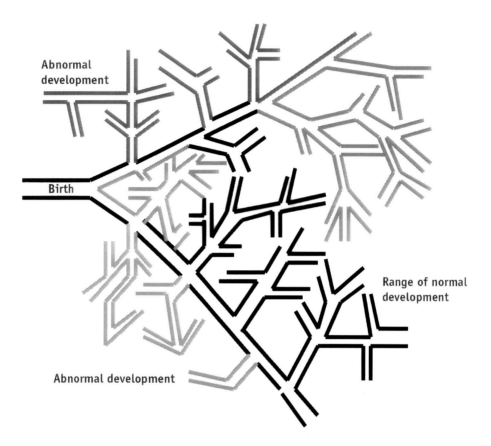

The majority of pathways lead to good outcomes, but a substantial minority lead to poor outcomes. Once started on a trajectory, deviation from that pathway becomes more difficult. A wrong turning inevitably leads further and further from the relatively wide range of pathways where conditions of survival are optimal, much in the way that Waddington described when he wrote of 'canalisation' (the groove gets deeper as the water wears it down, the water therefore runs faster and wears the groove further). Some have likened this model to a tree (e.g. Sroufe 1996) with four or five interwoven trunks (labelled A, B, C, D). Some parts of the tree are healthier or more robust than others. The metaphor might be extended to a whole forest in which strong healthy saplings head up towards the light. Those overshadowed by larger-leaved light-blocking trees and crowded in by other healthy saplings, without rapid adaptation, re-planting or other assistance, despite their healthiness, will struggle to survive. Less robust plants face even greater challenges.

In fact, although the analogy of a tree captures a notion of the inter-dependence of environmental influences and individual development quite nicely, it fails to capture the principle that Bowlby was actually putting forward when he used the branching pathways metaphor. One weak branch in a tree rarely endangers a whole tree whereas one wrong turn, especially if taken early, is likely to lead to long-lasting consequences. Bowlby's use of the branching pathways analogy was, at that time, rather more deterministic than the tree analogy would imply. In a sense, the tree analogy may have evolved as more empirical evidence has been added to Bowlby's early theorising. It may also be valuable in drawing attention to the possibility that each individual may have, both at the outset and later in life, the potential to develop along multiple, interlinking trajectories. These considerations aside, in the early days of Bowlby's Attachment Theory, it was certainly not known for sure whether different patterns of attachment represented different levels of robustness or simply different kinds of 'plant'. Soon, many studies were being undertaken to test whether pathological conditions were more likely to be associated with one developmental trajectory, or attachment pattern, rather than another.

Several studies of pre-schoolers began to provide evidence to support the notion that insecure attachments are more closely associated than secure attachments with poor outcomes, especially with respect to behaviour problems (e.g. Lewis et al. 1984, Erickson et al. 1985, Greenberg et al. 1993, Burgess et al. 2003).

Some researchers, however, did not find that Strange Situation attachment classification predicted behaviour problems at age three, five or six years (Bates and Bayles 1988), even though mothers of a very small number of avoidantly attached (A1) boys reported more problems. However, they concluded that, rather than there being no association, their measure of problems may have been at fault, since they had relied chiefly on mothers' reports.

Disorganisation is known to be more prevalent among children living in high-risk environments, e.g. where parents are violent, abusive, alcoholic or depressed (Carlson et al. 1989, Teti et al. 1995, O'Connor et al. 1987). It has also been consistently found to be associated with more behavioural problems in pre-school and early school years (Lyons-Ruth et al. 1993, Shaw et al. 1996), as well as with social-emotional and cognitive deficits in older children (Lyons-Ruth and Jacobvitz 1999, van IJzendoorn et al. 1999).

Different types of attachment disorganisation (e.g. controlling-punitive, controlling-caregiving, etc.) appear to be associated with a wide range of negative outcomes (Teti 1999). In infants with attachment patterns classified A/C (Avoidant/Ambivalent) by Crittenden (1985, 1988), one pattern appeared to be associated with older children who were more severely abused while a second pattern was linked with serious neglect rather than abuse. Because of the difficulties (mentioned in Chapter Three) that are associated with making sense of findings using different coding systems, it will not be possible to give more than a brief account of outcomes for children classified in infancy as disorganised. However, in the next two chapters, we do present more research evidence concerning the kind of parent-child relationship apparently associated with this pattern of attachment. We also re-visit this group of children when we consider treatment approaches in Chapter Seven.

Middle childhood

Family interactions

Studies of children in middle childhood show that, as in earlier childhood, secure attachment relationships seem to set children on track for better relationships generally. This applies both within the family and beyond. Teti and Ablard (1989), for example, reported that siblings who are each securely attached to their parents interact together more harmoniously than siblings who are not each securely attached. Also, as with younger children, securely attached older children have higher self-esteem and greater self-confidence as well as better social skills in interaction with other children (Elicker et al. 1992). Elicker et al. (1992) conclude that important experiences of reciprocal interactions with key figures at home may have generalised to relationships outside the home, a conclusion which also gained support from the findings of Ziv and colleagues (2004). These researchers observed that seven- or eight-year-olds with secure attachments anticipated more sensitive reactions from their mothers and were also more likely than insecure children to expect other children to be kind to them and to like them. Thompson (1999), though, cautions against over-confident causal claims and points out that it is difficult to be sure whether differences arise as a result of early attachment security or, more generally, from continued confidence-producing parenting.

Social interactions

Interestingly, some researchers have found that children with histories of secure attachment can, at times, appear less socially competent than other children. Belsky and his colleagues, for example, found that securely attached five-year-olds had fewer close friends and were less sociable than less secure children (Youngblade and Belsky 1992, Youngblade et al. 1993). In explaining these findings, Youngblade and Belsky (1992) raised the possibility that more securely attached children at this age, which is a key transition stage (from home to school) in many cultures, may have less motivation than insecurely attached children to engage in the task of making new friends. This might be particularly true of children who are temperamentally inhibited or shy. The implication here is that, during major childhood transitions, other factors may come into play that alter the quality of social interactions and differentially affect the adaptive strategies adopted by children with different attachment histories.

At later ages, the benefits of earlier secure attachment have tended to re-emerge. In early middle childhood, both teacher ratings and observations by researchers in the Minnesota study indicated that children with secure attachment histories formed closer friendships, were more effective in peer groups (Pancake 1985, Sroufe 1983), were more outgoing and positive in interaction with other children (Sroufe et al. 1984) and were better accepted by their peers (Kerns et al. 1996). They were also observed to show more empathy and interest in other children.

By age ten, securely attached children in both US and German longitudinal studies, were found to have greater social competence, more close friends and stronger friendships (Freitag et al. 1996, Grossmann and Grossmann 1991, Elicker et al. 1992) and to be less dependent on summer school camp counsellors (Urban et al. 1991) than non-securely attached peers.

At age 12, on a sentence completion task, securely attached children again described their primary caregivers significantly more positively and, on a projective story task, described more positive peer relationships and were more creative in solving interpersonal problems (McCrone et al. 1993, cited in Carlson and Sroufe 1995). Children who had been classified as avoidant again conveyed more aggression, negativity, victimisation themes and lack of conflict resolution (McCrone et al. 1993).

Insecurely attached children fared less well. Insecurely attached six-year-old boys were less popular and were perceived as more aggressive by their peers (Cohn 1990) and tend to be rejected by their peers more frequently (Granot and Mayseless 2001). Reviewing a number of studies, Thompson (1999) reported that older insecurely attached children are also prone to problems relating to social competence, aggression, self-esteem, self-efficacy, popularity, self-control and autonomy (Thompson (1999).

As with younger children, studies of older children show that children with histories of avoidant attachment tend to victimise other children (Troy and Sroufe 1987) while ambivalently attached children evaluate their own social status lower than their peers evaluate it (Granot and Mayseless 2001), tend to label themselves as victims in social interactions (Wright et al. 1995), accept the role of victim when interacting with peers (Cassidy and Berlin 1994, Troy and Sroufe 1987) and expect peers to be less kindly disposed towards them or to reject them (Ziv et al. 2004).

Interestingly, children with histories of disorganised attachments have not, as might have been expected, consistently been found to be less competent socially than other children (Goldberg et al. 1995, Jacobvitz and Hazen 1999), which suggests, as Crittenden has commented (Crittenden and Claussen 2000) that the disorganised category may need to be further subdivided in order for it to be well understood.

Exploration, play and aggression

Generally, differences in the quality of play and exploration between securely and insecurely attached younger children have been found to persist at later ages. Securely attached children show greater interest, explore more intensely and stay on task for longer than insecurely attached children (Main 1983), though the difference between securely and avoidantly attached children is less marked than that between ambivalently attached children and others.

Compared with ambivalently attached children, avoidantly attached older children explore more and show greater persistence and competence in object manipulation (Frodi et al. 1985, Belsky et al. 1984a). However, Cassidy and Kobak (1988) suggest that this attention to objects might reflect a strategy of using exploration to distract themselves from negative interpersonal experiences.

Cognitive skills

Although cognitive ability is not expected to vary as a function of attachment security, some researchers have found differences in attentional strategies that appear to result in secure children being better disposed to learn effectively (Maslin-Cole and Spieker 1990). However, there is little evidence that children with avoidant strategies are less able academically than children with histories of secure attachment and few significant differences have been found in this respect. It is conceivable that children with histories of insecure attachment but with high IQ may compensate for lack of positive feedback in the social sphere by putting more effort into academic or non-social skills. More research is needed to establish whether this might be the case, particularly in relation to artistic, creative or IT skills. Surprisingly, no research appears to have addressed the question of whether 'geeks' (people who are highly invested in exploration of ideas) are more likely to have histories of avoidant than of secure or other types of attachment.

Some researchers have begun to investigate the relationship between attention disorders and quality of attachment and have theorised a link between ADHD (Attention Deficit Hyperactivity Disorder) and avoidant attachment (e.g. Ladnier and Massanari 2000). However, opinions vary on the question of what the nature of this connection might be and other researchers have pointed to a link between ADHD and the ambivalent attachment style (e.g. Clarke et al. 2002). Another theory that has been put forward is that insecure attachment may be due to dysfunctional attentional strategies and that a neurochemical problem (e.g. problems related to the neurotransmitter, serotonin) may underlie both patterns (Smith 1994).

This proposition certainly seems worth further exploration but it is important not to jump to premature conclusions. More work is needed to investigate the nature of links between attachment patterns, attentional strategies, and neurological and neurochemical activity. It is not currently clear how or even whether any causal relationships may obtain.

Self-control and sense of self

This kind of debate also stretches into consideration of the mechanisms through which children's capacity for self-regulation develops. Many theorists and researchers, both before and after Bowlby, have surmised that it is within close relationships between infants and their carers that infants gain a sense of their own agency and their capacity to cope with intense emotions. Bowlby points to this awareness in the work of Freud who drew attention to the difficulties posed for infants as they confront "the conflict – the inevitable conflict – which develops within us" (Bowlby 1958c/1979c, p.5) when love and hate are directed at the one person who is most important. Bowlby links resolution of this kind of conflict with healthy development and non-resolution with problems; "when a young child lacks confidence in his ability to control his threatening impulses, there is a risk that unwittingly he will turn to one or more of a multitude of primitive and rather ineffective psychic devices to protect his loved ones from damage and himself from the pain of a conflict that seems insoluble by other means" (Bowlby 1958c/1979c, p.6).

Bowlby proposed that the recipe for coping with this inevitable conflict came through the love and acceptance of one's parents: "Nothing helps a child more than being able to express hostile and jealous feelings candidly, directly and spontaneously, and there is no parental task more valuable, I believe, than being able to accept with equanimity such expressions of filial piety as 'I hate you, Mummy' or 'Daddy, you're a beast'. By putting up with these outbursts we show our children that we are not afraid of hatred and that we are confident that it can be controlled; moreover, we provide for the child the tolerant atmosphere in which self-control can grow" (Bowlby 1958c/1979c, p.12).

Because this process of tolerance and containment begins very early in life, well before children have begun to use language to convey their feelings, some theorists have speculated that it becomes encoded into the workings of the nervous system and so influences the way in which structures within the brain develop (e.g. Schore 1994). Beguiling though such speculations may be (being able to attribute anti-social behaviour, for example, to the ineffective working of the amygdala, lack of neurons in the frontal cortex, malfunction in a neurological network, etc.), the task of gathering evidence in support of them is no small one. We might be tempted to call kids 'pea-brained' when they annoy us but it is quite another matter to prove that their maddening behaviour is really due to the unique size, weight, shape or workings of their individual brains! The search for simple solutions may continue[2] but their capacity to yield verifiable evidence has to be seen, even with the assistance of brain-imaging or other 'new brain science' techniques, to be currently still quite limited.

Another view that is sometimes put forward as though it were a well-established fact is the notion that an insecure (avoidant or ambivalent) child "will have a weaker sense of self than a securely attached child, because he or she will have lacked optimum 'social biofeedback'" (Gerhardt 2004, p.27). Without getting embroiled in conceptual details concerning

---

2   As it has for decades in the generally less well-illuminated corners of the field of forensic science and as it has in psychiatry and witch medicine when bits of brains were severed/trepanned/lobectomised/leucotomised in order to correct 'faulty' behaviours.

how strength of sense of self may be defined or measured, it seems important to mention here that any pattern of attachment, no matter how organised or disorganised, is likely to involve awareness of self in interaction with others. Attachment theory does not predict that insecure attachment 'weakens' the child's sense of self. Some children with highly disorganised patterns of attachment may even have such strong senses of self that this sense causes them considerable psychological pain. Highly avoidant children may have a strong, idealised sense of themselves and they may also be aware at times of the discrepancy between their own view of themselves and that of others. Children with highly ambivalent patterns are likely to be the most self-focused and the most aware of the discrepancy between who they are and who they want to be, or how they would like to feel and how they actually do feel. It is difficult, however, to prove any of these speculative notions. They may turn out to be unsupported. In addition, it seems important to note that one's sense of self comes from a number of sources.

Psychologists working in the field of social cognition have long understood that one's sense of self emanates both from external (self-awareness) and internal (self-consciousness) processes (e.g. Fenigstein et al. 1975, Scheier and Carver 1977, Scheier and Carver 1980). Both self-awareness and self-consciousness can be publicly observable or privately experienced. Self-awareness arises directly in relation to the situation, for example, as a lecturer, I could be more or less aware of the sound of my voice, its content, whether it is buzzing into the microphone, whether it can be heard above the noise of traffic, where I am standing in relation to the students, how warm the room is, etc. These aspects can be experienced by others present too, so they constitute my public self-awareness. At the same time, perhaps seeing my reflection in a window or noticing how students are looking at me, taking notes, etc., I will be drawing upon another level of information to gain a more private self-awareness. The degree to which I attend to either of these sources of information also depends on my personality, that is how self-conscious I am, in other words, both on my personal disposition and how attentive I normally am to my own emotional state (my private self-consciousness) and on my judgement of how I am performing (my public self-consciousness). At any one time, I may be more or less aware of the task I am undertaking, my feelings about it, and the impact on the students.

In other words, my sense of self is *contextually dependent*. In relation to that situation, it will be tied in with many dimensions over and above whether or not I am securely or insecurely attached. It could also depend, more or less, on how shy I am, how I look, how self-confident, socially skilled or competent I feel, what the students are like, the history of my interactions with that class and as a lecturer, etc. Attachment theory is nearing the stage where, on the basis of evidence of differences accumulated from a growing number of investigations, it can make begin to make hypotheses about expected associations between different patterns of attachment and attention to different sorts of information relevant to a sense of self but, at this stage, there are few relevant studies and little conclusive evidence. Therefore, the assumption that secure attachment equates to a stronger sense of self seems highly disputable. What evidence there is suggests that more securely attached children may be better able to tolerate frustration, more empathic, have greater ego control, ego resiliency and self-esteem, but how these qualities translate into a sense of self is unclear. Nor is it yet altogether clear whether these associations are direct consequences of attachment history or of other continuing influences (Thompson 1999).

Securely attached children, however, do tend to be both more self-accepting and, possibly, more realistic in their self-appraisals. Cassidy (1988) found that securely attached six-year-olds describe themselves generally positively but that they can admit flaws. Insecure six-year-olds, on the other hand, tend to see themselves either as all bad or all good. She also found that securely attached children engaged with experimental tasks with more genuine pleasure and responded to the researcher more cooperatively. As a result, the atmosphere between these children and the researcher was more relaxed, personal, warm and intimate and securely attached children imitated the researcher more readily. Avoidantly attached children tended to avoid engagement and to respond in a neutral though non-confrontational manner. Although they were not hostile, they did limit interaction. Children classified as ambivalent/resistant also avoided talking about their feelings, but came across as sad, fearful, hostile at times and ambivalent about seeking proximity. Children classified as disorganized-controlling adopted two general strategies: they either positively rejected assistance and were confrontationally controlling, or they insisted on being in the carer role and attempted to comfort or placate the researcher.

Coping

As with younger children, attachment-related differences are evident in how children in middle childhood cope with uncomfortable situations. Mary Main and her colleagues (Main et al. 1985) observed six-year-olds as they viewed photographs of stressful separation situations. They rated securely attached children higher on emotional openness and also found that these children offered the most constructive ideas about how to cope. Along the same lines, Cassidy and Kobak (1988) tested six-year-olds with a story completion task and found that the accounts given by children judged as avoidant (on the basis of a separation-reunion procedure) tended to downplay the amount of distress that the child in the story might have felt and also did not include as many references to parents as sources of comfort or support.

Finnegan et al. (1996) have linked insecure attachment patterns to distinctively different styles of coping. They suggest that the avoidant coping style involves a denial of need for attachment figures and avoidance of them when stressed and that the ambivalent/preoccupied style involves strong need for attachment figures but inability to be soothed by them. Using a specially designed questionnaire to assess the presence of different styles of coping in 229 eight- to twelve-year-old children, Finnegan and her colleagues examined how styles of coping related to children's assessments of each other along dimensions such as aggression, argumentativeness, withdrawal, anxiety, etc. They found that the preoccupied style of coping was associated with internalising problems (anxiety/depression), immaturity and victimisation (for boys though not for girls) while avoidant coping was associated with externalising problems (aggression, disruptiveness) and dishonesty for both girls and boys.

Behaviour problems

The notion that avoidant and ambivalent/resistant attachment insecurity will be linked through qualitatively different pathways to specific pathological outcomes is known as the 'specific-linkage hypothesis' (Figure 4.6). The argument here is that the ambivalent/resistant pattern is underpinned by the child's urgent sense of a need to connect to a caregiver (maintained by unpredictable experiences of emotional connectedness) which detracts from their ability to connect with and explore the outside world. As a result, the child feels helpless and dependent and becomes vulnerable to fear and self-doubt. This self-directed negativity can, under stress, become transformed into internalising problems, such as anxiety, panic attacks and depression. Avoidantly attached children, by contrast, turn away from the caregiver and, in order to cope with their sense that their desire for emotional connection is inappropriate, disconnect from it by diverting their attention elsewhere. Residues of the need for connection, however, remain but, rather than directing their negativity inward, they direct it outward. As a result their negativity manifests as externalising problems, including aggression and anti-social behaviour.

Although there appears to be some evidence that ambivalent children are more dependent and withdrawn and suffer from internalising problems whereas avoidant children are more aggressive and evince externalising problems (Cassidy and Berlin 1994), relatively little work has so far been done to test the specific-linkage hypothesis. In addition, there are indications that links may be mediated or moderated by factors such as income level and child abuse: whereas the link between avoidant attachment and aggression has been found in some predominantly low-income, socially disadvantaged samples (e.g. Renken et al. 1989), others have not found the same effect in higher-income samples (e.g. Fagot and Kavanagh 1990, Lewis et al. 1984). Similarly, one study of abused and neglected children indicated a link between avoidance and higher aggression in abused children but a link between ambivalence and low aggression for emotionally neglected children (Finzi et al. 2001). A link between the disorganised pattern of infant attachment and aggression, both in infancy and at later stages throughout childhood, has been more consistently reported (e.g. Lyons-Ruth et al. 1993, Shaw et al. 1996, Carlson 1998).

Figure 4.6: The specific-linkage hypothesis

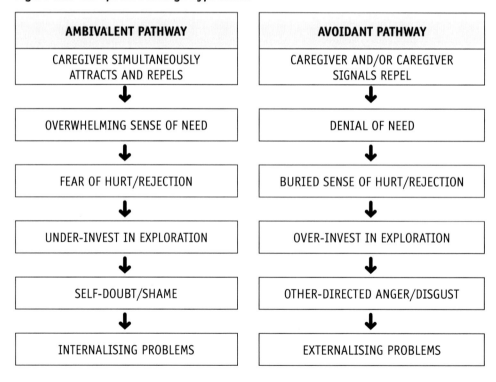

Adolescence

Relationships with parents

Adolescence is widely believed to be a time when children come most strongly under the influence of peer pressure and, for that reason, can be feared by many parents who anticipate that their stroppy teenager will thwart their authority, fail to attain their potential and become exposed to unnecessary dangers. However, most recent research points to the fact that parents, as their key attachment figures, usually remain very important to most teenagers, as sources of advice, friendship, practical and material support, comfort and reassurance. In confirmation of this, Simons et al. (2001) found that adolescents' perceptions of the quality of their attachment to their mother correlated negatively with their reported aggressiveness. Though based only on self-report, these findings therefore seem to underscore the need for mothers even during the teenage years to provide a secure base for their children.

Allen et al. (2003) propose that security of attachment in adolescence is indicated by four independent markers of the relationship between teenagers and their mothers:
- the extent to which the young person and his or her mother are able to stay in discussion over issues upon which they disagree
- lack of idealisation in the adolescent's perception of his or her mother
- the degree to which mothers can estimate their child's responses on a self-perception questionnaire (designated 'maternal attunement') and
- maternal supportiveness assessed by adolescent's responses to two subscales from the Inventory of Parent and Peer Attachment (Armsden and Greenberg 1987).

Also according to Allen et al. (1989), those adolescents who are judged by teachers and by peers as most socially competent tend to hold views that are independent of their parents. However, while their outlooks do differ, they tend to differ on relatively superficial rather than on fundamental levels, for example, while the teenagers might choose, contrary to their parents' preference, to flout a school rule, they would generally agree with their parents on more important matters, such as the value of an open, trusting relationship or good communication.

Allen and Land (1999) point out that adolescence, because it is a time when young people are expected to become more independent and autonomous, can also put a strain on the relationship between parents and teenagers. Incipient problems within insecure relationships that may have lain dormant throughout earlier stages of childhood may emerge as a result of additional stresses placed both on the child and the parent as the adolescent seeks to become more self-reliant. This and the possibility that avoidantly attached children may be the least likely to check back with their parents or to tell their parents if they are feeling out of their depth raises the likelihood that adolescence may be a time when some youngsters are particularly vulnerable as they may not have the knowledge or motivation to access appropriate support networks (we discuss this further in Chapter Seven).

Sroufe et al. (2001) point out that certain outcomes, e.g. teenage sexual promiscuity, appear to be better predicted by a measure of generational boundary dissolution, assessed at two, three and 13, than by quality of attachment. Although assessments of attachment security in the past have not systematically included measures of generational boundary dissolution (which is tied in with the balance of power between adults and offspring), arguably, there is a theoretical basis for the assumption that the two influences are necessarily independent. Certainly, the disorganized attachment pattern has incorporated the notion that child-parent roles may be reversed while avoidant attachment, which involves precocious detachment from parental authority can also be accompanied by early sexual forays, according to Belsky's account of the potential evolutionary origins of attachment patterns (Belsky 1999). This observation may highlight the need for further refinement of assessment of attachment in infancy.

Relationships with peers

Most findings in relation to the role of attachment security in social interactions in early and middle adolescence have tended to repeat findings at earlier ages. A meta-analytic review of studies of attachment in adolescence (Rice 1990) concluded that there was evidence that secure attachment in adolescence is associated with higher self-esteem, social competence, ego identity and psychosocial adjustment.

Follow-up studies of the Minnesota sample into adolescence have shown that 15-year-olds assessed as securely attached at age one were judged to be less dependent on camp counsellors, competent with peers, generally more socially competent and more likely to be in leadership positions (Sroufe et al. 1993, 2001, Weinfield et al. 1999). Adolescents with secure attachment histories were also the most likely to be in steady dating relationships by late adolescence and appeared to have a better understanding of the nature of close relationships (Collins and Sroufe 1999). Collins and Sroufe speculate that secure attachment may have predisposed young people to take more confident steps toward dating partners and that the associated superiority in social skills may have enabled them to negotiate close relationships more successfully than their insecurely attached counterparts.

However, research on the relationship between adolescent attachment and experiences in romantic relationships is still sparse and support for these hypotheses is not strong. Nevertheless, there are some indications that anxious-resistant attachment in adolescence may be associated with fewer experiences of dating relationships.

Emotional self-regulation

Kobak and colleagues (1993), examining mother-teen interactions in a problem-solving task, observed that abortive strategies appeared to be associated with attachment insecurity, particularly in boys. In this study, they found some evidence to support their prediction that securely attached children would be able both to control their emotional responses and to use them in order to elicit assistance from mothers; mothers of securely attached teenagers were also expected to be better able to pick up on their children's emotional state and use it to guide appropriate interventions. The interventions by mothers of insecurely attached teenagers were observed to be less effective. These children were also less able to moderate angry responses and to remain constructively involved in problem-solving.

Kobak et al. (1993) propose a control theory model to account for the differences between securely and insecurely attached adolescents and suggest that there may be underlying psychophysiological correlates and attentional biases. Their model is based on a model outlined by Scheier and Carver (1988) who attempted to account for attentional and attributional biases in appraisals and actions within different social contexts. However, Kobak et al. appear to have abstracted the bare bones of the Carver and Scheier model and to have arrived at a schematic representation of adolescent problem-solving strategies which leaves considerable room for further investigation and refinement. The account they give is premised on the notion that attachment strategies in a challenging situation will be kicked into play by a process that starts with evaluation of attachment figure availability. When the attachment figure is assessed as not sufficiently available, the young person attempts to reduce the resulting discrepancy between desired and actual availability. If the attachment figure responds satisfactorily, the young person, reassured, is able to re-engage with exploration and problem-solving. If not, a second stage of evaluation commences during which the young person inspects their mental representation of the caregiver's ability and concludes from this inspection whether or not there is hope of eventually obtaining reassurance. When hope is retained (the preoccupied strategy), the attachment behaviour system becomes hyper-activated and the young person, now hypervigilant, steps up their demand for assistance. Where there is no hope (avoidant strategy), the attachment behaviour system becomes de-activated, the young person avoids proximity seeking and diverts their attention from the attachment figure. In other words, only when the attachment figure responds appropriately is the young person left free to return to the problem. Further, hypervigilance is associated more strongly with ambivalence than avoidance. We would dispute both of these propositions.

While the resonance of this model with Bowlby's notions of the attachment behaviour system as a control system seems seductive, certain aspects do not inspire confidence. Because so much of the mechanism proposed involves covert processes, the possibility of testing it as a theory is much reduced. In addition, there are difficulties associated with the fundamental premise that, when challenged during any kind of problem-solving task, all adolescents should and would turn to attachment figures for assistance. For some adolescents, for example, those with a history of maternal inadequacy or intrusiveness, it seems that such a strategy may well be prohibited, not because the young person has chosen to forgo the possibility of assistance but because they are only too keenly aware that such a request is highly likely to result in their feeling a hundred times more helpless, incompetent and humiliated. For these adolescents, turning to mother is unlikely to be a strategy still within their armoury. Rather, they may be more likely to be aware of the risks involved in being shown up as unable to complete the task in the presence of their mother: this will put them in direct line of the kind of fire that they have spent most of their lives trying to evade. Small wonder that "dysfunctional anger" emerges in this kind of situation! But, as Kobak et al. (1993) remark, this anger is likely to be qualitatively very different from that evinced by ambivalent/preoccupied children who have a history of employing a diametrically contrasting strategy. For these children, 'dysfunctional anger' is more likely to be an exaggeration of their normal fussiness. Figure 4.7 illustrates a re-formulation of a control systems understanding of adolescent-mother interaction within the context of 'problem-solving', taking into account the emotional context prevailing at the outset.

Figure 4.7: Alternative account of adolescent problem-solving

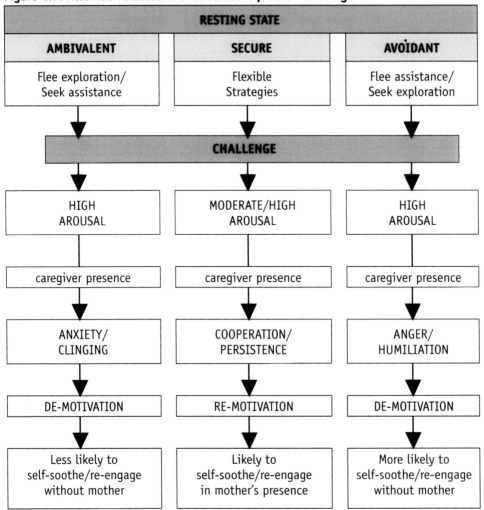

This hypothetical representation of teenagers' responses differs from that proposed by Kobak and colleagues, primarily, in situating the mother-teen problem-solving task more overtly within the context of the young person's relationship history. Although we agree that the Attachment Behaviour system, as Bowlby (1969/1982) proposed, is operative throughout the lifespan and that, under challenging circumstances, most individuals will seek appropriate assistance, we would question the assumption of equivalence across attachment class with regard to the desirability of the attachment figure's availability and the significance of mother's presence. For avoidantly attached adolescents, the 'availability' of a relatively unsupportive attachment figure may actually disrupt normal modes of coping or learning, and so impede attentional processes. The assumption that these individuals would need to go through a process that involved checking that their mother was available therefore seems questionable. The proposal that, as a result of this process, adolescents should de-activate their attachment system and also desist from exploration seems even more questionable. It seems more likely that the adolescents only cease exploration within this context because the attachment figure's presence inhibits their exploration. However, there does not yet appear to have been much work done that could either support or refute these arguments.

The possibility that ambivalently-attached children might be more prepared than securely attached children to tolerate mothers' intrusions into their personal space was explored by Bar-Haim and colleagues (2002) in a study of 11-year-olds. These researchers used Hayduk's stop-distance procedure in which the researcher, with a neutral facial expression, silently approaches the participant looking at his or her knees until the participant tells them to stop at the point when (a) s/he feels 'slightly uncomfortable' and again when (b) s/he feels 'considerable discomfort'. This procedure was repeated with both male and female researchers and then children were asked to fill in an Adolescent Interpersonal Competence Questionnaire (Buhrmeister 1990). This provides a measure of how willing the children are to self-disclose, to initiate relationships, to provide emotional support to others, and the strategies they use to manage conflict and to assert themselves (i.e. positively or negatively). They found that children who had ambivalent attachments to both mother and father allowed more intrusion than children who were securely attached to both parents. It would be useful to extend this kind of research to include older children and children with other attachment styles.

Psychosocial adjustment and risk-taking

How, or even whether, attachment security in infancy might be related to later development has been much discussed. As we mentioned earlier, a number of clinicians, theorists and researchers assert that patterns of relating established in early years can direct individuals along pathological developmental pathways so that insecure attachment in infancy and early childhood provides not just a fair estimate but a strong prediction of maladaptive behaviour and psychosocial problems in later life (e.g. Cicchetti and Howes 1991, Costello and Angold 1993, Hinshaw et al. 1993, Genuis 1995). Others, however, (e.g. Kagan 1998, Harris 1998) contest these claims, arguing that later events and reparative experiences in close relationships outside the family can alter the original trajectory enough to prevent the development of pathological conditions.

A high incidence of attachment insecurity is commonly found among clinical populations (e.g. Bakermans-Kranenburg and van IJzendoorn 1993, Lessard and Moretti, 1998). Fewer psychological problems (e.g. depression, anxiety, attention difficulties, behaviour problems) tend to be found in securely attached adolescents (Nada-Raja et al. 1992) while the presence of psychosocial problems has been linked with young people's perception of poor child-parent relationships.

In one study, adolescents who rated their relationship with both their peers and parents positively had the fewest problems and, conversely, adolescents who had insecure relationships with both parents and peers had the most problems. Adolescents who rated themselves as secure with peers but insecure with parents had more problems than adolescents who were securely attached to parents but not secure with peers (Laible et al. 2000). The measure of attachment adopted in this study almost certainly did not tap the same aspects of attachment relationships as is captured by the Strange Situation.

There is some evidence, too, from other studies that the expected link between a very difficult family background and 'acting out' (e.g. being anti-social, aggressive or conduct-disordered) is weaker if children have a wide circle of friends (Criss et al. 2002). Overall, therefore, it is not yet clear exactly how much poor outcomes might be attributable to early attachment insecurity as opposed to ongoing relationship difficulties.

Some workers have found that internal working models constructed on the basis of multiple relationships (as in Israeli children raised in kibbutzim) predict socio-emotional development five years after Strange Situation assessment better than attachment models based on one figure alone (van IJzendoorn et al. 1992). However, Thompson (1999) concludes that less evidence has emerged from long-term than from short-term follow-up studies of the benefits of a secure attachment in infancy for subsequent close relationships. He suggests that perhaps the mother-child relationship constitutes a prototype for a few years but does not necessarily do so for the whole lifespan. Both he and Belsky acknowledge the lack of consistent findings in relation to behaviour problems, "In general, therefore, it is hard to find reliable, consistent personality sequelae of a secure or insecure attachment in infancy, largely because so few hypothesized correlates have been replicated in more than one sample... the prediction of complex personality sequelae is likely to require multi-variate longitudinal analyses" (Thompson 1999, p.278).

Belsky (Belsky et al. 1991, Belsky 1999) proposes that some children may be more vulnerable than others to effects of the quality of caregiving. While some seem resilient regardless of how good or bad their experiences are, others are more sensitive and prone to difficulties.

Quite a lot of evidence has now been gathered to indicate that attachment security status is generally only stable throughout childhood if nothing dramatic happens in the child's social life. Major changes, both positive and negative (such as parental separation, re-marriage, death, birth of a sibling, a parent's recovery from illness, improved family or child support, amelioration of financial circumstances leading to a significantly less stressful family atmosphere, etc.) can impact on children's outlook and social behaviour to the extent that securely attached children may become insecure, while insecurely attached children may develop more trusting relationships. In these cases, early attachment classification fails to predict later outcomes (Vaughn et al. 1979, Erickson et al. 1985). We return to this issue in Chapter Six.

As mentioned above, adolescence is often conceptualised as a time of "sturm und drang", when teenage hormones are raging and when parents expect to have difficulties relating to rebellious youth who are determined, sometimes in responsible ways but at other times precociously or immaturely, to demonstrate their independence. There is also some evidence that adolescence is a time when experimentation and boundary-challenging may be most likely to result in infringement of social codes. This has led policy-makers to seek greater understanding of how processes resulting in youth crime or lawlessness might be stemmed.

Again, opinions differ over how much attachment relationships might contribute to different outcomes (Rutter 2002, Harris 1998). Allen et al. (1990, p.458) assert that "attachment theory fits much of the available data on the correlates of adolescent problem behaviors". They argue that insecurely attached adolescents can account for most youth crime and explain how dismissing adolescents engage in delinquent acts as a form of rebellion against the norms and values of attachment figures while ambivalent/preoccupied adolescents misbehave in order to draw attention to themselves (Allen et al. 1997). While these hypotheses seem, on the face of it, reasonably plausible, considerably more evidence is needed than is currently available to substantiate the claims.

Associations have been found between attachment insecurity in adolescence, use of illegal drugs and behavioural problems (Vicary and Lerner 1986, Brook et al. 1993, Rosenstein and Horowitz 1996, Elgar et al. 2003). However, a more recent study (Marsh et al. 2003) suggests a rather more complex model in which pathways to adolescent risk-taking, like pathways to other anti-social behaviour outcomes, are multiply determined. They produce evidence which supports the notion that a preoccupied style of attachment may pre-dispose to either internalising or externalising (acting out) problems and that the way the adolescents behave will depend upon their mother's style of self-assertion. Specifically, adolescents classified as 'preoccupied' will be more likely to 'act out' if they have mothers who are relatively assertive and forthright in their views whereas adolescents whose mothers are less sure of themselves will tend to manifest more internalising problems (anxiety, depression, etc.).

Adulthood

It is well beyond the scope of this book to summarise findings from the enormous body of research on patterns of adult attachment. Not only the sheer number of self-report questionnaires that have been developed to tap different aspects of attachment but the number of published papers generated even in relation to single instruments[3] render this a task of prohibitive proportions. Also, as mentioned in Chapter Three, we suspect that there is a long way yet to go before it is conclusively established that all, or any, of these instruments really taps the same construct as each other, let alone the same aspect of attachment relationships as the Strange Situation. Even though it has usually been demonstrated that the majority of tests of adult attachment have sound psychometric properties in terms of internal consistency, face validity and test-retest reliability, many difficulties still surround interpretation of findings. Many self-report inventories depend on elicitation of information about attitudes toward current or important relationships in adulthood. It is not clear that they provide information about more general patterns of attachment behaviour across the lifespan.

Some studies, which we review in Chapter Six, have included both Strange Situation assessments in infancy and follow-up assessments in adulthood. A larger number of studies (which we consider in Chapter Five) has included Adult Attachment Interview assessments of maternal attitudes prior to or around the same time as Strange Situation assessments of infants. Rich and interesting though the findings are from each set of studies, neither can resolve the problem created by the lack of an agreed operational definition of attachment security across the lifespan. This makes it difficult to draw the findings together in any very coherent manner. In collating information from some of the more well-known studies, we must stress that, in our view, many of their claims are still in need of extensive corroboration and substantiation. At best, they should be viewed as 'work in progress'.

Bearing these reservations in mind, in the following section, we present a selection of findings in relation to manifestations of attachment security in adulthood. First, we summarise some of the findings from studies of students. Next, we consider how or whether different attachment patterns might be linked with any more or less positive aspects of couple relationships. Finally, we briefly touch on the question of relationships between attachment security and mental health outcomes, to which we devote more attention in Chapter Seven.

Young adulthood/late adolescence: Studies of students

Since self-report measures of attachment lend themselves easily to being tested on captive populations of undergraduate students, a large proportion of adult attachment investigations

---

3   e.g. since its inception in 1987, Hazan and Shaver's measure alone has been used in well over 1,000 published papers.

has focused on this group, presumably on the grounds that findings from this relatively homogeneous group can generalise reasonably well across other adult populations. Reports generally provide scant detail regarding the make-up of student groups (e.g. relationship status or history, ethnicity, parity, family background).

Undergraduate students rating themselves as securely attached have been found to differ from non-secure students in that they are/have:
- higher self-esteem (Armsden and Greenberg 1987, Feeney and Noller 1990)
- a higher sense of self-worth, greater confidence and are more expressive (Collins and Read 1990)
- greater life satisfaction (Armsden and Greenberg 1987)
- more likely/ready to seek assistance from both mother and father (Armsden and Greenberg 1987)
- more comfortable with closeness, feel more able to depend on others, unworried about being abandoned or unloved (Collins and Read 1990)
- lower on depression/anxiety, on resentment/alienation and on irritability/anger (Armsden and Greenberg 1987)
- perceive their mothers to be caring, loving, affectionate and responsive (Mikulincer and Nachson 1991)
- view people as trustworthy and dependable, altruistic, willing to stand up for their beliefs and having control over outcomes in their lives (Collins and Read 1990)
- report positive early family relationships and trusting attitudes toward others more frequently (Feeney and Noller 1990)
- better at solving relationship difficulties (Shi 2003)
- most likely to attempt 'problem-focused' coping strategies, and to seek instrumental and emotional support from close friends and family (Florian et al. 1995, Larose et al. 1999)
- more willing to compromise to reach solutions to relationship problems (Shi 2003)
- unlikely to describe themselves as cold or introverted (Bartholomew and Horowitz 1991)
- unlikely to be described by friends as cold (Bartholomew and Horowitz 1991)
- likely to describe themselves as nurturant and autocratic (Bartholomew and Horowitz 1991)
- lower scores on frustration, jealousy, clinginess, self-reliance and ambivalence (Brennan and Shaver 1995)
- higher scores on trust and proximity-seeking (Brennan and Shaver 1995).

In comparison with students classified as secure, students classified as 'dismissing' or 'avoidant':
- were thought, by peers, to be more anxious (Kobak and Sceery 1988)
- showed more (peer-rated) hostility (Kobak and Sceery 1988)
- were more sensitive to criticism (Kobak and Sceery 1988)
- tended to view themselves in a more positive light than others saw them (Kobak and Sceery 1988)
- were less likely to be willing to talk about their feelings to their mothers, fathers or same-sex friends (Mikulincer and Nachson 1991)
- were uncomfortable with closeness and intimacy, not confident of others' availability, though not particularly worried about being abandoned (Collins and Read 1990)
- were less likely to talk about their feelings to their lovers (Mikulincer and Nachson 1991)

- were least likely to oblige others (Shi 2003)
- were unlikely to describe themselves as warm (Bartholomew and Horowitz 1991)
- were likely to be described by friends as cold, introverted, non-nurturant and non-expressive (Bartholomew and Horowitz 1991)
- scored higher on frustration, self-reliance and ambivalence (Brennan and Shaver 1995)
- scored lower on trust and proximity-seeking (Brennan and Shaver 1995).

In comparison with students classified as secure, students classified as 'preoccupied' or anxious-ambivalent were/had:
- less likely to talk about their feelings to their lovers (Mikulincer and Nachson 1991)
- likely to describe themselves as expressive and warm (Bartholomew and Horowitz 1991)
- likely to be described by friends as autocratic, expressive and not introverted (Bartholomew and Horowitz 1991)
- higher scores on frustration, jealousy and clinginess (Brennan and Shaver 1995)
- lower scores on trust (Brennan and Shaver 1995)
- comfortable with closeness and intimacy, fairly confident of others' availability, and very worried about being abandoned and unloved (Collins and Read 1990).

Other adults

Similar findings have been found in other samples of adults. Adults who describe themselves as secure also describe themselves as:
- happiest about job security, the amount of recognition they receive at work, their co-workers, prospects of career advancement, highest on work satisfaction, most confident that co-workers would rate them highly (Hazan and Shaver 1990)
- least likely to say that love interferes with work, that they fear failure or disapproval, that work harms health or relationships, and most likely to say that relationship gives more pleasure than work (Hazan and Shaver 1990)
- experiencing fewer symptoms of loneliness or depression (crying easily, feeling hopeless), anxiety (feeling nervous, worrying), psychosomatic illness (muscle tension, intestinal problems), physical illness (cold, flu) (Hazan and Shaver 1990).

Couple relationships: Satisfaction and stability

Considerable effort has been devoted by researchers to the task of discovering how attachment style in adulthood might predict the stability of couple relationships. Comparisons on numerous dimensions, including conflict resolution, communication style, support-giving and receiving, and self-disclosure have been made between couples with same or different 'states of mind with respect to attachment' (in Mary Main's terms).

Couples who describe themselves as secure have been found to be:
- more ready to self-disclose, to be responsive to their partner's self-disclosure and to prefer a high self-disclosing partner (Mikulincer and Nachson 1991, Pistole 1993)
- more likely to communicate openly and to discuss things with each other (Collins and Read 1990, Feeney et al. 1994)
- less likely to display aggression or anger (Cohn et al. 1992)

- more likely to persist longer when seeking resolutions to problems though also more likely to compromise in order to reach mutually agreeable solutions (Pistole 1989, Corcoran and Mallinckrodt 2000, Mikulincer and Shaver 2003)
- least likely to resort to verbal aggression or withdrawal (Senchak and Leonard 1992, Creasey et al. 1999)
- most likely to be sensitive to their partner's needs and to give and receive care (Kunce and Shaver 1994).

Partners who self-classified as dismissing were:
- most likely to display negative moods and to withdraw from conflict situations (Creasey et al. 1999)
- most likely to employ 'distancing' strategies to cope with stress, i.e. strategies that minimise the importance of problems and distract from them
- least likely to self-disclose and most likely to be uncomfortable with high self-disclosing partners, that is, most likely to engage in 'compulsive closure' (Mikulincer and Nachson 1991)
- least likely to use compromise or integrating strategies (Corcoran and Mallinckrodt 2000)
- least likely to seek useful support when in difficulty (Collins and Feeney 2000)
- least likely to report pleasure-related feelings, orgasmic experiences or feelings of love towards partners during sexual activities (Mikulincer et al. 2002)
- least likely to engage in or approve of casual sex (Brennan and Shaver 1995, Fraley et al. 1998)
- most likely to 'mate-poach' and to engage in non-monogamous sexual relationships (Schachner and Shaver 2002).

Partners classifying themselves as 'preoccupied' or anxious-ambivalent were:
- most likely to try to dominate their partners (Corcoran and Mallinckrodt 2000)
- showed the most hostility (Simpson et al. 1996)
- most likely to self-disclose to relative strangers or to low-disclosing partners, and least likely to be responsive to other people's self-disclosures (Mikulincer and Nachson 1991)
- likely to use 'hyperactivating strategies' that escalate conflict (Shaver and Mikulincer 2002)
- most likely to use 'emotion-focused' coping strategies that exacerbate and 'awfulise' problems
- most likely to say that relationships cause them more pain than work (Hazan and Shaver 1990).

Interestingly, the correspondence between attachment style in couples has been calculated to be almost as low as some estimates of the incidence of same-sex partnerships: only about one in ten adults choose same-attachment-style relationships (Table 4.2).

Studies of domestic violence (e.g. Kesner et al. 1997) suggest that domestic violence is most likely to arise in heterosexual couples where both partners have a dismissing style of attachment though the combination of a dismissing female and an ambivalent/preoccupied male also appears to be fairly explosive.

Table 4.2: Partner choice

		FEMALE		
		Avoidant	Secure	Anxious/Ambiv
MALE	Avoidant	+.10	-.14	+.18
	Secure	-.05	+.12	-.14
	Anxious/Ambiv	+.13	-.17	+.09

Dutton et al. (1994) argue that intimacy anger may be the direct result of chronically unmet attachment needs which, in consequence of enduring failures to cope with frustration, have resulted since early childhood in constantly simmering protest and rage. They describe both the ambivalent and the avoidant attachment styles as being associated with high levels of subjective distress and hypersensitivity to criticism, and hypothesise that, in individuals with these styles of attachment, there will also be a chronic inability to cope with strong feelings and self-doubt, as well as a distrust of others' reliability and/or goodwill. These attributes, in whatever combination, will predispose to very high intimacy anger. Dutton et al. go on to speculate that, due to their earlier attachment difficulties, men who become violent may be constantly primed to link intimacy itself with extreme anxiety and anger. As a result, rather than attributing any changes in their arousal to their own fundamental anxiety about close relationships, they may perceive the partner as the problem.

While this account might provide an explanation for high levels of anxiety and frustration and for a tendency to misattribute uncomfortable feelings, why these high levels of anxiety should tip over into physical violence seems unclear. In the next chapter, we consider this question further in relation to effects of chronic stress on children's development.

Older people

Although attachment behaviours are often more visible in infants and were first examined in relation to infants, Bowlby was at pains to stress that attachment relationships are important throughout the lifespan. It is nevertheless commonly believed that being securely attached is more important in infancy than at other times and also that patterns of attachment formed in infancy are so deeply ingrained that they will last throughout the lifespan. No evidence supports either of these beliefs.

To date, relatively little research has focused on patterns of attachment in elderly people though, given the huge mass of research in other areas, this does not mean that there have not been a lot of studies. There is not space here to discuss this work in detail but nevertheless, in passing, we will attempt to highlight some key issues. Perhaps the most fundamental point to make is that the challenges associated with old age are often enormous. They can cover a range of loss experiences, through death of acquaintances, friends and relatives, declining physical and mental abilities, social status, ability to self-care, as well as other challenges associated with health, finances, social changes and life events that may or may not involve major transitions (moving house, maintaining contact with families in transition, etc.).

Caring for elderly parents plays a large part of the role of many parents in the twenty-first century and is set, with an aging population and a growing number of 'beanpole' families,[4] to play an even larger part. In addition, as mothers have become absorbed in greater numbers into the labour market and as divorce and parental separations have increased, the role of many grandparents has become increasingly important for many children and young people. To our knowledge, very little research has yet touched on the question of how children's relationships with grandparents might buffer the effects of poor relationships with parents, although there are indications that many grandparents play important parts in the lives of their grandchildren (Drew et al. 1998, AARP 2001, Clarke and Roberts 2002, Smith and Drew 2002).

The findings that are emerging from this growing body of research seem to indicate the possibility that Attachment Theory, used carefully, could prove valuable in helping offspring to manage their own feelings in relation to their elderly parents as well as in helping carers to understand people who may at times be very anxious and demanding. The elderly parent with a secure attachment style may tend to be easier to care for, because they are more open and appreciative, the parent with a preoccupied style may be much more difficult to satisfy while the dismissing parent may be difficult to 'read' due to their tendency to conceal their needs and to experience any 'help' offered by others as intrusive. Carers with secure attachment styles may also find it easier to cope with the demandingness of a very frightened or confused elderly parent or spouse whereas anxious/dismissive carers might try to 'fight' the symptoms and to panic rather than to engage with problems in a more realistic way (Ingebretson and Solem 1997).

Predictable attachment-related differences have also been found in adult children's responses to the death of a parent. Generally, the grief response of securely attached individuals eventually leads to a capacity to come to terms with their distress and is thought to involve 'unconflicted grieving' characterised by low anxiety, high self-confidence and a belief that attachment figures will be supportive and available when needed. By contrast, insecurely attached adult offspring, particularly ambivalent/preoccupied individuals with very high dependency needs, will be highly prone to 'conflicted grieving'. This is characterised by far greater felt distress, high anxiety, low self-confidence, the conviction that no-one will be available when needed, and that no-one really cares. It may also include a sense of rejection and an associated belief either that 'I am worthless' or that everyone else is, or vacillation between both these positions.

Clearly, the latter pattern is less adaptive than the former and can also become, like insecure patterns of relating in other circumstances, self-reinforcing and self-perpetuating. Such a grief reaction can therefore have a negative impact on current adult relationships and, in turn, on relationships between the grieving parent and their own children (if they have any). Not only will the parent become less available for the children but they are likely to also be temporarily less available to their partners. It is far more difficult for a spouse to stay close to a grieving insecure partner whose unspoken communications include messages such as 'I can't trust anyone', 'No-one is good enough', 'Everyone hates me', etc. than it is to stay close to a person whose grieving is less conflicted.

---

4   Beanpole families are characterised by few individuals in each generation (low numbers of offspring), in contrast to 'pyramid' families where there tend to be far more younger than older generation individuals.

Summary

What seems clearer from even this most brief perusal of the adult attachment literature is that couples in which both partners describe themselves as having a secure attachment style appear to be characterised by their ability not so much to avoid conflict or disagreement, but to resolve and repair the rifts caused by their disagreements. As a result, securely attached males and females are more likely to maintain intact, viable relationships. Common sense might suggest that these relationships should provide better role models and a more stable setting in which to bring up children, a question that we also explore in Chapter Five.

Before leaving this topic, it seems important to draw attention to the fact that most studies of couple relationships have used self-report rather than interview-based measures of attachment and have relied on cross-sectional or short-term longitudinal designs that have not spanned the lifespan. As there is some debate about the degree to which current relationship experiences influence self-reported adult attachment style and some indication that attachment classification is not stable across different relationships, it is not easy to ascertain exactly how large a contribution attachment security might make to the maintenance of stable relationships. There are certainly indications that its role may be substantial but, equally, it is possible that other factors play an important part, for example, stage in relationship formation, the existence of social support networks, shared values and attitudes, problem-solving style. Further, as research has shown that there are associations between attachment security and these other variables, it has proved quite difficult to tease apart the independent contributions of all factors.

Mental health

One of the key aims that Bowlby had in developing his Attachment Theory was to provide insight into the origin and nature of psychological problems. In this section, we outline some of the main findings from research on the relationship between patterns of attachment and mental health in adults with the aim of setting the scene for more detailed discussion in later chapters of the relationship between patterns of attachment, emotional wellbeing and psychological distress at other stages of development.

As described in earlier chapters and as evidenced in this chapter, Internal Working Models constructed on the basis of secure attachment relationships are thought to involve representations of positive self-other interactions, where disagreements, misunderstandings or other unpleasant experiences have generally been addressed and resolved. Such experiences not only deepen understanding of social interactions and decrease the likelihood of inaccurate perceptions of social situations, they also lead to better social skills. These, in turn, result in higher self esteem, greater self-confidence and other positive pre-dispositions that are not associated with diagnoses of mental ill-health.

Insecure attachments, by contrast, are identified within the context of less optimal close relationships. By definition, therefore, they involve less satisfactory IWMs of self and other in interaction. These, in turn, result in tendencies to reproduce more difficult social interactions with inevitable repercussions on mental health status.

Given that avoidant attachment is thought to be underpinned by down-regulation of attachment-seeking behaviour and up-regulation of exploratory activities, combined with suppression of negative emotional information, it follows that symptoms of stress in avoidant adults are unlikely to be directly or clearly expressed. By contrast, ambivalent attachment is maintained through up-regulation of attachment-seeking, down-regulation of exploration and a strong bias towards ready expression of negative emotional states of all sorts. It is not surprising therefore that adolescents and adults with a self-reported and other-assessed ambivalent or preoccupied style of attachment are more highly represented among clinical samples in which disorders relating to anxiety or depression are diagnosed (Warren et al. 1997, Dozier et al. 1999). We will expand further on this theme in Chapter Seven. Meantime, we conclude this chapter with a consideration of the question of the discriminant validity of the construct of attachment security.

What attachment security is not related to: the question of discriminant validity

As discussed at the beginning of this chapter, there are a number of attributes that are not predicted by Attachment Theory to be closely associated with how securely attached a child is. In the early days when Bowlby was just beginning to introduce his ideas, it was crucial for him to be able to demonstrate that the construct of attachment security was a real, independent phenomenon, not simply a side-effect either of a broader set of attributes (such as intelligence) or of a complex trait (such as temperament). Attachment behaviour and, in particular, the construct of attachment security had to be shown to be associated with effects that were all clearly attributable to itself and which could not be explained away as being due to other influences. With a construct as ubiquitous in its effects as attachment behaviour, this is actually rather a tall order which, as has been attested since its inception, has led to several trenchant critiques, some of which have resulted in notable advances in theory.[5]

Attachment, intelligence and perceptual ability

In spite of these difficulties, it is now fairly well established that intelligence and attachment behaviour are independent constructs. Very few studies report associations between infants' performance on tests such as the Bayley Development Quotient (the infant equivalent of an IQ test) and either concurrent or subsequent assessments of attachment (Thompson 1999). In a meta-analysis of 12 studies (with a total sample of 514 participants), van IJzendoorn and colleagues found a very weak relationship ($r = 0.09$) between attachment security and cognitive ability (van IJzendoorn et al. 1995a). These findings reflect most research in this area.

Attachment and biological sex

Since the first research began to be carried out on attachment, it has been rare to find associations between biological sex and attachment behaviour in infants and young children (e.g. Cassidy 1988). Similarly, few measures of adult attachment have reported consistent gender differences (Hazan and Shaver 1987, Brennan et al. 1991, Feeney and Noller 1990, 1992, Feeney et al. 1994). Nowadays, this lack of an association is so well established that it is quite difficult to find papers that report tests for potential associations.

---

5 e.g. Rutter's classic 'Maternal Deprivation Reassessed' (Rutter 1972a); also, Lamb et al. 1984's important critique (Lamb et al. 1984, 1985), which appeared to lead to a certain closing of ranks but also enabled serious and valuable debate.

This might surprise some readers, particularly those who are aware of the gender biases that still operate in many social situations and gender differences that emerge over the course of development, for example, the tendency for girls to learn to talk before boys, differences in emotional expression, etc. It is also notable that most other psychoanalytic theories do propose qualitative differences between boys and girls in respect of relationships with parents and social development. But gender differences have not been found to influence the type of attachment relationship formed between mothers and babies, and this would appear to support the notion that attachment behaviours are part of an independent system of behaviour that operates independently of other aspects of social relating. Nevertheless, it may also be worth bearing in mind the possibility that studies may not have contained samples large enough for fine-grained analysis of attachment sub-groups since, typically, cell sizes (particularly numbers of C- or D-group children) have been too small to permit reliable analysis of gender differences. It is therefore conceivable that, with larger samples, a different picture may yet emerge.

Attachment and temperament

It has proved somewhat more difficult to establish that attachment behaviour and temperament are separate phenomena. For some researchers (e.g. Kagan et al. 1994, Kagan 1998, Goldsmith and Harman 1994), this task has not yet been completed, in spite of the many attempts by workers in the field of attachment to prove their independence. As Vaughn and Bost (1999) recognise, if it is shown that differences in mother-infant interactions can be attributed to within-person characteristics that are independent of the mother-infant relationship, this would represent a serious challenge to the construct of attachment security.

In his book called *Galen's prophecy*, Kagan (Kagan et al. 1994) sets out many arguments in support his view of temperament. He reviewed much of the work then available and described his own longitudinal study of 89 Caucasian-American children, born between 1929 and 1939. Kagan was particularly interested to find out what might account for the behaviour of a very small group of children who he identified as extremely 'behaviourally inhibited'. These children scored very highly on measures of reactivity, had fast and strong physiological responses to unfamiliar events and their arousal levels dropped only very slowly back to pre-arousal levels. Such highly reactive children tend to be more tense, dour, serious and fearful than low reactive children who, conversely, are more joyful, fearless and relaxed about engaging in new social situations. However, there is a complex relationship between physiological reactivity responses and emotional states over the lifespan and not all highly reactive individuals become fearfully inhibited (Table 4.3).

Table 4.3: Temperamental variability in infants (in a hypothetical middle-class Caucasian sample)

	LOW REACTIVE	HIGH REACTIVE
4 MONTHS	c 40%	22%
1 YEAR	25%, low reactive, low fear	14% high reactive, high fear
	18% low reactive, low fear, + frequent smiling	8% high reactive, high fear, + infrequent smiling

In any healthy middle-class sample of Caucasian children, it is likely that, by chance, only a very small proportion of extremely fearful children will be found. This is an argument for large samples and a reason, according to Kagan, to distrust many conclusions from attachment research. This makes it very difficult to identify accurately the very small group of individuals who, according to Kagan (Kagan et al. 1994, p.xxii), "begin life with a physiology that will make it a bit difficult for them to be as relaxed, spontaneous, and capable of hearty laughter as they would like" whether or not they have all the advantages of a healthy, attractive personality or a comfortable, caring family. Kagan further added that, although about one-fifth of four-month-olds react strongly to an unfamiliar object, showing high arousal, distress and motor activity (kicking, etc.), by two years, only about two-thirds of these children will still show the same 'high reactivity' response. Conversely, only just over half of three-year-olds who are behaviourally inhibited will have shown high reactivity at four months (four months usually being the earliest time that a reliable response is elicited). Kagan spent years trying to understand what it might be that causes or explains this variability in behaviour.

In Kagan's view, extreme temperamental differences arise from physiological and psychological processes that operate independently of each other and result in a complex network of interdependent relationships between various components. Not only, as we mentioned above, is there is no one-to-one correspondence between temperament traits (the individual's fundamental disposition) and temperament states across the lifespan but, also, there is no evidence that differences in levels of behavioural inhibition emanate from the same neurological source. Kagan argued that the behaviour of extremely inhibited children is qualitatively different from that of non-inhibited children (i.e. behavioural inhibition phenomena do not lie along a continuum) and that very different underlying processes appear to be implicated. This is instanced by the fact that the ease with which a child becomes aroused does not correspond with their emotional state: some easily aroused children cry a lot, others do not, and the same applies to slow-to-arouse children.

Taking into consideration a range of physiological measures including average heart rate, heart rate variability and magnitude of response, pupillary dilation, urinary norepinephrine, cortisol levels (at home and in the university laboratory), quality, quantity and pitch of vocal utterances, Kagan emphasised that, typically, only half of the children identified as inhibited show high levels of responsivity on all measures. His investigation, which included taking multiple physiological and psychological measures over time, soon brought him to the conclusion that multiple measures do not produce simple results. On the contrary, the pictures they produce are not neat at all: "There will be some correspondence among behavior, physiology, and subjective feelings in some children on some occasions but never most of the time" (Kagan et al. 1994, p.122). In the end, Kagan argued, the attempt to find neural substrates for temperament differences is like trying to plot the relationship between economic conditions and heart rate in individual community members – such an exercise would be pointless because it would be based on a conceptualisation of the nature of individual-environment interactions that is far too simplistic. It is largely on the basis of the penchant of attachment researchers and theorists for simplistic views and methodologies that Kagan stands as one of its major critics.

Kagan's arguments have subsequently become known as the 'temperament hypothesis'. He proposed that the Strange Situation, being strange and unfamiliar, would elicit extreme fear in a proportion of infants. This fear, he maintained, would be more indicative of the infants' temperamental disposition. Further, he argued, elicitation of this response in a short 21-minute session could not possibly capture the true nature of the relationship between infants and their primary caregivers.

Some people have argued that support for the temperament hypothesis can be found in the resemblance between distributions of infants among Ainsworth's major attachment categories and distributions of profiles across the major temperament profiles proposed by Thomas and Chess (1977): in each taxonomy, the largest group of children are those who are most sociable (securely attached or 'easy' temperamentally); the smallest group is made up of the most socially awkward infants (ambivalent/resistant in attachment terms and 'difficult' in temperament classification); and in the middle are the group of children who are socially avoidant (avoidant in attachment terminology, 'slow to warm up' in temperament terminology).

Empirical support for a one-to-one correspondence between major categories of temperament and attachment, however, has not been found. In fact, no direct, strong evidence has yet appeared to emerge in support of the role of temperament in attachment (Lamb et al. 1985, Thompson 1986, Vaughn and Bost 1999).

Failure to find a relationship, though, does not necessarily preclude the possibility of there being one and, given the complexity of assessing attachment relationships and temperament profiles across the lifespan (Rutter 1982, 1987), challenges such as Kagan's must be taken seriously and addressed. Much attachment research, particularly that which has aimed at understanding the relationship between physiological and psychological processes, has relied on very small samples (which, even if they include the full range of temperaments, may not contain sufficient extreme cases to test hypotheses adequately). It has also tended to use designs and methods that may not capture effects on parent-child interaction of more subtle variations in infant or parent temperament. More usually, in research on attachment, temperament is measured through mothers' reports and/or by observations (that may not necessarily monitor relevant dimensions). Kagan (1998) has eschewed reliance on parental reports, though other workers have argued that they can provide extremely valuable insights into the parent-child dynamic, and also, in some respects, may be more accurate than observer reports (e.g. Mebert 1991, Rothbart and Bates 1998, Pesonen 2004).

Although there have been more sophisticated study designs (e.g. Fox and Calkins 1993), attachment studies that have incorporated other behavioural and physiological measures have been relatively rare and have tended to be carried out by only a few groups of researchers. These workers generally rely on measures such as salivary cortisol[6] or those pertaining to heart rate activity, which are relatively easy to take but have the disadvantage of being ambiguous[7] indicators that vary considerably according to factors such as the child's age, circadian rhythms, physical and psychological state (Fox and Card 1999). Most findings are therefore still in need of further investigation and replication.

In research on temperament, agreement between maternal reports and observations of infant behaviour has typically been low, though concordance has been found to increase over multiple assessments, taken from both mothers and fathers, and at later ages (Pesonen 2003a). Also, higher levels of agreement have been found when temperament characteristics have been measured as continuous, higher ordinate entities rather than as discrete phenomena (for example, 'negative emotionality' as opposed to 'fussiness' or 'anger', etc.; Pesonen 2003b). A key task for temperament researchers has therefore been to understand the relationship between multiple influences and descriptions of infant temperament.

The range of influences can include:
- the parent's own state or trait emotionality/temperament
- parents' attitudes and beliefs about children

---

6   The use of salivary cortisol for assessing stress levels, though still not very prevalent, has been undertaken in some research groups – this will be discussed further in later chapters.
7   This ambiguity is exacerbated in the absence of adequate measures of baseline rates.

- parents' relationship with each other and the extent to which their joint narratives may impact on their behaviour towards their children
- parents' behaviour in interaction with children
- children's behaviour
- parents' perception of children's behaviour
- when measures are taken (e.g. multiple measures over time and situation)
- how and which measures are taken (e.g. which observations, which questionnaires, which physiological indicators, etc.).

What seems to have emerged from this work are models of development that are complex and not yet fully determined. Infant temperament has been conceptualised as emanating from and manifesting at three levels (Bates 1989):
- *the biological level* – relating to the individual's genetic endowment and to prenatal gene-environment effects
- *the neurological level* – relating to the functioning of the individual's central nervous system
- *the behavioural level* – relating to observed patterns of individual behaviours across social contexts.

Several different models of how temperament might interact with environmental influences have also been proposed, for example, Scarr and McCartney (1983) suggest three possible ways in which the child's genetic endowment might correspond to or interact with the kind of parenting he or she receives:
- the child and the parents may share the same genetic endowment
- the child's genetic endowment may produce particular responses/behaviour in caregivers (and others)
- the child's genetic endowment may influence the child to engage selectively with different social situations (e.g. a shy child might avoid large group situations or situations that will focus attention onto him- or herself).

Temperament is therefore not a static, deterministic entity. Not only are children of similar temperament likely to have very different experiences of interactions with their parents but these interactions can have more or less impact on how the child's initial endowment might manifest throughout life.

Attachment research, though premised on the notion that the quality of attachment is about the relationship between at least two people, is often interpreted as though the relationship element were peripheral and the quality of infant attachment is entirely independent of the mother's (or other caregivers') input. This has sometimes led to rather odd arguments with respect to relationships between attachment and temperament, for example, in the early 1980s, it led to the notion that the way to test whether attachment and temperament are related is to demonstrate either concordance or non-concordance in the infant's pattern of attachment to mother and to father.

The logic here was, apparently, as follows:
A Temperament is a trait
B Traits are stable across time and situation
C If attachment is synonymous with temperament, it will be stable across time and situation
D Therefore, non-concordance between infant-mother and infant-father attachment provides evidence that attachment security is an independent construct

E Conversely, if attachment is found to be stable across time and situation, then the challenge to attachment theory would stand.

It appears to be on the basis of this kind of reasoning that Belsky and Rovine (1987) decided to examine whether concordance of infant-mother and infant-father attachment ratings, which had until then been found to be low, might be increased if classification of attachment patterns were to reflect variations of infant temperament more closely. Picking up on Frodi and Thompson's observation (Frodi and Thompson 1985) that infants classified A1, A2, B1 and B2 differed in pattern of arousal (i.e. less separation distress, longer onset and peak time, quicker recovery) from infants classified B3, B4, C1 and C2, and were also rated by their mothers as easier to manage, Belsky and Rovine examined the effect of re-grouped attachment patterns in two samples of infants (one of 42 infants and the other of 92 infants) on rates of concordance. Although they failed to find significant levels of concordance among A, B, C patterns, they did find significant associations, in both samples, between infant-mother and infant-father attachment classifications when infants were grouped into A1-B2 versus B3-C2 patterns. This suggested that there may be a connection between attachment and temperament type. Belsky and Rovine concluded from this exercise that infant temperament may have an effect on how attachment security is expressed rather than on whether the infant is secure or insecure. They further speculated that the kind of attachment that emerged may be likely to depend on the mother's response to her baby's disposition.

Figure 4.8: Patterns of arousal and strange situation classification (hypothetical relationships

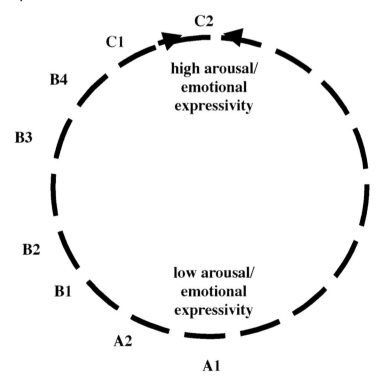

Subsequently, Belsky et al. (1995a), in view of further information about the relationship between expressivity and quality of attachment, did eventually move away from this position. Even so, given the extent to which this study was cited at the time, it seems important to consider some conceptual aspects of their design and arguments.

In respect of design, four points urge for caution. First, infants were tested twice in the Strange Situation with only one month between times of testing, first with mother, then with father (no counter-balancing). Given Ainsworth's strictures about sensitisation effects, it seems possible that this aspect of the procedure may, in itself, have had some impact on continuity estimates. Second, there are questions to be asked about the use of chi-squared tests in repeated measures designs: even if the infant is with mother on one occasion and father on the next, the contribution of the infant to the assessment of attachment would suggest that tests for change might be more appropriate, not tests that assume that data is drawn from independent samples. The third point relates to the fact that, within the major attachment categories, there was a very uneven distribution of infants, with around three-quarters assessed as securely attached to mother. Division into two groups is therefore likely to have produced a comparison based on sub-group classifications within the B category. Given the traditional roles of mothers and fathers, one could speculate that most children might interact slightly more distally with fathers than with mothers, with the possible result that securely attached children might be assessed as B1/2 with fathers and B3/4 with mothers. If so, results might have reflected this tendency rather than any differential effects of temperament (though this is a purely speculative notion). Fourth, the report provided no indication of variability around infants' mean scores either on newborn behaviour ratings or on maternal temperament reports at three months. Thus, there are no grounds for confidence that analysis of variance tests were either appropriate or sufficiently sensitive.

The tenability of the conceptual basis seems even more important to think about. The fundamental premise that non-concordance of infant attachment classification with mother and father must, inevitably, prove that attachment patterns are nothing to do with temperament appears distinctly doubtful. First, even if traits are stable across time and social situation, this does not mean that at any point in time or in any situation they will be manifest at the same level: even the shyest of children is usually more at ease with familiar than with unfamiliar people. Similarly, the finding that a timid child is more nervous in a strange setting when in the presence of father than in the presence of mother cannot be taken either as evidence that the child is not timid, nor as proof that timidity is not a trait, nor as evidence that the child's timidity bears no relation to the quality of their attachment. All that can safely be concluded is that we do not yet know what role it may or may not have. The same arguments apply to the status of attachment patterns as traits. Even if the same quality of attachment was found to be associated with attachment to mother and to father in absolutely every recorded case, the conclusion that attachment security must depend on an infant trait could not be said to be sound. There are just too many potential influences involved for such simple accounts to be considered safe or sound.

As already mentioned, Belsky and colleagues have moved away from the views expressed in the Belsky and Rovine paper. More recently, they have examined the extent to which shared environment and genetic influences might contribute to attachment security (Bokhorst et al. 2003), a question that is discussed further in Chapter Five. Belsky has also suggested that individual variability in temperament may pre-dispose children to differential susceptibility to parenting influences (Belsky 1997a, 1997b). This view possibly takes more account of findings from workers such as Grazyna Kochanska who has studied relationships between shyness and attachment (e.g. Kochanska 2001), studies of 'irritable' infants (e.g. Crockenberg 1981,

Miyake et al. 1995, Goldsmith and Alansky 1987, van den Boom 1994) and observations of relationships between Strange Situation behaviour and psychophysiological measures (e.g. Spangler and Grossmann 1993).

The latter study indicated that, in spite of superficial appearances of calmness or coping, heart rate measures during the Strange Situation betrayed stress in avoidantly attached infants while cortisol measures taken after the SS indicated that both avoidant and other insecurely attached infants found the SS more stressful than securely attached infants. Since this early study, more links have been made between work on temperament (most notably, work carried out by Mary Rothbart and her colleagues), peer rejection (e.g. Rubin and colleagues) and on the development of emotional self-regulation (e.g. Vondra et al. 2001), while a number of investigators have pursued the question of how reactivity, self-regulation, parenting influences and patterns of attachment might be related.

Some key messages to emerge from this work include the realisation that the relationship between self-regulation and reactivity is complex, that the phenomenon of reactivity itself is tremendously difficult to quantify as different types of it arise from so many different neurological sites (Siegel 1999) and that the relationship between parental influence, genetic influences and the development of temperamental characteristics is also very complex.

All these considerations point to the potential value of further research to investigate in greater depth relationships between combined infant and parent temperamental characteristics and assessments of attachment security. Strange Situation assessments are based, after all, not just on the infant's behaviour but on the interaction between the infant and its carer (Ainsworth et al. 1978). This means that, to test whether temperament and attachment are independent constructs, it is necessary to examine the contribution not just of the infant's temperament but also that of the other person involved in the Strange Situation assessment. This investigation, to our knowledge, has not yet been carried out.

This discussion of the relationship between attachment and temperament has been necessarily sketchy. In it, we have attempted to give some indication of the complexity of the phenomena involved and of directions in which future research might proceed. Like attachment, temperament is very difficult to measure. Its effects on patterns of relating have to be seen to be complex, multi-directional and so very challenging to discern. One thing is certain. It cannot possibly be adequate to assess infant temperament and infant behaviour in isolation from its context within the social context of the mother-father relationship and the caregiving setting. The development of temperamental traits in infants, like the development of patterns of attachment, is likely to be susceptible to the rearing environment (differentially so if Belsky's thesis is proved correct). This rearing environment includes the parents' (i.e. the principal carers') own temperamental and social relational styles as well as the psychological resources available to them, that is, it will be informed by several histories of social interactions and the sense that all main protagonists make of them. These (more or less) shared family narratives affect how parents understand and respond to their children as well as how the children are able to interact with key people in their social context.

The practice of taking readings only of the baby's state and traits seems destined, therefore, to capture only a very small part of the picture. In respect of the Strange Situation assessments, the carer's temperament and attachment style are also likely to contribute. Agreement between independent raters on assessments of children's temperament tends usually to increase as children get older, perhaps because the traits become more evident as they evolve, or because environmental influences (e.g. parenting) become more predictable, or because children make more active choices about which social situations to engage in, or because genetic potential takes time to be realised, etc. As a result, the best temperament measures taken in infancy are likely to have a rather limited capacity to predict relationship history, or other outcomes for children.

This would seem to suggest that more complex longitudinal designs employing larger batteries of measures with a wider span (and thus with greater capacity to monitor more comprehensively potential sources of influence throughout the child's hierarchy of attachment figures), are needed if it is to be possible to tease out, definitively, whether temperament and attachment are really independent constructs. Our view on this matter, therefore, is not just that the jury is still out but that, so far, key witnesses may have been missing from the trial.

Concluding comments

The absence of key witnesses is, in fact, rather pertinent to an overview of this chapter. Most of the evidence presented relates to outcomes associated with patterns of infant-mother attachment assessed at age one, or, in a few cases, at age six. The predominant message of this literature is that children who have been assessed as securely attached to mother at age one tend to do better on most social outcomes at later ages. These data are correlational only. They do not provide evidence of causal relationships and nor do they take much account of the influence of attachment figures other than the mother. They imply that it is usual for each individual to have one predominant pattern of relating, that attachment security remains stable over the lifespan and that the 'secure' attachment pattern is optimal for good social development. Whether there is really strong evidence to support any of these inferences, though, seems questionable.

The first inference is difficult to test, largely due to the cumbersomeness of the Strange Situation procedure and to the difficulty of determining what exactly might be involved in attachment security both as assessed in the Strange Situation as age one and later on throughout the lifespan. Although some studies did include an assessment of attachment to both mother and father, few reported on either the separate contribution of father-child attachment or of the combined influences of mother-child and father-child attachments (not to mention the influence of attachments to other figures such as grandparents, day care workers, nannies, other family relatives and friends, etc.).[8] It is possible that children develop a range of relationship strategies and that the most socially successful children are not those who have learned to apply one optimal strategy regardless of social context but those who have learned to know which strategy to use in which relationship context. Whether mother-infant 'security' provides this adaptive capability more than any other relationship experience or combination of relationship experiences has not yet been tested, although the data may seem to suggest this conclusion. The testability of the second inference is hampered by similar assessment problems which we discuss further towards the end of Chapter Six when we review evidence from a number of longitudinal studies.

It seems important also to regard the third inference, that the 'secure' attachment pattern is optimal for social development, with caution. Even greater caution seems appropriate with respect to the views of those who hold more deterministic interpretations of Attachment

---

8 Some studies have indicated that security of attachment to both mother and father is associated with more positive outcomes than security to mother alone, though these studies have tended to be small-scale and cross-sectional in design.

Theory and who assert that only the secure pattern of attachment is healthy. Other organised patterns are likely to be more adaptive when rearing conditions are more challenging and, as we show in Chapter Six, there is no substantial evidence to support the argument that individuals go through life using the same attachment pattern in all circumstances and all relationships.

There is still a need for further refinement of research methodologies and concepts. It is not safe to conclude that, even with longitudinal study designs, particular social outcomes are due to attachment security as opposed to other social processes. Alternative explanations also need to be investigated. For example, is it possible that attachment security is simply another name for conformity to social norms? It is a sad but true fact that children who are seen as conforming to social norms, i.e. children who are relatively attractive physically (without visible disability) and relatively similar to their peers (not in a minority on the basis of linguistic or cognitive ability, temperamental characteristics, or on ethnic, religious or cultural grounds), are also those who are likely to be most popular and so most at ease with their peers. They may also be those whose mothers find least difficulty in forming close and loving relationships, perhaps, who knows, due to the fact that they have these socially desirable attributes.

Quite apart from the fact that it is an error to regard one particular pattern of attachment as more adaptive than others (Hinde 1982b), it seems worth considering the possibility that there may be other reasons for questioning the assumption that the 'secure' pattern is what everyone should be aiming for. Children with histories of secure attachment are likely to be easier to get to know, more comfortable to be with, more open and relaxed, and more obviously interested in other people. Some children with histories of less secure attachment may be more prickly and more prone to feel slighted, more reserved, sceptical and introverted, less trusting and, certainly until they are well known, likely to be more awkward to be with. Assuming that their attachment style is less than optimal, that they have inferior social understanding, that they have less good will toward others, that their way of processing social information and their very character needs to change, seems likely to reinforce their sense of inferiority and may possibly force them into more and more constricted modes of relating. As we argued before, just as left-handed children were not given appropriate instruction in the past to teach them to write, dubbing children 'insecure' may risk stigmatising them and increasing their disadvantage. This is clearly not what Bowlby would have intended. Rather, he aimed to extend advantages to as many children and parents as possible by seeking to elucidate the processes that lead to psychological well-being. In the next chapter, we explore what is known about the conditions that might facilitate the formation of secure attachments.

Meanwhile, it seems important to acknowledge that, at this stage in the history or attachment research, there is still a lot to be learned about the nature of Internal Working Models across the lifespan. As Belsky (2004) commented, "To this day I remain surprised that we know so little about what processes constitute the internal working models." Due to the central 'fuzziness' of conceptual definitions of attachment security both in the first year of life and across the lifespan with concomitant problems of measurement, there is still a lot to be discovered about the significance of one-year-olds patterns of attachment for later development. The assumption that the majority outlook is optimal under all circumstances, on logical grounds alone, does not hold water. A variety of outlooks is, in an evolutionary sense, highly desirable. For this reason, it seems important that, in our efforts to improve quality of life for everyone, we do not lose sight of the adaptive value of non-secure organised patterns of attachment. Perhaps it is important that we are not all secure all the time, but that we retain a capacity to flexibly adapt our mode of relating according to the currently available opportunities. To do this, it may be necessary to reach greater agreement on operational definitions of attachment security and to further refine measures of it so that we can track even more closely its role and significance.

5 Links between quality of parental care and attachment security

"When a mother is perceptive of her child's signals and responds promptly and appropriately to them her child thrives and the relationship develops happily. It is when she is not perceptive or not responsive, or when she gives him not what he wants but something else instead, that things go wrong... Disturbances of attachment behaviour are of many kinds. In the Western world much the commonest, in my view, are the results of too little mothering, or of mothering coming from a succession of different people"

(Bowlby 1969/1982, p.422).

The importance of quality of care

As will be apparent from Chapter Four, securely attached children are more socially competent and more comfortable with others than less securely attached children. They come across as having more positive attitudes towards others, more optimism, higher self-esteem and more confidence in interactions with others. They are also better able to control their emotions and to tolerate frustration and are generally thought of as more mature, empathic and responsible. In addition, they bounce back more readily in the face of difficulty and react less adversely to criticism or rebuff. As a result, they tend to be more popular and are often judged to have more mature and appropriate social and coping skills. So why aren't all children like this?

According to Attachment Theory, these qualities do not appear accidentally. They are neither incidental, arbitrary nor pre-existing attributes. Rather, they are present, like dormant seeds, in all children. All that is needed for the seeds to set down roots and to begin to flourish are the social conditions and experience afforded by a particular kind of caring relationship. From these basic premises, it doesn't take much to work out that Attachment Theory stipulates that some caring relationships produce secure children and others do not. Put more bluntly, as we saw in the Introduction to this book, Bowlby (1988g) asserted that about 60 per cent of parents are good at looking after their children and enabling them to develop well. The other 40 per cent are not.

In this chapter, we explore whether there are any identifiable qualities that can provide a reliable recipe for the establishment of secure attachment relationships between infants and their caregivers. In doing this, we bear in mind the early work of Mary Ainsworth as well as that of John Bowlby and the others on which Bowlby based his view that, "What is believed to be essential for mental health is that the infant and young child should experience a warm, intimate and continuous relationship with his mother (or mother-substitute) in which both find satisfaction and enjoyment" (Bowlby 1969/1982, p.12). We also recall that Attachment Theory evolved for the specific purpose of understanding why mother-child relationships should be so important for later mental health. At the outset, Bowlby set out to discover why it might be that "loss of mother-figure, either by itself or in combination with other variables yet to be clearly identified, is capable of generating responses and processes that are of the greatest interest to psychopathology. Not only so, but these responses and processes, we concluded, are the very same as are known to be active in older individuals who are still disturbed by separations that they suffered in early life" (Bowlby 1969/1982, p.14).

When Bowlby expressed these views, he was also aware that very little empirical research had directly addressed the question of exactly what quality of care children might need in order to develop well. He hypothesised, from his knowledge of work with animals as well as from observations of young children separated from mothers (e.g. Heinicke and Westheimer 1965), that continuity, emotional availability, warmth and responsiveness may all be implicated. By the time he died and after, researchers were still debating what it might be that contributes most to secure attachment relationships between children and parents. In this chapter, we consider some of the arguments that have been advanced, beginning first with a closer look at the concept of maternal sensitivity proposed by Mary Ainsworth and going on to consider some of the alternative or, possibly, complementary theories.

Maternal sensitivity

Mary Ainsworth (Ainsworth 1969, Ainsworth et al. 1971) soon came to the conclusion, based on her observations of mothers and infants in interaction, that some mothers were much better able than others to 'read' their babies' cues and to interact with them warmly and calmly. These mothers were also the most likely to have infants who were securely attached to them. To measure the differences between these other mothers, Ainsworth began to construct a measure of the qualities that she identified as contributing to 'maternal sensitivity' (fuller details of ratings on this scale can be found in Appendix 5.1).

Ainsworth's scale measured mothers' behaviour along four dimensions:
- *sensitivity vs. insensitivity:* the mother's ability to read and respond to her baby's cues
- *cooperation vs. interference:* the mother's willingness to allow the infant to pursue her/his own agenda and not to intrude too much with her own
- *accessibility vs. ignoring and neglecting:* the extent to which the mother allows herself to be psychologically and physically available for the baby (and, conversely, the extent to which she does not ignore or neglect her baby)
- *acceptance vs. rejection:* the mother's acceptance and non-rejection of the infant's demands and needs.

By rating mothers along each of these four dimensions, Ainsworth aimed to arrive at a fuller picture of the processes involved in creating an emotionally secure child. The scale that she created, though, was not formally standardised, that is, there were no publicly agreed formulae for decisions about ratings. Given the naturally subjective nature of judgements about mother-infant relationships, this lack of formalisation might be expected to lead to "noisy data".

Take the following example of a piece of observational material:

Janine has just heard that her husband has lost his job. She has three children and the youngest is sixteen-month-old Celine. Janine puts the phone down and sits looking blank and shocked. During the phone call, Celine has been playing with her plastic carpentry set, knocking cylinders into holes in a play work-bench. As her mother puts the phone down, Celine stops playing and looks, wide-eyed, at her mother. Still holding a plastic hammer in one hand and picking up the work-bench, she toddles over and tries to get her mother to play with her. She pushes the work-bench onto Janine's lap, saying, "Mum" in an urgent-sounding voice. She begins to hammer again, looking at her mother and appearing to seek reassurance. Janine rather vacantly smiles at Celine, then gently puts the work-bench back on the floor beside Celine, saying "Clever girl". She stands up and goes to make herself a cup of tea. Celine sits still for a few seconds, watching her mother's retreating figure, then, leaving the playbench and hammer, begins, half-crawling, to follow her.

Data like this are ambiguous. In order to rate this sequence along the four Ainsworth sensitivity dimensions, observers need to add inferences about the potential effect of Janine's behaviour on Celine. A small snippet of behaviour like this would also need to be judged in the context of other observations taken over a longer space of time. The sense the observer makes of their other observations will also contribute to their later judgements. It is not difficult to appreciate that, even if raters are given guidelines on how to rate particular situations, differences in subjective judgements will arise. One observer's 'crass intrusion' (rated '9' on intrusiveness) may be another's 'well-meant mistake' (rated '6'). Even if all studies adopted Ainsworth's Sensitivity Scales, it is therefore likely that researchers might reach different conclusions.

As it turns out, not all studies purporting to measure maternal sensitivity have used these scales. Rather, a number of alternative measures have been developed, e.g. Crittenden's C.A.R.E. Index (Crittenden 1998), Biringen's Emotional Availability Scale (Biringen et al. 1998), the Empathic Understanding procedure (Oppenheim et al. 2001; recently re-named the Parental Insightfulness Scale – Oppenheim 2005, personal communication). More research is needed before it will be known how these alternatives (additional information about which can be found in Appendix 5.2) map onto Ainsworth's conceptualisation.

Maternal sensitivity has generally been linked to a range of positive outcomes in children, including school achievement and a variety of cognitive and socio-emotional skills (Beckwith et al. 1999) as well as better emotional self-regulation in infancy (Spangler et al. 1994). However, it is not altogether clear whether these associations reflect causal or incidental links or what the relationship might be between maternal sensitivity and attachment security. Numerous studies have reported associations between maternal sensitivity and infant attachment security in both low- and high-risk samples (e.g. Grossmann et al. 1985, Isabella 1993, Egeland and Farber 1984, Belsky et al. 1984b, 1984c, Miyake et al. 1985, Goldberg et al. 1986). Typically, these studies suggest that mothers of secure babies are more responsive to infants' vocalisations and distress signals, are more likely to interact with their babies without either under-or over-stimulating them (Belsky et al. 1984b, 1984c), that they show more physical affection (Bates et al. 1985), and that they hold their babies more often and interrupt the baby's ongoing behaviour less (Miyake et al. 1985).

However, others have noted that these associations are often not very strong. Allen et al. (2003), for example, commented that most studies have only found a modest relationship between maternal sensitivity and attachment security with, at most, only about a quarter of the variability in infant security being linked to this aspect of mothers' behaviour (r = 0.24). This estimate was possibly based on the meta-analysis of 66 studies carried out by De Wolff and van IJzendoorn (1997) which found a combined effect size of .24 from the 16 studies (n=837) that had used the Ainsworth scales to measure maternal sensitivity. Studies using other measures (30 studies, n=1,666) produced an effect size of .22. Also, in contrast to the original Baltimore study which reported a correlation of .78 (n=21) between maternal sensitivity and attachment security or .85 when statistical corrections for measurement error were considered, the combined effect size from replication studies (n=1097) appeared to be only .24 while the combined effect over all 66 studies (n=7,223[1]) was only .17. De Wolff and van IJzendoorn argued that even this small effect size might still indicate the existence of powerful causal mechanisms and justified their argument by citing results from their meta-analysis of intervention studies (van IJzendoorn et al. 1995b) in which they had found a "moderate effect" on attachment security (d =.48)[2] for interventions that focused on maternal sensitivity to infant cues.

While defending the role of maternal sensitivity as a causal factor, De Wolff and van IJzendoorn conceded that sensitivity had "lost its privileged position as the only important causal factor" (De Wolff and van IJzendoorn 1997, p.585). They identified the need for multidimensional approaches to the investigation of parental antecedents to attachment security and drew attention to the role of other factors such as cooperation, mutuality, interactional synchrony, stimulation, physical contact, support and contiguity of response (Table 5.1). As Table 5.1 shows, all effect sizes were small: the largest one (r = 0.32) emanated from only three studies containing an overall sample of 168 participants and, in this case, the authors suggest that there may have been a 'file drawer problem' (i.e. a failure to find this effect in most other studies that may have led to non-publication of studies in which the factor was measured). They suggest that this might have applied to the majority of factors listed while the difficulty of computing probability levels points to considerable variability in the data-sets.

A more recent meta-analysis of 41 studies of mother-infant dyads (Atkinson et al. 2000) also found that there was an overall effect size of r = 0.27 linking sensitivity to attachment security but that the length of time between assessments moderated this effect: the effect size when assessments were concurrent was far larger than when they were non-concurrent, although small effect sizes did still appear with non-concurrent assessments.

It is important, though, to be cautious when interpreting results of meta-analyses: they do not provide evidence of causal relationships and, by combining results relating to variables that purport to be the same from studies using very different methods, samples and measures of variables, can often be rather misleading. This seems very likely to limit the usefulness of the findings relating to 'attitude' and 'support', for example, both of which are likely to have been measured in a variety of ways. Even so, these findings undoubtedly lend strong support to De Wolff and van IJzendoorn's argument for the relevance of a multi-dimensional approach. They also lend support to the notion that, particularly in the early days of research in any field, there is a clear need for publication of non-significant outcomes. This seems particularly urgent in relation to intervention studies.

---

1 This figure includes reports that contain overlapping samples – the actual total was 4,176 from all 66 studies.
2 Though Cohen's criteria for a medium effect size is 0.50-0.79 while .020-0.49 is considered small (Cohen 1988).

Table 5.1: Potentially important dimensions of parenting (from De Wolff and van IJzendoorn, 1997)

PARENTAL BEHAVIOUR	NUMBER OF STUDIES	NUMBER OF PARTIC-IPANTS	EFFECT SIZE (r)	p	FAIL SAFE (number)
Sensitivity	30	1,666	.22	9.12 E-15	861.8
using Ainsworth's scales	16	837	.24	1.55 E-09	238.9
Contiguity of response	14	825	.10	.01	38.7*
Physical contact	9	637	.09	.04	14.1*
Cooperation	9	493	.13	.007	17.2*
Synchrony	6	258	.26	.0001	35.5*
Mutuality	3	168	.32	.00003	17.6*
Support	22	1664	.16	7.41 E-06	328.2
Attitude	21	1092	.18	3.02 E-08	273.2
Stimulation	9	422	.18	.0001	32.0*

* Possible file-drawer problem

Whatever the size of the contribution of maternal sensitivity to attachment security, as several reviewers have commented, there is even less evidence of a positive association between maternal insensitivity and secure attachment (Goldberg 2000) and more reason to suppose that caregiver insensitivity is associated with insecure attachment in infancy (see Weinfield et al. 1999 for review). Much of this evidence comes from studies that involve clinical populations of caregivers (for example, mothers with postnatal depression) or of samples of infants and children where there is evidence of or reason to suspect abuse. Such samples can be expected (hopefully!) to include caregivers who are more or less outside the typical range of sensitivity-insensitivity. While it may be reassuring to think that measures of maternal sensitivity are able to reflect effects on infants of extremes of caregiver insensitivity (this suggests that they are not *completely* 'up the spout' at least!), the real challenge for attachment researchers may be to find more subtle indicators of early relationship difficulties.

Antecedents to attachment

Infant researchers have devoted considerable time to analyses of early mother-infant interactions. Some have attempted to specify, in minute detail, ways in which infant and mother vocalisations, facial expressions and movements relate to each other, in quality, timing and spatial location (e.g. Papousek and Papousek 1977, Trevarthen 1977, Murray and Trevarthen 1985, Stern 1985, Isabella et al. 1989, Hobson 2002). What tends to come out of such studies besides detailed descriptions of often very complex interactions is an awareness of wide variations in degrees to which dyadic responses relate to each other and appear to cue each other.

Intersubjective synchrony

Trevarthen has termed this quality of interaction 'intersubjective synchrony'. From a starting point where he defines 'subjectivity' as the capacity to show at least the rudiments of individual consciousness and intentionality (e.g. by focussing attention on things, orienting towards them, handling or exploring them), he describes communication as involving the adaptation of this subjective control to take account of the subjectivity of others, a capacity that he calls 'intersubjectivity' (e.g. Trevarthen 1979, 1993). Trevarthen suggests that intersubjectivity develops through stages. 'Primary intersubjectivity' emerges at about two months when infants appear to begin to distinguish between people and things by using more expressive movements to communicate with people (as opposed to chewing on them, or manipulating them). A qualitative change in the way that infants interact with people is thought to take place at around nine months when 'secondary intersubjectivity' or 'person-person-object relating (Trevarthen and Hubley 1978) takes over.

Trevarthen (e.g. Trevarthen 1989, p.51) stresses that the newborn "baby is not vacuous 'biological' material waiting to be socialized, but a being adapted, in the course of evolution, to function intersubjectively, in communication". At this stage, which begins in late pregnancy, the baby "enters into an intimate 'being in contact'". By now, according to Trevarthen, the baby already shows interest in orienting towards the source of sound, smell and visual stimuli, seeks physical contact and, in the first weeks, shows preferences for the mother's voice and smell, and can imitate eye and mouth movements. This basic interest in others and the early-developed capacity to imitate is thought by Trevarthen to be shared by non-human primates and to be an important skill that enables infants to reference others' emotional states and helps them to learn how objects or actions are valued by others and what they might mean. From week six at least, Trevarthen claims that babies show distress in response to a break in contact and have identified a "main, most affectionate caregiver, who is given preferential attentiveness in expressions of greater happiness and readiness to make 'utterances'" (Trevarthen 1989, p.43).

In response to these sociable overtures of the baby's, the mother "finds herself attuning her behaviour in appropriate supportive ways, pacing her brief, evenly spaced expressions of motherese (baby talk) ... to fit with the periodic utterances and gestures of the infant" (Trevarthen 1989, p.42). Noticing "an increased awakening of interest and focusing of attention on the part of the infant, a change which occurs at about 46 weeks of gestational age", the mother sets up 'protoconversational exchanges' on the "shared beat of moving, and both mother and infant adjust intensity of emotion in movements of face, voice, hands, and body posture" (Trevarthen 1989, p.42). Mothers of two-month-old infants interpret the baby's gestures and facial expressions as meaningful: their responses "are stimulating, attentive, confirmatory, interpretative and highly supportive. They inject meaning into the infants' expressions, but at this stage verbal meaning has no influence on the infants' minds" (Trevarthen 1979, p.338). Even at this stage, although there is asymmetry in interactions, the mother does not always take the lead and babies show a functioning ability to direct communications: to some extent, babies "control the social stimulation on which their own development depends" (Trevarthen 1979, p.343). According to Trevarthen, the basis of attachment relationships may be being created in this social context, not by a simple process of imprinting but through mutual enjoyment of communicative exchanges.

By three months, Trevarthen argues, infants show increased self-regulation and initiative and can engage in cheeky, defiant, humorous exchanges. Mothers are then obliged to increase their communicative repertoires to keep track and, to do so, often introduce traditional nursery rhyme tunes "in which the beat and rhythms of interaction and the qualities and melodic forms of voice that signal feeling are brought out clearly" (Trevarthen 1989, p.44). Trevarthen explains that mothers' ability to tune in to their infants at this stage is not culturally determined. The mother does not impose cultural values. She simply follows the infant's lead. It is not until about nine months, due to a change in the quality of attention that infants pay to other people (Trevarthen and Hubley 1978), that mothers might begin to teach culture-specific behaviours.

What it is that effects the transition to the stage of 'secondary intersubjectivity' at around nine months is not clear. What is clear is that the quality of the infant's interactional exchanges alters. Diagrammatically, they become capable of triangular relationships as opposed to two-dimensional ones, as relationships between self, other and object assume greater importance (Figure 5.1). Trevarthen rejects the notion that infants are essentially egocentric (Piaget's idea) and proposes that intersubjectivity develops from the outset because (a) infants have an innate interest in relating to others, (b) this is both self-reinforcing and increases exposure to rewarding experiences and (c) from this basis, their skills at relating simultaneously become increasingly sophisticated through experience.

Trevarthen emphasises that the infant's capacity for relating to both people and objects is motivated by a fundamental neurologically-based pre-disposition to relate to others. He later endorsed the view that the concept of a 'virtual other' may be pre-wired (Aitken and Trevarthen 1997) or, as Bråten (1987, 1992, 1998, 2003) proposed, that "within the central nervous system of the newborn, there are circuits which specify the immediate co-presence of a complementary participant, which are termed the 'virtual other', in place of which the actual other may step" (Bråten 1987, p.221). Trevarthen (1990, 1996) argues that this pre-wiring appears to provide the impetus for meaningful communication and relationships between children and adults: "Finally, completing the picture, we find evidence that the intrinsic regulators of human brain growth in a child are specially adapted to be coupled, by emotional communication, to the regulators of adult brains of people who know more. This seems to be the key generic brain strategy for cultural learning that takes place not in single brains, but in communities of them" (Trevarthen 1990, p.357).

The possibility that the 'virtual other' may be multiple others has been further explored in the work of Elizabeth Fivaz-Depeursinge and her colleagues who have developed the Lausanne Trilogue Play (LTP) paradigm, a technique initially designed for observing triadic interactions in parents and neonates but subsequently adapted for parents with older children and for prenatal parent-doll figure enactions (Fivaz-Depeursinge et al. 1996, Corboz-Warnery and Fivaz-Depeursinge 1999, Fivaz-Depeursinge 2005). Research using this technique is showing that even babies of a few weeks old appear to anticipate, make sense of and utilise two-way other-person exchanges and are able to engage in three-way interactions. It has also demonstrated that 70 per cent of triadic communications appear to be characterised by mis-communications which, in the remaining 30 per cent of the time are, more or less, repaired (Fivaz-Depeursinge 2005). This work seems likely to throw considerable light in future on the question of what the optimal role of interactional synchrony may be in the development of parent-child relationships.

Figure 5.1: The development of intersubjectivity

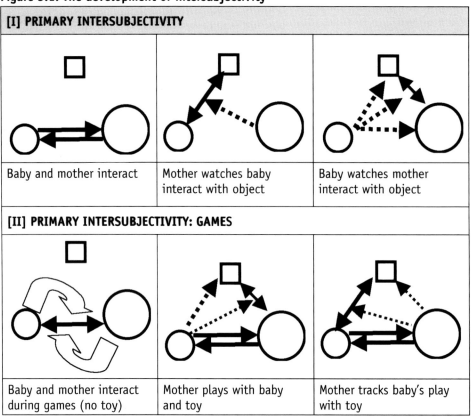

Interactional synchrony

The concept of 'interactional synchrony' proposed by Isabella and colleagues (Isabella et al. 1989, Isabella and Belsky 1991) is, in some ways, similar to Trevarthen's notion but this group of researchers used rather different observational methods and explored the relationship between mother-infant interactions in the home and in the Strange Situation. The earlier study (Isabella et al. 1989) involved 51 mothers and first-born infants who were participating in the Pennsylvania Infant and Family Development Project (IFDP) while the later replication (Isabella and Belsky 1991) extended the study to 153 mother-infant dyads (51 from the second and 102 from the third wave of the IFDP).

Mothers and infants were observed in their homes when infants were aged three and nine months. When the babies had reached their first birthday, they and their mothers were assessed in the Strange Situation. During home observations, observers were instructed not to interact with mothers or infants but to record infant-mother interactions over a 45 minute period. Every fifteen seconds, observers counted the frequency of occurrence of 14 types of mother-infant interaction (e.g. infant sleeping, fussing or crying, vocalisation, exploration, looking at mother, en face interaction, maternal vocalisation to infant, responding to infant, soothing, stimulating, looking, not interacting). All co-occurring mother and infant behaviours were classified according to whether they were synchronous or asynchronous with synchronicity being defined as "an interactive experience reflecting an appropriate fit of mother and infant behaviour, presumed to derive from maternal sensitive responsiveness and to foster a state of social harmony" (Isabella and Belsky 1991, p.374). Synchronous interactions were coded if mothers responded in a contingent way to their infants, for example, by taking action to soothe an infant who is fussing or crying, or by talking back to an infant who vocalises, or paying visual attention to an infant who is looking or approaching the mother. Asynchronous interactions were coded if the mother's response appeared inappropriate, for example, if they made no attempt to soothe a crying baby, or appeared to be following their own agenda rather than that of the infant so that they interrupted or ignored rather than facilitated the baby's activities.

In both studies, infant-mother interactions in the home appeared to predict later behaviour in the Strange Situation and subsequent attachment classification. Infants and mothers in secure dyads showed the highest levels of interactional synchrony. Mothers of infants classified as insecure-avoidant showed more non-contingent responses, for example, some talked almost continuously 'at' rather than to their babies and they tended as a group to be more over-stimulating and intrusive. Isabella et al. (1989) remarked that it was as if the reaction of these mothers to being observed was to "'put their best mothering foot forward' for the sake of the observer, thus displaying a good many noncontingent, misguided interactive behaviors" (Isabella et al. 1989, p.19). Mothers of insecure resistant infants seemed less inclined to 'fake' being good mothers: they tended to be under-involved or inconsistently involved with their infants and the interactions between them and their babies gave the impression of being poorly coordinated. Isabella et al. (1989) speculated that the interactive strategies employed by mothers of avoidant infants might lead directly to the distinctive defence strategies adopted by their infants: the infants may also be 'playing the game' of covering up and defensively distancing thoughts of mothers' shortcomings. This strategy might pave the way for the development of defensive idealisation (the tendency, thought to be common among avoidantly attached individuals, to portray their parents as faultless).

Isabella and Belsky's concept of interactional synchrony did not emerge in isolation and, in fact, it is difficult to tell whether the close observational work of several other groups of researchers around this time (e.g. Brazelton et al. 1974, Stern et al. 1977, Tronick et al. 1982) set the main precedent for identification of the importance of a role for interactional synchrony in the development of attachment relationships. Certainly, a number of workers were reporting on very similar relationship qualities.

Affective attunement

Stern (1985), for example, proposed that mothers' capacity to tune in to their baby's emotional state, or their 'affective attunement', could enable the developing child to make sense of and to begin to take control over his or her experiences. He suggested that mothers who are good at 'tuning in' to their babies, resonating with them and encouraging them to share attention, impact on the development of their infants' abilities in all areas: their social competence (including language and communication), emotional understanding and cognitive ability. Stern argued that far greater affective attunement was found in mothers of securely attached infants than in those with non-securely attached children.

He further argued that because mothers of securely attached infants are affectively attuned to their babies, they are more able to accept and acknowledge both the negative and positive states that infants experience. This acceptance gradually enables the infants to acknowledge, share and regulate their experiences which, in turn, helps them to know how to recognise and anticipate when they and others might again experience particular feelings.

Lester et al. (1985), again along similar lines to Trevarthen, suggest that the process of becoming affectively attuned involves both awareness on the part of both infant and carer of each other's characteristic rhythms and mutual synchronised co-regulation, mostly led by the carer but in response to the infant's cues and stage of development. By contrast, the non-acceptance, discomfort, rejection or denial of particular states of arousal (e.g. demands for attention and comfort, or expressions of distress) by mothers of avoidant infants encourages their children to defensively exclude non-accepted, and so unacceptable, feelings and states from consciousness. In consequence, avoidantly attached infants do not learn how to cope well with states of high arousal and consequently are unable to acknowledge their impact either on their own responses or on those of other people. This clearly restricts their capacity to empathise and to engage closely with other people. Lester et al. also suggest that mothers of ambivalent/resistant infants do tune in to their infants' emotional states, but only on an inconsistent and unpredictable basis. This prevents the baby from learning to control themselves and, as a result, the ambivalent infant is keenly aware of potential discomfort and ultra-quick to seek attention and reassurance. But it is important to remember that their urgent demonstration of need will usually be simultaneously accompanied by anticipation that their needs will not be met.

Stern's notion of affective attunement clearly has much in common with concepts of maternal sensitivity, interactional synchrony and intersubjectivity. Like them, it is difficult to be sure whether it better describes than rather than explains attachment security or whether it is a separate motivational system as Stern has implied (Stern 1985, 2005). Work by Jaffe and colleagues (Jaffe et al. 2001) suggest that the relationship between maternal affective attunement and attachment security may resemble an inverted U rather than a positive linear relationship. In this optimal midrange model, both mothers who are hyper- and those who are hypo-responsive to their infants' cues fall outside the optimal mid range associated with attachment security. In other words, it is possible for parents to be both too much and too little attuned to their babies: in the first case, the infant's capacity to initiate interactions will be undermined; in the second case, the infant's ability to control the course of interactions will be undermined. Both strategies therefore are likely to prevent infants from having a sense of executive control in social interactions.

Helpfulness

Another quality that has been identified as associated with attachment security is helpfulness. Crowell and Feldman (1988) observed mothers and children as they interacted during a problem-solving task and concluded that mothers who self-classified as having a secure attachment style were best at giving help. Dismissing mothers were cool, controlling and very task-focused while preoccupied mothers were inconsistent in their help-giving and presented at different times as confused, confusing, warm or angry. Secure mothers were much better able to interact calmly with their children, balanced their attention more evenly between the needs of the child and the demands of the task and focused more on seeing things from the child's perspective. Other researchers have found similar differences between fathers too: secure mothers and fathers provide their children with more structure on problem-solving tasks and come across as warmer and more effectively engaged with their children (Cohn et al. 1992, Pearson et al. 1994). Avoidant parents seem to be least likely to provide their children with effective support in teaching settings (Rholes et al. 1995).

Again, there does not appear to be any widely agreed definition of what might constitute helpfulness: while some researchers focus on adults' ability to see the problem from the child's perspective, others emphasise the presence of aggressive and defensive reactions. Few have investigated the possibility that the mothers who are most helpful might also be those who are most aware of and appropriately responsive to their children's mental state though it seems likely that researchers might agree that this factor plays an important role. For example, in one study of mothers reading books to their children, Bus and van IJzendoorn (1988) found that secure mothers, unlike others, tended to use book-reading as an opportunity to teach their children about reading, not just to read. Such attention to their children's mental development might be expected to impact on emergent literacy skills.

In more stressful contexts, such as during inoculation, marked differences have been found in the way secure and insecure mothers help their children to cope. Perhaps rather too predictably, in this situation parents with avoidant tendencies stood out as being particularly unhelpful: the more distressed their children became, the more detached and unsupportive they were (Edelstein et al. 2004). Findings such as these raise the question of what relationship, if any, there might be between ability to handle stress, experience of stress and attachment history.

Psychobiological regulation

Early in his formulation of Attachment Theory, Bowlby came to the view that mothers might in some way help infants to make sense of their experiences: "… a mother by her mere presence and tenderness can act as an 'organizer' on the mind of a child, still in the quite undeveloped stages of very early growth" (Bowlby 1953/1965, p.62).

Here, as elsewhere in his writings, Bowlby's language failed to reflect his keen awareness of the importance of affective exchanges between mothers and children. This awareness has often not been fully appreciated, as Bowlby himself sensed: "In writing this lecture I have throughout been aware that, by using terms such as 'information', 'communication', and 'working models', it would be easy for the unwary reader to suppose that these terms belong within a psychology concerned only with cognition and one bereft of feeling and action… There are, in fact, no more important communications between one human being and another than those expressed emotionally, and no information more vital for constructing and reconstructing working models of self and other than information about how each feels towards the other. During the earliest years of our lives, indeed, emotional expression and its reception are the only means of communication we have, so that the foundations of our working models of self and attachment figure are perforce laid using information from that source alone" (Bowlby 1977b/1988b, pp. 156-157).

Much that Bowlby wrote about in describing the formation, maintenance and breakdown of attachment bonds relates to the important role of the mother (and other attachment figures) in acting as a reference point by which the developing child can assess how to proceed. By providing continuity, reassurance and guidance, the attachment figure who provides a secure base does considerably more for the infant than the petrol pump does for the car. In addition to providing the conditions for re-fuelling, the attachment figure helps the infant to know when it is safe to explore, closely monitors the child's state, assists them to prepare for action and gradually helps them to learn how to increase their scope for future self-management. In Bowlby's words, "this strong and consistent support from parents, combined with encouragement and respect for a child's autonomy, so far from sapping self-reliance, provide the conditions in which it can best grow" (Bowlby 1973b/1979c, p.124).

Although the concept of the attachment figure as providing a homeostatic function for the developing child was implicit throughout Bowlby's writing, it was largely left to other researchers to spell out exactly how this regulatory function might operate. A number of attachment researchers (e.g. Sroufe and Waters 1977, Gunnar et al. 1989, Cicchetti et al. 1991, Sroufe 1995, 1996, Reite and Capitanio 1985, Thompson 1994, 1998, Zahn-Waxler et al. 1992), researchers investigating stress response mechanisms (e.g. Collins and Depue 1992), psychologists and neuropsychologists investigating cognitive, perceptual and social development in infancy (e.g. Johnson, 1999, 2001, Trevarthen 1989, 1990, 1993) and developmental psychologists working in many areas such as the development of social and emotional understanding (e.g. Block and Block 1980, Lamb and Sherrod 1981, Field and Fox 1985, Saarni and Harris 1989, Campos et al. 1989, Barrett and Campos 1987, Tronick 1989, Garber and Dodge 1991, Applegate et al. 1992, Fogel 1993, Kochanska 1995, 1997, 1998, 2001), temperament (Bates et al. 1985, 1998, Kagan et al. 1994, Posner and Rothbart 1998, 2000), the development of concepts of self (e.g. James 1890/1983, Lewin 1935, Mead 1934, Bertenthal and Fischer 1978, Lewis and Brooks-Gunn 1979), and the development of language and communication (e.g. Papousek et al. 1985, 1992, Nelson 1989) have all contributed to this line of enquiry and have helped to build up a more detailed picture.

Like Bowlby himself, many of these workers, particularly those within the field of social cognition and its related field of cognitive development, have seemed at first glance to portray the developing child as if he or she were an organism independent of any socio-affective context or feelings. Perhaps for this reason, though doubtless for other reasons too,[3] ideas generated within the vast field of mainstream psychology have tended to filter through to more clinically- or psychoanalytically-oriented theorists in a somewhat piecemeal way. In the other direction, ideas generated within the psychoanalytic tradition have often been positively out-ruled. This is not the place to address this problem but it nevertheless seems important to remark that, in spite of the work of notable individuals whose names begin with S (Stern, Sroufe, Schore), there still remains huge potential for further cross-fertilisa-

---

3   This process seems likely to be a continuation of the same processes through which Bowlby during his lifetime became alienated from the psychoanalytic community and also distanced from much of 'mainstream' academic psychology. It may stem from within mainstream psychology as much as from the boundary of psychoanalysis and psychology, from marked tendencies for workers within and outside empirical scientific conventions to distrust and even to de-value each others' conclusions.

tion (though it may be difficult to agree upon the best way to ensure that evidence is not taken out of context during transfer).

Putting this problem aside for the time being, it seems fair to say that, from the initial conceptualisation of attachment relationships as being concerned with infants growing up with other, relatively independent carers, it has increasingly become recognised that the young child's self-and-other-awareness emerges within the socio-affective context of co-dependent relating. As Sroufe (1996, p.172) puts it, "Attachment, which refers to a special relationship between infant and caregiver that evolves over the first year of life and beyond, is inherently an emotional construct. Not only does it imply an 'affective bond' between parent and infant, it also is properly characterized in terms of the regulation of infant emotion. In fact, it is the apex of dyadic emotional regulation, a culmination of all development in the first year and a harbinger of the self regulation that is to come".

Along the same lines as Reite and Capitanio (1985, p.235) who described the attachment relationship as essentially functioning "to promote the synchrony or regulation of biological and behavioral systems on an organismic level" and Field (1985) who used the term 'psycho-biological attunement' to describe the emotional relationship between infants and their cares, Sroufe (Sroufe and Waters 1977, Sroufe 1995, 1996) have detailed the way that emotional self-regulation in pre-schoolers gradually emerges through experiences of joint attention and affective sharing with more or less attuned caregivers. He argued (Sroufe and Waters 1977) in favour of viewing the attachment relationship as an organisational construct on the grounds that it centrally involves co-regulation which is more or less mutual, reciprocal or effective. Secure attachment, Sroufe (1996, p.189) maintained, "is the effective dyadic regulation of emotion in infancy *(which)*... is predicted to have consequences for emerging expectations concerning emotional arousal and, at the behavioral level, consequences for the expression, modulation, and flexible control of emotions of the child".

The recipe, therefore, for secure *organising* attachments, according to Sroufe, is:
- repeated experiences of others as available and responsive at times when the baby is aroused
- extremely rare or brief experiences of being left out of control and in the grip of strong emotions
- repair and re-stabilisation of emotional equilibrium after upsets or over-excitement.

Sroufe (1996, p.189) explains how, based on such experiences, a child with a secure attachment history should readily engage with "situations having the potential for emotional arousal and should directly express emotions, since emotions themselves are not threatening and are expected to be treated as communications by others". By contrast, an insecure attachment history does not provide children with experiences that enable them to organise themselves or to deal with emotional arousal so effectively.

While the concept of emotional regulation and the related organisational processes that operate at all levels (physiological, affective, conscious/subliminal, etc.) seems intuitively appealing, as Thompson et al. (1995, p.267) point out, there is a "tendency to conclude that clear or consensual definitions of emotional regulation exist among developmental scientists when, in fact, they do not". They also stressed that much remained to be discovered about the complex neurophysiological processes underlying the development of capacities for emotional self-regulation, the extent to which this development is dependent on biologically pre-programmed maturational processes and real life experiences, and the interplay between these influences.

Thompson et al. (1995) outline a general framework within which the relationship between infants and carers develops under the influence of multiple and multiply-determined constraints that permit a huge number of potential developmental trajectories (Table 5.2).

Table 5.2: Early development of emotional self-regulation (Thompson et al. 1995)

EXCITATORY PROCESSES	INHIBITORY PROCESSES
• increasing stability of HPA* arousal system in early months • therefore infant begins to calm more rapidly • increased parasympathetic regulation (more positive vagal tone) • arousal becomes less all-or-none, more 'graded' • increased emotional and motivational complexity • baby becomes better able to self-soothe (e.g. by non-nutritive sucking or rocking) • baby becomes more responsive to carer's attempts to calm or arouse	• by c2-4 months, rudimentary forebrain inhibitory centres begin to mature • more control leads and more regularity of emotional and behavioural state • more smiling in response to outside stimuli • more laughter and more contingent responses • by 9-10 months, frontal lobe maturation enables more control over emotional expression and experience • this particularly affects control over negative emotional experiences • speedier reactions, more capacity to manage stronger emotions • greater control leads to greater complexity of emotional experience, e.g. blending of primitive emotions • beginnings of strategic use of emotional expressions to manage social interactions

* The hypothalamic-pituitary-adrenal axis is thought to be a central system that co-ordinates responses to stress (Gunnar 2000).

Within this framework, Thompson et al. (1995) particularly emphasised how, in normally developing infants, this pattern of development leads to greater control both on the part of the infant and of the carer of the interactive experience, a phenomenon that can be expected to lead to increased motivation to invest in the relationship. They also described situations where excitatory or inhibitory processes may not develop in this more satisfactory way, due, for example, to within-child factors (e.g. temperament, premature birth, conditions such as Down syndrome, autism, problems with attentional focusing, coping strategies, etc.), to factors within the caregiving environment (e.g. maternal depression) and to possible interactions between child, caregiver and wider social contextual influences. Throughout, they emphasise the complexity of the processes subsumed under the term 'emotional regulation', the fact that it is not a unitary phenomenon and the potential for emotional difficulties to arise for very many different reasons.

Elucidating their understanding of the relationship between emotional regulation and attachment, Thompson et al. (1995, p.282) assert that "the development of emotional regulation and the growth of close relationships must be regarded as concurrent, mutually influential processes", on the grounds that "from early in life, a major task of successful parenting is managing and guiding the emotional experience of offspring".

They list a number of ways in which parents do this, e.g.:
- by directly intervening to relieve distress and to avert negative experiences
- by selectively reinforcing and modelling desired emotions and behaviours
- by sharing emotional experiences (reflecting on them, directing attention to them, etc.)
- by being empathic and sympathetic
- by giving support and guidance, and resources for coping with emotions
- by monitoring and regulating the children's social experience (e.g. exposure to other people)
- by the use of shaming, blaming or other guilt-inducing strategies to place markers on unwanted actions (this, in turn, leads to the child internalising the parents' values).

Summing up, Thompson et al. (1995, p.283) state that close relationships "not only provide a context for mastering and exercising the skills of emotional management but also, because these relationships impose emotional demands (of richly varying emotional valence) that require emotional self-control, they become important developmental laboratories for the growth of emotional self-regulation". However, they were also careful to point out the presence, throughout the lifespan, of many other influences besides that of the infant-parent relationship and recommend that understandings of children's emotional development need to also explore how these additional relationships might enhance or detract from the parent-infant relationship. Finally, they drew attention to the potential problem (also raised by Rutter, 1995) of the circularity of argument that is incurred if emotional regulation or dysregulation are defined so broadly that they become synonymous with well-functioning or poorly-functioning personalities, or if the definition is not sufficiently cognisant of the ways in which any one child's capacity for self-regulation may fluctuate according to the situational demands that they face. In other words, their definition is a multi-dimensional and dynamic one, determined by many different influences throughout the lifespan.

This rather complex conceptualisation of emotional regulation and how it develops seems to resonate well with recent conclusions from the Minnesota longitudinal study: "Our 25-year study has underscored two major features of development: its complexity and its dynamic nature. It no longer makes sense to us to ask questions such as, is one or another influence or one or another developmental period more important? Repeatedly, we find that current and past experience, current and past stresses and opportunities are complexly interactive... Either/or questions are recognized as being limited. Complex transactional views prevail." (Sroufe et al. 2001, no page numbers). Rather nervously, they add, "We are pleased to be a part of this movement, although it must be noted that it risks being vacuous; that is, simply concluding that everything is complex and everything interacts isn't very interesting."

Not all theorists or commentators have been so circumspect in their conclusions. In the next section we briefly consider some of the arguments advanced by Allan Schore whose views, recently popularised in the UK (Gerhardt 2004), have been very enthusiastically received in some psychodynamic circles.

Schore and the development of the 'social brain'

Allan Schore, like Daniel Stern ten years earlier and Bowlby himself, has been praised by many people in the psychoanalytic community for his ability to synthesise concepts across disciplines, including psychiatry, psychoanalysis, neurobiology, evolutionary biology and developmental psychology. Unlike Bowlby, though, Schore's writings are somewhat opaque, being couched in extensive anatomical descriptions, and the links between his ideas and the research evidence upon which they draw seem sometimes to involve rather greater leaps of faith. In this section, we briefly (and for reasons of space somewhat cursorily) outline the main arguments put forward in his major work (Schore 1994).

Essentially, Schore contends that:
- the primary carer is essential for regulating every aspect of infant functioning
- this regulation influences the development of the infant's brain, specifically the development of two limbic circuits that mature in the first two years of life
- it determines how genetic predispositions are expressed
- it involves the infant imprinting the mother's gaze
- it permanently affects the part of the brain responsible for social understanding and action
- it permanently sets the balance between inhibitory and excitatory mechanisms
- this brain development in the first years is critically important for all later development
- it involves both parents.

In other words, in Schore's view, later development is largely determined by the nature of the relationship between the infant and his or her primary carer in the first two or three years of life and particularly depends on visual experience. Throughout his book, the word 'critical' recurs frequently, revealing a deterministic philosophy which is well reflected in the account given by Gerhardt (2004).

A few examples provide a flavour of Schore's thesis and style:

"mother's modulatory function is essential not only to every aspect of the infant's current functioning, but also to the child's continuing development ... Her essential role as the psychobiological regulator of the child's immature psychophysiological system directly influences the child's biochemical growth processes which support the genesis of the structure." (Schore 1994, p.7)

"The interval between 10-12 and 16-18 months is a critical period for the final maturation of a system in the prefrontal cortex that is essential to the regulation of affect over the rest of the lifespan." (Schore 1994, p.24)

"I present evidence to show that just as the postnatal growth of posterior cortical neural networks underlying developing visual capacity requires appropriate forms of visual stimulation during a critical period (refs), the postnatal emergence of anterior cortical neuronal systems mediating affective processing also requires adequate caregiver-provided intensity and variety of affective stimulation during a time-window of plasticity in early postnatal development." (Schore 1994, p.60)

"Socioaffective stimulation at the end of the first year induces permanent morphological changes in each of the cellular components of the orbitofrontal cortex." (Schore 1994, p.167)

"I suggest that... the offset of the maternal attachment-regulated orbital-frontal critical period is followed by the onset of a paternal attachment-regulated critical period for the maturation of the other prefrontal system, the dorsolateral prefrontal association cortex." (Schore 1994, p.234) "early affective experiences critically and permanently influence the development of the psychic structures that process unconscious information." (Schore 1994, p.280)

"The caregiver influences the parcellation of the two limbic circuits in the infant's maturing orbitofrontal cortex, and thereby the permanent excitation-inhibition (autonomic) balance of his prefrontolimbic regulatory system. This dyadic psychoneurological mechanism ontogenetically sculpts the enduring temperamental features of the child's emerging personality." (Schore 1994, p.284)

Schore argues that the development of the two limbic circuits that occurs within the first two years fits well with Mahler's theorisation of stages of infant development (Mahler et al. 1975). In Mahler's account, infant development proceeds in four developmental sub-phases: first, an early 'autistic' or 'symbiotic' sub-phase (which starts tapering off at around seven or eight months); second, a 'practicing' sub-phase (c10-16/18 months); third, the 'rapprochement' sub-phase (during the early part of which, at c18-24 months, the child is thought to experience intense conflicts between their contrary needs for both independence and dependence); fourth, an 'emotional object constancy and individuality stage (mainly during the third year of life). The 'practicing' sub-phase is characterised by delight in mastery and much positive emotion while the 'rapprochement' sub-phase is characterised by greater self-mastery and restraint but also more negative affect.

According to Schore, the development of the limbic circuits responsible for control of sympathetic and parasympathetic responses maps very closely onto the 'practicing' and 'rapprochement' sub-phases (Figure 5.2). The first limbic circuit to develop (the A10 ventral tegmental circuit, or VT circuit, for short) governs the production of deliberate actions (and so is associated with activation of the sympathetic nervous system). Its development coincides with Mahler's 'practicing sub-phase' (from about ten to 16 or 18 months). The second limbic circuit (the lateral tegmental, or LT, circuit) is involved with the control of the newly learned actions (associated with activation of the parasympathetic nervous system). Its development starts at the end of Mahler's late 'practicing' sub-phase when the 'rapprochement' sub-phase begins. By the time both limbic circuits have matured, according to Schore, the pattern of emotional regulation in the infant has become set for life.

Figure 5.2: Development of limbic circuits (Schore 1994)

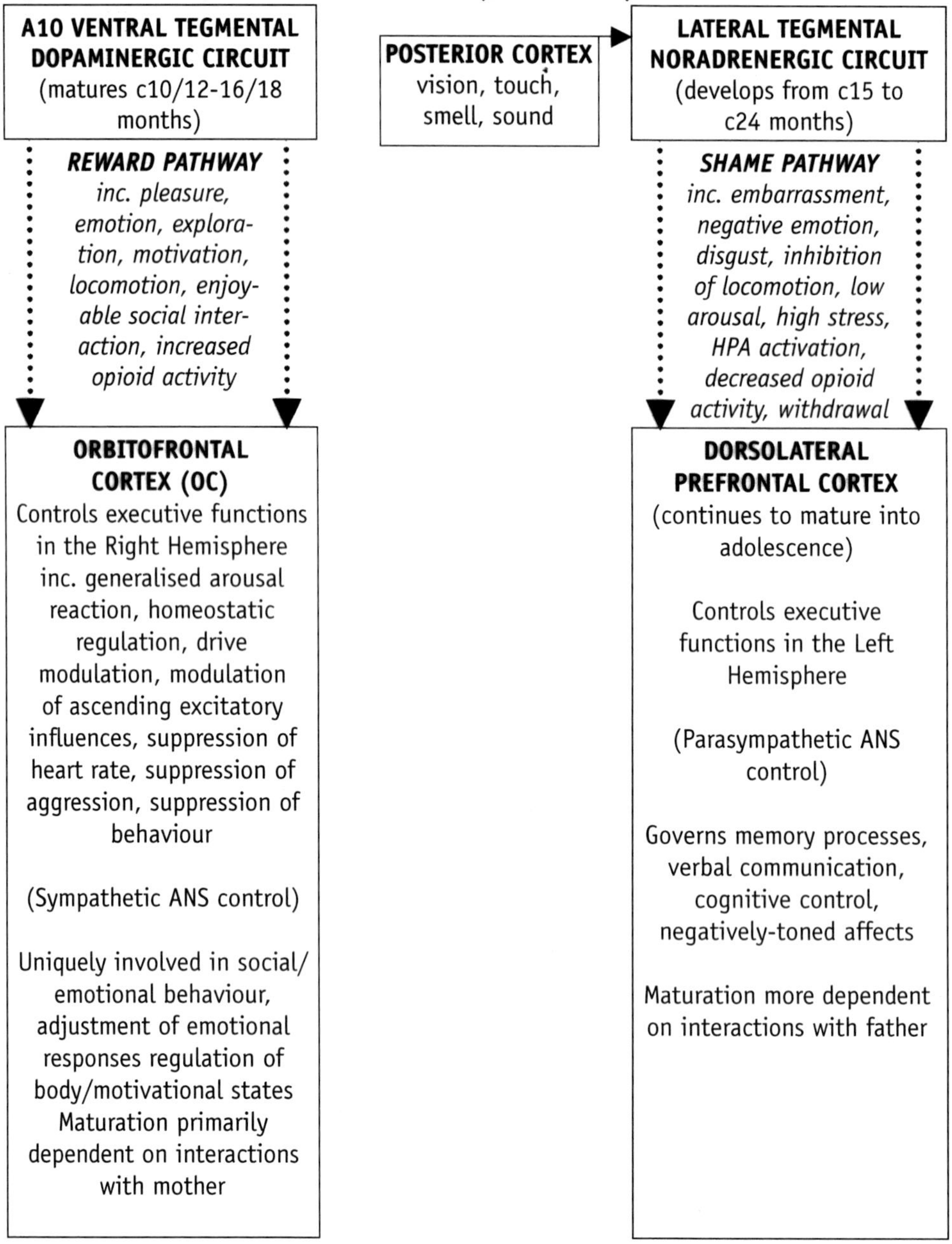

A10 VENTRAL TEGMENTAL DOPAMINERGIC CIRCUIT (matures c10/12-16/18 months)	POSTERIOR CORTEX vision, touch, smell, sound	LATERAL TEGMENTAL NORADRENERGIC CIRCUIT (develops from c15 to c24 months)
REWARD PATHWAY inc. pleasure, emotion, exploration, motivation, locomotion, enjoyable social interaction, increased opioid activity		**SHAME PATHWAY** inc. embarrassment, negative emotion, disgust, inhibition of locomotion, low arousal, high stress, HPA activation, decreased opioid activity, withdrawal
ORBITOFRONTAL CORTEX (OC) Controls executive functions in the Right Hemisphere inc. generalised arousal reaction, homeostatic regulation, drive modulation, modulation of ascending excitatory influences, suppression of heart rate, suppression of aggression, suppression of behaviour (Sympathetic ANS control) Uniquely involved in social/emotional behaviour, adjustment of emotional responses regulation of body/motivational states Maturation primarily dependent on interactions with mother		**DORSOLATERAL PREFRONTAL CORTEX** (continues to mature into adolescence) Controls executive functions in the Left Hemisphere (Parasympathetic ANS control) Governs memory processes, verbal communication, cognitive control, negatively-toned affects Maturation more dependent on interactions with father

The way this is accomplished, according to Schore, is that, during the 'symbiotic' and more intensely during the 'practicing' sub-phases, mutual gazing accompanied by a symbiotic state of mutual heightened affect between infants and mothers provides infants with output from the mother's right hemisphere visual system that serves as the template for imprinting the infant's own anterior temporal cortex. Interactions such as mirroring, attunement and interactional synchrony, are sought after by both infant and mother because they are reinforced by opioids and so give rise to a psychoneurobiological mechanism which is "essential to an imprinting phenomenon in the child's developing right hemisphere, thereby enabling the maturation of limbic areas in this cortex that are involved in socioemotional function" (Schore 1994, pp. 71-72).

Put very simply, Schore maintains that, because it is associated with reward pathways, the first limbic circuit will only develop satisfactorily if visual exchanges between mothers and babies are sufficiently positive and mutually rewarding (Figure 5.3): "It is hypothesised that maternal regulated high intensity socio-affective stimulation provided in the ontogenetic niche, specifically occurring in dyadic psychobiologically attuned, arousal-amplifying, face-to-face reciprocal gaze transactions, generates and sustains positive affect in the dyad. These transactions induce particular neuroendocrine changes which facilitate the expansive innervation of deep sites in the orbitofrontal areas, especially in the early maturing visuospatial right hemisphere, of ascending subcortical axons of a neurochemical circuit of the limbic system – the sympathetic ventral tegmental limbic circuit. This imprinting experience initiates the maturation of a frontolimbic excitatory system that is responsible for the ontogenetic adaptations in the inceptive phase of practicing critical period-behavioural hyperactivity, high levels of positive affect and play behaviour, and subsequently the establishment of the capacity to form an interactive representational model that underlies an early functional system of affect regulation" (Schore 1994, p.65). In other words, mothers who look miserably at their babies prevent their babies' brains from growing. Watch it, Mums!

Figure 5.3: Mechanism for experience-dependent brain development associated with VT limbic circuit

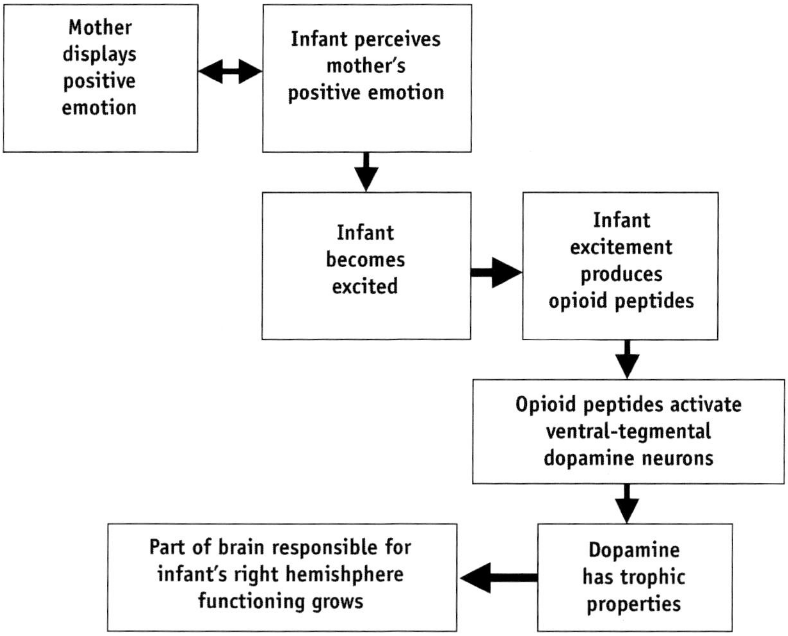

```
┌──────────────┐       ┌──────────────┐
│   Mother     │       │   Infant     │
│  displays    │ ←───→ │  perceives   │
│  positive    │       │  mother's    │
│  emotion     │       │ positive     │
│              │       │  emotion     │
└──────────────┘       └──────┬───────┘
                              │
                              ▼
                       ┌──────────────┐       ┌──────────────┐
                       │   Infant     │       │   Infant     │
                       │  becomes     │ ───→  │ excitement   │
                       │  excited     │       │  produces    │
                       │              │       │ opioid       │
                       │              │       │ peptides     │
                       └──────────────┘       └──────┬───────┘
                                                     │
                                                     ▼
                                             ┌──────────────────┐
                                             │ Opioid peptides  │
                                             │ activate         │
                                             │ ventral-tegmental│
                                             │ dopamine neurons │
                                             └────────┬─────────┘
                                                      │
                                                      ▼
      ┌────────────────────────────┐          ┌──────────────┐
      │ Part of brain responsible  │          │  Dopamine    │
      │ for infant's right         │ ←──────  │  has trophic │
      │ hemisphere functioning     │          │  properties  │
      │ grows                      │          │              │
      └────────────────────────────┘          └──────────────┘
```

Alarming though this sounds, it does appear to be fairly widely accepted that eye gaze perception plays an important role in mother-infant interaction and in infant social development. Even newborns prefer face-like stimuli and are sensitive to whether eyes are open or shut, averted or straight-on (Johnson and Farroni 2003). There is also some evidence from studies of the development of foveation in the eye that the way infants look at others influences and/or is influenced by how their eyes and, possibly, the neural connections to the eyes develop. However, gaze perception does not usually occur independently of perception of other body movements or facial aspects (Johnson and Farroni 2003). Early in development, gaze perceptions become integrated with other perceptions in complex ways that are not yet fully understood (Beebe et al. 2000) and it is likely that the areas of the brain that become activated during mutual gaze may vary considerably according to the social context. More research is needed to discover exactly which areas and processes are involved. For this reason, it would appear somewhat premature to assume that imprinting of visual experiences, no matter how salient these exchanges might be for the infant, will prove to be an accurate way to describe the mechanism or mechanisms involved. It may be, but at this stage the relevant research has yet to be carried out that will indicate just how near or far Schore's account may be from the truth.

It does seem possible that patterns of mutual eye contact may very early in life become more predictable and rewarding for some infants than for others and that this might lead to wide individual variations in both the amount of mutual gazing and the sort of looking that infants engage in. Whether this means that the brains of infants who come to prefer less full-on visual experiences develop differently to those of infants who take more interest in and obtain more enjoyment from exchanging looks, again, is not something that researchers even at the 'cutting edge' of human brain research have yet ascertained. However, it also seems possible that other sensory modalities also play important roles (Jaffe et al. 2001) and that the processes underpinning attachment formation in humans may have evolved to support greater chances of survival success, i.e. they would be unlikely to be characterised by a principle of 'all eggs in one basket'. This, though, constitutes one of the key tenets of Schore's argument: that the development of the right hemisphere and of the structures within it that are dominant for processing non-verbal socio-emotional information depends critically upon positive visuo-affective experiences with the caregiver.

The centrality of visual experience in Schore's account of the development of attachment relationships leads to him to conclude that children who have visual impairments will be prone to attachment problems.[4] In support of his thesis, he cites a study by Freedman (1981) as having shown that congenitally blind children have severe emotional problems associated with impaired representational and affective functions.

The possibility that autistic and congenitally blind children might experience similar difficulties in social relating has also been explored by Hobson and colleagues (Hobson et al. 1997, 1999; Hobson 2002). Hobson and his colleagues found both differences and similarities between severely visually impaired children and sighted children: they noted that while it was rare for sighted children to manifest 'autistic-like' symptoms, it was relatively more common for these to be found in congenitally blind children. The autistic-like symptoms included, for example, echolalia (repeating other people's words as opposed to responding dialogically), pronoun confusions (inappropriate use of 'I' and 'you') and instances of stereotypy and obsessive play with objects.

Hobson observed: "it seems that, when children are blind from birth, they are predisposed to autism even if their social impairment is somewhat less profound than in sighted children

---

4 To our knowledge, Schore does not appear to contend, by the same argument, that parents with serious visual impairments would afford equally limited opportunities for effective imprinting experiences while parents and children who are both blind or severely visually impaired would, theoretically at least, stand almost no chance of forming secure attachments.

with autism. Their lack of vision plays a role in causing the picture of autism, even when their intrinsic social disability is not so sufficient to cause autism" (Hobson 2002, p.195). However, he conceded that, "On the other hand, one can also see that blindness per se is not sufficient to cause autism... because many blind children are remarkably like sighted children in their development" (Hobson 2002, pp. 195-196). On balance, he suggested that there may be many routes to autism, that information obtained through visual experience is very important but possibly not exclusively so (other sensory and verbal experiences play a role too) and that more research on the role of sightedness in the development social interactive problems is needed.

Conclusions such as these as well as logical objections to 'putting all ones evolutionary eggs in one basket' raise doubts about the central role given by Schore to the imprinting of gaze in the development of social relationships. But what about Schore's account of the nature of memory in infancy? How does this stand up to the research evidence?

Schore asserts that, by the end of the first year onwards, the infant has developed the capacity to retain a schematic representation of the mother's face in her absence, that "The stored image of the mother's face, distributed in part over the visual processing areas of the cortex, represents a prototypical primordial flashbulb memory" (Schore 1994, p.181). He also claims that "This representational model contains a permanent abstract prototype of the mother's emotionally expressive facial expressions that is linked to the child's interoceptive response to this input" (Schore 1994, p.175) and that "internal representations of the self-in-interaction-with-other are more precisely abstractions of the infant's autonomic physiological-affective responses to the visual perception of the emotionally expressive face of the attachment object" (Schore 1994, p.178).

Why it is necessary to speculate with quite such specificity about the nature of infant mental representations at this age is rather puzzling. Even techniques such as functional magnetic resonance imaging seem unlikely to prove successful at testing hypotheses about 'primordial flashbulb memories' in pre-verbal infants. On the other hand, it does perhaps seem reasonable to suggest that the encoding of visual experiences will not be segregated from their affective context. Even so, ascertaining how memories are stored and what effect processes of storage might have on the development of neurological circuitry seems more likely to be accomplished once the relevant research has been done.

This brings us to a consideration of the more controversial arguments that Schore puts forward about the existence of direct relationships between positive and negative emotionality and brain growth in infancy. Schore explains that, at around 12-14 months, the emergence of shame/embarrassment in infants signals the end of the critical period for mother-child attachment-related imprinting. From about 15 months onwards, as infants becomes more mobile and independent, mothers usually begin to place more restrictions upon them and to expect them to take more control over their impulses. Having previously spurred their babies on to extend themselves as far as possible, mothers start setting limits. The affective tone of the relationship between mother and babies alters. Their role begins to change from primary caretaker to primary socialiser. At around the same time therefore, in the middle of the second year, according to Schore, the critical period for mother-child attachment offsets and that for father-child attachment onsets: "I suggest that the child first imprints the developing right hemisphere to affective interchanges with the mother, thereby constructing non-verbal working models. This is followed in later infancy by the imprinting of his or her left hemisphere to affective transactions with the father, thus initiating the construction of verbal IWMs" (Schore 1994, p.238).

Infants who now, on the basis of their previous experience, have come to expect congruency between their own and their mothers' excitement, are taken aback by new experiences of non-congruency. From a state of positive high intensity high arousal (primary grandiosity or narcissism), they shift to one of negative low or high intensity low arousal. This emotional state, which Schore contends involves embarrassment or shame, puts the brakes on the positive affect and interest that are associated with their previous self-assertion and delight in exploration, and leads to a stressful hypo-activated state. The VT limbic circuit becomes de-activated and the LT limbic circuit becomes activated. As a result, cortisol is released which assists with the development of the LT limbic circuit and, in moderation, with growth in the dorsolateral prefrontal cortex (Figure 5.4). As a result, "Dyadic shame regulating transactions in the practicing critical period... generate permanent effects in the frontolimbic cortex" (Schore 1994, p.252).

Figure 5.4: Mechanism for experience-dependent brain development associated with LT limbic circuit

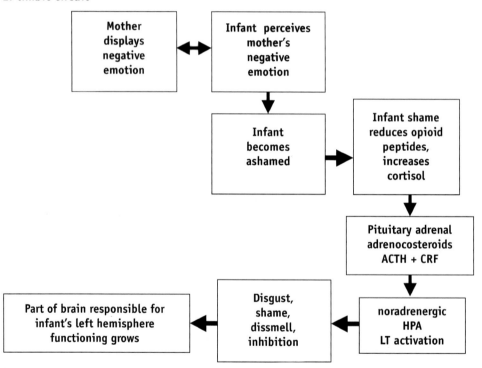

Schore argues that, crucially, in their first years, infants are not able to regulate their own state of emotional arousal: "Without access to the mother's affect regulating function, the child remains stuck fast for long periods of time in a parasympathetic-dominant state of conservation-withdrawal, a state in which dysphoric cognitive-affective patterns color all subjective experience" (Schore 1994, p.247). He explains that this can happen when babies are separated from their caregivers. If there is no-one available to help them to recover, infants may remain stuck in the position of thinking that their affective needs are somehow unacceptable or shameful. With assistance from the mother, the balance between the dual limbic systems comes under control so that "The developing individual's particular socioaffective imprinting-dependent parcellation process fine-tunes the final, mature distribution of the innervation pattern of orbitofrontal columns, emphasizing either early practicing, sympathetic, excitatory, VT dopaminergic inputs, or later practicing, inhibitory, para-sympathetic, LT, noradrenergic inputs, thereby influencing the excitation-inhibition balance of the prefrontal limbic regulatory system" (Schore 1994, p.277). In other words, the pattern is set for the infant to begin to be able to keep their feelings under control. This pattern also becomes hard-wired into the brain. Schore provides evidence of causal relationships between cortical function and behavioural control systems from research on patients with damage to the orbitofrontal and dorsolateral cortices (Table 5.3).

Table 5.3: Links between cortical damage and behavioural control

ORBITOFRONTAL CORTEX	DORSOLATERAL CORTEX
Ventrolateral caudate Medial pallidum Centromedial nucleus Hypothalamus Septal nucleus	Anterodorsal caudate Lateral pallidum Subthalamic nuclei Hippocampus
OC PATIENTS	**DC PATIENTS**
Sexual disinhibition Inappropriate social behaviour Impulsiveness Self-indulgence Explosiveness Inc. motor activity	Flat emotional expression Depression Lack of behavioural spontaneity

Schore's thesis raises many interesting and valuable questions. That opponent processes governing sympathetic and parasympathetic control exist within the autonomic nervous system, that limbic circuits can be described (though not always in the same way by everyone) and that they play a fundamental role in human behaviour seems undeniable. It is also increasingly accepted, as Schore (1994, 1996, 1997, 2001a, 2001b) recognised, that recent research and technological advances have highlighted the need to update theories about the nature of gene-environment relationships (e.g. Rutter 2002). But it is also important to recognise that Schore is not a primary researcher in the field of neuroscience and that his speculations about the development of limbic circuits and their relationship to social experience in human infants are just that.

The fact that most of Schore's speculations about the relationship between brain development and the nature of mother-child interactions are yet to be tested obviously does not invalidate his account. However, it does suggest that uncritical acceptance of all, or even any, of his postulates is not sensible. At this stage, it is important to recognise that Schore draws largely upon work with a variety of non-human animals, with a sprinkling of data from human infants and older humans hardly any of which has directly examined the relationship in healthy human infants between brain growth, brain function and the nature of social abilities. That pre-verbal sensory and affective experiences occurring within the same time frame as maturation of physical structures are likely to be encoded somewhere or somehow is not a matter for dispute. Much more debateable are Schore's assertions about (a) the existence of direct and simple causal relationships between physical and socio-emotional processes, (b) the nature of mental representations in infancy, (c) the nature of sensory processing in infancy and its role in the development of different patterns of attachment, (d) the role of fathers in the development of attachment relationships and internal representations of these and, finally, (e) the huge question of whether the development of social understanding relates in any way to brain shape or size (any more than it does to physical attributes such as height, weight or hair colour, though it could be speculated that unusual extremes of these might impact to varying extents on patterns of social relating).

The complex issue of brain growth aside, it may be true that both the quality of encouragement given to babies by mothers in the first year or so, and of mothers' and babies' enjoyment of each other during the same time (hinted at in Ainsworth's initial observations), may be associated with later attachment security. Much of the research reviewed in previous sections would seem to support these hypotheses. These qualities are multiply-determined, by attributes within mothers and infants as well as within current and past social contexts, and it is not clear whether they might make independent or interactive contributions to attachment outcomes. Nor is it yet clear whether underlying psychobiological processes result from, contribute to or interact with the quality of ongoing social relationships. Until more is known about these matters, it is only possible to speculate very tentatively about how the formation or stability of attachment relationships might be constrained by psychobiological influences. This is not to say that speculations, especially ones that are as acrobatic and lively as Schore's, should not be entertained. But it is to say that far more work is needed before relationships between mother-infant ecstasy/depression, attachment security, right or left hemisphere function and brain growth, and so on, are fully understood. This fact must deter over-confident assumptions about the veracity of Schore's conclusions. To treat his words as though they were gospel truths is something that Bowlby, with his respect for empiricism and scientific method and his distrust of hermeneutic truths, would almost certainly have resisted.

Antecedents to poor social relationships: Autism

Similarities between patterns of autism and of attachment

Drawing upon work in the field of autism, several groups of researchers have explored potential connections between processes that underlie attachment relationships and those underlying autistic spectrum disorders. The number of theories proposed to account for autism and definitional issues surrounding autistic spectrum disorders make for great complexity in this field of research. However, if autistic behaviour is conceptualised as primarily characterised by problems with making social relationships and attachment behaviour as ability to make close social relationships, it seems, logically, a possibility that the two outcomes could emerge from the same basic propensity, adequate quantities of which produce more or less effective social behaviours and lack of which produces autistic spectrum disorders.

This kind of conceptualisation seems even more plausible when descriptions of autistic people are compared to those of individuals with avoidant and ambivalent/resistant/preoccupied patterns. Frances Tustin wrote about autism as "a state in which auto-sensuousness holds sway, attention being focused almost exclusively on bodily rhythms and sensations" (Tustin 1981, p.3). She suggested that autism might arise from a failure to cope with early stages of self development: "In my experience, the crux of the psychotic child's damaged condition is that he has had an agonising awareness of the 'not-self' before he had a sufficiently integrated self to cope with the strain" (Tustin 1981, p.5). Two defensive strategies assist the baby to recoil from the outside 'not-self' world, negation and confusion. The former produces 'encapsulation' reactions that shut out the 'not-self' outside world while the latter produces 'confusional' reactions which blur the 'not-self' outside world.

Tustin describes 'encapsulated' or 'shell-type' children as looking like fairy children, otherworldly and aloof. They avoid looking at people, make no distinction between animate and inanimate objects, rarely use language (although may repeat words spoken to them) and go rigid if cuddled: "They are fascinated by mechanisms… spin certain objects obsessively… take hard objects… to bed with them instead of the soft cuddly toys enjoyed by normal children… are usually faddy about food in that they will only eat soft foods… They will often use another's person's hand to open doors or even to spin objects" (Tustin 1981, p.21). Tustin speculated that the psychological development of 'encapsulated' children might have been halted at an earlier stage than that of 'confusional' or 'entangled' children who she described as "teetering on the verge of becoming aware that they are flesh and blood… they occasionally experience and express this experience as a 'wound'" (Tustin 1981, p.39); they play in a way that draws in the people around but "the discerning person has an uneasy sense that this is not healthy involvement and participation, but that it engulfs and entangles" the child (Tustin 1981, p.40); they speak but "in an incomprehensible stream of words in which important words may be left out. Their talk seems to engulf the listener and has the effect that he ceases to attend to the meaning of what is being said" (Tustin 1981, p.40).

Unlike Bettelheim, whose theories are associated with the term 'refrigerator mothers' (e.g. Bettelheim 1967), Tustin did not attribute autism to particularly unhelpful parenting but did suggest that different types of parenting might be linked with 'encapsulated' and 'confusional' children: parents of 'encapsulated' children are more likely to be controlling while those of 'confusional' children are more likely to be entangled both with the child and each other. It was not clear whether Tustin considered that these characteristics preceded or evolved in response to the difficulties of bringing up a child with autistic characteristics. Tustin very tentatively speculated that different kinds of autistic spectrum disorders might be attributable to early development, almost as though self or brain development in the 'encapsulated' child had prematurely formed like an unopenable shell to keep external pressures out while the 'entangled' child had not been able to form an effective skin at all. However, she recognised that her theories about aetiology could not easily be tested.

The chief reason for spending so much time on Tustin's theory is that her descriptions of the two types of autistic behaviour, superficially at least, appear to have much in common with the two 'typical' insecure attachment patterns (Figure 5.5). Similar difficulties pertain, too, with regard to attachment relationships in establishing how the development of children's sense of self might correspond to their relationship with their parents. Tustin, in essence, suggests that whatever it is that causes children's sense of self to develop, in making the distinction between self and other and between animate and inanimate objects, some children see more 'thinginess' in people than others while, conversely, other children see more 'peopleness' in things. This idea seems to resonate loudly with the notion that some insecurely attached children are predisposed to avoid close contact and to attend to more 'thing-y' aspects of the social environment (the balance for these children is tipped in favour of exploration and away from close social interaction) while others are predisposed to attend to more 'people-y' aspects (the balance for these children is tipped towards the person providing the not-so-secure base). It is difficult to tell whether these differences arise in the same way that handedness arises, from genetic predispositions which are shared between parents and offspring to greater or lesser degree or, as Tustin suggests, from early developmental experience or, as Bowlby's theory suggests, more directly from opportunities provided by parents, or through maturational processes, or from various combinations of these explanations.

Figure 5.5: Similarities between autistic 'types' and insecure attachment patterns

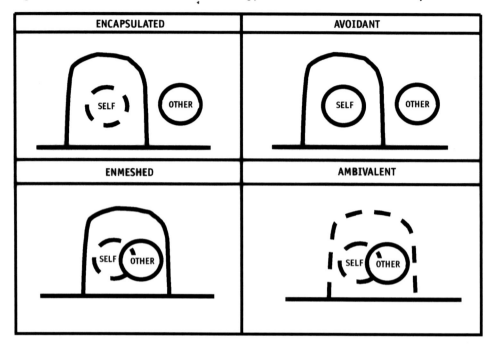

A number of theories besides those of Frances Tustin have been proposed to account for the nature of the pathological processes involved in autism. Some of these have also begun to be incorporated into thinking about the development of attachment relationships. While most theorists have acknowledged the possibility of a role for chromosomal or genetic influences, it seems to be increasingly recognised that there may also be some role for psychogenic influences in maintaining different degrees or types of autistic functioning.

Baron-Cohen and Theory of Mind

One explanation proposed by Simon Baron-Cohen is that autistic people may lack a 'theory of mind'. Baron-Cohen (Baron-Cohen et al. 1985, 1993, Baron-Cohen 1995, 2004) suggested that autistic problems may arise from a lack of the ability to impute intentions, desires or beliefs to other people. Autistic individuals may not have developed the computational capacity to envisage either a 'virtual other' and or a 'virtual self' and to include these in helping them to understand or predict social interactions or how to behave in them. This could account for difficulties associated with distinguishing between social objects (people) and non-social objects. The autistic child who takes a mother's hand and uses it like an inanimate tool to open a door does not do this for innately selfish purposes, or because they are manipulative or self-centred. Rather, for some reason, they experience the hand as a thing rather than as 'peopled'. Why they should perceive the hand in this way is, according to 'theory of mind', because they are unable to 'mentalise', that is, to see below the surface and to 'read' other people as people in the same way that non-autistic people can.

These difficulties are also thought to be integrally linked with the way people with autistic spectrum disorders view themselves. If the sense of self is seen as being constructed not just through direct physical experiences of one's own body but also through processes of interacting with others (as Trevarthen suggested), then it can also be seen to depend on the capacity to see oneself in interaction with others. This involves some kind of mental representation not only of dyadic but of triadic relationships (self-other-object). If these mental representations are to be used to inform understanding of social relationships, they also need to be available for conscious inspection (though it may not be necessary for all aspects to be fully conscious). Theory of mind accounts suggest that a breakdown somewhere in this mental processing may explain the difficulties that autistic people experience in forming mental pictures of themselves and others. As a result, they are unable to reflect on their own behaviour or to form a picture of themselves as beings with hopes, beliefs or intentions and, similarly, are unable to understand other people's mental states.

In this sense, autism can be thought of as a kind of 'mind-blindness' which involves restricted access to mental representations of social interactions. As a result, some autistic children may experience people as too complex, too overwhelming and too unpredictable, perhaps somewhat in the way that spiders are experienced by people with arachnophobia. Something seems to prevent them from holding in mind important formulae that enable them to reflect effectively on their own and others' behaviours and to make sense of the dynamic relationships between them. Quite what might have produced this outcome is unknown, although many theories are currently being explored to find out (e.g. the role of genetic factors, empathising-systemising theory, executive function theory, central coherence theory, etc.). Also unknown is the role of temperament or emotional responses in exacerbating difficulties, at primary or secondary levels.[5]

Variations in ability to understand other people's feelings, beliefs and intentions, that is, in 'mentalising capacity', are also observable among people who have not been diagnosed as having autistic spectrum disorders. Some people are much better than others at taking other people's feelings into account or at empathising with other people. Some teachers, for example, are able to pick up on the most effective way of speaking to particular children so that they bring out the best in them, encourage them and motivate them to improve their performance. Others, though they may be aiming for exactly the same outcomes, fail to tune into the children's emotional state and manage only to increase the children's sense of incompetence and shame, effectively crushing potential improvement.

These qualitative differences in 'perspective-taking' begin to appear at an early age. As indicated in the previous chapter, one of the distinctive differences between children with histories of secure attachment and children with histories of less comfortable relationships with attachment figures appears to be that they are better at taking other children's feelings into account, are more self-confident and so are calmer and more prepared to arrive at mutually satisfactory compromises when conflict situations arise.

Recognising the parallels between autistic and non-autistic, securely and non-securely attached people, some researchers have hypothesised a shared origin for differences related to capacity to 'mentalise'. Drawing on 'theory of mind', Peter Fonagy and his colleagues (1997) devised a measure, named 'Reflective Functioning', that could be applied to the narrative

---

5 Secondary level difficulties are those that arise in response to primary difficulties, for example, a child who finds it difficult to learn to read might aggravate their primary difficulty by avoiding situations where they have to read. This emotional response will mean that they get less practice than their peers at reading and so put them at further disadvantage.

transcripts obtained from Adult Attachment Interviews. At about the same time, Elizabeth Meins was developing a measure of mothers' mentalising capacity termed 'maternal mind-mindedness' with the aim of assessing whether this might predict infant attachment security more successfully than available measures of maternal sensitivity.

Reflective Functioning and Maternal Mind-mindedness

The Reflective-Functioning Scale was developed with work on metacognitive functioning in mind (though psychoanalytic interpretations appeared to feature more prominently than ideas from more experimentally-based and social cognitively-oriented developmental psychology) and drew upon ideas presented by Mary Main (Main 1991). Fonagy et al. (1997, p.6) proposed that "The emergence and full development of the reflective function depends upon the caregiver's capacity to more-or-less accurately perceive intentionality in the infant. The capacity for reflection is seen as influencing the quality of psychic reality experienced by the individual, and accounts for the richness and diversity of inner experience."

By commenting aloud on their children's behaviour, Fonagy et al. (1997) argued, parents provide and confront children with the contents of their own minds. In addition, because the contents of parents' thoughts are both like and unlike the contents of the children's minds, they:
- encourage the development of effective communication
- enable children to build up a picture of reality and to distinguish between appearance and reality
- help children to know what to expect and how to make sense of other people's actions
- enhance children's capacity for self-control and emotional self-regulation and, in doing so, promote and maintain attachment security
- make more meaningful connections between inner and outer realities so that children are afforded deeper and richer relationship experiences.

People with high or moderately high capacities for reflective functioning are considered to:
- demonstrate more awareness of the nature of mental states
- make more effort to understand the meaning of other people's behaviour
- recognise that different ages, stages and states of development will influence how people understand and relate to each other
- vary their speech appropriately to accommodate for the person they are speaking to and the situation they are in.

Some examples of the kind of evidence that might support a judgement of high or moderately high reflective functioning are shown in Table 5.4. Poor reflective functioning was identified partly by lack of evidence of good reflective functioning but also by features such as refusal to discuss questions related to mental states; inability to answer questions about why parents behaved as they did; failure to focus on the questions asked; highly egocentric recollections; self-aggrandizing gestures or "extraordinarily arrogant claims to insight"; "naive or simplistic reflective functioning" (indicators include use of clichés, self-contradiction, idealised or denigrated portrayals of parents, superficiality); overly-analytical or hyperactive reflective functioning (like Main's criteria for the AAI, this refers to meaningless and unconvincing wordiness); bizarre or inappropriate responses (e.g. attempts to change the subject, non-sequiturs).

Table 5.4: Dimensions of Reflective Functioning

AWARENESS OF THE NATURE OF MENTAL STATES	
Dimension	Example
Opaqueness	I think he meant to hurt me, but maybe he didn't really
Dissembling	I think she was really mad at me but she was acting all sweet and nice
Mis-attribution	That food was horrible but perhaps it's because I'm in a bad mood today
Over-identifying	She looked uncomfortable to me but perhaps it was just me who was embarrassed
Different perspectives	I thought she misunderstood me and that hurt, but she probably meant well
Own impact	I suppose I was difficult for her to care for, I was very highly strung
Others' pre-suppositions	People always think I'm younger and sweeter than I am, a pushover. It comes as a surprise to them when I won't back down – they can get aggressive and indignant
Ongoing reflection	The speaker conveys a sense that their reflections are being updated as they speak

Judgements about the existence of reflective functioning therefore involve decisions about speakers' ability to appreciate multiple perspectives as well as an assessment of whether the account that has been given is a valid one. There is an assumption that analysts have privileged insight into the lives of interviewees and that there are certain 'right' ways to behave in the interview situation. It is not clear how individual differences in handling the interview might be interpreted. Is it the case, for example, that individuals who are very shy, who do not find it easy to talk about themselves to strangers, who are reserved, or just uncomfortable with a particular interviewer will be judged as having poor reflective functioning? How tenable is the assumption that the perspective of the analyst is valid?

These reservations aside, as Peter Fonagy and his colleagues astutely recognised, there is obvious value in attempting to systematically assess differences in ways of thinking about social relationships and the impact of such differences on willingness to engage in and ability to sustain positive close relationships. If it is possible to identify how particular sets of metacognitive skills predict the development of particular types of attachment in parents and children, it might then be possible to encourage the development of those considered more desirable.

Elizabeth Meins, working along the same lines as Fonagy's group, has proposed that the concept of maternal sensitivity should be re-defined to take more account of the appropriateness of mothers' responses (Meins 1997, 1998, Meins et al. 2001). She argues that research on antecedents of attachment security may have been limited by lack of consensus about which aspects of mothers' behaviour reflect sensitivity and that many researchers appear to have been measuring aspects that are only tangentially related to the most important qualities: "Unfortunately, much of the research on maternal behavioural antecedents of attachment... paid insufficient attention to Ainsworth et al.'s distinction between mothers' responsiveness to infants' emotional cues and the appropriateness of each response" (Meins et al. 2001, p.638). Measures that focus exclusively on aspects such as contiguity, synchrony, stimulation or supportiveness, Meins asserts, are likely to omit consideration of the context in which interactions occur or the appropriateness of maternal responses.

In her own re-conceptualisation, Meins (1997) "coined the term maternal *mind-mindedness* to describe the mother's proclivity to treat her infant as an individual with a mind, rather than merely as a creature with needs that must be satisfied" (Meins et al. 2001, p.638). Two separate studies of mothers' talk about their young children indicated that mothers of securely attached infants appear spontaneously to focus on their children's mental states more readily than mothers of insecurely attached children, that is, the mothers of securely attached infants appeared to be more 'mind-minded' (Meins 1998, Meins et al. 1998).

To test whether the quality of mind-mindedness might pre-date the formation of secure attachments, Meins (Meins et al. 2001) observed 71 mother-baby dyads at six and again at 12 months. At six months, mothers and babies were observed during a 20-minute play session in a university laboratory. Their interactions were coded using both the Ainsworth et al. (1971) maternal sensitivity scale and a measure of mind-mindedness that consisted of:
- *Maternal responsiveness to change in infant's direction of gaze*
    - whether the mother changed her gaze, looked at, touched, or talked about the same object as the infant
- *Maternal responsiveness to infant's object-directed action*
    - whether the mother changed her focus of attention to the same object as the infant
- *Imitation*
    - e.g. of sounds that the infant makes, including their affective tone
- *Encouragement of autonomy*
    - i.e. gently encouraging the infant to extend their capacity to do things for themselves
- *Appropriate mind-related comments*
    - based on analysis of mothers' speech (see below).

Analysis of mothers' speech involved categorisation and quantification of the extent to which mothers' comments reflected attention to:
- ▶ infants' mental states (their thoughts, desires, interests, knowledge, preferences)
- ▶ mental processes (memories, thoughts, etc.)
- ▶ their emotional engagement (comments about whether the baby was bored, worried, etc.)
- ▶ the nature of infants' interaction (e.g. "You're joking!", "You're playing games with me!")
- ▶ putting words in the baby's mouth and reflecting on what the baby might say if s/he could (e.g. s/he says "Mummy, roll me back over").

A further stage of coding involved an assessment of the appropriateness of mothers' mind-related comments (Table 5.5).

Table 5.5: Appropriateness of mind-related comments

APPROPRIATE COMMENTS	INAPPROPRIATE COMMENTS
Accurate reading of infant's mental state: e.g. the mother says, "I see, you want the toy" and observers agree that baby is indicating this	Inaccurate reading of infant's mental state: e.g. the mother says, "I see, you want the toy" and observers agree that baby is NOT indicating this
Relevant link between past and current activity e.g. "Do you remember seeing a camel?" while baby is playing with toy camel	Irrelevant link between past and current activity e.g. "Do you remember seeing a camel?" while baby is engaged with an unrelated toy/activity
Helping the baby to carry on playing e.g. Suggesting an appropriate activity during a lull	Interrupting baby e.g. Intervening with an inappropriate activity

Unclear comments were also coded as inappropriate and, to control for differences in the amount that mothers talked, the number of mind-related comments was computed as the proportion of total comments made. In coding the extent to which mothers made mind-related comments, Meins et al. (2001) noted that this did not appear to relate directly to other measures such as contiguity, responsiveness or sensitivity.

At 12 months, the infants were tested in the Strange Situation and given an intelligence test. Analyses showed that the fifth dimension of mind-mindedness (appropriate mind-related comments) was a significant predictor of attachment security (accounting for 12.7% of the variance) even after maternal sensitivity had been accounted for (maternal sensitivity accounted for 6.5% of the variance). Also, appropriate mind-related comments appeared to discriminate between the three attachment patterns somewhat better than maternal sensitivity did: the differences on mind-related comments between secure and avoidant, secure and ambivalent/resistant, avoidant and ambivalent/resistant comparisons were significant whereas maternal sensitivity did not discriminate between mothers of avoidant and ambivalent/resistant infants. These findings suggest that the way mothers talk about their children may be an even more important aspect of secure attachment relationships than their sensitivity to children's cues alone. Meins et al. (2001, p.646) further speculated that "a mother's tendency to frame interactions in terms of her infant's desires, intentions, beliefs and emotions may provide us with a naturalistic measure of the mother's internal working model of self with child". They suggested that growing up in a context where feelings and mental states are discussed a lot might also give children with histories of secure attachments an advantage over other children in being able to anticipate how people will feel in different sorts of social situation. Meins' research group is currently investigating these possibilities in a longitudinal study of a larger sample of families.

Growing up in a stressful family environment

Numerous studies have established that among families living in poverty (which is usually associated with multiple difficulties) the incidence of insecure attachments is high (e.g. Waters et al. 1980, Egeland and Sroufe 1981, Spieker and Booth 1988, Shaw and Vondra

1995, Barnett et al 1998, Ackerman et al. 1999). It is also evident from many studies that stressful life events, such as parental divorce, marital conflict, teenage pregnancy (e.g. Lamb et al. 1987), illness, abuse or maltreatment (Main and Hesse 1990) are associated with higher incidence of insecure attachments.

Despite the fact that stress is notoriously difficult to define (Engle 1985), it has for some time been known that chronic stress increases the risk of physical and mental ill-health, and may also play a role in the aetiology of some developmental disorders.[6] However, the link between insecure attachment and a stressful parenting context is by no means direct. For example, insecure attachments have not been found to be directly associated with poverty and social disadvantage, rather, they appear to be more closely associated with maltreatment and inadequate care. In their examination of a high-risk sample, Spieker and Booth (1988) found that although there initially appeared to be a higher incidence of insecure attachments in lower- than in higher-income groups, with cases of known maltreatment and inadequate care removed from analyses, there were similar proportions. Also, when Egeland and Sroufe (1981) sub-divided their Minnesota sample according to the quality of care provided, they found that, in the 'excellent' care group, three-quarters of children were securely attached when assessed in the Strange Situation at 12 and again at 18 months. In the 'inadequate' care group only 38 per cent of children were assessed as secure at 12 months and 56 per cent at 18 months.

Studies such as these indicate a clear link between poor care and insecure attachment. That the very poor outcomes associated with raising children in difficult social circumstances may only obtain in combination with poor care has now been corroborated from many studies (Figure 5.6). To some policy-makers the implications may seem obvious: improving social conditions alone may not be enough to ensure children's wellbeing. Rather, parents need to be encouraged to provide optimal care. But what kind of care should they be giving?

Figure 5.6: Hypothetical links between adversity, parenting practices and outcomes for children

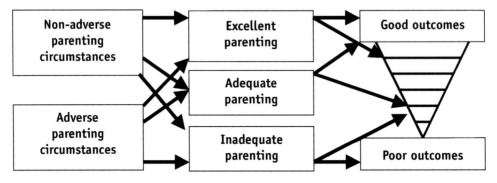

Clues as to the kind of parenting most helpful to children have emerged from research in a number of areas but particularly in connection with studies devoted to stress responses and coping in children and parents. These have highlighted the possibility that relationships with parents, even in catastrophic situations such as natural disasters or war, can mediate and influence the effects on children as well as helping to shape children's coping strategies

---

6   It seems important to emphasise that this is a controversial area in which research is still ongoing.

(Figley 1985, Anthony and Cohler 1987, Garbarino et al. 1992, Garmezy and Rutter 1983). For the majority of children, possibly as many as 80 per cent (Garbarino et al. 1992), exposure to major stressors seems to encourage resilience and competence rather than otherwise (Werner and Smith 1982, Rutter 1979). One view is that parents of resilient children may have been models of resilience themselves or may in some way have enabled the children to view both their parents and themselves in a positive, encouraging light (Ressler et al. 1988).

These within-family processes appear to mirror and magnify processes present in less extreme situations. It seems that it is not so much the way a parent copes with stress but children's beliefs about how well their parents or other significant figures are coping that determine whether or not they develop competent coping strategies. The chances, of course, of perceiving one's parents as coping well are likely to decrease as risks, such as poverty, poor health, mental and physical illness, inadequate social support, lack of material resources, low self-esteem, etc. increase (Bradley et al. 1994, Sameroff et al. 1987).

Another consistent finding is that competent coping is more closely associated with flexible approaches to problem-solving than with one particular style (Lazarus and Launier 1978, Folkman et al. 1986a, 1986b, Compas 1987). Coping strategies have broadly been grouped into those that involve paying attention to the problem itself (external factors) and those concerned with managing one's own emotional response (internal factors). In situations where children perceive themselves as having no control and where they actually do not have any control, an emotion-focused strategy, such as withdrawal or distraction, may be the most effective solution. Where taking action is an option, problem-focused strategies are more appropriate. Researchers have sought to discover how effective coping strategies develop in children in widely varying social contexts, and how context and coping might relate to the development of pathological (e.g. immune system disorders, physical illness, etc.), psychopathological or healthier outcomes.

Much of the research devoted to identification of vulnerability and protective factors and to understanding the phenomenon of resilience (defined as the capacity for normal healthy development despite extreme adversity; Rutter 1990, Fonagy et al. 1994) has focused attention on individual differences in handling stress as well as upon the nature of stress response mechanisms more generally. It has been particularly concerned to understand how effective coping might develop throughout the lifespan and, especially, what the role of parents might be in promoting healthy responses to stress in their children.

Perhaps the first point to make in discussing how healthy responses to stress develop in children is that stress, in itself, is not damaging. Correspondingly, stress responses are not, in themselves, a health risk. In many ways, they are what gives life its 'zip'. Some level of stress or arousal is not only an almost inevitable part of family life, it can be positively beneficial. Stress responses are essential in mobilising the body's resources, mental, emotional and physical, and helping to focus the mind on the problems in hand. In dealing with the constant challenges that surface during everyday family life, big and small, stress response mechanisms are called upon, first to appraise the situation and to decide how to respond, then, according to the attributions made, to take action (Figure 5.7).

Figure 5.7: Coping with stress

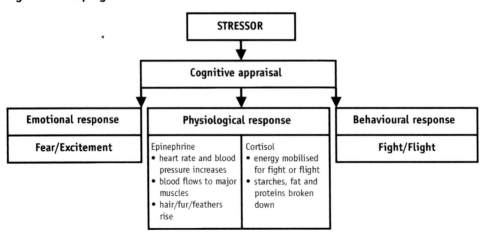

As Figure 5.7 illustrates, it is not just the nature of the threat or stressor that matters. The appraisal process is in many ways just as important in terms of health outcomes. Having said that, generally, the two aspects are not completely independent. Parents faced with multiple problems, including perhaps a child with a difficult temperament, are less likely to have spare resources at their disposal than parents with a similarly difficult child in more comfortable circumstances. For these reasons, it has been suggested that, although there may not be a direct connection between family stress and insecure attachment, there may be indirect links that are mediated by the way in which experiences are made sense of within the family, or within family stories, self-narratives or shared experience.

Although it is perhaps somewhat counter-intuitive to view stress responses as mediated by cognitive appraisal processes, a large body of research has shown that we do, more or less consciously, decide whether or not to panic! When a new experience produces a state of arousal, it needs to be interpreted before we identify ourselves as either fearful or excited (Schachter and Singer 1962). Further processing is needed to reach a decision about whether or not to stay and fight, or to flee. These decision-making processes are very rapid and informed by our history of responding as much as, if not more than, the actual new experience. They are also often very much influenced by observation of other people's responses in the same or similar situations.

Within the literature on coping and the development of ineffective responses, it has long been recognised that having a sense of control is one of the best predictors of effective coping (e.g. Langer 1983, Seligman and Maier 1967, Seligman 1975), though there has also been a longstanding debate about the psychosocial and neurochemical underpinnings of this phenomenon (e.g. Weiss et al. 1976). From Seligman's well-known observations of dogs in shuttle-boxes, in which dogs shocked for trying to escape electric shock learned to stay still and stayed still even when shocks were not given, came the concept of 'learned helplessness' (Seligman and Maier 1967). This concept was considered a prime candidate in the search for explanations of processes underlying depression in humans: if attributions of uncontrollability rather than actual uncontrollability are responsible for the depletion of nervous energy and the pervasive sense of despair and hopelessness in depression, then perhaps it might be possible, by simply getting people to alter the way they think about themselves and the world, to beat the depression (Beck 1976). These 'faulty' attributional processes were also thought potentially capable of explaining why some patients, despite being given drugs known to make potent alterations in brain chemistry, either failed to recover or swiftly relapsed.

Research focusing on attributional processes has also provided useful insights into many childhood problems, including attention deficit hyperactivity disorder (Carlson et al. 1993, Barkley 1998, Hoza et al. 1993), aggressive or anti-social behaviour (Crick and Dodge 1994), bullying (Sutton et al. 1999), extreme shyness, social phobia or social anxiety (Buss and Scheier 1976, Rubin et al. 1990). Although much of the initial research in this area took place nearly a quarter of a century ago, it has continued to reverberate throughout the literature on developmental psychopathology and to influence conceptualisations of social behaviour, including conceptualisations of the formation of different patterns of attachment. The debate over which comes first, insurmountable difficulties, 'faulty' attribution processes or depleted neurochemical reservoirs, which has for a long time perplexed researchers in the field, occasionally disappears from more popular accounts, particularly those that hold most closely to the view that psychobiological processes are 'set' in infancy.

Put in as simple terms as possible, the argument put forward by those who hold this more deterministic view seems to be that the advantages that accrue to children who have formed secure attachments emanate directly from psychobiological mechanisms which become set to function as a direct result of how parents deal with the difficulties in their lives and of how they have taught their children to cope. In this view, the explanation for the success in social interactions enjoyed by children with experience of secure attachments is that they are underpinned by sound psychobiological responses to stress. This has led some workers to postulate that security of attachment may be no more than optimal emotional self-regulation defined as "the flexibility of adaptiveness of the individual, reflected in the ability to use a range of possible strategies, depending on their appropriateness in given contexts" (Bridges and Grolnick 1995, p.203). Less resilient children with experiences of maltreatment or chronically adverse care, or insecurely attached children with experiences of insensitive care, develop less adequate psychobiological stress response mechanisms, and all the inferior neurological networks that support them. These less than optimal stress response systems can explain why these children mis-attribute both other people's behaviour and their own physiological states, and why, as a result, their social interactions are far less pleasing or in tune with other people's perspectives.

Stress responses involve many psychobiological systems that interact with each other in complex ways. Two systems are particularly implicated in mounting stress responses: the sympathetic-adrenomedullary (SAM) system and the hypothalamic-pituitary-adrenocortical (HPA) axis which seems to play a central role in co-ordinating stress responses in humans (Gunnar 2000). Since these systems, and others, are inter-dependent, dysregulation can produce changes in the neuroendocrine system, in serotonergic functioning, in thought processes and in behaviour. Although it is possible to speculate about the nature of dysregulation that might underlie overt pathology, there is still much that remains unknown about the exact relationship between the development of healthy stress responses and growing up in a stressful family environment (Repetti et al. 2002, Gunnar and Vasquez 2001).

Chronic stress or 'accumulated allostatic load' (McEwen and Stellar 1993) has been associated with a huge range of pathological outcomes, including signs of HPA axis dysregulation (though it is important to note that HPA dysregulation can occur for other reasons, too, such as congenital disorders or in utero distress). HPA dysregulation is indicated by abnormal cortisol responses to stressful events and, because cortisol is relatively easy to collect, has become an important focus for the study of stress responses in early childhood. Interpretation of data yielded by cortisol assay, however, is complicated due to the variability both within and between individuals in any sample and the ambiguity of information drawn from a stress response system that operates differently at different sites within the body. For these reasons, in order to be confident that interpretations are correct, ideally, more than one method of assessment is needed. Because other methods tend to be more invasive, the current status of knowledge still remains, in many respects, rather tenuous.

Putting these reservations temporarily aside, several potentially fruitful lines of inquiry are being pursued and some interesting hypotheses are under investigation. One line of argument stems from the premise of 'use it or lose it' and the belief that, since patterns of excitation shape the way the brain grows, the social interactive and emotional experience of babies is biologically embedded (Schore 1994, Hertzman 1997). Another, not unrelated, argument leads to the conclusion that chronic stress can result in permanent HPA dysregulation, namely, over-activation, indicated by low thresholds for cortisol release, or under-activation, indicated by lower cortisol levels, slower responses or higher thresholds for responding. Both patterns will lead to difficulties with social interaction, due either to over-readiness to appraise situations as threatening or to disengagement.

HPA dysregulation has been linked to high-conflict family life, families characterised by harsh or erratic discipline and low warmth (Flinn and England 1997, Chorpita and Barlow 1998), child maltreatment (Hart et al. 1996), and a range of physical and psychological problems, including cognitive (memory and attention) problems, immune system impairment, and delayed or inhibited growth and sexual maturation.

Given the close relationship between emotional self-regulation and patterns of attachment, it is not difficult to appreciate the attraction of theories about relationships between patterns of insecure attachment and patterns of activation in stress response systems. Specifically, it has been hypothesised that the ambivalent and disorganised patterns may be associated with lower thresholds for stress reactivity ('up-regulation') and avoidant patterns with higher thresholds ('down-regulation').

In a graphic and rather dramatic account of the processes leading to different patterns, Gerhardt (2004) describes how stress causes high levels of "corrosive cortisol" to circulate around the brain and body of the infant. According to her account (based on a number of studies, mainly of rats and other non-human animals), this "corrosive cortisol" deters the growth of healthy neurological pathways at a critical point in development and leaves the growing brain permanently set to produce dysfunctional coping responses. The extent to which damage is done depends both on the absolute level of stress hormones in circulation but, more importantly, on the way that responses to stressful experiences are managed. According to Gerhardt, infants lacking appropriate assistance from regulating caregivers are more vulnerable to the damaging effects of "toxic" levels of stress hormones, because they are unable to regulate their own stress responses in the first months of life.

While this account sounds plausible, it seems important to make several cautionary remarks:
1) the relationship in humans between attachment style and stress response patterns is still relatively unexplored
2) complex relationships obtain within and between the various physiological, behavioural and psychological processes involved in stress responses and coping
3) many hypotheses tested and conclusions generating further research are based on work with non-human animals whose responses to stress may differ in important ways from humans

4) findings from studies of non-human species (particularly rats and non-human primates) have too readily been over-attributed without qualification to humans
5) there has been an, often associated, tendency for speculative ideas to be enthusiastically promulgated as though they were well-established facts borne out by extensive empirical evidence.

Further, it also seems important to note that the 'up/down regulation account' of attachment patterns seems (a) lacking in power as an explanation for the nine or more patterns of attachment described throughout the attachment literature, (b) to conflate reactivity and with regulatory processes (high cortisol levels are often observed in the absence of high reactivity), (c) in danger of producing circular causal arguments with respect to process and outcome such that the physiological correlates could be conceptualised as epiphenomenal, and (d) potentially over-simplistic, reductivist and restrictive in terms of implications for treatment.

Having made these points, it also seems fair to remark that many of the hypotheses being put forward, whether on the basis of pure speculation or deductively inferred from non-human animals, seem very much in tune with lines of enquiry that Bowlby was eager to pursue. For this reason alone, it seems important to continue to investigate them carefully. But it is also essential to take on board the full complexity of the processes under investigation and to defer facile or premature conclusions.

Links between attachment insecurity and environmental stress

In some ways, it seems odd that stressful circumstances should be associated with less secure attachment behaviour. If, as Bowlby (1969/1982) has often been described as asserting, attachment behaviours are designed to protect the species and to promote survival, why, under conditions of severe threat, do our natural instincts not lead us toward the pattern tagged secure which would, presumably, afford us the greatest protection? Why, instead, do difficult circumstances tend to produce more insecure attachment behaviour?

Resource-rich and resource-poor environments

One explanation has been proposed by Belsky (Belsky et al. 1991) who suggested that each attachment pattern is an adaptive strategy designed for qualitatively different environmental conditions (Figure 5.8). This account recognises that behaviours that are tagged 'secure' in benign circumstances may in fact be very risky under less favourable conditions.

Figure 5.8: Life history account of attachment (Belsky et al. 1991)

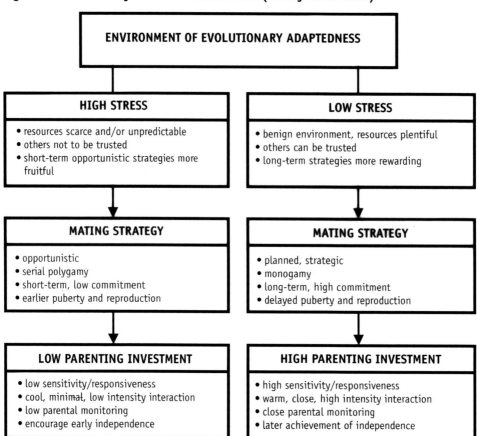

Belsky et al. (1991) predicted that more stressful parenting circumstances in the early lives of children (particularly those associated with father absence and parental disharmony) would be likely to produce fundamental differences in attitudes to social relationships which could impact on individual reproductive strategies. More specifically, children in father-absent households might be expected to begin dating earlier and to adopt the *r* child-rearing strategy which involves little parental care and many offspring, as opposed to the *K* strategy which involves few offspring and much parental care (MacArthur 1962). It follows from this account that stressful environments are associated with less cerebral activity and more fight/flight responses (insecure attachments) whereas less stressful circumstances afford the luxury of a more ruminative 'lovey-dovey' style (secure attachments). The preference for secure attachments might therefore simply be a function of more fundamental preferences for a comfortable life.

Belsky et al. (1991) also stressed that these patterns were theorised as having evolved throughout the history of the human race rather than specifically within the lifespan of each individual. For this reason, although there may be a degree of environmental stability and continuity over many generations, their theory would not necessarily predict that the degree of stress in current parenting circumstances would map directly onto attachment security or mating strategy, though some overlap may be found. Later, in a vein which seems to depart somewhat from Bowlby's position (e.g. Bowlby 1980a, Belsky 1999, p.157) suggested that some children might be more 'environmentally reactive' than others, that is, some children appear almost immune to the quality of their caregiving environment and are "strongly disposed to develop secure, avoidant, or resistant attachments almost regardless of the quality of care they experience" while others are much more vulnerable to its effects.

In commenting on Belsky et al.'s 1991 paper, Hinde (1991) applauded their attention to detail and their attempt to incorporate and to explain diverse facts, but emphasised the need for more theoretical refinement. He drew attention to the possibility that adapting to lack of resources or stress could be predicted to involve different (and possibly opposite) parenting and mate selection strategies in males and females. He further emphasised that not all behaviour is adaptive ("we must at all costs avoid the extreme sociobiological assumption that all behavior is adaptive": Hinde 1991, p.674) and stressed the challenges to theory-development posed by the impossibility of providing objective proof of how behaviour might have evolved. Finally, he suggested that the two alternative pathways (which Belsky and colleagues acknowledged to be extremes of a continuum) might be better viewed as multidimensional. This question of how adaptive different patterns of attachment behaviour might be has been a source of some contention in discussions about the significance and nature of disorganised attachment behaviours. In our view, there is still some way to go before these important debates are resolved, as our discussion in the next section may indicate.

Attachment disorganisation

"...adverse childhood experiences have effects of at least two kinds. First they make the individual more vulnerable to later adverse effects. Secondly they make it more likely that he or she will meet with further adverse experiences" (Bowlby 1982a/1988b, pp. 36-77).

A meta-analysis of almost 80 attachment studies reporting on distributions of disorganised attachments in over 100 samples (van IJzendoorn et al. 1999) yielded the information displayed in Table 5.6. At least two systems of classification were used, the Main and Solomon (1990) system in which D attachments are assigned in addition to the Ainsworth et al. (1978) A, B, C categories and other systems such as those that use the A/C category.

Table 5.6: Distribution of disorganized attachments (from van IJzendoorn et al. 1999)

	TOTAL NUMBER OF PARTICIPANTS		PERCENTAGE OF DISORGANISED ATTACHMENTS	
	Other system	Main and Solomon	Other coding systems	Main and Solomon coding system
Non-clinical samples				
Non-risk US samples	2,104	–	15%	–
Other non-risk Western samples	3,024	812	18%	17%
Low socio-economic status samples	586	338	25%	34%
Non-risk non-Western samples	–	2,302	–	21%

Clinical samples				
Known child maltreatment	165	31	48%	77%
Mothers with alcohol/drug abuse	144		43%	
Children with neurological problems	248	–	35%	–
Teenage mothers	282	248	23%	23%
Depressed mothers	340	212	21%	19%
Severe physical problems	186	–	20%	–
Severe physical problems	186	–	20%	–

Disorganised attachment has been described as "the breakdown of an otherwise consistent and organized strategy of self-regulation" under stress (van IJzendoorn et al. 1999, p.226). Soon after the disorganised attachment category was identified, several researchers began to report higher incidences of disorganised attachments in clinical and high-risk samples (e.g. Carlson et al. 1989, Cicchetti and Barnett 1991, Lyons-Ruth et al. 1987, 1990, 1991, Rodning et al. 1991).

Main and Hesse (1990), noting a link between maltreatment and disorganised attachment, suggested that disorganised behaviour possibly reflects an aborted attempt on the part of infants to seek comfort from people who might be expected to provide a potential place of safety but who have, for some reason, become a source of fear. They further suggested that, at its core, disorganisation is associated with the experience of fright without solution and is linked with parental behaviour that is either frightened and/or frightening for the child, for example, baring of teeth, glaring, etc., often within a context where more friendly behaviour might be expected.

This kind of characterisation appears at times to have led to an assumption that disorganised attachments are inextricably linked to experiences of child mistreatment or abuse, that is, that all children classified as disorganised will have had some sort of abusive experience. This is not, in fact, the case. Rather, the kind of potentially puzzling or frightening parental behaviours described by Main and Hesse have been observed in some maltreating but also in non-maltreating parents, for example, parents who have experienced abuse, trauma, unresolved loss, parental discord or mental problems such as depression. Patterns of attachment that resemble disorganisation can also occur in association with clinical conditions such as autism or Down's syndrome, although the Main and Solomon 1990 coding system precludes the use of the disorganised classification in cases where these conditions have been identified.

It is not yet clear to what extent parents' lack of control over their own strong negative emotions is implicated in the development of disorganised attachment relationships. One theory is that the parent may have 'split off' in some way from their own emotional state and that it is exposure to this dissociated state that obstructs attachment organisation in infants (Liotti 1992, Main and Morgan 1996). Processes like these are thought to be responsible for the lapses in monitoring of discourse or reasoning that occur while talking about traumatic events in adults classified as Unresolved/Disoriented in the AAI (Hesse and van IJzendoorn 1999). While this theory seems to offer a plausible explanation for the association between disorganised infant behaviour and frightened or frightening parental behaviour, evidence in support of this kind of link has not been entirely consistent (Lyons-Ruth and Jacobvitz

1999). Nevertheless, this explanation does seem to account for a certain proportion of cases (Lyons-Ruth et al. 1999, Schuengel et al. 1999, Abrams 2000, True et al. 2001).

In a related field of investigation, a broader range of maternal communicative behaviours that are also thought to interfere with the more optimal, open communication observed in secure parent-child interactions is also being identified (Lyons-Ruth and Spielman 2004). Some of these are shown in Table 5.7.

Table 5.7: Problematic affective parent-child communication (from Lyons-Ruth and Spielman 2004)

AFFECTIVE COMMUNICATION ERRORS
• Contradictory cues, e.g. open arm invitation to approach while baring teeth • Inappropriate or mismatched responses to infant cues or bids for attention
DISORIENTATION
• Appears frightened or confused by infant's bid for attention • Goes off into trance-like state or appear disassociated while in interaction
NEGATIVE/INTRUSIVE/FRIGHTENING BEHAVIOUR
• Verbal negative intrusion – e.g. mocks or teases distressed infant • Physical negative intrusion – e.g. follows own infant-cleaning agenda regardless of infant response, rough-handles child, etc.
ROLE AMBIGUITY
• Usual adult-child caregiver-caregiving roles reversed • Sexualisation, e.g. over-intimate tone
WITHDRAWAL
• Verbal distancing – e.g. does not greet on reunion • Physical distancing – e.g. holds at arm's length or too stiffly, etc.

Lyons-Ruth and Spielman (2004) further suggest that, among the mothers of disorganised infants, there may be a dynamic that produces two opposite types of parenting profiles: 'hostile/self-referential' and 'helpless/fearful' mothers. Although both groups of mothers are markedly out of synchrony with their children and both have difficulty maintaining role boundaries, the former tend to intrude upon their children more and to impose their own agenda while the latter are more passive, anxious and distant. Patterns of disorganised behaviour seem correspondingly polarised in infants, with the infants of 'hostile-self-referential' mothers showing more intrusive or conflicted approach/withdraw behaviours and infants of 'helpless-fearful' mothers being more prone to seek contact but equally unable to draw comfort from it and prone to 'freeze', turn away or huddle while in contact. Lyons-Ruth and Spielman (2004) suggest that because 'helpless/fearful' mothers can come across as more caring than 'hostile/self-referential' mothers, particularly if their children are not seeking emotional support, their relationship difficulties may be less apparent. Although this paper gives the impression that disorganised behaviour in the Strange Situation can be classified relatively easily into two distinct subtypes and that cause-effect relationships between infant and caregiver behaviours can be discerned, further investigation is needed before these patterns can be said to be confirmed.

Crittenden and Claussen (2000) take the view that 'disorganised' behaviours can be seen as an adaptive response to particularly difficult circumstances. They propose that attachment behaviours are multiply determined but see non-secure patterns as likely to have arisen in response to specific types of danger that have occurred within the context of relationships between parents and children. They propose that almost all types of danger can be described in terms of timing, location and probability of occurrence and that these aspects will combine to elicit different attachment patterns. Avoidant strategies are more suitable when children can predict when the danger is going to be present, ambivalent strategies when danger is unpredictable (for example, because interaction depends on the parent's transient moods rather than on the child's own behaviour). If the danger is predictable, children can take more focused action to avert it, for example, by compulsively complying to rules and inhibiting forbidden behaviours. If the danger is not predictable, the "best self-protective strategy is to attend closely to the changes in the parent's state (wary fearfulness), to threaten if the parent can be intimidated or made to feel guilty (anger), and to seek parental assistance frequently (desire for comfort)" (Crittenden and Claussen 2000, p.235-6).

Crittenden (e.g. Crittenden 1995, Crittenden and Claussen 2000) departs most pronouncedly from other interpretations in her conceptualisation of the nature and role of disorganised patterns of attachment. Most other attachment researchers designate disorganised attachment as maladaptive and as indicative of the breakdown of organised behaviour, or as showing inability to marshal an organised strategy (e.g. Main and Solomon 1990). Crittenden, by contrast, has argued that it is possible to see the majority of behaviours subsumed within this category as serving a self-protective function. She has also pointed out that, using Ainsworth's system of classification, although most maltreated children are classified as insecure avoidant, a minority is classified as secure whereas, using Main and Solomon's system of classification, most (though not all) maltreated children are classified as disorganised (Carlson et al. 1989). In addition, she suggests that signs of disorganisation tend to be less apparent in association with the eight original Ainsworth sub-groups and rather more closely evident in children with obsessive or compulsive types of behaviour. In developing her own system for extending the system of classification of attachment behaviours, therefore, Crittenden attempts to specify as precisely as possible how a much wider range of infant and carer behaviours interact to produce specific outcomes. The system that she has developed is still in process of being developed and tested.

Crittenden recommends that, rather than treating all maltreatment contexts as though they were homogeneous, it may be more useful to view them as at least three types: "the under-responsiveness of neglectful parents, the hostile intrusion and control of physically abusive parents, and their combination in abusive-and-neglectful parents" (Crittenden and Claussen 2000, p.238). Each of these parenting situations might be expected to produce different, more or less effective, strategies for self-protection, for example, physically violent parents might induce compulsively compliant children who try not to display negative affect whereas neglecting parents might evoke compulsive caregiving in children, inhibition of negative affect and displays of false positive affect. Crittenden and Claussen speculate that such organised behaviours, because they serve specific functions within the context of dynamic parent-child relationships, may not generalise outside those situations. Rather, in less threatening social situations, they might transmute into more generalised aggression or disorder.

How disorganised behaviour in the Strange Situation generalises beyond the infant-carer dyad seems unclear. Steele and Steele (2005) point out that in their sample of 96 infants assessed with mothers in the Strange Situation and 90 assessed with the mothers' partner (the biological father), no infant was assessed as disorganised with both parents. While it might seem reasonable to predict that disorganisation within the context of the carer who spends most time with the infant would have the greatest influence on personality development, this hypothesis has yet to be tested. In fact, there is no clear agreement on the subject of whether disorganisation is environmentally determined (i.e. it is the result of the parent's influence) or influenced by within-child factors. Steele and Steele propose, in line with the argument from research on temperament, that the fact that children are very rarely found to have disorganised attachment to both parents indicates that the pattern is "arguably social in origin, relationship-specific, and stemming from messages internalised by the child concerning how to regulate emotional conflict" (2005, no page number). We have already discussed the possible problems with this line of argument elsewhere: non-concordance of mother-child and father-child attachment, in our view, need not preclude a contribution from within-child factors. This touches on a debate over the extent to which attachment disorganisation might be genetically driven, a debate that seems set to rumble on for some time as larger samples and more complex models of potential genetic transmission and gene-environment correlations and interactions are explored (Lakatos et al. 2000, 2002, Bakermans-Kranenburg and van IJzendoorn 2004, Gervai and Lakatos 2004). Arguably, genetic theories could be seen as about the 'hardest' form of attachment theory possible. Alternatively, since genetic predispositions often require environmental input of some sort to effect genetic expression, it does not seem entirely sensible to view genetic and environmental explanations as reciprocally excluding or opposing arguments. Both levels of investigation are important.

It seems fair to say that much is still to be discovered about the nature, origin and consequences of attachment disorganisation in infancy. One thing that does seem fairly well established, though, is that disorganised patterns of attachment do appear to be linked with the highest levels of stress in the Strange Situation (Spangler and Grossmann 1993, Hertsgaard et al. 1995) and are also not homogeneous, that is, children who show disorganised behaviour in the Strange Situation do not resemble each other very closely and are not likely to have identical caregiving experiences. There has been some suggestion, though, that the parents of these children may be more likely to be classified as 'unresolved' with respect to trauma in their own lives.

The effect of parents' own histories on patterns of attachment in children

"...however she may accomplish it, when a woman manages either to retain or to regain access to such unhappy memories and reprocess them in such a way that she can come to terms with them, she is found to be no less able to respond to her child's attachment behaviour so that he develops a secure attachment to her than a woman whose childhood was a happy one" (Bowlby 1988b, p.135)

"...the family experience of those who grow up anxious and fearful is found to be characterized not only by uncertainty about parental support but often also by covert yet strongly distorting parental pressures: pressure on the child, for

example, to act as caretaker for a parent; or to adopt, and thereby to confirm, a parent's false models- of self, of child, and of the relationship. Similarly, the family experience of those who grow up to become relatively stable and self-reliant is characterized not only by unfailing parental support when called upon but also by a steady yet timely encouragement toward increasing autonomy, and by the frank communication of parents of working models – of themselves, of child, and of others – that are not only tolerably valid but are open to be questioned and revised... the inheritance of mental health and of mental ill health through the medium of family microculture is certainly no less important, and may well be far more important, than is their inheritance through the medium of genes"
(Bowlby 1973a, pp. 366-367)

"Of the many types of psychological disturbance that are traceable, at least in part, to one or another pattern of maternal deprivation, the effects on parental behaviour and thereby on the next generation are potentially the most serious"
(Bowlby 1982a/1988b, p.37)

In this lecture, Bowlby went on to describe how mothers may be unable to respond to their children's demands because they themselves lacked a mental image of having their own needs met, but, he emphasised, this does not happen in all cases.

The sense that, whether parents like it or not, their own experience of being parented has an influence on the relationships they have with their children, is not uncommon: "Oh no! I sound just like my mother!" "The older I get, the more I seem to be turning into my father!" "I couldn't believe what I just heard myself say!" While some parents are comfortable about following in their parents' footsteps ("Well, it never did me any harm, I do the same with my children." "Now that I've got my own children, I can appreciate more how much my parents did for me"), others are less comfortable. Also, while some people are very aware of ways in which they emulate their parents and some patterns of influence are very near the surface and obvious, others are far more subtle. The following case study, which is a true story, provides an illustration of these processes.

> May, the oldest child of Gwen and Morgan, was born within two years of the end of World War I. For the first years of May's life, the family grew and prospered. There was a second child, Tom, three years younger than May. Morgan, a highly intelligent man whose university career had been forestalled by the outbreak of the First World War, was doing well in his chosen profession, both May and Tom were doing well at school, and Gwen provided a secure and comfortable home environment.
>
> Then troubles began. In the early 1930s, Morgan resigned his post when his boss altered his contract of employment. Had he realised the difficulty he was then to have in securing another job in what turned out to be a major economic recession, he may have swallowed his pride and stayed on. As it transpired, with a third child on the way and no income, the family was forced to make serious economies. One of these involved sending May to live with her grandmother, a move that lasted throughout most of May's teenage years. By the time World War II broke out and Tom had been called up, May had returned home and was working for the Post Office.
>
> Within months of the outbreak of war, May received news that her father had been taken to hospital. Even today, she recalls freshly her feelings as she sat beside her mother and her father's body. Not long after this, news came that Tom was missing

in action. She accompanied her mother to the War Office and remembers talking to the officers there about her brother while her mother sat outside. She cannot explain why she and not her mother spoke to the officers. Next, she recalls getting home from work to be told that her mother had been taken to the same hospital where her father had died the year before. The news she dreaded soon came. She, now as much as then, believes her mother literally died of a broken heart. She describes how the loss of her parents devastated her and destroyed her confidence in herself. She remembers feeling for years as though she was living in a cupboard, a very dark place.

Feeling that the family had been broken up too much, she turned down relatives' offers to look after her younger sister, Flo, then only eight years old. At 21, she became her sister's guardian, prevented by this responsibility from taking up the more prestigious war work that her contemporaries were engaging in.

By 25, she had married another Post Office worker and gave birth to the first of her own four children when she was 28. By now, Tom had returned to the UK having been released from a Japanese prison-of-war camp and he too had married and had a child. However, shortly after May had given birth to her second daughter, both Tom and Flo emigrated to New Zealand.

May still says she worshipped her parents. She understood why she had had to go away and felt that her father may have regretted his resignation but bore no resentment towards him. She quite liked the grandmother she went to live with and didn't remember feeling particularly homesick.

At times, though, she rather ruefully wonders whether perhaps she might have made her own children too independent. Determined to protect them from the pain of loss that she had experienced and possibly also to avoid the painful re-experience of feelings associated with caring for a demanding younger sister while herself struggling with bereavement, she strongly encouraged early and precocious self-reliance, particularly in her two older children.

This case illustrates how parents' own experiences of loss can, without necessarily reducing their sense of the value of close relationships, impact on relationships with their children. What it does not explain, though, is what mechanisms might underlie this impact, how parents' own childhood experiences might be predicted to affect their ability to support and nurture their children or why it might be that some underlying messages seem to permeate the boundary between generations while others do not. Nor does it explain how it is that some parents with past experiences of trauma, loss and abuse cope with these experiences in a way that preserves their ability to relate closely to their children, while others cope far less effectively.

A large number of studies has now begun to address the question of intergenerational transmission of attitudes toward attachment. One early study (Main et al. 1985) indicated an association between parents' attitude of mind towards attachment relationships, as classified by the AAI, and children's attachment classification at age one in the Strange Situation as well as at age six in a separation-reunion test. Parents who spoke freely about their childhood relationships and whose transcripts indicated that they valued attachment relationships tended to have children also classified as secure at both assessments. Parents of children classified as avoidant, conversely, were described as devaluing the importance of attachment relationships, for example, they claimed to have forgotten more than other parents about their past and were inclined to present idealised images of their parents.

Parents of children classified as ambivalent/resistant were also found to have more children who were classified as preoccupied while parents of children classified as disorganised often had unresolved issues concerning loss of their own parents in childhood. Similar findings have subsequently emerged from other studies in which parents' and parent-child attachment were measured concurrently (e.g. Grossmann et al. 1988, Ward and Carlson 1995) or prospectively, that is, the parents were assessed before the birth of the child and the child was assessed some time later (e.g. Heinicke et al. 1983, Zeanah et al. 1993, 1994, Fonagy et al. 1991).

One report, on a predominantly middle- to upper-middle class, married group of mothers and maternal grandmothers (Benoit and Parker 1994), showed 81 per cent concordance between mothers' AAI classification during pregnancy and infant SS classification one year later comparing across three categories of attachment and 68 per cent comparing across four categories. Across all three generations, comparing across three categories, 65 per cent of grandmother-mother-triads were concordant (Table 5.8).

Benoit and Parker drew attention to the fact that, although they had appeared to find stability of attachment classification both for mothers across time (mothers were assessed with the AAI before pregnancy and when the baby was 11 months) and across generations, the majority of adult participants in their study were assessed as secure/autonomous. It seems that this fact ought to preclude confidence in their conclusion that "the present study provides compelling evidence for Bowlby's (1969/1982) contention that internal working models of attachment tend to be perpetuated across generations" (Benoit and Parker 1994, p.1454) but rather ought to encourage caution, as they advised elsewhere in the paper.

In fact, as Table 5.8 indicates, looking in detail at the patterns across generation, the picture appears actually rather complex. First, the four-category system did not appear to produce very high concordance across grandmothers and adult daughters, particularly in respect of preoccupied and unresolved/disorganised classifications, which were much more common in the grandmothers. Only when the three-category system was used did there appear to be higher concordance and this seemed to be much more closely associated with autonomous than with insecure classifications. A similar picture emerged from comparison of mothers' AAI to mothers-infant SS. There appeared to be less evidence of intergenerational transmission of attachment classification when the four-system category was used and almost none in respect of dismissing/avoidant attachment. Even when the three-category system was used most of the continuity appeared to be associated with the larger number of mothers labelled secure.

An interesting finding emerges when infant classifications are compared directly with those of grandmothers (of course, it should be borne in mind that these comparisons include 'outside the family' comparisons so could not be said to be due to intra-familial transmission). Considerably more secure attachments exist in the youngest generation than in the oldest generation. An optimistic interpretation might be that the population under study had become more secure across generations! A more realistic view might be to question this use of statistics and to seek alternative explanations. This position is very much in line with ours, as we later discuss. For the present, we turn to an important meta-analysis of two-generation studies carried out by van IJzendoorn (1995a).

Van IJzendoorn's meta-analysis included 14 studies in which parents' representation of their attachment experiences had been assessed using the AAI and the attachment relationship between parents and children had been assessed using the SS. The 14 studies reported on 18 parent samples (854 parents in total, ranging from 20 to 96) and included four data-sets from fathers, one from adolescent mothers, one from mothers of very low socioeconomic status and one where children had oppositional behaviour problems. In five of the studies, parents' attachment had been assessed before the birth of the child; in most of the others both assessments were carried out at the same time, though in some the adult assessment was carried out after the SS.

Initial inspection of the data indicated that the relation between parent and child attachment was very strong, explaining about 35 per cent or more of the variance (with a combined effect size of 1.06). However, effect sizes were not homogeneous, which means that the relationship was not found in all samples and could, hypothetically, have come from only a handful of samples (though in fact it appeared to be present in the majority of them).

The relationship between parent and child attachment appeared to be much stronger for mothers than for fathers, on whom reports varied considerably, from no association at all to a strong association. Timing of AAI assessment (before birth or at the same time as the parent-child attachment assessment) did not affect the strength of the relationship although the relationship was weaker for older children. Effects appeared to be stronger for US samples than for samples drawn from Australia, the Netherlands and the UK. This may have been partly due to the fact that some of the biggest discrepancies in findings emerged from the UK and the Dutch samples: both included reports on fathers but, whereas the UK study showed a very strong association between fathers' AAI and subsequent parent-child attachment, the Dutch sample found no association. Weaker associations were also found in lower-income samples and, conversely, the strongest effects appeared to be associated with higher-income samples, which are likely to be characterised by greater economic stability over time.

Van IJzendoorn examined relationships between AAI and SS results in three ways: first, he looked at whether AAI security/insecurity predicted SS security/insecurity (the results outlined above); next, he looked at whether AAI dismissiveness predicted SS avoidance (13 samples); then he looked at whether a preoccupied AAI style predicted SS ambivalent/resistant classification (10 samples); he also considered whether the unresolved AAI category was related to disorganisation on the SS. While outcomes on the dismissive-avoidance and unresolved-disorganised dimensions appeared very similar to outcomes on security, outcomes on the preoccupied-ambivalent/resistant were less consistent and, in studies where disorganisation had also been coded, were only marginally related. Less training in AAI and SS procedures was associated with lower effect sizes and effects also tended to be negatively correlated with parents' age. But, overall, van IJzendoorn concluded: "The stable and large overlap between autonomy of the parent and security of the child is impressive because the measures are different" (1995a, p.396). He explained that the weaker findings in respect of the preoccupied-ambivalent dimension may have been possibly due to the relatively small numbers involved but also pointed out that boundaries between C and D categories might be less strict than those between other categories and D categorisation and that this might have introduced category slippage due to measurement variability.

In the same paper, van IJzendoorn (1995a) tried to reveal what the mechanism might be for this apparent intergenerational transmission of attachment styles. Exploring to see whether, as Ainsworth's and Bowlby's work suggests, maternal responsiveness or sensitivity mediates parent and infant attachment, he discovered what he subsequently called the 'transmission gap', that is, that there is no direct link from AAI to SS scores via maternal sensitive responding. In fact, he found that maternal sensitivity could account for only around 23 per cent of the variance linking AAI and SS classifications, a finding that has subsequently been confirmed by other researchers (e.g. Pederson et al. 1998, Raval et al. 2001).

Table 5.8: Transmission of attachments across three generations (Benoit and Parker 1994)

MATERNAL GRANDMOTHERS (AAI): 4 CATEGORIES															
AUTONOMOUS				DISMISSING				PREOCCUPIED				UNRESOLVED			
26				7				4				44			
16	3	2	5	2	4	0	1	0	1	1	2	23	1	4	16
Aut	Dis	Pre	Un	Aut	Dis	Pre	Un	Aut	Dis	Pre	Un	Aut	Dis	Pre	Un
61.5%				57.1%				25.0%				36.3%			

EXPECTANT DAUGHTERS (AAI) Per cent in same category

MATERNAL GRANDMOTHERS (AAI): 3 CATEGORIES								
AUTONOMOUS				DISMISSING			PREOCCUPIED	
51				14			16	
45	3	3		7	5	1	3	2	8
Aut	Pre	Dus		Aut	Dis	Pre	Aut	Dis	Pre
88.2%				35.7%			50.0%	

EXPECTANT DAUGHTERS (AAI) Per cent in same category as mother

EXPECTANT DAUGHTERS (AAI): 4 CATEGORIES

AUTONOMOUS				DISMISSING				PREOCCUPIED				UNRESOLVED			
48				9				7				24			
0	40	1	7	2	4	1	2	1	0	4	2	1	8	1	14
A	B	C	D	A	B	C	D	A	B	C	D	A	B	C	D
	83.3%				22.2%				57.1%				58.3%		

INFANTS (SS) Percentage of infants in same category as mothers

EXPECTANT DAUGHTERS (AAI): 3 CATEGORIES

AUTONOMOUS			DISMISSING			PREOCCUPIED		
55			10			12		
2	51	2	4	4	2	1	4	7
A	B	C	A	B	C	A	B	C

INFANTS (SS)		
SECURE/AUTONOMOUS	AVOIDANT/DISMISSING	AMBIVALENT/PREOCC
Percentage of infants in same category as mother		
92.7% (51/55)	40.0% (4/10)	55.3% (7/12)
Percentage of infants in same category as both mother and grandmother		
80.4% (41/51)	15.4% (2/13)	46.2% (6/13)
Percentage of infants compared with grandmothers in each category		
115.6% (59/51)	53.8% (7/13)	84.6% (11/13)

What else, van IJzendoorn asked, might explain the connection between the two sets of scores. Could it be due to:
- maternal sensitivity all the same, but missed because measures of maternal sensitivity were not sufficiently well calibrated to capture its effects?
- shared parent and child genetic influences, perhaps those related to temperament?
- shared environmental influences on both parents' and children's behaviour?
- or a combination of the above?

We have already explored some of these questions earlier in this chapter and will take up the remainder in the next chapter. Here, though, we would like to draw attention to a further possible explanation, namely, that in spite of van IJzendoorn's assertion (which many other workers in the field also espouse) that "the predictive validity of the AAI is a replicated fact" (1995a, p.387), there may still be a possibility that its status is questionable. Many researchers assume that measures of adult attachment taken at any point in relation to the birth of an infant and subsequent assessment of infant attachment jointly produce information about the stability and transmission of attachment not only across the lifespan but across generations. In our view, this assumption seems questionable.

First, even if the adult attachment measures do relate to the same construct as assessments in infancy, which is difficult to prove though, in theory, possible, there are no logical grounds for assuming that styles of attachment have been 'transmitted' across generations, by some kind of osmotic principle. Despite their intuitive appeal (why, after all, shouldn't children follow in their parents' footsteps?), such assertions go rather a long way beyond the data. Most humans move around on two legs after a certain age. Finding that both mothers and offspring do this does not mean that the ability to move on two legs is transmitted by the mothers to the children. Rather more evidence is needed to substantiate a transmission hypothesis.

Second, given that mothers' behaviours are also assessed in the Strange Situation and that this assessment, like that of the AAI, is based on a search for behaviour related to patterns of attachment and the elusive entity 'attachment security' which, it will be recalled from previous discussions, was not operationally defined, it seems highly likely that the maternal interactive behaviours that are sorted and classified in relation to their children in the Strange Situation may not just be similar to the behaviours being sorted and classified in the AAI but, possibly, another aspect of the same maternal qualities. If this is the case, then the SS and the AAI may actually tap the same maternal qualities and it may be this fact that produces such high concordance between assessments. The contribution from the infant could, conceivably, be relatively small. If this is the case, then concordance or "predictive validity" may be more artefact than fact.

This brings us to another query, which is perhaps rather more of a quibble. In many reports, particularly earlier ones (naming no names), that present analyses of maternal AAI and infant-mother SS data, data is treated as though it came from two independent populations and evidence for associations is sought using chi-squared tests. Tables of probabilities for these tests are calculated on the understanding that the same people are not being tested repeatedly and so consider similarity to be highly unlikely by chance. While this is a reasonable assumption when comparing AAI classifications from mothers and grandmothers, who are separate groups of people, it seems less appropriate when comparing mothers' AAIs with mother and baby classifications from the SS. The more appropriate test here would seem to be a test for change which assumes that data is drawn from the same population. Having said this, some studies have used change tests and some data sets have now also been analysed using both types of test. As similar conclusions have been arrived at with both types of test, this point appears somewhat academic.

Even so, it does seem that, while there may eventually prove to be some evidence of correspondence between attachment security from one generation to the next, only large-scale longitudinal studies that take account of many other sources of influence are likely to be capable of establishing whether the mechanism underlying this correspondence involves transmission. Other methodologies run the risk of simply re-asserting the now well-established finding that, in most 'representative' samples, around two-thirds of the population are assessed as secure. This fact in itself could account for the appearance of continuity which may have more to do with regression towards the mean (the tendency towards homeostasis) than has previously been acknowledged: when there are strong pressures to conform, like a sort of centrifugal force, these pressures are likely to support majority group preferences more than less normative ones. This might account for the tendency for 'secure' attachments to be more stable than 'insecure' ones.

To illustrate this point more sharply, we can draw an analogy to the question of whether parents determine the sexual orientation of their offspring. Let us suppose that approximately 90 per cent of any sample of the adult population self-reports a heterosexual sexual orientation. Let us also suppose that we find that 98 per cent of parents who self-identify as heterosexual have children who also self-identify as heterosexual whereas two per cent have children who self-identify as gay, lesbian or bisexual. Does this mean that heterosexual parents transmit their heterosexuality to their children or does it simply mean that the default mode for sexual orientation is heterosexuality? Without considerably more investigation, we have no real way of knowing. Crude head counts across samples drawn from different generations simply do not address the essential question of whether sexual orientation is socially, genetically or socio-genetically influenced. In-depth, large-scale longitudinal studies are needed if enough relevant data is to be available to take account of all potential influences that might affect particular outcomes. The same problem applies to attachment security.

Nevertheless, intuitively, the notion that parents' own experiences of being parented will influence the way they parent their own children seems sensible. And it seems clear that, as in May's case and in the case of many parents, childhood experiences of loss and difficulty can and will carry over more or less consciously into relationships with their own children. What seems less clear is what form this carry-over might take and what influences may shape transmutations of experience across generations. As Byng-Hall (1995a, 1995b) describes, the family script adopted by some parents is 'replicative' while that of others is 'corrective' and it is not yet clear which parents will repeat the mistakes and successes of their own parents and which might make appropriate corrective alterations, or why these differences might arise. For this reason, there does not seem yet to be sufficient evidence to assume that 'dismissing' parents will breed avoidant children or that children whose parents have not managed to come to terms with their own difficult experiences, i.e. children whose parents have 'unresolved' attitudes toward their own attachment experiences, will be unable to form secure attachments to their parents. The processes involved appear to be far more complex than such a simple linear, 'pipeline' transmission model would suggest.

Other caregivers besides mother

Most of the information presented so far in this chapter has been heavily focused on relationships between mothers and children. This is more to do with the preponderance of studies of mothers and infants within the attachment literature, particularly in the earlier literature from which most of the longitudinal data presented in this chapter is drawn, than to do with a view that other relationships are not important. It is also rather unfortunate because there are now so many studies of attachment to draw upon, including studies of father-child attachment, sibling attachments and studies of attachment figures in other parts of the family and community (e.g. grandparents, godparents, day care providers, teachers, etc.). However, within a general introductory text, it is very difficult to include the broader view of attachment as the Grossmanns have termed it (Grossmann et al. 1999) or to satisfy those who gently complain that "From a family therapist's perspective, it appears as if attachment researchers have a professional working model of the dyad, not of the family. With no disrespect meant, a reappraisal and extension of the model may take some time, especially as the dyadic model has proved to be so successful" (Byng-Hall 1999, p.643).

As this comment hints, there is a sense in which Attachment Theory research has become something of a victim of its own success. As attachment research has gained momentum, as we mentioned in Chapter Three, the research tools have multiplied. While the picture that emerges using most tools is of secure attachments being more closely associated than insecure attachments with positive outcomes in many areas, the question of how different attachment relationships might relate to each other within the hierarchy of attachments available to each child is much less clear. Is it, for example, the case that children who are securely attached to their primary caregiver have found a recipe for the formation of positive attachments or meaningful relationships across a wider span than children who are less securely attached? If so, then the effect of secure attachments might accrue not only to the quality of the primary relationship but to the quantity of similar relationships available to securely attached children.

As Byng-Hall (1999), again, points out, to explore this possibility is to complicate the research design enormously: while a relationship involving two people (one dyad) is captured by the Strange Situation, relationships involving three people (a triadic or three dyadic relationships) is not. For example, the infant-mother and the infant-father relationship can be separately assessed (though not easily simultaneously) in the Strange Situation, but the mother-father relationship needs a separate assessment. In this sense, the Strange Situation can be seen to fail to take account of the effect of the father-mother relationship both on the mother-child relationship and on the father-child relationship. It is also rather limited (due to constraints of timing already mentioned in Chapter Three) in the degree to which it can assess the separate influence of father-child and mother-child relationships as well as the effects of these on each other. Adding another family member into the picture (a grandmother perhaps) produces 15 possible influences of one dyadic relationship upon another while adding a teacher, a day care giver and a sibling (eight people in total) would produce 378 possible effects of one dyadic relationship on another (Emde 1988, cited in Byng-Hall 1999). Given the potential complexity of any one child's social context, it seems possible that monotropic tendencies may be all that saves attachment researchers focused on only one, two or at most three dyadic relationships from being powerless to capture any meaningful patterns. And this raises the question of the extent to which a primary focus on mother-child relationships may have led to a rather superficial and over-simplified account of attachment relationships.

In the next section, we will briefly consider this issue in relation to a very highly selected portion of the literature on father-child attachment.

Fathers as attachment figures

In the early days of attachment research, both mainstream developmental psychology and many psycho-analytic theories were still very matrocentric. In fact, it is now widely agreed that research on the role of fathers did not really begin to feature very highly within academic or policy arena until the 1980s, although models of parenting had emerged from other fields such as anthropology, ethology and sociology. Within these fields, as reflected in Bowlby's and Freud's theories, the dominant notion has tended to be that fathers and mothers serve mutually complementary but separate functions and that they are naturally designed to be biologically and psychologically distinct.

When fathers first began to appear in the attachment research literature, a view seemed quickly to emerge that they may be more fittingly seen as children's playmates or as having an affiliative function as opposed to vying with the mother for an important role as caregiver or attachment figure (Lamb 1981, Lewis 1987); at best, they were seen as secondary caregivers or 'allomothers' (Hrdy 1999).

This view of the role of fathers was based on evidence from a number of areas of research including attachment research itself in which studies of fathers and infants in the Strange Situation showed fairly consistently that mother-child and father-child attachment patterns were independent of each other (e.g. Main and Weston 1981, Belsky et al. 1984b, Oppenheim et al. 1988, Bridges et al. 1988, Fox et al. 1991, Volling and Belsky 1992, Freitag et al. 1996) although two meta-analyses have now indicated small but significant patterns of concordance both in respect of security/insecurity distinctions, and in relation to major categories and sub-categories (Fox et al. 1991, van IJzendoorn and de Wolff 1997).

Studies have also tended to show that, unlike patterns of mother-child attachment, father-child attachment patterns do not appear to be systematically related to child outcomes (Miljkovitch et al. 2004). More recently, on re-examining data in relation to fathers' style of play with children from their longitudinal studies, the Grossmanns have confirmed that the way that fathers play with their young children appears to predict later outcomes far better than early father-child attachment (Grossmann et al. 2002)

While these findings may appear to suggest that the role of fathers as attachment figures is relatively unimportant or that the nature of child-father attachment is secondary to that of the child-mother relationship, there may be good reasons for distrusting these conclusions. First, in the relatively few studies where child-father attachments have been measured, it would appear that children with secure attachments to both parents fare better than those with only a secure attachment to mother (Main and Weston 1981). More important, though, is the second point that comes loud and clear from all research on fathers, that models used to assess father-child relationships need to be designed specifically for that task and not for the task of assessing mother-child relationships. Using tools designed to assess mother-child relationships, almost inevitably, produces a 'deficit model' of fathers (Richards 1982) particularly in respect of the quality of fathers' involvement with their children which, in most families, is mediated by processes very different from those that mediate the mother-child relationship (Palkovitz 1997, Biller 1993, Hawkins and Dollahite 1997).

In other words, the use of the Strange Situation to capture the nature of attachment relationships between fathers and children may be inappropriate not just on the grounds that it necessitates repeat testing, with the potential problems that this entails, but, more directly, because the coding system which is designed to capture mother-child relationships may be less sensitively attuned to subtle qualitative differences in father-child patterns. Only an assessment procedure evolved, like the Strange Situation procedure was for mothers, from close observation of father-child relationships seems likely to capture these subtleties. Such an instrument may be able to capture the effect of the fact that the influence of fathers on the nature of the child's attachment is usually more or less mediated by both the mother-child and the father-child relationship, and their social context, rather than being an independent primary influence that is relatively easy to isolate from its social context. Perhaps, before assuming that father-child attachment patterns are not related to later child outcomes, as has tended to be the conclusion from many studies, it is now time to acknowledge the daunting possibility that the research tools may need to be re-constructed if they are really going to be capable of assessing different qualities of father-child relationship?

Other relatives and day care

As shown in Chapter Three, the most widely used assessments of attachment in infancy and childhood have been almost exclusively designed to assess dyadic relationships. Adding fathers to research designs has often been accomplished by repeating the Strange Situation rather than by using an alternative assessment designed to capture the relationship that a child might have with attachment figures who are not also the main caregiver. This has also tended to be the case where researchers have been interested to assess relationships with other attachment figures outside the immediate family, for example, in studies of relationships between infants and alternative mother figures, such as the metapelet in Israeli kibbutzim (e.g. Fox 1977, Oppenheim et al. 1988, Sagi et al. 1985, Aviezar et al. 1994, 1999).

While the focus on dyadic relationships has produced rich information capable of predicting important later outcomes for children, it seems unfortunate that it has often failed to capture the full picture of children's early attachment relationships. Bowlby was clearly aware that the benefit of a secure attachment with mother (or father, if he is the primary caregiver) was often maximised because of the availability of other supportive adults in the primary caregiver's social network (Bowlby, 1969/1982). Children with secure attachments to one key figure tended also to be more likely to have good relationships with other less central figures. Children with less secure primary attachment relationships, according to Bowlby, would be less likely to be able to form good relationships with other available attachment figures. From Bowlby's writings it is possible to deduce two possible underlying assumptions. The first is that the further down the attachment hierarchy a good relationship occurs, the less potency it has in terms of laying foundations for positive social relationships. The second is that unless the primary attachment relationship is secure, the chances of attachments further down the hierarchy being secure are negligible. These assumptions, neither of which appears yet to have been systematically tested, can be illustrated in simple numerical terms as in Figure 5.9 below. This shows a simple one-to-one relationship between the value of a primary relationship and those further down the hierarchy.

Figure 5.9: The value of attachment relationships – Possible assumptions of Attachment Theory

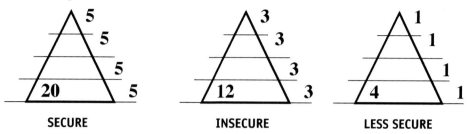

This pattern is, of course, not the only possible pattern that could be deduced from the attachment literature. There is also the possibility, for example, of the patterns shown in Figure 5.10. All these patterns would produce the result that, over all the relationships within any hierarchy of attachment relationships, opportunities for good relationships systematically decrease as the primary relationship becomes less secure.

Figures 5.10: The value of attachment relationships – More possible assumptions of Attachment Theory

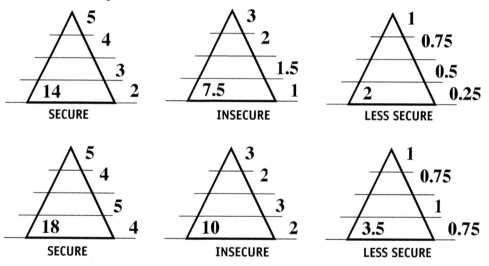

It is possible that assumptions that patterns like these exist may fuel concerns about leaving very young babies with secondary caregivers, particularly if the secondary caregivers are not biologically related. The chief concern seems to revolve around the dual possibility that a secure primary relationship will have less opportunity to form and that, because of this, children will not be able to form secure relationships at any other level in their hierarchy of attachment figures. While these are understandable concerns, they have yet to be fully tested. It seems more likely that valencies of relationships within attachment hierarchies will turn out to be far more labile, dynamic and complex than the conjectured formulae (e.g. Figure 5.11).

Figure 5.11: The value of attachment relationships – Alternative possibilities

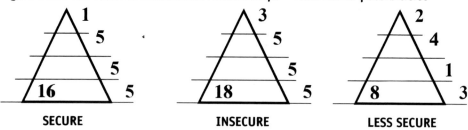

Following this line of argument, there do appear to be indications that secure attachments with other adults beyond the parent-child constellation can be beneficial, for example, grandparents (particularly maternal grandmothers) in situations where marital relationships are strained (Jenkins and Smith 1990). There also appears to be evidence that siblings can play a role as attachment figures, though (unless there are very exceptional rearing conditions such as those reported by Burlingham and Freud (1944) their role is unlikely to assume great importance until later in life (Cicirelli 1995, van IJzendoorn et al. 2000, Bank and Kahn 1997, Berlin and Cassidy 1999).

Evidence from a growing number of studies has shown that, where the relationship between mother and baby is not secure (perhaps due to maternal depression, or due to other difficulties emanating from the mother's history, the child or the social context of parenting), children can form secure relationships with other adults, such as other relatives, foster carers, daycare providers, teachers or therapists (Egeland et al. 1988, Honig 1998, Stovall and Dozier 2000, Cairns 2002). Howes (1999, p.678), for example, describes how daycare providers can be attachment figures, especially if they provide physical and emotional care, continuity or consistency in child's life, and have an emotional investment in the child: "Children with prior relationship difficulties, when moved to settings with sensitive caregivers, appear to be able either to reorganise their attachment representations… or to construct independent relationships based on experiences with the new caregivers." This outcome is obviously less likely in settings where the ratio of children to adults is too high (Goossens and Melhuish 1996).

Perhaps because of the limitations of attachment assessment measures, very little research has yet been carried out to explore how, in cases where there have been initial attachment difficulties between mothers and babies, the presence of another attachment figure who can provide the child with a more secure base impacts on the mother-child relationship. Conceivably, a warm, supportive daycare giver, grandparent, aunt, foster carer, etc. can not only take the strain off the parent but might enable them to re-engage at a later stage. On the other hand, it is also possible that some mothers, resenting the relationship that their child has been able to form with other people, may attempt, more or less subtly and more or less consciously, to undermine the child. The effect of this kind of dynamic on the child might be to increase the likelihood of problem behaviours and to discourage the formation of close relationships. As Rolfe (2004) points out, little is yet known about the conditions that might enable professional caregivers to function most effectively as attachment figures (Constantino and Olesh 1999).

In sum, there is still much to be discovered about how attachments beyond the mother-child relationship influence children's development, how they impact on the most important attachment relationship(s) and how the network of relationships impacts on children's developing sense of self and others.

Cultural considerations

Concern about the sensitivity of attachment assessments to the nature of relationships between children and parents within heterosexual relationships can be and has been extended to other social contexts too. One of the most central questions here has been what the significance of attachment security might be within different cultural contexts. Perhaps even more fundamental though is the question of what the significance of attachment security might be in Western cultures.

Numerous books and websites attest to the growing popularity of the view that creating secure attachments in children is to be aspired towards (e.g. Biringen 2004). The value label itself confers a higher status to secure over insecure patterns. It also firmly dichotomises the relationship between the 60 per cent or so 'secures' and the 40 per cent or so 'insecures' to be found in most populations. The message for parents is clear. If their children are securely attached, they must doing well. If their children are insecurely attached, they are probably doing less well. If their children show signs of disorganised attachment, they are not doing well at all, in fact, they may be child abusers. Taking stock of the fact that in any representative sample the chances are that between ten and fifteen per cent of children will be assessed as disorganised, both parents and people working with parents may feel distinctly worried. It would seem that at least one in ten, if not considerably more, parents are seriously failing their children.

Fortunately, according to popular accounts of Attachment Theory, there are several ways in which parents of insecurely attached children can comfort themselves. First, as they may have had poor experiences of having been parented themselves, they need not feel entirely to blame: at worst they are misguided not wicked and, if they can only be helped to understand themselves better, they may become better parents (Gerhardt 2004). Second, help is at hand: parents can learn how to make their children more secure, though this may require assistance from trained professionals, i.e. psychotherapists or psychoanalysts (Gerhardt 2004) or allegiance to certain doctrines and practices, such as extended lactation, co-sleeping or baby-wearing (this is discussed further in Chapter Six). Third, professionals with understandings based on attachment theory may be better able to help anti-social or otherwise disturbed children: instead of giving children negative labels or being prone to reject or damage children further, they may be able to offer more constructive support. From the children's point of view, therefore, the negative impact of being identified as being insecure could lead to more sympathetic understanding than might otherwise have been the case.

Nevertheless, glamorisation of 'secures' and demonisation of 'insecures' seems to be the rule (this is put rather strongly, to emphasise the value-laden dichotomisation). From most corners of the literature, securely attached children come out the winners and insecurely attached children as losers. Just occasionally there is a dissenting voice, e.g. "I fear we have taken a deficit approach to thinking about 'anxious' attachment... Recognizing the accomplishment and adaptation implied in the non-B patterns and placing them in the ecological context of family, culture and history can help us understand human relationships better and change the negative value placed on Type A and C patterns" (Crittenden and Clausen 2000, p.10). More usually, arguments such as the following are heard: "...it is secure attachment – with all its positive developmental sequelae, including prosocial skills and empathy – that represents the ideal to which we should all aspire in our caregiving of children" (Rolfe 2004, p.187).

Rolfe (2004), like Karen (1994), reaches this conclusion after a careful consideration of the literature on cross-cultural differences in distribution of attachment classification. In an extensive critique of attachment theory which, as Karen (1994) purports, went down 'like a lead balloon' with his senior, Mary Ainsworth, Lamb (Lamb et al. 1985) suggested that attachment patterns might be far more vulnerable to culture than had been previously recognised. Specifically, he suggested that the B pattern, labelled secure in US samples may not signify either normative or necessarily the most adaptive pattern in all cultures. This assertion was based on a perusal of findings from ten studies carried out in six countries, including the US, Japan, Germany, Sweden, Israel and the Netherlands. Figure 5.12 provides an illustration of the variations that Lamb found among these samples although even within countries he pointed to differences between high- and low-income, urban and rural, kibbutzim and town samples. He suggested that the relatively high proportion of avoidant infants in the German samples and the relatively high proportion of ambivalent/resistant infants in the Japanese samples (two of the three had no avoidant infants and all had almost twice as many 'C' babies as in other samples) may reflect differences in normal socialisation processes within each culture. He also raised the possibility that, as Japanese infants were not used to being separated from their mothers due to the prevalence of co-sleeping and baby-carrying in that culture, the Strange Situation may have been not just unfamiliar but terrifying, adding that the procedure had been curtailed in some cases because a number of infants could not tolerate the separation; he explained that these infants had also been classified 'C'.

Figure 5.12: Cultural variations in distributions of attachment patterns (after Lamb et al. 1985)

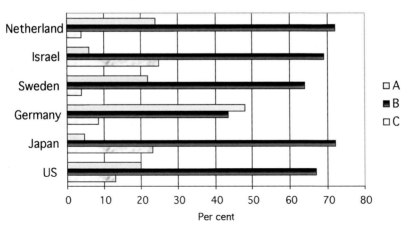

These findings led Lamb, as others were later to do in relation to day care, to ask what the meaning of Strange Situation classifications might be in each culture. Was it possible that, if in some cultures infants become self-reliant earlier than in others, the Strange Situation might simply reflect differential rates of achieving independence? Or did these results prove, as Kagan had argued, that differences in the Strange Situation could largely be accounted for by cultural variations in temperament that had also been revealed in his own research?

The German research team argued against the early maturation interpretation on finding that, although samples within Germany appeared to vary, overall, the B pattern appeared to be associated with better social outcomes than the avoidant pattern, which was found to be linked with similar patterns to those found in the Minnesota sample. Others also flagged up the failure of data to support a temperament explanation.

Nevertheless, even if the secure attachment pattern appears to be associated with benefits in most cultures (and attachment research may have some way to go yet before this conclusion can be said to be sound), it seems important to remember that these findings are only associations. This means that there is no proven causal relationship between secure patterns of attachment and positive outcomes: just as there may be advantages for right-handed people of growing up in societies that are predominantly designed for right-handed people (e.g. finding it easier to use scissors designed for right-handed people, learning to write especially when taught by right-handed teachers, opening doors designed for right-handers, using tin-openers, playing musical instruments, etc.) and disadvantages for left-handed[7] children, so the social environment may advantage 'secures' over 'insecures'. Recalling the teaching practices that were prevalent until only very recently in the UK, where left-handed children were punished for using their left hands to write and so, quite literally handicapped, it seems even more important to take care that Attachment Theory is not used in a way that increases tendencies to simplistically dichotomise and fuel discriminatory practices rather than to recognise, celebrate and support the diversity that is part of our evolutionary heritage.

It has consistently been found that the A and C insecure patterns can predispose towards negative outcomes (e.g. Sroufe 1983, Greenberg 1999). If this is true and if these associations are not due to additional non-identified influences, then it seems important to consider how negative outcomes might arise. Might the advantage for secure attachment be based on discriminatory processes that mitigate against diversity rather than on sounder health grounds? Is it similar to the discrimination so prevalent in many cultures against minority groups (including minority ethnic communities, people with same-sex partnership preferences, people with 'disabilities' or different abilities, etc.). Is the B attachment style really the optimal style in terms of the reproductive fitness of the species? Or is it simply a socially-constructed gimmick equivalent to the leggy ultra-thin fashion model? If so, perhaps it would be valuable to consider the possibility that, as in physical health and ability, some physiques are superior to others for accomplishing some tasks while others are better for others. Ultimately, it seems, the question becomes a philosophical one about the meaning and value of individual variations across species.

Logically, it seems very sensible to have an assortment of types within the communal pool (e.g. tall, short, muscly, lean, plump, spare, long-legged, short-legged, far-sighted, short-sighted, etc.) and all sorts of combinations of such traits. It also seems that it may be more adaptive for the bulk of these types to be 'normally' distributed, that is, for there to be more non-extreme than extreme exemplars. But is this an argument for everyone to aspire towards the middle B bunch in attachment style terms? Or is there not an argument for cherishing the less common variations?

The picture that seems to have emerged, particularly from the adult attachment literature, is that everyone should aspire for a secure attachment style and shun insecure styles. Avoidantly attached individuals are portrayed as cold, dismissive, arrogant, lacking in empathy and subconsciously hostile. Preoccupied individuals are portrayed as needy, emotionally

---

[7] Semantically, too, there are interesting parallels between the value labels used in Attachment Theory and relative values placed on the words 'left' and 'right' (e.g. 'gauche' or 'droit' in French) in many languages.

demanding, shallow, and myopically fixated on past, present and future negative emotional experiences. Disorganised individuals are seen as deeply damaged and traumatised. Secure individuals, by contrast, are everybody's best friend. Corresponding stereotypes of parents emerge from the infant attachment literature, with only parents of securely attached infants being seen as in any way competent as carers.

The overall impression is that only one style is truly adaptive and of value to society. This view seems worth questioning. While it seems quite possible that, in many ways, individuals with secure attachment styles are likely to be more rewarding and easy to be with, it also seems likely that individuals with other organised attachment styles may have an important contribution to make. Just as people who are socially inhibited tend, as adults, to opt for careers suited to their temperament (Kagan et al. 1994), perhaps individuals with avoidant or ambivalent attachment styles find niches that suit their particular adaptive style better. It may be time to re-visit the research bases from which very negative stereotypes have emerged and examine whether it is true that avoidant attachment styles are underpinned by latent hostility, or whether it might be equally possible that (mis)attributions of hostility may cast avoidant individuals, Pygmalion-like, into roles that constrain them even more towards reticence or further increase their tendency to turn to things rather than to people for experiences that do not wound their self-esteem. Not all attachment styles are adaptive and it does seem possible that disorganisation does, in a very substantial proportion of cases, reflect serious difficulties in parent-child relationships. This may also be true for at least some individuals with histories of avoidant or ambivalent attachment. Even so, having identified three different adaptive, organised attachment patterns, it seems important not to assume that the two minority-group styles are completely redundant.

6 | Early experience, infant determinism, social brain development: What do we really know?

"The evidence is that if the first phase of development – that of establishing a relation with one particular person recognized as such – is not satisfactorily completed during the first twelve months or so, there is the greatest difficulty in making it good: the character of the psychic tissue has become fixed (the limit for many children may well be a good deal earlier)."

(Bowlby 1953/1965, p.62)

"A principal variable in the development of each individual personality is, I believe, the pathway along which his attachment behaviour comes to be organized and further that that pathway is determined in high degree by the way his parent-figures treat him, not only during his infancy but throughout his childhood and adolescence as well."

(Bowlby 1981a/1988b, p.59)

The importance of the earliest years

That Bowlby viewed the earliest years of life as important for laying down foundations for later relationship formation is not in doubt. He maintained that patterns of attachment observed in one-year-olds, once developed, tend to persist and explained that "One reason for this is that the way a parent treats a child, whether for better or for worse, tends to continue unchanged. Another is that each pattern tends to be self-perpetuating. Thus a secure child is a happier and more rewarding child to care for and also is less demanding than an anxious one. An anxious ambivalent child is apt to be whiny and clinging; whilst an anxious avoidant child keeps his distance and is prone to bully other children. In both of these last cases the child's behaviour is likely to elicit an unfavourable response from the parent so that vicious circles develop" (Bowlby 1988b, pp. 126-127).

However, while in some of his earlier writings he made very definite assertions about the effects of specific early experiences, such as prolonged separation, on later personality development, as more evidence emerged and he became more and more aware of the complexity of adaptive processes, Bowlby modified his views in order to take better account of research evidence. This shift was reflected particularly clearly in his writings about how critical it was for mother-child attachments to develop in the first two years of life. While, in the 1950s, he maintained that good mothering would be almost useless if a child did not experience it by the age of two-and-a-half (Bowlby 1953/1965), by the 1970s and 1980s, he had accepted that, though it may become steadily more difficult to form secure attachment relationships as children grew older, the sensitive period for formation of attachments might last even into adolescence: "sensitivity in this regard persists during the decade after the fifth birthday" (Bowlby 1973a, p.202).

Meantime, although Bowlby's own understanding, which was always considerable, had deepened and expanded, certain of his more controversial earlier assertions were being adopted, extended and, sometimes, misrepresented by theorists and, more noticeably, by campaigners eager to enlist Attachment Theory to advance their particular causes. These developments, along with the fact that research in the field of Attachment Theory, though prolific, still has much ground left to till, have led to continuing controversy and to a certain degree of confusion about what really was claimed by John Bowlby and, more confusingly, by Attachment Theory.

Hard and soft models of development: Determinists and Constructivists

In this chapter, we explore the question of how important early experience is for later development, what Bowlby's most considered position appeared to be, especially with regard to the link between poor outcomes and early care, and what more recent research appears to have contributed to this debate. The nature and importance of early experience is perhaps one of the most controversial areas within Attachment Theory and one on which theorists of different persuasions diverge most widely. Some, who espouse 'harder' models of Attachment Theory (for ease, we refer to these as 'AT Determinists'), consider the first two or three years of life as a critical period with irreversible consequences for social development. In their view, infants need particular social interactive experiences in the early years in order to develop satisfactorily. Lack of such experiences, for example, not being held in the first few days of life, or not being given enough sensitive and contingent care in the first two years of life, leads to very serious consequences, such as failure of mothers to bond with babies, failure of infants to form secure attachments to caregivers, or failure to develop vital parts of the brain essential for good social functioning.

In another camp are those who hold less deterministic views (we refer to these as 'AT Constructivists'). AT Constructivists may also view the early years as important but only to the extent that they see interactions in the early years as tending to set patterns for later interactions. Unlike Determinists, Constructivists are less inclined to see the early years as the only time that key lessons about social interactions are learned. As the label implies, they conceptualise the infant and growing child as a constructor, playing an active part in engaging with social situations and being highly creative in making sense of social experiences. They do not see the infant as a passive organism programmed only to survive if particular social conditions obtain. They also tend not to ascribe to the view that psychological growth is related to physical growth in a simple one-to-one fashion.

Four recurrent controversial themes and their more recent reincarnations

In this chapter, we look at the arguments of AT Determinists and Constructivists and consider which, if either, view appears best supported by research findings. In doing this, we consider evidence in relation to what we identify as four recurrent controversial themes in the history of Attachment Theory.

The four controversial themes relate to:
1) The effects of early deprivation of maternal care or early prolonged separation on later development
2) The question of whether there is a critical period for the formation of attachment bonds
3) The relationship between physical contact or holding and attachment security
4) The effects of real-life experiences on socio-emotional and personality development

All of these themes except the third arose directly from Bowlby's own work. During his lifetime, as we show in this chapter, in the light of research evidence, Bowlby modified his views in relation to the first two themes. The fourth, which to most readers today will hardly seem controversial at all, was met with great resistance from Bowlby's contemporaries.

In spite of Bowlby's position in relation to the controversial themes, it is remarkable that all have been 're-incarnated' recently in slightly different guises, sometimes alongside claims that Bowlby's early views or 'Attachment Theory' have been vindicated by findings from neuroscience (e.g. Schore 2002, Gerhardt 2005: "Current neurobiology is in fact confirming the insights of attachment thinking first developed by John Bowlby in the 1940s.").

In this chapter, taking each of the four controversial themes in turn, we attempt to establish what the evidential status of Attachment Theory might really be.

Early separation experiences and later development

In his early work on thieves, in his report to the World Health Organization and on the basis of later studies of institutional care, Bowlby (1944, 1951, 1953/1965, 1969/1982) hypothesised that many psychological problems, including delinquency and a range of other negative psychosocial outcomes would be traced to relationships that had been disrupted by prolonged separation (maternal deprivation) in early life (Figure 6.1).

Figure 6.1: The effects of separation on later outcomes for children (Bowlby 1944, 1951, 1953/1965)

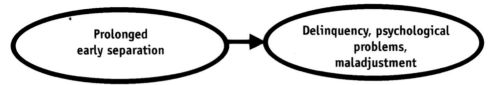

At this point, it seemed that Bowlby had in mind experiences of being separated for fairly substantial lengths of time early in life from mother's care, perhaps due to mothers' incapacitation (e.g. illness, imprisonment, financial circumstances[1]) or for other reasons such as evacuation or the child's illness (it was common at that time for children with infectious diseases such as tuberculosis to be isolated for long periods in sanatoria). It occurred to Bowlby that these separation experiences might present the ideal 'natural experiment' by which he could test his hypotheses about the nature of attachment relationships.

In practice, setting up these 'experiments' proved to be far more complex than Bowlby had initially thought.

While the length of time that a child is physically separated from a parent (if it can be recalled) may be quantifiable, it is often not constituted as a 'clean' break and can be more or less presaged by surrounding events. As a result, this more quantifiable aspect can be both overlapped and over-shadowed by psychological aspects that do not map neatly onto linear time-lines. In addition, separation experiences often involve more than physical separation, for example, they can include a range of other negative or difficult circumstances such as:
- illness and exposure to higher rates of infection
- poor physical care/nutrition
- lack of opportunity to learn (motor, perceptual, cognitive and social skills)
- multiple caregivers
- inconsistent care
- harsh or punitive discipline from substitute caregivers
- emotional neglect
- exposure to aggression from peers.

Research has also indicated that the processes most likely to interfere with children's capacity to sustain or to form meaningful relationships may be those tied to children's beliefs about carers' emotional responsivity or availability rather than the actual physical availability or preparedness to be available on the part of the carer (Sroufe and Waters 1977). These beliefs can be moderated and mediated by other characteristics of the child (e.g. his/her age, temperament and cognitive ability, previous relationship history, the 'chemistry' of the child-caregiver interaction) which are likely to influence both the degree to which key attachment figures can be kept alive in the child's mind (and therefore their capacity to sustain a sense of connectedness when apart) and the child's ability to make subsequent relationships.

---

1 We are not aware of any research on this phenomenon but suspect that sending children to live with wealthier relatives during times of financial hardship, for example, during the period of economic depression in the thirties in the UK, may not have been an unusual way of coping with relatively large families.

Towards the end of his life, Bowlby had modified his earlier views quite considerably, and had begun to realise that separation, in itself, may be less important than the quality of relationships before, during and after separations. This realisation, though, does not seem to have deterred the re-emergence more recently of views very similar to Bowlby's earlier assertions in respect of effects of early experiences of separation on later development (Figure 6.2). In the remainder of this section, we consider these assertions in the light of more recent research on effects of institutional and day care on outcomes for children.

Figure 6.2: The effects of separation on later outcomes for children (Recent re-incarnations of Bowlby's views)

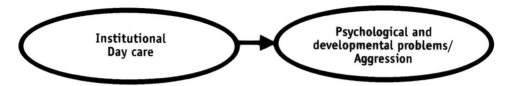

Institutional care

Bowlby's early studies of effects of institutional care drew together findings from many sources. Workers such as Heinicke and Westheimer (1965) and Spitz (1945, 1946, Spitz and Wolf 1946) had observed that infants in institutions appeared, literally, to waste away for no obvious physical reason, despite strenuous efforts to maintain excellent standards of hygiene and physical care and to provide close monitoring. They termed this condition hospitalism or 'marasmus' and ascribed it to lack of maternal care. Though it has also been attributed to lack of physical holding (e.g. Solter 2001), the exact identification of the underlying cause of this mysterious failure to thrive would require an experimental approach in which all potential influences are teased apart, isolated and manipulated in order to assess the independent effect of each on outcomes. For ethical and practical reasons, such experimentation is virtually impossible. Even so, quasi-experimental circumstances can naturally arise that, in some ways at least, mimic the more controlled conditions required for rigorous testing of hypotheses.

In the World Health Organization monograph, remarking upon the deleterious effects of institutional care on children's later social and emotional development, Bowlby issued a special note of warning about children who respond apathetically or with cheerful undiscriminating friendliness, stating that often the children who are most damaged are those who are "quiet, obedient, easy-to-manage, well-mannered and orderly, and physically healthy; many of them even appear happy" (Bowlby 1951, p.25). In later works, too, he drew attention to the tendency of institution-reared children to be indiscriminately friendly and to be capable only of forming superficial relationships (though it is also important to note that he never argued that all institutionalised children would manifest the same behaviours). To lend strength to his arguments, he likened the effect on psychological health of lack of mother's love during infancy to the effect on physical health of lack of vitamins. This rather reductive but compelling metaphor has become known as one of the chief conclusions that Bowlby drew from his consideration of research on the effects of institutional care.

Needless to say, his conclusions did not go unchallenged. One of Bowlby's most strident critics was Michael Rutter (e.g. Rutter 1972a, 1972b, 1981) who, reflecting more recently on the period from the 1950s to the 1970s, argued that it had become fashionable at that time to over-attribute the role of environmental influences on development and that, "there was a serious neglect of the need to provide rigorous tests of the environmental mediation hypothesis... and a failure to appreciate the substantial continuities in environmental disadvantage and, therefore, an exaggeration of the extent to which persistent sequelae derived from the early environment, rather than from continuing psychosocial adversity" (Rutter 2002, p.9).

Gradually, in light of research on the aetiology of delinquency (e.g. Rutter and Giller 1983, Farrington 1986) as well as on adoption and fostering (e.g. Hodges and Tizard 1989, Clarke and Clarke 1976), Bowlby realised that his earlier account might stand in need of modification and, indeed, that it had sometimes been taken more literally than he had intended. In his later writings, he acknowledged the complex interplay of environmental and individual effects and the likelihood that multiple influences were responsible for anti-social behaviour. He also recognised a role for high-quality substitute care and for a network of support, particularly in situations where the principal carer was indisposed: "It is an excellent plan to accustom babies and small children to being cared for now and then by someone else – father, for instance, or granny, or some other relation or neighbour. Then if a mother is suddenly taken ill or there is some other family emergency, the child will be used to someone else looking after him and will not be as frightened as he might be with a stranger. And in this way mothers can have some freedom too." (Bowlby, 1958b, p.6). However, he did not shift from his original opinion of the importance of sensitive, responsive care, of the difficulty of providing this within an institutional setting, and of the likelihood that prolonged institutional care would seriously limit the chances that children might be able to form meaningful relationships.

According to Rutter (2002), it has only been recognised relatively recently that adoption studies can provide suitable 'natural experimental' conditions for hypothesis-testing (though Bowlby's associates might suggest that he had long been aware of this potential). Comparisons can be made of outcomes for children with similar post-adoption experiences but with differing lengths of pre-adoption experience or different types of pre-adoption experience (e.g. Duyme et al. 1999, Gunnar et al. 2003, Ames 1997, Ames and Chisholm 2001). They can also be made between children with pre-adoption experiences of extremely poor institutional care and those with better quality home-based foster care (e.g. Roy et al. 2000). They can be made between children with and those without experiences of early institutional care (e.g. Rutter and Quinton 1984, Verhulst 2000a, 2000b, Cederblad et al. 1999, Zeanah et al. 2003). And they can be made between children restored or not restored to the care of their biological parents (e.g. Hodges and Tizard 1989, Rutter et al. 1990). As a result, a huge literature now exists documenting outcomes from such comparisons. These reports tend to converge on the opinion that the incidence of social, emotional, relational and behavioural difficulties among children who have experienced extended periods of poor quality institutional care is, rather unsurprisingly, considerably higher than among children with no such history. Somewhat more surprisingly, though, they also point to the fact that in most samples there is a substantial proportion of children who appear to be relatively resistant to even the most severe conditions.

These studies have tended to leave certain questions unanswered concerning effects of timing on outcomes, for example, whether later experiences of institutional care might be more or less damaging than earlier experiences, how much time spent in poor-quality institutions might be needed to influence later development or whether there might be critical periods during the lifespan of most infants when being in a poor-quality institution is likely to inflict more lasting damage. Drawing upon evidence from studies of socially deprived animals, deterministic attachment theorists have hypothesised that deprivation of one-to-one care in the first years of life inevitably compromises brain development (Schore 1994, Gerhardt 2004). Gerhardt has further claimed that recent evidence from studies of Romanian orphans shows that "those who were cut off from close bonds with an adult by being left in their cots all day, unable to make relationships, had a virtual black hole where their orbitofrontal cortex should be" (Gerhardt 2004, p.38). In the following section, we examine the evidence for this alarming assertion.

Orphan studies

Just as Bowlby and Spitz attempted to document effects of institutional care in the 1950s, more recently institutions in Russia, China, Romania, and elsewhere, have become a focus for attention. The design of these studies is as problematic as it ever was: not only are records of children's day-to-day experiences in the institution rarely available but, usually, there is little information about their precise age or physical condition on admission, parental characteristics, or the circumstances surrounding their births. It may be safe to assume that these institutions often offer conditions of global deprivation which "means that children experience social, perceptual, nutritional, medical, and intellectual deprivation simultaneously" (Ames and Chisholm 2001, p.129) but, as Ames and Chisholm point out, it is not possible to pinpoint which of these types of deprivation might produce differences between institution- and family-reared children. There is also some evidence that, even in conditions of severe global deprivation, individual children can be singled out for special treatment or favouritism by staff (perhaps due to particularly good looks, ease of management, easy temperament) and that this, to some extent, can spare them from some of the worst effects (Ames 1997).

The author's observations of an institution near the front line in 1996 post-war Bosnia illustrate this. Conditions in this institution closely resembled those described by others elsewhere in Eastern Europe (e.g. Johnson 2000). In some wards, frail old people lay passively alongside each other. In another, men who were described as violent and dangerous were made to sit still all day on low benches against walls as white-coated guardians with long sticks stood by. Other wards housed babies and very young children varying in age from a few months to several years. The range of clinical conditions represented was enormous and included those with no obvious medical condition, those with skin problems, a baby with very mild Downs syndrome (never visited by her parents who were doctors), and children with disabilities such as epilepsy, acromegaly, hydrocephalus, gross physical deformity, etc. From the description provided by Johnson (2000), it seems that this mix may have been typical of institutionalised children.

Metal cots with narrow vertical bars and wide gaps were jammed up against each other. Though the sides of cots were high, some of the older children were large enough to climb over. Arms could easily stretch from one cot into another. Only a few children had acquired language and those who had had little opportunity to use it. At any one time, there was a ratio of one care staff to a minimum of 20 children and an almost complete absence of evidence of toys or of playful stimulation.

Perhaps most striking was the fact that the children were not socially isolated. On the contrary, provoking a reaction from a defenceless infant in a neighbouring cot was a distinct option for some of the larger children. The chances of a guardian noticing a bit of aggression were slim. It was as if some crazy scientist had set this up as the human equivalent of Seligman's learned helplessness experiments. But these were not dogs that had been conditioned not to expect to be able to avoid electric shocks in a shuttle box. They were babies who may have learned that the semi-animate body in the next-door cot made noises if it was prodded or stared at hard enough, or who may have learned to shut down their responses in order to block out their awareness of constant unpredictable threats or even persecution, perhaps, from 'the monster' next door. They were not the equivalent of young kittens brought up in the dark with no social contact whatsoever. This kind of institutional care was very different. These children were clearly at risk of emotional neglect but, perhaps equally importantly, they were even more at risk of experiencing unusual levels of unpleasant, intrusive, non-reciprocal and non-reciprocatable social exchanges.

In the 'natural experimental' conditions within institutions, there is almost never any scope for rigorous testing of causal hypotheses. As a result, it is difficult to test theories about critical periods of development. This would require several samples of children matched on indices of physical and psychosocial health status at birth and a design in which length of time spent in institutional care, conditions within the institutions and age at entry and exit from institutional care were controlled. Without this kind of design, aspects such as length of time and age are likely to be confounded and this will limit the kinds of conclusion that can be drawn. It may be safe to conclude that the development of social skills in children who have spent 100 per cent of their time in very poor-quality institutional care might be affected in a negative way. It is unlikely to be safe to conclude that the negative effects on development of spending the first months of life in very poor quality institutional care constitute evidence for a critical period for social development. Such an interpretation clearly constitutes an extrapolation beyond the data given. Nevertheless, these considerations have not deterred some commentators from making this claim in relation to Romanian orphans. Other researchers' conclusions, though, as we show in the next section, tend to be rather more carefully qualified.

Romanian orphans: early reports and the UK study

In the wake of the Ceausescu regime which ended with the execution of the Ceausescus in 1989, groups of researchers based in England and Canada have been tracking the progress of infants adopted at different ages from Romanian orphanages during 1990 and 1991 (sample details are given in Table 6.1).

Table 6.1: Sample details in British and Canadian Romanian Adoption Studies

UK (ERA Study)	CANADA
Rutter, O'Connor and the ERA team (1998)	Ames (1997)
58 0-6-months instit. care 59 7-24 months instit. care 48 24-42 months instit. care cf 52 UK-born adoptees	43 8+ months instit. care 43 matched Canadian-born non-adoptees 43 matched Early adopted (< 4 months)

In the first reports of the Canadian study (Ames and Carter 1992, Chisholm et al. 1995, Morison et al. 1995, Ames 1997, Fisher et al. 1997), researchers compared two groups of Romanian adoptees (one group of 46 children who had spent at least eight months in an orphanage and a second group of 29 children who were adopted before the age of four months and who had no experience of institutional care) with a group of 46 never-institutionalised non-adopted children born in Canada. Across these three groups, 29 children were matched by age and sex and, as some children were lost to the study, others were later added in.

Ames and Carter (1992) reported that institutionalised infants had spent at least 20 hours a day without attention.

At the time of adoption, 59 per cent of adoptees were below the fifth percentile for weight (Ames 1997) and were shorter than children in the other groups; many showed signs of developmental delay and most had major health problems such as anaemia, intestinal parasites and hepatitis B (most but not all of these conditions were cured by the time of the second assessment). Many of the children with longer experiences of institutional care had eating difficulties and showed signs of behavioural disturbance (their behaviour included stereotypies such as rocking, engaging in ritualistic actions, etc.).

Assessments were carried out when children had spent 11 months in their adoptive homes and again when they were aged about four-and-a-half years. Differences were found between adoptive homes and on children's performance according to their institutional experience: adoptive homes containing later-adopted children tended to be the least stimulating or supportive (and were probably those who faced the most serious challenges) while, at four-and-a-half, the mean IQ of later-adopted children was only 90, as compared with 109 in the Canadian born children and 98 in the early-adopted group. The lowest scores on the Stanford Binet IQ test were associated with children who had spent more than two years in an institution and with families that had adopted two children at the same time. On second assessment, later-adopted children continued to show more behavioural disturbance than children in either of the other two groups and were rated as having more externalising problems on a Child Behaviour Check List (though this difference was not significant in comparison with the other adopted children).

Since, at four-and-a-half, the range of IQ scores among later-adopted orphans was wide, from 65 to 127, with the lowest scores being associated with older children who had spent the longest time in institutional 'care', it is important not to over-generalise these findings. Ames (1997) also pointed to the role that adoptive family circumstances might play in helping later-adopted children to increase their potential and suggested that more serious problems tended to be associated with lower income families, families that had adopted two children at once and families where only the father had visited Romania during the adoption proceedings (i.e. the mother was not involved when the child was selected).

The British researchers (Rutter et al. 1998, Rutter 2000, O'Connor et al. 2003, Rutter et al. 2004) drew upon a total sample of 324 children adopted into the UK from Romania between February 1990 and September 1992. They used a stratified random sampling process to identify three groups of Romanian adoptees (those adopted under six months of age, those adopted between 6 and 24 months, and those adopted from 24 to 42 months). Although 165 children were identified in this way, some were adopted from a home setting and later reports focused on the 144 who were reared in institutions (45 adopted under six months, 54 at six to 24 months and 45 between 24 and 42 months). The 52 comparison group UK adoptees had been placed for adoption before the age of six months and none had experienced abuse or neglect or institutional care. By contrast, like the Canadian sample of Romanian orphans, most of the Romanian adoptees in the British sample were severely malnourished (O'Connor et al. 2000, Rutter et al. 1998): more than half weighed less than the third percentile of weight for their age; three-fifths performed at a developmental level considered to reflect severe mental retardation.

Adoptive families were described as mainly middle-class and better educated than the general UK population. There were demographic differences due to UK fostering and adoption policies: parents who had adopted from Romania tended to be about two years older, were more likely to have older biologically-related children (33 versus 2 per cent) and were less likely to have adopted before (4 versus 48 per cent).

Follow-up assessments of children were made when the children were aged four, six and again at age eleven (though reports of eleven year assessments are not yet published). Results on a measure of attachment at age four suggested that length of institutional care was associated with disturbed attachment patterns. O'Connor et al. (2003) carried out a modified separation-reunion assessment (Marvin and Rutter 1994, cited in O'Connor 2003; Cassidy and Marvin 1992) on a home visit to 58 (47 per cent female) children placed for adoption by the age of six months, 59 (56 per cent female) placed between six and 24 months, and a comparison group of 52 (35 per cent female) UK-born children adopted before the age of six months. Details of the procedure are shown in Table 6.2.

Table 6.2: Separation-reunion procedure used at age four (O'Connor et al. 2003)

EPISODE	DESCRIPTION	LENGTH
1	Semi-structured play (parent and child with Etch-a-Sketch toy)	10 mins
2	Researcher/Stranger takes child to another room, without parent, and measures child's weight, height and head circumference	10 mins
3*	Reunion: Child rejoins parent	3 mins
4	Parent leaves room. Child is administered a number of standardised measures	30 mins
5*	Parent returns	3 mins

* Researcher is in room, filming reunions and "busying herself with paperwork"

This assessment yields information about the patterns of attachment shown in Table 6.3. An additional judgement was also made of 'normative' children's reunion behaviour using a system developed by Greenberg and Marvin (1982), primarily because, as the Strange Situation was developed on the basis of observations of children whose rearing environments were more congenial, it was considered that there was a need to extend the classification to include a wider range of behavioural sequences, for example, unexplained switches from stranger approach to avoidance, or vice versa, or confused sequences of behaviours with no discernible pattern.

A further rating of 'disinhibited' attachment behaviour was made on the basis of a semi-structured interview in which children's behaviour towards parent and other adults in familiar and unfamiliar contexts were assessed. Disinhibited attachment behaviour was indexed by:
1) Definite lack of discrimination between adults
2) Clear indications of readiness to go off with a stranger
3) Definite lack of checking back with the parent in anxiety-provoking situations.

Table 6.3: Separation-reunion classifications (Cassidy and Marvin 1992)

PATTERN	DESCRIPTION
Secure	Children use parent as a secure base for exploration, show a positive, engaged and open style of verbal and nonverbal interaction, and little or no insecure behaviour on reunion
Insecure-avoidant	Children typically downplay involvement with parent, do not seek comfort when distressed, minimal/impersonal conversation, gaze minimal/fleeting, tendency to neutral affect, often clear evidence of affect inhibition
Insecure-dependent/ ambivalent	Children exhibit either a passive, helpless or immature style or an angry, resistant, petulant manner of interaction with parent, especially on separation and reunion
Insecure-disorganised	Children do not use either secure or insecure strategies; instead they show disordered behavioural sequences such as including severe confusion, apprehension, depression or withdrawal on reunion
Insecure-disorganised-controlling	Children attempt to control the parent or structure and organise attachment-caregiving interactions in a way that suggests role reversal
Insecure-Other	Children do not appear secure but behaviour does not fit into any other 'insecure' category

Each of these indicators was rated on a three-point scale (0 = no evidence; 1 = some/mild evidence; 2 = marked/pervasive evidence) and scores over all three indicators were summed. Severe disinhibition was identified as a total score of four or above.

Among all Romanian adoptees, patterns of attachment for children who had been reared in institutions differed from those of home-reared children, with institution-reared children showing considerably more disturbed patterns of attachment (Figure 6.3). For this reason, the small sub-group of home-reared children was excluded from the remainder of analyses reported.

Figure 6.3: Patterns of attachment among Romanian adoptees (O'Connor et al. 2003)

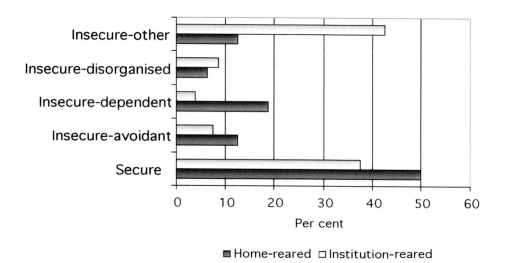

In the remaining analyses, comparisons were made of institution-reared children grouped according to age of placement. At age four, as later at age six, duration of institutionalisation was found to be associated with lower rates of all organised forms of attachment (secure and insecure) and with higher rates of atypical attachment, most particularly 'insecure-other' classification. At age four, O'Connor et al. (2003, p.33) noted that children classified as 'insecure-other' tended to approach the stranger and attempted to maintain contact with her almost the same extent as to their parent. They also commonly showed "extreme forms of emotional overexuberance, nervous excitement, silliness, coyness, and excessive playfulness more typical of a much younger child". Whether this kind of behaviour is similar to the over-exaggerated, excessive sociability observed in some small children during the initial phase of separation (Robertson and Robertson 1976; Barrett 1997) is unclear. If so, this would suggest that, even in children who have been subjected to prolonged severe early deprivation, some vestiges may remain of the experience-expectant social orienting behaviour that may possibly be associated with a critical period in social development.

At age six, general cognitive abilities were measured using the McCarthy Scale of Children's Ability (GCI: this provides information about verbal, mathematical, perceptual and memory ability) and attachment behaviour was assessed using a semi-structured interview measure devised by the Maudsley team (validated against the modified separation-reunion procedure used when the children were four). Rutter et al. (2004) again reported that 'disinhibited attachment' was both more common among Romanian adoptees and that it was associated with duration of institutional deprivation. They noted that it also appeared to be linked with other distinctive behaviours, including an apparent inability to pick up on cues for socially acceptable behaviour (e.g. noticing others' discomfort or disapproval), quasi-autistic features (e.g. markedly limited and rather obsessional interests, behavioural stereotypies, etc.), and problems with attention and over-activity that appeared to stem mainly from the challenge of dealing with group situations and to be more closely associated with patterns of social disinhibition than with cognitive ability or impairment.

By age six, the Romanian orphans who had been adopted before the age of six months were performing very much like the UK adopted children on tests of psychological adjustment and cognitive ability, and this was so whether or not they had shown signs of severe subnutrition. Indeed, catch-up was quite remarkable among the Romanian children as a whole: by age six they had almost caught up to UK population means on cognitive tests, weight and head circumference. However, looking separately at the children who had spent more than six months in severely depriving institutional care, a very different picture emerged: whether or not these children had been severely malnourished when adopted, they were performing significantly worse at age six on cognitive tests. The children who were performing least well were those who had spent more than two years in institutions and who had experienced severe malnutrition. There was a positive correlation between head circumference and scores on cognitive tests and these differences were not thought to reflect differences between adoptive parents in level of education.

Overall, the findings of the study of Romanian orphans adopted to the UK seem to point to the possibility that conditions in the Romanian institutions may, like those in the Bosnian institution, have encouraged some Romanian orphans, particularly those with greater exposure to institutions, to retract from close social interaction. Further, it seemed that they may have retained elements of these defensive strategies even when they were no longer appropriate, perhaps much in the way that a dog might limp long after an injury has healed or that a sensation of pain will persist long after its function as a signal of injury has become redundant. On the other hand, a number of children also appeared to engage in displays of rather 'over-the-top' pro-social behaviour that could also be deemed superficial, immature or otherwise inappropriate. One could speculate that the function of this kind of behaviour may be to signal that no assistance is needed or, alternatively, it may constitute an attempt to ward off an attack by flagging up 'no foe' status. Speculation aside, the ecological and psychological significance of both kinds of behaviour seems currently unclear. These findings do not appear to provide evidence that prolonged, very poor quality institutional care precludes the formation of secure attachments. Indeed, a substantial proportion of the children with this experience did appear able to form secure attachments to their adoptive parents. Nevertheless, as would perhaps be expected, the kinds of attachment relationship that they made appeared to be qualitatively different from those of home-reared children. What the implications of these differences may be for longer term outcomes remains to be seen.

Later reports from Canada

Table 6.4 gives details of some of the later reports from the study of Romanian children adopted to Canada.

Table 6.4: Later Canadian reports of Romanian adoptees

Chisholm 1998	Marcovitch et al. 1997	Gunnar et al. 2003	Chugani et al. 2001
43 8+ months instit. care	19 >6 months instit. care	29 Canadian-born	10 Romanian children, no sample details given
43 matched Canadian-born non-adoptees	37 <6 months instit. care	16 early-adopted	
30 matched Early-adopted (< 4 months)	cf 38 Canadian-born non-adoptees	22 late-adopted	cf 'normal' adults and children with epilepsy

From the first reports, a picture similar to that in the UK arose. Ames and Chisholm (2001) observed that just over one-third (37 per cent) of children with extensive institutional experience (more than eight months) were securely attached when assessed at age four-and-a-half. They noted that "This would certainly argue against Goldfarb's (1945, 1947) conclusion that early deprivation of the opportunity for a close contact with a specific caregiver necessarily produces permanent damage of the capacity to attach later" (Ames and Chisholm 2001, p.137).

However, in the two comparison groups of children,[2] secure attachment patterns were far more common and appeared to resemble distributions in other non-clinical samples: 58 per cent of non-adopted Canadian-born children were classified as securely attached and two-thirds (66 per cent) of the Romanian children who had been adopted before they were four months old were classified as securely attached. Among the remainder, distributions of 'typical' insecure patterns (ambivalent/resistant or avoidant) were similar (30 per cent of both samples of Romanian children with institutional experience were assessed as having 'insecure typical' patterns compared with 35 per cent of the Canadian-born children).

The main difference therefore between Romanian children with extensive institutional experience and the other two groups lay in the incidence of 'atypical insecure' attachment: only four per cent of early-adopted Romanian children and seven per cent of never-adopted Canadian children exhibited these patterns compared with one-third (33 per cent) of the later-adopted Romanian children. While it is possible that the pre-school attachment measure (Crittenden 1992) may not tap exactly the same construct as the Strange Situation and it is certain that Crittenden's method of classifying insecure attachment departs from the system developed by Mary Main, Ames and Chisholm (2001) propose that the high incidence of 'atypical insecure' attachments found in late-adopted Romanian children would rarely be found in a non-clinical sample, may have a lot in common with patterns of disorganised attachment found in maltreated children and is very likely to be a risk factor for the development of psychopathology.

Summing up their assessment of whether there might be a sensitive period for the development of attachment relationships, Ames and Chisholm (2001) concluded that, as attachment patterns in early-adopted children and non-adopted children appeared similar, this seemed to support Bowlby's notion that the first few months of life were not critical for the development of attachment. They also concluded that they had not found any evidence of an upper age limit for the development of attachment but admitted that the nature of their sample was not ideal for testing a sensitive period hypothesis (being as only five children had spent more than 39 months in institutional care and five is too small a sample). However, after consideration of data from other studies, they concluded that "In summary, studies are fairly consistent in indicating that after children have been in institutions for many months with little or no opportunity to attach, they do show the capacity to attach to their adoptive parents. Such attachments may, however, be slow to develop, and a higher proportion of previously institutionalised children than family-reared children form insecure attachments, with some of those insecure attachments taking forms that are unusual in family-reared children" (Ames and Chisholm 2001, p.141).

Another group of Canadian researchers also attempted to assess patterns of attachment among a separate group of Romanian adoptees (Marcovitch at al. 1997) using the Cassidy

---

2   Children in each of the comparison groups were described as individually matched by age and sex to children in the group of later-adopted children though, as group sizes were not equal, it is not quite clear how this was achieved for the early-adopted children.

and Marvin system for attachment classification when children were aged between three to five years. They compared 37 children who had spent less than six months and 19 children who had spent more than six months in institutional care with 38 healthy four-year-olds. No significant differences in patterns of attachment were found between the two groups of children with experience of institutional care and no relationship between length of time spent in institutional care and attachment security. Combining results for all children with experience of institutional care showed that significantly more of these children were insecurely attached (67 versus 50 per cent) and that they were more likely to show an atypically insecure pattern (42 versus 15 per cent were judged to have atypical 'controlling or other' styles which have been described as approximate to the 'disorganised' pattern identified by Mary Main). Interpretation of data from this study is complicated by the fact that some of the adopted children were not placed in institutions at birth. This, combined with unequal numbers of children in each group, the type of assessment, the rather wide range of ages at which children were tested and the associated large variation in length of time since adoption all make it difficult to draw any firmer conclusion from this study other than the rather obvious one that being placed in an institution is likely to make for less secure attachment relationships. Longer-term follow-up is needed to address the question of whether early disruption makes for permanent relationship problems.

Stress responses in Romanian adoptees

An interest in discovering whether severe stress in the early years of life might permanently affect the way that stress response mechanisms develop and operate has been the focus of a group of researchers led by Megan Gunnar. This group of researchers has been investigating relationships between chronic stress (induced through 'natural' events such as day care or institutional care experiences) and later difficulties such as problems with impulse control, attention, concentration or emotional self-regulation.

Very poor-quality institutional life means that most children's physical and psychological systems will have been subjected to chronic stress (the exceptions perhaps being those who have been treated as favourites). These deprivations usually mean that it is not uncommon for children who have grown up in institutions to show signs of severe malnutrition. They will be less well physically developed than similar-aged well-tended children and this can show in various ways, including head circumference, height, weight, coordination or motor ability; some may also have poor perceptual abilities due to non-diagnosed perceptual problems (eyesight, hearing, etc.). The physical manifestations of neglect are likely also to be reflected in the ways that the children think, feel, see, hear and interact socially.

Many controlled experiments on the effects of various sorts of deprivation have been systematically studied in animals. Some of these experiments have used methods such as magnetic resonance imaging and PET scans that have given access to an understanding of biochemical and electrophysiological processes. They have also used more crude methods involving sacrifice, dissection and examination of animals' brains and other tissues. This kind of invasive, controlled intervention and measurement is not permissible on a routine basis in humans and, until the advent of less invasive technology, has been almost exclusively limited to the study of individuals with severe pathological conditions.

However, in the last decades, cortisol assay has, as mentioned in the previous chapter, become available and slightly more popular in research with children. Collecting salivary cortisol is a relatively straightforward task though analysis is still fairly costly and, unless the collection is done carefully, the data that is obtained can be very difficult to interpret. Simply taking samples of salivary cortisol at one point in the day (e.g. the afternoon) is unlikely to provide sufficient information about baseline levels (patterns of cortisol variability that are characteristic of individual children) or about diurnal variability. Also, taking samples without regard for the physical state of the child (e.g. whether they are tired, hungry or ill) will introduce extraneous sources of variability that make for 'noisy' data (that is, data that reflects influences that the study was not designed to measure). For these reasons, it is usual to obtain morning and afternoon samples of salivary cortisol over several days in order to get as accurate as possible a picture of how children are coping. The normal diurnal pattern is of highest levels of circulating cortisol in the mornings followed by a gradual decline over the course of the day.

Gunnar's team (Gunnar et al. 2003) studied daily cortisol patterns in a subsample of Romanian orphanage-reared children drawn from the British Columbia sample (Ames' study, mentioned above). The subsample included 16 early-adopted children (with four months or less orphanage experience), 22 later-adopted children (with eight months or more orphanage experience) and 29 Canadian-born family-reared non-adoptees. Children's salivary cortisol was collected while children were at home at three times during three days: on waking, at noon, and before bed. The team reported that, although all children showed the normal decline in cortisol levels over the day, the later-adopted children had higher cortisol levels across all time points. Further, cortisol levels were correlated with length of time spent in institutions and children who had spent more than two years had substantially higher cortisol levels than any of the other children. Gunnar also reported that children with secure attachments, even if they had spent a lot of time in institutional care, appeared to have cortisol levels that were similar to home-reared children. However, she added a caution about the very small sample, the impossibility of knowing whether this was a reliable or generalisable result and the need for far more research before jumping to any unsound conclusions: "While the animal research would suggest that early privation may have long-term impact on stress-sensitive physiological systems, we do not know that this will be true in children. The data that we have to date, while consistent with research on rats and monkeys, are too meager to form firm conclusions" (Gunnar 2003, p.4).

On the basis of these studies, it would seem that firm conclusions about the long-term effects of even the most terrible institutional conditions on children may be inadvisable at this point in the history of research. Gunnar points out that it is well-known that outcomes for humans are often far more diverse than for animals. Few animals moved from the laboratory where they were so stressed into a therapeutic social situation and, in addition, while the early history of laboratory-stressed animals is known intimately, very little is known about the early history of institution-reared children (i.e. what it was that prevented their parents from caring for them, how stressful the prenatal environment was, whether teratogenic substances such as drugs, pollutants, may have impacted on foetal development, or the nature of the children's experience in the institution). Until more is known about these aspects, it is not wise to assume that children and laboratory-tested animals will share identical fates or that all institution-reared children are likely to be socially defective. Such assumptions may, Pygmalion-like, be extremely detrimental to vulnerable children who may *(who knows?)* turn out to be highly sensitive to others' expectations.

"Virtual black holes where their brains should be"

The source of this alarming statement is purported to be a report by Chugani and colleagues (2001) of PET (positron emission tomography) imaging using 2-deoxy-2-[^{18}F] fluoro-glucose (FDG) in ten Romanian orphans, six boys and four girls. By mapping patterns of glucose uptake, Chugani et al. compared patterns of brain activity in this 'group' of ten children with that in 17 'normal' adults and seven children with uni-lateral temporal lobe epilepsy. They produced images showing that brain activity in the orphans was less than in the other participants in specific parts of the brain. Darker coloration indicated lower activity (NB, *not* no activity and NO black holes). They drew the following conclusion: "In summary, children exposed to early social deprivation show long-term cognitive and behavioral deficits, associated with dysfunction (indicated by decreased glucose utilization) in a group of limbic brain regions known to be activated by stress and damaged by prolonged stress. We suggest that chronic stress endured in Romanian orphanages during infancy in these children resulted in altered development of these limbic structures and that altered functional connections in these circuits may represent the mechanism underlying persistent behavioral disturbances in the Romanian orphans" (Chugani et al. 2001, p.1300).

This suggestion can clearly only stand as a hypothesis to be tested. Data from ten children about whom no sampling details are provided can in no way constitute conclusive evidence of any kind (although some information is given about exclusion criteria, no explanation is offered as to how these ten children were selected from a larger pool of children). Chugani et al. (2001) do give the following information: the children had a mean age of 8.83 years at testing (the youngest was 7.1 and the oldest 11.3 years), they had been transferred from hospital to institutions at approximately 4-6 weeks of age, had been in an orphanage for between 16 months and seven-and-a-half years and had been in their adoptive homes between 15 months and nine years and four months; in addition, they had not all been in the same institution and historical data on the children and the institutions was sparse; at the time of adoption all the children were small for their age, malnutrition was suspected in nine of ten children, five had evidence of having been physically harmed (scars), three were left-handed, all were severely developmentally delayed. No information is given about the explanation given to children for the study and no details of the language in which tests were carried out (though since only one child was speaking at the time of adoption, it could be assumed that the tests were not carried out in Romanian). It is difficult to know what sense the children might have made of the tests and no details are given of children's emotional states during testing. It seems possible that the children may have found the test situation extremely frightening.

Chugani et al. argue that it is reasonable to compare the performance of ten children (average age nearly nine) with adults (nine men and eight women with an average age of 27.6 years) because ethical constraints prohibit obtaining this information from healthy children, general patterns of glucose uptake are usually fixed by age one and are similar to those seen in adulthood. Nevertheless, it may have been useful to have been given more details about individual differences between the ten children before merging them together. Given the wide variety of age, institutional and adoptive experiences among so small a sample, the practice of lumping them all together seems likely to have the potential to produce a rather unusual group picture. Also, the logic of comparing the orphans' brain activity with that of the non-affected lobe of a small number of older children (average age 10.74 years) suffering from unilateral epilepsy did not seem clear, although the authors claimed that the patterns of orphan brain activity differed from those of epileptic children in the same way as they differed from adults. Not knowing enough about this field, we are not in a position to comment further at this stage.

As Gunnar advised in relation to her own work, it seems distinctly premature to base any firm conclusions on the findings of this study: "The psychobiological science of early deprivation in human children is just beginning" (Gunnar 2003, p.4). The biggest concern perhaps is an ethical one. Given such a small sample and the likelihood of any generalisable results, is there any real justification for subjecting healthy but already severely traumatised children to this kind of invasive procedure? The next most serious concern is the use that might be made of conjectures about underlying brain processes in young children who have already endured major challenges in their early years and who are likely to need considerable understanding if their physical and psychic wounds are to be allowed time to heal. How helpful is it to describe these children as having virtual holes where their brains ought to be? Cognitive neuroscientists have only just begun to have access to the tools that will enable them to interrogate let alone to answer questions about relationships between patterns of brain activity and social behaviour. Perhaps the biggest problem for non-neuroscientists and policy-makers is to discover who to believe?

Further studies of Romanian orphans in Bucharest

Taking stock of evidence from the many studies of Eastern European orphans (e.g. Johnson 2000, the UK and the Canadian studies), earlier reports of effects of institutional care (e.g. Goldfarb 1945, Dennis and Najarian 1957, Provence and Lipton 1962, Tizard and Hodges 1978) and Chugani et al.'s work,[3] in 2000 Charles Zeanah and his team embarked on a more carefully controlled study of Romanian orphans. Their aim was (and is) to collect longitudinal data from three groups of Romanian children: a group in institutional care (IG), a group randomly assigned to foster care (FCG), and a never institutionalised comparison group (NIG). They have been particularly interested in gathering information about brain electrophysiology though have also measured children's performance on a wide range of tests of physical, social, emotional and cognitive abilities (including three assessments of attachment – Strange Situation, Attachment Q-Set, Disturbances of Attachment, temperament, social communication and interaction, behaviour problems, emotion and face recognition, attention, language and cognitive ability, physical development and the nature of the caregiving environment). So far, reports have been published in respect of brain electrophysiology and of recognition of facial expressions of emotion.

The EEG report (Marshall et al. 2004) describes differences in patterns of brain activity between 104 children in six institutions in Bucharest (the IG group) and 46 never-institutionalised children (the NIG group) when children were aged between nine and 31 months (mean age for IG children = 22.4 months; mean age for NIG children = 21.0 months). They found between-group differences both on measures of absolute power, on distributions of relative power within the power spectrum and on hemispheric asymmetries. Specifically, IG children showed more low-frequency (theta) power in posterior scalp regions and less high-frequency (alpha and beta) power particularly in frontal and temporal sites. Patterns of EEG activation in IG children were also more symmetric across hemispheres, particularly across temporal lobes.

In discussing what these differences might signify, the authors described the findings for IG children as being consistent with patterns of EEG activity in children who have learning disorders as well as with patterns found in children exposed to extreme environmental challenges. They explain that increased relative theta power and decreased relative alpha

---

3   About Chugani et al.'s report, Zeanah et al. (2003, p. 888) comment, "Collectively, results from this study, the first of its kind, points to the serious neurobiological sequelae of early and prolonged institutionalisation... Unfortunately, this study suffers from the same shortcomings as other postadoption studies noted earlier, making it unclear to whom the results generalize."

and beta power have been associated with disorders of attention and impulse control (as in attention deficit hyperactivity disorder/ADHD) and add that the pattern of EEG activity in IG children bore some resemblance to that found for ADHD children (though it was not exactly the same). They also raise the possibility of some similarities between patterns of EEG in IG children and those found for children with autism, and for children exposed to extreme poverty or other environmental risks.

With regard to the relative absence of right hemisphere asymmetry in IG children, Marshall et al. (2004) point out that these patterns of EEG activation are not easy to interpret: they bear some resemblance to infants of depressed mothers and to patterns in autistic children but they also differ in ways that may be important. Marshall et al. also wonder whether the EEG results might reflect unusual patterns of approach and withdrawal to unfamiliar objects/situations which are prevalent in the IG group. However, these vary so widely within the group that the overall group pattern may not actually mirror individual idiosyncrasies. This seems to suggest that an individual case study approach might be of value.

Marshall et al. also tried to decide which explanation of the IG's children's developmental status might best account for the differences that they had discovered: delayed or distorted development. Reasoning that excess relative theta power might indicate a maturational lag in the development of the central nervous system whereas reduced absolute beta power might indicate stimulation-seeking due to chronic low levels of arousal, they concluded that the patterns of EEC activity observed in IG children did not appear to fit either picture neatly. They also drew attention to the fact that debates over these matters were still going on in respect of more widely identified groups of children, such as those diagnosed as having ADHD.

In their report on recognition of facial expressions of emotion, Parker et al. (2005) compared 72 institutionalised infants (35 boys) aged between seven and 32 months with 33 never-institutionalised infants (16 boys) aged between eight and 32 months. Each baby had 16 electrodes placed on his or her scalp (Parker et al. 2005, p.58): "Following gentle abrasion, a small amount of electrolyte conducting gel was inserted into each of the electrode sites" and impedances were measured as babies sat on their carer's lap. They then looked at colour photographs of a Caucasian woman posing expressions of four emotions: happiness, sadness, anger and fear. Each facial expression was presented 25 times (100 pictures in total) and three different women were included in the stimulus set. Event-related potentials were recorded in response to the four expressions at different electrode sites.

Large differences were found between institutionalised and never-institutionalised infants both in speed and amplitude of responses and in patterns of hemispheric asymmetry. Specifically, the institutionalised infants appeared to be primed to respond much faster to fear expressions than never-institutionalised infants, a finding which prompted the authors to suggest "the role of early institutionalisation in potentially overemphasizing the perceptual importance of fear recognition or vigilance in this type of environment, thereby leading to an overly, or more easily, activated amygdalar circuitry" (Parker et al. 2005, p.67). One might wonder perhaps about the appropriateness of the judgement that institutionalised children *overemphasise* the perceptual importance of fear expressions. Is it not possible that this response may be adaptive and that home-reared children may be relatively unprepared for the occurrence of danger?

Commenting on other differences between groups, Parker et al. (2005, p.68) claim that their own and both Marshall et al.'s and Chugani et al.'s studies provide "tremendous support for the possibility of a type of hypoactivation resulting from early institutional rearing" (which, it will be recalled, was not the conclusion drawn by Marshall et al.). As their study was cross-sectional and therefore not appropriate for testing the alternative maturational model, this conclusion seems somewhat premature (which is not to say that it may not eventually prove correct). Another of their conclusions, that the IG and NIG children appear to be following distinctly different developmental trajectories, seems more reasonable.

Like Marshall et al. (2004), Parker et al. (2005) also found little or no evidence of hemispheric asymmetry in institutionalised infants in comparison with never-institutionalised infants. They speculated that, as the institutionalised children are likely to have been systematically deprived of opportunities to make sense of social and emotional stimuli, their lack of hemispheric asymmetry might indicate that their brains were not receiving appropriate stimulation for the left hemisphere to develop its specialisation for language functions or for the right hemisphere to develop its specialisation for emotional recognition. They further speculated that this disadvantage may specifically involve dysfunction of the amygdala. However, without the use of more invasive techniques such as neuro-imaging, these speculations seem difficult to substantiate.

In sum, the ongoing Bucharest study is unique in its attempt to resolve some of the most problematic methodological aspects involved in studying the effects of early experiences of institutionalisation. It is also important in the scale of its effort to advance knowledge of relationships between social development and patterns of brain activity. So far, it is demonstrating that children with extensive experience of low-quality institutional care do not develop in the same way as never-institutionalised children and is providing a data-base that should add considerably to existing knowledge about effects of institutionalisation on children's development. However, there is, as yet, insufficient data to justify generalisations about long-term effects of early institutional deprivation (or privation) on the development of neural circuitry. It is clear that severe early deprivation affects current and some aspects of later physical development (Rao and Georgieff 2000) though most studies have shown fast catch-up in this respect. It is also clear that severe early deprivation affects current psychological health status but whether there are mechanisms that sustain long-term psycho-social effects in the absence of continuing environmental challenge and, if so, what these might be remains a mystery.

Day care

Concern about the effect of maternal employment on developing relationships between mothers and very young babies has been highly prevalent in the UK throughout the twentieth century (Yudkin and Holme 1963, Moore 1964, Stroud 1967, Prince 1967, 1968, Hood et al. 1970, Garner 1972, Jackson and Jackson 1979, Bryant et al. 1980, Mayall and Petrie 1983, Melhuish et al. 1990a, 1990b). Whether this concern stems from genuine worries about the needs of young babies or more pragmatic considerations is debateable the presence of strong underlying ambivalence towards day care as the "Cinderella of the education system" (Pugh 2003, p.186) seems undeniable.

During the Second World War, women were encouraged to work and to leave their children in nurseries that were billed as positively good for children: nurseries enriched children's lives, encouraged their mental development and gave them a head-start by preparing them early for school. By the early 1950s until the 1980s, this message had changed. Nurseries had dwindled in number, fewer mothers with young children were in paid employment and mothers with young babies were strongly encouraged to stay at home. Even where there were serious concerns about the capacity of mothers to care for babies, local authorities were reluctant to provide nursery places for children under two. Registered childminders in many parts of the country were instructed not to take in babies under one year old.

That these practices would have met with Bowlby's approval seems evident from the following assertions: "Any move that separates children from their mothers needs scrutiny, for we are dealing with a deep and ancient part of human nature" (Bowlby, BBC broadcast on "Security and Anxiety," 1968); "...psychologists have, usually without intending it, amassed evidence that to start nursery school much before the third birthday is for most children an undesirably stressful experience. The records, indeed, make it apparent that ignorance of the natural history of attachment behaviour, coupled with a misguided enthusiasm that small children should become independent and "mature," has resulted in practices that expose children, and their parents, to a great deal of unnecessary anxiety and distress. Nevertheless, for scientific purposes the resulting records have the great advantage that there is no danger that the degree of upset has been exaggerated; indeed, the reverse is probably the case" (Bowlby 1973a, p.54); "Clinical experience suggests that, whereas there are children who enjoy attending a very small playgroup a few mornings a week towards the end of their third year, there are strong reasons for caution about full-time attendance, the more so when it begins soon after the second birthday" (Bowlby 1973a, p.261).

However, local authority officers responsible for registration and supervision of childminders and other day care providers in the 1980s were in a prime position to observe at close quarters the inconsistent and piecemeal day care provision that ambivalent attitudes produced. While encouragement of registration facilitated access for the purposes of monitoring care standards and providing support, there was often little officials could do to deter unsatisfactory care practices. Restrictions on care of very young babies fuelled the market for private foster care which was often the only option for minority ethnic mothers, particularly young mothers from the African sub-continent, many of whom were single parents working long hours for low wages. It also discouraged those friends and neighbours caring informally for this youngest group of babies from cooperating closely with local authority workers.

As a result, unregistered childminding flourished, largely unchecked and uncheckable by local authority officials or police[4] (Jackson and Jackson 1979). Even though many of the women who offered their services as registered childminders were kind, highly committed and offered practical, emotional and informational support (Barrett 1991, Davie 1986), childminding was seen as a risky business (Owen 1988-89, Barrett 1991) and day care generally was scarce and costly. The risks to children of poor-quality day care were emphasised in a number of studies, though these typically employed small samples and non-rigorous methodologies.

Of particular concern were the risks faced by relatively recently immigrated African-Caribbean mothers and their infants (Stroud 1967, Prince 1967, 1968, Graham and Meadows 1967, Gregory 1969). Several studies identified a link between day care and poor developmental outcomes. Prince (1967, p.484) described 21/23 West Indian children seen in his clinic in 1966 as "aloof, apathetic, withdrawn, scarcely speaking or speaking not at all". He identified some as having experienced grossly inadequate care or multiple fostering and assessed 20 of the 23 mothers as clinically, and often seriously, depressed. In a later paper, Prince (1968) described a condition of 'pseudo-autism' among the children with a picture of unresponsiveness and lack of spontaneous activity which was particularly evident in children born in the UK.

---

4   It is still the case currently in the UK that it is almost impossible to provide sufficient proof to prevent non-registered childminders from caring for children not related to them on a regular basis – whether the incentives to register have increased is also in question – since it is not a criminal offence, police cannot be called upon to assist with obtaining proof and local authority officers have no rights of entry to properties where it is suspected.

In another study of 100 West Indian mothers admitted to a maternity unit, Stroud (1967, p.489) reached similar conclusions: "There is no doubt from what we have seen of children being child-minded that many of them are left to their own devices – and these are the children we see referred to us as possible cases of mental retardation of organic aetiology, but in whom we find evidence of emotional deprivation…The mother is forced to go out to work leaving the child with a child-minder who will give it no emotional stimulus; the same child is collected by an overtired mother who returns to her overcrowded and expensive home where she and the child are isolated in a non-English culture and where her child will have no experience of the English children with whom he will later be educated."

Jackson and Jackson's study of the conditions of care among unregistered childminders reiterated these concerns and extended them to a wider community, describing childminders who worked for a pittance and children who sat, day after day, with no stimulation of any kind (Jackson and Jackson 1979). The same picture was painted by Mayall and Petrie (1983) whose work is perhaps best described by an extract from Jack Tizard's foreword: "The picture we get from this study is of sad, passive children, of anxious, harassed mothers, and hard-pressed minders insensitive to the children's needs and distrustful of the mothers…who in turn are resentful of the minders …. Mrs. Mayall and Mrs. Petrie, who write in restrained terms, describe much of what they saw as deplorable. No one could disagree with that judgement" (Mayall and Petrie, 1977, p.11).

Working as a childminding officer in the 1980s and simultaneously studying for a doctorate on the social experiences of childminded children, Barrett (1991) was puzzled by these portrayals. At any one time, it was possible to visit a sample of registered childminders and to find, in the majority of homes, warm, busy childminders caring for children who appeared bright, happy and well-entertained. These childminders generally reported that they enjoyed working with parents and were very keen to talk about the children's progress. Were most of these children in the later stages of detachment, superficially sociable but deeply damaged by their early experiences of separation? It was hard to believe.

By contrast, a minority of childminders was clearly over-stressed, for reasons connected with their own home lives, or because they were working for parents they found difficult, or because they were caring for children who worried them. At any one time in the location supervised by any one childminding officer, among around 60 childminders who were actively caring for between 100 and 150 children, there were at least three or four children who, no matter how hard the childminder tried to enliven him or her, was dramatically withdrawn, sad and non-responsive.

In semi-structured interviews with 21 ex-childminders (Barrett 1991), childminders recalled all the children they had cared for and reported having had worries at some time about 30 of the total of 90 children they talked about. Of these, 12 children (13.3 per cent) were described as anxious, withdrawn or passive, seven (7.8 per cent) were considered disruptive or disturbed in some way, and 11 (12.2 per cent) were less obviously distressed but were considered by the childminders to be unhappy in some way, for example, having stressful relationships with their parents (parents of six children were described as being too "close" or "possessive").

Descriptions and explanations for the behaviour of the anxious, withdrawn or passive children varied considerably. Some childminders attributed the children's difficulties to their home lives, "…she was, like, a poor little thing. The mother, as I say, P was OK but, as I say, the home life – I don't know what it is but, when kids are put out to childminders, the home life isn't always a bed of roses…" Others attributed the problems to the children's personality, or developmental stage, "I think there's probably lots of children that really shouldn't be childminded"; "It was silent tears, it was really upsetting, he wouldn't make a lot of noise, screaming, he would just sit there and there would be these tears coming down his eyes... he'd look sort of blankly... and then even the crying would stop... I said I think it's me, he doesn't get on with me, but I don't think it was, he just wanted to be at home with his Mum, that's what I think." Other childminders attributed the difficulties to a combination of mother and child characteristics, for example, "he was like an out-of-space child. I couldn't take it, that's why I gave him up... his mother didn't seem to care".

These accounts, along with the accounts given by mothers of their experiences of using childminders, pointed to the existence of a minority of children who, for a variety of reasons, did not cope in the day care situation. However, from both childminders' and mothers' interviews, an impression emerged that, for a small number of children, some of the difficulties may have been nascent prior to the parents' decision to return to work. In some cases, parents' work relieved pressure on strained relationships. In others, pressures appeared to increase, on relationships between parents as well as between parents and children.

During the time that the author was working with and researching childminders in the UK, the 'Day Care Wars' broke out in the US. Since his 1984 review, Belsky had taken an about-turn. The 1984 report had covered two waves of US day care research, one that ended around 1978 and mostly involved high-quality university day care centres often used either by more privileged families or by under-privileged families participating in special programmes designed to provide enriching environments and a second that included community-based day care more representative of day care generally and was, according to Belsky's account, focused on organisational issues (group size, staff:child ratio, etc.).

Reviewing the first wave of studies which identified effects on intellectual, social and emotional development, Belsky concluded that no differences were to be found between day care and home-reared children in terms of intellectual development although, in the case of disadvantaged children participating in enrichment programmes, there was some evidence that on IQ and language scores, day care children fared better than home-reared control children. Findings relating to social development were more complex, with some evidence that day care experience increased self-reliance and both negative and positive social interactions with peers including egocentric, impulsive, aggressive, attention-seeking and troublesome behaviour, and non-compliancy with adults. At this point, Belsky (1984) suggested that day care-reared children may tend to orient more towards peer than to adult values and that this could be seen as a potentially disturbing effect of day care on social development. However, he argued that it did not emerge in every study and could possibly be associated with specific aspects of individual day care settings (e.g. permissive environments) as opposed to being an inevitable consequence of all day care experiences. With regard to effects on emotional development, Belsky pointed to methodological flaws in many studies and to the importance of controlling for length of day care experience when studying emotional effects since, he argued, many children go through a period, which may last as long as five months or more, of stressful adaptation to day care.

He finally concluded that supplementary child care exerted little influence on children's emotional ties to their mothers other than transient distress, except under certain conditions such as when children are enrolled in unstable or poor-quality day care prior to their first birthday. These children, he suggested, may develop avoidant behaviour towards their mothers and may be more likely to show emotional and social problems later. Unlike an earlier paper where he had qualified his conclusions by stating that the absence of evidence for deleterious effects of day care in existing research did not mean that no such effects occur (Belsky and Steinberg, 1978), Belsky (1984) emphasised that effects might be neither long-lasting nor inevitable and drew attention to the fact that early day care entry in itself had not been shown to be associated with adverse effects where day care facilities were of a high quality.

At this stage, then, whilst noting that there were contradictory findings concerning effects of day care upon child development, Belsky did not consider that popular beliefs or predictions from attachment theory received sufficient support from empirical investigations to give cause for concern. However, it was clear that much remained unknown about the effects of day care and much was obscured by the difficulty of separating out what was an effect of the day care setting itself and what was an effect of the way in which the day care facility was being used or was operating.

Soon after, Belsky again reviewed studies of day care effects and concluded in a non-peer-reviewed article (Belsky 1986) that his earlier opinion needed revision. He now considered that there was evidence that the reunion behaviour of infants of working mothers differed from that of infants of non-working mothers and that five studies had indicated that maternal employment was associated both with stress and with the risk of emotional insecurity in infants, particularly where day care was used for more than 20 hours per week and began in the first year of life. Further, he considered that this risk factor was not reduced by considerations of quality or consistency of care but might better be seen as attributable to the ecology of day care.

In a carefully-worded article, he proposed that, "If one does not feel compelled to draw only irrefutable conclusions, however, a relatively persuasive circumstantial case can be made that extensive infant day care experience may be associated with increased avoidance of mother, possibly to the point of greater insecurity in the attachment relationship. In addition, such experience may also be associated with diminished compliance and co-operation with adults, increased aggressiveness, and possibly even greater social maladjustment in the preschool and early school-age years" (Belsky 1988b, p.256).

Belsky's initial claims were greeted with considerable resistance. They were challenged by many workers on a number of grounds, perhaps the most notable being that unsound conclusions had been drawn from attachment data (Clarke-Stewart 1988; Fein and Fox 1988) and that conclusions rested upon non-representative, poorly controlled studies, or unreliable findings (Thompson 1988; Richters and Zahn-Waxler 1988; Roggman et al. 1994).

Subsequently, many of these issues were addressed by studies employing more careful sampling controls and alternative methodologies. A major longitudinal study, carried out by the National Institute of Child Health and Human Development Early Child Care Research Network (NICHD ECCRN) of 1,364 children on ten sites has emerged in the US (NICHD ECCRN 1997, 1998, 1999, 2000a, 2000b, 2001a, 2001b, 2001c, 2002, 2003a, 2003b, 2003c). In this study, a range of selection effects was monitored, including parents' education, child-rearing beliefs, race, economic and marital status and health-related measures such as parenting stress, maternal depression and separation anxiety. Analyses have enabled consideration of factors such as children's gender and temperament, as well as many aspects of day care including type, quality, stability, quantity and age of entry. Outcome measures are based where possible on multiple sources (observations, Strange Situation test, standardised questionnaires, parent and teacher reports) with careful checks for inter-rater reliability. This increased design sophistication has made it possible to examine more closely relationships between parent, child and day care variables and their effects on children's development.

While this study did not find any direct effects of day care on attachment security, some interactive effects were found. Insecure attachments were associated with poor-quality care in combination either with more than ten hours of care per week or with changes of child care during the first 15 months of life, but only in the case of infants whose mothers had been assessed as least sensitive; this relationship between attachment insecurity and quality of care did not obtain among infants with mothers who scored more highly on the measure of sensitive responsiveness. A relationship was also found between the amount of time spent in non-maternal care and incidence of externalising behaviour problems, suggesting, as Belsky (e.g. 2001) has consistently maintained, that more time away from maternal care might put children at risk.

Whether this might be an alarmist interpretation of the data is not easy to evaluate. On one level, all Belsky is saying is something remarkably similar to Bowlby's views, namely that, for a small minority of vulnerable children, early separation experiences appear to be linked to disrupted patterns of attachment and poor social relationships. While it is not clear exactly what it is that might make these children vulnerable, or even, for that matter, whether they might have developed these problems in the absence of experiences of day care, the fact that this vulnerable minority exists raises concern. So far, though, there is no clear evidence that day care, in itself, is the cause of the problem. By far the majority of infants who experience high-quality day care appear to cope well and there is clear evidence that infants from more disadvantaged backgrounds can benefit from the experience of high-quality care (e.g. Campbell et al. 2001, NICHD ECCRN 2003b). However, there is also evidence, particularly from studies of poor-quality care (e.g. the University of Haifa study; Sagi et al. 2002) of negative effects on cognitive and socio-behavioural development and some indication that high child-carer ratios, particularly in combination with low-quality care, can be detrimental (Vandell 2004).

Further evidence that day care may put children under greater strain than home care has also come from studies of daily cortisol levels in children. Work on LHPA (limbic hypothalamic-pituitary-adrenocortical) activity in young children has suggested that stress response mechanisms may operate differently for infants of different ages in out-of-home preschool settings. The importance of efficient activation and deactivation of the HPA axis is well established (though the complexity of links between HPA and other systems is often under-emphasised in popular accounts; Schwartz et al. 1998, Gunnar and Donzella 2002). Inefficiency has been linked with negative effects on metabolism as well as long-term effects on cardiovascular and immune systems. There is also evidence that chronic over-activation can impact upon capacities for emotional self-regulation, memory and learning.

Of particular interest to the question of early day care effects is the finding that, normally, over the course of the first year, a hypo-responsive phase develops during which it becomes increasingly difficult to elicit cortisol elevation responses to potentially threatening events. This phase has been observed both in non-human species and in human infants (e.g. de Kloet et al. 1996, Gunnar et al. 1996) and is considered to be strongly associated with the availability of maternal protection (Levine and Wiener 1988). A question therefore arises as to how stress response patterns might evolve in infants for whom maternal protection is not continuously available at very early stages of development.

Using carefully trialled methods for salivary collection and assay (Gunnar 1989, Spangler 1991, Larson et al. 1998), a number of studies now suggest that patterns of HPA activity in children in day care or entering new pre-school classes differ from home baselines. Contrary to normal circadian decreases, three- to four-year-old children in day care have shown increases in cortisol levels (Tout et al. 1998, Dettling et al. 1999). Watamura et al. (2003) showed that increases only occurred in association with day care, did not occur on days when the same children were at home, nor in school-aged children and tended to be present in toddlers who were more fearful and less inclined to play with other children in the day care setting. Other researchers have found that larger increases appear to be linked with lower-quality day care (Legendre and Kortinus 1996, Lane et al. 2000), and with insecure attachment, negative temperament attributes and poorer self-control (Gunnar et al. 1996).

Valuable though these studies are, many point to the need for further exploration, for example, to discover more about the significance of variations in response between older and younger children (Gunnar and Donzella 1999, 2002), factors underlying individual variability, the role of cognitive evaluation in appraisal of threat (Stansbury and Harris 2000), and whether patterns of cortisol increase might be related to positive or negative adaptation (i.e. linked to positive experiences such as increased motivation, interest or learning, or negative, stressful or over-taxing experiences). These outstanding questions make it difficult, not to say inappropriate, to draw any very definite conclusions at this stage about the long- or short-term effects of day care on very young children. Further, most samples have drawn predominantly upon middle/upper-income parents using relatively high-quality group care and, due to their non-homogeneity in respect of cultural background, day care and sibling experience, have tended toward cell sizes which are too small for fine-grained analysis. Thus, their scope has been limited in the sense of being able to provide insights into the small minority of vulnerable children identified by both Belsky and Bowlby as being at risk.

Research has thrown light on the importance of quality of day care (see Love et al. 2003, Vandell 2004 for recent reviews), and of the value of continuity particularly in the early years (Howes 1999). Less agreement has been found on the effects of number of hours per week and timing of start of day care, which are usually correlated, and which are highly influenced by the social and cultural context and quality of care (Vandell 2004, Harrison and Ungerer 1997, 2002). Overall, therefore, there seems to be a lack of convincing evidence that high-quality day care is either particularly bad or particularly good for the majority of very young children. There is even less substantial evidence of long-term effects on children's development or on the development of relationships between parents and children, and a need for more research in this area. Nevertheless, it is also clear that a substantial minority of children in day care settings do not cope well and that these experiences may set them at a disadvantage for later social development. Perhaps a key 'take-home' message, therefore, should concern the need to put strategies in place so that these children can be identified as early as possible and to ensure that adequate assistance is available for them and their carers.

Social policies that put pressure on parents to work long hours and force them to rely on day care regardless of their children's capacity to cope are likely to exacerbate the difficulties of the vulnerable minority. It is therefore imperative that checks and balances are in place, to ensure that these children and their parents are protected from potential risks.

Is there a critical period for the development of attachments in humans?

"If growth is to proceed smoothly, the tissues must be exposed to the influence of the appropriate organizer at certain critical periods. In the same way, if mental development is to proceed smoothly, it would appear to be necessary for the unformed mentality to be exposed, during certain critical periods, to the influence of a psychic organizer – the mother." (Bowlby 1953/1965, pp. 60-61)

"So it is wise to remember that the most vulnerable stage for children is roughly between the ages of six months and three years (and it must be said that there is much controversy about the lower limit." (Bowlby 1958b, p.13)

"As time goes on, the best solutions will become clearer. Meanwhile, we are wise to be wary. Any move that separates children from their mothers needs scrutiny, for we are dealing with a deep and ancient part of human nature." (Bowlby, BBC broadcast on 'Security and Anxiety', 1968)

As discussed in Chapter Two, early in the development of his theory of attachment, Bowlby wondered whether imprinting in animals might provide a model of attachment in humans. If so, he speculated that there may be a critical period within which certain types of experience would be essential if secure attachments were to form and if healthy trajectories were to be set for later personality development (Figure 6.4).

Figure 6.4: The early critical period hypothesis (Bowlby 1944, 1953/1965)

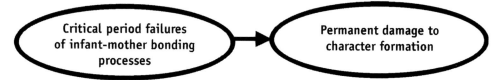

In his earlier work, while recognising that the course of development of attachments in humans did not appear to follow that in other animals exactly, Bowlby (1953/1965) suggested that there did appear to be certain phases for which it was "imperative to have regard" for (Bowlby 1953/1965, p.61). These included:

a) the phase up to five or six months during which the infant establishes an attachment relationship
b) the phase from that point until about three years when the infant needs the attachment figure as an "ever-present companion"
c) the phase where the young child begins to cope more independently: only for days or weeks, in favourable circumstances, without mother, during fourth and fifth year; not until after seven or eight for longer periods, though even then with difficulty.

One of the most trenchant critiques of Bowlby's maternal deprivation hypothesis was delivered by Michael Rutter (Rutter 1972a). In this work, Rutter re-examined the available evidence on the importance of early experience and questioned several of Bowlby's conclusions, e.g. "There are age-specific effects, and early learning will influence later learning. Because of its primacy early learning may in some ways disproportionately influence development. Yet it is essentially reversible and in some cases the effects of later experience will predominate. There can be no general rule. Whether or not 'maternal deprivation' in infancy has a long-term effect depends in large part on environmental conditions in later childhood" (Rutter 1972a, p.60).

In response to challenges of this kind and in the light of further evidence, Bowlby gradually came to the conclusion that imprinting processes did not appear to account for attachment formation in humans: attachments formed more gradually over a number of years, did not appear to be governed by the same principles that applied to responses in precocial birds, for example, and were capable of being altered by later experiences. For these reasons, Bowlby moved to the view that the early years appeared to be a sensitive period for the development of patterns of secure attachment but recognised that later relationships could also be very important: "Although for these reasons patterns, once formed, are apt to persist, this is by no means necessarily so" (Bowlby 1988b, p.127); "The model of developmental pathways regards an infant at birth as having an array of pathways potentially open to him, the one along which he will eventually proceed being determined at every moment by the interaction of the individual as he now is with the environment in which he happens to be" (Bowlby 1988b, p.136). Therefore, while seeing responsive care in the early years as potentially laying the foundation for later emotional wellbeing, Bowlby did not ascribe to the view that it could 'inoculate' against later life events or that it would be impervious to later experience. His move from a critical to a sensitive period hypothesis and to increasing recognition that later experiences could also have important effects seems often to be overlooked by those propounding the more deterministic 'hard' accounts of Attachment Theory.

It seems particularly remote from the school of thinking prevalent among those who have resurrected the critical period hypothesis in their account of early brain development (Figure 6.5). These theorists, essentially, posit that there is a critical period, within the first two years of life, or earlier, during which lack of attuned interactions between infants and key carers permanently affects brain development, specifically, the part of the brain responsible for emotional self-regulation and understanding of others (e.g. Schore 1994, 1999; Gerhardt 2004, 2005), for example: "...nothing can change the fact that the house is not well built and will continue to be high maintenance. Likewise with human beings whose foundations have not been well built. Although extensive repairs may be undertaken later in life, the building stage – when adjustments can be made – is largely over. For prevention to be effective, it needs to be targeted at the point when it can make the most difference. These foundations are laid during pregnancy and in the first two years of life. This is when the 'social brain' is shaped and when an individual's emotional style and emotional resources are established" (Gerhardt 2004, pp. 2-3); "children are most vulnerable to adversity at a time when the brain is developing rapidly and is at its most plastic" (Gerhardt 2005).

Figure 6.5: Re-incarnation of critical period hypothesis (Schore 1994, 1999; Gerhardt 2004, 2005)

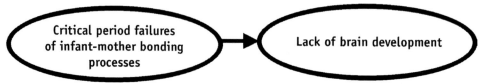

We have already discussed some of these ideas in Chapter Five. In this chapter, we take a further look at the conceptual basis upon which such views appear to be founded. First, we discuss what is meant by the notion of critical periods and consider why Bowlby, and others, considered the distinction between critical and sensitive periods to be important. Next, we discuss some more general principles of development and draw attention to different views on the role of experience in 'bringing out' inherent predispositions to social interaction. Finally, we consider some of the evidence on effects of maternal postnatal depression on children's development since this is often cited in support of more Deterministic accounts of Attachment Theory.

The distinction between critical and sensitive periods

The term 'critical period' is not used in the same way across all disciplines. Since this can lead to conceptual confusion, it seems important to clarify what our understanding of the term entails. According to Bruer (2001), the notion of 'critical periods' of development has been extant in various branches of science since at least the 1920s and is thought to have originated in the field of embryology with the work of Charles Stockard on fish embryos. Stockard (1921), though, tended to use the terms 'critical moments' or 'sensitive periods' synonymously, to refer to points when disruptions in embryo development (for example, due to extremes of temperature or exposure to toxic substances) caused specific birth defects.

In the 1930s, the term 'critical period' began to be used slightly differently by embryologists to denote points in cell development at which cells could be induced to take one pathway rather than another and after which no such inducement could influence them to revert or change direction (Spemann 1938). According to Bruer (2001, pp. 6-7), it is this understanding of the term that appears to have been adopted in the current field of developmental neurobiology where it is associated with:

- very short time periods (e.g. 24 hours in respect of frogs' eyes)
- very strong effects of environmental conditions
- irreversible and permanent effects.

Lorenz (Lorenz 1937) reintroduced the term in his descriptions of imprinting phenomena in precocial birds, stating that imprinting phenomena occurred within a critical period which was:

- extremely short in duration
- during which development is susceptible to specific influences
- and effects are totally irreversible.

Gradually it became apparent that development rarely conformed to this pattern: not only could most effects be reversed but very few aspects of development could be limited to specific critical times. For this reason, many scientists chose to relinquish the term 'critical period' in favour of terms such as 'sensitive' phases or periods (e.g. Bateson 1979, 1983; Bornstein 1989). 'Sensitive phases' were characterised by:

- longer, far more variable and ill-defined time periods
- greater susceptibility to particular environmental influences
- effects that could be modified or even reversed by subsequent experiences.

More recently, the term 'window of opportunity' has also appeared in the literature. Currently, Bruer (2001) emphasised, there is no formally agreed use with respect to any of these terms and consequently much scope for confusion and mis-information. He warned that this situation can create a context for misguided policy-making: "A *critical period* connotes that as the twig is bent, so inevitably grows the tree. Such deterministic, and possibly dire, connotations and implications are particularly compelling in the policy arena, in which they prompt interest in policy reports, garner media attention, and engender public interest. Qualified talk about ill-defined sensitive periods, with modifiable effects, lack the same emotive and rhetorical force" (Bruer 2001, p.11). He added that, in the interests of sound policy-making principles, it may be important to pay more attention to less florid arguments since "the highly qualified sensitive period claims are more likely closer to the scientific truth than are the dramatic window slamming claims of critical periods narrowly constructed" (Bruer 2001, p.11).

Experience-expectant versus experience-dependent development

The distinction between experience-expectant and experience-dependent development (Greenough et al. 1987) is an important one which is sometimes overlooked in popular accounts of child development. It is implicated in some of the most common misconceptions about the nature of learning in the early years. These include beliefs such as:
- infancy is the time when we learn the most efficiently
- because infancy is associated with the period of most rapid brain growth
- more neural connections mean cleverer children
- environmental enrichment in infancy means more neural connections
- if brains are not used in the early years, abilities are forever lost
- social learning in infancy forms the basis for all later social development
- the early years are the most critical for development.

All these beliefs point to a general sense that brains have a 'sell-by' date which is reached so early in life that it should only take a few timely injections of the correct kind of experience to immunise against all future problem development. An understanding of the distinction between experience-expectant and experience-dependent development suggests that such a view may be misguided.

The first point to make is that only experience-expectant development is thought to be associated with critical or sensitive periods. On these grounds, by definition, experience-expectant development could be said to be a fourth characteristic of critical or sensitive periods.

Bruer and Greenough (2001, pp. 210-211) explain that "Experience-expectant development is limited to developing skills and neural systems that are characteristic of a species. Typically, sensory and motor systems (e.g. vision, audition, first language learning in humans) develop in part via experience-expectant processes. In the overwhelming number of cases these systems develop normally because the expected, required experiences are reliably present in any typical human environment and readily available to all typical members of a species in their typical environments." From this explanation, it is possible to deduce that more complex, non-universal skills, such as tipping your cap to the boss, playing the ukulele, being mindful not to burp or pass wind in company, learning to read, etc. would not fall within the remit of experience-expectant development. Such skills develop only through experience of more specific and non-universal conditions which are best described as 'experience-dependent'. Several aspects of experience-dependent development are thought to distinguish it from experience-expectant development: first, it has a different evolutionary history; second, it does not have the same biological function; third, it has a different neurological basis; fourth, there is no evidence of critical or sensitive phases in experience-dependent development; fifth, it is relatively age-independent; sixth, it is unique to each individual and their social context. To describe some of these differences more clearly, it is necessary to look a bit more closely at the nature of each kind of development.

Experience-expectant brain development begins before birth when, under genetic control, neural cells have begun to form and the connections between them (synapses) have begun to send messages throughout the neural network. Though there is already some sensitivity to environmental conditions, this kind of brain development is predominantly 'hard-wired', that is, most of it occurs regardless of experience. This is not to say that experience plays no part at all in 'fine-tuning' the neural circuitry involved in experience-expectant development but the kind of experience required is non-specific and rarely absent from human societies world-wide (e.g. exposure to light, sound, warmth, space, other people): "Experiences like these are so overwhelmingly likely to occur that nature has bet successfully on them for eons...It is only when there are severe genetic or environmental aberrations from the normal that nature's expectations are frustrated and neural development goes awry" (Bruer, 1999, pp. 108-9). It is precisely because these experiences are so ubiquitous that this part of human development can afford to be almost exclusively 'hard-wired' or programmed on the expectation that the final processes will be kicked into play by experience.

Genetically-programmed experience-expectant development is thought to involve all sensory and motor systems, to continue after birth and to be responsible for the rapid period of brain cell proliferation (synaptogenesis) and the selective pruning of synapses which takes place in the first four or five years of life in monkeys but over the first *sixteen* years of life in humans (Table 6.5). In other words, experience-expectant learning in humans is not thought to be confined to the first years of life. Indeed, important experience-expectant changes occur in adolescence in association with further myelination, synaptic pruning and maturation of important executive functions (Steinberg 2005, Paus 2005).

Table 6.5: Time span for cortical development[5]

	PHASE OF DEVELOPMENT		
	SYNAPTOGENETIC PEAK	PLATEAU	ADULT LEVELS
MONKEY	From 2 months before birth until about 2 or 3 months after birth	2 or 3 months to 3 years	Between 3 and 4 or 5 years
HUMAN	Auditory cortex: c3 months Visual cortex: 8-12 months Frontal cortex: 2-3.5years	c 1 year to 2-16 years (for different parts of brain)	Visual cortex: 11 yrs Auditory cortex: 12 years Frontal cortex: c16 yrs

It is popularly believed that there is a strong correlation between rapid learning and the rapid increase in brain cells that occurs during infancy. Contrary to this belief, though, the relationship between synaptic density and intelligence has been found to be considerably more complex. Greenough et al. (1987) suggest that, while experience-expectant development appears to be more closely associated with synaptic pruning, experience-dependent development may rely more heavily on the development of new connections between existing neurones. Also, because some cells die back while other more specialised cells grow, measurements of synaptic density alone (as opposed to tracking the development of specific neurones) are unlikely to pick up on qualitative changes like this, which are possibly more important in respect of developing abilities and specialisms. Moreover, such changes are likely to occur during childhood and adolescence at points that do not coincide with 'synaptic blooming' and that have not yet been fully investigated and so are not yet well understood. Bruer (1999) further emphasised that some mental defects (e.g. Fragile X syndrome) are associated with over- not under-production of brain cells and argued that most learning in children and adolescents occurs more rapidly and more effectively during the much longer

---

5 The information contained in this table pertains to data from studies by Huttenlocher and colleagues (Huttenlocher 1979, Huttenlocher et al. 1982, Huttenlocher and De Courten 1987, Huttenlocher and Dabholkar 1997) reported in Bruer (1999).

period when excess synapses are gradually being lost from the frontal cortex rather than in the period when brain cell proliferation is at its height (i.e. the first two years).

In sum, according to this account, only very unusual circumstances should prevent pre-programmed experience-expectant development from taking place, for example, a child brought up *completely* deprived of sensory experience, of the capacity to move, or of experience of social interaction might be expected to have developmental problems associated with the specific organs or systems affected. There does, however, appear to be a further difficulty in relation to theories of social development in that no consensus appears to have been reached on which aspects are designated experience-expectant and which experience-dependent. According to Bruer's arguments (Bruer 1999), social development is socially constructed and experience-dependent. According to Thompson (e.g. Thompson 1999), attachment-formation is experience-expectant. Other workers have suggested that the sensitive period for the formation of secure attachments may be earlier than that for insecure attachments. And those espousing the 'hard' form of Attachment Theory appear to propose that all social development is experience-expectant and critically determined within two years of birth.

These divergent views suggest the need for clearer conceptualisation and for more careful evaluation of research findings. What seems possible is that the initial social orienting responses observed and listed by Ainsworth as attachment behaviours may, in large part, provide evidence of experience-expectant social development, that is, these responses are elicited in response to even the most insensitive parental care and may only be extinguished in very unusual circumstances where no social interactions at all are experienced. The likelihood of babies surviving in conditions where no social interactions at all are possible seems very low. Most babies will therefore begin to develop socially no matter how appalling the care is that they are given and their later social development may well involve experience-dependent development, i.e. it may not be subject to 'critical' or even 'sensitive' periods. This is not to say that social experiences during the early years will not be important, nor that they will be less important than later experiences. It simply underlines the point that little appears to be certain about how 'fixed' any individual brain might be as a result of them, if it is at all. In the next section, we consider this problem in relation to research on postnatal depression.

Postnatal depression

It has been estimated that about 12 per cent of all mothers experience postnatal depression (Cooper et al. 1988, O'Hara and Swain 1996) and that rates are far higher in low-income samples (Hobfoll et al. 1995) and among teenage mothers (Koniak-Griffin et al. 1996). Possibly as many as one in four low-income teenage parents is likely to suffer from postnatal depression while at least one in five women will be affected in high-risk samples (i.e. those characterised by poverty and multiple social disadvantage).

It is well established that having a parent who suffers from depression increases the risk that children will also develop depression[6] (Weissman et al. 1987, Downey and Coyne 1990, Dodge 1990, Dawson and Ashman 2000), although there is no clear consensus about which mechanisms produce these outcomes, that is, whether they are chiefly mediated through the quality of parent-child interactions, through shared familial predispositions to affective disorder, through associated social contextual influences, or by a combination of these

---

6 Orvaschel et al. (1988) reported depression in 21.3 per cent of children with depressed parents compared with 4.3 per cent in children whose parents were not depressed (cited in Hay and Angold 1993).

factors. In addition, parental and child depression are often accompanied by other difficulties, such as psychiatric conditions (e.g. anxiety, social phobia, etc.), problems related to substance abuse, poor physical health, behaviour or attention problems. Co-morbidity inevitably makes it difficult to identify the separate contribution of each disorder to eventual outcomes (Orvaschel 1983), and there has been considerable debate about whether it is specific disorders or more general psychological disturbance in parents that might be linked to children's difficulties (Rutter and Quinton 1984).

Studies of postnatal depression have indicated associations between mothers' depressed mood and subsequent problems in mother-child interactions (Murray 1992) and have confirmed findings from studies of maternal depression of lack of attunement or synchrony in interactions between depressed mothers and their babies and of more general problems with parenting (e.g. Weissman et al. 1972, Field 1984, 1992, 2000, Zahn-Waxler et al. 1984, Murray 1992, Murray et al. 1996a, 1996b, 1999, Dawson et al. 1997a, 1997b, 2000). These studies have pointed to different degrees of difficulty associated with depression according to its timing, duration (frequency of relapse and chronicity), its nature (bipolar or unipolar) and with the way it manifests, that is, whether it is accompanied by externalising symptoms (e.g. increased irritability, touchiness, negativity, hostility, harsh discipline, abuse, resentment, or paranoia) or internalising symptoms (e.g. feeling tired, overwhelmed, lethargic, unable to move, becoming socially withdrawn, etc.). Different mixes of symptoms have been thought to be associated with distinctly different styles of parenting (withdrawn or unresponsive cf intrusive and hostile; Cohn et al. 1986).

Mis-attuned parent-child interaction affects behaviour on all levels (Cohn and Campbell 2000), including non-contingent or non-existent responses to infant cues, fewer affectionate and more negative exchanges, and lack of engagement in meaningful communication (marked, for example, by poor quality and low rates of speech, decreased emotional expressiveness, lack of eye contact, etc.). Besides the increased risk of later mental health and psychological problems for children, there is also evidence of effects on security of attachment (de Mulder and Radke-Yarrow 1991, Murray 1992, Teti et al. 1995, Cicchetti et al. 1998) and on children's ability to regulate their own emotional state (Zahn-Waxler et al. 1984). Interestingly, while de Mulder and Radke-Yarrow (1991) found higher numbers of insecure attachments only among children of bipolar-depressed mothers (67 per cent compared with 42 per cent among children with unipolar or non-depressed mothers), they also found strong associations between attachment insecurity and displays of negative affect (seeming anxious, angry or irritable, or looking downcast) and of lack of positive affect (showing tenderness or affection), among both children and mothers, but most pronouncedly among children of unipolar mothers.

Negative consequences of maternal depression for children have been quite consistently found, particularly in association with the severity and chronicity of maternal depression (Teti et al. 1995). However, findings in respect of the long-term consequences of postnatal depression are less consistent and, for a number of methodological reasons, are generally more difficult to evaluate. While a report by Field et al. (1996) suggested that negative consequences for children may not accrue if postnatal depression lifts within six months after birth, other researchers have reported effects on children's cognitive development and play even where the mother's illness had remitted within six months (Cogill et al. 1986, Sharp et al. 1995). It also seems worthy of note that, where effects have been found, patterns of effects appear frequently to differ between boys and girls, raising further questions about the mechanisms involved. The likelihood of bi-directional influences was raised by Murray et al. (1996b) who drew attention to the possibility that mothers' symptoms may have been preceded by irritability or poor motor coordination in infants. In a similar vein, Field (1988) observed that infants of depressed mothers had appeared more apathetic and less smiley than other babies prior to the appearance of mothers' symptoms. Observations such as these suggest the need for researchers to be heedful of the way in which children's behaviour may have contributed to the development of relationship problems as opposed to simply having arisen in consequence of maternal pathology.

Further complications for researchers interested in isolating the effects of postnatal depression from more pervasive psychological disturbance include problems such as mothers' previous psychiatric history and the social context of parenting. Prenatal depression, for example, has been found to have independent effects on children's development (Field et al. 2004, Jones et al. 1998) while social contextual factors can differentially influence the course and nature of illness (Brown and Harris 1978). Small sample sizes and potential confounding of 'third factor' effects such as maternal education, socio-economic status, with illness status also limit generalizability of findings (Murray et al. 1996c). Finally, while many definitions of 'postnatal depression' would restrict it to depression that has remitted by six months and would distinguish it from maternal 'blues' and puerperal psychosis, there does not seem to be any clearly agreed consensus in the literature on this, with the result that it is not always clear what the term refers to (Wisner and Stowe 1997). All these issues can make for difficulty in reaching confident conclusions about the specific effects of maternal postnatal depression on children's development.

These problems have not prevented the appearance of confident assertions, particularly in lay literatures, concerning the deleterious effect of maternal postnatal depression on brain development. Whilst not pretending to be specialists in this area, given that such opinions appear to be promulgated as though they stem directly from Attachment Theory (which they do not, necessarily, although some may feel that they are implied within it), it seems important to attempt some sort of evaluation of this point of view.

Our impression from perusal of the literature is that many of these claims are based largely on findings from animal studies (e.g. Le Doux 1987, 1992), on studies of maternal depression more generally and on a few reports of studies in which brain activity in human infants with depressed or non-depressed mothers has been examined. Though we recognise the value of animal studies, it is outside the scope of this book to consider all relevant studies or to adequately address the complex question of how findings from animal studies might apply to humans. For this reason, we have confined the following discussion to a selection of the studies of humans.

To set the context for our discussion, it seems useful first to outline briefly the measure of brain activity involved. Although there are a number of ways of measuring brain activity, the one most used in the studies about to be discussed is the monitoring of electrical activity using an electro-encephalogram (EEG). This involves attaching electrodes to different points on the skull with a jelly or cream that permits vibrations to pass through to the electrodes. Since absolute levels of activity tend to be less informative because these, as might be expected, vary from person to person for all sorts of reasons, relative levels of activity within individuals are monitored from different parts of the brain, usually from more than one region, so that records from a number of sites and combinations of sites can be compared. These patterns of relative activity (e.g. more processing in one hemisphere than another when watching emotionally neutral, positive or negative stimuli) give an indication of specialisation in particular regions for specific types of processing (the assumption being that more activity is indicative of greater engagement with the task, not just greater effort).

EEG studies have been particularly popular in advancing understanding of emotions. For example, studies of frontal lobe activity while watching films or faces have suggested that more activity may be generated in the right hemisphere when experiencing or expressing more negative emotional states (e.g. fear, sadness) while the left hemisphere is more active when more positive states are being experienced, for example, when joy or interest are involved (Figure 6.6).

A series of studies by Fox and Davidson (e.g. Davidson and Fox 1982, 1988, Fox and Davidson 1986, 1988, Fox 1991, Davidson 1993, 1998) led to the proposal that different hemispheres might be involved at each end of the continuum of emotional states that range from joy to fear and that are associated with social approach or withdrawal. The left hemisphere, he suggested, is more involved in activities and emotions related to social approach (i.e. joy, pride, bliss, interest, concern, responsibility, anger, hostility and jealousy) while the right hemisphere deals with activities related to social withdrawal (i.e. distress, misery, agony, disgust, contempt, resentment, fear, horror and anxiety). It is worth noting that this conceptualisation does not depend on a sharp divide between positive and negative emotions and that transfer of information from one hemisphere to another, anyway, takes place in a matter of milliseconds in intact brains. However, findings such as these as well as information from studies of individuals who have suffered brain trauma or disease, have led to speculations about the significance of asymmetric electrical activation.[7] It is these patterns of hemispheric asymmetry that appear to have caught the headlines in respect of effects of maternal depression on the development of children's ability to regulate their own emotional state.

Figure 6.6: Frontal lobe activity and processing of positive and negative emotional stimuli

---

7   The need for further investigations to follow up work that is still largely speculative is stressed in a review by Davidson (1998).

Occasional reports of hemispheric asymmetries in infants with depressed mothers have appeared during the past decade or so (e.g. Field et al. 1995) and a series of papers has emerged from work carried out by Geraldine Dawson and researchers at the University of Washington. As there is not space here to discuss all the available work, we will confine ourselves to the work of Dawson's group which has been studying infants of depressed mothers with an effort to "demonstrate not only how the early social environment influences children's behavior, attitudes, beliefs, and thoughts, but also how it influences the neural processes that underlie them" (Dawson and Ashman 2000, p.246).

Dawson et al.'s initial study (Dawson et al. 1992) included 27 mothers aged between 15 and 21 years, from a low socio-economic background. Thirteen had clinically high levels of depression and fourteen were relatively symptom-free. Videotape observations were made alongside EEG recordings of frontal and parietal lobe activity in infants who were aged between 11 and 17 months while:
1) they watched bubbles cascading from behind a black curtain (baseline measure)
2) they watched a Sesame Street video interspersed with three ten-second segments of an actress silently modelling three emotions ('happy', 'sad' and 'neutral')
3) the mother played Peek-a-Boo for a minute
4) a stranger entered, loomed over the baby and slowly left the room
5) they played with the mother and again watched bubbles
6) mother waved goodbye and slowly left the room (ten seconds) and stayed out (20 seconds).

EEG recording ended when mothers, who had been required to maintain a neutral expression during all but the Peek-a-Boo episode, re-entered the room. Analyses showed greater left frontal lobe activity in infants with asymptomatic mothers during play (suggesting that they were experiencing positive emotions during this interaction) whereas no asymmetry was found for infants of depressed mothers in whom left hemisphere activity appeared depressed. Interestingly, these patterns of brain activity were not reflected in ratings of the video observations of infant affect. Also, no differences were found on parietal measures.

Significant differences in patterns of frontal lobe activation appeared during the conditions designed to produce negative emotions (when the mother was out of the room and when the stranger loomed over the baby). Whereas babies with depressed mothers showed greater left frontal lobe activation, those with asymptomatic mothers tended to have greater right frontal lobe activation (as might be predicted in view of the theory that the right hemisphere is more involved in processing negative emotion). Dawson et al. (1992) concluded that these findings might best be explained by the notion that infants with depressed mothers are thrown back on emotion-focused self-directed coping strategies in order to regulate their negative affect whereas infants with non-depressed mothers use more other-directed strategies. This led them to wonder whether these patterns of cerebral asymmetry may obtain only in relation to babies' relationships with their mothers or whether they would be found to generalise to other situations too.

This is an interesting question and one that has led to valuable further investigation. There seems a possibility, though, that there might have been an underlying assumption that, should the patterns be found to generalise outside the mother-infant relationship or across other samples of mothers, the authors might consider themselves nearer their stated goal of demonstrating that the social environment influences neural processes. It seems, therefore, important to bear in mind the fact that, so far, there is no firm evidence that any differences found are due to the mother-child relationship rather than to other influences or predispositions. They may be, but a different study design would be needed to demonstrate this conclusively.

After further analyses of the video data from this same study, Dawson et al. (1997a, 1997b) later reported that, at times when infants of depressed mothers were displaying anger, their patterns of brain activity again differed from patterns shown by infants of non-depressed mothers.

From this initial small study, Dawson proceeded to a longitudinal study of 159 mother-child dyads, mostly married, from a middle-income background, and not suffering from any known medical conditions or major psychiatric problems. In this larger study, reports of which are still emerging, Dawson et al. (1999) have taken measures of measures of electrical brain activity (EEG), heart rate and vagal tone when children were aged 13 to 15 months, and repeated these measures along with cortisol assay at 42 months and at six-and-a-half years. The team was interested here to explore how patterns of brain activation in infants of these older mothers might compare with those in the teenage mother sample:
1) would the same patterns be found?
2) would they be found in mothers with other forms of psychopathology?
3) would they be found in relation to interactions with adults as well as mother?
4) would they predict individual differences in infant behaviour?
5) would it be possible to conclude that they were dependent upon the mother-child interaction and nothing else?

Ninety of the mothers were assessed as depressed at Time 1 testing (when babies were 13-15 months) and inspection of EEG patterns indicated similar patterns to those found in infants of teenage mothers (Dawson et al. 1997a, 1997b). During play with a familiar experimenter who silently played peek-a-boo using toys and smiling animatedly, patterns of brain activity differed in the same way as during play with mother (Dawson et al. 1999). Again, no differences were found in videotape ratings of infant affect displays. This time, though, the researchers found that, across all conditions except for the stranger approach (episode four), infants of depressed mothers not only had lower activity in the frontal regions but that these differences appeared to be more pronounced under conditions where positive emotions might be expected. Infants with depressed mothers showed less left frontal lobe activity than infants of non-depressed mothers. Dawson and Ashman (2000, p.265) comment, "This suggests that maternal depression may have a more specific effect on altering left frontal brain activity that has been associated with approach behaviour." The comment implies an assumption that patterns must have arisen from the mother-child relationship, which is a possibility, though not the only one.

Dawson et al. (1999) also found individual differences in infant behaviour associated with infants with depressed mothers: they were less able to show affection towards their mothers, less able to amuse themselves while their mothers completed a questionnaire, and were described by mothers as having more problems associated with emotional self-regulation and concentration. Patterns of hemispheric asymmetry also reliably predicted social approach behaviour, negativity, hostility, aggression and tantrums though only in respect of infants with depressed mothers.

On considering the critical fifth question, Dawson and Ashman (2000, p.268) rightly concluded that "At this point, our evidence is not definitive because we cannot control for genetic effects (this would require something like a twin adoption study); rather, the data are highly suggestive that such postnatal effects exist." Unfortunately suggestion is not sound science and, until the more rigorous test is carried out, the evidence cannot be said to be either conclusive or reliable. Therefore, the critical question of what might explain the observed differences remains unanswered.

In a later paper (Ashman et al. 2002), Dawson's team reported on cortisol levels among seven- to eight-year-old children of 74 mothers in the same longitudinal study. In this subset of mothers, who were similar to the total sample on demographic characteristics, 29 had no symptoms of depression, 15 had symptoms that remitted after second year of child's life and 30 had chronic depression. All postnatally depressed mothers had also experienced prenatal depression (on average 4.5 months for chronically depressed mothers and 1.8 months for mothers whose symptoms had remitted by two years).

Children's cortisol levels were recorded on arrival at the university laboratory, after mild stress (a task involving measurement of fear-potentiated startle responses to white noise and an air blast to the throat), at home on waking up and at bedtime. Results showed that, as previous studies had found, children with chronically depressed mothers were rated by mothers as having more behaviour problems and by researchers as having more symptoms of major depression. The authors also claimed that their results provide preliminary evidence of sensitive periods in terms of the impact of maternal depression on children's stress responses since mothers' depression in the first two years of life was the best predictor of elevated cortisol levels at age seven: "It is conceivable that early exposure to the more negative and unpredictable caretaking of a depressed mother sensitizes the neural pathways that mediate the stress response and increases vulnerability to depression" (Ashman et al. 2002, p.346).

Caution is needed when considering these findings. First, for unexplained reasons, only time of day, mother's concurrent psychiatric symptoms (Brief Symptom Inventory), months of prenatal depression, months of depression in the first two years and months of depression in years three to seven were entered into analyses of effects of the timing of mothers' depression on children's cortisol levels. Only baseline laboratory cortisol levels and months of depression in the first two years were significantly associated (at only $p=.04$), not home levels or cortisol elevations due to the laboratory 'startle' task. These findings therefore, on the grounds of the design alone, cannot be said to have elucidated the relationship between months of maternal depression in the first two years and children's cortisol responses. In order to draw confident conclusions about sensitive period effects emerging from the first two years (which, according to some definitions may indicate more than postnatal depression anyway) comparisons would need to be made between a no-depression control group and seven other conditions (Table 6.6). This is nothing like the design from which Ashman et al. draw their conclusions. Rather, condition H, essential if inferences about the impact of maternal depression in the first two years are to be viable, appears in Ashman et al.'s design to have been conflated with at least three other conditions. The same problem applies with their analysis of chronicity: it is not clear whether this was chronic prenatal and postnatal depression, only 3-7 or 0-7. These problems make it very difficult to be confident about any conclusions drawn in respect of the timing of mothers' depression.

Table 6.6
Conditions needed to establish sensitive period effects for postnatal depression

	TIMING OF MOTHERS' DEPRESSION		
Condition	prenatal	0-2 years	3-7 years
A	Yes	No	No
B	Yes	Yes	No
C	Yes	Yes	Yes
D	No	No	No
E	No	No	Yes
F	No	Yes	Yes
G	No	No	Yes
H	No	Yes	No

Separate analyses were carried out to examine the relationship between mothers' symptoms of depression and children's behaviour problems (as reported by mothers using a Behaviour Check List). In order to perform these analyses, children's behaviour problem scores were sorted into two groups: those above a clinical cut-off point (nine children) on internalising symptoms (anxiety, worry, etc.) and those below (65 children). Eight of the nine children who scored above the cut-off point had chronically depressed mothers.

Although there was no main effect of internalising symptoms on cortisol levels, the researchers found that the nine children who had been described by their mothers as high on internalising problems had higher levels of cortisol after the laboratory startle task than other children. The temptation might have been to stop analysing data on these nine children and think, so, under stress, cortisol responses in children described as highly anxious by their depressed mothers reflect their reported personality – in this sample at least.

Instead, the researchers went on to perform tests for moderator variables using the mothers' diagnostic group and children's internalising symptoms as predictor variables. They found that these variables, as may perhaps be expected, both predicted baseline laboratory cortisol levels, post-laboratory startle task responses, and, less strongly, cortisol levels on waking, and that there was an interactive effect of mothers' diagnostic group and children's internalising symptoms on baseline laboratory cortisol levels. They reported no effect sizes which, given both the small number of children with internalising problems in the clinical range and the unequal cell sizes for comparisons, might be a matter for concern. They speculated that "Children of depressed mothers who also had elevated internalizing symptoms may have perceived the laboratory situation as threatening and themselves as less able to cope with the novel situation" (Ashman et al. 2002, p.346).

In a later paper, Dawson et al. (2003) followed up 116 mothers from the same sample when children were three-and-a-half years old. Of these, 59 mothers had never been diagnosed as depressed, 24 mothers had been depressed postnatally (some prenatally too) but their depression had remitted during the first two years of the child's life and 41 mothers had been chronically depressed (six of these had been hospitalised for psychiatric reasons while no mothers in the other groups had this experience). It was estimated that children of mothers in the 'remitted depression' group would have experienced maternal depression for about 20 per cent of their lives whereas 'chronically depressed' mothers had been depressed for approximately 50 per cent of their children's lives. The only demographic difference between groups of mothers was that fathers in the chronically depressed mother group were significantly older.

Similar arrangements were made for EEG recordings as when the infants had been tested at 13 to 15 months, and eye movements were also monitored. In addition, mothers and children were videotaped on a separate occasion during (a) free play, (b) clean-up, (c) an active hand-clapping 'gotcha' game, (d) a teaching task, (e) a waiting task. Mother-child interactions were coded according to mothers' affective behaviour (negative, flat, affectionate, body contact); mothers' verbal behaviour (praise, encouragement, amount of talk); and children's negative behaviour (aggression, non-compliance). Contextual risk factors were also noted using various measures of life events, parenting stress, social support, marital satisfaction and family conflict. Additional assessments of children's performance were also obtained using a version of the Child Behaviour Check List used before and another questionnaire designed for parents and teachers to record children's conduct, social and academic performance. These assessments were used to derive a score on internalising, externalising and all problems.

Complete EEG data was obtained for 89 children. No details are reported of numbers of children in each group. Graphs indicate lower brain activation in both frontal and parietal regions for children of chronically depressed mothers over all conditions, in comparison with children of mothers with no or remitted depression. Analyses were carried out to examine whether the mean number of months per year of maternal depression during the first two years, compared with the mean number of months per year of maternal depression during years three to seven, predicted EEG patterns. It was concluded that the latter measure was the strongest predictor of frontal and parietal EEG patterns at age three-and-a-half. No differences were found in respect of hemispheric asymmetry scores. No effect sizes are reported.

To examine the relationship between EEG patterns and children's behaviour problems, children were divided into those scoring one standard deviation above and those scoring below the mean on a composite measure of behaviour problems. Higher scores on externalising, internalising and total behaviour problems were associated with lower brain activation; internalising and total behaviour problems were associated with lower activation only in the frontal regions.

Dawson et al. (2003) also analysed the relationship between timing and duration (mean number of months per year), contextual risk factors, children's behaviour problems and quality of mother-child interaction and found higher levels of contextual risk factors among chronically depressed mothers as well as higher levels of parenting stress among both groups of depressed mothers. Chronically depressed mothers were no lower on warmth than other mothers but showed more withdrawn behaviours. A number of associations were found between children's behaviour problems and the duration and timing of depression (though, due to questions already raised concerning the adequacy of this study design for testing timing effects as well as the difficulty of determining the significance of a measure of average number of months of depression per year, these will not be discussed further here).

Summing up their findings, Dawson et al. (2003) suggest that differences in patterns of brain activity in children of depressed mothers might reflect less than optimal self-regulation and vulnerability to behaviour problems. However, they are careful to point out "that the mediational path between maternal depression and child brain activity was modest, suggesting that child brain activity is only one of many factors that can help account for variations in children's behavior" (Dawson et al. 2003, p.1172). They also recognised the need for more research before the significance of differences in patterns of brain activity can be determined, a point that is reiterated in a recent review of the literature on the significance and heritability of frontal EEG asymmetry (Coan and Allen 2004).

In another more theoretical paper, Dawson et al. (2000) take issue with many of Bruer's assertions about the relationship between early experience and social development, particularly his assertion that there is no proof of any direct causal relationship between rapid brain growth in infancy and the emergence of new skills, and his questioning of beliefs that particular kinds of interaction between parents and infants directly influence brain growth. They further agreed, contrary to the suggestion in the paper discussed above, that:

1. "it is unknown to what extent the early years of life, because of the tremendous changes in the sheer number of synapses that take place during this time, represent a particularly sensitive period for selecting and establishing preferentially active patterns of neural networks that are less susceptible to change later in life" (Dawson et al. 2000, p.699).
2. Sensitive periods for experience-expectant learning have been found in relation to first language acquisition and visual development but that "in most cases, it is not reasonable to consider one type of experience as having a permanent and specific effect on later outcomes" (Dawson et al. 2000, p.706).
3. There is a need for far more research on humans before a whole range of questions can be answered.

Among these questions, they included, for example, whether altered brain activity early in life constitutes a risk factor for later psychopathology, whether exposure to maternal depression within 14 months, or two years, of birth critically affects later development, whether the different patterns of brain activity in infants of depressed mothers are due to:
- imitation
- failure to learn effective self-regulation
- inadequate input that prevents optimal brain development
- less that optimal intra-uterine experiences
- other genetic factors.

The chief point on which Dawson et al. and Bruer would appear to disagree is in their understanding of which experiences might occur in an 'environment of evolutionary adaptedness' (EEA), that is, what kind of environment experience-expectant development has evolved within. While Bruer argues that the kind of environmental conditions that could produce experiences outside the EEA are, by definition, extraordinary and extremely rare, Dawson et al. argue that there are many common conditions that result in experiences being outside the EEA. This difference of opinion seems to stem from a philosophical rather than an empirical source but represents a fundamental divergence and produces two very different perspectives. Dawson et al. seem to identify as outside the EEA experiences that compromise any aspect of 'normal development' whereas Bruer's definition is restricted to experiences which, if missed, would terminate the processes leading to normal development. As a result, Dawson et al. consider experience-expectant development as in greater danger of being threatened than Bruer does and conceptualise early experiences as of greater, indeed, critical significance for later development. Bruer's tighter definition leaves the way open for most development to be conceptualised as experience-dependent and so not subject to critical, or sensitive, period effects. Disadvantages due to lack of experience, particularly social experience, can therefore, in Bruer's view, usually be remedied if necessary or desired, at a later time.

The two perspectives obviously lead to rather different strategies in terms of recommendations for early intervention. Dawson et al. opt principally (though not exclusively) for early intervention, with training focused on early identification of problems, early delivery of appropriate support and treatment, targeting of multi-problem communities, more practical, material and emotional support for parents who are experiencing difficulties and educational initiatives aimed to increase public awareness of prenatal risks, for example, from drug use, etc. Bruer, by contrast, argues that there are no grounds for prioritising early over later interventions and suggests that some early interventions may be mis-targeted, ineffective and, if they divert resources from necessary later interventions, counter-productive.

In this brief review of the literature on effects of postnatal depression on brain development, we have deliberately erred on the side of caution in drawing conclusions. The research so far does not seem sufficiently advanced to enable firm conclusions to be drawn as to the origin of differences in patterns of electrical brain activity, nor to determine what the effects of early remitting postnatal depression might be. On the other hand, there does appear to be good reason for fearing that infants cared for by mothers who are suffering from stress or depression will be at risk for experiencing less than optimal interaction. It has also been recognised relatively recently that fathers, too, can experience depression during the period immediately after childbirth (Ballard et al. 1994, Areias et al. 1996, Buist et al. 2003), a factor that may further impact on the quality of the parenting environment. There is evidence that appropriate support can be beneficial though further efforts are needed to discover which kind of support may be most effective for individual parents (Barnes and Freude-Lagevardi 2003, Barrett 2003). This would suggest the wisdom of continued funding of initiatives aimed to support parents experiencing difficulties early in the lives of their children.

Skin-to-skin contact and baby-carrying

Figures 6.7 and 6.8 illustrate the earlier version and its more recent re-incarnation of the controversial theme relating to the role of physical contact in the formation of attachment bonds.

Figure 6.7: The necessity of skin-to-skin contact for bonding (Klaus and Kennell 1976)

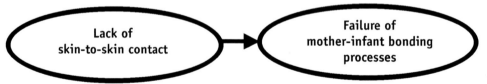

Figure 6.8: Re-incarnation of skin-to-skin contact hypothesis (Hofer 1984, Odent 1999)

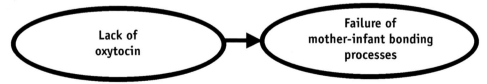

Skin-to-skin contact

The view that early skin-to-skin contact is important for the formation of bonds between mothers and babies does not appear to have emerged as a key message either from the work of Bowlby or of Ainsworth although questions about the role of physical contact were of great interest to them. While Bowlby may have encouraged the policy of rooming-in for mothers of sick infants and children in hospitals, and tended in his earlier work to stress that physical proximity-seeking (as opposed to emotional availability or 'felt security') was the 'set-goal' of attachment behaviour, and was certainly very adamant that prolonged mother-child separation in the first years of life was detrimental, he actually wrote relatively little about the relationship between the development of attachment security and physical contact. Even so, occasional references, particularly in his earlier papers, might be seen to support the view that he advocated close physical contact, for example: "In my experience a mother's acceptance of clinging and following is consistent with favourable development even in the absence of breast feeding, whilst rejection of clinging and following is apt to lead to emotional disturbance even in the presence of breast feeding" (Bowlby 1953/1965, p.370); "The role of close physical contact with mother during human infancy has been studied especially by Ainsworth who finds that children who develop a secure attachment to mother are those who, during early infancy, are held longest in a tender and loving way" (Bowlby 1984a/1988b, p.15).

Ainsworth, on the other hand, expressed more views on the role of physical contact. In her 1967 paper, she reported that security of attachment appeared to be associated both with the amount that mothers held their infants, the way that infants were held and the promptness with which mothers responded to infants' bids for attention. Mothers who were less tender and affectionate in their handling of their infants were more likely to have infants rated as being insecure. This opinion brought Ainsworth into some conflict with childcare 'experts' from the behaviourist perspective who were then advising that paying attention to infants' crying would reinforce bad behaviour and 'spoil' the child.

Later, she appeared to have accepted the view that the process of mother-infant bonding differed from that of infant-mother bonding: "the evidence reported so far suggests that the bonding of mother to infant may take place almost immediately after the infant's birth, provided that conditions are optimum, whereas there is every reason to believe that the attachment of infant to mother develops only gradually during the infant's first six months or so of life" (Ainsworth 1982, pp. 23-24). And, although carrying did not feature highly in her later work, in an interview with Karen (Karen 1994), Ainsworth re-affirmed her view that "It's a good thing to give a baby and a young child physical contact... especially when they want it and seek it. It doesn't spoil them. It doesn't make them clingy. It doesn't make them addicted to being held" (Karen 1994, p.170).

However, overall amount of holding or physical contact was not found by Ainsworth to discriminate between infants who were securely or insecurely attached. Rather, she identified important qualitative differences which have also been appreciated by other workers (Main 1977, Main and Stadtman 1981, Egeland and Farber 1984): "Ainsworth showed that mothers of babies who are later avoidant hold their babies as much as mothers of babies who are later secure. So if you just measure frequency of holding you get no differences. But there's one circumstance in which mothers of babies who are later avoidant do not hold them, and that's when the baby signals that it wants to be held. So you could have counted a lot of holding and you would have gotten nothing" (Interview with Sroufe, quoted in Karen 1994, p.165). Perhaps for this reason, studies of patterns of physical contact between mothers and children are almost as rare in the field of attachment research as is physical contact between patient and analyst in the psychoanalytic consulting room.

One exception to this rule is an experiment designed to test the effect of infant carrying on attachment formation which was carried out by Anisfeld and colleagues (1990). In this study, 23 mothers who carried their infants close to their bodies in soft carriers were compared with 26 mothers who used plastic seats which deterred close body contact. Both groups of mothers were described as coming from a low-income clinic population recruited on a postnatal ward. In the soft carrier group, 65 percent of mothers were Hispanic and 35 per cent were Black while the converse was the case for the plastic chair condition (38 per cent of mothers were Hispanic and 62 per cent were Black); also there were fewer first-time mothers in the soft carrier group (30 vs. 58 per cent). At the outset of the study, scores on a Maternal Attitude Scale (no details of this scale or its psychometric properties are given and each mention attributes it to different authors) showed no differences between mothers. It is unclear from the information given whether maternal qualities such as state of mind in respect of attachment or attitudes toward infants' need for physical contact were measured. There remains a possibility, therefore, that the two groups may have differed in important ways at the outset of the study.

Results showed a lower proportion of secure relationships in the plastic seat group (38.5 versus 83 per cent) with ten (38.5 per cent) of infants in the plastic seat group being classified at 13 months as insecure-avoidant and six (23 per cent) being classified as insecure-resistant. Mothers in the soft carrier group were also judged to be responding more contingently to their babies' vocalisations at three-and-a-half months: they joined their infants more readily in vocalising and interacted more proactively (this measure was labelled 'maternal responsivity' and involved different items to 'maternal sensitivity' on which no significant between group differences were found at three-and-half months).

While this study may appear to show the benefit of one type of carrier over another, several considerations call into question the reliability and generalisability of findings. First, the size of the sample was very small and attrition rates, which were generally rather high, affected the two conditions differently: complete data could not be obtained for seven out of 30 mothers in the soft carrier condition and four out of 30 in the plastic seat condition; the effects of these differential attrition rates on outcome are not known. Second, from the information given, it appeared that the majority of mothers in both conditions had not complied with instructions to use the equipment every day. The actual extent of usage seems unclear: plastic seat mothers were described as having used the seats for 5.3 months on average in comparison with 8.5 months for soft carrier mothers; four 'soft carrier' mothers were still using their carriers at 13 months though no information is presented about 'plastic seat' mothers at this stage. Pedometers measured use of slings but not plastic seats though no details were given about what these showed and no statistical analysis of length of product use was presented. In addition, four mothers in the plastic seat condition, three of whom were assessed as having securely attached babies, also began to use soft carriers after the start of the study but were neither dropped from the study nor re-assigned. Thus, there is a possibility that the benefits of soft carrier use may have been under-estimated. Third, there was no true control condition (i.e. no 'no carrier' or 'no seat' condition) and, although the authors maintained that the plastic seat could not be considered an intervention because "they are ubiquitous in this culture" (Anisfeld et al. 1990, p.1619), the possibility that encouragement to use a plastic seat may have had a disruptive effect cannot be discounted. Fourth, mothers and infants in each group were fairly well matched on a number of relevant criteria but were not matched on ethnicity, parity, or mode of feeding.

More mothers in the soft carrier group breastfed their babies (48 vs. 38 per cent). Although the authors state that method of feeding was not related to sensitivity or attachment, their credibility is not helped by the fact that this claim is unaccompanied by details of analyses and is in the same sentence as a misprinted and incompletely reported non-significant association between feeding and mothers' verbal responsivity at three-and-a-half months (".20 >p >.10"; Anisfeld et al. 1990, p.1622).

Overall, these problems point to the need for further replication of this study, with a larger and better controlled sample and a study design capable of examining in more detail the effects of different types of carrying for mothers from different social and cultural backgrounds. The value of such an investigation is underscored by the fact that, in their recent meta-analysis of attachment interventions, Bakermans-Kranenberg et al. (2003) calculated that one of the most substantial effect sizes for attachment security came from this intervention (.62).[8] Now that the 'disorganised' attachment pattern has also been identified, there may also be a therapeutic benefit in discovering whether or not the use of soft carriers might reduce the incidence of these patterns among mothers in populations identified as at risk of abuse or neglect.

Skin-to-skin contact for full-term babies

The real source of popular beliefs about the benefits of skin-to-skin contact between newborns and parents is difficult to track down but seems to have been quite independent of Attachment Theory. Some have traced their origins to interpretations of studies of animals, particularly non-human primates. Others have traced them to the influence of the 'natural' childbirth movement (possibly introduced towards the end of the 1950s in Britain) and, in particular, to the advice of Ferdinand Leboyer who advocated that babies should be born in near darkness, in a peaceful environment, and placed immediately after birth on the mother's body and massaged by her (Oakley 1979).

In a slightly different vein, Jean Liedloff (1977) outlined her theory of the 'Continuum Concept'. On the basis of her experiences of life among the Yequana Indians in South America, Liedloff had come to the view that modern Western childbirth practices, which routinely separate mothers and babies post-partum, are an evolutionary anathema. The Yequana way, in contrast, involves constant physical contact between babies and their caregivers, breastfeeding on cue, parent-child co-sleeping, almost continuous carrying of infants and small children, and acceptance that infants' bids for attention are legitimate. Identifying an early "in-arms" phase of infant development, she believes that babies are "programmed by millions of years of evolution to signal his or her own kind by sound and action when care is incorrect... Unanimously, they let us know by the clearest of signals that *they should not be put down at all*" (Liedloff 1989, pp. 17-18). Though closely related, this concept is rather different from the notion that early skin-to-skin contact in the first hours of life is important for the formation of attachment bonds and has received relatively less attention from researchers, although work by Tiffany Field's team at the Touch Research Institute in Miami is gradually addressing this question.

---

8   Rather curiously, Bakermans-Kranenburg and Van IJzendoorn also report an effect size of .53 for maternal sensitivity although Anisfeld et al.'s report states that maternal sensitivity was only assessed during a play session at three-and-a-half months and that between-group differences, though favouring soft carrier mothers, were not statistically significant.

Field et al. (2004), in a recent review of stimulation programmes for preterm infants (primarily baby massage employing stroking with light pressure as opposing to light stroking which can be experienced as aversive and tickly) pointed to evidence of benefits including greater weight gain, greater alertness and subsequent financial savings as babies are discharged earlier from hospital, though only if it is used as an intervention with babies that weigh between 900 and 1500 grams. The mechanism for these benefits, they suggest, may be associated with facilitation of metabolic efficiency linked with increased activity or with an increase in vagal nerve activity which might both enhance gastric motility and increase the rate of food absorption by making growth-facilitating, such as insulin, available. They further speculate that the insulin growth factor (IGF-1) might decrease levels of circulating cortisol and increase the likelihood of growth in the nervous tissues associated with brain development. Finally, they suggest that the benefits of baby massage might be associated with increases in endogenous opioids such as oxytocin which might also be linked with pleasurable growth-promoting experiences, although they admit that there is as yet no substantial evidence to support this idea.

Investigations of the effects of immediate, postnatal contact on later outcomes for mothers and children have been rather more common. Reviewers (e.g. Lamb and Hwang 1982, Sluckin et al. 1983, Anderson 1991, Eyer 1992) have generally concluded that benefits, if any, tend to 'wash out' quite soon over the first year or two of life, that evidence for benefits is inconsistent and that many studies are methodologically flawed. For example, Sluckin et al. (1983) considered claims in relation to the role of skin-to-skin contact and mother-to-infant bond formation. They drew particular attention to the well-known study by Klaus and Kennell (1976) which claimed to have demonstrated that during the first few days of neonatal life, in humans as in monkeys, there was a critical period during which skin-to-skin contact was essential for the later development of close mother-infant bonds.

Klaus and Kennell assigned mothers of full-term babies to one of two conditions, a 'routine care' group and an 'extended contact' group. Mothers in the extended contact group were given one hour of close physical contact with their naked baby within the first three hours of delivery and another 15 hours in the first three days. Results suggested that, one month after birth, mothers in the extended contact group fondled their babies more during feeding and spent more time in eye contact with them; one year later, extended contact mothers were reported to be more attentive to their infants and more responsive to them during a physical examination but there were no differences between mothers in four other situations, including free play; another year later, it was claimed that the extended contact mothers' speech to their infants was richer and more appropriate. Subsequent reviews of this study (e.g. Lamb and Hwang 1982, Goldberg 1983) cast serious doubts on the claims made, both on the grounds that, on many measures, no differences had been found but, more seriously, because of flawed methodology. Mothers in the extended contact group, which focused on 28 high-risk young black single mothers, not only had more contact with their infants, they also received more attention from researchers than their counterparts in the control condition. In addition, the sample was small and idiosyncratic.

Subsequently, de Chateau and Wiberg (1977a, 1977b, 1984) attempted to replicate the original Klaus and Kennell study in a more controlled study. They compared 22 middle-class Swedish primiparous mothers given just 15 minutes of skin-to-skin contact and suckling time within hours of birth with 20 matched controls who received routine care. Results suggested that mothers given extended care did not differ from routine care mothers on most measures at 36 hours, three months, one year and three years but that, where there were differences, these indicated closer and more cooperative relationships between extended contact mothers and their infants. Also, extended care mothers breastfed for longer and were more likely to have had other babies while routine care mothers tended to feel that they had not been given enough time with their babies after delivery.

Findings from other studies have been inconsistent: some studies failed to find any effects of extended care or skin-to-skin contact (e.g. Carlsson et al. 1978, Svejda et al. 1980, Craig et al. 1982); a number have indicated that the practice of permitting mothers only very limited immediate postnatal contact with their infants (common in hospitals at the time) might reduce either the mother's readiness to have physical contact with her baby in the early weeks after birth or the quality of her interactions, though usually in limited ways rather than in all situations (e.g. Carlsson et al. 1979); other studies have indicated that there may be some benefits for infants of early skin-to-skin contact, such as prevention of temperature loss, improved breathing, higher blood glucose, less crying and more quiet sleep and benefits for mothers, such as increasing their sense of confidence and pleasure in engaging in close physical contact, breastfeeding and other aspects of baby care (e.g. Christensson et al. 1992, 1995; Karlsson 1996).

The qualified conclusion offered by Sluckin et al. (1983) was that, while there may have been some benefits of early skin-to-skin contact for some mothers, there was little evidence to support the view that it played a critical role in the quality of mother-infant attachment bonds over longer times. They drew attention to the fact that, since many studies were flawed methodologically, more evidence was needed before definitive conclusions could be drawn. This cautious conclusion would also seem to be supported by evidence from more recent studies, though there are indications that inclusion of different outcome measures may have produced an even more patchy and varied picture. It is difficult to surmise whether a more thorough and extensive review might produce different conclusions.

Kangaroo care for preterm infants

More systematic reviews are available of the studies of the effects of close body contact on preterm neonates or 'kangaroo mother care' (KMC) as this practice of baby care is now more widely known. KMC is thought to have been first introduced by Dr. Edgar Rey in response to overcrowded postnatal wards and high numbers of low birthweight babies[9] in Bogotá, Colombia (Tessier et al. 1998). It includes constant skin-to-skin contact between mothers and their newborns, who are usually positioned ventrally between their mothers' breasts and, as far as possible, exclusive breastfeeding as often as the baby will feed. Once KMC babies reach a certain target, e.g. 1700 kg, the mother and baby are discharged from hospital, earlier than would be the case for an incubator-reared premature infant. The aim of KMC is that KMC mothers, like mother kangaroos, take the place of incubators for their pre-term babies, helping the babies to maintain a stable body temperature. This in turn ensures optimal feeding and breathing conditions and can provide additional protection by both colonising baby with the mother's skin flora and reducing exposure to hospital infections. Obviously, this practice considerably reduces the cost of hospital care and has the additional benefits of 'de-medicalising' the care of LBW babies and of maximising the involvement of the mother.

Most studies focusing on the use of KMC with premature babies are designed to ascertain whether this regime can reduce the likelihood of infant death and improve the baby's physical condition rather than to track longer-term effects on the relationship between

---

9 LBW babies are usually considered to be those who weigh less than 2000 grams at birth.

mothers and young children. Nevertheless, a number of studies have included an assessment of maternal attitudes and have included measures of maternal sensitivity (not usually Ainsworth's measures).

One study by Tessier et al. (1998) is mentioned in the meta-analysis of intervention studies by Bakermans-Kranenburg et al. (2003) as one of the four studies that did not use personal contact as a means of intervention. These four studies (which included Anisfeld et al. 1990, discussed above, a study that used a workbook and one that used a video) are described as tending, surprisingly, to show the largest effect sizes and Bakermans-Kranenburg et al. (2003, p.205) comment: "It is somewhat paradoxical that the interventions with the smallest investments in terms of time and money tended to be the more effective." However, they did qualify their positive remarks with the reservation that the subset was rather small, the difference in effect size for them compared with the other studies did not reach statistical significance. For this reason, they urged against over-confidence in this result as the variability in the data was large. In fact, the effect size estimate for the Tessier et al. study was only 0.08 and the study only included an assessment of maternal sensitivity, not of attachment security.

The Tessier et al. report describes a randomised controlled trial that compared outcomes for 488 LBW (<2001 grams) infants (246 given kangaroo mother care and 242 given traditional care) with those for 258 non-participating mother-infant dyads (infants in this group were on average 56 grams heavier at birth but did not differ on any other socio-demographic or birth-related variable). Allocation to the KMC (kangaroo mother care) or TC condition was random.

Baseline assessments of infants were taken at birth and outcome measures were based on analysis of interview and videotape data focusing on mother-infant interactions. Structured interviews with mothers took place after 24 hours in the hospital and when babies reached 41 weeks conceptional age. They were based on a questionnaire (Mother's Perception of Premature Birth) that focused on three areas: the mother's social and family background and perception of social support, her sense of stress and worries about the baby and her sense of competence. When infants reached 41 weeks gestational age, mothers were videoed feeding their babies for 15 minutes. Videos were scored using an instrument called the Nursing Child Assessment Feeding Scale. This scale was described as measuring the emotional bond between mother and child and consists of 76 binary items designed to tap six factors, including the mother's sensitivity to the infant, her response to infant distress, her behaviour in relation to the baby's socio-emotional and cognitive needs, and the infant's response the mother (clarity of cues, responsiveness). From these subscales, a measure of maternal sensitivity can be derived.

Results suggested that the main benefit in reduction of length of hospital stay was for the lowest birthweight infants (<1501): there was no difference in length of stay for KMC or TC mothers with infants above this birthweight. At the 41 week conceptional age interview, KMC mothers reported that they felt more competent although they also reported having less social support than TC mothers. These differences were associated with the length of time mothers spent in the hospital: TC mothers became more stressed the longer they stayed in the hospital whereas the opposite tended to be the case for KMC mothers. KMC mothers were assessed as more sensitive to their infants and, though this effect was slightly moderated if interventions began later, it did not appear to depend on timing. Concerns about the babies' health moderated the group differences on sense of competence and on maternal sensitivity. KMC scores were higher on all measures of maternal sensitivity and infant responsivity if babies had needed intensive care at birth.

The authors remarked that, although the mothers in the KMC group felt more competent, the psychological impact of KMC was more complex than they had initially thought and concluded that "The observations of the mothers' sensitive behavior did not show a definite bonding effect, but rather a resilience effect (mothers in the KMC group were more sensitive toward an at-risk infant whose development has been threatened by a longer hospital stay)... the infant's health status may be a more prominent factor in explaining a mother's more sensitive behavior, which overshadows the kangaroo-carrying effect" (Tessier et al. 1998). However, they also concluded that, from a subjective perspective, the empowering nature of KMC appeared to effect a change in mothers' perception of the child. They also observed short-term benefits in terms of mothers' perceptions and behaviour (lasting for up to one month) for both TC and KMC mothers compared with control group mothers. In conclusion, the authors recommended that KMC should be promoted actively but that it should include an element of support.

A recent meta-analytic review of studies of the use of KMC with premature infants, which identified nine studies, three of which were randomised controlled trials, however, drew a rather different conclusion: "Although KMC appears to reduce severe infant morbidity, there is not enough evidence to recommend its routine use in LBW infants" (Conde-Agudelo et al. 2003, p.6). The authors did acknowledge that there might be some benefits of KMC in respect of less severe illness, nosocomial infection, maternal dissatisfaction and greater preparedness to exclusively breastfeed but stated that it was not possible to be confident that these were real effects due to methodological limitations (non-blind assessment, non-random allocation to trial, etc..). The authors recommended that further, better controlled evaluations were warranted and stressed the value of including longer-term follow-up of development. As mentioned above, this latter recommendation would also seem very apposite in relation to studies that use KMC with full-term babies.

The role of oxytocin

The notion that the hormone oxytocin plays an important role in the neurobiological processes that underpin the formation and maintenance of social bonds, most specifically pair bonds in adults and parent-child bonds, has recently been used to support the argument that emotional bonding processes depend upon physical contact. While it was formerly believed that oxytocin was only peripherally implicated in the action of muscles used during labour and lactation (hence the use of exogenous oxytocin, or pitocin, to bring on and oxytocin antagonists, such as atosiban, to delay labour), some workers now believe that the release of oxytocin in mother and child during breastfeeding in particular but also during physical contact more generally may be a key factor that promotes mother-infant and infant-mother bonding. They also argue, as Bowlby did, that this bonding process has a direct function in respect of the survival of offspring.

One of the most widely cited studies in this connection is that of Hofer (1984) who proposed, on the basis of studies of rats, that mothers appear to act as 'hidden regulators' of all the physiological systems developing in their offspring. At birth, rat pups are unable to self-regulate or to self-calm. At this stage therefore, they are dependent on contact with their mothers in order to maintain body temperature and all other physiological functions, including heart rate, respiration, protein synthesis, endocrine activity, etc. Separation from mothers evokes squealing and distress which can be reduced by administration of either exogenous oxytocin (OT) or vasopressin (AVP) but which more usually stops when the pups are in contact with mothers. During the first weeks after birth, oxytocin in the rat pups begins to be genetically transcribed and both OT and AVP receptors rapidly appear. Surges of oxytocin in the mother are thought to be responsible for the emergence of maternal caregiving. Although it has been suggested that OT secreted in the mothers' milk, once ingested by offspring, is absorbed into the gut and into the infant's brain and that it is this process that is responsible for calming the infant, there is little evidence to support this view (Insel 1997).

In greatly over-simplified terms, the argument appears to be that endogenous (produced by one's own body) oxytocin is produced in mothers and babies during labour and lactation as well as in association with physical contact and warm, close social encounters. Oxytocin is intrinsically linked with reward pathways which involve natural opiates and so produces a calming effect in both mothers and babies (which has been demonstrated in many species including rats, sheep, dogs and chicks). This in turn increases the strength of preferences for particular people because it makes their company enjoyable. In fathers, or at least among a substantial subset of them, it appears that exposure to babies can also increase blood levels of oxytocin in much the same way as in mothers (Light et al. 2000), though it is not clear whether the ways in which oxytocin reinforces paternal and maternal behaviours are exactly the same. Figure 6.9 indicates the relationship between oxytocin and its naturally occurring antagonist, argenine vasopressin.

It appears that oxytocin has been singled out for special attention as an 'attachment hormone' largely on the basis of findings from animal studies such as the one mentioned above but also from studies of two different species of vole and their patterns of mating and family formation. Unlike montane (meadow) voles, prairie (pine) voles engage in affiliative social behaviour, show selective preferences for con-specific partners and form monogamous pair-bonds that last throughout their lives. Adult males take on the role of protector to female partners and offspring, show selective aggression towards intruders and are involved in parenting. By contrast, montane voles are social isolates. The males are sexually promiscuous and polygamous. They do not form pair bonds and do not stay with the females that they have impregnated. Female montane voles leave their young to fend for themselves soon after birth and do not parent them. Neurobiologically, the two species differ in that the prairie voles have more OT receptors in their prelimbic cortices (PLC) and particularly in their nucleus accumbens (NAcc), an area in which no or hardly any OT receptors are to be found in montane voles (Shapiro and Insel 1990). They also have more AVP receptors in the ventral pallidal areas of their brains (which output to the nucleus accumbens) and in the ventral striatal areas. For a very brief period only after they have given birth, the pattern of OT receptors in montane voles appears to become more like that in prairie voles but otherwise patterns are distinctly different (Insel 1997).

Since both the nucleus accumbens and the ventral pallidal areas are thought to be key components of reward pathways, within the mesolimbic dopamine circuit and other opioid systems, it has been further hypothesised that OT and AVP play a key role in modulating the reward pathways that facilitate social attachment and affiliation (Young et al. 2001). It has also been noted that the linked mesolimbic dopamine pathway is the reward pathway thought to be associated with addiction, an observation which has led some workers to postulate some commonality of origin between addictive dependency and the kind of social dependency involved in attachment behaviour (Nelson and Panksepp 1998).

Figure 6.9: The relationship between the two nonaminergic peptides

OXYTOCIN (OT)	BOTH	VASOPRESSIN (AVP)

• ONE known receptor (but binds to AVP receptors)
• The most abundant neuropeptide in the hypothalamus (mRNA)
• Associated with
  – birth
  – lactation
  – sexual behaviours
  – HPA down-regulation
  – affiliative behaviours
• Can produce calming (both behavioural and physiological manifestations)
• Released during social interactions without fear
• Attenuates fear responses to social stimuli
• Facilitates growth and restoration
	• Possibly originate from a common genetic pathway
	• Are made up of nine amino acids (seven same, two different) and are closely related
	• Are present in the same regions though not in the same cells
	• Are released into bloodstream through posterior pituitary (neurohypophysis), hence called neurohypophyseal peptides
	• Are made in and act on the brain, especially the hypothalamus and areas that regulate the autonomic nervous system but also the central nervous system
	• Interact with each other
	• Have roles in
	  – modulation of memory
	  – regulation of fluid balance
	  – response to hypothermia
	  – complex social behaviours
		• THREE receptor subtypes
		  – V1a related to social bonding
		• Reduce social anxiety
		• Can facilitate social bonding
		• Associated with HPA up-regulation
		  – increases alertness
		  – increases behavioural reactivity
		  – increases arousal
		  – increases defensive behaviour
		• Males produce more than females, in association with androgens
		• Associated with mate-guarding and male parenting in monogamous species

Evidence in support of the hypothesised relationship between OT, AVC, monogamy and parenting comes from experiments on voles, other rodents and animals such as sheep. Some of these experiments involve blocking AVC and OT receptors with antagonists at selected stages of development and in selected sites to see whether mating and caregiving patterns alter. Blocking AVC receptors, for instance, in male prairie voles appears to reduce paternal caregiving. Blocking OT receptors in the nucleus accumbens and in the prelimbic cortex of prairie voles terminates selective preferences for partners and can lead to severely reduced levels of caregiving including attacks on offspring. However, injecting the same OT antagonist into the caudate putamen does not appear to affect parenting or partner preferences. Nelson and Panksepp (1996) demonstrated that giving exogenous OT to rat pups facilitates recognition, discrimination and preference for the smell of the mother rat while OT antagonists delay this conditioning. In mice, though, it has been found that knocking out the gene that expresses endogenous OT does not alter pair-bonding or parenting behaviours in any way: the only effect of lack of OT in 'knock-out mice' appears to be that they no longer produce milk (Nelson and Panksepp 1998).

These findings raise questions about what other compensatory mechanisms may be involved in pair bond formation and caregiving, what the role of oxytocin really is, how it interacts with other opioids and peptides (such as dopamine and norepinephrine) and how neuro-biological processes in humans might relate to those in other species. Insel (1997), along with other researchers in this field, stress that "oxytocin is only one link in a very complex neurochemical chain necessary for maternal behaviour" (p. 731) and that neither oxytocin nor vasopressin should be thought of as 'attachment hormones': "In a sense, then, oxytocin and vasopressin provide interesting case studies for investigating the neural substrates of attachment, but neither peptide should be thought of as pre-potent or even pre-eminent for these behaviours" (p. 733). He further warns against generalisation across species and emphasises that "Both the pathways *(OT and AVP)* and their regulation by gonadal steroids change markedly across species, precluding a simple extrapolation from mouse to monkey to human" (p. 733). What's more, he suggests, since OT receptors are found in so many sites throughout the body and since they do not appear to operate in the same way at all sites, it may be some time before the role of oxytocin in human behaviour is fully understood. Nevertheless, he concedes that both OT and AVP are likely to be important in the development of social behaviour and that they may be somehow implicated in autism.

Taken altogether, it seems rather difficult to evaluate the significance of all these findings in relation to humans. Some interpretations have led to the conclusion that the mother's brain is organised by the oxytocin rushes that she experiences during pregnancy and the first years of motherhood, and that this 'hard-wires' her brain for life, with high levels of oxytocin producing the most sensitive, responsive maternal care, the greatest understanding of infant cues and the strongest bonds both with the baby's father and with the child. In similar vein, it has been suggested (e.g. Carter 2003) that infants who are not breastfed, held or enjoyed enough may be at risk of beginning life with a peptide history already set on a dangerous track towards less optimal brain growth, poor emotional self-regulation and all the inevitable long-term consequences of a disregulated stress response system. While not being able to entirely dismiss such alarming possibilities, interpretations such as these do seem rather to reduce human development from a highly complex, multiply determined and often surprising phenomenon to a relatively meagre single thread. What seems more likely to be the case is that physical contact, including breastfeeding, skin-to-skin contact and carrying are each possible contributors to a much more complex array of influences, and that the importance of each single factor will depend on the overall 'symphony'. However, until more data is available to enable us to understand more fully the nature of that symphony, it seems likely that many parents will feel the safest choices may be those most similar to the animals closest to us in evolutionary terms. But which animal do we pick? Even within non-human primates, there are tremendous variations in relationships between mothers and fathers, and in how the tasks of child-rearing are carried out and shared.

The effect of the caregiving environment on personality development

The fourth controversial theme concerns effects of early experience on later development. At the time Bowlby put it forward, the view that children's personality development might be directly influenced by experiences within the family (as illustrated in Figure 6.10) was highly controversial. Figure 6.11 shows it in a more recent guise with the emphasis on the mechanism for parental influence being portrayed as very much centred on the extent to which parents regulate their children's emotional state and the consequences of this for children's physical and psychological wellbeing. The question we address here, then, is whether what parents do in the first few years of children's lives will have a lasting effect, whether, for example, when on the odd occasion parents 'lose it' and shout at their toddlers, or fail to pick up cues that their toddlers are unwell, tired or hungry, or lose them at a village fete, they may do permanent damage to their relationship or to the child's basic sense of trust.

Figure 6.10: The fourth controversial theme (Bowlby's entire work)

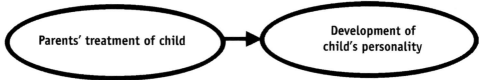

Figure 6.11: Recent re-incarnation of the fourth controversial theme

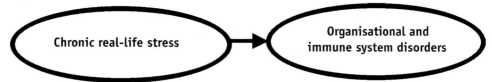

We have already touched on this question to some extent in Chapter Five, where we considered how patterns of attachment and children's subsequent social development might be shaped by influences from parents. In that chapter, we discussed a number of theories about the different qualities of parenting that may be associated with attachment formation. We also discussed the potential long-term effect of a stressful childhood family environment on children's social and emotional development. Earlier in this chapter, too, we discussed research on the impact of parenting practices (holding, carrying) and postnatal depression on outcomes for children.

In this section, we look more closely at two bodies of research that we have not so far considered: research on the influence of mothers' emotional state during pregnancy on the development of offspring and research that addresses the question of what the relationship might be between patterns of attachment established in the first years of life and later social relationships and development.

Prenatal stress and depression

It has long been popularly believed, more in some cultures than others, that a mother's mood during pregnancy has the power to influence the fate and/or personality of the baby growing within her. It has even been supposed by some that, in some magical way, the mother's deepest hopes and beliefs somehow infuse themselves into the foetus embedded within her. However, as Herschkowitz, a Swiss neuroscientist commenting on the effects of prenatal stimulation on later development, remarks, "If a mother's thoughts alone were enough, how different parenting would be!" (Herschkowitz and Herschkowitz 2002, p.21). Yet he acknowledges that research has shown that there may be a grain of truth in the common truism.

Results of few small, controlled studies of the effects of stress during pregnancy on infant development are available. These seem to converge on a conclusion that there may be an association between postnatal maternal stress and infant irritability though, as we shall show below, methodological problems urge for some caution before accepting these conclusions. Also, it is important to note that long-term effects are not yet clear and that there is no agreement about effects on infant cognitive development.

Van den Bergh (1992) found a positive correlation between mothers' level of anxiety in the third trimester of pregnancy and mothers' assessment of their infants' 'difficult' temperament at ten weeks and seven months, but no effects on infant mental or motor development. The possibility that mothers' anxiety may have contributed to the assessment of infant difficulty cannot be ruled out.

Another more recent study, employing a large sample of women who participated in the Avon Longitudinal Study of Parents and Children (ALSPAC) also claimed to have found that level of maternal stress during pregnancy could predict behaviour problems in offspring at age four (O'Connor et al. 2002). Logically, it would seem that the design needed to test such a prediction would be that shown in Table 6.7. If outcomes for offspring of women in condition A were to be found to differ from those of women in other conditions, then the conclusion could be drawn that prenatal stress or anxiety may predict later outcomes. With a small sample, this design would be over-ambitious. With the ALSPAC sample size of 7,448, it would seem more feasible. Yet, for unexplained reasons, this was not the design that the authors employed.

Table 6.7: Design required to test effects of prenatal stress on postnatal development

CONDITION		BEFORE BIRTH	AFTER BIRTH
A	+/-	Stress/anxiety	No stress/anxiety
B	-/+	No stress/anxiety	Stress/anxiety
C	-/-	No stress/anxiety	No stress/anxiety
D	+/+	Stress/anxiety	Stress/anxiety

Instead, O'Connor et al. (2002) measured levels of anxiety and depression in mothers antenatally (at 18 and 32 weeks gestational age) and postnatally (at eight weeks, eight months, 21 months and 33 months). They then collected parents' reports on children's emotional and behaviour problems at 47 months. They also gathered information about mothers' parity and obstetric history (including foetal risk status, mode of delivery, etc.), as well as their smoking and drinking behaviour (no mention of maternal health otherwise). High anxiety was identified as the 15 per cent of mothers who rated themselves highest on anxiety at each time of testing. Bivariate and multivariate analyses, controlling for co-variates and for postnatal anxiety and depression, indicated that mothers with elevated anxiety at 32 weeks gestation were more than twice as likely to have children with high levels of behavioural and emotional problems at age four. These effects appeared to be associated most closely with hyperactivity or attentional problems for boys but with a wider range of problems in girls. The authors concluded that "There could be a direct effect of maternal mood on foetal brain development, which affects the behavioural development of the child" (O'Connor et al. 2002, p.502). However, the design employed did not appear to have adequately tested for this effect.

O'Connor's conclusion was questioned by Oates (2002, p.479) who suggested that "it seems to be a case of the statistical tail wagging the clinical dog" and quipped: "The modern Western pregnant woman must not drink more than four cups of coffee a day, drink alcohol, smoke cigarettes, change cat litter trays, eat soft cheese, uncooked eggs or packaged salads or go into the lambing sheds. They should not work too hard or too long, or at night or be ambivalent about their pregnancies. Now it seems they must not become anxious either." As suggested above, she argued that the design of this study and its conclusions appear unsound. Oates further points out that the notion that stress stops at the point of delivery seems hard to imagine and that the authors' claim to have demonstrated that the effects of antenatal anxiety and depression were independent of postnatal effects is unconvincing. She adds that the move from discussing anxiety and depression as continuous variables to the conclusion that neuro-endocrine processes must have adversely affected brain development in the foetus is not a cautious one. O'Connor et al.'s conclusion seems clearly to move beyond the data given (as the authors themselves appear to acknowledge when they state that the data do not allow them to determine what physiological mechanisms might account for associations). We would further add that reliance on mothers' self-report and on parental report of children's behaviour is a serious limitation and also question the wisdom of not assessing maternal stress when the final measure of children's behaviour was made at 47 months. Although the authors argue that the dip in anxiety and depression ratings postnatally argues against the existence of reporter bias, as Oates points out, this dip has also been found in other studies (Green and Murray 1994). Both the possibility of reporter bias and of a genetic explanation for outcomes seem real and call out for further investigation.

Another research team, led by Jan Buitelaar, arrived at similar conclusions to O'Connor's team. They had monitored levels of cortisol in mothers' saliva at regular intervals during pregnancy and, on the basis of these tests, divided mothers into two groups according to whether mothers' cortisol levels were higher or lower. At the outset of the study, 230 women satisfied inclusion criteria (i.e. they were first-time mothers of singletons with no major pregnancy or birth complications, near full-term infants with good health and had APGAR scores higher than seven);[10] by follow-up at eight months, 170 women remained in the study, most having been eliminated because they gave birth before the late pregnancy cortisol test had been carried out. Tests of infants' mental and motor development were carried out when the infants were aged three and eight months. In another part of the study, Buitelaar's team videotaped infants in interaction with their mothers at home, between one and 20 weeks after birth.

---

10 APGAR scores provide an indication of the integrity of a baby's central nervous system and are routinely carried out in most cultures within hours of the baby's birth.

Results showed that babies of mothers in the 'high cortisol' group scored somewhat lower on developmental tests than did babies of mothers in the 'low cortisol' group though this finding only applied to comparisons between infants whose mothers' cortisol levels were the top and bottom quartiles; no linear relationship was found across the whole group of infants (Buitelaar et al. 2003). More 'high cortisol' group mothers described their babies as "difficult" and mothers who were fearful of giving birth also tended to have infants who scored lower on tests of psychomotor development. However, this only applied to measures of maternal stress taken early in pregnancy (no relationship was observed between measures taken later and infant temperament) and, once mothers' postnatal stress and depression was taken into account, only the correspondence between infant temperament measures at three months, not at eight months, was significant. This finding clearly indicates the need for replication before it is safe to conclude that the results are reliable or further generalisable. While effects on infant temperament in the Buitelaar et al. (2003) study were not assessed by independent observers, another study which included independently assessed videotape evidence confirmed that babies of 'high cortisol' mothers showed more signs of irritability: the infants were observed to fuss and cry more and to show more negative facial expressions (De Weerth et al. 2003).

Another study, with a smaller sample and a slightly less ambitious design, also reached similar conclusions to those of O'Connor's team and claimed that their "results link the findings of preclinical studies to humans by showing that exposure to early maternal stress may sensitize children's pituitary-adrenal responses to subsequent stress exposure" (Essex et al. 2002, p.776.) From an initial pool of 570 women recruited from prenatal clinics, 282 participated in the study which involved an assessment of maternal stress one year and four-and-a-half years after birth. The 282 women had a total of 135 sons and 147 daughters, as well as other siblings.

Maternal stress was assessed using a composite measure derived using principle components analysis (PCA) from maternal self-reports based on items taken from whole or part-measures relating to maternal depression, expressed anger in the family, parenting stress, role overload and financial stress. Children's mental health over the six months before they were four-and-a half (internalising and externalising symptoms) was assessed using PCA on combined scores from reports given by teachers, mothers and children. In addition, afternoon cortisol was collected from children (86 per cent between the target times of 3 and 7pm, the rest between 12 noon and 10pm). Data from 59 children on medication (for physical ailments) was included in analyses (although these children had higher cortisol levels), no data was excluded that was collected outside the target times (although, as might perhaps be expected, a significant negative correlation was found between time of collection and cortisol level) and no logarithmic transformation of scores was used (a normal procedure with the usually highly variable data obtained through cortisol assay). Usual practice when collecting samples of cortisol is to collect several samples over at least two days at different times of day (morning and evening). This establishes baseline levels and provides some indication of whether variations across the day might be due to within-child changes rather than between child differences. The method adopted by Essex et al. essentially confounded intra- and inter-child differences (that is, it muddled variability due to traits such as temperament with states such as illness).

Children's salivary cortisol levels were analysed in three ways:
1) by level of concurrent maternal stress (divided into the highest 25 per cent, the middle 50 per cent and the lowest 25 per cent)

2) by whether mother was judged to have been highly stressed both concurrently and in the past (when the child was one), only in the past, only now, and never
3) by level of symptom severity at the end of first grade.

Results showed a significant overall effect of concurrent maternal stress on children's cortisol levels: cortisol levels in children of highly stressed mothers were significantly higher than those in children of low and of moderately stressed mothers (no difference between children of moderately stressed and low stressed mothers though). This finding appeared also to obtain among the siblings in the study.

A significant effect of time of exposure was found which indicated that those children whose mothers were highly stressed both concurrently and in the past (i.e. at both times, which could indicate a continuity of stress since birth) had higher cortisol levels than children whose mothers were never stressed (though no details are given of how 'no maternal stress' was defined). No differences were found on *any* other comparisons of children's cortisol levels, i.e. no differences were found between children of mothers stressed at time two versus children of mothers stressed at time one, and no differences between children whose mothers were stressed at both times and either children whose mothers were only stressed at time one or those whose mother were only stressed at time two. The authors' overall conclusion therefore seems to fly in the face of these important null findings which do not suggest sensitization effects. An indication of these might have been evident had it been found that children of mothers stressed at both times had higher cortisol levels than both children of mothers stressed only at time one and those of mothers stressed only at time two. This is not what was found.

Correlations were found between levels of externalising and internalising symptoms at the end of first grade and cortisol levels but, once overlapping scores were taken into account, only a non-significant tendency remained on internalising symptoms ($p = 0.056$). This result therefore clearly requires replication before its importance can be assessed. Children living in low socio-economic status (SES) families also had significantly higher cortisol levels than children in high SES families.

Overall, then, the only conclusions that can safely be drawn from this study are that both concurrent and enduring maternal stress throughout childhood may be may be positively associated with cortisol levels in children. The possibility that these associations could be due to socio-economic conditions or to genetic influences most certainly cannot be ruled out. In sum, the authors' claim to have presented data to justify either the title of their paper or the claim that "our study suggests that early exposure to stress sensitized later HPA and behavioural responsivity" (Essex et al. 2002, p.782) seems highly questionable. As they rightly state, design limitations do not permit causal interpretations. The same limitations should also have precluded them from claims to have demonstrated sensitisation effects. All that was demonstrated was that enduring maternal stress may be associated with higher cortisol levels in children (leaving open the possibility that there may be no common underlying cause of this association).

Numerous animal studies have also suggested that there may be effects on brain development of high prenatal levels of maternal cortisol, for example, studies of monkeys (Lyons et al. 2000) and of rats (Caldji et al. 2000) have indicated that parts of the brain may develop differently if high levels of maternal cortisol are present during pregnancy. How these results might apply to humans is as yet unclear and the fact that different parts of the brain appear to be affected in different species underlines the need for caution before results are assumed to apply to humans. This caution does not seem to have been much heeded either by Schore (1994) or by Gerhardt (2004) who both appear rather uncritically to have assumed that sufficient evidence already exists to indicate that similar principles apply to infant development, for example, Schore (1994, p.7), whilst acknowledging that most of the research upon which he draws comes from animals, claims that "these studies uniquely reveal the biological and chemical changes that comprise the internal processes underlying the complex affective and cognitive capacities that come to be so highly developed in humans". Perhaps he is right to assume this, but no-one can be sure until neuroscientists have carried out the requisite studies in humans.

It appears to be on the basis of generalisations of this kind that both Gerhardt and Schore seem rather prematurely to have reached more deterministic conclusions than current evidence might support, e.g. "There is a remarkably strong weight of evidence that has now accumulated in this field. It suggests that the HPA stress response can be programmed to be hypo- or hyper-responsive through early social experience, and that cortisol can have permanent effects on the developing baby's central nervous system" (Gerhardt 2004, p.84). This view leads Gerhardt to the conclusion that very good parental management can keep even babies whose high irritability may be genetically based free from stress (Gerhardt 2004, p.68). But does research really support such conclusions?

Turning back to the work of Buitelaar and colleagues, it is important to note that these studies cannot definitively establish a causal relationship between prenatal levels of maternal cortisol and infants' later development. Only if it is assumed that no possibility of genetic influence exists can it confidently be concluded that infant outcomes depend exclusively upon prenatal experience. It is not yet seem safe to make this assumption in respect of humans. The reality is far more complicated than this.

It has been recognised for a very long time that there are very wide variations in infant irritability that may have a genetic basis (Thomas and Chess 1977, Kagan et al. 1994). Jerome Kagan, who has carried out painstaking, extensive and detailed studies of temperamental variability in children (albeit a rather small sample) over a long period of time, reached a view diametrically opposed to that of Gerhardt: "I confess to an occasional sadness over the recognition that some healthy, attractive infants born to affectionate, economically secure families begin life with a physiology that will make it a bit difficult for them to be as relaxed, spontaneous, and capable of hearty laughter as they would like... More troubling is the possibility that, for a very small group of children, neither family love nor personal effort will be able to tame every bout of acute, intense anxiety" (Kagan et al. 1994, p.xxii). What might have led to such different conclusions?

It seems possible that the divergence of views may stem from rather different ways of conceptualising the relationship between genes and environment. Having possibly taken on board Schore's argument that much of the way that genes are expressed depends upon experience in the first years of life, Gerhardt appears to take the view that all behaviours can be traced back to early experience (whether in the womb or in the two years after birth). Kagan, by contrast, comes across as much more puzzled about how to explain differences in temperament that can be discerned from very early in foetal development but which do not always follow predictable patterns across the lifespan. Far from making generalisations, Kagan argues in favour of an appreciation of individuality, "There is a human addiction to superordinate categories that submerge the obvious differences among phenomena that share a small number of qualities so that a maximum number fit into the same class" (Kagan et al. 1994, p.184). He further suggests that individual variations in susceptibility to environmental influence may serve an evolutionary function: "Environments do not influence all children in the same way; this is the fundamental premise in evolution" (Kagan et al. 1994, p.207).

Patterns of attachment across the lifespan

In this section, we consider results from a selection of longitudinal studies which have included measures of patterns of attachment in infancy and examine how stable patterns of attachment might be across the lifespan. The rationale for this discussion emanates from dialogues between AT Determinists and AT constructivists about the long-term impact of early attachment history on later social and emotional development. Specifically, we are interested in exploring what evidence there might be that failure to form a secure attachment relationship in the first years of life might lead to poor psychological adjustment, a question to which we return in Chapter Seven.

Sroufe (1983) argued that coherence in development across the lifespan can be expected if it is accepted that development is hierarchical, i.e. that later stages are super-imposed on earlier ones, because vestiges of earlier adaptation are bound to remain. He further argued (1988) that much of later development of child is determined by what child brings to situation. A child with previous positive experiences is likely to build on these in making sense of current social context, constructing a reality that is consistent with expectations. But, even if this pattern is accepted, does this mean that attachment classification will be stable across the lifespan or that the patterns of adaptation to early caregiving settings will linger on vestigially regardless of later experiences? Perhaps the only way to answer this question is to look at follow-up studies of individuals. However, as already discussed, there have been serious challenges to this kind of study as it has not been definitively established that measures used to assess adult attachment tap the same construct assessed by Ainsworth and colleagues in the Strange Situation.

Some attachment literature has tended to assume that attachment assessment in infancy can produce a valid account of an individual's attachment status. This assessment is usually based on the relationship between the infant and his or her mother or other principal carer. Studies that have also assessed attachment relationships between infants and fathers have generally concluded that mother-infant and father-infant attachment classifications are independent (e.g. Main and Weston 1981, Youngblade and Belsky 1992, Belsky et al. 1984b, Oppenheim et al. 1988, Bridges et al. 1988). An exception to this, though, was a meta-analysis by Fox et al. (1991) which included 11 studies (ranging in sample size from 32 to 132; total number of participants = 710). In this study, it was found that "security of attachment to one parent was dependent upon security to the other parent, that type of insecurity (avoidant/resistant) to one parent was dependent upon type of insecurity to the other, and that subcategory classification within the secure category (B1 B2/B3 B4) to one parent was dependent upon subcategory classification to the other" (Fox et al., 1991, p.210). Fox et al. concluded this from data that showed that three-quarters of children judged secure with mother in the Strange Situation were also judged secure with father (354 infants/76 per cent) although only just over half of the children judged insecure with mother were also judged insecure with father (135 infants/55 per cent).

This does raise the question of how to identify the reference point from which to judge stability of attachment classification: using only mother-infant classification might fail to capture the relationship dynamic that contributes most to the Internal Working Model being formed by the developing child: children who are secure in relation to both parents may be more likely to have developed the kind of positive self and other images upon which adult attachment classifications are built; those who are insecure with mother but secure with alternative caregivers may (or may not) develop qualitatively different IWMs to those who are secure with mother but insecure with father/others. These conceptual difficulties have not been widely addressed by attachment researchers perhaps largely because mother-infant Strange Situation classifications have been thought to predict child outcomes rather well, unlike father-infant SS classifications, a situation which has encouraged some intellectual 'free-wheeling' as opposed to more rigorous investigation. As a result, there has been a general tendency to assume not only that mother-infant SS classifications are the 'gold standard' by which attachment stability can be assessed but that it is unusual for them to change much at all. As Lewis et al. (2000, p.708) comment, "By assuming that attachment remains stable, these studies and their interpretations mistakingly *(sic)* promote the view that infant attachment status is a trait-like attribute of an individual throughout development." Perhaps the only way to examine or challenge such fallacies is within longitudinal research designs which explore the effect of as many influential variables as possible.

Six longitudinal studies (from infancy to adulthood)

In the next section, we consider a number of longitudinal studies in an effort to evaluate the extent to which they appear to have tackled what can perhaps be viewed as a fundamental challenge to the establishment of attachment theory as a testable scientific account of human development. Although we are aware of the existence of two other studies (the Berkeley longitudinal study: Main et al. 2005 and the Haifa study: Sagi-Schwartz and Aviezer 2005), the former has not been published in enough detail for us to include it here while the latter focuses on very specific cultural circumstances (kibbutzim and poor day care). Instead, we have selected those studies that have included SS assessments at 12-18 months and which have followed the same group of people into early adulthood. This yields six studies, four conducted in the US and two in Germany, with sample sizes varying from 30 to 125.

Table 6.8: Longitudinal studies

AUTHORS	SAMPLE	ASSESSMENTS	STABILITY
Lewis et al. 2000	84/113 white, middle class (48 female)	1 year, 13 years, 18 years	No concordance
Waters et al. 2000	50/60 lower to upper middle class (29 female)	1 year, 20-22 years	Concordance
Hamilton 2000	30/205 selected on basis of infant attachment class	12 months SS, A^{d}AI at 17-19 years	Concordance
Grossmann et al. 1985	Bielefeld (N. Germany) 44/49 middle-class at 16 yrs	Many assessments, in home and lab, inc. SS + AAI	No concordance
Grossmann et al. 1999	38/49 at 21/22 years		No concordance
Grossmann et al. 1999	Regensburg (S. Germany) 38/51 non-risk at 21/22 years	Mainly lab. assessments inc. SS and AAI	No concordance
Weinfield et al. 2004	125/169/267 high-risk young mothers	SS at 12 and 18 months + multiple assessments until AAI at 19	No concordance

The first study, by Lewis et al. (2000), used a modified Strange Situation within three weeks of infants' first birthday, followed up by assessments at 13 years which required participants to reflect on their childhoods, and further assessments at 18 years which included the Adult

Attachment Interview, coded using a Q-sort method. Full data-sets were obtained from 84 of the initial sample of 113 and, of these, 17 children had experienced parental divorce.

Figure 6.12 illustrates outcomes and shows that, while change from secure to insecure status was slightly elevated among children of divorced parents, lack of stability could not reliably be attributed to this one factor. Of children classified as securely attached at age one, only just over a half were classified secure (56.7 per cent) at age 18; of children classified as insecurely attached at age one, an even smaller proportion, just over a third (37.5 per cent) were classified as insecurely attached by age 18. In other words, overall attachment security classification remained the same across time points for only 51 per cent of the sample and classification as insecure was less stable than classification as secure.

These results would appear to caution against the assumption that attachment security will be stable across the lifespan. However, as noted elsewhere, failure to find consistency between different tests at different times may reflect methodological problems rather than real changes in individuals' attachment security status. In this study, both the assessments at one and at 18 years were modified versions of 'standard' SS and AAI procedures. In addition, the sample was relatively small (though not as small as many). But, as the sample was middle class, with rates of divorce no higher than might be expected among the general population, which might suggest levels of environmental stability at which *lack of* stability of attachment classified would not have been anticipated. For this reason, the lack of stability seems remarkable and the study suggests a need for replication.

Figure 6.12: (In)stability of attachment (Lewis et al. 2000)

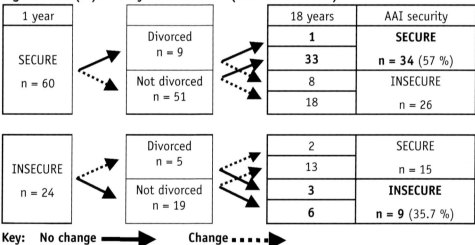

Two other US longitudinal samples,[11] by contrast, claim to have found relative stability from infancy to adulthood. Waters et al. (2000) used the Ainsworth et al. (1978) Strange Situation to assess attachment security at one year (during 1975 and 1976, before Main had identified the 'disorganised' attachment category) in 60 infants. They managed to re-contact 50 of the original sample (83 per cent) who were then aged between 20 and 22 years and described, as the original sample, as from lower- to upper-middle classes. The majority of parents of these young adults (78 per cent) had remained married; two participants had lost a parent

---

11 Main et al. (2005) also report high levels of stability in the Berkeley sample, though do not provide statistical details to support their conclusions.

before the age of six. Figure 6.13 illustrates the patterns of change across attachment classification from infancy to adulthood.

Overall, the attachment classification of 32 of the 50 participants (64 per cent) remained the same and change was not found to be more strongly associated with attachment insecurity although there was a slightly greater tendency for individuals who had been classified as ambivalent/resistant in infancy to have changed classification (of individuals classified as avoidant in infancy, 33.3 per cent were differently classified in adulthood; of individuals classified as secure in infancy, 31 per cent were differently classified in adulthood; of individuals classified as resistant in infancy, 56 per cent were differently classified in adulthood). Although attachment security classification for the majority of individuals did not change, it is worth noting that, for at least a third of participants overall, it did and, among participants classified as insecure in infancy, this proportion was slightly higher (43 per cent). It may be worth noting, too, that the type of statistical analysis differed between the Lewis et al. and the Waters. et al. studies. While Lewis et al. used chi-squared analyses (which assume independent samples), Waters et al. used a change test (which assumes that scores are drawn from the same sample). It seems unlikely that this would have affected conclusions to any great extent, but it does seem worth noting that concordance in the Waters et al. sample was not as high as might have been expected if, as some people have claimed, early attachment patterns persist throughout the lifespan. Waters et al. comment on a further analysis taking into account negative life events and suggest that, while a certain amount of instability may be due to measurement error, they also found evidence that "experiences beyond infancy also play a role in adult security" (Waters et al. 2000, p.686).

Figure 6.13: Stability of attachment (Waters et al. 2000)

INFANT CLASSIFICATION	20-22 YEARS	ADULT CLASSIFICATION
(A) Avoidant (N = 12)	**8** (67 %)	Dismissing (D)
	2	Secure (F)
	2	Preoccupied (E)
(B) Secure (N = 29)	6	Dismissing (D)
	20 (67 %)	Secure (F)
	3	Preoccupied (E)
(C) Resistant (N =9)	2	Dismissing (D)
	3	Secure (F)
	4 (44 %)	Preoccupied (E)

Key: No change ⟶   Change ▸▸▸▸▸

Hamilton (2000) selected 30 adolescents from a sample of 205 families (51 two-parent conventional and the remainder 'non-conventional') taking part in an ongoing longitudinal study, the Family Lifestyles (FLS) Project. Her subsample was selected to reflect the larger FLS sample, to represent the FLS distribution of attachment categories and to over-represent infants who had been classified as insecure at 12 months in the Strange Situation (see Figure

6.14). A version of the Adult Attachment Interview (George, Kaplan and Main 1984) adapted for adolescents was used to assess attachment status at age 17-19.

As Figure 6.14 shows, in adolescence, two-thirds of children classified as insecure in infancy retained the same major group identity and only just over a tenth (0.11 per cent) of these children were re-classified as secure; of those classified as secure in infancy, 58 per cent were re-classified as secure. Hamilton (2000) examined the number of life events associated with change and stability of attachment classification and argued that she had found some evidence that negative life events appeared to be associated with attachment instability for people classified as securely attached in infancy while they were associated with continuity of insecure attachment. Although Hamilton (2000), like Waters et al. (2000), reported continuity, it should be noted that this was the case for somewhat less than two-thirds of participants in each of the two samples.

Figure 6.14: Stability of attachment (Hamilton 2000)

INFANT CLASSIFICATION		17-19 YEARS	ADULT CLASSIFICATION
(A) Avoidant (N = 12)	→ ┈▶ ┈▶	8 (67%) 1 3	Dismissing (D) Secure (F) Preoccupied (E)
(B) Secure (N = 12)	┈▶ → ┈▶	4 7 (58%) 1	Dismissing (D) Secure (F) Preoccupied (E)
(C) Resistant (N =6)	┈▶ ┈▶ →	1 1 4 (67%)	Dismissing (D) Secure (F) Preoccupied (E)

Key: No change ⟶   Change ┈▶

Small-scale longitudinal studies have also been carried out in two separate non-risk samples in Germany. In both studies, attempts were made to replicate the intensive observational design instigated by Mary Ainsworth. The first study began in 1976 and 1977 in Bielefeld, a middle-sized town in northern Germany, and involved a sample of 49 middle-class two-parent families (26 girls and 23 boys). Observations were carried out at regular intervals during the first six years (though not at age four) at home, in the Strange Situation and in kindergarten, then children were followed up again at age ten, 16 and 22 when they were assessed using the Adult Attachment Interview. A second study of 51 non-risk middle-class families based in Regensburg, in southern Germany, began in 1980. This study involved laboratory-based assessments which included the Strange Situation at 12 months and 18 months (with both mother and father) and follow-up assessments at five, six, eight, 16, 18 and 20 years. Adult attachment style was assessed in this study using the Adult Attachment Projective (George et al. 1999). Grossmann et al. (1999) report that they found no concordance between attachment classifications in infancy and in adulthood for either sample. However, analyses are still in process which will take account of a wider range of measures of effects of parent-child interactive experience on later representations of close relationships in adulthood. Grossmann et al. (1999) suggest that, since attachment behaviour is an adaptive process, stability of attachment organisation from infancy to adulthood should only be expected where the care environment is also stable. Where childhood involves adversity or change in the stability of the care environment, non-concordance may be expected but this would not necessarily indicate maladaptation. They further argue that adaptation may be indicated by patterns of exploration as much as by patterns of attachment and that there is a need to pay more attention to this wider view. According to Main et al. (2005), follow-up of the German samples at 26 years now indicates greater continuity.

Weinfield et al. (2004) reported on a follow-up study of a high-risk sample of primiparous women from the Minnesota Parent-Child Project (Egeland and Brunnquell 1979). The 267 women who had initially been recruited during the third trimester of their pregnancies were young, poor and socially-disadvantaged. Among the 125 young adults who participated in the Adult Attachment Interview, 116 had been tested in the Strange Situation at both 12 and 18 months. Of these, only 59 (51 per cent) had received the same classification at both times. In eight of the 57 cases that had received different classifications, further information from a 24-month assessment was used to determine attachment category while for the remaining 49, the 12-month classification was used. A further nine infants had only been tested once in the Strange Situation. As can be seen in Figures 6.15 (a) and (b), the correspondence between attachment classification in infancy and at 19 years was low.

Looking overall at the extent of change from secure to insecure classification (and treating the three AAIs which could not be classified as insecure), 71 of the 125 (57%) cases received the same classification at both times. Change of category was more common where participants had received secure classifications in infancy: among this slightly smaller group almost two-thirds had slipped from secure to insecure whereas only just over a quarter of those classified as insecure appeared to have 'earned' security as young adults.

In trying to understand what this apparent instability might signify, Weinfield et al. (2004) pointed out that some of the discrepancy was likely to be attributable to the method used to assess attachment[12] at both times, particularly in view of the fact that some of the participants may have had multiple important attachment relationships, only one of which had been included in analyses. They further suggested that age 19 may well be a time when these young people, most of whom were growing up in adverse social contexts, might be expected still to be in transition between adolescence and adulthood. They emphasised that, in their view, stability should not be expected in such circumstances: "Within this challenging environment attachment relationships continued to evolve in a dynamic fashion, suggesting that attachment is not a static personal quality, but an adaptive, context sensitive, relational quality" (Weinfield et al. 2004, p.90). They added that it is quite conceivable that the attachment patterns of their participants may have changed several times between infancy and young adulthood, in response to changing life events and relationship opportunities, and implied that, if this were the case, timing of assessments may have produced artefactual results. However, they also drew attention to the fact that their study was the first to report comparisons including the disorganised attachment category and that this

---

12 Discrepancies may have been due to the way the SS had been coded, or the nature of the data compared, or the fact that inter-rater agreement on a random sample of AAI codings (90 per cent for unresolved cases but 82 per cent for D, E and F cases which, one might have thought, ought to have produced higher than barely over 4 in 5 agreement) may have introduced too much measurement error.

infant classification appeared most closely associated with later insecure attachment. They, like the Grossmanns, advocated a wider view of attachment, to include closer attention to the more complex influences of life circumstances on overall patterns of attachment.

Figure 6.15a: (In)stability of attachment (Weinfield et al. 2004)

INFANT CLASSIFICATION	19 YEARS	ADULT CLASSIFICATION
(A) Avoidant (N = 17)	**5** (29.4%)	Dismissing (D)
	8 (47.1%)	Secure (F)
	0 (0 %)	Preoccupied (E)
	4 (23.5%)	Unresolved (U)
(B) Secure (N = 48)	28 (58.3%)	Dismissing (D)
	15 (31.3%)	Secure (F)
	2 (4.2%)	Preoccupied (E)
	3 (6.3%)	Unresolved (U)
(C) Resistant (N =15)	7 (46.7%)	Dismissing (D)
	5 (33.3%)	Secure (F)
	1 (6.7%)	Preoccupied (E)
	2 (13.3%)	Unresolved (U)
(D) Disorganised (N =42)	27 (64.3%)	Dismissing (D)
	6 (14.3%)	Secure (F)
	0 (0 %)	Preoccupied (E)
	9 (21.4%)	Unresolved (U)

Key: No change ⟶   Change ▪▪▪▶

Figure 6.15b: (In)stability of attachment (Weinfield et al. 2004)

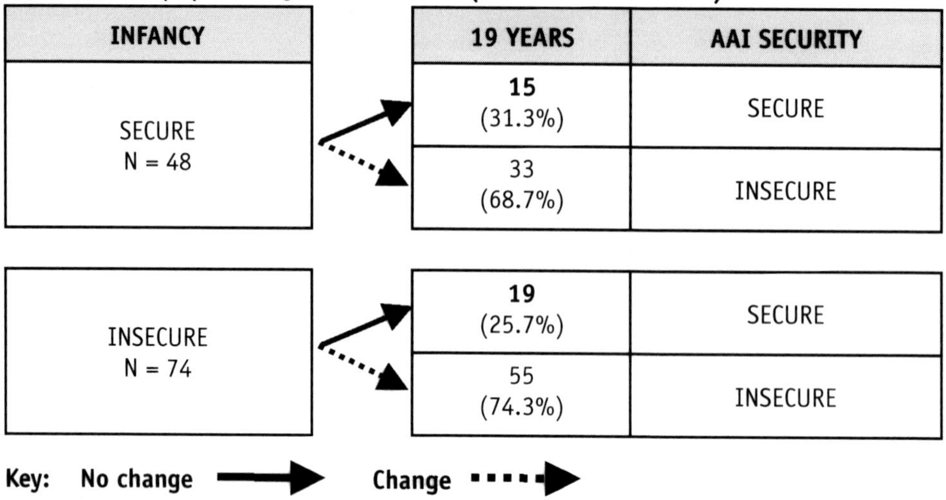

INFANCY	19 YEARS	AAI SECURITY
SECURE N = 48	15 (31.3%)	SECURE
	33 (68.7%)	INSECURE
INSECURE N = 74	19 (25.7%)	SECURE
	55 (74.3%)	INSECURE

Key: No change ⟶   Change ┅▶

In this section, we have deliberately chosen to consider longitudinal studies that have lasted from infancy to adulthood and that, in the main, employed the two assessments perhaps considered the most valid and reliable and so most likely to be comparable. In general, the picture yielded through this exercise is one that does not confirm a view that one pattern of attachment established with one main caregiver in infancy necessarily remains the predominant pattern even in low-risk samples. The extent to which this may be due to measurement problems is still unclear (partly due to the issue of non-definition of attachment as a construct across the lifespan). However, even over shorter spans of time, instability has been found, particularly in samples where negative life events or an unstable social context are high on the agenda (e.g. Vaughn et al. 1979, Belsky et al. 1996, Vondra et al. 2001). Nor is instability confined to studies of infancy since a number of studies has now indicated that attachment patterns in adulthood also fluctuate (e.g. Zhang and Labouvie-Vief 2004).

Some researchers (e.g. Kobak 1999, Sroufe et al. 1999) have argued that, since attachment style is a product of experience within salient relationships and not a personality trait, it may be rather misguided to anticipate stability. Kobak (1999) argues that, on this basis, more attention should be paid to current relationships than to hypotheses about internal working models. However, given that it is this experience in close attachment relationships that is hypothesised by Attachment Theory to inform the 'working model' of relationships and, also, given that these working models have been described in such broad terms (two, three or four boxes for the complete gamut of human experience), it does not seem entirely unreasonable to be surprised that tracking the development and establishment of stable strategies appears so far to have eluded researchers. Does this mean that the primacy of early attachment relationships and their role in informing internal models may have been over-estimated or that, in order for these patterns to be maintained, some other process also needs to be in place, such as maternal sensitivity (Belsky and Fearon 2002, Erickson et al. 1985)?

We tend to take the view that there is still a lot to be learned in this area. We would also tentatively conclude that the complexity of internal working models is likely generally to be far too great for it to be sensible to attempt to reduce them to the product of one (or even two) main close attachment relationships, even if that/those relationship/s do/es play a major role during infancy.

That this should be so seems intuitively not only plausible but necessary. If attachment relationships have evolved to ensure maximum survival potential, whether at the level of the individual gene, the individual person, the social group or the species, they are hardly likely to achieve this if they induce a sense of security that is impervious to social circumstances. The survival value of a strategy which assumes that, regardless of the nature of relationship opportunities available, 'all is well with me and with everyone else, thank you very much', seems distinctly dubious! Internal working models that have evolved on the basis of even the most positive experiences of self in relation to others need to be informed by accurate social evaluations if they are to be adaptive. As Bowlby suggested (Bowlby 1980a), IWMs of securely attached individuals are likely to be more "permeable", i.e. open to inspection, than IWMs that have been constructed more for the purpose of self-defence, as might be the case for some insecurely attached and rather inflexible individuals.

The fact that the requirements of a secure base will change over the lifespan also needs to be taken into account. How we relate to key attachment figures and how they influence us, either directly or indirectly through our internalisation of past experiences, will also be qualitatively different as we grow older. In simple terms, as adults, we usually operate a certain amount of choice over the company we keep. We will probably spend more social time with our close friends and confidants than with people less congenial to us, though this may not apply quite so much to work time. If we have a fair number of people close by who make us feel valued, the chances are that we will not spend massive amounts of time feeling that we are despicable or worthless. However, unless we are unusually thick-skinned, if we happen to have to be in close proximity to people who systematically undermine and belittle us, without recourse to alternative support or reassurance, we may well begin to imbibe the negative information to some degree.

The extent to which we 'let it get to us' will depend on a number of factors, such as:
- concordance between current and past experiences
- the amount of attention we pay to the incoming information
- our intellectual evaluation of the incoming information (its credibility, potency and valency)
- our emotional response to the incoming information (e.g. do we allow ourselves to be goaded into defensive behaviours that risk further alienation, do we become de-motivated to the extent that we move ourselves closer to the imaginary target of the offensive information, etc.)
- the effect of the incoming information on our relationship with the person/s at its source (is it coming from someone we want to impress, someone whose opinion we hold in high esteem, or would we prefer not to be engaged)
- our predictions about the future effect of the information on others' valuation of us
- the availability of alternative, contradictory sources of information.

Similar processes, with opposite valences, are also likely to operate in relation to positive feedback. The question of whether individuals with histories of secure attachments, to mother and to father, as well as good relationships with teachers and peers, would cope better than those with histories of predominantly insecure attachments with difficult circumstances, such as, for example, workplace bullying, or an abusive sexual experience (rape, domestic violence, etc.), natural or man-made disasters, has barely begun to be investigated. Nor has the hypothesis that early secure attachment can immunize against later adversity, however popular it may be in 'attachment mythology', been systematically investigated. It is not yet clear, for example, whether individuals who 'earn' security by gaining insights into the nature of their earlier insecure attachments might have more or less experience relevant to coping with later difficulties than secure individuals who might (or might not, of course) have sailed through life with relative ease.

Concluding comments

Where, then, does this leave us in respect of resolving the battle between the Determinists and the Constructivists? Perhaps frustratingly for many readers, we have to admit that, at this stage in the history of attachment research, it would seem that there are still too many unknowns for us to comfortably take either side. Although, as readers will have gathered, we tend to the view that there remains considerable scope throughout the lifespan for individuals to engage in relationships that correct earlier scripts without the need for radical reconstructive measures (e.g. chemotherapy, psychotherapy, behaviour therapy, etc.) and, erring on the side of the Constructivists, agree with Bowlby (1988b, p.152) that, although early experiences will play an important role in opening up opportunities for development, "Fortunately, the human psyche, like human bones, is strongly inclined towards self-healing."

What prevents or enables recovery from disruptions in parent-child relationships, whether major as in parental divorce, abuse, serious illness, emotional absence or death, or relatively minor and/or transient, clearly depends on a whole range of factors, both within the individual and in the use that he or she can make of available opportunities within his or her social network. Logically, the longer an individual remains stuck on a pathological trajectory, the less likely it is that opportunities will arise that enable them to change track. The effort required to be motivated to change may also be lacking. But that change is possible at almost any point throughout the lifespan, either from a position of strength to one of relative weakness, or from a position of insecurity to greater security, seems evident from the data so far gathered in longitudinal studies, as indicated in this chapter, as well as from reports of interventions, which we will describe in the chapter that follows.

Part Three

Applications/Implications

7 | Attachment difficulties and therapy

"…when an individual is confident that an attachment figure will be available to him whenever he desires it, that person will be much less prone to either intense or chronic fear than will an individual who for any reason has no such confidence."

(Bowlby 1973a, p.202)

In this chapter, we first present a brief overview of key research findings with regard to links between attachment security and psychological health. We go on to outline some of the debates that have arisen about the definition and aetiology of attachment disorders and describe some of the opposing arguments in this area. This debate leads us to pose two questions: first, whether Attachment Theory should be interpreted as upholding the view that parents are responsible for children's attachment difficulties and, second, whether Attachment Theory offers any solutions for problems associated with attachment difficulties. In this second section, we include consideration both of Bowlby's views and recommendations and examine approaches that purport to stem from Attachment Theory. In doing this, we outline some UK initiatives that appear to have successfully incorporated an Attachment Theory perspective but also draw attention to some US initiatives which, despite their self-advertised allegiance to Attachment Theory, appear to arise from rather different perspectives.

Links between patterns of attachment and mental health problems

It is now widely recognised, as indicated in Chapter Six, that any links between mental health problems and attachment history are usually complex and not well described as simple one-to-one correspondences. Any links that emerge tend to be mediated and moderated by a host of social-contextual and within-individual factors. However, some studies have indicated a greater proneness for individuals with particular patterns of relating to manifest particular forms of difficulty. For example, in one of the earliest longitudinal studies, conducted in Minnesota, it was found that both the organised non-secure attachment patterns were associated with externalising problems (e.g. disruptive and anti-social behaviour or aggression) in middle childhood (Sroufe 1983). Garber et al. (1985) also reported that the avoidant pattern appeared to be associated with depression. In a separate study, Cassidy (1994) reported links between infant attachment insecurity and recklessness and accident proneness. Ambivalent/resistant infants tended to be the clumsiest but they might also, if they were assessed as having 'controlling' or 'compulsive caregiving' tendencies, be precociously self-protective.

Different mechanisms have been proposed as underlying the emergence of problem behaviours in relation to the two non-secure patterns of attachment: aggression or anti-social behaviour has been linked to poor self-regulation in children with ambivalent attachments while suppressed (or not so well suppressed) hostility has been linked to the avoidant pattern. Adding temperament and quality of parenting to this picture, Rubin et al. (1991) propose that the combination of child temperament and anxious, unresponsive parenting might produce externalising problems and avoidant attachments in children capable of emotional self-regulation but that the same combination produces internalising problems and ambivalent attachment in children of less stable temperament. Others have suggested that highly reactive children, with poor self-regulation, and pronounced tendencies toward negative emotionality may be differentially susceptible to rearing influences. For example, Belsky and colleagues (Belsky et al. 1991, Belsky 1997a, 1997b, 1999, 2004) have suggested that children with positive, easy-going temperaments may be relatively unaffected by the quality of parenting that they receive while children high on reactivity and negative emotionality may be more susceptible. Specifically, they propose that the psychological health of this group of children will either be compromised by poor parenting (however defined) or positively influenced by good parenting.

Understanding the nature of the relationship between infant attachment patterns and mental health outcomes for children has, in some ways, been complicated by the introduction of the disorganised classification which a number of studies have shown to be linked with infant psychopathology (Hesse and van IJzendoorn 1999). The plethora of adult self-report instruments, some of which produce continuous scales relating to avoidance and anxiety and others of which produce either three or four categories (and not always the same three or four categories),[1] has also led to a certain degree of confusion or even, in Greenberg's words, to something of a "measurement roadblock" (Greenberg 1999, p.486).

Nevertheless, in line with the conceptualisation of the preoccupied style as involving maximisation of attachment needs, there appears to be a stronger association between preoccupied attachment, help-seeking and incidence of psychological problems using self-report measures, while the evidence in relation to avoidant attachments is less consistent. A similar pattern emerges in respect of associations between AAI classification and type of psychological disorder: classification as avoidant tends to be more closely associated with schizoid-type disorders while classification as unresolved/disoriented has been associated with anxiety, substance abuse and borderline personality disorders (using four-way classifications) and with the preoccupied classification using the three-way classification (Dozier et al. 1999; Figures 7.1 and 7.2). These patterns, however, have not always been found consistently, partly due to variations in diagnostic practices and in methodology (e.g. some researchers exclude participants who have more than one psychological problem whereas others include those with mixed diagnoses), but also, Dozier et al. (1999) suggest, due to non-homogeneity among patient groups in respect of internalising and externalising problems (for example, while some depressed patients might 'act out', others may become more withdrawn). Also, although, in general, adults assessed as securely attached on the Adult

---

[1] Some use the Bartholomew and Horowitz negative/positive model of self/other which produces secure, preoccupied, avoidant-dismissive and avoidant-fearful (described in Chapter Three), others use just three categories (secure, preoccupied, avoidant) and others include a measure of disorganised/unresolved attachment.

Attachment Interview (AAI) are less likely to report psychological problems, the so-called 'earned secure' proportion who have a history of insecure attachment (40-70 per cent) is thought to be more prone to depressive symptoms (Pearson et al. 1994).

Figure 7.1: Distribution of three category AAI classification by diagnostic group (after Dozier et al. 1999; *numbers in parentheses refer to number of studies*)

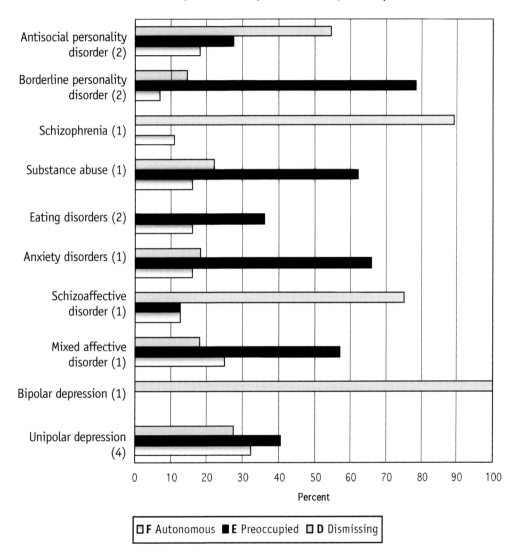

Figure 7.2: Distribution of four category AAI classification by diagnostic group (after Dozier et al. 1999; *numbers in parentheses refer to number of studies*)

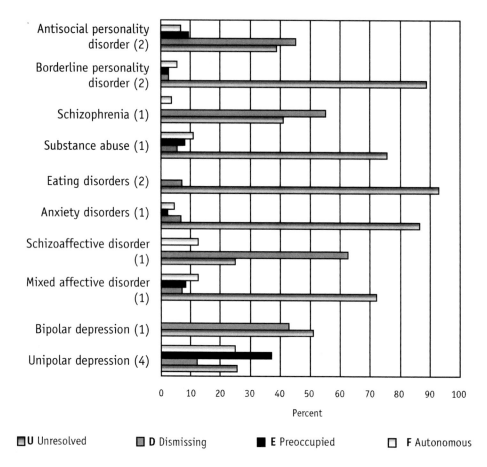

Inconsistent evidence has also been found for associations between organised attachment patterns in infancy and the development of attachment disorders. It is important to recognise that insecure attachment is not the same as attachment disorder: "it should be made quite clear that an insecure attachment is not in itself a measure of psychopathology. In some cases an insecure attachment may set a trajectory that, along with other risk factors, increases the risk for either externalizing or internalizing psychopathology" (Greenberg 1999, p.477). This fact has sometimes been overlooked by some groups of practitioners who have assumed that attachment insecurity is directly linked with disorder. Parallel to physical problems, as Greenberg points out, "Even in the case of disorders in which a biochemical or genetic mechanism has been discovered, the expression of the disorder is influenced by other biological or environmental events" (Greenberg 1999, p.473). In other words, although insecure attachment may increase the likelihood of problems, particularly if very challenging circumstances arise, there is no proof of direct causal links, either from insecure attachment to psychopathology or from psychopathology to insecure attachment.

It follows from this that it is not safe to assume, as some clinicians appear at times to do (e.g. Marrone 1998, Randolph 2000, Gerhardt 2004), that anyone seeking psychological help will have a history of insecure attachment, nor is it valid to assume that they will currently be assessed as insecurely attached. This assumption possibly arises from over-generalisations based on data gathered on clinical populations, for example, from outcomes of meta-analyses that indicate distinctly different patterns of distribution of AAI classifications among at-risk or clinical and non-clinical populations (Table 7.1). Further analysis would be helpful to distinguish between clinical and at-risk populations.

Table 7.1: Distribution of AAI classifications based on meta-analysis (Bakermans-Kranenburg and van IJzendoorn, 1993)

	D **DISMISSING**	**F** **AUTONOMOUS**	**E** **PREOCCUPIED**	**UR** **UNRESOLVED**
Non-clinical	24%	58%	18%	19%
At-risk/Clinical	26%	8%	25%	40%

It seems important to recognise that, even where experiences of intrusive, inconsistent, rejecting or abusive parenting are recalled, such retrospective material cannot be relied upon for assessing with any confidence the nature of the adult's attachment history. What seems more likely is that people seeking help will often have some experience of relationship difficulties, either currently or in the past. Nevertheless, it would be a mistake to assume that these experiences inevitably involve attachment difficulties. As Zeanah et al. (1993) point out, there are many different types of parent-child relationship problem (for example, parental over- or under-involvement, child conduct disorders, etc.) which, though potentially related to attachment difficulties in some way, would not be accurately classified as attachment problems. They suggest that the critical difference between attachment disorders and other relationship problems might be the degree to which the child or adult feels unsafe and the extent to which they feel able to use other people to inform safe exploration or to seek reassurance.

How this capacity develops is not yet fully understood. As indicated by the differential susceptibility hypothesis (Belsky et al. 1991, Belsky 1997a, 1997b, 1999, 2004), the relationship between negative life events, attachment difficulties and psychopathology is complex. Harris et al. (1986, 1990), for example, noted that, although childhood separations or experiences of parental loss were a vulnerability factor in relation to risk of depression in adulthood, the actual occurrence of depression was far lower where these experiences were accompanied by adequate parenting. Inadequate parenting before and after loss experiences was more closely linked to later depression.

Attachment disorders – definitions and debates

"Here, in brief, are many of the typical features: superficial relationships; no real feeling – no capacity to care for people or to make true friends; an inaccessibility, exasperating to those trying to help; no emotional response to situations where it is normal – curious lack of concern; deceit and evasion, often pointless; stealing; lack of concentration at school" (Bowlby 1953/1965, p.37).

Although Bowlby's descriptions of children with serious attachment problems had become quite widely accepted within his lifetime, the diagnostic criteria for attachment disorders has only been developed relatively recently. As Zeanah (1996) points out these diagnoses are almost unique as psychiatric diagnoses in being applicable to extremely young children and there continues to be considerable debate over conceptual and definitional issues (Greenberg 1999).

According to Greenberg (1999), earlier definitions of Reactive Attachment Disorder (RAD) identified three major characteristics: pervasive disturbance across all relationships, commencement before the age of eight months and associated Non-organic Failure to Thrive (NFTT). These were revised in *DSM-III-R*[2] (APA 1987) and *ICD-9*[3] (WHO 1975) which omitted the NFTT criterion and revised the age criterion to read "Starts before the age of five years." By the time *DSM-IV* (APA 1994) and *ICD-10* (WHO 1992) were compiled, two types of Reactive Attachment Disorder had been identified, an *inhibited* and a *disinhibited* type (Table 7.2; see also Appendix 7.1 for fuller details). Other causes of social difficulties, such as developmental delay (as in mental retardation), autism or any other pervasive developmental need to be eliminated before a diagnosis of RAD is made.

The disinhibited type will be familiar to readers of Bowlby's descriptions of non-discriminate friendliness in children reared in institutions: "A special note of warning must be sounded regarding the children who respond apathetically or by a cheerful undiscriminating friendliness, since people ignorant of the principles of mental health are habitually deceived by them. Often they are quiet, obedient, easy to manage, well-mannered and orderly, and physically healthy; many of them even appear happy. So long as they remain in the institution there is no obvious ground for concern, yet when they leave they go to pieces, and it is evident that their adjustment had a hollow quality and was not based on a real growth of personality" (Bowlby 1951, p.25).

Table 7.2: Two types of Reactive Attachment Disorder (*DSM-IV* criteria, 1994)

INHIBITED	DISINHIBITED
Hypervigilance, fear	Indiscriminate friendliness
Withdrawal	Absence of selective attachment figure
Inaccessibility	Seek and accept comfort non-discriminately
Ambivalence	
Rarely seek comfort	Pathogenic caregiving

Greenberg (1999) points out that the DSM definitions remain problematic because they place inappropriate emphasis on the individual and take insufficient account of the fact that attachment disorders are related to relationships between the individual and others. Whether this is a consequence of the label 'reactive' is unclear since this label seems rather to exclude the possibility of endogenous influences. In similar vein, Greenberg (1999) takes issue with the assumption that the diagnosis of RAD is only made where there is a history of poor care (i.e. neglectful, abusive care or frequent changes of caregivers due to institutional or foster care) and points out that attachment disorders can occur in the absence of such a history (Boris et al. 1998). He also remarks that, using the DSM definition, no attachment

---

2 Diagnostic and Statistical Manual of Mental Disorders
3 International Classification of Diseases

problem would be diagnosed if major difficulties were present in relation to just one key attachment figure but not with other people.

In a recent study, Zeanah et al. (2004) attempted to develop distinct operational definitions of inhibited and disinhibited RAD as defined by the *DSM-IV* criteria in order to examine the nature of attachment problems in maltreated toddlers. Having rated children's behaviour on the two sets of criteria identified (Table 7.3), Zeanah et al. concluded that the two categories might overlap since many of the children in their sample exhibited symptoms of both types of disorder.

Table 7.3: Criteria for two types of Reactive Attachment Disorder (Zeanah et al. 2004)

INHIBITED	DISINHIBITED
1) absence of a discriminated, preferred attachment figure 2) lack of comfort-seeking when distressed 3) failure to respond to comfort when offered 4) lack of social and emotional reciprocity 5) emotion regulation difficulties	1) absence of a discriminated, preferred attachment figure 2) failure to check back after venturing away from the caregiver 3) lack of reticence with unfamiliar adults 4) willingness to go off with relative strangers

In an earlier paper, O'Connor and Zeanah (2003) suggested that, while there appears to be consistent evidence of the disinhibited pattern, the inhibited pattern, which is less common, seems both less clearly defined and more easily confused with disorganised attachment. They concluded that considerably more refinement of diagnostic criteria is needed and regard the ICD-10 and DSM-IV criteria as inadequate for guiding clinical decisions. They further recommend that greater effort should be made to base diagnoses on multiple assessments, including observations of children in interaction with caregivers and peers and measures of behavioural, cognitive and neuropsychological functioning. In assessment of older children, diagnosis should also take account of how children talk about themselves in relation to others as behaviour alone may not pick up on restricted capacity to mentalise (acknowledge their own or other people's internal states). They also stressed the need to take account of co-occurring problems and to make very clear distinctions between these and attachment disorders.

Rather in the way that Belsky and colleagues (Belsky and Rovine 1987, 1988, Belsky et al. 1995) suggested that temperament might influence the manifestation of attachment insecurity, Zeanah and Fox (2004) raised the question of how, if at all, the manifestation of the disinhibited and inhibited types of RAD may be related to temperament. Considering how reactivity, emotional self-regulation and care experiences might interact, they suggest three potential models: an exogenous-effects model, an endogenous-effects model and an interactive-effects model. The exogenous-effects model describes caregiver effects which are independent of child temperament, for example, the inhibited pattern may be hypothesised as resulting from neglect or abuse whereas the disinhibited pattern appears as a consequence of limited opportunities to form continuous relationships with specific caregivers. The endogenous-effects model describes child effects which are relatively independent of experience, with children who are highly reactive, prone to be irritable and high on negative affect tending to display the inhibited pattern and children who are more impulsive, less reactive and more outgoing showing the disinhibited pattern. The interactive-effects model, which describes child and caregiver attributes as capable of dynamically influencing each other, reflects the possibility that different combinations of child and caregiver attributes might interact with social contextual factors to produce particular outcomes. These models have yet to be tested.

Lieberman and Pawl (1988) proposed an alternative taxonomy which hinted at different aetiological roots for attachment disorders (Table 7.4). While this taxonomy paid more attention to the child's relationship history and acknowledged the possibility that attachment difficulties might emerge within a wider range of care contexts, Greenberg (1999) questioned whether all loss reactions in young children should be considered pathological and so argued that this categorisation also needed further refinement.

Table 7.4: Alternative typology proposed by Lieberman and Pawl (1988)

	TYPE	CRITERIA
A	Non-Attachment Disorder	• No preferred attachment figure • Cognitive age between 10-12 months – Might be manifested as withdrawal or indiscriminate social behaviour
B	Disordered/Distorted Attachments	• Extreme inhibition (clinginess, passivity) • Reckless self-endangerment (no checking back) • Role reversal
C	Loss Reactions	• Applies to children under three

Other workers, recognising the difficulties that clinicians have in agreeing upon diagnoses, have suggested that a wider range of behaviours might need to be taken into account and that batteries of tests for problem behaviour assessment might be needed (e.g. Sheperis et al. 2003, Kay Hall and Geher 2003). Still others have suggested that the current diagnostic criteria may place too much emphasis on discrete problem behaviours at the expense of capturing the aspects most relevant to disturbed relationships (Stafford et al. 2003). Stafford et al. (2003) also question whether it will ever be possible to satisfactorily disentangle the processes of disturbed attachments from their effects, since early disturbances in attachment relationships are likely to have been implicated in the development of most psychiatric disorders. Steele (2003, p.219) concludes that "the very concept of 'attachment disorders' is a controversial one because of the substantial remaining questions about assessment and diagnosis".

These diagnostic problems appear to have been further compounded by the development of 'diagnostic' tools, freely available on the WorldWideWeb, which are based on the erroneous assumption that insecure attachments are pathological (for example, the Randolph Attachment Disorder Questionnaire: RADQ; Randolph, 1997, 2000, or the Becker-Weidman Attachment Disorder Checklist more details of which can be found in Appendix 7.2). Some practitioners using these diagnostic criteria have not only departed from the *DSM-IV* criteria for RAD but have described Attachment Disorder (AD) as a more severe form of disorder which includes other anti-social behaviours listed under Oppositional Defiant Disorder in *DSM-IV* (Randolph, 2000). Although developers of such tools claim that they are directly derived from Attachment Theory, these claims seem both questionable and in need of challenge. Attachment Theory, in a way that is curiously redolent of the development of religious belief systems, seems to be open to multiple interpretations. Even so, Bowlby's approach, in its very essence, was founded upon his determination to avoid empirically questionable speculation and unwarranted assumptions. When empirical research failed to support his theories, he modified the theories though, unfortunately, not in as systematic a way as might have been preferable. This appears to have left the door open for very varying interpretations and for the emergence of 'therapeutic' approaches that purport to be true to Attachment Theory but which may well bear more resemblance to a religious movement than Bowlby would have liked.

As well as the check lists associated with the Randolph approach, diagnostic criteria also stress the child's deviousness and malicious cruelty, evidenced mostly when alone in the company of their mother but also in anti-social acts like fire-setting and torturing animals. Mercer (2002) draws attention to other worrying aspects of diagnostic practices associated with this approach, such as the acceptance of the mother's unverified report of the child's behaviour and the reliance on dubious criteria, such as difficulty making eye contact when adults want him/her to (Randolph, 2000). "Presumably", Mercer argues "only the adults themselves can know whether they wanted the child to make eye contact at a given moment" Mercer (2002). She points out that the Randolph approach, labelled 'Attachment Therapy' and also known as holding therapy, rage-reduction therapy, Z-process therapy (Zaslow and Breger 1969, Zazlow and Menta 1975) and re-birthing, includes therapeutic practices that have no empirical validation and have been associated with serious negative consequences. This issue is further discussed later in this chapter, under the heading *'Controversial practices'.*

Are parents to blame for attachment difficulties?

There seems to be a popular sense that we live nowadays in a culture of blame. In the field of Attachment Theory, although it is recognised that problems grow out of a complex interplay between the social context of parenting, with varying contributions from attributes of parents and children, there has often been a tendency to see the responsibility for avoiding problems as resting with parents, or more specifically, with the mother. Mothers stressed or anaemic during pregnancy, mothers with postnatal depression, mothers with histories of insecure attachment or abuse, mothers with histories of mental or addictive problems, mothers unable to handle infants who are highly irritable, pre-term or otherwise medically at risk (e.g. infants with congenital visual impairments, epilepsy, autism, cerebral palsy, cystic fibrosis, etc.), all these mothers, as discussed in Chapters Five and Six, have been identified at some time as potential sources for elevated risk of attachment problems.

The emphasis on the crucial importance of mothers[4] in the welfare of young children has been one of the most controversial aspects of Attachment Theory (AT). Currently, as in the past, it continues to evoke strong objections, on several grounds:
- because cause-effect relationships between outcomes for children and input from mothers are rarely simple and linear
- because all the evidence points in the direction of a much more complicated picture, with multiple influences leading to specific outcomes but also with many routes to the same and different outcomes (equifinality and multifinality)
- because the relationship between the number of risk factors (e.g. maternal depression, social deprivation, lack of social support, etc.) and poor outcomes for children tends to

---

4   Or on other key significant Attachment Figures, who could stand in almost any relationship to the developing child, but who even today are most still likely to be the child's mother.

- be exponential rather than linear (due, as much as anything, to the propensity of risk factors to interact among themselves to produce their strong negative impacts)
- because so much credibility has been accorded to theories about a critical period for attachment formation and there has been relatively little recognition of the fact that risks can occur at all levels in the history and evolution of individual families
- because, due to the above emphasis, there has been a tendency among many AT devotees to espouse a belief in the inoculatory powers of early intervention targeting naive mothers.

The following extract from an essay critiquing the hard form of Attachment Theory serves as an example of such criticism:

> "Did you know that there is no such thing as a 'difficult baby', only 'difficult parents', who are either 'neglectful or 'intrusive'? ... So argues psychoanalytic psychotherapist Sue Gerhardt in *Why Love Matters: How affection shapes a baby's brain'* ...
> The reality is that it is far from obvious how early attachments shape our development... The mistake often made is to conflate occasionally clumsy or unresponsive parental behaviour, with systematic abuse and neglect... It will not help parents if they are loaded with guilt for being insensitive to their children's every need – and it will do children no good to think they can blame their bad behaviour today, and whatever problems they may encounter in future, on their parents. It will also be bad for all of us if intervention into our family and private lives is made the norm."
> (Guldberg 2004)

It is true that Gerhardt (2004) asserts very emphatically that an extremely wide range of difficulties stems from interactions between mothers (or other primary caregivers) and offspring either during pregnancy or in the first two years. These difficulties include addictions, depression, post-traumatic stress disorder, personality disorder and a number of behavioural and medical problems generally associated with chronic stress. It is also true that the same argument could lead to the conclusion that almost any disorder could be attributed to the same rather non-specific origins. And it is clearly true that Gerhardt strongly advocates the value of sensitive, responsive care during the early years and extends this to the need for carers to have plenty of support and encouragement both before and after giving birth. However, rather than holding parents directly responsible, Gerhardt diffuses the responsibility across generations of parents by stressing that the care that parents offer to their children will be predominantly influenced by their own childhood experiences of being cared for. This view closely reflects that of Bowlby (1988b). However, it also plays into a common and rather simplistic belief about lack of change across generations, that is, the belief in 'cycles of abuse' or 'cycles of violence'.

Around the time that Bowlby began to develop his Attachment Theory, the subject of child abuse had also begun to feature in academic disciplines and in practice. This issue, previously taboo, only gradually began to be acknowledged and theorised in the UK during the twentieth century. Early hypotheses about origins and explanations produced the view that abusive behaviour runs in families. Those who hold this view, which is based on a simple unilinear model of intergenerational transmission derived from a behaviourist account of development, postulate that abusers abuse because they themselves have been abused ('violence begets violence'). Evidence from many different studies have been brought in to support this position including reports on clinic populations of violent patients, on prison populations of violent offenders, cross-sectional studies of abusing versus non-abusing parents, longitudinal studies of at-risk children and of children of 'battered mothers', retrospective studies of youth offenders, and others.

In a wide-ranging review of these studies as well as of a small number of studies of effects of television violence, Spatz Widom (1988) concluded that none of the studies convincingly supported the hypothesis that 'violence begets violence'. She pointed out that many were methodologically flawed, that evidence was rather inconsistent, that definitions of abuse and access to information about it were problematic, and that there was a need for carefully controlled longitudinal studies to examine the question of why some children appeared to be more vulnerable to effects than others. However, she stressed that, as other workers have also found, the majority of children (well over two-thirds) who experience abusive caregiving did not become abusers even though there did appear to be some evidence that a slightly higher proportion[5] were more at risk of becoming abusers than children growing up in non-violent homes. She concluded (Widom 1988, p.24) that "It is likely that our conceptualization of the relationship between child abuse and violence has been overly simplistic… it is important to draw attention to the persistent transmission of confident conclusions in this literature with little regard to data or lack thereof." Since this paper has been written, it has become much less common for researchers to reflect the view that this simple causal model is accurate. Attachment research in general is no exception to this rule although pockets within it, particularly reports of clinical cases written from a psychoanalytic perspective, still tend to reflect the earlier model.

In several respects, Gerhardt's thesis fails to reflect the more complex aetiological models that tend to be favoured by psychologists and medical sociologists studying social and emotional development. These models recognise the multiplicity of influences on development over the lifespan and the fact that single measures of children's behaviour in the early years (e.g. of anti-social behaviour) do not reliably predict later outcomes. A number of additional assumptions are also discernible in Gerhardt's thesis. These can be extended and summarised as follows:
1) Attachment Theory provides the diagnostic tools to assess attachment relationships.
2) The goal of therapy (and of society) should be to promote secure attachments.
3) Attachment problems are intergenerationally transmitted.
4) Therapy needs to influence under-developed non-verbal, right-hemisphere processes.
5) The earlier the intervention, the more effective therapy will be.
6) Shorter, simpler interventions are possible in infancy.
7) Attachment Theory can inform therapy for attachment-related problems.
8) Only properly trained experts can identify, understand and treat attachment-related problems.

Readers may recall our questioning of the first assumption in Chapter Three where we outlined the problems still associated with classification of patterns of attachment across the lifespan. We have further discussed problems related to diagnostic criteria on attachment disorders in this chapter. We questioned the second assumption in Chapter Four where we argued that, while a reasonable goal might be to facilitate as much security as possible, it is also necessary to be wary about the potential for negative stereotyping and to keep open the possibility that most organised patterns of attachment may have some adaptive potential. We reiterated this argument in Chapter Five. In Chapter Six and again in our

---

5   Estimates vary according to different studies, but it appeared from longitudinal studies that around 20-30% of children growing up with family violence later became violent as opposed to about 18% of children growing up in non-violent homes.

discussion of research on abuse, we emphasised the need for more evidence to support the third assumption and showed that, even across the lifespan, there may be less evidence for stability of attachment status than previously believed.

In the remainder of this chapter, we examine the status of the other five assumptions, first by discussing the view that therapy needs to address right hemisphere processes, second, by examining the evidence for the effectiveness of therapy informed by Attachment Theory and, third, by considering some of the ways in which Attachment Theory has been applied to therapy.

Therapy and right-hemisphere processes

The view that brains are hard-wired during critical periods of development and can only be re-programmed by trained therapists is perhaps the most contestable strand of Gerhardt's thesis. It can be seen to derive directly from Schore's speculations about the relationship between the development of neural structures in the right hemisphere and the development of social and emotional abilities or understanding. As we have suggested elsewhere in this book, there is still considerable debate over the relationship between physical growth and abilities. It seems not only unlikely but, as yet, unproven that any simple one-to-one mapping of these processes exists.

On logical grounds also, there are reasons for disputing the view that only therapy can re-programme a brain that has been hard-wired during a critical period of development. The first major problem is that, if a brain really has been hard-wired during a critical period of development, by definition, it cannot be re-wired. If it can, then it cannot have been 'hard-wired' in the first place. Having said that, even a 'hard-wired' brain could possibly be re-wired, or de-wired, if it were to be physically re- or de-constructed. This would not require any techniques that have not already been perfected within the repertoire of psychiatrists and brain surgeons. Brain surgery has been shown to alter behaviour: a few twiddles during leucotomy can alter some people's brain patterns dramatically while more radical lobectomies have influenced recalcitrants who are insufficiently responsive to leucotomy. Re-patterning of neural connections has also been achieved using drugs known to have effects on neurotransmitter pathways, or by electroconvulsive therapy which has observable effects through relatively unknown mechanisms (perhaps because random damage forces compensatory activity, or because under-used pathways are energised, or because over-used pathways are blitzed...). Was Gerhardt meaning to imply that only people trained and empowered to use physical methods such as these can influence patterns that are fixed in infancy or before? Or is the implication that these hard-wired patterns, which are presumed to have had generations of practice at going wrong, can be altered by particular therapeutic interventions capable of effective re-wiring by non-physical means?

Perhaps the most plausible and positive aspect of the view that right hemisphere processes need to be involved in and influenced by therapy is the fact that it draws attention to the need to consider non-verbal processes within client-therapist interactions, to understand that behaviour might be influenced by important earlier social experiences that are no longer verbally accessible by the patient but which may become more accessible if less speech-dependent interactions are encouraged (e.g. drawing, imaging, drama-therapy, etc.). It may also be valuable in that it may flag up the need for therapists to consider the possibility that their patients' perspective may be 'legitimately' different from outlooks considered appropriate, maybe because they are influenced by experiences that the patient was unable to manage, either as a young child or later (since experiences that disrupt one's ability to make sense of social relationships can happen later in life, for example, the development of inappropriate sexual relationships within an otherwise seemingly 'normal' family). Bowlby was keenly aware of these influences, of the difficulty of understanding their derivation and of the value of using the dynamics of the patient-therapist relationship to explore and understand the meaning of non-verbal behaviour (Bowlby 1988b).

However, whether framing explorations of this kind in terms of a communion between the therapist's and the patient's right hemispheres really adds anything to the therapist's toolkit seems questionable. On the one hand, it seems that any theory that increases the likelihood that therapists will try to make sense in a non-judgemental manner of the significance of patients' non-verbal communications must have potential value. On the other, reductively explaining the patient's outlook as due to hypothetically arrested brain development does not seem to hold much promise for the development of the kind of respectful power dynamic that Bowlby recommended. We return to this later in this chapter when we outline some of Bowlby's ideas about the therapeutic relationship. Meantime, we turn to studies of the effectiveness of therapy using an attachment orientation.

Effectiveness of therapy

There is now a huge number of reports of interventions using an Attachment Theory approach. In this section we consider findings from meta-analyses. These meta-analyses involve pooling results from reports that have used different statistical procedures and, often, different designs (e.g. longitudinal, cross-sectional, observational, experimental) and outcome measures, by computing a statistic that takes account of the nature of findings and of the source (i.e. sample size) and that calculates an overall estimate of effects and their size.

Meta-analyses of therapy interventions

Two meta-analytic studies of interventions using attachment approaches have been reported in the last decade, both carried out by the research group based in Leiden and led by Marinus van IJzendoorn (van IJzendoorn et al. 1995b, Bakermans-Kranenburg et al. 2003). The first included 16 reports of attachment interventions while the second extended this to 70 reports (as some of these reports were of multiple studies or samples, the total number of studies and the total number of attachment measures considered was considerably larger than this). Although there was substantial overlap between the studies included in each report, not all the studies in the first report were retained in the second analysis.

Interventions adopting an attachment theory perspective are premised on the assumption that secure attachment is associated with more optimal social and emotional development. In view of this, they aim to prevent the development of insecure attachments, to transform insecure into secure attachment patterns and to promote attachment security.

Within the studies included in the meta-analyses, the methods used to achieve these aims varied considerably, for example, Anisfeld et al. (1990) encouraged mothers to carry infants more while other inventions involved either home visits, individual psychotherapy, or parent education using group, video and/or written material. Home visits, usually by trained nurses, offered various blends of social support, advice or skills training, for example, Barnard et al. (1988) offered social support and encouragement to develop social skills, Barnett et al.

number of sessions, intervenor, location, use of video feedback, child's age at start, outcome measures and focus of intervention).

Table 7.6 indicates the focus of interventions in relation to the outcome measures taken and shows that the majority of interventions attempted to alter mothers' sensitivity or responsiveness to infant cues or did this in conjunction with offering some form of social support. Relatively few studies focused predominantly on trying to alter mothers' mental representations, that is, the way mothers think about past or current experiences of attachment relationships. Only five of the 88 studies did not involve measurement of maternal sensitivity or responsiveness (which was measured using a variety of scales including, amongst others, Ainsworth's scales, the HOME inventory and the Nursing Child Assessment Teaching Scale). In 21 of the 29 studies in which it was measured, infant attachment status was measured using the Strange Situation procedure (using three- or four-way methods of classification[7]).

Table 7.6: Focus of intervention by outcome measure

FOCUS OF INTERVENTION	OUTCOME MEASURES		
	Sensitivity	Attachment	Sensitivity and Attachment
Maternal sensitivity	27	1	10
Maternal sensitivity + Social support	23	1	4
Maternal sensitivity + Representations	1	–	3
Maternal sensitivity + Social support + Representations	4	–	3
Social support	1	2	2
Social support + Representations	1	–	–
Representations	1	1	2
Not stated	1	–	–
Total number of studies	59	5	24

Combined effect sizes were computed for studies which had used randomised controlled designs. For studies which measured changes in maternal sensitivity, Bakermans-Kranenburg et al. (2003) again found moderately strong effects both for interventions focusing directly and exclusively on maternal sensitivity ($d = 0.45$) and for those focusing on maternal sensitivity, social support and mental representations ($d = 0.46$). They found smaller but still statistically significant effects for those focused on maternal sensitivity and social support ($d = 0.27$). Contrasting interventions focused only on sensitivity with all the others, they concluded that those focused on sensitivity alone were most effective. However, it is important to note that interventions that included maternal sensitivity and social support appeared to be as effective as those focused on maternal sensitivity alone and effects from this small group of studies would have been occluded in this contrast.

---

7   Three-way = A, B, C; four-way = A, B, C, D

Bakermans-Kranenburg et al. (2003) also found that interventions using video feedback tended to be more effective in altering maternal sensitivity than those not using this method (though only at p = 0.04) and, as we discussed in Chapter Six, they suggested that physical interventions (e.g. provision of a baby carrier or specific way of infant-carrying) appeared to be more effective than personal interventions, though they did qualify this finding by remarking that only two studies were involved and neither involved a large sample.

Bakermans-Kranenburg et al. (2003) also found that sensitivity-oriented interventions lasting more than 16 sessions were less effective than those lasting 5-16 or fewer than five sessions (which were equally effective). They found interventions that started when children were over six months were more effective than those starting earlier and that interventions with clinically referred samples were more effective than those conducted with non-referred groups. Effects on maternal sensitivity outcomes appeared to be more consistently associated with some measures of sensitivity than others and were also positively correlated with success in retaining participants.

With regard to attachment security, as in the earlier meta-analysis, only a small combined effect size was found (of $d = 0.19$ for three-way and $d = 0.20$ four four-way classifications). Individual effect sizes ranged between -.061 to +0.83. However, a subset of ten studies (total sample size 463) focused only on maternal sensitivity yielded a slightly larger combined effect size ($d = 0.39$). A benefit for studies focusing only on sensitivity was again found when these studies were contrasted with the remaining 13 studies which focused either on support only, maternal attachment representations only, sensitivity and support, sensitivity and representations and sensitivity, representations and support. Whether this is a truly reliable finding or why it should arise seems worth further investigation.

As with sensitivity outcomes, attachment outcomes were more effective when interventions started after the first six months. Unlike sensitivity outcomes, though, positive attachment outcomes were not associated with interventions using video feedback and were most closely associated with interventions of less than five sessions duration. Outcome measures based on Ainsworth's Strange Situation procedure appeared least likely to yield positive effects.

Bakermans-Kranenburg et al. (2003) carried out further analyses on studies of 'multi-problem' families which they defined as a combination of multi-risk and clinically referred samples (multi-risk having been described as "high risk parents or infants e.g. drug dependent, impoverished, socially isolated, minority group, single parents, adopted infants, irritable infants"). They found similar patterns in respect of number of sessions: programmes lasting longer than 16 sessions were less effective than those of either less than five or five to 16, which were equally effective. Programmes that focused solely on maternal sensitivity were again found to be more effective than those which included other components. Interestingly, they also unexpectedly found that non-professional intervenors produced greater effects on maternal sensitivity outcomes with these multi-problem samples than professional intervenors.

In sum, these analyses appeared to support and extend the findings of the earlier meta-analysis (Table 7.7). Length of follow-up was not discussed and it may be useful to bear this omission in mind when considering both these conclusions and those from future meta-analyses and intervention studies. It also seems worth bearing in mind the fact that neither meta-analysis directly addressed either the question of whether earlier interventions are more effective nor that of whether shorter, simpler interventions are more feasible in infancy than later. In fact, the second meta-analysis suggested that interventions that commenced very soon after the baby's birth appeared to be less effective.

Table 7.7 Summary of findings from second meta-analysis (Bakermans-Kranenburg et al. 2003)

- Showed moderate effects of interventions focused on altering mothers' sensitive responsiveness to infants' behavioural cues
- Showed relatively small effects of interventions on infant attachment security
- The studies that were most effective in altering mothers' responsiveness tended to be those that also impacted on infant attachment security
- Shorter-term programmes (less than 16 weeks) may be the most effective
- Interventions of less than five weeks can be as effective as those between five and 16 weeks
- Interventions starting after baby is six months appear to be more effective than those starting before this time
- Interventions focused on mothers' sensitive responsiveness alone may be most effective
- For some multi-problem families, non-professional intervenors may be more effective
- But it is unclear whether shorter, less complex interventions are actually most effective in the long term, as long-term outcomes were not examined

In the next part of this chapter, we examine in more detail therapeutic approaches that have adopted an attachment perspective, bearing in mind the question of whether Attachment Theory can inform therapy for attachment-related problems, what kind of training might be needed in order to identify, understand and treat attachment-related problems and what the role of non-verbal processes might be in therapy.

Therapeutic approaches

In this section, we consider, first, one of the most effective early intervention studies so far reported that has used an attachment theory approach, the study of irritable babies conducted by Van den Boom (1988). Next, we outline some of the key principles proposed by Bowlby as having a therapeutic application and go on to describe an attachment-based intervention called the *Circle of Security programme*. Fourth, we describe some UK-based projects and programmes, in the community and in schools, that have adopted similar approaches, and consider the need for professional trained intervenors or facilitators. Fifth, we touch briefly on the vast topic of family therapy and consider the special case of children in care. Finally, we turn to the vexed question of 'Attachment Therapy', a form of 'therapy' which, in our view, is mis-named, bears very little relationship to Attachment Theory and has involved the use of techniques which are neither therapeutic nor safe.

Therapy with irritable babies

Dymphna van den Boom's study (van den Boom 1988, 1989, 1991) involved a longitudinal study of 30 mothers and their first-born children from shortly after birth until 12 months of age. The families involved were intact two-parent families of lower socioeconomic status in which the mother was the primary caretaker. The babies were healthy, full-term, Caucasian and not considered to be at risk for developmental problems. The Brazelton Neonatal Behavioral Assessment was used to assess infant irritability ten and 15 days after each baby was born.

This has three items from which information relevant to irritability can be derived: peak of excitement, rapidity of build-up and irritability. By combining these items and averaging across the two administrations, 15 babies were identified as irritable (scoring six and over) and another 15 (scoring under six) were recruited as the comparison group.

Observational data was gathered once a month, morning and evening, on unstructured mother-infant interactions. At six months and again at 12 months, a temperament questionnaire (the ICQ/Infant Characteristics Questionnaire; Bates et al. 1979), which contains a rating of negative emotionality, was filled in by mothers and researchers. At 12 months, the Strange Situation procedure was used to assess attachment security. This study indicated a relationship between irritability and avoidant attachment as well as a tendency for mothers of irritable babies to be less responsive than average while the opposite was true for mothers of non-irritable infants. From this study, Van den Boom surmised that interactions between mothers and irritable babies might be characterised by a two-way process in which the babies' behaviour discouraged maternal responsiveness and irritability was also encouraged because mothers of irritable babies used less effective strategies when trying to sooth their babies. Nearly all the babies classified as secure in the SS were not irritable while nearly all those classified as avoidant or ambivalent-resistant were.

Looking at the interactions between mothers and irritable infants, Van den Boom observed that mothers of avoidant infants tended to communicate with their babies from a distance. They ignored their babies' crying more and responded similarly to the babies whether or not the babies were distressed and whether or not they were showing positive affect. Mothers of ambivalent infants were very variable in their responses: sometimes they totally ignored the baby or tried ineffectively to soothe the baby by distracting them and in consequence made the baby more distressed; at other times their responses were more contingent and effective. The most sociable babies had mothers who were rated highly on sensitive responsiveness. On the basis of these observations, Van den Boom concluded that an appropriate intervention for lower-class mothers with irritable infants should aim to enhance three aspects of sensitive responding: contingency (avoidance of distance interactions), consistency and appropriateness (avoidance of general responses that are not cued by the infant's state).

Table 7.8: Design of intervention study (Van den Boom 1994)

	PRE-TEST (6 months)	**INTERVENTION**	**POST-TEST (9 months)**	**POST-TEST (12 months)**
1	Yes (n=25)	Home visits plus intervention	Yes	Yes
2	No (n =25)	Home visits plus intervention	Yes	Yes
3	Yes (n=25)	Home visits only, no intervention	Yes	Yes
4	No (n =25)	Home visits only, no intervention	Yes	Yes

In the intervention study, 100 irritable infants (47 girls and 53 boys) were identified using the same methodology as in the previous observational study from a sample of 588 infants (17 per cent were therefore identified as irritable, suggesting that the criterion used to identify irritability in this study might have been reasonably close to the high reactivity criteria used by Kagan). The 100 mother-infant dyads were randomly assigned to one of four conditions: pre-test plus intervention, no-pre-test plus intervention, pre-test without intervention, no pre-test no intervention. This design was used in order to ensure both that there were no differences between mother-infant dyads before the intervention and to check that the pre-intervention assessment had not contributed to the effectiveness of the intervention. All four groups were assessed post-intervention (Table 7.8 presents more details of the timing of tests and intervention).

Pre-treatment tests consisted of a measure of the quality of mother-infant interaction (assessed on two home visits, one in the morning and the other in the afternoon, during which routine interactions were observed for 40 minutes at each visit) and of infant exploration during a free-play task (babies seated on mothers' laps were shown toys for a minute, then offered three sets of toys to play with for five minutes each). These observations were coded by researchers blind to experimental conditions. The same tests were repeated post-treatment by different observers who did not know which experimental group the dyad they observed was in. In addition, at each assessment and on each home visit, all 100 mothers were asked to record life events on an inventory designed for this purpose. When the babies were 12 months, they were video-ed in interaction with their mothers in the Strange Situation. In total, therefore, the study involved seven home visits (four focused on pre- and post-treatment assessments and three on intervention) and a Strange Situation test.

The intervention, or treatment, began three weeks after pre-intervention assessments and consisted of three intervention sessions at three-weekly intervals when the babies were aged between six and nine months. The same intervenor made three two-hour home visits during which four aspects of mothers' responses to infant cues were addressed: noticing the infant's signals, correctly interpreting signals, selecting an appropriate response, carrying out the response effectively. To increase perception of signals, mothers were encouraged to imitate their babies, to repeat their own verbal expressions, and to be quiet when the baby's eyes were averted. This was intended to slow down and simplify the mothers' behaviour in response to irritable babies who often signal a lot. Mothers were also taught to use more effective methods for soothing fussing babies and were encouraged to engage in satisfying play activities in order to increase the likelihood of pleasurable interactions (since mothers of irritable infants may otherwise be more attentive to negative baby behaviour). These interventions were tailored to suit individual mothers, depending on the mother's interactive style (e.g. mothers who were rather inactive might be encouraged to be more active whereas very active mothers might be encouraged to slow down). Mothers in the comparison group received the same number of visits though not from the same person.

Analyses showed no differences between intervention and comparison group mothers or infants on pre-treatment scores. Post-test comparisons showed that intervention group mothers were significantly more responsive, more stimulating, more visually attentive and more controlling of their babies' behaviour than non-intervention group mothers. Although both groups of mothers increased the amount that they controlled their babies behaviour from pre- to post-test, non-intervention mothers became less responsive, stimulating and visually attentive over the three months (as might be expected given that previous research had shown the tendency for mothers of irritable babies to withdraw from non-rewarding interactions). Babies in the intervention group were also found to be significantly more sociable, to engage in more self-soothing, to explore more and to engage in more sophisticated exploration than non-intervention group infants; they also directed more positive social behaviour at their mothers and showed less negative emotionality. Babies in the no pre-test intervention group seemed particularly likely to be sociable. A Strange Situation assessment at 12 months indicated that the proportion of irritable infants in the intervention group who were insecurely attached was well within the normal range (38 per cent). By contrast, 78 per cent of babies in the control group were insecurely attached and two thirds of these were avoidantly attached (Table 7.9).

Table 7.9: Effects of intervention on Strange Situation classification of irritable infants (Van den Boom 1994)

		A Avoidant	B Secure	C Ambivalent	D Disorganised
1	Pre-test + intervention	8 (32%)	14 (56%)	1 (4%)	2 (8%)
2	No pre-test + intervention	4 (16%)	17 (68%)	2 (8%)	2 (8%)
3	Pre-test, no intervention	13 (52%)	6 (24%)	4 (16%)	2 (8%)
4	No pre-test, no intervention	13 (52%)	5 (20%)	3 (12%)	4 (16%)
	Total	38 (38%)	42 (42%)	10 (10%)	10 (10%)

In discussing these results, Van den Boom (1994, p.1474) cautioned against over-generalisation, pointing out that "Without the use of a comparison intervention group, the possibility cannot be ruled out that, in some way, the intervention dyads showed an improvement in their behaviour simply because they received a great deal more attention than the control dyads." However, later follow-ups (of 82 mothers and infants when the infants were aged 18 months and 24 months and of 79 dyads when the child was three-and-a-half) indicated that the positive effects of the intervention had endured over time, although the authors were hesitant about attributing these positive effects to changes in mothers' sensitivity as opposed to more general attitudinal change, that is, they considered it possible that the improvements may be due, for example, to mothers' greater enjoyment of the relationship rather than to sensitivity alone (Van den Boom 1995).

Since this study was carried out, it has often been cited as evidence of the power of interventions focused on maternal sensitivity to produce lasting positive change in outcomes for children. Effect sizes have been calculated as sufficiently large to justify confidence in this approach. However, as the author cautions, it is not safe to make generalisations on the basis of one study, particularly since this study did not involve high risk participants. Currently, Jude Cassidy and colleagues are carrying out a replication and extension of Van den Boom's study.

Bowlbian principles and therapy

Bowlby's ideas about how Attachment Theory can inform therapy can be found throughout his writings but most noticeably, perhaps, in the third volume of his trilogy (1980a) and in the later collection of papers (Bowlby 1988b).

In these texts, Bowlby describes how processes involved with experiences of loss and trauma that can lead to unresolved states of mind and to what Winnicott (probably early 1950s: Winnicott et al. 1989, p.43) described as the development of a 'false self':"...there is a premature taking over of the nursing functions of the mother, so that the infant or child adapts to the environment while at the same time protecting and hiding the true self... In typical cases the imprisoned true self is unable to function, and by being protected its opportunity for living experience is limited. Life is lived though the compliant false self, and the result clinically is a sense of unreality". Bowlby (1979b/1988b, p.57) comments, "To provide, by being ourselves, the conditions in which a patient of this kind can discover and recover what Winnicott calls his real self, and what I call his attachment desires and feelings, is not easy: On the one hand, we have really to be trustworthy and we have also genuinely to respect all those yearnings for affection and intimacy that each of us has but which in these patients have become lost. On the other, we must not offer more than we can give and we must not move faster than the patient can bear. To achieve this balance requires all the intuition, imagination, and empathy of which we are capable. But it also requires a firm grasp of what the patient's problems are and what we are trying to do."

Bowlby strongly emphasised the need to understand what the patient's symptoms mean and, in this connection, quoted one of Freud's last papers which urged the need to fully reconstruct a picture, accurate in all respects, of the patient's forgotten years. To this end, Bowlby was very much in favour of careful and meticulous note-taking and observations of patient-doctor interactions during therapy, to see whether any 'hidden agenda' could be revealed and to gain a better understanding of what might underlie processes of change. He was also firmly convinced of the immense value of child-parent observations and the vital need for as full as possible an understanding of normal and abnormal development.

Summing up the therapist's task, Bowlby (1988b) suggested that it involves five elements:
1) the provision of a secure base from which the patient can explore current and past painful feelings, that might not be bearable without a "trusted companion to provide support, encouragement, sympathy, and, on occasion, guidance" (p. 138)
2) helping the patient explore expectations and unconscious biases about close relationships and current significant figures
3) encouraging the patient to examine the relationship between him/herself and the therapist and the way that the patient thinks about the therapist as an attachment figure
4) supporting the patient in thinking about how childhood experiences, particularly in relation to parents and family, influence or limit current perceptions and outlook, a task which can involve 'permitting' the patient to consciously express feelings that were not acknowledgeable hitherto
5) helping the patient to acknowledge and re-evaluate images of self and of others that derive from real life experience of interactions with key figures.(6)

In elaborating on these five principles, Bowlby likened the therapist to a mother who provides a secure base for exploration but drew attention to the possibility that this could set up false expectations as well as real fears. He also stressed the need for the therapist to recognise his or her own contribution to the therapeutic relationship, to focus on the here and now more than on the past, and not to assume that *all* the patient's current experience is governed by 'ghosts from the past'. Even where the patient's perceptions appear to be mis-construals, Bowlby made it clear that these intrusive thoughts or feelings should not be treated as illogical but should be viewed as having roots in a reality that needs to be respected in order to be understood.

Whilst emphasising that his theory must not be seen as a parent-blaming exercise (on the grounds that most parents are doing their best but may be misguided due to their own experiences of being parented), Bowlby also listed some parental malpractices. These included:
- threatening not to love a child as a means of control
- threatening to abandon a child as a means of control
- threatening suicide
- denying a child's reality by disclaiming or disconfirming the truth.

Bowlby explained how these highly frightening and confusing parental behaviours might be 'defensively excluded' from a child's memory so that, although their effects may linger on, the patient may not be able without help to trace the real source of the strong emotions associated with such negative experiences.

In essence, the role of the therapist in Bowlby's account is to be reliably, consistently and patiently 'there' in the real world as a companion, for however long it takes to enable the patient to build a trusting relationship: "Whilst some traditional therapists might be described as adopting the stance, 'I know, I'll tell you', the stance I advocate is one of 'You know, you tell me'. Thus the patient is encouraged to believe that, with support and occasional guidance, he can discover for himself the true nature of the models that underlie his thoughts, feelings, and actions and that, by examining the nature of his earlier experiences with his parents, or parent substitutes, he will understand what has led him to build the models now active within him and thus be free to restructure them. Fortunately the human psyche, like human bones, is strongly inclined towards self-healing. The psychotherapist's job, like that of the orthopaedic surgeon's, is to provide the conditions in which self-healing can best take place" (Bowlby 1988b, pp. 151-152).

We have quoted at length from Bowlby himself in the above passage because, for reasons that we think will become more apparent towards the end of this chapter, we feel that it is very important to convey exactly what Bowlby's views were, rather than our interpretation of those views. We now proceed to a description of a programme which seems to be largely in line with the principles outlined by Bowlby.

The Circle of Security project

The Circle of Security intervention protocol is a group-based intervention for caregivers and children that aims to:
1) increase caregivers' sensitivity and responsiveness to their children's signals, particularly in relation to exploration and the use of a secure base
2) increase caregivers' ability to reflect on their own and their children's behaviour, thoughts and feelings regarding attachment and caregiving
3) enable caregivers to reflect on aspects of their own life that might have influenced their caregiving.

It does this by:
1) creation of a 'holding environment' or 'secure base' within which parents can explore their own parenting
2) provision of the Circle of Security concept which acts as a "user-friendly map of attachment theory"
3) facilitation of reflective group discussions that parents can internalise and adopt (this is seen as the key to effective change)
4) supporting parents in making a shift from limited defensive strategies that limit their empathic understanding of their children to more child-relevant strategies
5) helping parents to read and respond to children's cues or miscues, i.e. developing their observational skills.

The programme (Table 7.10) involves group work with, usually, high-risk caregivers and pre-schoolers (one to four years of age), for an hour and a quarter a week, for 20 weeks. Videotape records are made of each parent and child (in the Strange Situation) before the group begins and analysis of these tapes is used to determine the aspects of the parent-child relationship to be focused on during the course. Selected video-vignettes are used in group discussions throughout the course. At the end of the course, a further videotape is made of parent-child interaction to use in assessing change.

Table 7.10: The Circle of Security programme (Marvin et al. 2002)

TIMING	FOCUS/ACTIVITY
Introduction & theory-building – Week 1	Establishing a 'holding environment'
	Focus on parents' competence and positive intentions
	Use video of parent and child interaction with song 'You are so beautiful' super-imposed; Parents are told "This is the song your child is singing to you"
	Benefits of secure attachment are discussed
	Parents view pictures of their children moving between proximity-seeking and exploration and are given 'The Circle of Security' picture
– Week 2	Enhancing observational skills and understanding children's needs
	Use more videos of parent and child interaction
	Parents begin to identify children's primary need (exploration or attachment)
	Try to identify what children are thinking and feeling
Phase 1 Tape reviews – Weeks 3-8	Each week a different parent-child video is watched – this parent is in the 'hot seat' for week
	All parents assess parent's ability to meet child's exploration and attachment needs
	- identify 'under-used capacities' and 'over-used strengths'
	4 video-clips are used: (1) distressed child wanting parent (2) parent using least-used capacity well (3) parent using least-used capacity not so well (4) parent and child interacting well
	Parent receives a picture that illustrates the central lesson or 'lynchpin issue' of the week, i.e. a print from the video of the parent doing what they need to do more of
Transition & theory-building – Week 9	Theme: All parents struggle
	Group leader reads essay "Welcome to the Club" which illustrates everyday problems and 'shark music'
	Educational videotape introduces 'Limited Circles of Security' and dynamics behind non-secure attachment patterns
	Discussion of defensive processes

TIMING	FOCUS/ACTIVITY
Phase 2 **Tape reviews** – Weeks 10-15	Watch Strange Situation tapes to focus on 'under-used capacities' and difficulties – focus on parent's vulnerability and issues relating to emotional regulation 4 video-clips used again: 1) parent caregiving well 2) parent's greatest problem with caregiving 3) parent overcoming this problem 4) parent and child interacting well Parent receives a picture that illustrates the parent being successful in area that causes them greatest caregiving difficulty
Transition & review – Week 16	Review of previous weeks Preparation for final weeks Discuss 'unfinished' group process issues
Phase 3 **Tape reviews** – Weeks 17-19	Two parent-child videos reviewed each week to celebrate changes that have been made Again use four edited video vignettes to emphasise parents' increased success
Final session – Week 20	Graduation and celebration Parents share experiences of group Group leader shows appreciation of parents and shows video montage, with music, of salient moments of each parent-child dyad Parents are given certificates, completed workbooks, a take-home children's story and copies of video tapes; arrangements are made for post-intervention assessment

Central to the Circle of Security protocol is the belief that "It is the ability to repair a disruption that is the essence of secure attachment, not lack of disruptions" (Marvin et al. 2002, p.109). This is also referred to as the 'Circle of Repair'. Parents are therefore taught to identify disruptions in interactions between themselves and their children and to try to understand what processes might be maintaining them. To assist with this identification, pictures of two different types of circle are used, one illustrating the 'Circle of Security' and the other illustrating 'Limited Circles of Security' (Cooper et al. 1999 and 2000). Parents are encouraged to help their children to trust that, in the safe and secure relationship between them and their parents, they will (almost) always set things right (Cooper et al. 1999 and 2000).

The Circle of Security is safe and containing only when the parent supports the child both as s/he moves away to explore and as s/he returns back to the safe haven of the secure base. On the moving away side of the Circle of Security, children are depicted as needing parents' support in order to explore with confidence and as specifically needing parents to watch over them, help them and enjoy their exploration with them. On the coming back side of the Circle of Security, children are depicted as needing parents who welcome their coming back, by protecting them, comforting them, delighting in them and organising their feelings. The alternative picture shows that Limited Circles of Security arise when parents fail to support the child's exploration adequately (which disrupts exploration, encourages over-dependency and creates a short-circuit in the Circle of Security) and when parents fail to welcome the child's return (which disrupts the child's comfort-seeking, encourages premature self-reliance and again short-circuits the Circle of Security). In this Limited Circles of Security picture, the running child figure is therefore shown as being diverted from the task of running around the larger circle by two extraneous loops, one interfering with exploration and the other interfering with approaches to the parent. Each extraneous loop is portrayed as arising from mutually supported parent-child interactions, with the child, who picks up on the discomfort that both parent and child feel, miscue-ing the parent about his/her needs: disruptions in exploration result in the child acting as though they need comfort and protection (mis-cueing the actual wish to explore); disruptions in approaches to the parent result in the child acting as though they want to be distant or to explore (mis-cueing the actual need to be welcomed).

The pictures, which are displayed during the course of the project, are accompanied by the following message, described as '(almost) everything I need to know about being a parent in 25 words or less', which exhorts parents to:

- *Always:* **be BIGGER, STRONGER, WISER, and KIND**
- *Whenever possible:* **follow my child's need**
- *Whenever necessary:* **take charge**

Although the pictures depict the child as mis-cueing, parents are also taught to recognise their own contribution to this process and the fact that they too mis-cue the child due to their own defences against painful feelings arising not from the child's situation but from their own histories. In addition, the parent is encouraged to recognise that this mutual mis-cueing prevents them from picking up on direct information from the child, for example, they may have failed to realise how unusual the behaviour is of a child who is disrupting approaches by averting their gaze, over-focusing on toys and lacking emotion-expressiveness.

In order to help parents to understand their feelings, part way through the course they watch two video clips: first, of a rainforest and coastline accompanied by soothing music; second, of the same scene accompanied by more menacing music (e.g. a soundtrack from *Jaws*). After each clip, parents discuss the feelings evoked and ways in which their own agitation and anxiety can be transferred to their children: "It is as if the parents had learned from their own parents that certain needs are like shark-infested waters and must be avoided" (Marvin et al. 2002, p.112). Subsequently, as parents discuss with other parents the videos depicting their interactions with their children, they use the term 'shark music' which is thought to help them to increase their tolerance for the painful feelings that have caused them to mis-read their child's cues.

Besides the secure, avoidant and ambivalent patterns depicted by the circles, other insecure 'disordered' patterns are also acknowledged which may involve parents' abdication of their caregiving role, role reversal, mixtures of avoidancy and ambivalence, intimidation, compulsive caregiving, or mutual disengagement. Some of these parents may be so far from engaging in supportive or welcoming circles of interaction that they may have difficulty relating to the concepts involved. Marvin et al. (2002) recommend that it may most beneficial to help these parents to follow the child's lead in the first instance.

The *Circle of Security* project can be seen to incorporate Attachment Theory both directly, in the sense that Attachment Theory terms are discussed during the course, and indirectly, in that the experience of sharing and reflecting on parent-child interactions within a supportive group is, like a caregiver-child relationship, potentially capable of facilitating emotional co-regulation and enabling the internalisation of positive memories of experiences in relation to other people. Although the 'graduation' ceremony (distinctly Western Atlantic!) has an element of behavioural conditioning (since it involves reward-giving), this component is peripheral to the more central ingredient that directly engages with current and past relationships.

The use of video feedback in work with parents and very young children, though still fairly uncommon, has also featured in some of the UK-based interventions adopting Attachment Theory as a framework.

UK-based interventions influenced by or based on Attachment Theory

Evidence from numerous sources has encouraged the development of initiatives aimed at improving the quality of infant-carer relationships in the early years. Much of the impetus for these initiatives is derived from 'commonsense' beliefs that early intervention must be more effective than later interventions, which may arrive only after serious problems have become entrenched. These beliefs have encouraged major projects around the world as well as nationwide projects in the UK (e.g. routine ante- and postnatal Health Visitor programmes, Home Start, Sure Start, and attachment-oriented day care services such as that of the Soho Centre in London). These larger-scale projects have not, in general, included systematic application of findings from attachment research, although the way services are monitored makes it difficult to ascertain the exact extent to which Attachment Theory may be reflected in the practices of service deliverers. Relatively few services offer support to parents of older children and much that is on offer tends to come through schools as opposed to health services. Within schools, evidence of the value of initiatives, such as nurture groups, circle time and mentoring, and projects such as the UK *Place2Be*, that recognise the value of making provision for individual children's emotional and relational needs, tends to be sparse.

A few small-scale projects have been trialled that have a more specific focus on attachment relationships and aim to incorporate findings from attachment research as well as findings from related research. These tend to emphasise the need to strengthen support networks and to take account of the social context of mothers and children as well as looking at the dynamics of parent-child interaction. Although some evaluation of these programmes has been undertaken, systematic comparisons with other treatment approaches have not yet been carried out. In the next section, four of these programmes will be briefly outlined:

- PIPPIN (Parents In Partnership – Parent Infant Network)
- Newpin
- SIP (The Sunderland Infant Programme)
- OXPIP

PIPPIN (Parents In Partnership – Parent Infant Network)
PIPPIN states its aims as to facilitate the transition to parenthood and to safeguard family relationships. It does this by offering accredited training to professionals who deliver services to new parents and by running programmes for parents. PIPPIN argues that its approach

differs from conventional parenting classes, which may focus more on practical or management aspects of parenting, because it draws upon attachment research (especially Daniel Stern's work on mother-child attunement) and focuses on the building of strong two-way attachments between parents and babies.

Some aspects that PIPPIN workers will emphasise include:
- encouraging parents to talk about their feelings about being a parent
- helping parents to recognise and respond to their baby's emotional state
- encouraging parents to reflect on how their sense of emotional connectedness to their baby might be influenced by their own experiences of being cared for
- enabling parents to reflect on their new roles as partners and carers
- facilitating the growth of communication, observation and listening skills
- encouraging discussion of developing relationships.

PIPPIN stresses that its approach is not prescriptive nor based on any one model of how a family should be. Rather, it can apply to diverse family forms and all cultures. PIPPIN classes have been evaluated to some extent, although results of controlled trial follow-up studies are not yet available. Comparisons between parents who did and did not attend classes have suggested benefits of attendance in respect of:
- greater relationship satisfaction (with babies and partners)
- more confidence as parents
- fewer affective problems (less anxiety and less depression)
- more child-centred attitudes to childrearing
- greater flexibility in coping with routine family situations.

Information on the PIPPIN website also suggests that there is evidence that children whose parents have attended PIPPIN classes are more likely to be securely attached to their parents and, as a result, are less likely to be disruptive and anti-social (though, in the absence of controlled trial follow-up studies, the status of this evidence must be indicative rather than conclusive).

NEWPIN

While PIPPIN works with parents with or without difficulties, the 15 NEWPIN centres (based mainly in London but also in Chesterfield and Northern Ireland and now affiliated with the Family Welfare Association) aim more specifically to help parents who are experiencing difficulties, particularly where there may have been a family history of abuse. Referrals are accepted from both parents and professionals for a wide range of problems that might interrupt parent-child relationships, for example, depression, feeling unable to cope with raising children or with giving children the care and attention they need, hurting or taking anger out on children, feeling socially isolated or feel unvalued as an individual or as a parent.

NEWPIN services are comprised of four complementary strands which include attachment and befriending, group work and counselling, family play programmes, and personal development and learning-for-life programmes. There is also a London-based network of antenatal classes run by volunteers, a project specifically geared towards fathers and one for teenage parents. Underlying each component is an interest in building up available support networks for parents and children and so empowering parents and children to take greater control over their lives, by developing self-esteem and emotional maturity. It is hoped that this will bring about lasting improvements in quality of life. NEWPIN projects have been evaluated positively several times though ongoing evaluations are also in progress.

NEWPIN also runs several accredited courses one of which includes parenting skills. Overall, although there is an attachment orientation within NEWPIN programmes, it is not altogether clear what the impact of this element might be and it does not appear to be a central feature of the programme which emphasised support needs more generally. The next two programmes to be described are more overtly focused on attachment relationships though neither has been running for long enough for evaluation reports to be publicly available.

THE SUNDERLAND INFANT PROGRAMME (SIP)

The Sure Start-funded[8] Sunderland Infant Programme has been set up in a way that enables close monitoring and evaluation exactly along the lines recommended by Bowlby, of parent-infant interactions and development. The programme consists of video-based screening of parent-infant interaction at 8-16 weeks which is used to provide the basis for an intervention programme in which participants either simply view the video, or are offered different levels of intervention: information about child development, guidance aimed at increasing responsive, attuned interaction or psychotherapy focused on difficulties that might prevent parents from interacting well with their baby.

The intervention is carried out by a team of workers but principally by health visitors trained in the use of Crittenden's CARE-Index (Appendix 5.2). Mothers are followed up when the baby is aged six and 12 months. At 12 months, the mothers and babies are assessed in the Strange Situation and the CARE-Index is again carried out. Evaluation reports are almost complete. Preliminary analyses indicate positive effects of interventions with regard to maternal sensitivity and attachment security. Despite the social disadvantages that might otherwise have been expected to produce higher levels of non-securely attached infants (Shaw and Vondra 1995, Shaw et al. 1997), rates of secure attachment in the intervention group were almost in the normal range (55 per cent compared with 30 per cent in the non-intervention group) while the proportion of non-normative patterns (i.e. the extra categories identified in Crittenden's system beyond the three major organised A, B, C groups) was considerably lower in the intervention group (14 cf 43 per cent). The distribution of organised non-secure attachment patterns was similar for intervention and non-intervention infants (A1-2: 18 versus 17 per cent; C1-2: 14 versus 11 per cent).

Although the programme appears to show distinct promise, more detailed evaluation is needed to identify precisely which programme elements might have been effective. Also, refusal rates for participation were fairly high, though perhaps not exceptionally so given the nature of the social group: almost 40 per cent of parents declined to participate while some professionals were also initially unwilling to cooperate. This suggests that more work is needed to ascertain whether alternatives to video-based intervention might be needed to complement this type of programme or perhaps more gradual induction into the programme by some other means.

OXFORD PARENT INFANT PROGRAMME (OXPIP)

OXPIP, which was founded in 1998, aims to offer counselling to parents with a child under the age of two years, either on an individual or a group basis. It accepts referrals from par-

---

8   Sure Start funding was made available to families living in areas considered, by the Department of the Environment Index of Multiple Deprivation to be the two per cent most deprived; it is not clear how long it will continue to fund this kind of programme.

ents and through professionals for problems of varying degrees, perhaps because the parent is uncertain about their parenting, worried about the baby's development or suffering from emotional problems including anxiety, depression, post-traumatic disorders, etc.

Like PIPPIN, OXPIP works with parents to help them understand their relationship to their baby and to develop new ways of responding to each other. Its philosophy is very much that of the more deterministic interpretation of Attachment Theory, along the lines outlined by Gerhardt (2004), who is one of the directors: "OXPIP believes that secure attachments made during the first two years of life are crucial for the development of emotional health. Help given during this time can prevent or lessen psychological problems in later life. Parents need to feel nurtured themselves before they can nurture their babies" (OXPIP website, 2005). They emphasise that "A baby who is understood and whose needs are met will be securely attached to its parent (this can be either or both parents, or the key caregiver) and will have a basic unconscious expectation that its feelings will be regulated and that its attachment figure will restore its well-being. An insecure child will not feel this" (OXPIP website, 2005).

OXPIP literature explains that, informed by animal research and particularly studies of rats (e.g. Panksepp 1998 and Hofer 1984), they see the parent as having an important role in regulating babies' emotional state. Parents are therefore taught how they can respond to and regulate the baby's state physically through feeding, speech, contact and temperature control, and psychologically by teaching very young infants to name their feelings, to think about them and to gradually gain greater control over negative emotional states.

This emotional regulation, according to OXPIP, is related to attachment security which, in turn, is related to children's self confidence, ability to cope with new experiences, lack of antisocial behaviour and increased social skills. OXPIP places particular emphasis on the capacity of extensive holding to correct faulty stress response systems, especially where there are chronic problems. OXPIP literature also claims that their work is informed by brain research that has demonstrated a relationship between secure attachment, stress response systems, neurotransmitter pathways and brain growth.

Therapy consists of an initial introductory session during which the client and counsellor agree whether counselling is appropriate and, if so, over how many sessions. This can take place at any point around the baby's birth, before or after. Counselling sessions, which last 50 minutes, are usually on the same day at the same time each week and held at the clinic, although home visits may be made in certain exceptional circumstances. A major focus of therapy is on observation of parent and baby together and video feedback can be included, with the parent's agreement, where indicated.

All therapists, or clinicians as OXPIP prefers to call them, are professionally qualified counsellors or psychotherapists and employ a psychodynamic approach, but will work flexibly in response to the particular needs of the parent and baby. Clinicians are in regular supervision. Due partly to funding problems, the work of OXPIP has not yet been evaluated.[9] While it is likely that similar results may be found, possibly pertaining to a wider sample of parents given that there is no requirement for all OXPIP parents to be video-ed, as in the Sunderland Infant Programme, currently no objective assessments are available. It is our view that full

---

9   This situation seems to highlight a loophole in the monitoring of service provision: new organisations can start up with no requirement to provide evidence of efficacy. They are also impeded by lack of financial support to obtain this important evidence. Given the potential for some forms of therapy to be harmful, this situation is a matter of some concern.

evaluation of this programme with detailed publicly-available reports containing both quantitative and qualitative material could prove of immense value in building a picture of the true worth of attachment-oriented approaches. However, it does seem important to separate out which programme elements are and which are not informed by attachment theory.

Attachment oriented family therapy

As Bowlby emphasised, and as Ainsworth was keen to stress, there is a distinction to be made between attachment behaviours and attachment relationships. Attachment behaviours are the behaviours elicited when there is a threat that, usually, lead a child to seek out an attachment figure or when there is a threat that leads a child to fear that the attachment figure is not going to be available. Attachment relationships, according to Bowlby, always involve at least dyads (if not more people).

If, as Gerhardt (2004) and the OXPIP approach suggests, attachment behaviour systems are conceptualised as underpinned by dysregulated stress hormone responses then it might be considered appropriate to attempt to alter patterns of non-secure attachment in children by focusing on the way that individual children cope with difficulties and manage their emotions. This conceptualisation might well, in the case of older children, encourage clinicians to consider that a behavioural or cognitive behavioural approach would be suitable. In this work, the focus might be the child's attributional or coping style and work might involve encouraging the child to appraise threatening situations differently, for example, the aggressive child might be taught to construe social situations that provoke anger in them as less threatening. The immediate aim would be to enable the child to have more control over the regulation of their own negative emotional states while the ultimate aim would be to increase their capacity to engage in rewarding social relationships. In work with very young babies, though, even this kind of conceptualisation would be unlikely to lead to a treatment approach that focused on the baby in isolation from its caregiver.

An alternative conceptualisation, more along the lines suggested by Bowlby (e.g. Bowlby 1980a, 1988b), is to view a focus of treatment as attachment relationships rather than specific attachment behaviours. In work with children, this conceptualisation almost invariably brings the social context of attachment relationships, that is, the whole family, into the clinical picture. However, as Byng-Hall points out (Byng-Hall 2005), although he wrote one of the earliest papers on family therapy (Bowlby 1949a) and saw great value in working with children and parents together, Bowlby chose to concentrate his efforts on understanding individual and dyadic infant-mother relationships rather than the whole family constellation. This decision was a pragmatic rather than an ideological one. Bowlby viewed the mother-child relationship as of central importance and, in contrast to complex family relationships, relatively easy to study in a controlled way. For these reasons, he chose this as a starting point. He left others to extend the study of attachment relationships across the family.

As mentioned in Chapter Five, observational studies have now begun to extend the focus of attachment research beyond the dyad, though systematic observation of the development of infants within triadic relationships is still at a relatively early stage. In the 1980s, serious attempts were made to draw fathers into the picture (though we would argue that methods have yet to be devised that can accurately reflect the nature of the father's influence on internal representations of attachment relationships). In the late 1980s and early 1990s, workers like Marvin and Stewart (1990) began to explore the nature of conceptual links between Attachment Theory and family systems theories. This discussion continues and is providing a rich vein of valuable and challenging ideas (e.g. Rothbaum et al. 2002, Kozlowska and Hanney 2002, Akister and Reibstein 2004, Dallos 2004). Byng-Hall (1991, 1995a, 1995b, 1999) has introduced the concept of attachment-oriented family therapy and has suggested that families may be more or less able to function as secure bases for individual members. More recently, Jonathan Hill and colleagues (Hill et al. 2003) have begun to pilot the use of a Family Attachment Interview though little information about the psychometric properties or the nature of this interview is as yet available in the public domain.

Intuitively, it seems that there should be much in common between family systems theories and attachment theory, since both focus on relationships between individuals and others, and both appear to be premised on the notion that these relationships can be described as located within systems of relationships, that is, that each individual sub-system contributes to a whole that is greater than the sum of its parts (von Bertalanffy 1968).

Certainly, on first consideration, some of the best-known family systems models such as Minuchin's systemic family theory (Minuchin 1974, 1984), the Circumplex Model of Olson (e.g. Olson 1993), the McMaster Model of Family Functioning (summarised in Barker 1992) identify dimensions of relating that appear to map directly onto the relationship patterns identified by attachment research (Figure 7.3). They emphasise the importance of agreed boundaries between individuals, optimally set so that they are neither too close (enmeshed), nor too distant (disengaged), nor too over-organised (inflexible, rigid, over-controlled), nor under-organised (chaotic, disorganised). Since the family is not a completely closed system, that is, it is open to influences from outside itself, having a certain amount of flexibility enables adaptation both to changes that affect individuals and those that affect the family as a whole.

ATTACHMENT DIFFICULTIES AND THERAPY

Figure 7.3: The Circumplex Model of Family Functioning (Olson 1993)

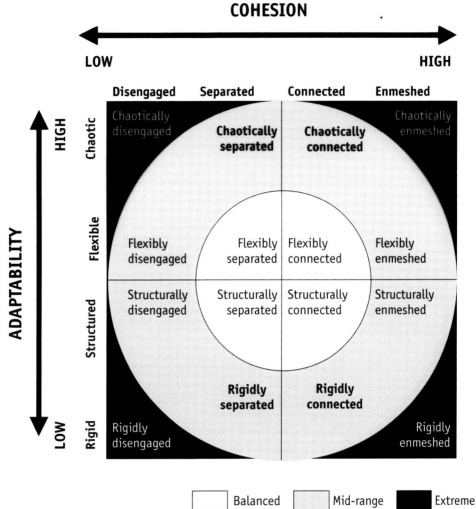

Optimal boundaries also facilitate the development of more effective communication. Given that a fundamental characteristic of communication is that meaning-making is generally individual, local and idiosyncratic rather than predicated on universal semantic laws (Harre 1986, Parker 1992), i.e. there is no one-to-one correspondence between one person's understanding of a string of words and another's, a certain amount of between-people reflective space is needed if communication is to be effective: too little space (as in enmeshed families) is likely to constrict opportunities for reflection and negotiation of meaning-making while too much space (as in disengaged families) is likely to over-stretch capacities for joint meaning-making. In enmeshed families, where there may be false expectations that all members will share the same understanding, the experience of non-shared meanings is likely to cause considerable friction. The experience of non-shared meanings is likely to be more commonplace for members of disengaged families and this may mean that the effort to negotiate share-able meanings atrophies. In families where tendencies toward separation and connection are more balanced and responsive to social events and influences, there will be more room for reflection upon and negotiation of meanings that are more likely to

be shared or, rather, respected as being different but as having legitimate currency. There is also likely to be as much misunderstanding, but more 'effort after meaning' and more attempts to repair mis-communications.

One strand of theory-building in relation to the forging of connections between family systems theories and attachment theory has pointed to the possibility that optimally-functioning families may share scripts or narratives (e.g. Byng-Hall 1995b, Hill et al. 2003). This line of enquiry generally postulates the existence of shared 'family scripts' or shared narrative experiences and tends toward the view that, within families where communication and interaction is most harmonious, individual members may produce similar stories. This possibility is yet to be fully explored as the methodology for coding and comparing scripts is barely begun (e.g. Hill et al. 2003). However, given the fundamental principle of non-shared meanings and negotiated realities (Harre 1986), it may be more likely that, where families are more harmonious, there may tend to be greater recognition of individual variations in understanding, dependent upon individual attributes related to age, maturity, intelligence, temperament, etc. Along with this may go a greater acceptance of the possibility that different family members will have their own 'takes' on family life. An analogy may be drawn with music-making, in which the most coordinated and synchronous orchestra or group of players can be appreciated as being not groups where everyone tries to play exactly the same but those where members have become sufficiently aware of individually different voices to know when to mimic, when to contrast, when to be quieter, and when to allow other instruments to dominate. It is perhaps only at this level of meta-awareness that playing together really becomes possible.

Another strand of theory-building has emerged from consideration of the possibility that more optimally-functioning families have attributes that resemble attributes of securely-attached mother-infant dyads or securely attached adult romantic partners. Marvin and Stewart (1990), for example, propose that more or less optimal levels of family cohesion map onto different patterns of attachment (Figure 7.4) while many workers have proposed that parents' own childhood experiences of close relationships influences their capacity both to relate to each other and to provide, as a caregiving couple, a secure base for the rearing of children.

Figure 7.4: Relationship between patterns of attachment and family structure (Marvin and Stewart 1990)

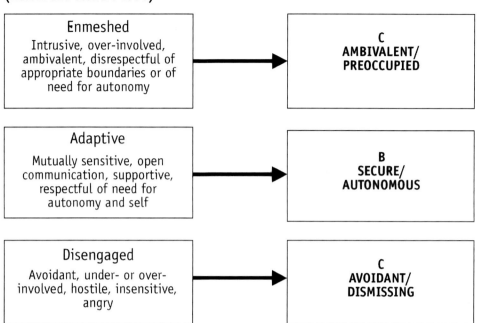

While the extent to which childhood experiences produce replication of one's own childhood rearing environment as opposed to 'corrective scripts' (Byng-Hall 2005) is, as yet, unknown, there does appear to be more agreement about the prominence of the 'enmeshed mother/disengaged father' pattern in less than optimally-functioning families (Nichols and Schwarz 1998). This relationship is thought to produce the 'distancer-pursuer' pattern identified by Minuchin (1974) in which a proximity-seeking mother (ambivalent/preoccupied or enmeshed) chases a partner who prefers considerably less proximity and feels uncomfortable in very close relationships (avoidant or disengaged). The result is that each step taken by either partner leads to an even more intense reaction on the part of the other. The children oscillating between such parents are, almost literally but certainly metaphorically, as if on shifting sands. In an attempt to incorporate this lack of stability into an attachment framework, Byng-Hall (1997, p.27) suggested that a secure family base might be defined as: "a family that provides a reliable and readily available network of attachment relationships, and appropriate caregivers, from which all members of the family are able to feel sufficiently secure to explore their potential".

Plausible though attempts to integrate Attachment Theory and family systems theories and straightforward though the extension of research from dyadic to more complex family relationships may seem, in many ways, this task tends to bring into even sharper focus fundamental and unresolved conceptual problems.

Specifically, it highlights at least four central questions:
1) what exactly is the construct that is measured in the Strange Situation and how might this construct be measured at different ages and in relation to multiple social interactions?
2) what elements really constitute a 'secure base' and how might the nature of the secure base change over the lifespan?

3) can we be sure that methods currently used to assess 'state of mind in respect of attachment' capture enough information about individual internal representations to anticipate or explain behaviour in all close family relationships?
4) how do the attachment and caregiving behaviour systems as observed in dyadic interactions in early infancy develop across the lifespan and how are they influenced by experiences at other levels within the nest of systems (i.e. family, local community, culture, race, etc.) as described by ecological theory (e.g. Bronfenbrenner 1979, 1986)?(5)

Arguably, the origin of all these questions is the more fundamental question of whether the full complexity of Internal Working Models has ever been reliably captured at all or whether the best that has been managed so far is some kind of distorted approximation. Inge Bretherton, perhaps to a greater extent than any other worker within the field of attachment research and, true to the spirit of Bowlby, with great persistence, has addressed the question of how these internal representations evolve or are constructed. As early as 1985, she raised the question of whether the infant-mother attachment pattern should be seen as the prototype for all other relationships or whether alternative models might provide a better account (e.g. Bretherton, 1985, 1987, 1990a, 1990b, 1991, 1994, Bretherton and Mulholland 1999). These debates are at the centre of the problem of how or even whether attachment theory and family systems theories can be profitably integrated, or whether they should be viewed as complementary but distinct perspectives.

Attachment Therapy

It is not accurate to attribute any one type of therapy to Bowlby's theory of attachment. Bowlby advocated that individuals should be perceived as uniquely influenced by their background and circumstances. He also, as indicated earlier, recognised the complexity of family relationships and was adamant that the notion of regression was not appropriate. His theory of development was not a stage theory and he did not agree with the view that individuals get stuck at certain points in their development: "There is one further way in which attachment theory differs from traditional types of psychoanalytic theory, namely its rejection of the model of development in which an individual is held to pass through a series of stages in any one of which he may become fixated or to which he may regress, and its replacement by a model in which an individual is seen as progressing along one or another of an array of potential developmental pathways" (Bowlby 1988b, p.135). For this reason alone, Bowlby would have strongly disagreed with simplistic views that construe individuals as needing to regress to earlier points of development in order to move forward. In other ways, too, he would have been against certain methods that have been associated with some of the people who call themselves 'Attachment Therapists'.

According to Maloney (2005), around 500 Attachment Therapists currently practice in the US and offer what they call Attachment Therapy (AT), a therapy that "has a frightening history, a devastating present, and, if legislatures and mental health licencing boards don't get more involved, a deadly future". Maloney describes how parents who engage with this form of AT become members of an attachment community which operates a cult-like brainwashing process. She and Mercer (2001, 2002, Mercer et al. 2003) comment that many parents who approach Attachment Therapists do so after having consulted other therapists without success. Some are adoptive parents who, on experiencing some difficulties in their relationship with an adoptive child or even before, consider Attachment Therapy principles as of value for their personal and professional training.

Maloney recounts that the 'attachment community' tells parents that (a) things are not their fault, (b) the only effective treatment for RAD (Reactive Attachment Disorder) is AT, and (c) their child is terribly sick and, if untreated, could go on to be the next serial killer. She cites the source of this information as Magid and McKelvey (1987). Both she and Mercer (2001, 2002, Mercer et al. 2003) argue that AT deviates from accepted ethical principles of psychological practice in not providing opportunities for informed consent, in the use of excessive touching, in the use of restraint, in the provocation of rage, and in telling children what they are feeling on the basis of the therapist's account of what the child needs to feel. Both Mercer and Maloney are also aware of the connection between the AT view of the child and practices more commonly associated with 'casting out demons'. They and others (e.g. O'Connor and Zeanah 2003) also point out that this kind of approach (rage-reduction therapy) derives from work with autistic children with whom it was found to be ineffective.

As indicated in our earlier discussion of diagnosis, AT therapists use checklists that do not reliably detect RAD but, rather, identify a disorder that is not based on standard diagnostic criteria and that they consider to be more serious. They describe the child as a manipulative con artist, not to be believed and not to be charmed or seduced by. At the basis of AT approaches therefore appears to be a deficit model of the child which leads to invalidation of the child's contribution. At worst, Attachment Therapists demonise the child. At best, they view children as needing to be put in touch with their own feelings on the assumption that the therapist has superior insight into these feelings. Lack of close monitoring of therapy practices makes it difficult to be absolutely sure of the nature of Attachment Therapy but, besides Mercer and Maloney, over the past decade, concerns have been being expressed by groups of workers worldwide (e.g. James 1994, Hunt 2000, Wilson 2001, Speltz 2002, Sroufe et al. 2002, Steele 2003, O'Connor and Zeanah 2003).

Controversial practices

Three particularly controversial practices have been linked to AT: 'rebirthing', 'holding therapy' and 'therapeutic foster parenting'. None was a practice that Bowlby recommended and it is highly unlikely that he would ever, under any circumstances, have supported them. They appear to be used to 'tame' or control the child rather than to provide understanding, comfort or care, or, as is advocated by Attachment Theory, to facilitate the emergence of a relationship based on trust. As we discuss below, many Attachment Therapists work from a perspective that is definitely not child friendly and employ methods, some of which are potentially lethal, that are designed to disempower and humiliate.

Re-birthing

Rebirthing is a practice that departs radically from Bowlby's recommended approach. It involves enacting a birth with the aim of enabling a new start in an individual's psychological life. This is premised on the view that healthy development can only proceed if a kind of symbolic re-winding of the individual's history and circumstances takes place, as though the past history can be over-written. This 'mumbo-jumbo' flies in the face of relevant research evidence relating to the nature of memory and experience and so is clearly out of line with Bowlby's views.

The link between re-birthing and AT came very much into public awareness in connection with the death of Candace Newmaker in 2000.[10] Candace Newmaker was one of several children born to a teenage mother who was living in a home for mentally ill children. Her father had a record for being violent and the family had for some time been known to social services. In view of this background, she had been adopted by a paediatric nurse, Jeane Newmaker who, soon after the adoption, began to seek help from professionals because she was having trouble relating to Candace. These professionals (psychotherapists and doctors), offered a number of diagnoses including post-traumatic stress disorder and manic depression and prescribed psychotropic drugs. No formal caseworker was involved and nobody tracked Candace's progress as Jeane consulted different services.

Eventually, Jeane attended a workshop at the Guilford Attachment Center in High Point, North Carolina, went to group meetings and took Candace for individual sessions with an AT practitioner. Candace was given 'holding therapy', which was practised in a degrading and abusive manner, and, during two weeks of intensive therapy at Evergreen, Colorado and the eight days leading up to her death, experienced 'therapeutic foster care' (described in the next part of this chapter). Candace also received 'compression therapy' which required Jeane to lie on top of her and to lick her face. To these brutalising practices was added 'rebirthing' during which Candace was to wriggle her way out of a flannel sheet, wrapped tightly around her to form a symbolic birth canal and hemmed in by pillows that were leaned on by the presiding adults, so that she could be 'reborn' as Jeane Newmaker's true daughter. These events were videotaped and showed Ponder, Watkins, and Newmaker taunting Candace for 40 minutes while she struggled to get out of the blanket, screamed and begged for air. Once Candace had stopped 'resisting treatment' and gone quiet, the three adults leaned on her motionless body and chatted for a further 30 minutes before unwrapping her. Candace had choked on her vomit. Attempts to resuscitate the now brain-dead child were unsuccessful.

Mercer et al. (2003) comment that practitioners of rebirthing claim that it would normally only involve a five- to ten-minute procedure. However, they also emphasise the extent to which beliefs underlying the practice of re-birthing, a substantial component of which is the conviction that prenatal experience impacts on later relationships, deviate from Attachment Theory. While parents' experiences of pregnancy are likely, as we have discussed elsewhere, to correspond closely with the parent-child relationship that later develops, there is currently no way of assessing how or even whether pre- or perinatal experiences influence the child's capacity or motivation to relate. Nor is there any empirical evidence that it can help with 'bonding'. From the child's point of view, it seems to have more potential to further confuse and traumatise than to increase the likelihood of their being able to make more meaningful emotional connections with 'carers'.

In sum, re-birthing is not a practice that has any conceptual basis in Attachment Theory. What's more, it goes against fundamental principles inherent within Bowlby's arguments and is counter to the model of development put forward by him.

Holding therapy

"Holding therapies have not been shown to be an effective clinical tool, and according to some practices may be seriously harmful and counter-therapeutic"

(Steele 2003, p.219).

---

10 A more detailed analysis of this case and of the ways in which Attachment Therapy beliefs diverge both from Attachment Theory and from psychological research is presented by Mercer et al. (2003).

There appear to be no clear rules about how holding therapy should be practised, how often or why. It can involve imposing physical restraints on a child, with one or more therapists pinning the child down or holding them on their lap, to prevent movement. This might be in response to a child's tantrum but not necessarily. The aim is to provoke the child to express their anger directly towards the therapists who are controlling them through intense physical experiences (body and eye contact). This subjugation forces the child into compliance and enables the therapist to operate from a position of greater control. The belief, for which there is no empirical support, is that forcible expression of rage will cause latent anger to dissipate, much as lancing a boil reduces inflammation.

During the restraint phase, the therapist might provoke rage in the child by insulting them or giving them 'rib cage stimulation' (poking or prodding at them). If the child asks for this treatment to stop, the therapist interprets this as resistance to treatment and steps up restraints until the child finally gives up struggling. This can take hours. Even when the struggling has ended, the therapist continues the session by bringing up for discussion the child's real or imaginary misdemeanours. If the child denies these, the 'stimulation' might re-continue. In short, the child is goaded into submission. At the end of the session, he or she is usually hugged and congratulated for "good work". In return, the child is expected to thank the therapist (or else!).

This use of touch alongside humiliation and enforced compliancy seems almost inevitably likely to produce fear and a very confused emotional state in most children. The only way for the child to escape further humiliation is to give in. This alone is insufficient since the therapist also needs to be convinced that the child has made a choice to comply. The practice therefore infringes not only the child's rights and subjects them to unsolicited touch but also challenges the child's self-integrity. It is very different from the non-touch techniques approved by conventional psychoanalysts and also very different from more gentle touch that may occur in other therapeutic settings.

O'Connor and Zeanah (2003) list some additional erroneous beliefs associated with holding therapy including:
- attachment-disordered children do not experience holding therapy as intrusive (Fearnley 1996)
- holding needs to be intrusive if it is to force re-attachment (e.g. Cline 1992)
- holding therapy re-activates delayed development (Keck and Kupecky 1995).

In sum, the effects of holding therapy have not been systematically researched but, to date, there does not appear to be any empirical support for it. It is not based on and indeed deviates from fundamental principles of Attachment Theory. It can be dangerous and is likely to compromise rather than promote development of children's capacity to trust others and to feel that others respect, value or trust them. However, as indicated by the website of ATTACh (the Association for Treatment and training in the Attachment of Children), an organisation that represents Attachment Therapists, there is a difference between coercive restraint and therapeutic or nurturing holding (Kelly 2003). Until there is more knowledge about the extent and nature of physical contact in therapy settings, it will not be possible to determine whether, for some individuals and in some circumstances, there might not also be some benefits. It therefore seems imperative that research is undertaken and that more efforts are made to monitor the use of physical contact by therapists.

Therapeutic foster care

Therapeutic foster parenting (Thomas 2000) is described by Mercer (2002) as the second consistent component of Attachment Therapy. It involves separating children from their parents and from day school (clearly not a practice that Bowlby would have supported) and sending them to live in foster homes. The foster 'care' is based on punitive behaviourist principles that bear no relationship to attachment theory and consist of 'boot camp' training schedules (e.g. 'strong sitting' or sitting upright and motionless on the floor for long periods, withholding food, forced labour, etc.). In short, a therapy less based on Attachment Theory principles would be difficult to find. However, Attachment Therapists, such as Thomas, assert that strong sitting is not punitive but, like yoga or other meditational techniques, relaxing and re-invigorating.

Essentially, these procedures involve goading children into submission, with the 'therapist' very much in the role of powerful bully rather than co-explorer. The energy of the child's anger is more or less captured by the therapist who manipulates it, revving it up and down so much that the child relinquishes any attempt to control it for him or herself. Once the therapist has fully impressed upon the child that the therapist is in control of the child's will, then control is gradually handed back to the child. The impact of this kind of treatment on children is not known. It seems possible that it may impinge on the child's self-image enough to force them into paying more attention to powerful adults than might otherwise have been the case. But it also seems only too likely that forced compliance on these 'quick and dirty' terms may be at the price of causing further damage.

The influence of 'Attachment Therapy' in the UK is currently unclear. Also unclear is the extent to which people who offer therapy for attachment-related problems adopt approaches that are out of line with basic principles of Bowlby's Attachment Theory. This situation is a matter of some concern, particularly with regard to very vulnerable looked-after children, who are known to be at high risk of being as well as having been abused.

Children in care

The value of Attachment Theory to professionals working in the care system has been widely recognised. The realisation of the importance of enabling children to maintain a positive image of a parent who is no longer available to care for them, the need to keep experiences of separation to a minimum and to ensure that contact with siblings and other family members, so far as possible, is maintained, the recognition that children separated from important caregivers may be likely to attribute the cause for separation to their own lack of lovability or to a sense of being wronged, etc., these and other insights have informed decision-making processes around placement and around the support and training needs of carers. However, too often, these needs are not met and when problems arise, carers are thrown back on personal resources which may or may not be adequate.

Children in care, by definition, have histories of disrupted or disordered attachment relationships and may sometimes have had very few consistent opportunities to form close, trusting attachment relationships. For this reason, the incidence of attachment difficulties among this population of children is often high. Yet it would be a mistake to expect the difficulties manifested by children in care to be uniform or predictable, either in the way the children behave or in the way they respond to attempts to help them. Rather, how each individual child experiences and copes will depend upon many factors, including:

- attributes of the child, e.g. temperament, social skills, cultural background, intelligence, academic and other skills, physique, attribution style, hobbies
- attributes of the child's family of origin, e.g. nature and history of problems, nature of current contact, if any
- attributes of the care situation, e.g. continuity, quality, opportunity for close relationships with adults and other children, length of time in care, age at start, whether adopted, short- or long-term fostered, relationship between current care family and previous home, etc.
- attributes of the wider social context, e.g. availability of support from older people including extended family, friends, mentors, attachment to school and or other organisations, etc..

Children who, from a young age, have been unable to form trusting relationships with adults or who have had to protect themselves against adults who may have been incapable of caring for them or may have put them in danger are likely to have developed strategies that, at a deep level, warn them against relying on anyone but themselves. Where this basic level of distrust exists, it can be very difficult for adults to break through the barriers. Immense patience can be needed over many years before children begin to realise that it may be safe to lower redundant defences and begin to rely in a more relaxed way on their new carers.

Often, this process will be hampered because children will have built up a long history of distrust or even resentment of adults who, probably not always at a conscious level, they perceive as potentially frightening, dangerous or otherwise antagonistic. Children who have this degree of basic distrust behave in a variety of very complicated ways in relation to adults. Almost undoubtedly, they repeatedly test their carers out, to the point of being self-destructive and/or of appearing destructive towards relationships that might be growing between themselves and their carers. These behaviours are bound to provoke strong feelings in carers who may find it very difficult to imagine or understand what the child's behaviour might signify.

Living with this degree of anxiety and uncertainty can be very frustrating and humiliating. Being able to view the child as very sick and in need of radical treatment can therefore be very reassuring. Being able to locate the problem as residing in the child rather than in the carer can also bring immense relief. And being able to have faith in a qualified professional must also be a source of greater optimism. Unfortunately, such simple analyses are rarely appropriate and evidence that quick, easy remedies exist is equally hard to find.

Howe (2003) describes how, while researching the needs of looked after children and their carers in the 1980s, he became aware of a number of adoptive parents who, feeling that their parenting skills were being held responsible in the UK, were finding solace in Attachment Therapists in the US who diagnosed their children as attachment-disordered. Howe flags up the likelihood that the difficult behaviour of children with histories of abuse or neglect will be more closely associated with the development of aggressive, controlling strategies associated with ambivalent or disorganised attachments rather than with lack of ability to form selective attachment relationships. Nevertheless, however their behaviour is described, the children are often difficult to relate to and they do present particular challenges for carers. However autonomous the carers are with respect to attachment, their efforts to engage the children in reciprocal, loving relationships are often rebuffed and, no matter what they do, the situation only seems to get worse. Howe makes a plea that the definition of attachment disorder be extended to recognise this problem and to enable carers to feel understood. Certainly, this might reduce their need to take recourse to radical treatments.

Daniel Hughes, an Attachment Therapist who appears to have gained a sizeable following in the UK and whose books (e.g. Hughes 1997, 1998) have been widely read, makes a similar plea (Hughes 2003) and also outlines seven principles which he considers important with regard to therapy:

1) Where carers have secure, not non-secure or unresolved, attachment strategies, the therapist can immediately involve them in the therapy, by modelling and directly facilitating carer-child relationships; where this is not the case, separate sessions will be needed with carer and child.
2) Interactions between carer and therapist need to reflect their experience of the child's subjective experience so that as a pair they co-regulate the child's emotional state and communicate with the child about this experience.
3) Carer-therapist interactions should resemble those of securely attached couples, that is, they should be characterised by acceptance, empathy, curiosity, playfulness, sensitivity, responsiveness and availability.
4) To ensure effective communication, the carer and therapist may need to exaggerate non-verbal expressions through eye contact, voice, facial expression, movement, gestures, touch, etc. to make their significance clearer to children who may have difficulty 'reading' them and to enable children to experience valuable joyful, playful interactions; this must not involve force.
5) Any misattunements or conflict within the triangle should be addressed directly and ruptures repaired; in particular, the child's experience of shame or fear should be co-regulated by the carer and therapist using strategies characterised by empathy, reassurance, acceptance and curiosity.
6) Specific strategies are needed that involve the carers' own organised inner state to structure the child's experience: "Essentially, the parents allow the child to rely on their own organized inner states, until he is able to gradually develop a more fully defined and integrated state himself. The central stance of the parent is to be able to maintain a vision of the child's inner strength – or at least potential – to resolve trauma and find a more adaptive developmental pathway. If the parent loses this vision, the child will never discover it within himself" (Hughes 2003, p.275).
7) Cognitive-behavioural strategies can also be used by carer and therapist but only after "the intersubjective states of attunement, interpersonal motivation, and meaning-making" have been established as these are "crucial for facilitating the secure base necessary to utilize these strategies" (Hughes 2003, p.276).(8)

While the major tenor of these strategies seems sensible and in line with attachment theory and research, what their practical implications might be is not entirely clear.

Elsewhere, Hughes (e.g. Hughes 2004) provides more explicit detail of his approach in action. He indicates that "With many children, the therapist's empathy is experienced more deeply if the therapist guesses what the child might want to say, speaking for the child" (Hughes 2004, p.270) and illustrates the technique of matching the intensity, cadence and duration of a child's speech while discussing how hard it was for the child to live with six different families:

Child (yelling): "Don't TALK about that! It **wasn't HARD**!"

Therapist (ditto): "Of COURSE you don't want to talk about it! ... Who WOULD?... It's the PAST!"

The therapist stays quiet and breathes in time with the child, looking at him but looking away from time to time to give the child "some sense of privacy in his attempts not to feel" (Hughes 2004, p.271).

Therapist (gently)	"What were you able to do… so that moving… so much… **wasn't**… **hard** for you?"
	(Five seconds gap)
Child (quietly):	"I just didn't think about it."
	(Five seconds gap)
Therapist (matching):	"Ah."
	(Five seconds gap)
Therapist (matching):	"I am sad that there was so much in your life… that you had to… not… think about."

Later in the same paper, Hughes describes a session during which he is treating a four-year-old child referred for being violent towards his adoptive mother. The session consists of Hughes telling the child that, when he was two, a big person lied to him and told him that it was OK to hit mothers. Hughes recounts this with gestures, looks and changes in volume and tone of voice that grab the child's attention yet leave little scope for disagreement or disconfirmation. Part-way through, the child starts whispering to his mother. When Hughes' reaches the grande finale where he shouts out who it was that lied and that it wasn't right, the child "suddenly sat backwards in his chair as if I had pushed him. He continued to stare at me for 10 seconds and then he climbed into his mother's arms and buried his head against her chest. Then his hand reached down to her stomach and he began to knead her stomach as is frequent with nursing babies" (Hughes 2004, p.274).

Hughes claims that this experience had enabled the child to make sense of his inner life because the therapist co-regulated his affect in a way that enabled him to re-experience and to think about a possible new meaning for his inner life "and he was able to immediately shift his joint experience of self-and-other with respect to his relationships with both of his adoptive parents as well as his relationships with his birth mother and stepfather" (Hughes 2004, p.274). From this point, the child stopped hitting the mother.

Critiquing this paper, Trowell (2004) cautions against uncritical use of the techniques outlined and observes that they may be inappropriate for particular client groups. She argues in favour of prioritising the need to involve carers and stresses the need for therapists to be supervised. However, she makes no mention of the possibility that therapists may need guidelines on how to present child patients with their conjectures about the child's unspoken experiences. Nor does she mention the need for research into the use of the particular techniques adopted by Hughes (though this may be implicit in her approach which respects the rule 'no service without research, no research without service').

Despite Hughes' insistence that all the strategies he proposes have precedence within attachment theory and research, it seems debateable whether this style of therapy would enable him to function as a 'secure base' in the sense that Bowlby might have intended. His instruction that carers should impose their organised attachment patterns on children who have no integrated, organised pattern seems rather more to reflect the view of Attachment Therapists who assume that all adopted children are attachment disordered than the possibility that children may find it difficult to transfer affections from biological parents, no matter how inadequate, to new carers. Though Hughes does appear, like Bowlby (1988b, p.136), to accept the "continuing potential for change", implicit within his approach there seems to be an assumption that this change needs to be effected by ensuring that adoptive parent and child relationships develop along the same lines as patterns of attachment at a much earlier age. The model of the child in this appears to be a deficit model. The child is conceptualised as immature, unformed and in need of shaping in much the way that relationships with very young infants have been observed to develop. Parents are encouraged to take control of the child's proximity-seeking and exploration and to require the child to stay within a distance acceptable to them. They are also encouraged to use 'affective attunement' techniques, including touch and eye contact, as demonstrated by Hughes.

The appropriateness of this infantilisation of older adoptive children seems questionable. What evidence is there that this kind of exaggerated speech is relevant to work with older children, that it is similar in quality to interactions between adults and infants with rather different perceptual and attentional capacities, or that the child will benefit from this kind of treatment? Hughes, as the powerful therapist, takes control of the agenda in a way that seems considerably more directive than the 'follow the patient' principle recommended by Bowlby. In doing this, he offers adoptive parents 'quick fixes' that are not necessarily in the child's long- or short-term interest and that suggest behaviourist rather than Attachment Theory informed principles. The agenda is much more heavily weighted towards the parents' rightful desire for an instant close and rewarding relationship. Any reservations or uncertainty that the child may have appear to be considered inappropriate. This assumption that the child should go along with the adults' wishes is, of course, exactly what children with experience of sexual abuse have been accustomed to. Helping them to become more comfortable about who they are, about how they relate to their own bodies and how they and their bodies relate to other people seems likely to require a rather different approach.

There are, of course, questions about what the principle of following a client's or patient's lead might, in practice, involve. Bowlby's view was that, although internal working models develop through experience and may be adaptive under certain circumstances, over the lifespan, some become more flexible and more capable of incorporating new experiences than others. As a result, some individuals might repeatedly construe social interactions in ways that offend or that in other ways diminish the potential for positive or mutually reciprocal exchanges. Dozier (2003, 2005) comments on the tendency of looked after children to react with distrust and contempt towards their new carers and on their propensity to 'lead the interaction dance' rather than to relinquish control and engage in reciprocal relationships. She suggests that it may be necessary for foster carers to respect the child's apparent rejection but at the same time to retain a sense that this is not what the child really wants and so to persevere in the attempt to engage with the child. However, rather than forcing the child to engage via direct head-on methods, she recommends a more crab-like approach that affords the child room to choose to re-orient. She illustrates this approach with an example of a therapist puppy that persisted in being physically available to a grieving older dog despite the older dog's reluctance to tolerate approaches. Eventually, a strong companionable relationship developed. Research by Dozier and her colleagues (e.g. Stovall and Dozier 1998, Dozier et al. 2001) also indicates that foster carers who are autonomous with respect to attachment (securely attached according to assessments such as the AAI or the Adult Attachment Projective) may be more able to provide this kind of care than those who are not.

This leads to the question of whether, where carers experience difficulties in caring for adoptive or foster children, it is more appropriate to work with the parents and children separately or together. Hart and Thomas (2000) propose that, rather than working directly with the child, carers might be used as co-therapists (they name this model Parent Co-Therapy or PCT). The advantages of this approach include a potentially more economic use of carer's skills and availability, as well as greater recognition, inclusion and status for carers. However, given that the Jeane Newmaker scenario emerged from a very similar set of circumstances, it seems that such a model would need to incorporate independent checks on the veracity of the carer's view.

Concluding remarks

That Attachment Theory has been found useful in work with children at risk and looked after children is well illustrated by the rapidly growing number of publications in the UK (e.g. Howe et al. 1999, Cairns 2002, Fahlberg 2002, Schofield 2002, Schofield and Beek 2005) as well as abroad. Attachment Theory has enabled considerable advances to be made in understanding reactions to grief, separation and loss. It has also provided insights into the value for children of consistent, sensitively responsive and continuous care, as well as of opportunities to form close, confiding relationships with carers who are able to help children to feel valued and understood within safe, predictable home environments. And it has provided insights into the nature of parent-child relationships and, to some extent, what might be needed if parents are to be able to provide a secure base from which their children can safely explore. These insights have now become well established as principles that inform the work of professionals at all levels within the care system (social workers, workers in fostering and adoption agencies, mentoring schemes, as well as court welfare officers, guardian ad litem and other court officers). It is also widely accepted that the internal working models of looked after children are likely to reflect their experiences of contradictory, disrupted or confusing relationships and may make it difficult for them to form trusting relationships with new caregivers. But it is equally clear that many children do manage to come through and weave more sense into the chaotic scripts bequeathed to them by their parents.

What is less clear, though, is the kind of assistance that each individual child might need in order to do this, how best a secure base might be created and whether there might be any reliable way of protecting unsuspecting foster or adoptive parents from dangerous but alluring Attachment Therapy practices. It is not the case that all therapists calling themselves 'Attachment Therapists' are dangerous (though it might be wise to treat all with great caution) nor is it true that all therapists who describe themselves as taking 'attachment-oriented approaches' are safe. There is currently no way of discriminating easily between those therapists who use the respectful, patient, exploratory hypothesis-testing approach recommended by Bowlby and those who purport to draw directly upon a huge range of theory-building within the field of attachment research but who might, in seeking simple and quick solutions, have extrapolated beyond the data or lighted upon an approach that is not suitable.

For these reasons, it seems urgent that steps are taken to remedy this situation. Not panic measures that involve turning all the existing systems inside-out as if in an attempt to re-invent the wheel. But more efforts to improve procedures for monitoring the effects of different treatment interventions and more research designed to explore what children with non-secure patterns of attachment really need in order to be able to make the best use of adults who are available to them. Perhaps most importantly, strategies need to be developed so that the information that is publicly available to parents and carers becomes more open to inspection. Parents and carers need to know how to judge whether or not there really is evidence that a particular type of therapy might be safe or effective for children they are concerned about, and they need to be able to consult sounds sources of advice on these matters. This will not be possible unless there are sound sources of advice, built on reliable and extensive research evidence.

The tendency of funding strategies for intervention projects in the UK to be small scale, short-term and piecemeal rather than long-term, large scale and rigorous seems more likely to increase than to decrease the dangers for vulnerable parents and children. One way to avert these perils for parents would be to ensure that programme evaluations are carried out routinely, rigorously and universally and that no new programme or treatment initiative takes place outside a centralised system of inspection. Such a draconian measure is likely to meet with resistance, but perhaps it is time to consider both the need for this and the viability of more flexible alternatives.

8 | Summing up: How secure are the foundations of Attachment Theory?

The conceptual status of Attachment Theory

As we have already suggested, not all aspects of Bowlby's theory of attachment were fully worked out by the time of his death. Like any scientific theory grounded upon available evidence, Bowlby's theory of attachment is perhaps better viewed as a set of 'working models' or as a theory under development rather than as a fully worked-out doctrine 'set in stone'. Certainly, throughout his lifespan, Bowlby added, modified and scrapped parts of his account as new ideas and evidence came to his attention.

This kind of approach is essential if a new account of behaviour is to be effectively trialled, tested and refined. It only becomes a problem if the theory needs so much modification that it or substantial parts of it need to be replaced completely. In the long term, even this is not necessarily a bad thing, especially if the theory has functioned as a vehicle for the development of better theories.

In this chapter, we consider how Attachment Theory seems to have fared as a theory, according to criteria that are generally agreed within the social sciences as necessary for a good theory. Before doing this, though, we will examine in more detail one aspect of Bowlby's theory that we have not so far discussed at any length, that is, his account of human behaviour systems, their function and the general principles that govern their development and organisation. We consider what advantages there may or may not be in conceptualising human behaviour and development in this way and try to determine how watertight this aspect of Bowlby's theory is, how useful it is, and whether it really matters anyway. Having done this, we go on to outline the criteria for a good theory and consider Attachment Theory in the light of these requirements.

Characteristics of human behaviour systems

In trying to understand the nature of the special relationship that emerges between infants and their principal carers, Bowlby (1969/1982) drew heavily on his knowledge, from engineering, physiology, psychology and ethology, of control systems. A control system is a dynamic system that is set to reach one goal but which has the capacity to modulate itself according to available resources in order to reach that goal (Figure 8.1). A simple system consists of a sensor mechanism that picks up cues relevant to the goal and a central comparator that determines whether and what action needs to be taken in order for the goal to be reached.

Figure 8.1: A behaviour control system

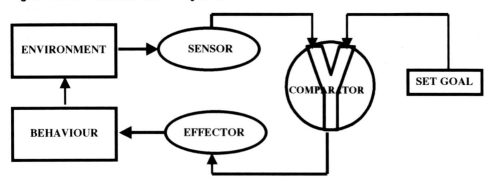

Bowlby (1969/1982) used the term 'behaviour system' to apply to a range of behaviours, including simple reflexes, chains of behaviours with no overall organisation, chains of behaviour organised hierarchically, and mixed chains. He argued that attachment can be viewed as a behaviour system which has a specialised biological function independent of, though in dynamic interaction with, other behaviour systems, that is, "a fundamental form of behaviour with its own internal motivation distinct from feeding and sex, and of no less importance for survival" (Bowlby 1982a/1988b, p.27). At different points throughout his writings, he indicated that a number of organised behaviour systems may exist (Table 8.1).

Table 8.1 : Hypothesised behaviour systems

SYSTEM	ACRONYM
Affiliation/Sociability	SBS
Attachment	ABS
Caregiving/Caretaking	CBS
Exploration/Play	EBS
Fear/Wariness	FBS
Eating/Feeding/Nutrition	NBS
Parenting	PBS
Sexual/Sexual reproduction	RBS

In the first volume of his trilogy, Bowlby explained how children's attachment behaviours and their antithesis (exploratory and play behaviours) related to the mother's caretaking behaviour as well as to behaviours of the mother that were not related to parental care or care of the infant (Bowlby 1969, Chapter 13). Elsewhere, he consistently described a dynamic relationship between the Attachment Behaviour System and other systems and this theme was also reiterated in the work of Ainsworth (e.g. Ainsworth et al. 1978, Ainsworth 1982). However, Bowlby did not outline a comprehensive description of all behaviour systems, nor, with the exception of the Attachment Behaviour System in infancy, did he formally specify which behaviours belonged to which behaviour system or why, nor did he clearly make a distinction between behaviours and behaviour systems.

In some respects, perhaps this should not matter. Bowlby was, after all, primarily concerned with understanding what might underlie individual differences in the quality of relationships between babies and their mothers and how these might impact on later social development. The rather tedious task of making a systematic inventory of all human behaviours and their relationships to each other would have held little interest for him. Yet, logically, it seems to follow that if Bowlby wished to present a convincing case for the existence of control systems, and for the superiority of attachment theory over, for example, Freud's theories of drives and instincts, this task could be seen as essential to his thesis. We have seen that attachment style is thought to be predictive of positive outcomes in terms of children's social and emotional development. But, in the absence of a comprehensive taxonomy of control systems, how can it be proved that particular outcomes are associated with one system and not with others? How can we be sure that it is the quality of the attachment relationship that has been responsible and not some other closely associated aspect of family relationships which has neither been identified nor measured?

In considering this question, we will also consider some more general characteristics of human behaviour systems outlined at various points by Bowlby including the propositions that:
- human behaviour systems have evolved for the benefit of the species
- human behaviour systems operate in certain lawful ways
- human behaviour systems can respond to the external environment
- the development and organisation of human behaviour systems changes observably across the lifespan
- there is a dynamic pattern of relationships between different behaviour systems.

We will discuss each of these propositions in turn.

Human behaviour systems have evolved for the benefit of the species

Bowlby described each behaviour system as complete in itself and as having evolved to fulfil a specific biological function. He further proposed that each system is, in essence, motivational so that the separate behaviours comprising each system have the same shared, overarching goal. There has been some debate about what the goal of the Attachment Behaviour System (ABS) might be. Initially, with mothers and infants at the centre of his thoughts, Bowlby asserted that the function of the Attachment Behaviour System was to promote species survival by protecting the young from predators. However, there were problems with this explanation. First, it could not account for the function of the ABS across the lifespan, that is, it did not comprehend the need for adults to form attachments to each other. Second, this set goal could be seen as more appropriate to the caregiving behaviour system. What, then, is the distinctive goal of the ABS?

Belsky (1999) offers one solution. He points out that the view that the purpose of the ABS was to afford protection to the young is misguided and that Bowlby, in the second edition of volume two of his trilogy, revised his theory. Now the target was not the survival of the "interbreeding population" but, rather that, "through the process of differential breeding success, individuals that are carrying certain genes increase in numbers whilst individuals that are carrying others diminish... the ultimate outcome to be attained is always the survival of the genes an individual is carrying" (Bowlby 1969/1982, p.56). In other words, the target of the ABS is not simply to protect the young from predators but to preserve the young because they carry genes.

Taking as his starting point, therefore, the premise that "Genetic replication is the goal of (all) life; and thus the ultimate target of natural selection" (Belsky 1999, p.141), Belsky describes how different patterns of attachment behaviour may have evolved to maximise reproductive capacities within particular 'environments of evolutionary adaptedness' (EEAs in the language of evolutionary theory). Each pattern (with the exception of disorganised attachment which did not fit into this conceptualisation, perhaps because, of all the patterns, it is the least coherent or adaptive)[1] can be seen as a component part of an overall reproductive strategy. Secure patterns, Belsky argues (Belsky 1999, Belsky et al. 1991), may reflect an adaptation to environmental conditions where resources are abundant and where life is relatively comfortable. In this kind of setting, parents can afford to commit to longer relationships and to produce fewer offspring because health risks are lower and the likelihood of having to flee to another setting is smaller. Avoidant patterns, on the other hand may have evolved as adaptations to environments where predation risks were high and resources in short supply: many short, uncommitted relationships under these conditions could maximise the chances of impregnation and of reproduction; the offspring from such relationships in such uncompromising contexts would need to learn much earlier to stand on their own two feet and to fend for themselves. In the latter circumstances, where individuals need to be constantly on the alert, watching their backs, quantity rather than quality of offspring might be the rule. In the former context, where there are fewer risks and others can be trusted, quality rather than quantity of offspring may be the rule. Belsky's account of the 'ambivalent/preoccupied' pattern involves a rather greater stretch of the imagination. He suggests that the high dependency needs of these individuals may have evolved as the equivalent of the 'helper in the nest' pattern: "In the most speculative comments to be made in this reinterpretation of the evolutionary basis of attachment in humans, especially patterns of attachment, we propose that the capacity for developing resistant attachments evolved as a means of fostering indirectly reproductive 'helper-at-the-nest' behaviour" (Belsky 1999, p.156). Belsky supports this argument with the observation that some researchers (e.g. Kunce and Shaver 1994) have linked the ambivalent/resistant pattern with compulsive caregiving.

Does this mean, therefore, that the only function in life of any individual whose life is not organised around the aim of reproduction of his or her own genes is to facilitate the selective reproduction of the genes of anyone who is biologically related? It would seem not, since Belsky does not include those with 'disorganised' patterns within this imaginary scenario. Although this particular speculation may be consistent with an interpretation of evolutionary theory that perhaps has firm roots in theoretical argument and empirical evidence, it nevertheless seems to fly in the face of common sense. How useful are ambivalent/resistant characters as 'helpers-in-the-nest'? Common sense alone seems to suggest that their self-focused attention, their tendency to over-emphasise negative events and their own dependency needs might render them the least likely candidates for the task! This is not a good reason, of course, to reject the hypothesis, especially if there are strong grounds supporting it.

This incredulity, however, is not helped by the fact that Belsky (1999, p.149) also argues that, because different patterns of attachment behaviour have evolved from environmental circumstances that no longer obtain, "It would be a mistake to presume that the evolutionary interpretation of patterns of attachment to be advanced requires for confirmation evidence that reproductive fitness is currently associated with different patterns of attachment." One cannot help wondering whether this stance might not grant permission to propose any old theory! This objection aside, the notion that the preoccupied pattern might be the

---

1   Though, as indicated elsewhere, Crittenden (2000, 2002) disputes this interpretation.

least altruistic and the best disposed to serve to help raise other people's offspring seems somewhat counter-intuitive.

Although not in a position of sufficient authority to dispute basic tenets either of evolutionary theory or of Attachment Theory, these doubts, both about the evolutionary significance of, particularly, the ambivalent/resistant style and the apparent assumption that replication of one's own genes necessarily requires non-cooperation with others in their self-replication, led us to ponder on alternative possibilities.

To many students of Attachment Theory, the lack of gender differences in distributions of patterns of attachment comes as something of a surprise. It is popularly believed that most boys and girls have different qualities of relationship with their mothers and grow up with different ways of being in the world, for example, boys are more likely to be diagnosed as autistic, to manifest externalising disorders, to acquire language at a slower rate than girls and to be better than girls on right hemisphere, spatial tasks. Men and women have also, in traditional hunter-gatherer societies (Hewlett 2004), had fairly clearly delineated roles, with the father, as hunter, having responsibility for exploring beyond the home base to secure provisions to support the family and protect the nest from predators, and the mother having responsibility for looking after and raising the children. In this context, men and women develop different attentional strategies and focuses of interest, for example, women might be expected to be more attentive to the quality of life for children while men might be more concerned, particularly where the context of family life is challenging, to attend to the nature of the terrain beyond the immediate family and to ensure that their knowledge of how the world outside functions is capable of identifying ultra-efficiently elements that will benefit as well as those that might threaten the family. In this way, men might have a tendency to focus on distal relationships whereas women may be expected to focus more on proximal ones and on cues that will provide insight into both the physical and the emotional state of family members.

That these gender role differences are not reflected in patterns of attachment may seem somewhat puzzling, especially if one accepts the premise that the ABS has evolved on the basis of reproductive requirements. Even so, failure to find gender differences has now been so extensively confirmed that, nowadays, comparisons are rarely reported. Nevertheless, it seems theoretically possible that some differences may exist that have not so far been detected, perhaps due to the relatively small numbers of people representing non-B group patterns even in the largest studies. Is it possible, for example, that a weak overall tendencies toward avoidant strategies among males and toward ambivalent/resistant strategies among females could have been overlooked? Given the typically small cell sizes in most studies of attachment and questions about the validity of self-report measures, this does not seem too far-fetched a speculation.

Some support for this line of argument may perhaps be found in the literature on autism. In Chapter Five, we pointed to a potential connection between the 'encapsulated' autistic pattern and avoidant attachment strategies. Baron-Cohen (2005) has further suggested that some forms of autism may be associated with a 'male brain', that is a tendency to pay more attention to logical connections, local details and literalism, as opposed to the global aspects which can be more strongly influenced by cultural values and socially constructed meanings. While not suggesting that autism and patterns of organised, insecure attachment are synonymous, it seems worth considering whether more general species-specific adaptive strategies might not be linked with these different qualities of relating.

Is it possible that the avoidant pattern may have evolved from the need to look beyond the perimeters for sustenance and to be hyper-attentive to more distant possibilities that are less dependent upon the meanings bestowed by one's own culture whereas the ambivalent/resistant pattern, in contrast, evolved from the need to focus on immediate, own-family-oriented interests?[2] It would follow from this that distinct attentional strategies would underlie each pattern, with avoidant patterns being under-written by more abstract logic and reasoning and pre-occupied patterns by more immediate, less reflective modes of action or reaction. Both patterns, in this view, could be conceptualised as extreme kinds of behaviour that would not be expected to occur in every male or female. For this reason, they may not be easy to detect, particularly in samples that include only small numbers of individuals who manifest the more extreme behaviours (statistical analyses that emphasise measures of central tendency, which most do, seem likely also to miss picking up on these 'non-normative' effects). That other adaptive styles might also exist, hidden perhaps within sub-groups that are rarely large enough to be closely inspected, also seems theoretically possible. Perhaps some of these, contrary to more common assumptions, may include alternative survival strategies, for example, strategies premised on recognition of the value of preserving good relationships with non-biologically related neighbours or of the value to the reproductive human community of members who are not reproductive. These hypotheses may eventually prove unfounded but, we would argue, so far, they have not been adequately tested.

With regard to the larger question of the function of the ABS, therefore, there also seems to be room for debate. Conceptualising its purpose as replication of one's own genes seems theoretically problematic in that it raises the question of how, then, the goal of the ABS might differ from goals of other behaviour systems. Arguably, all human behaviour systems could be seen as having this very specific aim, some, for example, the sexual reproductive system, more obviously than others. Might this imply a hierarchical organisation of behaviour systems all aimed at one over-arching goal? If so, would such a conceptualisation also imply that individuals who do not reproduce must, by definition, be viewed as dysfunctional? This conceptualisation seems rather more restrictive than an alternative conceptualisation in which each system may be viewed as having a more proximal goal, or goals, which, possibly, change over the lifespan. It is not our intention here to resolve any debates over what the ultimate or proximal goal of the ABS might be but it does seem important to acknowledge that there still appears to be room for further consideration of this issue. This seems to be an aspect of Attachment Theory that may not yet be convincingly established.

Human behaviour systems operate in certain lawful ways

This principle of behaviour systems specifies that each system is activated and de-activated by conditions or events unique to itself. It is therefore activated by particular cues or stimuli (sometimes called 'triggers') and de-activated when the activating stimuli are no longer salient (for example, because a system goal has been attained, because the activating stimulus is no longer present or because a perceived change in the environment has triggered a different behaviour system which has over-ridden the first). The Feeding Behaviour System, for example, is triggered both by the sight and smell of food and by internal cues. It is de-activated when over-ridden by the Fear Behaviour System. There has

---

2   For example, a number of mothers, when confronted by any potential challenge to their children's interests, will manifest an otherwise uncharacteristic degree of hostility and self-assertiveness, almost as if their own adult identity becomes subsumed by a more basic protective response.

been considerable debate about what triggers the ABS at different ages but there seems to be general agreement that, when triggered, in most people, it produces behaviour aimed at ensuring a sense that trusted other people are available when needed. There also appears to be general agreement that, when it is activated, the Exploration/Play behaviour system becomes de-activated, though this hypothesis has never been systematically tested. This brings us to the question of how independent each behavioural system might be and also again draws attention to the fact that, without clear specifications about the parameters of each system, it is difficult to test such hypotheses.

Additional questions also arise, for example, is it possible that, in some individuals or in some circumstances, systems might be recruited to subserve each other's goals or that systems operate equally effectively but more independently and in a less complementary fashion in some individuals than in others? If this were the case, then it is likely that there would be implications both for aims and for processes within therapy. Might it be that the general aim to promote greater felt security, which most clinicians already know requires a range of strategies, could become more understandable if the relationship between different systems were to be better understood? Might it be the case that individuals with histories of secure attachment have behaviour systems that operate more or less independently of each other and in a complementary fashion or that the different systems in these individuals operate alongside each other with relatively little conflict? By contrast, insecurely attached individuals may have behaviour systems that are less clearly specified and which may take over parts of each other's roles. If this is the case, it may be that the securely attached infant with an activated ABS may behave in a way that is easier to understand and relate to because their behaviour is cued in a less complex way. By contrast, individuals with insecure patterns may be more difficult to 'read' because their behaviour systems are cued in more complex ways. For example, in individuals with histories of avoidant attachment, it seems possible that the play/exploration system may be activated more readily alongside the ABS partly because they have had to recruit this system to service their attachment needs instead of the ABS. If this were the case, then it is also possible that attachment-related cognitions might be more available to conscious inspection in avoidantly attached individuals in association with play- or exploration-related goals rather than when considering attachment-related issues. This might be more pronounced where the individual has resorted to addictive or obsessive-compulsive types of behaviour in order to meet inexpressible attachment needs.

These speculations could perhaps, but have not yet, been tested. We put them forward tentatively but with the deliberate intention of making the point that there is still considerable scope for further development and testing of the parameters of Attachment Theory and its applications. If behaviour systems were more clearly specified in the way that we are suggesting, and if it were to be found that they operate differently in individuals with different attachment histories, then the implications of Attachment Theory for therapy might become clearer. It might, for example, be possible to trace the development of problems such as anorexia, obsessive-compulsive disorders, kleptomania (compulsive stealing) to states in which individuals have come, for some reason, to displace the goal of the ABS onto another system, for example, onto the feeding behaviour system in the case of anorexia or onto the exploration/play system in the case of stealing. Whether conceptualising problem behaviours in this way would increase the ease with which therapists could relate to clients and facilitate transition to more optimal ways of functioning seems debatable, but the possibility that greater insights could be gained in respect of understanding the client's perspective seems worth considering all the same.

Human behaviour systems can respond to the external environment

Although each behaviour system is biologically programmed, Bowlby argued that behaviour systems are not completely 'closed' systems: their development is to some extent dependent upon influences from the environment and individual experience. To facilitate adaptation, systems are both geared toward their own specific overarching goals but, at the same time, have multiple means at their disposal to reach those goals. This means, first, that there is nearly always an element of choice about how goals may best be arrived at, that is, that there is a certain degree of flexibility built into the system and, second, that this flexibility will give rise to a variety of variably adaptive behaviours that will be more or less effective in different circumstances. This principle seems to underpin the contention that diversity is necessary for the system to be maximally adaptive and also seems to bring into question the notion that the goal of each system will be set for life soon after, if not before, birth.

The development and organisation of behaviour systems changes across the lifespan

In his description of the general characteristics of behaviour systems, Bowlby (1969/1982) drew attention to the fact that, over the lifespan, providing that no catastrophic event intervenes, behaviour systems become modified according to certain basic principles, that is, they become more organised, better co-ordinated, more specialised, more clearly goal-oriented, more reliant on habitual/automatic processes (and therefore more speedy and efficient) but, at the same time, somewhat less capable of adapting to environmental demands (because they become more rigid). Behaviour systems in more mature individuals therefore become capable of operating in a 'goal-corrected' fashion, that is, they are organised so that they can take different environmental conditions into account as they seek to achieve their goal.

Bowlby further observed that while immature systems tend, on the one hand, to be more 'open' to the effects of experience and less rigid than more mature systems, their basic structure and operation is partially dependent upon automatic biologically pre-programmed responses over which the immature individual has little control. For example, a hungry human neonate, guided by smell and contact with the nipple, may be more or less successful at rooting, suckling and swallowing but has very little control over its own reflex responses. As a result, once a neonate's Feeding Behaviour System is activated, termination will depend almost entirely upon the state of Caregiving Behaviour Systems in others close by.

This extreme vulnerability in human infants, along with observations of 'critical periods' in the development of the young of other species, led Bowlby to consider the possibility that the first few years of life are crucially important for later development. He formed this opinion early in his career: "In my experience a mother's acceptance of clinging and following is consistent with a favourable development even in the absence of breast feeding, whilst rejection of clinging and following is apt to lead to emotional disturbance even in the presence of breast feeding. Furthermore, it is my impression that fully as many psychological disturbances, including the most severe, can date from the second year of life when clinging and following are at their peak as from the early months when they are rudimentary" (Bowlby 1958a, p.370). As we have already discussed in Chapter Six, these speculations are still very much open to debate.

There is a dynamic pattern of relationships between different behaviour systems

A further characteristic of behaviour systems is that, although they operate independently of each other, some systems will be turned on while others are turned off. Thus, lawful relationships between patterns of activation can be expected and, following on from this, big departures from expected patterns can be used to indicate dysfunction (i.e. the possible existence of pathology). To demonstrate this point, we will use a description of hypothetical observations at a playgroup over the space of three minutes:

Maisie, a lively, sociable three-year-old, sits down happily to lunch at the playgroup, next to her best friend, Harriet. It's food that both she and Harriet like and they tuck in eagerly, imitating each other playfully as they take individual mouthfuls. Maisie's mother, Sue, sits nearby, deep in conversation with other mothers and, seemingly, not at all concerned about what Maisie is doing.

Suddenly, there is a loud noise and the building begins to shake violently. Maisie stops eating and, like several other children, looks worried and fearful. She looks toward her mother who runs over, picks her up and carries her to an open doorway. Maisie, who briefly cried as her mother ran towards her, clings tightly to her mother, quiet and tense, all thoughts of eating forgotten. Her mother comforts her, saying, "It's only a little earthquake, nothing to worry about."

Dorothy Heard and Brian Lake have developed a time-chart method to portray this kind of sequence (Heard 1999).[3] Along the same lines, we have charted these three minutes in the lives of Maisie and her mother (see Figure 8.2). The time-chart gives some indication of how different behaviour systems might interact with each other as individuals respond to stressful events.

We have identified five behaviour systems in relation to Maisie's behaviour (feeding: NBS; affiliation/socialising: SBS; play/exploration: EBS; attachment: ABS and fear/wariness: FBS) and four in relation to that of her mother (affiliation/socialising: SBS; caregiving: CBS; attachment: ABS and fear/wariness: FBS).

Just looking at the profile for Maisie, in the first minute before the earthquake started, three systems were highly activated: feeding, socialising and play/exploration. Two systems were relatively inactive: attachment and fear/wariness. The low level of activation reflects something of Maisie's personality: her outgoing nature, her growing self-reliance and her confidence. She was relaxed and excited, enjoying the company of her friend and her lunch, safe in the knowledge that her mother was near at hand. Then came the earthquake. As a three-year-old, Maisie had no previous experience of this kind of event. She is not, at first, sure what is going on or what to make of it. However, she stops eating and stops paying attention to her friend. Both her fear/wariness system and her attachment system become more ready for full activation. She looks at her mother, notices the serious expression on her face and that she is moving with urgency. Her attachment behaviour system now becomes fully activated as she clings to her mother for comfort. Her fear/wariness system is also almost fully activated but is held in check by the approach of her mother. Gradually, as her mother reassures her, both fear/wariness behaviours and attachment behaviours decline.

Maisie's mother's profile is quite different. Sue's attachment behaviour system, though mildly activated as the earthquake occurs, soon gives way as her fear/wariness and caregiving sys-

---

3   Unpublished talk given to International Attachment Network, London

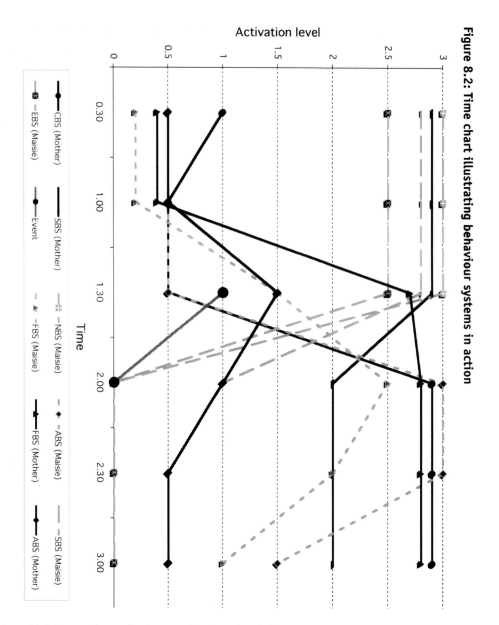

Figure 8.2: Time chart illustrating behaviour systems in action

tems kick into action and take over. She stops socialising and, even when she has managed to soothe Maisie, continues herself to be quite fearful and wary for some time. She knows that the danger may not yet be completely past.

This portrayal of Maisie's and Sue's behaviour illustrates the hypothetical response of different behaviour systems to the same event. In our scenario, the event was interpreted by both Maisie and Sue as a sign of danger and so triggered Fear/Wariness, Attachment and Caregiving systems but de-activated Exploration/Play, Affiliative/Sociable and Feeding/Nutritive systems. Before the event, when no threat was present, Exploration/Play, Affiliative/Sociable and Feeding/Nutritive systems were activated while Fear/Wariness, Attachment and Caregiving systems were de-activated. Even though we have not included all possible behaviour systems for Maisie and her mother, and have only described three minutes, we have produced a rather complicated account of behaviour systems in action. That so much complicated information arises from such a small amount of time might make readers wonder how easy it might be to use information of this kind to inform understanding of the nature of the relationships between children and their mothers. In Chapter Two, we showed how Mary Ainsworth succeeded in isolating a significant chunks of parent-child interactive behaviour in order to assess the quality of their attachment relationship. Ainsworth, though, tended to focus mainly on three systems (Attachment, Exploration and Caregiving), asserting that the way, in particular, that Attachment and Exploration interacted with each other "is even more significant for development (and for survival) than either in isolation" (Ainsworth 1972, p.118).

Evolutionary theory anticipates diversity among adaptive behaviours within species since complex and varied responses are needed to accommodate life's challenges which are also complex, variable and all too often unpredictable. This depiction of Maisie and Sue does not emerge from a true account and many other mother-child reactions could have been described. Variations will depend on state and trait characteristics within each individual (e.g. their current state and their characteristic modes of response), on the nature of the relationship between them, as well as on their perception of alternative sources of support. For example, a more timid or tired, less sociable or less confident child might have taken a more active role in running to her mother as soon as she sensed the first tremor. A less protective or less assertive mother might have hesitated longer before taking action to safeguard her child and a more fearful or insecure mother might have become too preoccupied with her own need for reassurance to be free to take prompt or effective action to look after her child, and so on.

Some patterns of responding may be assessed as more or less adaptive but the criteria for assessing quality of adaptation cannot be said to be a biological given. Different cultures and environments support different forms of adaptation. What's sauce for the mother goose can be poison for the mother hoopoe. Further, under adverse conditions, some forms of adaptation that may be highly effective in the short term, can be at a cost to the individual, for example, because they involve prolonged over-activation of certain behaviour systems, with associated wear and tear, or prolonged under-activation (sometimes involving suppression) of other systems which can also be associated with eventual loss of optimal functionality. These points raise the question of cultural variability and how optimal functionality might be determined. There is a risk that criteria for optimal functionality may be too 'culture-bound' or stereotyped, that is, overly determined by the cultural perspective of one group and so prejudiced against others.

Another point that we should make here in relation to our time-chart is that, although it indicates that one system (Maisie's Explorative/Play system after the event) has become completely de-activated, there is some justification for believing that, in their resting state, systems are never completely inactive, unless they have become severely dysfunctional. The reason for this is that systems always need to be maintained at some minimal level (i.e. to 'tick over') if they are to retain any potential for rapid re-activation. This means that, even when there is no outwardly observable or measurable evidence of activity, the system should be in a state of readiness, for example, the Fear/Wariness system will always need to be on the look-out for danger even when no danger is present. Bearing in mind Bowlby's eagerness to ensure that his theory could be supported by observational evidence, this point hints at a practical problem which, though to some extent acknowledged in the literature, may only now be beginning to be addressed in studies which include measures taken of less covert processes (e.g. measures of electrical brain activity, neurochemical state, sweating, blood pressure, respiratory state, etc.).

Other practical difficulties are associated with operational definitions[4] of behaviour systems. For researchers to be sure that they are each talking about the same phenomena, behaviour systems need to be clearly defined. We described above the case of the insecure mother who had become too preoccupied with her own need for reassurance to look after her child. It might be possible to describe the Caregiving Behaviour System of this mother as having been activated. However, because it only has herself and not her child as the target of attention, to describe her as caregiving is misleading. Bowlby's theory, which was more concerned to develop specifications for the Attachment Behaviour System than for other systems, does not provide a very complete description of the Caregiving Behaviour System and did not specify how this fundamental qualitative difference might be conveyed. More recently, Cassidy (1999) has proposed a more circumscribed definition of caregiving, suggesting that it should include only parenting behaviours which are aimed at promoting proximity and comfort at times when the parent perceives the child to be in danger. George and Solomon (1999), however, have warned that cultural variations in caregiving practices may preclude very precise specification of the behaviours to be included in a universal Caregiving Behaviour System.

A similar problem arises in relation to distinctions between the Exploration/Play and the Affiliative/Sociable systems. Bowlby does not appear to have supplied operational definitions for either system and the potential for confusion seems high. Does the behaviour of a child on starting a new school and making new friends count as exploration, affiliation or both at once? These questions reflect the fact that Bowlby's theory left quite a number of 'untied ends' and that, despite his intention to bind the theory as closely as possible to testable observations, may inadvertently have left rather a lot of room for idiosyncratic interpretations.

In order to draw together some of the theoretical points already hinted at, we can consider the example of feeding. The Feeding Behaviour System becomes activated by a number of 'triggers', such as hunger pangs, and the sight, taste or smell of food. The goal of feeding behaviour could be conceptualised as hunger reduction. There are numerous possible ways to reach that goal, depending on individual capability, choice of strategy, and resources available. We might, for example, choose to get someone else to make us a meal, procure our own food (healthy/unhealthy, a lot /a little, etc.), ignore the hunger pangs, satisfy them by drinking instead of eating, persuade ourselves that we are not hungry but greedy, realise that we are only reacting to the smell or sight of food, etc. Should a tiger stroll between us and the food, it is highly likely that our Feeding Behaviour System will be de-activated and that our Fear/Wariness System will spring into action (and our fate is likely to depend almost entirely on the state of the tiger's Feeding Behaviour System).

This example shows that, until the tiger arrives at least, options for attaining the goal of the Feeding Behaviour System are relatively unrestricted. It also gives an indication of the difficulties, from a research perspective, associated with objective observation and measurement of behaviour systems in action. First, the triggers and responses to them are subjectively

---

4   As we have already explained in Chapter Two, in the absence of an operational definition, it is difficult to measure an abstract construct, such as attachment or self-esteem, accurately. In order to determine the degree to which the abstract entity is present, researchers need first to determine which overt, observable behaviours can be used to indicate its presence reliably. This is known as creating an operational definition, i.e. a list of descriptors or conditions that need to be met for the construct to be said to be operative. By comparing the observed behaviour against this set of criteria, it is possible to assess the status of the abstract construct.

experienced and so are not easy to measure objectively. Individuals vary considerably both in their behavioural response to triggers and in their persistence in pursuing system goals. While some people may feel the need to completely assuage their appetites, others may be content to stop eating before they reach satiation point. Some individuals might be savannah grazers (a little and often) while others might be camels (a lot and not at all often), and so on. Alternative more or less adaptive variations are also possible.

This brings us to a second area of difficulty concerning both how best to conceptualise system goals and how to judge whether they have been effectively reached. We suggested above that the goal of the Feeding Behaviour System could be identified as reduction of hunger. We might, perhaps equally plausibly (or implausibly?), have identified it as the maintenance, within particular limits, of a state of physical strength or wellbeing, or of a particular relationship between body mass and body weight. Alternatively, on a broader scale, we could have identified the ultimate goal as self-preservation or, in line with different strands of evolutionary theory, as the preservation of the human species, the reproduction of our own genes, or the attainment of optimal fitness. Although these goals might appear mutually compatible and the differences between them inconsequential, it seems important to recognise that the way a system goal is defined inevitably has implications for our assessment of the efficiency of that system. If the goal is not appropriately defined, then the assessment process is in danger of being flawed. A car designed for speed is likely to differ considerably from a car designed for carrying large objects. Accordingly, two separate sets of criteria will be needed if the efficiency of each type of car is to be appropriately assessed.

Similarly, still using feeding patterns as our example, Bowlby's theory would anticipate that adults living in a well-resourced society would almost certainly have a far greater range of options and control, in relation to their response to Feeding Behaviour System triggers, both than less mature humans in the same society and than adults in a less well-resourced social environment. Even so, as individuals, they might be expected to behave in fairly predictable ways that reflect particular patterns of response to unique environment-biological contexts. In a well-resourced habitat, savannah grazing which keeps animals in a state of constant readiness for quick escapes from predators may be most adaptive. In a desert, the camel's pattern is more likely to promote survival. It is only by taking into account the environmental context that adaptive success can be accurately assessed. This mean that judging all behaviours by their relation to one goal (e.g. achievement of secure attachment status) is likely not only to be inappropriate but to give rise to unsuitable interventions and ones that will have the potential to disrupt rather more than to facilitate self-understanding.

Having said this, defining system goals in very broad terms results in all systems ultimately having the same goal, for example, survival of the species (Ainsworth et al. 1978, Bowlby 1969) or differential gene replication (Simpson 1999; Belsky 1999). It inevitably then becomes difficult, and possibly irrelevant, to assess the relative contribution of each behaviour system to the overall outcome. Lacking proximal goals for individual behaviour systems, there are no clear criteria by which to judge optimal function in individual behaviour systems. In the end, the choice of goal seems rather arbitrary and the mechanisms for determining how successfully that goal has been reached seem equally arbitrary. For example, even if, as Belsky (1999, p.141) asserts, "the ultimate target of natural selection is genetic replication because this is the goal of (all) life", it does not automatically follow that only the genes of the individual (as opposed to the gene pool of the social group or even of the species) are the target of natural selection. Altruistic behaviour may be relatively rare but it is not pathological, though defining the target of natural selection very narrowly suggests that it might be. Besides, if genetic replication is all that matters, should not the universal target be to produce the greatest number of offspring capable of reproducing, regardless of their fitness or their cost in terms of parents' quality of life? Belsky acknowledges that reproductive aims are moderated by environment: parents in well-resourced settings tend to have fewer and fitter offspring than parents in environments where resources are scarce. But why, if genetic replication is really the aim, should better-off parents be content with replicating fewer genes? These parents would seem to be in the best position to produce and sustain the highest number of healthy offspring. The question, therefore, of what the ultimate goal of human behaviour might be, and more specifically, what the goal of the Attachment Behaviour System is, seems still to be in need of a satisfactory answer.

As already mentioned, a third fundamental area of difficulty arises if the behaviour system is not defined sufficiently clearly. Although Bowlby always maintained that attachment bonds are important across the lifespan, his initial theorising focused heavily on infancy and early childhood. Only towards the end of his life did he and other workers begin to give more attention to adulthood and to the way in which behaviour systems changed over the lifespan. By this time, other workers in the field were contributing to the development of attachment theory so that, by the middle of the nineties, an interesting debate had begun on the subject of the relationship between different behaviour systems in adulthood (e.g. the special edition of *Psychological Inquiry* 1994, volume five). Key to this debate was the question of how attachment bonds might alter across the lifespan, how they differ from other adult affectional ties (e.g. spousal relationships) and where the cut-off point between attachment and sexual relationships might be drawn. By the time this debate had really got under way, Bowlby was no longer alive to referee its outcome.

Summary: general characteristics of behaviour systems

In summary, a number of conceptual issues arise in connection with Bowlby's account of behaviour systems. These centre upon:
- the definition of system goals (i.e. the biological function of each system)
- operational definitions and parameters of specific behaviour systems
- the measurement and identification of activating events
- the changing form of individual behaviour systems over the lifespan
- consequent difficulties in assessing the effectiveness of individual behaviour systems.

The question that now seems to emerge is how viable Attachment Theory might be in view of lack of resolution on these matters. Is it, for example, the case that the theory still needs to be refined in order for it to become more powerful and more capable of fully encompassing the data, is it possible that the systems theory aspect of it is in some way extraneous to the more central part of the account, or might these outstanding problems constitute an important theoretical limitation? Although it is not yet clear how easy it might be to reach firm conclusions on these matters, for any psychological theory to be considered tenable or adequate as an account of human behaviour, there are certain generally agreed criteria by which it can be assessed. In the next section, we outline these criteria and consider how well Attachment Theory fares in relation to each of them in turn.

What is a good theory?

Table 8.2 shows some key criteria by which the adequacy of a theory can be assessed. These criteria are drawn from a number of sources and are widely accepted within the social sciences, and particularly the discipline of psychology, as important markers.

Table 8.2: Criteria for assessing the value of a theory

CRITERION	DESCRIPTION
Testability	Can the theory be falsified? Can it be tested at all?
Fertility	Does it generate further hypotheses (new ideas and directions for testing)?
Generalisability	Does it specify clearly which behaviour it is attempting to explain? Is it based only on normative data? Can it account for new discoveries?
Explanatory power	Is it coherent and understandable? Is it useful? Is it parsimonious? Can it predict future as well as past behaviour? Can it account for interacting variables?

Testability

As shown in Table 8.2, testability refers to whether a theory can be falsified and whether it can be tested at all. Unless a theory is capable of being tested, its status as fact or fiction cannot be established. It can neither be proved nor disproved.

One of the major criticisms of psychoanalytic theory has been the problem that many of its claims, particularly those in relation to the existence of unconscious processes, are not amenable to empirical verification. How, for example, do you test Melanie Klein's theory of early development which posits views such as that, in the first year of life, an infant will "try to destroy its mother by every method at the disposal of its sadistic trends – with its teeth, nails and excreta and with the whole of its body, transformed in phantasy into all kinds of dangerous weapons" (Klein 1932/1989, p.130). She also described sexual development in baby girls in the following way: "As a result of the oral frustration she experiences from her mother, the girl turns away from her and takes her father's penis as her object of satisfaction" (Klein 1932/1989, p.194). Such hypotheses are very difficult to test. Until we have the means either to inspect directly the contents of the minds of six- to 12-month-old babies or the unconscious phantasies of older children, or can use some other method for assessing the images that they are entertaining, these theories cannot be tested.

One of the fiercest critics of psychoanalysis was Hans Eysenck (Eysenck and Wilson 1973, Eysenck 1985) who firmly believed that unless a theory is based on observable facts and can be tested using empirical scientific methods, it cannot qualify as a scientific theory. Eysenck dismissed Freud as a non-scientist and claimed that "He was, without doubt, a genius, not of science, but of propaganda, not of rigorous proof, but of persuasion, not of the design of experiments, but of literary art. His place is not, as he claimed, with Copernicus and Darwin, but with Hans Christian Anderson and the Brothers Grimm, the tellers of fairy tales" (Eysenck 1985, p.208).

In defence against such attacks, some have argued that psychoanalysis should not be viewed or judged as a theory or set of theories to be subjected to the same kind of rigorous proof as physical sciences. Rather, it should be considered a 'hermeneutic' discipline (this has nothing to do with hermits – it means that the substance of the discipline relates to interpretations, as opposed to facts which can be more objectively specified and measured), which has its own internal consistency but the truths of which are not capable of reduction to externally observable phenomena. The danger here, though, is that disciplines in which theories are not testable rather too readily come to resemble religious dogma with unchallengeable beliefs.

Testability: How Attachment Theory weighs up

One of Bowlby's prime motivations in developing Attachment Theory was his desire to create a sounder, empirically testable base for psychoanalytic theories. He argued, "There will be endless feuds and schisms and schools of thought or whatever, until we can get our discipline on to a scientific basis, and I think it's a priority job to do that. I've always held that view" (Bowlby et al. 1986, p.56). That his theory of development should be seen as a hermeneutic discipline was also, quite emphatically, not Bowlby's view: "I believe that our discipline can be put on to a scientific basis. A lot of people either think you can't or don't know how to. There are people who think psychoanalysis is really a hermeneutic discipline. I think that's all rubbish quite frankly" (Bowlby et al. 1986, p.55). But how successful was Bowlby in achieving his aim to create a scientifically testable theory of attachment?

That some aspects of Attachment Theory can be tested seems indisputable. As Bowlby remarked, "It is a little unexpected that, whereas attachment theory was formulated by a clinician for use in the diagnosis and treatment of seriously disturbed patients and families, its usage hitherto has been mainly to promote research in developmental psychology" (Bowlby 1988b, p.ix).

However, it also seems important to recognise that the use of AT concepts to guide empirical research does not automatically confer the status of testability. This requirement can only be considered to have been met if all relevant hypotheses are testable. While some aspects of AT have been tested to some extent and are relatively amenable to experimentation, for example, hypotheses relating to effects of separation and loss, for both ethical and other practical reasons, there have often been limitations on the extent to which rigorous tests can be employed. As Chapter Four illustrated, many of the studies inspired by AT have been observational in nature rather than experimental so, although they may have had a covert aim of hypothesis-testing, they rarely tested cause-effect relationships. This focus on descriptive, correlational relationships between patterns of attachment, or clusters of attachment behaviours, and performance in other spheres has undoubtedly begun to build up an extremely rich data base and has opened doors to an exceptionally wide arena of investigation. However, it cannot be taken as an unambiguous test of all aspects of Attachment Theory.

A central concern throughout this book has been the question of what the significance might be of different patterns of attachment. We have constantly returned to this question and have queried fundamental, supposedly well-established, 'facts', such as whether 'secure' attachment is really more secure than insecure attachment, particularly the avoidant pattern. We have raised these questions out of a concern to ensure that Attachment Theory does not become used as a means for reinforcing majority-group prejudice against minority groups and also because of the potential risk of AT turning into exactly the kind of dogma that Bowlby was so anxious to avoid.

While the early days of attachment research were dominated by a search for empirical evidence, during 'the move to the level of representations' in the mid-1980s (Main et al. 1985), the nature of investigations altered radically. Research became more theory- than data-driven as the focus on 'Internal Working Models' gave rise to many new measures to be applied to the study of attachment in adults and adolescence and, to a lesser degree, in middle childhood. This more theory-driven research does not appear to have had the same capacity to achieve what was arguably the most distinctive aspect of the infancy research, namely, the ability to 'home in' on patterns of infant-carer relationships.

Ainsworth's new technique for observing relationships (the SS) was one of the key attractions of attachment research for developmental psychologists. Prior to this, within traditional mainstream psychology, there had been a tendency for individuals to be studied as though they were in a social vacuum, in spite of the fact that prominent theorists and researchers had consistently emphasised the need for both systemic and social constructivist approaches (e.g. Mead 1934, Lewin 1935, Bronfenbrenner 1979, 1986, Higgins et al. 1983).

Unfortunately, much of the work in adult attachment seems to have reverted to the more traditional, relatively impoverished questionnaire-based approach, on the assumption that adequate information about attachment relationships and attitudes towards attachment relationships can be obtained directly from individuals in the absence of observation of interactions. This kind of approach undoubtedly yields huge quantities of data, but what the significance of this information is, particularly in respect of Internal Working Models that have evolved as the result of the individual's history of interactions, seems unclear.

We would argue, therefore, that this aspect of AT still stands in need of empirical verification. If, as Bowlby intended, AT is to be put onto a firm scientific footing, the tendency throughout the adult attachment research literature for assumptions to be made about relationships attachment styles and interpersonal skills in the absence of sound evidence needs to be challenged. Further investigations are needed to test and substantiate hypotheses such as that insecure patterns are more inflexible, less modifiable, less open to inspection, etc. More tests need to be directed at the question of how organised patterns of attachment, particularly the insecure strategies, relate to past experience, performance and outlook.

A major obstacle is still the lack of a satisfactory operational definition of attachment security across the lifespan. Possibly, it will only be through continued labour-intensive observational research that the data base will be expanded sufficiently to arrive at a satisfactory definition. Meantime, the lack of a definition has led to confusion about how the different systems for tapping the construct might relate to each other. As a result, definitions of attachment security in adulthood have tended to become somewhat circular. It seems rather too often to be assumed that one unchanging pattern of attachment characterises each individual and that this pattern will be applied to all social situations and contexts within each person's experience. It has also been assumed that adults classified as insecure will be relatively incompetent at self-analysis and will also be relatively incompetent when it comes to responding to and understanding other people's emotional states largely, it seems, on the grounds that this is how the transcripts of their interviews are classified.

Longitudinal studies have not yet adequately addressed these questions nor tested many of the assumptions that have come to be associated with, in particular, adult attachment classifications, largely because of the fundamental lack of operational definitions and associated measurement problems. The way in which AT research has gathered momentum over the past two decades seems possibly to have taken it out of the sphere in which it was originally developed and may be threatening to take it back into the realms of a value system that is not sufficiently anchored in empirical validation. It seems to us that the time to may be ripe to redress this situation, to cut away super-imposed value judgements, to subject unsubstantiated assertions to more stringent tests and to develop a more consistently defined central construct that can be measured with well-calibrated instruments. This phase of testing, though, might require a far larger longitudinal study than hitherto, one that takes account of 'third-factor' variables (social contextual and socio-demographic variables) and that includes assessment of a wider range of relationships. It might also involve re-visiting some of the most highly favoured methodologies with a view to gaining a deeper understanding of their significance and of increasing their capacity to assess the significance of more fine-grained variations in qualities of attachment.

Fertility

Even theories that cannot be tested can be valuable if they generate ideas for future research. The more ways in which a theory can be tested, the more situations to which it applies and the more aspects of it that can be tested, the more fertile it is. For example, although some aspects of psychoanalytic theory may not be testable, this does not automatically preclude the possibility that they might provide a springboard for the development of more testable theories. However, there is a danger that fertile but untestable theories might stem more from group prejudices that can be very damaging.

Fertility: How Attachment Theory weighs up

That Attachment Theory generates further hypotheses, that is, new ideas and new directions for exploration, is perhaps its greatest strength. Although there is still much that is not well understood, the essential premise of Attachment Theory, that how children are cared for influences how they develop, continues to generate almost infinite hypotheses. These hypotheses extend to all aspects of development across the lifespan, and all social and cultural contexts.

Attachment Theory is almost unique in its focus on relationships. This focus has given rise to another sort of fertility: it has generated and continues to generate new methods for the study of relationships. However, as already argued in the previous section, it may now be time to bring those measures back to heel and to ask whether it is possible to identify more exactly what it is about the relationship between infants and carers that the Strange Situation taps, whether there might be additional ways in which the same construct can be assessed at later ages, or whether alternative methods might need to be developed if the quality of attachment relationships across the lifespan is to be captured. The AAI (Adult Attachment Interview) does appear to capture a similar or related construct, but the 'transmission gap' (van IJzendoorn 1995a, 1995b, 1995c) suggests that the construct it taps may not be identical.

Generalisability

In order for a theory to be applied in any systematic way or to be generalisable across different situations and populations, it is necessary for it to clearly specify which behaviour it attempts to explain. This kind of specification usually requires clear identification not only of which *behaviours* are the subject of the theory, but also which *populations* and which *situations* the theory is intended to apply to.

Taking a theory about separation anxiety as an example, this would need to entail clear specification of the behaviours to be included, the particular population involved and, possibly, the situations in which separation anxiety might be expected to arise. Specification of behaviours can often be achieved with reference to previously existing literature, for example, most child development textbooks describe separation anxiety as indicated by fear of separation from key caregivers as well as by fear of strangers and by dislike of being left alone, as having an onset at around six months, and as being particularly intense between approximately ten to 18 months. Textbooks often also contain the information that this form of anxiety appears to be linked to cognitive development since its emergence seems to coincide with the time that infants begin to succeed on cognitive tasks requiring them to hold in mind a mental image of objects that are no longer physically present (i.e. when their cognitive ability enables them to achieve what Piaget termed 'object permanency'). However, separation anxiety occurs not only in human infants but also older people and animals too and any theory would need to specify whether all forms of separation anxiety were to be encompassed or only the form that occurs as part of normal development in infancy.

It is important for the definition to be both precise and capable of discriminating between the phenomenon to be explained and related phenomena. Obviously, it would be important to distinguish separation anxiety from related behaviours such as shyness, more general anxiety or more specific fears, for example, fear of the dark, heights, looming objects, animals, etc. A theory lacking a sound definition of the behaviour it aims to account for will be more likely to confuse than to advance understanding. Imagine developing a theory of the mechanism required to jump but failing to distinguish between jumping and falling!

If a theory specifies clearly the behaviour that it aims to explain but fails to set limits on the populations or situations to which it applies, it can be assumed by default that it was intended to cover all related behaviour. This may mean that the theory gets extended so far beyond the data upon which it was originally based, and which it was originally intended to account for, that it becomes irrelevant. It explains everything and yet nothing.

Combine this problem with a weak definition of the behaviours being explained and it is likely that the theory will suffer one of two equally disastrous fates: either it will become applicable to behaviours for which it was not intended (e.g. it is conceivable that a *very* general explanation such as over-excitement might account just as well for jumping as for separation anxiety) or it will fail to generalise to behaviours that it was intended to explain when they are shown in new situations or populations (e.g. it might account for separation anxiety in human one-year-olds but not in other animals or in older humans).

This brings us on to the question of how comprehensive a good theory needs to be. If a theory can only explain why or predict how humans will behave under normative, or optimal, conditions but has no capacity to account for behaviour in more unusual circumstances, its usefulness will be somewhat limited. For example, if a theory of separation anxiety fails to account for the behaviour of children who do not show separation anxiety at the expected ages, then it cannot be said to explain the phenomenon well.

Finally, theories need to be able to account for new data or information. Bowlby argued that separation anxiety stems directly from the nature of the child's tie to its mother which involves "a number of instinctual response systems, each of which is primary and which together have high survival value" (Bowlby 1960b, p.93). He proposed that, very soon after birth, these instinctual response systems lead infants to seek contact and proximity with their mothers and, when frightened or alarmed, to look to their mothers for comfort and protection. Separation anxiety therefore, according to Bowlby, results from the activation of a biologically pre-programmed defence mechanism, triggered by external cues (danger signals) and/or internal cues (e.g. fears of abandonment or loss). However, it can also arise when neither internal nor external cues appear to be present. How does Bowlby's theory account for these situations? He reasoned that "Clinical evidence suggests that a principal reason why some individuals grow up prone to pathological *(separation)* anxiety is that, during childhood, they have been exposed either to long or repeated separations in strange settings or else to frequent threats of such. Given those experiences in childhood a person is apt to grow up over-reactive to any kind of separation or loss" (Bowlby 1969b, p.85). In other words, he suggests that the same process which gives rise to 'normal' separation anxiety can also explain 'abnormal' separation anxiety. In normal separation anxiety, the activation of defence mechanisms results in the infant accessing one (or more) protective other, or mother figure, whose presence de-activates the defence mechanism and enables the infant to return to a state of relative calm. Failure to access a protective other leads to over-activation of the defence mechanism which, because it is not under conscious control, continues to be inappropriately turned on.

Generalisability: How Attachment Theory weighs up

Attachment Theory, in most respects, meets the criteria for a good theory on grounds of generalisability, even in the absence of a standardised operational definition of the behaviour it is attempting to explain. This is perhaps because, even in the absence of a standardised definition, it has distinct 'face validity', that is, it seems plausible. For this reason, it has been possible to extrapolate from Bowlby's original formulations, possibly, to a greater degree than alternative theories that have emerged from the field of psychoanalysis.

Attachment Theory has now been applied to almost every conceivable social group and context, including dyadic and triadic relationships within families across the lifespan, schools, the workplace, other institutions, and in a growing number of cultures. It has also been incorporated into literary criticism, and into discourses within the field of religious experience, philosophy of self, sociology, ethology and anthropology. It has been applied to 'normal' and 'abnormal' development and to a wide number of clinical populations. Some steps have begun to be made in investigating the neurobiology of attachment though, as we have repeatedly stressed, there is still an enormous amount to be discovered in this respect.

In some senses, though, Attachment Theory may be in danger of being a victim of its own success. It is, in essence, a beguilingly simple view of social development and some have interpreted its central thesis, that children's experiences of being cared for have important consequences, as though it were context-free and prescriptive. The notion that there is only one acceptable way to develop and that all must aspire towards this pattern is not consonant with our interpretation of Bowlby's understanding. His view was that there are many pathways towards healthy development and considerable individual variability within the normal range. It will be remembered that he was initially very hesitant about calling particular styles of attachment 'insecure' and preferred to use value-free descriptions.

Bowlby also thought it important to cross disciplines and to bind Attachment Theory closely to other data-rich fields of understanding. Linking Attachment Theory to other disciplines, though, needs to be done with care. While a confused attachment to neuroscience may be more helpful than no attachment at all, it may well lead to ill-advised strategies if it does not involve a systematic, informed and organised relationship that is attuned to and respecting of the authority of better informed neuroscientists. The 'move to the level of representations' in the 1980s has involved some alliance with investigations in the field of social cognition but perhaps an even closer, more systematic, alliance with the wider field of cognitive, social and developmental psychology might prove fruitful, especially in respect of theories of self development, attributional processes, self-monitoring and motivation.

The need for research on Attachment Theory to move beyond the dyad has been heeded by a growing number of workers in the field. It seems clear that there is still an enormous amount of work to be done in this area and it is not obvious that the tools used hitherto to assess attachment relationships between mothers and infants will prove the most efficient or effective for assessing relationships between fathers and infants, between parents and older children, or across different family types.

Without minimising the achievements so far, which have been considerable, it seems that attachment researchers may now be on the brink of moving into an era where new tools will be developed to observe and document even more complex models of family relationships. These research instruments may then become capable of assessing the impact on individual development of multiple relationships. Whether this kind of extension would yield very different conclusions about the nature of individual development is unclear. Possibly, in situations where the influence of the primary carer is predominant over other influences (i.e. where monism and monotropy predominate), it would not, but other situations might produce different outcomes. The value of this kind of extended investigation seems obvious given increasing tendencies for children to grow up in families where parents have made new relationships and where important attachment figures no longer live with the child.

A central interest of Bowlby in developing his theory of attachment was to see whether there are universal patterns that humans share with other mammals. Work so far tends to indicate that, in all cultures, attachment figures play a vital role. However, relatively little is known about variations in the quality or nature of this role, according to social and political conditions. As a result, although it seems evident that Attachment Theory can generalise across cultures and social situations, there is still a need for more attention to be paid to increasing our knowledge base and extending studies more widely.

Explanatory power

Most of the attributes of good theories that we have already discussed lead to increased explanatory power, but the following additional sources are also important to mention:
- A good theory needs to be coherent, understandable and internally consistent, that is, free from contradictions and convoluted language.
- A good theory is also a useful one. This generally means that it explains behaviour that is relatively common. The usefulness of a psychological theory is often also judged by its usability, for example, it will not only explain what gives rise to particular problem behaviours but will, in doing so, give an indication of the action that might resolve the problems.
- The principle of parsimony is probably one of the most important criteria for a good theory. There is no need for a long, complicated account if a simpler account is adequate – longer accounts will be superfluous.
- Greater explanatory power is achieved if the theory can accurately predict future as well as past behaviour. It can only do this if the theory is testable of course.
- Finally, because human behaviour is so complex, almost every theory of psychological behaviour will need to include an account of the effect of interacting variables. This

usually means paying careful attention to the social context in which the behaviour that the theory is attempting to explain occurs. If insufficient account is taken of potential alternative influences, there is even a danger that a theory will become invalid. This will happen if it is subsequently proven that the other factors are influencing outcomes more than the few factors that the theory has acknowledged.

Explanatory power: How Attachment Theory weighs up

In considering the explanatory power of AT, therefore, we consider the following five questions:
- Is it coherent and understandable?
- Is it useful?
- Is it parsimonious?
- Can it predict future and explain past behaviour?
- Can it account for interacting variables?

– coherency and comprehensibility

With regard coherency and comprehensibility, particularly as expressed through the writings of Bowlby, AT seems, on the surface, able to meet the criteria for a good theory. However, it was a theory in progress and Bowlby always stipulated the need to test his hypotheses against evidence. In practice, it seems that AT's quality of being almost intuitively understandable may have made it vulnerable to misappropriation, for example, by those who consider practices such as holding therapy and skin-to-skin contact to be logical applications of it. To some extent, then, in spite of the cogency of Bowlby's writings, the evolving nature of AT has meant that it has, to some extent, lacked internal consistency as a theory. While, as a general framework characterised by the need to subject hypotheses to empirical test and to eschew dogma, its central message is and does still seem very clear, easily understandable, consistent and persuasive, there are perhaps questions about whether it can or will in the future be viewed, overall, as a coherent theory. This perhaps is an important matter for further debate.

– usefulness

The fact that AT can be misappropriated is a kind of negative testament to its usefulness. More positive indications come from its ability to generate hypotheses, its emphasis on the importance of relationships as organisational structures and the framework that it provides for investigating the nature of relationships and their impact on social and emotional wellbeing, both in respect of individuals' lives and self-understanding, and of societies and social policies more widely.

However, again, it is important to emphasise that AT is only likely to be useful if it is not seen as a set of rules and regulations 'set in stone'. AT points to the importance of relationships in enabling individuals to gain a sense of their own value in relation to their social context. At the same time, it suggests that individuals who gain a sense of not being valued or of being of questionable worth are less likely to become well-integrated into society and are more likely to contribute to society in a negative way. AT, in this sense, can be seen to be of use both on an individual and a social level. As Bowlby intended, it can valuably inform social policy and medical practice.

Currently, applications and interpretations of Attachment Theory are prolific. Its influence has become increasingly extensive across social, political, professional and personal arenas. It has been interpreted as offering clear prescriptions about how parents should and should not interact with their young children, and hard-and-fast rules about what kind of family and home care children need to develop into successful and socially responsible adults. Even when viewed in a less prescriptive light, it has been thought to provide evidence of the value to children of consistent, sensitive, responsive, attuned parents. But, however it is interpreted or used, whether as a form of social policing, as a guide for parents, as the impetus for greater self and other understanding, or in other ways, if Attachment Theory is to be in keeping with the vision that Bowlby had for it, it is essential that it should continue to be seen as a set of hypotheses capable of being empirically tested. If it is reduced to an overly prescriptive set of rules, its value as a framework for understanding social relationships within ever-changing social and cultural contexts is likely to diminish.

– parsimony

In order to assess whether Attachment Theory is parsimonious, it is necessary to consider both whether there are aspects of the theory that are redundant and whether other theories provide a simpler but equally comprehensive account. The latter argument has been debated extensively elsewhere and tends to conclude that Attachment Theory does provide a cogent explanation that can at least rival other accounts (e.g. Rajecki et al. 1978, Fonagy 1999).

Some aspects of AT, though, do appear to be rather problematic. Perhaps one of the most conceptually challenging aspects, as discussed earlier in this chapter, is the notion that attachment constitutes an independent behaviour system. At the level of metaphor, this terminology does seem to increase explanatory power. But at the level of objectively measurable behaviours, although some headway has been made and although some would argue that neural correlates have been discovered, considerably more work is yet needed.

– explanation of past and prediction of future behaviour

Whether AT can explain past and predict future behaviour is another area of contention. On a theoretical level, there can be little doubt that it does provide explanations of past and predictions of future behaviour. Particular types of psychopathology are theorised as due to quality of past experiences of being parented while quality of parenting is theorised as predictive of pattern of attachment and later development. These effects can occur within one lifespan or across generations. In this sense, therefore, AT is extremely potent as a theory.

In practice, though, the difficulty of measuring relevant effects does seem to limit the potential explanatory power of AT. Only once it is possible to be certain that measures of patterns of attachment really do measure the same entity across the lifespan will it be possible to have complete confidence in these explanations. As things stand, AT seems to be a theory with tremendous explanatory potential but one that still has some practical hurdles to overcome.

– account of interacting variables

Accounting for interacting variables is not a problem for AT. In fact, because it is in essence a systemic theory and because it sets out to trace emotional development 'from cradle to grave', it is well designed to take stock of a huge variety of influences on development. However, again, as mentioned above, there is still a need for its research instruments to evolve further if it is to be able to reflect the full complexity of the nature of individual relationships within their wider social context. Without these further extensions, there is a danger that AT will be restricted to being predominantly an account of normative patterns of attachment only.

Summing up: how secure are the foundations of Attachment Theory?

Attachment Theory is an ambitious theory founded in several disciplines. In this chapter, we have attempted to evaluate its status as a theory and have paid particular attention to the difficulties associated with its testability. Our general conclusion is that AT has very considerable potential as a theory, but that more work is needed in order for it to be convincingly tested. We have borne in mind the aim that Bowlby had of ensuring that his theory did not become seen as a 'hermeneutic discipline' and his strong determination to adhere to scientific principles in developing and testing his ideas. For these reasons, we have proposed that now may be an appropriate time for the concept of behavioural systems to be reconsidered and have suggested that questions about how different measures relate to each other should continue to be addressed.

We have also argued that the 'move to the level of representations' that began in the mid-1980s, although it created a huge wealth of data, can also be seen in a sense to have cut AT adrift from its empirical, observation-based moorings. This, we feel, has left open the possibility that AT may be used to discriminate against rather than to empower individuals who have not been in the position to enjoy the advantages conferred by a history of secure attachment. To guard against these developments, it seems important that insights from AT are used not just to maximise opportunities for attachment security but also to guard against tendencies to make premature or derogatory assumptions about the nature of the processes that might underlie interpersonal strategies adopted by people with histories of non-secure attachment.

We cannot be confident that the instruments employed in attachment research to date have been sufficiently refined to capture the true adaptive significance of the full range of variability in patterns of attachment. Until instruments are developed that do have greater capacity to throw light on these matters, value-laden assumptions or attributions seem not only premature and ill-founded, but potentially damaging. Such assumptions seem highly likely to foreclose discussion, to limit the chances of increasing understanding of minority group perspectives, and to automatically relegate idiosyncratic adaptations to the status of dysfunction. As stressed throughout this book, this approach is uncomfortably close to that associated with past assumptions and practices towards children who are left-handed and, for that matter, for current assumptions that attribute inferiority to minority group members and so lead to discrimination against people from minority populations, whether on grounds of race, sexual preference, disability or other characteristics. Attachment Theory does have a potential for increasing understanding of different perspectives but conversely, if not firmly tied to detailed empirical observations, it also has the capacity as a superficially rather too coherent value system, to become a weapon which could increase the disadvantages to a substantial proportion of the population.

Bowlby was determined that his ideas, from those that were most closely rooted in observation to the most speculative, should be tested against empirical evidence. He was also passionate about the potential that parents have to respond to the emotional needs of their children, and so to understand and improve their children's life chances. And he was adamant that there was a need for social policies to maximise the chances for relationships between parents and children to form the basis for healthy development.

Bowlby's theory was not fully fleshed out in every respect and certain aspects have not withstood rigorous tests. In a sense, because Bowlby does not appear to have intended it to be a static account but one that could, like his concept of 'working models' evolve in response to new evidence, it may be more aptly described as a framework than as a theory. As a framework for exploring further and for seeking to understand more deeply what the conditions are that promote the healthiest social and emotional development, it still seems to hold much promise. Its central message, that both children and adults need others to inform their constantly evolving sense of who they are and what they have to offer, seems sensible on both intuitive and logical levels. That parents and carers, whether biologically or non-biologically related, may be key players in the sense-making experiences of their children is also a notion that can be realistically subjected to empirical tests. However, as we have suggested in this chapter and throughout this book, there are still many questions that have not been answered and there is still considerable room for further work to be carried out if the full value of Bowlby's approach is to be realised.

Premature acquiescence in the view that Attachment Theory affords prescriptions about how to live or how to treat disorderly individuals would seem almost to be a travesty of the approach advocated by both Bowlby and Ainsworth. It seems doubtful that they would have intended Attachment Theory to become some kind of creed to be incorporated into social policing policies designed to root out the insecurely attached. Nevertheless, Attachment Theory does offer useful directions for policy decisions around the welfare of young children and it does recognise children's need for consistent protection, guidance and care. It also acknowledges the difficulties that many parents have in providing adequate qualities of care and their need for appropriate support if they are to be able to carry out the role and to fulfil the responsibilities that society, perhaps somewhat unreasonably given the traditionally unequal distributions of material and personal resources across society, expects of them as parents.

Despite the fact that children can become public testimonies to their parents, child-rearing in the UK is predominantly a private matter. Many hesitate to step in even in very public circumstances when a parent is clearly in difficulty with a child. Admitting that you are struggling is not easy and the advice that might be proffered consequent upon such an admission is often at odds with what is needed. The question therefore tends to be how best to ensure that accessible and congenially presented information and support is at hand. Perhaps the most important message that has arisen from Attachment Theory in this respect is the need to ensure that parents are free and able to make informed choices when it comes to making decisions about the wellbeing of their children. But, even more importantly perhaps, is the fact that Attachment Theory has provided a framework within which vital and crucial questions can be asked, questions such as when should children be separated from their primary caregivers, how and why, what kind of care do children need when, for any reason, their primary caregivers cannot be available to them, how to determine whether parents are failing their children, what to expect in the wake of severe trauma or loss. Whilst it is not always easy to give firm, categorical answers to such questions, the very fact that they are asked should at least give pause for thought and might avert any tendency for governments to impose child- and family-unfriendly policies.

The value of Attachment Theory as a lobby for children and parents is visible in many spheres, though there is still scope for further progress. It has been influential, for example:

- in changing *hospital practices* where, in the past, it has resulted in vastly improved hospital practices though, even now, these are not always as congenial as they could optimally be
- it has influenced ante- and post-natal care programmes for parents and babies
- it has encouraged serious questions to be asked about the extent, quality and timing of *day care* facilities, though, in our view, these questions have not so far produced a satisfactory response in respect of reconciling the needs of children and families to the considerably less humane demands of business; there appears, also, very little evidence of any attempt to put in place a system of checks that could forestall or prevent the kind of distress seen in some young children placed in inappropriate day care
- in respect of *foster and adoptive care,* it has been of clear assistance in decision-making processes by court welfare officers, other officials and social workers, though, again, it could probably be used far more effectively if it were incorporated into support and training of foster parents (particularly support with individual children on an ongoing basis, the provision of which is all too often woefully inadequate or absent)
- however, as demonstrated by Zeanah (2005), policies on foster care placement, particularly the currently popular kinship care about which there is cause for considerable concern, are not always as well informed by attachment research as they could be
- it is beginning to inform policies around care of the elderly, though, again, this is an area where it tends to show how inadequate the systems are that purport to safeguard the emotional wellbeing of this vulnerable group
- as mentioned in Chapter Six, it has begun to influence some aspects of school organisation and research has clearly shown the importance of children's attachment to school, though, again, with tremendous pressures on teachers to form-fill and to reach child competence targets that place scant emphasis on children's emotional needs, its influence is as yet not nearly as great as might be desired
- it could be of considerable use within prison and probationary services where its influence is sometimes apparent in decision-making but where its scope could be increased still further
- its value has increasingly been recognised by therapists practising within a wide range of perspectives
- it has informed the work of many people working with bereaved, traumatised or displaced people
- it is beginning to inform understanding of family members where there has been domestic violence or relationship breakdown; unfortunately, insights from Attachment Theory have not yet been incorporated into coherent strategies to facilitate maximum support to parents and children in these situations

Attachment Theory has relevance to most of the difficulties and dilemmas that parents face. Some interpretations of it may leave parents feeling inadequate, guilt-ridden and out of control, blaming themselves for not having protected children from negative experiences. But the most important messages of Attachment Theory for parents, in our view, do not involve blame or negative labels and stereotypes. They are the messages that encourage parents and carers to be patient, not to feel that they will lose face or control if they seek support from outside the family occasionally, to know where to find appropriate support, and to realise that the way to provide a sound basis for children's development is as much concerned with making repairs and clarifying miscommunications as it is with smooth transactions.

But if parents are to be able to seek the support that they need, it seems that, as a society, we may need to re-prioritise, so that the emotional needs of both parents and children are better served and so that the principle of shared care becomes dominant above that of competitive materialism. As Bowlby (1984a/1998b, p.2) put it: "Paradoxically it has taken the world's richest societies to ignore these basic facts. Man and woman power devoted to the production of material goods counts a plus in all our economic indices. Man and woman power devoted to the production of happy, healthy, and self-reliant children in their own homes does not count at all. We have created a topsy-turvy world."

9 | Attachment myths and the perils of parenting: Summary and conclusions

In attempting to write this book, we undertook what some may consider an almost foolhardily ambitious enterprise. Our main aim was, in an exceedingly short space of time, to explain what messages for parenting have emerged from Attachment Theory, how these messages are supported by research, how sound the research findings are and how they can inform policy and practice.

On the surface, this may sound a straightforward task. In truth, it requires a grasp of a now massive volume of research and opinion. This body of information emanates from an enormously wide range of theoretical disciplines (developmental, biological, social and cognitive psychology, neurology, psychiatry, sociology, ethology, anthropology, philosophy, and more) as well as from more practical arenas (e.g. social work, therapy, criminal justice, education, nursing, medicine). It is also, as much as it ever was, literature pertaining to a theory that is in many ways still highly controversial.

Distinguishing features of Bowlby's approach

Theories of attachment are, in essence, theories about the basis of human relationships, about what makes us want to be close to others, why some of us find it more difficult than others to feel comfortable in close relationships and how our experiences in close relationships impact on social relationships more generally. As explained early in this book, not all theories of attachment have linked the nature of attachment formation in early life with later development. This notion was perhaps the most controversial aspect of the theory that John Bowlby put forward, on the basis of observations made by his close colleagues, his trainees, his students and other workers in the fields of ethology (studying animals), cognitive psychology (studying how we make sense of our experiences), medicine, anthropology and biology. Bowlby's theory of attachment, and of the nature and importance of the relationship between infants and their caregivers, distinguished him from those in his own profession, psychoanalysis, who fiercely argued that real life experiences were relatively unimportant in comparison with inner realities or 'fantasies'. It also departed from the then prominent behaviourist approach among 'mainstream' psychologists who distrusted any assertion that could not be supported with hard, preferably experimentally derived, evidence. Many still do, of course.

The Bowlby/Ainsworth theory of attachment

Even though Bowlby's Attachment Theory was not the first, nor is it even now the only, theory of attachment, it has now become so influential that it is often referred to as though no other theories exist. It is also spoken of as though it is one set of ideas 'writ in stone', a myth that we hope this book has gone some way to dispel. Chief among Bowlby's characteristics, pugnacious and forthright though he may sometimes have seemed in the expression of his views, was his respect for individuals, his deep conviction of the importance of checking clinical intuitions against hard evidence and his aversion to ill-founded dogma. Bowlby, despite his rather impatient assertions in the *World Health Organization* monograph: "True, the evidence presented in this book is at many points faulty, many gaps remain unfilled, and critical information is often missing; but it must be remembered that evidence is never complete, that knowledge of truth is always partial, and that to await certainty is to wait eternity (Bowlby, 1953/1965, p.241), wholeheartedly espoused the principle that theories need to be subjected to rigorous tests and was, for this reason, eager to set his theory to the proof. He encouraged research and, in his lifetime, benefited greatly from it, most particularly from the work of his research assistant and colleague, Mary Ainsworth. Possibly, had Mary Ainsworth not developed the Strange Situation procedure, which enabled Bowlby to test out and further develop his early theories, his Attachment Theory may now be consigned to history. As it is, Ainsworth's painstaking observations have formed the 'secure base' from which most later exploration and theorising have developed.[1]

The 'working model' of an Attachment Theory

The legacy that Bowlby left was not therefore, despite what many people seem to think, a fully-worked-out theory that can be used to generate creed-like rules and regulations for parents to follow. Rather it was more like a 'working model' of Attachment Theory, a system of beliefs that was, in Bowlby's lifetime, and still is now, open to modification. This in no way means that it has not generated hypotheses about optimal forms of child-rearing nor that it has not produced conclusions about what children need in order to develop well. It has. It is now, for example, well established that being securely attached at any age and using any measure for assessing attachment has advantages in terms of mental health and social adjustment. There is also some indication that certain ways of looking after young children are far less likely to be associated with secure attachment than others. But these findings are not unchallengeable, nor are they necessarily evidence of cause-effect relationships since most of them are arrived at by observational rather than experimental methods. Their significance can and should be explored further. The findings can and should, as has been happening, be extended to new situations. This was encouraged by Bowlby.

---

[1] Even so, as children get older the ingredients required for a 'secure base' alter. Throughout this book, we have suggested that the time may now be ripe for the 'secure base' provided by the Strange Situation test to be re-visited in the light of more complex relationship networks and extended to provide a picture of the wider context of children's development.

The first part of the book

In the first three chapters of this book, we set out our understanding of the roots of the Bowlby-Ainsworth ethological theory of attachment and described some of the methods that have been developed to observe and assess different patterns of attachment. In Chapter One, we described Bowlby's own background and asked how the fact that he came from so privileged a social circle in which there was no little evidence of sexism might be reflected in the theory of attachment that he developed. Next, we looked at how Bowlby's Attachment Theory evolved, on the basis of his sense that, like in other animals, the close attachments formed between human infants and their caregivers seem likely to have a biological function to promote the continuation of the species. We showed how his perusal of literature on the effects of separation convinced him of the need of young children for consistent, responsive care and of the likelihood that deprivation of this kind of care in their early years would disrupt children's capacity to form meaningful social relationships and to develop a sense of their own agency. This lack of capacity to feel valued in at least one close, consistent relationship, Bowlby postulated, would also explain the development of anti-social behaviour and psychological vulnerability, due to a reciprocal distrust and an associated de-valuing of social relationships on the part of the developing child. Feeling valued, on the other hand, would enable the child to develop a trusting relationship in which they would learn to respect others, understand and manage their own feelings, and be highly motivated to understand, empathise and cooperate with others.

As already suggested, this early form of Attachment Theory was unwelcome, to most of Bowlby's own colleagues in psycho-analytical circles, to both behaviourist and genetically-oriented psychologists, and to certain feminists who saw it as a not-so-subtle plan to subjugate women and to ensure that mothers took full responsibility for absolutely everything to do with how their children turned out. To Bowlby, the strength of this opprobrium came as something of a shock. However, perhaps because his background had taught him to rely strongly on his own judgement but to make sure that that judgement was supported by evidence, rather than backing down at this point, he clung to a sense that, though he may not have all details correct, his theory was worth serious consideration. In the years that came after, up until his death in 1990, he encouraged research designed to test and extend Attachment Theory, in particular the notion of Internal Working Models (the sets of expectations, beliefs and understandings about social interaction that develop as a result of real life experiences). By 1990, Bowlby had modified, clarified and complexified some of his earlier theorising. He had become increasingly aware that Nature rarely 'puts all her eggs in one basket' and that it might, after all, not be quite accurate to conceive of any simple linear causal chains linking early care experiences to later development (such as the earlier hypothesised direct link between early separations and delinquency). Rather, he tended more to the view that there are multiple pathways to healthy, and to unhealthy, development.

Nevertheless, he retained his conviction of the potential importance of attachment relationships for physical and psychological health across the lifespan. He also continued to explore the nature of attachment formation in infancy and the relationship between this and later development. And he continued to believe that a sense of 'felt security' was vital for children's psychological wellbeing and could only come through direct experience of at least one relationship in which the child has experienced sensitive and responsive care.

Even so, by Bowlby's death, his theory was still relatively young and untested. Research on it was rapidly gaining momentum and, in the last years of his life, Bowlby had witnessed the very beginnings of work in adult attachment. What's more, the 'move to the level of representations', celebrated in his eightieth birthday conference, seemed completely in tune with his theories about Internal Working Models, while developmental psychologists were carrying out more and more painstaking observational studies that were very much in line with the kind of work that he recommended.

The second part of the book

In the second part of the book (Chapters Four to Six), we presented some of the many findings from attachment research. In Chapter Four, we described findings in relation to links between patterns of attachment assessed in the Strange Situation and development from early childhood to adulthood. We showed how systematic links have been found between children's social and emotional development and the three organised patterns of attachment. We questioned what the real significance of these associations might be in terms of social and emotional wellbeing.

In Chapter Five, we discussed what parents' contribution might be to the development of different patterns of attachment and scrutinised the research evidence to ascertain, mainly, what the mother's contribution might be (since this has been the focus of most attachment research); however, we also considered the effect of stressful family environments on the development of attachments in children and briefly considered what is known about the role of fathers and other people in the child's immediate environment. In this chapter, too, we considered the question of what is really known about the effects of stress on early brain development.

In Chapter Six, we turned to some of the most controversial aspects of Attachment Theory and considered whether, as those espousing the 'hard' form of Attachment Theory believe (those who we refer to as Attachment Theory Determinists), the early years critically determine future development or whether, as the Attachment Theory Constructivists who take a less deterministic approach would argue, social development is influenced by experiences throughout the lifespan. In this chapter, we considered evidence on several much debated questions, including effects of maternal prenatal stress and depression, postnatal depression, holding and skin-to-skin contact, day care and institutional care on children's capacity to form close attachment relationships. In doing this, we touched on the question of how and whether 'Attachment Parenting' really can be seen to be informed by the Bowlby-Ainsworth theory of attachment.

The third part of the book

The third part of the book (Chapters Seven to Nine) is more theoretical. In Chapter Seven, we described some of the attempts to use Attachment Theory to improve the quality of care given to children. First, we discussed findings from meta-analyses of interventions informed by Attachment Theory and questioned whether there really is evidence for the effectiveness of this kind of approach. We concluded that there might be but that more evaluation is needed, particularly using randomised controlled trials in which attachment theory informed approaches are compared with alternatives such as cognitive behaviour therapy or non-talk approaches such as body massage, reflexology or sacro-cranial osteopathy. We then went on to outline some of the ways in which Attachment Theory has been incorporated into parenting programmes (e.g. the Circle of Security programme) and into therapeutic work, particularly video-based work and family therapy. In this chapter, we also showed how some developments, such as 'Attachment Therapy', appear not only to be misnamed but to have seriously departed from the basic principle held by Bowlby of the need to respect the patient.

In Chapter Eight, we attempted to evaluate Attachment Theory, first, by devoting time to a consideration of the concept of behaviour systems and asking whether this conceptualisation really adds anything to our understanding of social and emotional development, then by considering the extent to which Attachment Theory can be seen to meet the well-established criteria used to determine the value of psychological theories. Throughout the book, we tried to assess what contribution Attachment Theory has made to an understanding of parent-child relationships. We also tried to tease out ways in which understandings of Attachment Theory may have departed from the principles that Bowlby put forward. In the next section of this chapter, we summarise some of our conclusions in relation to these questions.

Attachment Theory post-Bowlby

Many developments have taken place in the field of attachment research since or immediately around the time of Bowlby's death, including:
- the development of attachment measures beyond infancy
- the identification of 'disorganised' attachment
- disagreements over classification of infant attachment
- results of long-term follow-up studies
- larger-scale studies incorporating attachment measures
- meta-analyses of attachment studies
- 'new' data from Romanian (and other) orphans
- attachment mythology and 'the new brain science'
- video-based observational research
- video-based attachment-oriented therapy
- attachment-oriented family therapy
- the emergence of 'attachment therapy' and 'attachment parenting'

Bearing in mind that Bowlby was astute and perspicacious with respect to evidence and that the main reason for his ostensible ostracism from the psychoanalytic community during his lifetime was his determination to move beyond speculative approaches or anything resembling cultism, we consider the likelihood of Bowlby's approving of each of these more recent developments.

The development of attachment measures beyond infancy

As already mentioned, Bowlby clearly welcomed the attempt to extend assessment of attachment beyond infancy. He repeatedly expressed his belief in the importance of attachment relationships throughout the lifespan and stressed that our need to turn to other trusted people when we are confronted by difficult situations is a sign not of immaturity but of a sound and socially necessary mechanism. His concern to explore the nature of the relationship between the attachment behaviour system and mental health and his interest in finding out what might promote greater attachment security at all ages suggest that Bowlby would have welcomed all the research that has led to the plethora of adult self-report instruments and the Adult Attachment Interview, as well as assessments geared for younger children.

However, currently, it is not clear how all these instruments relate to each other. The fact that they all seem to produce, almost to the point of tedium, the well-known conclusion that securely attached individuals have all sorts of advantages over insecurely attached individuals suggests but by no means proves that they are all measuring the same construct. There remains the possibility that they are simply sorting larger and larger populations of people into three or four crude categories, much as one might sort any population into huge boxes – lesbian/gay, straight, bisexual, asexual; left-handed, right-handed, ambidextrous, disabled; black-skinned, brown-skinned, pink-skinned; red, blue, green, etc. The question of why these variations might occur and what their significance is for personal and social organisation, development and wellbeing still needs to be better understood. Whether Bowlby would have been comfortable with the new attachment language that is so replete with pejoratives also seems highly debatable. For there is a distinct tendency towards the vilification of the non-secure which too few researchers are resisting (e.g. Crittenden 2000, Fraley and Brumbaugh 2005) and which in the current 'attachment mythology' seems to be growing at a rather alarming pace.

Throughout this book, we have presented evidence that secure attachments are associated with advantages but have questioned what the significance of this association might be and have stressed the need to bear in mind that associations are not evidence of cause-effect relationships. Right-handed children find life easier in a society set up for the majority of right-handers. Left-handers have been in the past (and possibly still are to some extent, in some places) called 'clumsy', 'sinister', 'not right'. They have been punished for using their dominant hands and have been found to have more problems with reading and writing than right-handers. It would be easy to conclude that people with right hemisphere dominance for handedness are inferior. But it would be both prejudiced and unfair to do this, and it would lead to greater, not less, disadvantage.

The same argument can apply to any minority group. Non-secure individuals are not in a majority. Many are clearly less easy to be around than self-confident, outgoing 'secures' who make others feel as valued as they feel themselves. But diversity makes good evolutionary sense and the assumption that non-secure patterns are maladaptive and in need of correction seems a premature and possibly ill-advised conclusion (one that brings only too readily to mind the attempts of psychiatrists to correct homosexuality). Some patterns of non-secure attachment may be very closely associated with interpersonal difficulties and with histories of frightening experiences, but it seems equally plausible that less proximal forms of interaction, perhaps under-written by different neurological pre-dispositions in a minority of individuals, may need to be retained in a species that, even in our global 'Nike-ified' culture, needs to be maximally adaptive.

Perhaps we do need some people to be more focused on things and abstract concepts than on people. Or, perhaps we need avoidant people with 'eyes in the sides of their heads', looking behind and around, much as we need the more front-focused secures? The fact that they don't look straight at us may not mean that they think we are rubbish! Some might, but more rigorous research is needed to be sure of this, research that avoids circular arguments or pre-judgement. Many adult attachment measures are top-heavy with theory and premised on assumptions about the inferiority of insecure patterns. It seems unsurprising that, having defined insecure patterns by their presumed association with relatively superficial negative attributes, more negative attributes are found in association with them. This kind of circularity of argument seems unlikely to advance understanding. This point seems important with regard both to interventions for parents and children, and for work with individuals. The assumption of the moral superiority of security, like the assumption of the moral value of being financially comfortable, may be questionable. Clearly, there are advantages, but perhaps, as Crittenden (2000, p.10) points out, "To understand anxious attachment, I think we must both understand a child's situation and feel for him or her… in spite of all our existing attachment research, we do not yet fully understand the meaning of the patterns, the full range of meaningfully different subpatterns, or the full implications of the interactions of history, maturation, context, and person that produce the patterns."

So much data has now been amassed that points to the likelihood that individual differences in patterns of attachment are a real phenomenon. But it still seems important to question whether we really know what the significance is of these differences in terms of mental health and well-being. It seems that we may be in danger of using Attachment Theory to inform some kind of social policing policy, in which the advantage to 'secures' is increased at the same time as the disadvantages to 'non-secures' are increased. This seems to risk turning Attachment Theory into exactly the kind of dogma that Bowlby so passionately fought against. The research certainly does seem to indicate that attachment security has benefits in terms of access to desirable social skills. Maternal sensitivity explains only a small part of this outcome. Maternal mind-mindedness (the tendency to think and talk in terms of feelings and internal states) possibly explains a little more. Stressful family contexts seem, in a substantial proportion of children, to be linked to insecure attachments. But exactly what kind of processes might underlie these outcomes is not yet fully understood.

We need more research, conducted within the same spirit of inquiry that characterised Bowlby's approach, and we need, meantime, to tread carefully if we are, as Bowlby recommended, to respect individuals and the sense that they make of their lives. There are many things that are still unknown about the nature of 'Internal Working Models' of attachment relationships: whether we all hold in mind the possibility of different modes of social interaction and keep a stock of mental maps of the full range of attachment patterns permanently at our disposal or whether, as popular accounts of attachment often suggest, but as longitudinal research tends to contradict, we are much simpler beings, wedded to one almost immutable pattern by the age of two. More research is needed to examine these two very different possibilities, as well as the range of potential alternatives in between.

The identification of 'disorganised' attachment

The realisation that the original attachment classification system proposed by Mary Ainsworth resulted in a substantial proportion of unclassifiable cases and the further realisation that, even when over 200 of these unclassifiable cases from different studies were examined, no consistent pattern emerged among them gave rise to the notion that, alongside the classifiable organised patterns, there exists a group of infants who, for some reason, cannot organise consistent strategies in interaction with their caregivers. There has been a lot of debate about what this disorganisation might signify and what seems to have filtered into the attachment mythology is a widespread belief that attachment disorganisation is indicative of abusive or severely dysfunctional caregiving. This is not always the case.

In the largest study to date that has assessed attachment security among a representative sample of over one thousand 15-month-olds in the US,[2] almost 15 per cent of infants were classified as disorganised. Whether it is safe to conclude that all of these infants were at risk for maltreatment is questionable. A safer conclusion seems to be that there is a need for further investigation into the significance of attachment disorganisation. In this connection, studies of adult attachment representations using the Adult Attachment Interview (AAI) suggest that there may be an equivalent adult state of mind in respect of attachment and that this is linked for some people to experiences of unresolved loss or trauma, a finding that would have been of clear interest to Bowlby. That these parental experiences of lack of resolution might translate into disrupted infant-parent attachment seems logical and the implications for intervention seem clear: enable resolution of the parent's state of mind in respect of their loss or trauma (closure) so that they become able to interact with their babies free of the 'ghosts from the past' (Fraiberg et al. 1975). As yet, this promising line of investigation is still in its infancy. No precise instrument capable of assessing degrees or qualities of lack of resolution has yet been devised and no formal operational definition of lack of resolution has been arrived at. The development of such a tool, it seems, must now be possible and is likely to be as valuable in work with new mothers as in work with parents more generally.

More work is also needed to specify exactly what relationship might obtain between mothers' state of mind, infant attachment and other family dynamics. Another tale told in the attachment mythology is that there is strong evidence of intergenerational transmission of attachment patterns. Interestingly, this is often the evidence used by 'hard' attachment theorists (those who believe that pregnancy and the first two years are critical for attachment formation and all that happens later in life). We have argued that much of this evidence appears to hinge on findings of concordance between a mother's way of talking about her own childhood experiences, assessed either before giving birth or at the same time as assessing her way of interacting with the baby in the Strange Situation procedure, and the infant attachment classification (the mistaken assumption often being that this classification is not about the mother, which it obviously is). That high levels of concordance should be found in two different ways of assessing the mother's attachment style (attachment-related behaviour or ways of talking about attachment) might be reassuring to the devisers of the measures: it does, after all, suggest that the construct of attachment is being captured by both methods.

However, the notion that intergenerational transmission of attachment patterns is in evidence seems almost unquestionably to be an extrapolation beyond the data. Whether it would ever be possible to prove that transmission had definitely occurred using observational approaches of this sort seems doubtful. To reach such a conclusion, it would be necessary to separate out the contribution of the mother from the contribution of the infant as well as to demonstrate continuity of attachment patterns over individuals' lifespans. All that it seems possible to conclude from this kind of study is that the way mothers talk about their own childhood when they are pregnant appears to predict, to a substantial degree, the nature of their relationship with their babies.

This, of course, is not unimportant. In fact, it seems to indicate that the AAI may be a potent diagnostic tool. However, it is very labour-intensive and the prohibitive cost of training as well as the inaccessibility of training for most UK-based practitioners today might mitigate

---

2 A six-year longitudinal study carried out by the National Institute of Child Health and Development Early Child Care Research Network (see references to NICHD ECCRN).

against its widespread adoption. Also, more work is needed before we can be confident that it can be used as a guide for interventions.

Both these considerations may point to the value of developing a diagnostic instrument that is capable of monitoring lack of resolution more precisely. Whether this could be done satisfactorily before further steps are taken to reach agreement about how to measure attachment across the lifespan seems, at present, difficult to tell.

Disagreements over classification of infant attachment

While Bowlby was still alive, he and Mary Ainsworth were both aware of the possibility that the ways in which patterns of attachment were identified and classified would change as larger samples and different cultures were studied. Because the forced classification method that Mary Ainsworth and her colleagues had developed could not classify all infants even in the small samples already studied and because some workers had already suggested new patterns (e.g. infants with depressed mothers often seemed to fit equally well, or not well, into both avoidant and ambivalent categories; Radke-Yarrow et al. 1985), it seemed very likely that, eventually, more than the original three patterns would emerge. According to Patricia Crittenden (Crittenden 2000), this has begun to happen but, according to Mary Main, it has not happened in the way that Crittenden asserts.

This disagreement over whether particular patterns are evidence of disorganisation or of limited, restricted but adaptive responses to challenging and aversive caregiving contexts has led to the development of two systems of classification in infancy. In some respects it seems inevitable and valuable that different researchers will reach different conclusions. However, it would be a shame if the measurement problems that pervade the adult attachment literature were, because of these disagreements, to emerge in another form within the infancy research literature. If the two separate classificatory systems are not overtly comparable in the published literature, it seems almost inevitable that the value and quality of infancy research may be seriously compromised. Already, the expense of training, the need for special facilities and labour-intensive methodology lends an air of mystery to the Strange Situation. Given the overwhelming amount of attachment literature, some may be relieved at some sort of constraints, but nevertheless, there may also be a danger that this cabal-like shroud of mystery may eventually lead to loss of information unless some agreement is reached over how results using the different systems are to be compared.

Having said this, it also seems possible that the rift may be symptomatic of a bigger problem that we have already touched on earlier in this chapter, namely, it may reflect the possibility that the Strange Situation test and its classificatory system are now outliving their usefulness as a secure base for early 'Attachment Theory' research and that, being outgrown, the time may now be ripe for replacement, with measures that take are capable of cognising more than mother-infant, or dyadic-only relationships, and that can comprehend patterns of attachment relationships across the lifespan. The processes involved in developing such measures are likely to be complex and problematic. Meantime, question about the status of different classificatory systems remain unresolved.

Results of long-term follow-up studies

Controversy has also raged over whether or not there is evidence for stability of attachment over the lifespan. Fraley's recent meta-analysis, which included four studies, has suggested a lower rate of stability than previous research had indicated, with correlations between attachment classifications in infancy and those in adulthood (at ages from 17-19 to 21) ranging from 0.10 to .50 (Fraley 2002). Whether and how this lower level of stability relates to lawful discontinuities[3] (Ainsworth 1982, Kobak 1999, Sroufe et al. 1999), to changes that would be expected due to major life events (which could be expected to be high in families where there is a high level of disruption), or whether measurement problems play too large a part for comfort in these outcomes, is currently unclear. Also unclear is the question of whether stability is really due to attachment or to other concurrent personality variables that may contribute and be constant across the lifespan (Fraley and Brumbaugh 2004, Fraley and Roberts, 2005).

What does seem to be indicated is that there may be less support for what Guldberg (2004) and Kagan (1998) refer to as the 'myth of infant determinism' than some people have thought. This represents a serious challenge to those Determinists who espouse the 'hard' or 'strong' form of Attachment Theory which stipulates the existence of an early critical period during which patterns of attachment are set for life. Even more specifically, it brings into grave doubt the notion that the area of the brain responsible for social development, or the 'social brain' as it is called in the attachment mythology, becomes permanently wired within the first two or three years of life (a view that, as discussed in Chapter Six, has been queried by a number of neuropsychologists).

Larger-scale studies incorporating attachment measures

As already mentioned, the NICHD ECCRN study of day care is the largest-scale reported study to have incorporated assessments of attachment. This study involved 1,300 children followed up at five separate times from the age of six through to 54 months; 1,153 of these infants were filmed in the Strange Situation with their mothers at 15 months and a measure of maternal sensitivity was also obtained from two sources of observations. Unlike previous studies, analyses of data obtained from this study permitted control of ten potentially confounding variables (e.g. mother's education, family structure, family income, mother's beliefs about child-rearing) and generated sufficiently large numbers of non-secure infants for meaningful analyses to be carried out on the relationship between attachment status and outcomes such as problem behaviour. This kind of large-scale investigation enabled important questions about the importance of daily separations for very young babies to be addressed and, though more studies are still needed, particularly in view of the geographical and social differences in the nature of child care provision, appeared to confirm Bowlby's view of the fundamental importance of responsive care for infants' development, particularly where quality of day care is poor. There was also some indication that, for a small but substantial proportion of children who spend more than 30 hours a week in day care (17 per cent), day care might be more closely associated with more than the average amount of 'acting out' behaviour (aggressiveness, non-compliance, assertiveness) in comparison with children who did not spend much time in day care. Since in the 'norming' sample (the standardised sample of children on which the norms for acting-out behaviours are based), 17 per cent of children were also found to have behaviour problems and no main effects of day care were found on patterns of attachment, it seems fair to say that this study did not provide convincing evidence that day care is bad for children. Having said that, there is

---

3 'lawful discontinuities' refers to the notion that, since the Attachment Behaviour System is designed to be adaptive to the particular social context, where major life events take place that reduce the availability of key Attachment Figures, the predominant pattern of attachment may change, e.g. from secure to insecure, or vice versa.

still some concern about the small number of children who do not cope well with day care and a need to develop better ways of monitoring children in day care to ensure that they are not being put at unnecessary risk.

Both large and small sample studies have also been carried out using self-report measures of adult attachment in a rapidly increasing number of social contexts and social groups. In terms of extending knowledge about attachment and family relationships, this literature has begun to throw more light on the nature of couple relationships, in straight and gay couples, as well as on the nature of relationships between adult children and their aging parents, and between adult siblings. They have extended upwards to grandparent-grandparent relationships and carer-elderly person relationships, as well as sideways into more and more workplace, hospital and institutional settings, and into more and more social groups.

While this rapid extension of the compass of attachment research has in many ways been exhilarating, it has in other ways been rather bewildering. Measurement problems continue to dominate the adult attachment literature and, although it is now more than a decade since a series of articles appeared in the *Psychological Inquiry* debating the nature of the Attachment Behaviour System in infancy and in adulthood (Hazan and Shaver 1994), and since then there has been a steady trickle of articles addressing related questions, no very satisfactory resolution of these very real conceptual difficulties appears to have been reached. Instead, the subject seems to have become somewhat submerged under the ever-growing masses of research papers that report on findings relating to ever-widening social contexts.

Therefore a central question remains: what construct are all these measures really tapping and how do findings reached using each separate measure relate to other findings? This question applies as much to the AAI and to the Strange Situation procedure as to any other attachment measure. Until this fundamental puzzle is solved, some of the most emotive debates, such as those pertaining to the significance of early relationships for later development, seem unlikely to be satisfactorily resolved.

Meta-analyses of attachment studies

In this book, we reported on and summarised the results of a number of meta-analyses, on effects of mother's attachment status on that of the child, on the relationship between maternal sensitivity and infant attachment status, and on interventions aimed at increasing the likelihood of attachment security. These meta-analyses have been extremely useful in pulling together and making sense of some of the contradictory findings from a growing number of studies. However, as discussed earlier in this book, meta-analyses are not without problems, principle among which is the fact that they are often based on published studies which tend to over-represent significant findings (since researchers who fail to find support for their hypotheses are less likely to publish their results). Meta-analyses relating to maternal sensitivity also tend to pool information from studies that have small and idiosyncratic samples or have not used the same methods to assess the quality of mothers' responses to their infants.

Despite these problems, these meta-analyses can give a more or less fair indication of general patterns that appear to be emerging from attachment research. They tend to underscore the fact that effects are rarely large but that, in the larger picture of parent-child interactions, there are small but important effects of particular types of maternal care on infant attachment. These effects do appear to be along the lines first identified by Mary Ainsworth but, clearly, her concept of sensitive responsiveness does not explain that much of what goes into the creation of secure attachments. This points to the need for continued efforts to develop

'New' data from Romanian (and other) orphans

Our review of the research on Romanian orphans centred around the questions of whether these studies add anything to the conclusions drawn by Bowlby after his review of numerous similar studies which resulted in the 1951 World Health Organization report, and whether, as some claim, there is evidence that severe early deprivation results in a "virtual black hole" (Gerhardt 2004, p.38) where the brain ought to be.

We came to the conclusion that even the most carefully conducted studies of Romanian orphans could be criticised on similar grounds to those on which Bowlby had been criticised (e.g. Rutter 1972/1979/1981) with regard to his conclusions from his review of institutional care (Bowlby 1951, 1953/1965, 1969/1982). While it is undeniable that severe deprivation in early life is disadvantageous, it is still not clear exactly which aspects contribute to or which processes underlie later outcomes. Nor is it safe to assume that children raised in very poor institutions have responses comparable with non-human animals brought up in social isolation, particularly in view of the fact that possibly one of the most frightening aspects of early institutional life may be being exposed, from a very young age, to unpredictable, intrusive or aggressive approaches from other children and/or staff (though there is no way at present of knowing this for certain).

Having examined the evidence for 'virtual black holes', we came to the view that this may be a misinterpretation of what little scientific data there is and that far more work is needed before any sound conclusions can be reached, with larger and less idiosyncratic samples of children about whose history and development a lot more is known. To base such strong assertions on ten children is, in our view, misguided. Though no-one can deny that appalling conditions of rearing are associated with problems for most children, there is as yet no good reason for believing that brain development is permanently compromised in most children. Again, more research is needed in this area if we are to understand more deeply the full range of individual variations in development. The assumption that anyone with an early history of severe deprivation must be permanently, or even temporarily, brain-damaged by their experiences is not one that is likely to inform a respectful approach to the care of such individuals.

Attachment mythology and 'the new brain science'

It seems unquestionable that investigations into the neurological underpinnings of attachment relationships would have been of immense interest to Bowlby. However, whether he would have been as quick as some have been to jump to the conclusion that these investigations have already proved that there are critical periods for the development of social abilities seems highly debateable. Bowlby was very wary of insisting on the existence of critical periods in the absence of evidence. Nearly all the assertions that he made on this matter were qualified by considerations of inconclusive or contradictory findings. Though he eventually came to the conclusion that attachment formation in humans differed from imprinting and from other processes observed in other species because it appeared to start later than birth and to form very gradually during the first year of life, he was open to the possibility that alternative accounts may eventually emerge.

The point here is that Bowlby's speculative assertions were just that. They were not, in general, claims to authority beyond the data given. This means that he is unlikely to have reached simplistic or premature interpretations of neuroscientific or other scientific evidence. Where he had conjectures about the patterns that seemed to be emerging, he checked these against the data. This more humble approach that respects the experts as well as the data does not appear to characterise major proponents of 'attachment mythology'.

Currently, within psychotherapy circles, it seems to be fashionable to proclaim a passion for neuroscience and particularly for Allan Schore's account of this. Suddenly, people with no prior training in neurology or psychobiology appear to have become self-identified experts on the development of limbic circuits, stress hormone response systems, and the neural circuitry underpinning social development. Strangely, they seem to have acquired understandings far in advance of neurologists thought to be at the cutting edge in this field (e.g. Professor Mark Johnson in the Baby Lab at Birkbeck, University of London). In Chapters Five and Six of this book, we discussed some of these accounts of neurological development and raised doubts about specific aspects, such as the potential over-emphasis upon visual experience. It would require another book with contributions from greater authorities than ourselves to do full justice to this debate. Meantime, it is exciting that researchers are continuing to explore the neurological underpinnings of social development. It also exciting that they are continuing to advance understandings of highly complex stress response mechanisms and to investigate the relationship between the development of emotional self-regulation, coping and patterns of attachment, both in parents and in children, at all points throughout the lifespan. This kind of meticulous research promises to increase understanding of the highly complex relationship between temperament and attachment. But there is *very much* more to be discovered yet.

The notion that both organised insecure attachment patterns involve different kinds of dysregulation of stress hormone response systems is appealingly simple and appears to account for some of the evidence: the avoidant pattern, with associated suppressed anger and hostility, reflects an under-reactive and over-controlled stress hormone response system, the ambivalent/resistant pattern, with anxious feelings always close to the surface, reflects an over-reactive and under-controlled stress response mechanism. One is overly self-reliant, the other overly dependent on others, and all because automatic, unconscious stress response mechanisms have got out of kilter at an early age, perhaps even before birth. Plausible and testable as much of this theory is, so far, there have not been enough tests and nor have there been tests of sufficient rigour or substance to warrant unquestioning acceptance that patterns of insecure attachment are underwritten by dysregulated stress response mechanisms. They may be, but it seems important to hold in mind the possibility that other equally, or perhaps more, plausible alternative explanations might be found.

Further research is needed to explore how experiences in close relationships, the social context of those relationships, social cognitive processes (thoughts, attitudes, attribution biases etc.) and physiological responses all contribute to produce particular patterns of social interaction. Unfortunately (or perhaps fortunately), it is rarely possible to explain human social behaviour in terms of simple response chains. For this reason, all the diagrams of the HPA (hypothalamic-pituitary-adrenomedullary) system on the world-wide web are unlikely to supply anywhere near enough information to satisfactorily explain the differences between insecure and secure attachment patterns. The notion, popular in attachment mythology, that insecure attachments are more closely associated with higher quantities of cortisol circulating, out of control, in the body seems not only reductive and simplistic but, more importantly in terms of implications for therapy, to legitimise a deficit model of non-secure patterns of attachment. Distinct advances have been made by researchers in this field but more work is needed before links between physical processes, coping mechanisms and attachment patterns will be fully understood. Until this work is done, it is safer though less comfortable to live in uncertainty than to assume that solutions are already at hand.

Our examination of the literature on brain development and its relation to social development led us to conclude that the relevant research has not yet been done that can supply evidence of a critical period for the development of social understanding. It also led us to the conclusion that the notion of critical periods, so prevalent throughout Schore's work (e.g. Schore 1994, 1996, 1997) was, as Bowlby and many others had suggested a long time ago, unlikely to be the most accurate description of human attachment formation. While the initial social-orienting responses usually seen very early in infancy may possibly be experience-expectant, the emergence of these responses seems more likely to occur during a sensitive than a critical period. Most other aspects of social development are likely to be experience-dependent and so are unlikely to be subject to timing constraints. However many clever brain-scanning techniques have now become available, no researchers have yet been in a position to investigate these matters in non-clinical populations. Therefore, despite claims about what the 'new brain science' has shown, very little, in truth, is actually really known about the neurological underpinnings of social development. Speculations about critical periods of development may have a valuable place in theory-building, but it is important to recognise that, until the relevant research has been done, such speculations should not be broadcast as though they were fact. They simply are not.

Our repeated plea for more research must be becoming rather repetitive but, even at the risk of appearing over-cautious, we feel that these matters are far too important to treat lightly. As Ainsworth (1982, p.27) pointed out, "Attachment research focuses on some of the most complex and thorny (and significant) of all the riddles that we face in trying to understand human nature and development. Patience and persistence on the part of many investigators is required before we can incisively sort through the complexities of human attachments, bonds, and other aspects of relationships."

Admittedly, that statement was made nearly a quarter of a century ago but many of the conceptual questions raised in that paper have still not been resolved and many of the areas identified as in need of further research (effects of relationships beyond the mother-child dyad, the role of lifelong friends, the role of fathers, etc.) have only just begun to come into focus under the lens of attachment research.

Video-based observational research

Bowlby was keenly aware of the benefit to attachment research of observational research on mother-infant interactions (e.g. Trevarthen 1979, Murray and Trevarthen 1985, Stern 1985). Since his death, this work has continued and has been extended, very much as Ainsworth and he might have wished, to investigations of triadic interactions (e.g. Fivaz-Depeursinge 2005, Fivaz-Depeursinge et al. 1996).

This work has really only just begun to get under way, but is already indicating that assumptions about the need of infants for consistent, one-to-one attention in order to make sense of their social world may overlook the capacity of very young infants to take in a wider perspective. Even by eight weeks, it seems, babies begin to use information from three-way social exchanges. As more research of this kind is carried out, perhaps the role of fathers, so often missed out in the attachment literature and in child development more generally, will at long last come more into focus.

That fathers do have an important role in children's development has, almost serendipitously, emerged from the longitudinal studies carried out in Germany (Grossmann et al. 2002). Whether this role is more related to play and exploration than to attachment is not yet clear. Rather, what seems to be indicated is that research instruments need to be refined so that they are capable of assessing the role of the father as well as that of the mother with regard to attachment. Paying attention to observations of triadic interactions is an excellent start but also, as researchers working towards a greater understanding of fathers emphasise, it is necessary to recognise that fathers are not 'shadow-mothers', their contribution is usually qualitatively different and, in natural settings, more difficult to capture by direct observation.

This really seems to bring us back to the 'Internal Working Models' problem. How do we know what kind of internal representation an infant has of a Dad who is out at work most of the day? We do not have an answer to this question but feel it is important to stress that there are these gaps in understanding. The difficulty of accessing 'Internal Working Models' has been a problem for attachment research. Even though the problem has, to some degree, been addressed in respect of adult attachment, difficulties remain and need to be acknowledged. Failing to acknowledge the difficulties leads to simplistic assumptions about the nature of attachment representations across the lifespan, for example, the common assumption that individuals categorised as avoidant, ambivalent, secure or disorganised at age one will inevitably go through life with this one pattern of attachment. This is an area where, we hope, attachment research will in the future extend its scope.

Video-based attachment-oriented therapy approaches

In Bowlby's lifetime, it was already beginning to be realised that videotaped mother-child interactions could be used therapeutically. This fits in well with the notion that the capacity for self-other reflection, reflective functioning in Fonagy's terminology (Fonagy et al. 1998) or 'maternal mind-mindedness' in Meins' account (Meins 1997, Meins et al. 2001), is associated with attachment security. Videotaped material is now often included as an element in parenting programmes, for example, in the Circle of Security programme (Marvin et al. 2002) and in the Sunderland Infant Programme (Svanberg 2005) as well as in individual therapy (e.g. Cohen and Beebe 2002, Beebe 2003). Further evaluation of interventions using this kind of approach is needed before it will be known which parents are most likely to benefit from these techniques (Bakermans-Kranenburg et al. 1998). It seems possible that both qualitative and quantitative information will valuable and that alternative approaches may be needed to complement intervention programmes for parents who may be intimidated by requests to be video-ed.

Attachment-oriented family therapy

Some work in the adult attachment field, particularly that pertaining to couple relationships, has indicated the importance of extending the model of dyadic relationships which has tended (perhaps necessarily in a young field of investigation where assessment and measurement techniques are still in their infancy) to dominate attachment research. For example, research has suggested that the least stable and most volatile couples may be those made up of men who self-classify as ambivalent and women who self-classify as avoidant. In these couples, the woman does not want to be close, the man does: she needs more distance, he needs more proximity. With parents like this, the chances of a peaceful life for the children seem slim. The chances that children will be securely attached to either parent also seem small, but relatively little research has examined whole families. While there is suggestive information from a small number of studies, there is a need, in this area too, for more research.

Although Bowlby (Bowlby 1949a) expressed an interest in the potential value of family therapy, his preoccupation with infancy research left him little time to devote attention to the development of this approach, leaving other colleagues to explore this area (e.g. Byng-Hall 1990, 1995a, 1999, Byng-Hall and Stevenson-Hinde 1991). The emergence of attachment-oriented family therapy has begun to demonstrate the value of an attachment perspective in understanding the co-construction of 'family scripts'. It has also shown that, although attachment relationships are a central element, successful family therapy requires attention to many other aspects of parenting as well (the family's social context, parents' ability to engage with children as caregivers, playmates, advisors, etc., and to relate to each other as parents, friends and sexual partners). This raises the question of whether therapists who attempt to alter only attachment behaviour are likely to approach their patients in a way that is less than well informed by attachment theory and that may not be sufficiently mindful of the patient as a unique individual located within a complex social network (Byng-Hall 2005).

As described in Chapter Seven, Bowlby (1988b) emphasised the need to follow the patient's lead, to respect his or her account and to join in an exploration of its origin. He also recognised the therapist's contribution to this therapeutic journey and considered that the main focus of discussion should be on the significance of current relationships and on the emotional import of communications. This approach seems very different from some of the practices of 'attachment therapists'.

The emergence of 'Attachment Therapy' and 'Attachment Parenting'

Visitors to the world-wide web who are interested in the topic of attachment are very likely to come across many websites that offer information about Attachment Theory, 'Attachment Therapy' and 'Attachment Parenting'. The availability of this material, the rapidity with which new websites appear and the quality and extent of information on offer are an important testament to the tremendous influence of Attachment Theory. However, it may be difficult, not to say impossible, for visitors who are not trained in principles of social scientific inquiry or who are naive to Attachment Theory to discriminate between attachment myths, sound information and inaccuracies, etc. This points to a need for informed guidance if pitfalls which can be perilous are to be avoided.

In Chapter Seven, we highlighted the very serious concerns that are held by many therapists and researchers in the field of attachment with regard to 'Attachment Therapy'. As indicated earlier, therapists identifying as 'Attachment Therapists', despite their claims, are often not well informed about the essential messages of Attachment Theory and have been found to adopt approaches that, in some cases, put children's safety at risk.[4] Adoptive parents having difficulty relating to the children in their care appear to be especially vulnerable to such practitioners, not least because of differences of opinion on how to diagnose and treat attachment disorders. This is an issue that is being addressed to some extent but one that may need to be treated as a matter of greater urgency if risks to children and parents are to be minimised.

---

4   e.g. the death of Candace Newmaker, described more fully in Chapter Seven.

First, there appears to be a need for diagnostic criteria to be re-considered, for screening instruments to reflect the new criteria and for misleading check-lists to be formally identified and removed from clinical practice. Second, there is a need to explore the extent to which non-conventional practices are employed in clinical settings, and a need to gain a better understanding of the role of contact and holding where children have difficulties relating to adults. Third, there may well be a need for tighter controls over practices such as re-birthing, boot camp strategies such as 'strong sitting', rage reduction therapy and the use of physical restraint in therapeutic settings. Fourth, there may similarly be a need to consider how therapeutic approaches need to be adapted to take account of patients with histories of sexual abuse (Trowell 2004). Fifth, there is a need for guidance for parents seeking help with management of troubled or troubling children.

Turning to 'Attachment Parenting', various forms of this have emerged, some more influenced than others by what we have termed' hard' (more fundamentalist or Determinist) forms of Attachment Theory. A central concept within the 'Attachment Parenting' movement, asserted often with an urgency reminiscent of Bowlby's 'maternal care is as important for psychological health as vitamins are for physical health' claim, is the notion that physical contact and holding are essential for the wellbeing of babies and young children. As discussed in Chapter Six, research seems somewhat equivocal on this matter. In general, few reliable relationships between quantities of holding and security of attachment have been found, apart from the tendency for insecure avoidant attachment to be associated with less frequent touching (Ainsworth 1982). Having said this, and at the risk of boring readers to death, no extensive or thorough study of the relationship between quality and quantity of physical contact and outcomes for children has yet been conducted. We reviewed, briefly, some of the available research and concluded that it is not currently clear whether lack of physical contact, in itself, is likely to disrupt parent-child relationships or to compromise children's development.

Therefore, while we have far fewer concerns about 'Attachment Parenting' than about 'Attachment Therapy', it still seems worth pointing out that advice on websites headed with this title is generally not very highly informed by Attachment Theory and is likely to be far more prescriptive than evidence from attachment research could support. This leads us directly to the question of what Attachment Theory does, in the end, really offer by way of advice or guidance to parents and people working with parents. More specifically, in light of the evidence that we have presented throughout this book, we will now re-visit the interview excerpt presented at the outset:

Bowlby: About 60 per cent of mothers do a very good job, so the majority of women have a good model to follow, and there's an awful lot to be said for that.
Interviewer: So are you saying that 40 per cent of mothers don't do a good job?
Bowlby: I am.
Interviewer: (pause) What does that mean?
Bowlby: Well. It means a lot of mental ill-health and disturbance and delinquency and ... what have you.
Out of the Doll's House, BBC TV, October 9th 1988

Does this really mean that, according to Attachment Theory, two of every five parents or, more specifically, mothers are liable to produce children who are psychologically damaged and/or out of control? If this is the case and at least 40 per cent of the population is off the rails in this way, what hope is there of society ever rectifying this situation? Come to that, if this 40 per cent of terrible mothers are also the most promiscuous, perhaps more than 40 per cent of the population of children has been affected. Also, did Bowlby really mean to imply that all these mothers doing a bad job as parents are directly to blame for their children's, and society's, problems?

It seems relatively safe to deduce that, when he made this comment, Bowlby had in mind the 35-40 per cent of mothers that studies were showing did not have secure relationships with their children. Only subsequently has research begun to indicate that the relationship between insecure attachment as assessed in infancy and later psychopathology is far more complex than Bowlby may have realised.

First, as mentioned earlier in this chapter, attachment stability from infancy to adulthood does not appear to be as high as was previously thought. Bowlby was aware that there was some instability and, indeed, never anticipated or theorised that patterns of attachment would invariably stay the same across the life course. He was not a fundamentalist in this respect.

Second, since this time, with its slightly more refined infant classificatory system but its rather less tidy adult classificatory systems, evidence has emerged that, though non-secure attachment patterns may be a vulnerability factor, they are not inevitably associated with psychopathology. In addition, though there is some indication that people classified as 'earned secure' may be slightly more vulnerable to depression than others classified as secure, the actual experience of depression is likely to be linked to social contextual factors as much as to relationship history.

Third, research has not provided substantial support for the notion that insecure patterns of infant-mother attachment are directly attributable to mothers' behaviour (as opposed to infant or environmental attributes). This assumption seems to be based on an exclusively empiricist model of development as opposed to the interactionist models that seem to have won more support in recent years and that Bowlby himself may perhaps, under less stressful circumstances, have entertained.

Having championed Bowlby as an astute scientist, this interview, then, rather shows that his interpretation of research findings did occasionally run ahead of the data. By way of some explanation though, it might be that the television programme setting did not permit him to represent his view in quite as balanced a way as he may have chosen. Elsewhere he did emphasise that responsibility for insecure attachments could not be attributed wholly to mothers (Bowlby 1988b) and stated that to focus on the mother alone would only give a part of the whole picture.

Messages from Attachment Theory for parents and work with parents

We have now reached the point where we attempt to summarise some of the key messages that seem to emanate from Attachment Theory for parents and for work with parents. Before making this attempt, though, it seems important to re-state that Attachment Theory:
- is not 'set in stone'
- contains many hypotheses that are still under investigation
- has evolved and continues to evolve
- is therefore still open to debate and differing interpretations

- needs to develop more powerful instruments to capture the construct of attachment security across the lifespan
- is only just beginning to develop tools for examining more complex than dyadic relationships
- may need to be re-conceptualised as these instruments develop and more discoveries are made
- needs to develop instruments that can reflect in more detail and with more accuracy the evolution of 'internal working models' across the lifespan
- needs to be tested much more before its neurological underpinnings can be said to be known or understood

With these points in mind, we will now try to draw together our conclusions about how Attachment Theory can contribute to an understanding of parenting and of relationships between parents and children.

First, as stated at the beginning of this chapter, the central message seems to us to be that experiences in relationships will influence expectations about and perceptions of subsequent relationships. This does not mean that every single act a parent does will result in long-term effects on children's development. Rather, there is a lot of variability in development, since parenting and being parented is always carried out in circumstances over which no individual has complete control.

Nevertheless the research has indicated that reliable patterns of attachment are discernible, for example:

– distributions of patterns of attachment
- the majority of attachment relationships between mothers and babies can be classified into four major categories
- in representative, non-clinical samples across a number of cultures, secure attachments have been found in around 60 to 65 per cent of mother-infant dyads

– qualities associated with parents of securely attached children
- these secure attachments are thought to be associated with mothers' ability to pick up on their babies' emotional states
- they are also thought to be associated with mothers' ability to reflect on and communicate their own emotional states to others
- parents who are able to talk about their own childhoods in a coherent, reflective, rounded way (taking account of more than one perspective) are more likely to have securely attached children
- less is known about the role of fathers as attachment figures, possibly because appropriate observational tools have not yet been developed to capture the more distal attachment relationships between fathers and children
- the nature of the relationship between fathers and children, particularly as reflected in play, does appear to have measurable effects on long term outcomes
- the quality of parents' relationships with each other is likely to influence the nature of their relationship with their children, although more research is needed in this area

– qualities associated with children who are securely attached
- children who are securely attached appear to learn to regulate their emotional states better than non-securely attached children, and to 'read' other people's emotional states more accurately

- this may account for their superior social skills, their popularity with peers, their willingness to engage in social interactions, their greater enjoyment of social interactions and their perseverance in repairing disruptions in interactions

– *stability and significance of attachment status*
- there is still considerable debate about the extent to which patterns of attachment in infancy remain the same into adulthood
- major life events and major changes in relationships can alter how individuals think about or behave in attachment relationships, at any point in life (therefore, secure attachment in infancy is not a life policy)
- although there are obvious benefits associated with secure attachment, it is not clear that all these benefits are quality-of-attachment-driven as opposed to being consequent upon a socially constructed bias towards particular relationship styles

– *qualities associated with non-secure attachments*
- non-secure attachments have been associated with less optimal parenting practices
- avoidantly attached infants have mothers who are predictably less accepting of close contact, discourage dependency even in very young babies and can be intrusive, hostile or cold when they do attend to their children
- ambivalently attached infants have mothers who are unpredictable and inconsistent in their responses to infants' cues, sometimes they are ignored, at other times they are given unsolicited attention
- a variety of non-contingent or aversive behaviours have been associated with mothers of infants who fail to organise attachment behaviour when under stress
- there is considerable debate about how patterns of disorganised attachment or non-attachment can be understood or ameliorated

This selection of findings is intended to be illustrative or indicative rather than comprehensive. It shows that Attachment Theory offers an account of several different types of parent-child relationship and indicates that parents who have securely attached children may differ from parents of children with non-secure patterns in being better able to help their children to make sense of their experiences. It also suggests that security of attachment, by virtue of children's superior self-control and understanding of themselves and others, is more likely to be associated with sound mental health and unlikely to be associated with anti-social behaviour. A logical conclusion from this is that society would be much better off if all children were securely attached. The next logical step, then, obviously seems to be to identify the recipe for attachment security and to try to ensure that all or as many parents as possible are equipped to enable their children to form secure attachments.

While this seems a reasonable enough aim, we have questioned whether it will, ultimately, constitute the most adaptive solution. Specifically, we, like Crittenden (2000), make a plea for greater tolerance of diversity and for more efforts to be made towards understanding minority group attachment patterns. It would be a pity if a theory conceived so ambitiously with the aim of improving chances of psychological health and so potentially empowering of parents and children turned out only to make disadvantaged parents feel even more alienated.

Bibliography: John Bowlby

Bowlby, J. (1938) The abnormally aggressive child. *The New Era in Home and School*, **19**, 230-234.
Bowlby, J. (1939a) Jealous and spiteful children. *Home and School*, **4(5)**, 83-85.
Bowlby, J. (1939b) Substitute homes. *Mother and Child*, **10(1)**, 3-7.
Bowlby, J. (1939c) Hysteria in children. In R.G. Gordon (Ed.), *A survey of child psychiatry* (80-94). London: Oxford University Press.
Bowlby, J. (1940a) The influence of the early environment in the development of neurosis and neurotic character. *International Journal of Psychoanalysis*, **21**, 154-178.
Bowlby, J. (1940b) *Personality and mental illness. An essay in psychiatric diagnosis*. London: Kegan Paul, Trench, Trubner and Co..
Bowlby, J. (1940c) The problem of the young child. *New Era*, **21**, 59-63.
Bowlby, J. (1940d) The problem of the young child. *Children in War-time*, **21(3)**, 19-30.
Bowlby, J. (1940e) Psychological aspects. In R. Padley and M. Cole (Eds.), *Evacuation survey: A report to the Fabian Society* (186-196). London: Routledge.
Bowlby, J. (1944) Forty-four juvenile thieves: their characters and home life. *International Journal of Psychoanalysis*, **25**, 19-52; 107-127.
Bowlby, J. (1945/6) Childhood origins of recidivism. *The Howard Journal*, **7(1)**, 30-33.
Bowlby, J. (1946a) The future role of the child guidance clinic in education and other services. *Report of the Proceedings of a Conference on Mental Health* (80-89. London: National Association for Mental Health.
Bowlby, J. (1946b) Psychology and democracy. *The Political Quarterly*, **7(1)**, 61-76
Bowlby, J. (1947a) The therapeutic approach in sociology. *The Sociological Review*, **39**, 39-49.
Bowlby, J. (1947b) The study of human relations in the child guidance clinic. *Journal of Social Issues*, **3(2)**, 35-41.
Bowlby, J. (1948) Seven to fourteen (four broadcasts). *The Parents Review*, **59**, 403-406, 432-36, 456-463.
Bowlby, J. (1949a) The study and reduction of group tensions in the family. *Human Relations*, **2**, 123-128. [reprinted in 1972]
Bowlby, J. (1949b) The relation between the therapeutic approach and the legal approach to juvenile delinquency. *The Magistrate*, **8**, 260-264.
Bowlby, J. (1949c) Research into the origins of delinquent behaviour. Report of the conference *Why delinquency? The case for operational research,* on the scientific study of juvenile delinquency held at the Royal Institution, London, October 1, 1949. London: National Association for Mental Health.
Bowlby, J. (1949d) Psychology and democracy. In R.C. Snyder and H.H. Wilson (Eds.), *Roots of political behavior: Introduction to government and politics*. New York: American Book Co..
Bowlby. J. (1950a) Parents influence for good or bad. *Mother and Child*, **21(5)**, 135-136.
Bowlby, J. (1950b) Research into the origins of delinquent behaviour. *British Medical Journal*, **1**, 570-579.
Bowlby, J. (1951) *Maternal care and mental health*. World Health Organisation, Monograph Series, No. 2, reprinted in abridged version as *Child care and the growth of love*, 1953.
Bowlby, J. (1952) The childhood roots of loyalty. Contribution to symposium on the development of social responsibility within the family. *Social Work*, **9**, 632-627.
Bowlby, J. (1953/1965) *Child care and the growth of love*. Harmondsworth: Penguin.
Bowlby, J. (1953b) Some pathological processes set in train by early mother-child separation. *Journal of Mental Science*, **99**, 265-272. [reprinted in 1954a and 1954f]
Bowlby, J. (1953c) The contribution of studies of animal behaviour. In J.M. Tanner (Ed.), *Prospects in Psychiatric Research* (80-108). Oxford: Blackwell Scientific Publications. [Reprinted in 1953i]
Bowlby, J. (1953d) Discussion on the application of recent research to health visiting. *Journal of the Royal Sanitary Institute*, **73**, 596-598.
Bowlby, J. (1953e) Be frank with your child ... about DEATH. *Childhood*, **8**, 28-29.
Bowlby, J. (1953f) *The roots of parenthood. Convocation lecture of National Children's Home*. Reprinted in Convocation Lectures, vol. 2, Portway, 1966.
Bowlby, J. (1953g) Special problems: Problem families, neglectful parents, the broken home, illegitimacy. In *The family: Report of the British national conference on social work* (21-29). London: National Council of Social Service.
Bowlby, J. (1953h) The commonsense of motherhood. *Childhood*, **8**, 34-36.

Bowlby, J. (1953i) Critical phases in the development of social responses in man and other animals. In M.L. Johnson and M. Abercrombie (Eds.), *New Biology*, **14**, 25-32. Harmondsworth: Penguin.
Bowlby, J. (1954a) Some pathological processes set in train by early mother-child separation. In M.J.E. Senn (Ed.), *Problems of infancy and childhood* (38-90). New York: Josiah Macy Jr. Foundation.
Bowlby, J. (1954b) Children who are ill. *Family Doctor,* October. [Reprinted in *Child-Family Digest,* **12(1)**, 8-11]
Bowlby, J. (1954c) The diagnosis and treatment of psychological disorders in childhood. *The Health Education Journal,* **12(2)**, 59-68. [Reprinted in *Child-Family Digest,* **11(2)**, 13-23]
Bowlby, J. (1954d) Should a baby be left to cry? *Child-Family Digest,* **10(6)**, 37-40.
Bowlby, J. (1954e) Theoretical problems. *Child-Family Digest,* **11(3)**, 94-102.
Bowlby, J. (1954f) Some pathological processes set in train by early mother-child separation. *Child-Family Digest,* **11(1)**, 12-27.
Bowlby, J. (1955a) Introduction to papers presented at the 11th interclinic conference for the staffs of child guidance clinics, March 26. In *Family approach to child guidance: therapeutic techniques* (5-10). London: National Association for Mental Health.
Bowlby, J. (1955b) Mental health and animal behaviour. *Mental hygiene* (1), Copenhagen.
Bowlby, J. (1955c) A note on the selection of love-objects in man. *British Journal of Animal Behaviour*, **3**, 122-123.
Bowlby, J. (1956a) Mother-child separation. In K. Soddy (Ed.), *Mental health and infant development, Volume 1: Papers and discussions* (117-122). London: Routledge and Kegan Paul.
Bowlby, J. (1956b) The growth of independence in the young child. *Royal Society of Health Journal*, **76**, 587-591.
Bowlby, J. (1956c) Learning to be clean and dry. *Parents*, **11**, 6.
Bowlby, J. (1956d) Little savages. *Parents*, **October,** 40-42. [reprinted in *Child-Family Digest*, **16(1)**, 89-92]
Bowlby, J. (1956e) Practical advice on new baby jealousy. *Child-Family Digest*, **14**, 25-28.
Bowlby, J. (1956f) Psychoanalytic instinct theory. In J. M. Tanner and B. Inhelder (Eds.), *Discussions on Child Development, Volume 1: A consideration of the biological, psychological, and cultural approaches to the understanding of human development and behaviour* (182-187). London: Tavistock.
Bowlby, J. (1957a) Symposium on the contribution of current theories to an understanding of child development. I. An ethological approach to research in child development. *British Journal of Medical Psychology*, **30(4)**, 230-240. [Reprinted in 1979c]
Bowlby, J. (1957b) Does he wake at night? *Child-Family Digest*, **16(3)**, 6-8.
Bowlby, J. (1958a) The nature of the child's tie to his mother. *International Journal of Psychoanalysis*, **39(5),** 350-373.
Bowlby, J. (1958b) *Can I Leave My Baby*? London: National Association for Mental Health (now called MIND).
Bowlby, J. (1958c) Psychoanalysis and child care. In J. D. Sutherland (Ed.), *Psychoanalysis and contemporary thought* (33-57). London: Hogarth Press. [Reprinted in 1979c]
Bowlby, J. (1958d) Letter (1 March 1958). *Lancet*, **1**, 480.
Bowlby, J. (1958e) A note on mother-child separation as a mental health hazard. *British Journal of Medical Psychology*, **31**, 247-248.
Bowlby, J. (1958f) Foreword. In P. Marris, *Widows and their families* (ix-x). London: Routledge and Kegan Paul.
Bowlby, J. (1958g) Preface. In J. Balls, *Where love is: The fostering of young children*. London: Gollancz.
Bowlby, J. (1959a) The roots of human personality. In P. Halmos and A. Iliffe (Eds.), *Readings in general psychology* (108-129). London: Routledge and Kegan Paul.
Bowlby, J. (1959b) A psychoanalyst learns from animals. *Child-Family Digest*, **18(3)**, 3-10.
Bowlby, J. (1960a) Grief and mourning in infancy and early childhood. *The Psychoanalytical Study of the Child*, **15**, 9-52. [reprinted in 1965a]
Bowlby, J. (1960b) Separation anxiety. *International Journal of Psycho-Analysis*, **41(2/3)**, 89-113.
Bowlby, J. (1960c) Symposium on the contribution of current theories to an understanding of child development. II. Ethology and the development of object relations. *International Journal of Psycho-Analysis*, **41(4/5)**, 312-317.
Bowlby, J. (1960d) Comment on Piaget's paper: 'The general problems of the psychobiological development of the child. In J. M. Tanner and B. Inhelder (Eds.), *Discussions on child development, Volume 4* (35-47). London: Tavistock.
Bowlby, J. (1961a) Processes of mourning. *International Journal of Psycho-Analysis*, **42**, 317-340.
Bowlby, J. (1961b) Separation anxiety: A critical review of the literature. *Journal of Child Psychology and Psychiatry*, **1**, 251-269.
Bowlby, J. (1961c) Childhood mourning and its implications for psychiatry. The Adolf Meyer lecture. *American Journal of Psychiatry*, **118(6)**, 481-497. [Reprinted in 1979c]
Bowlby, J. (1961d) Comment on J. L. Gewirtz, A learning analysis of the effects of normal stimulation and deprivation on the acquisition of social motivation and attachment. In B. M. Foss (Ed.), *Determinants of infant behaviour, Volume I* (301-303). London: Methuen.
Bowlby, J. (1961e) Note on Dr. Max Schur's comments on grief and mourning in infancy and early childhood. *The Psychoanalytic Study of the Child*, **16**, 206-208.
Bowlby, J. (1961f) Foreword. In B.M. Foss (Ed.), *Determinants of infant behaviour, Volume I* (xiii-xv). London: Methuen.
Bowlby, J. (1961g) Theories of psychological development in children. In R. MacKeith and J. Sandler (Eds.), *Psychosomatic aspects of paediatrics* (54-70). London: Pergamon Press.
Bowlby, J. (1962a) *Defences that follow loss: causation and function*. Unpublished manuscript, Tavistock Child Development Unit, London.
Bowlby, J. (1962b) *Loss, detachment and defence*. Unpublished manuscript, Tavistock Child Development Unit, London.

Bowlby, J. (1963) Pathological mourning and childhood mourning. *Journal of the American Psychoanalytic Association*, **11(3),** 500-541.
Bowlby, J. (1964a) Note on Dr. Lois Murphy's paper 'Some aspects of the first relationship'. *International Journal of Psychoanalysis*, **45(1)**, 44-46.
Bowlby, J. (1964b) *Security and anxiety: Old ideas in a new light*. Proceedings of the 15th Annual Conference of the Association of Children's Officers.
Bowlby, J. (1965a) Grief and mourning in infancy and early childhood. In G.E. Daniels (Ed.), *New perspectives in psychoanalysis: Sandor Rado lectures, 1957-1963* (124-169). New York: Grune and Stratton.
Bowlby, J. (1965b) Darwin's health (letter). *British Medical Journal, April 10,* 999.
Bowlby, J. (1965c) Participant in discussion. In B. M. Foss (Ed.), *Determinants of infant behaviour, Volume III*. London: Methuen.
Bowlby, J. (1966a) Foreword. In C. M. Heinicke and I. J. Westheimer, *Brief separations* (ix-xi). London: Longmans Green, and New York: International Universities Press.
Bowlby, J. (1966b) Security and anxiety. *The Listener*, **17**, 383-385. [CMAC: PP/BPW/F.5/3]
Bowlby, J. (1967) Childhood mourning and psychiatric illness. In P. Lomas (Ed.), *The predicament of the family: A psycho-analytical symposium*. London: Hogarth Press and the Institute of Psychoanalysis.
Bowlby, J. (1968a) Effects on behaviour of disruption of an affectional bond. In J. M. Thoday and A-S. Parkes (Eds.), *Genetic and environmental influences on behaviour* (94-108). Edinburgh: Oliver and Boyd. [Reprinted in 1979c]
Bowlby, J. (1968b) Security and anxiety (talk). In BBC series, *The formative years*. London: BBC Publications 7404.
Bowlby, J. (1969a) Affectional bonds: their nature and origin. In H. Freeman (Ed.), *Progress in mental health* (319-327). London: Churchill.
Bowlby, J. (1969b) Disruption of affectional bonds and its effects on behavior. *Canada's Mental Health Supplement*, **59,** 12.
Bowlby, J. (1969c) Psychopathology of anxiety: the role of affectional bonds. *British Journal of Psychiatry*, **3**, 80-86.
Bowlby, J. (1969d) Foreword. In B. M. Foss (Ed.), *Determinants of infant behaviour, Volume IV* (xiii-xiv). London: Methuen.
Bowlby, J. (1969/1982) *Attachment and Loss, Vol. 1: Attachment*. London: Hogarth Press and the Institute of Psycho-Analysis.
Bowlby, J. (1970a) Disruption of affectional bonds and its effects on behavior. *Journal of Contemporary Psychiatry*, **2(2)**, 75-86. [reprinted in *Child and Family*, **9**, 43-53]
Bowlby, J. (1970b) Reasonable fear and natural fear. *International Journal of Psychiatry*, **9**, 79-88.
Bowlby, J. (1972) The study and reduction of group tensions in the family. In G. D. Erickson and T. P. Hogan (Eds.), *Family therapy: An introduction to theory and technique* (16-23). Monterey, CA: Brooks-Cole Publishing. [reprint of 1949 paper]
Bowlby, J. (1973a) *Attachment and loss, Vol. 2: Separation: Anxiety and anger*. London: Hogarth Press.
Bowlby, J. (1973b) Self-reliance and some conditions that promote it. In R. Gosling (Ed.), *Support, innovation and autonomy* (23-48). London: Tavistock. [Reprinted in 1979c]
Bowlby, J. (1973c) *The family for good or ill*. Report on a seminar given in the Department of Psychological Medicine, University of Otago Medical School, New Zealand.
Bowlby, J. (1973d) Affectional bonds: Their nature and origin. In R. S. Weiss (Ed.), *Loneliness: The experience of emotional and social isolation* (38-52). Cambridge, MA: MIT Press.
Bowlby, J. (1974) Problems of marrying research with clinical and social needs. In K. J. Connolly and J. S. Bruner (Eds.), *The growth of competence* (303-307). New York: Academic Press.
Bowlby, J. (1975a) Attachment theory, separation anxiety and mourning. In D. A. Hamburg and K. H. Brodie (Eds.), *Handbook of Psychiatry, Volume 6, New Psychiatric Frontiers* (292-309). New York and London: Plenum Press, second edition.
Bowlby, J. (1975b) Discussion of paper by R. J.Stoller on healthy parental influences in the earliest development of masculinity in baby boys. *Psychoanalytic forum*.
Bowlby, J. (1976) Human personality development in an ethological light. In G. Serban and A. Kling (Eds.), *Animal models in human psychobiology*. New York and London: Plenum Press.
Bowlby, J. (1977a) The making and breaking of affectional bonds: I. Aetiology and psychopathology in the light of attachment theory. An expanded version of the Fiftieth Maudsley Lecture, delivered before the Royal College of Psychiatrists, 19 November 1976 *British Journal of Psychiatry*, **130**, 201-210. [Reprinted in 1979c]
Bowlby, J. (1977b) The making and breaking of affectional bonds: II. Some principles of psychotherapy. The fiftieth Maudsley Lecture. *British Journal of Psychiatry*, **130**, 421-431. [Reprinted in 1979c]
Bowlby, J. (1978) Attachment theory and its therapeutic implications. In S. C. Feinstein and P. L. Giovacchini (Eds.), *Adolescent psychiatry: Developmental and clinical studies, volume VI* (5-33). Chicago: University of Chicago Press.
Bowlby, J. (1979a) On knowing what you are not supposed to know and feeling what you are not supposed to feel. *Canadian Journal of Psychiatry*, **24(5)**, 403-408.
Bowlby, J. (1979b) Psychoanalysis as art and science. *International Review of Psychoanalysis*, **6(3)**, 3-14.
Bowlby, J. (1979c) *The making and breaking of affectional bonds*. London: Tavistock.
Bowlby, J. (1979d) Continuing commentary on article by D. W. Rajecki, M. E. Lamb and P. Obmascher, 'Toward a general theory of infantile attachment: a comparative review of aspects of the social bond. *Behavioral and Brain Sciences*, **2**, 637-638.

Bowlby, J. (1979e) Note sur le contexte historique de la theorie de l'attachement. In R. Zazzo (Ed.), *Le colloque sur l'attachement* (55-57). Paris: Delachaux et Niestle.

Bowlby, J. (1979f) Seconde intervention. In R. Zazzo (Ed.), *Le colloque sur l'attachement* (127-139). Paris: Delachaux et Niestle.

Bowlby, J. (1979g) Troisieme intervention. In R. Zazzo (Ed.), *Le colloque sur l'attachement* (206-209). Paris: Delachaux et Niestle.

Bowlby, J. (1980a) *Attachment and loss, Vol. 3: Loss: Sadness and depression*. London: Hogarth Press and New York: Basic Books; also Harmondsworth: Penguin in 1981.

Bowlby, J. (1980b) By ethology out of psycho-analysis: An experiment in interbreeding. The Niko Tinbergen lecture. *Animal Behavior*, **28(3)**, 649-656.

Bowlby, J. (1980c) How will mummy breathe and who will feed her. *New Society*, **51**, 492-494.

Bowlby, J. (1980d) A symposium on parent-infant attachment in a changing culture: Introductory comments (editorial). In E. J. Anthony, C. Koupernik and C. Chiland (Eds.), *Yearbook of the international association for child and adolescent psychiatrists and allied professions, Volume 6* (23-26).

Bowlby, J. (1981a) Psychoanalysis as a natural science. *International Review of Psycho-Analysis*, **8**, 243-256. [reprinted in *Psychoanalytic Psychology*, **1**, 7-27, and as Freud Inaugural lecture, University College, London, and in *New Universities Quarterly*, **35**, 483-504]

Bowlby, J. (1981b) Perspective: a contribution by John Bowlby. *Bulletin of the Royal College of Psychiatrists*, **5(1)**, 2-4.

Bowlby, J. (1981c) Contribution to symposium, Emanuel Peterfreund on information and systems theory. *The Psychoanalytic Review*, 68, 187-190.

Bowlby, J. (1981d) The rediscovery of the family. In *Sister Marie Hilda Memorial Lectures, 1954-1973, Rediscovery of the family and other lectures* (1-7). Aberdeen: Aberdeen University Press.

Bowlby, J. (1981e) Jean Piaget: Some reminiscences. *Tavistock Gazette*, **5**, 17-21.

Bowlby, J. (1982a) Attachment and loss: Retrospect and prospect. *American Journal of Orthopsychiatry*, **52**, 664-678. [reprinted in 1983, *Annual Progress in Child Psychiatry and Child Development*, 29-47]

Bowlby, J. (1982b) A case of mistaken identity. *The New Universities Quarterly*, **36**, 328-332.

Bowlby, J. (1982c) Epilogue. In C. M. Parkes and J. Stevenson-Hinde (Eds.), *The place of attachment in human behaviour* (310-313). London: Tavistock, and New York: Basic Books.

Bowlby, J. (1984a) Caring for the young: Influences on development. In R.S. Cohen, B.J. Cohler and S.H. Weissman (Eds.), *Parenthood: A psychodynamic perspective* (269-284). New York: Guilford Press.

Bowlby, J. (1984b) Violence in the family as a disorder of the attachment and caregiving systems. *American Journal of Psychoanalysis*, **44**, 9-27. [reprinted in 1988a]

Bowlby, J. (1984c) Discussion of paper 'Aspects of transference in group analysis' by Mario Marrone. *Group Analysis*, **17**, 191-194.

Bowlby, J. (1984d) Psychoanalysis as a natural science. *Psychoanalytic Psychology*, **1(1)**, 7-21. [reprinted in 1989c]

Bowlby, J. (1984e) Darwin and developmental psychology (meeting). *Bulletin of British Psychological Society*, **37**, A6.

Bowlby, J. (1985a) The role of childhood experience in cognitive disturbance. In M.J. Mahoney and A. Freeman (Eds.), *Cognition and Psychotherapy* (181-200). New York: Plenum Press.

Bowlby, J. (1985b) Tributes to Noel Hunnybun. *Tavistock Gazette*, 27-28.

Bowlby, J. (1986a) Interview. In J. Munnichs and B. Miesen (Eds.), *Attachment, life-span and old age*. Deventer: Van Loghum Slaterus.

Bowlby, J. (1986b) Processi difensivi alla luce della teoria dell'attaccamento. *Psicoterapia e Scienze Umane*, **20**, 3-19.

Bowlby, J. (1987a) Defensive processes in the light of attachment theory. In D. P. Schwartz, J. L. Sacksteder and Y. Akabane (Eds.), *Attachment and the therapeutic process*, (63-79). New York: International Universities Press.

Bowlby, J. (1987b) Attachment phobias. In R.L.Gregory (Ed.), *The Oxford companion to the mind* (57-58). Oxford: Oxford University Press.

Bowlby, J. (1988a) Developmental psychiatry comes of age. *American Journal of Psychiatry*, **145**, 1-10.

Bowlby, J. (1988b) *A secure base: Clinical applications of attachment theory*. London: Routledge.

Bowlby, J. (1988c) *A secure base: Parent-child attachment and healthy human development*. New York: Basic Books.

Bowlby, J. (1988d) The thinker (letter). *Psychology Today*, **22**, 6.

Bowlby, J. (1988e) Changing theories of childhood since Freud. In E. Timms and N. Segal (Eds.), *Freud in exile: Psychoanalysis and its vicissitudes* (230-240). New Haven and London: Yale University Press.

Bowlby, J. (1988f) Defensive processes in response to stressful separation in early life. In E. J. Anthony and C. Chiland (Eds.), *The child in his family. Perilous development: Child raising and identity formation under stress* (23-30). New York/Chichester: Wiley.

Bowlby, J. (1988g) Interview. For *Out of the Doll's House, October 9 1988*. London: BBC.

Bowlby, J. (1989a) The role of attachment in personality development and psychopathology. In S. I. Greenspan and H. Pollock (Eds.), *The course of life. Vol. 1, Infancy* (229-270). Madison, CN: International Universities Press.

Bowlby, J. (1989b) Foreword. In D. Aberbach, *Surviving trauma: Loss, literature and psychoanalysis*. New Haven: Yale University Press.

Bowlby, J. (1984d) Psychoanalysis as a natural science. In J. Sandler (Ed.), *Dimensions of psychoanalysis* (99-121). London: Karnac.

Bowlby, J. (1990) *Charles Darwin: A new biography*. London: Hutchinson.

Bowlby, J. (1991a) The role of the psychotherapist's personal resources in the therapeutic situation. *Tavistock Gazette,* Autumn.

Bowlby, J. (1991b) Ethological light on psychoanalytical problems. In P. Bateson (Ed.), *Development and integration of behaviour* (301-313). Cambridge, England: Cambridge University Press.

Bowlby, J. (1991c) Post-script. In C. M. Parkes, J. Stevenson-Hinde and P. Marris (Eds.), *Attachment across the life cycle* (293-297). London: Routledge.

With other authors (in chronological order)

Bowlby, J., Miller, E. and Winnicott, D. W. (1939) Evacuation of small children (*letter*). *British Medical Journal*, December **16**, 1202-1203.

Durbin, E. F. and Bowlby, J. (1939) *Personal aggressiveness and war.* London: Routledge and Kegan Paul.

Bowlby, J., et al. (1948) Diagnosis and treatment of psychological disorders in childhood. *Medical Press,* **220**, 1-10.

Caplan, G. and Bowlby, J. (1948) The aims and methods of child guidance. *Health Education Journal,* **6**, 1-8.

Bowlby, J. and Tod, R. (1951) Families under world tensions. *Child Study,* **6-8**, 28-29.

Rosenbluth, D., Bowlby, J. and Roudinesco, J. (1951) Separation from mother as a traumatic experience, some notes on obtaining a relevant history. *Courrier de la Centre International de I'Enfance,* **1**, 3-18.

Bowlby, J. and Mackenzie, M. (1952) Juvenile delinquency and the health visitor. *Woman Health Officer,* April.

David, M., Nicolas, J., Roudinesco, J., Robertson, J. and Bowlby, J. (1952) Responses of young children to separation from their mothers: I Observations of children aged 12 to 17 months recently separated from their families and living in an institution. *Courrier de la Centre International de I'Enfance,* **2(2)**, 66-78.

Robertson, J. and Bowlby, J. (1952) Responses of young children to separation from their mothers. II. Observations of the sequences of responses of children aged 18-24 months during the course of separation. *Courrier de la Centre International de I'Enfance,* **2(3)**, 131-142.

Bowlby, J., Robertson, J. and Rosenbluth, D. (1952) A two-year-old goes to hospital. *The Psycho-analytical Study of the Child,* **7**, 82-94.

Robertson, J. and Bowlby, J. (1953) Some responses of young children to loss of maternal care. *Nursing Care,* **49**, 382-386. [Also published in *Courrier de la Centre International de I'Enfance,* **2(2)**, 131-142]

Ainsworth, M. D. and Bowlby, J. (1954) Research strategy in the study of mother-child separation. *Courrier de la Centre Internationale de l'Enfance,* **4**, 105-113.

Rosenbluth, D. and Bowlby, J. (1955) The social and psychological background of tuberculous children. *British Medical Journal,* **1**, 946-949.

Bowlby, J., Ainsworth, M. D. S., Boston, M. and Rosenbluth, D. (1956) The effects of mother-child separation: A follow-up study. *British Journal of Medical Psychology,* **29(3/4)**, 211-247.

Bowlby, J. and Robertson, J. (1956) A two-year-old goes to hospital. In K. Soddy (Ed.), *Mental health and infant development. Vol I. Papers and discussions* (123-124). London: Routledge and Kegan Paul.

Bowlby, J. and Carstairs, M. (1963) Psychiatric research: New mental million. *British Medical Journal,* **1**, 1342-1343.

Melges, F. T. and Bowlby, J. (1969) Types of hopelessness in psychopathological process. *Archives of General Psychiatry,* **20**, 690-699.

Bowlby, J. and Parkes, C. M. (1970) Separation and loss within the family. In E. I. Anthony and C. Koupernik (Eds), *The child in his family,* Vol. 1 (197-216). New York: Robert E. Krieger Publishing Company [reprinted in Bowlby 1979c and in the *International Yearbook of Child Psychiatry and Alhed Professions,* **1**, 197-216]

Klagsbrun, M. and Bowlby, J. (1976) Responses to separation from parents: A clinical test for young children. *British Journal of Projective Psychology and Personality Study,* **21**, 7-21.

Warme, G. E., Bowlby, J., Crowcroft, A. and Rae-Grant, Q. (1980) Current issues in child psychiatry: A dialogue with John Bowlby. *Canadian Journal of Psychiatry,* **25**, 367-376.

Bowlby, J., Figlio, K. and Young, R. M. (1986) An interview with John Bowlby on the origins and reception of his work. *Free Associations,* **6**, 36-64.

Bowlby, J., Fortuin, J. and Weeda, I. (1987) *Gehechtheid in relaties.* Deventer: Van Loghum Slaterus.

References

A.A.R.P. (American Association for Retired Persons) (2001) The A.A.R.P. grandparenting survey: The sharing and caring between mature grandparents and their children. Available on the web at http://research.aarp.org/general/grandpsurv.html

American Psychiatric Association (APA)(1987) *The diagnostic and statistical manual of psychiatric diagnoses (3rd edition, revised)*. Washington, DC: Author.

American Psychiatric Association (APA)(1994) *The diagnostic and statistical manual of psychiatric diagnoses (4th edition)*. Washington, DC: Author.

Abrams, K.Y. (2000) *Pathways to disorganization: A study concerning varying types of parental frightened and frightening behaviors as related to infant disorganized attachment*. Doctoral dissertation, Berkeley, University of California.

Ackerman, B. P., Kogos, J., Youngstrom, E., Schoff, K. and Izard, C. (1999) Family instability and the problem behaviors of children from economically disadvantaged families. *Developmental Psychology,* **35,** 258-268.

Ainsworth, M. D. and Bowlby, J. (1954) Research strategy in the study of mother-child separation. *Courrier de la Centre Internationale de l'Enfance,* **4**, 105-113.

Ainsworth, M. D. S. (1963) The development of infant-mother interaction among the Ganda. In B. M. Foss (Ed.), *Determinants of infant behaviour, Volume II* (67-112). London: Methuen.

Ainsworth, M. D. S. (1967) *Infancy in Uganda. Infant care and the growth of love.* Baltimore, MD: Johns Hopkins University Press.

Ainsworth, M. D. S. (1969) Object relations, dependency and attachment: a theoretical review of the infant-mother relationship. *Child Development,* **40,** 969-1025.

Ainsworth, M. D. S. (1982) Attachment: Retrospect and prospect. In C. M. Parkes and J. Stevenson-Hinde (Eds.), *The place of attachment in human behavior* (3-30). New York: Basic Books.

Ainsworth, M. D. S. and Bowlby, J. (1953) *Research strategy in the study of mother-child separation.* Paris: Courrier de la Centre International de l'Enfance.

Ainsworth, M. D. S. and Bowlby, J. (1991) An ethological approach to personality development. *American Psychologist,* **46(4),** 333-341.

Ainsworth, M. D. S. and Marvin, R. S. (1995) On the shaping of attachment theory and research: An interview with Mary Ainsworth (Fall 1994). In E. Waters, B.E. Vaughn, G. Posada and K. Kondo-Ikemura (Eds.), *Caregiving, cultural, and cognitive perspectives on secure-base behavior and working models: New growing points of attachment theory and research* (3-21). Monographs of the Society for Research in Child Development, **Serial No. 244, Vol. 60(2-3)**.

Ainsworth, M. D. S. and Wittig, B (1969) Attachment and exploratory behaviour of one-year-olds in a strange situation. In B. Foss (Ed.), *Determinants of infant behaviour,* Volume IV (113-136). London: Methuen.

Ainsworth, M. D. S., Bell, S. and Stayton, D. (1971) Individual differences in Strange Situation behavior of one-year-olds. In H. R. Schaffer (Ed.), *The origins of human social relations* (17-52). New York: Academic Press.

Ainsworth, M. D. S., Blehar, M. C., Waters, E. and Wall, S. (1978) *Patterns of attachment: A psychological study of the Strange Situation.* Hillsdale, NJ: Erlbaum.

Aitken, K. J. and Trevarthen, C. (1997) Self/other organization in human psychological development. *Developmental Psychopathology,* **9(4),** 653-677.

Akister, J. and Reibstein, J. (2004) Links between attachment theory and systemic practice: some proposals. *Journal of Family Therapy,* **26,** 2-16.

Allen, J. P. and Land, D. L. (1999) Attachment in adolescence. In J. Cassidy and P. R. Shaver (Eds.), *Handbook of attachment: Theory, research and clinical applications* (319-335). New York: Guilford Press.

Allen, J. P., Aber, J. L. and Leadbeater, B. J. (1990) Adolescent problem behaviors: The influence of attachment and autonomy. *Adolescence: Psychopathology, Normality, and Creativity,* **13(3),** 455-467.

Allen, J. P., McElhaney, D. B., Land, D. J., Kuperminc, G., Moore, C. W., O'Beirne-Kelly, H. and Kilmer, S. L. (2003) A secure base in adolescence: Markers of attachment security in the mother-adolescent relationship. *Child Development,* **74(1),** 292-307.

Allen, J. P., Moore, C., Kuperminc, G. and Bell, K. (1998) Attachment and adolescent psychosocial functioning. *Child Development,* **69(5),** 1406-1419.

Allen, J. P., Philliber, S., Herrling, S. and Kuperminc, G. P. (1997) Preventing teen pregnancy and academic failure: Experimental evaluation of a developmentally based approach. *Child Development,* **64(4),** 729-742.

Allen, J. P., Weissberg, R. P. and Hawkins, J. (1989) The relation between values and social competence in early adolescence. *Developmental Psychology,* **25**, 458-464.

Ames, E. W. (1997) *The development of Romanian orphanage children adopted to Canada. Final report to the National Welfare Grants Program: Human Resources Development Canada.* Burnaby, BC: Simon Fraser University.

Ames, E. W. and Carter, M. (1992) Development of Romanian orphanage children adopted into Canada. *Canadian Psychologist,* **33**, 503.

Ames, E. W. and Chisholm, K. (2001) Social and emotional development in children adopted from institutions. In D. B. Bailey, Jr., J.T. Bruer, F. J. Symons and J. W. Lichtman (Eds.) *Critical thinking about critical periods* (129-148). London: Paul H. Brookes.

Anderson, G. C. (1991) Current knowledge about skin-to-skin (kangaroo) care for preterm infants. *Journal of Perinatology,* **11(3)**, 216-228.

Anisfeld, E., Casper, V., Nozyce, M. and Cunningham, N. (1990) Does infant carrying promote attachment? An experimental study of the effects of increased physical contact on the develoment of attachment. *Child Development,* **61**, 1617-1627.

Anthony, E. J. and Cohler, B. J. (Eds.) (1987) *The invulnerable child.* New York: Guilford Press.

Applegate, J. L., Burleson, B. R. and Delia J. G. (1992) Reflection-enhancing parenting as an antecedent to children's social-cognitive and communicative development. In I.E. Sigel, A. V. McGillicuddy-DeLisi and J. J. Goodnow (Eds.), *Parental belief systems: The psychological consequences for children* (3-39). Hillsdale, NJ: Lawrence Erlbaum associates.

Archer, J. (1992) *Ethology and human development.* Hemel Hempstead: Harvester Wheatsheaf.

Areias, M. E., Kumar, R., Barros, H. and Figueiredo, E. (1996) Correlates of postnatal depression in mothers and fathers. *The British Journal of Psychiatry,* 169, 36-41.

Arend, R., Gove, F. L. and Sroufe, L. A. (1979) Continuity of individual adaptation from infancy to kindergarten: a predictive study of ego-resiliency and curiosity in preschoolers. *Child Development,* **50**, 950-959.

Armsden, G. C. and Greenberg, M. T. (1987) The Inventory of Parent and Peer Attachment: Individual differences and their relationship to psychological well-being in adolescence. *Journal of Youth and Adolescence,* **16**, 427-454.

Ashman, S., Dawson, G., Panagiotides, H., Yamada, E. and Wilkinson, C. W. (2002) Stress hormone levels of children of depressed mothers. *Development and Psychopathology,* **14**, 333-349.

Atkinson, L., Niccols, A, Paglia, A., Coolbear, J., Parker, K. C. H., Poulton, L., Guger, S. and Siteraneos, G. (2000) A meta-analysis of time between maternal sensitivity and attachment assessments: Implications for working models in infancy/toddlerhood. *Journal of Social and Personal Relationships,* **17(6)**, 791-810.

Aviezar, O., Sagi, A., Joels, T. and Ziv, Y. (1999) Emotional availability and attachment representations in kibbutz infants and their mothers. *Developmental Psychology,* **35**, 811-821.

Aviezer, O., Van IJzendoorn, M. H., Sagi, A. and Schuengel, C. (1994) "Children of the dream" revisited: 70 years of collective early child-care in Israeli kibbutzim. *Psychological Bulletin,* **116**, 99-116.

Bakermans-Kranenburg, M. J. and van IJzendoorn, M. H. (2004) No association of the dopamine D4 receptor (DRD4) and -521 C/T promoter polymorphisms with infant attachment disorganisation. *Attachment and Human Development,* **6(3)**, 211-218.

Bakermans-Kranenburg, M. J., Juffer, F., van IJzendoorn, M.H. (1998) Interventions with video feedback and attachment discussions: Does type of maternal insecurity make a difference? *Infant Mental Health Journal,* **19(2)**, 202-219.

Bakermans-Kranenburg, M. J., Jr. and van IJzendoorn, M. H. (1993) A psychometric study of the Adult Attachment Interview: Reliability and discriminant validity. *Developmental Psychology,* **29**, 870-880.

Bakermans-Kranenburg, M. J., van IJzendoorn, M.H. and Juffer, F. (2003) Less is more: Meta-analyses of sensitivity and attachment interventions in early childhood. *Psychological Bulletin,* **129(2)**, 195-215.

Ballard, C. G., Davis, R., Cullen, P. C., Mohan, R. N. and Dean, C. (1994) Prevalence of postnatal psychiatric morbidity in mothers and fathers. *British Journal of Psychiatry,* **164**, 782-788.

Bank, S. P. and Kahn, M. D. (1997) *The sibling bond.* New York: Basic Books.

Bar-Haim, Y., Aviezer, O., Berson, Y. and Sagi, A. (2002) Attachment in infancy and personal space regulation in early adolescence. *Attachment and Human Development,* **4(1)**, 68-83.

Barker, P. (1992) *Basic family therapy.* Oxford: Blackwell.

Barkley, R. A. (1998) *Attention-Deficit Hyperactivity Disorder: A handbook for diagnosis and treatment* (2nd ed.). New York: Guilford Press.

Barnard, K.E., Magyary, D., Sumner, G., Booth, C.L., Mitchell, S.K. and Spieker, S. (1988) Prevention of parenting alterations for women with low social support. *Psychiatry,* **51**, 248-253.

Barnes, J. and Freude-Lagevardi, A. (2003) *From pregnancy to early childhood: Early interventions to enhance the mental health of children and adults.* London: The Mental Health Foundation.

Barnett, B., Blignault, I., Holmes, S., Payne, A. and Parker, G. (1987) Quality of attachment in a sample of 1-year-old Australian children. *Journal of the American Academy of Child and Adolescent Psychiatry,* **26**, 303-307.

Barnett, D., Kidwell, S. L. and Leung, K. H. (1998) Parenting and preschooler attachment among low-income urban African American families. *Child Development,* **69**, 1657-1671.

Baron-Cohen, S. (1995) *Mindblindness: An essay on autism and theory of mind.* Boston: MIT Press.

Baron-Cohen, S. (2004) Autism: Research into causes and intervention. *Paediatric Rehabilitation,* **7**, 73-78.

Baron-Cohen, S., Tager-Flusberg, H. and Cohen, D. (1993) *Understanding other minds: Perspectives from autism.* Oxford: Oxford University Press.

Baron-Cohen, S., Wheelwright, S., Lawson, J. Griffin, R. and Hill, J. (2005) The exact mind: Empathising and systemising in autism spectrum conditions. In U. Goswami (Ed.), *Handbook of cognitive development* (491-508). Oxford: Blackwell.

Baron-Cohen. S., Leslie, A. and Frith, U. (1985) Does the autistic child have a 'theory of mind'? *Cognition,* **21**, 37-46.

Barrett, H. (1991) *Childminding experiences and early social development*. Unpublished doctoral thesis: Birkbeck, University of London.
Barrett, H. (1997) How young children cope with separation: Toward a new conceptualization. *British Journal of Medical Psychology,* **70**, 339-358.
Barrett, H. (2003) *Parenting programmes for families at risk: A source book*. London: National Family and Parenting Institute.
Barrett, K. C. and Campos, J. J. (1987) Perspectives on emotional development II: A functionalist approach to emotion. In J. D. Osofsky (Ed.), *Handbook of infant development* (555-578). New York: Wiley.
Bartholomew, K. (1990) Avoidance of intimacy: An attachment perspective. *Journal of Social and Personal Relationships,* **7(2)**, 147-178.
Bartholomew, K. (1991) *Attachment style prototypes*. Unpublished manuscript, University of British Columbia.
Bartholomew, K. and Horowitz, L. M. (1991) Attachment style among young adults: A test of a four category model. *Journal of Personality and Social Psychology,* **61(2)**, 226-244.
Bartlett, F. C. (1932) *Remembering*. Cambridge: Cambridge University Press.
Bates, J. E. (1989) Concepts and measures of temperament. In G.A. Kohnstamm, J.E. Bates and M.K. Rothbart (Eds.), *Temperament in childhood* (1101-1149). Chichester: Wiley.
Bates, J. E. and Bayles, K. (1988) Attachment and the development of behavior problems. In J. Belsky and T. Nezworski (Eds.), *Clinical implications of attachment* (253-299). Hillsdale, NJ: Lawrence Erlbaum Associates.
Bates, J. E., Maslin, C. and Frankel, K. A. (1985) Attachment security, mother-child interaction and temperament as predictors of behavior problem ratings at age three years. In I. Bretherton and E. Waters (Eds.), *Growing points of attachment theory and research, Monograph of the Society for Research in Child Development,* (No. 209), **50**, 167-193.
Bates, J. E., Pettit, G. S., Dodge, K. A. and Ridge, B. (1998) The interaction of temperamental resistance to control and restrictive parenting in the development of externalizing behavior. *Developmental Psychology,* **34**, 982-995.
Bates, J. E., Freeland, C. A. B., Lounsbury, M. L. (1979) Measurement of infant difficultness. *Child Development,* **50(3)**, 794-803.
Bateson, P. (1979) How do sensitive periods arise and what are they for? *Animal Behavior,* **27**, 470-486.
Bateson, P. (1983) Sensitive periods in behavioural development. *Archives of Disease in Childhood,* **58(2)**, 85-86.
Beck A. (1976) *Cognitive therapy and the emotional disorders*. New York: International Universities Press.
Beckwith, L. (1988) Intervention with disadvantaged parents of sick preterm infants. *Psychiatry,* **51**, 242-247.
Beckwith, L., Cohen, S. E. and Hamilton, C. E. (1999) Maternal sensitivity during infancy and subsequent life events relate to attachment representation at early adulthood. *Developmental Psychology,* **35,** 693-700.
Beebe, B. (2003) Brief mother-infant treatment: Psychoanalytically informed video feedback. *Infant Mental Health Journal,* **24(1)**, 24-52.
Beebe, B., Jaffe, J., Lachmann, F., Feldstein, S., Crown, C. and Jasnow, J. (2000) Systems models in development and psychoanalysis: The case of vocal rhythm coordination and attachment. *Infant Mental Health Journal,* **21**, 99-122.
Belsky, J. (1984) Two waves of day care research: Developmental effects and conditions of quality. Chap. 1 in R.C. Ainslie (Ed.) *The child and the day care setting: Qualitative variations and development*. New York: Praeger.
Belsky, J. (1986) Infant daycare: A cause for concern? *Zero to Three,* **6**, 1-7.
Belsky, J. (1987) Risks remain. *Zero to Three,* **7**, 22-24.
Belsky, J. (1988a) Annotation – Infant day care and socioemotional development: the United States. *Journal of Child Psychology and Psychiatry,* **29**, 397-406.
Belsky, J. (1988b) The "effects" of infant day care reconsidered. *Early Childhood Research Quarterly,* **3**, 235-72.
Belsky, J. (1997a) Variation in susceptibility to environmental influence: An evolutionary argument. *Psychological Inquiry,* **8**, 182-186.
Belsky, J. (1997b) Theory testing, effect-size evaluation, and differential susceptibility to rearing influence: The case of mothering and attachment. *Child Development,* **64(4)**, 598-600.
Belsky, J. (1999) Modern evolutionary theory and patterns of attachment. In J. Cassidy and P. R. Shaver (Eds.), *Handbook of attachment: Theory, research, and clinical applications* (141-161) New York: Guilford Press.
Belsky, J. (2001) Developmental risks (still) associated with early child care. *Journal of Child Psychology and Psychiatry,* **42**, 845-859.
Belsky, J. (4 June 2004) Are young children differentially susceptible to childrearing experiences? Keynote address to Fourth Annual Attachment Research Unit and the International Attachment Network Conference. London: University College.
Belsky, J. and Cassidy, J. (1994) Attachment: theory and evidence. In M. Rutter and D. Hay (Eds.), *Development through lives: A handbook for clinicians* (373-402). Oxford: Blackwell Scientific Publications.
Belsky, J. and Fearon, R. M. P. (2002) Infant-mother attachment security, contextual risk, and early development: A moderational analysis. *Development and Psychopathology,* **14**, 293-310.
Belsky, J. and Nezworski, T. (Eds.)(1988) *Clinical implications of attachment*. Hillsdale, NJ: Lawrence Erlbaum Associates.
Belsky, J. and Rovine, M. (1987) Temperament and attachment security in the Strange Situation: An empirical rapprochement. *Child Development,* **58,** 787-795.
Belsky, J. and Rovine, M. J. (1988) Nonmaternal care in the first year of life and the security of infant-parent attachment. *Child Development,* **59**, 157-167.
Belsky, J. and Steinberg, L. D. (1978) The effects of day care: A critical review. *Child Development,* **49**, 929-49.

Belsky, J., Campbell, S. B., Cohn, J. F. and Moore, G. (1996a) Instability of infant-parent attachment security. *Developmental Psychology,* **32,** 921-924.

Belsky, J., Garduque, L. and Hrncir, E. (1984a) Assessing performance, competence, and executive capacity in infant play: Relations to home environment and security of attachment. *Developmental Psychology,* **20,** 406-417.

Belsky, J., Gilstrap, B. and Rovine, M. (1984b) The Pennsylvania infant and family development project, I: Stability and change in mother-infant and father-infant interaction in a family setting at one, three, and nine months. *Child Development,* **55,** 692-705.

Belsky, J., Rosenberg, K. and Crnic, K. (1995a) The origins of attachment security: "Classical" and contextual determinants. In S. Goldberg, R. Muir and J. Kerr (Eds.), *Attachment theory: Social, developmental and clinical perspectives* (153-183). Hillsdale, NJ: Analytic Press.

Belsky, J., Rosenberg, K. and Crnic, K. (1995b) Maternal personality, marital quality, social support and infant temperament: Their significance for infant-mother attachment in human families. In C. Pryce, R. Martin and D. Skuse (Eds.), *Motherhood in human and nonhuman primates* (115-124). Basel: Karger.

Belsky, J., Rovine, M. and Taylor, D.G. (1984c) The Pennsylvania Infant and Family Development Project, III: The origins of individual differences in infant-mother attachment: Maternal and infant contributions. *Child Development,* **55,** 718-728.

Belsky, J., Spritz, B. and Crnic, K. (1996b) Infant attachment security and affective-cognitive information processing at age 3. *Psychological Science,* **7,** 111-114.

Belsky, J., Steinberg, L. and Draper, P. (1991) Childhood experience, interpersonal development and reproductive strategy: An evolutionary theory of socialization. *Child Development,* **62,** 647-670.

Belsky, J., Steinberg, L. D. and Walker, A. (1982) The ecology of day care. In M. Lamb (Ed.), *Childrearing in nontraditional families* (71-116). Hillsdale, NJ: Erlbaum.

Ben-Aaron, M., Eshel, Y. and Yaari, G. (1999) Mother and caregiver representations of toddlers in a kibbutz setting. *British Journal of Medical Psychology,* **72,** 189-201.

Benoit, D. and Parker, K. C. H. (1994) Stability and transmission of attachment across three generations. *Child Development,* **65,** 1444-1456.

Berlin, L. J. and Cassidy, J. (1999) Relations among relationships: Contributions from attachment theory and research. In J. Cassidy and P. R. Shaver (Eds.), *Handbook of attachment: Theory, research and clinical applications* (688-713). New York: Guilford Press.

Bertenthal, B. I. and Fischer, K. W. (1978) The development of self-recognition in the infant. *Developmental Psychology,* **14,** 44-50.

Bettelheim, B. (1967) *The Empty Fortress: Infantile autism and the birth of the self.* New York: Free Press.

Biller, H.H. (1993) *Fathers and families: Paternal factors in child development.* Westport, CT: Auburn House.

Biringen, Z. (2004) *Raising a secure child: Creating an emotional connection between you and your child.* New York: Perigree Publishers.

Biringen, Z., Robinson, J. L. and Emde, R. N. (1998) *The Emotional Availability scale* (3rd ed). Fort Collins: Department of Human Development and Family Studies, Colorado State University.

Blatz, W. E. (1966) *Human security: Some reflections.* Toronto: University of Toronto Press.

Block, J. H. and Block, J. (1980) The role of ego-control and ego-resiliency in the organization of behavior. In W. A. Collins (Ed.), *Development of cognition, affect, and social relations: The Minnesota symposia on child psychology, Vol. 13,* 39-51. Hillsdale, NJ: Lawrence Erlbaum Associates.

Bokhorst, C. L., Bakermans-Kranenburg, M. J., Pasco Fearon, R. M., van IJzendoorn, M. H., Fonagy, P. and Schuengel, C. (2003) The importance of shared environment in mother-infant attachment security: A behavioural genetic study. *Child Development,* **74(6),** 1769-1782.

Booth, C. L., Rose-Krasnor, L. and Rubin, K. H. (1991) Relating preschoolers' social competence and their mothers' parenting behaviors to early attachment security and high-risk status. *Journal of Social and Personal Relationships,* **8,** 363-382.

Boris, N.W., Zeanah, C.H., Larrieu, J. A., Scheeringa, M. S. and Heller, S. S. (1998) Attachment disorders in infancy and early childhood: A preliminary investigation of diagnostic criteria. *American Journal of Psychiatry,* 155, 295-297.

Bornstein, M. H. (1989) Sensitive periods in development: Structural characteristics and causal interpretations. *Psychological Bulletin,* **105(2),** 179-197.

Bradley, R. H., Whiteside, L., Mundfrom, D. J., Casey, P. H., Kelleher, K. J. and Pope, S. K. (1994) Early indications of resilience and their relation to experiences in the home environments of low birthweight, premature children living in poverty. *Child Development,* **65,** 346-360.

Bråten, S. (1987) *The Virtual Other: Accounting for protodialogue.* Talk at the Bergen Workshop on Intersubjectivity and Communication, Institute of Cognitive Psychology, University of Bergen. Published in: S.Bråten (2000) *Modellmakt og altersentriske spedbarn. Essays on dialogue in infant and adult* (204-212). Bergen: Sigma.

Bråten, S. (1992) The virtual other in infant's minds and social feelings. In A. H.Wold (Ed.), *The dialogical alternative: Towards a theory of language and mind* (77-97). Oslo: Scandinavian University Press.

Bråten, S. (1998) *Intersubjective communication and emotion in early ontogeny: Between nature, nurture and culture.* Cambridge: Cambridge University Press.

Bråten, S. (2003) Participant perception of others' acts: Virtual otherness in infants and adults. *Culture Psychology.* 2003; 9: 261-276.

REFERENCES

Brazelton, T. B., Kozlowski, B. and Main, M. (1974) The origins of reciprocity in mother-infant interactions. In M. Lewis and L. A. Rosenblum (Eds.), *The effect of the infant on its caregiver* (49-76). New York: Wiley.

Brennan, K. A. and Shaver, P. R. (1995) Dimensions of adult attachment, affect regulation, and romantic relationship functioning. *Personality and Social Psychology Bulletin,* **21(3)**, 267-283.

Brennan, K. A., Clark, C. L. and Shaver, P. R. (1998) Self-report measurement of adult romantic attachment: An integrative overview. In J. A. Simpson and W. S. Rholes (Eds.), *Attachment theory and close relationships* (46-76). New York: Guilford Press.

Brennan, K. A., Shaver, P. R. and Tobey, A. E. (1991) Attachment styles, gender, and parental problem drinking. *Journal of Social and Personal Relationships,* **8**, 451-466.

Bretherton, I. (1985) Attachment Theory: Retrospect and prospect. In I. Bretherton and E. Waters (Eds.), Growing points of attachment theory and research, *Monographs of the Society for Research in Child Development,* **50(1-2)**, 3-35.

Bretherton, I. (1987) New perspectives on attachment relations: Security, communication, and internal working models. In J. D. Osofsky (Ed.), *Handbook of infant development* (2nd ed., 1061-1100). New York: Wiley.

Bretherton, I. (1990a) Communication patterns, internal working models and the intergenerational transmission of attachment relationships. *Infant Mental Health Journal,* **11**, 237-252.

Bretherton, I. (1990b) Open communication and internal working models. Their role in attachment relationships. In R.A. Thompson (Ed.), *Socioemotional Development* (57-113). Lincoln: University of Nebraska Press.

Bretherton, I. (1991) Pouring new wine into old bottles: The social self as internal working model. In M. R. Gunnar and L. A. Sroufe (Eds.), *Minnesota Symposium on Child Psychology: Vol. 23. Self processes and development* (1-41). Hillsdale, NJ: Erlbaum.

Bretherton, I. (1994) Infants' subjective world of relatedness: Moments, feeling shapes, protonarrative envelopes, and internal working models. *Infant Mental Health Journal,* **15(1)**, 36-41.

Bretherton, I. (1995) Attachment theory and developmental psychopathology. In D. Cicchetti and S.L. Toth (Eds.), *Emotion, cognition and representation. Rochester Symposium on developmental psychopathology* (231-260). New York: University of Rochester Press.

Bretherton, I. and Mulholland, K. A. (1999) Internal working models in attachment relationships: A construct revisited. In J. Cassidy and P. R. Shaver (Eds.), *Handbook of attachment: Theory, research, and clinical applications* (89-111). New York: Guilford Press.

Bridges, L. J. and Grolnick, W. S. (1995) The development of emotional self-regulation in infancy and early childhood. In N. Eisenberg (Ed.), *Social development. Review of personality and social psychology, Volume 15* (185-211). Thousand Oaks, London: Sage.

Bridges, L. J., Connell, J. P. and Belsky, J. (1988) Similarities and differences in infant-mother and infant-father interaction in the Strange Situation: A component process analysis. *Developmental Psychology,* **24(1)**, 92-100.

Bronfenbrenner, U. (1979) *The ecology of human development: Experiments by nature and design.* Cambridge, MA: Harvard University Press.

Bronfenbrenner, U. (1986) Ecology of the family as a context for human development. *Developmental Psychology,* **22**, 723-42.

Brook, J. S., Whiteman, M.and Finch, S. (1993) Role of mutual attachment in drug use: A longitudinal study. *Journal of the American Academy of Child and Adolescent Psychiatry,* **32(5)**, 982-989.

Brown, G. W. and Harris, T. (1978) *Social origins of depression. A study of psychiatric disorder in women.* London: Tavistock.

Brown, R., Hobson, R. P., Lee, A. and Stevenson, J. (1997) Are there "autistic-like" features in congenitally blind children? *Journal of Child Psychology and Psychiatry,* **38**, 693-703.

Bruer, J. T. (2001) A sensitive and critical period primer. In D. B. Bailey Jr., J. T. Bruer, F. J. Symons and J. W. Lichtman (Eds.), *Critical thinking about critical periods* (3-26). London: Paul H. Brookes.

Bruer, J. T. and Greenough, W. T. (2001) The subtle science of how experience affects the brain. In D. B. Bailey Jr., J. T. Bruer, F. J. Symons and J. W. Lichtman (Eds.), *Critical thinking about critical periods* (209-232). London: Paul H. Brookes.

Bruer, J.T. (1999) *The myth of the first three years: A new understanding of early brain development and lifelong learning.* New York: The Free Press.

Bryant, B., Harris, M. and Newton, D. (1980) *Children and minders. Oxford Pre-School Research Project.* London: Grant McIntyre.

Buhrmeister, D. (1990) Intimacy of friendship, interpersonal competence, and adjustment during preadolescence and adolescence. *Child Development,* **61**, 1101-1111.

Buist, A., Morse, C. A. and Durkin, S. (2003) Men's adjustment to fatherhood: Implications for obstetric health care. *Journal of Obstetric and Gynecological Neonatal Nursing,* 32(2), 172-180.

Buitelaar, J. K., Huizink, A. C., Mulder, E. J., de Medina, P. G. and Visser, G. H. (2003) Prenatal stress and cognitive development and temperament in infants. *Neurobiology of Aging,* **1**, S53-S60.

Burgess, K. B., Marshall, P., Rubin, K. H. and Fox, N. A. (2003) Infant attachment and temperament as predictors of subsequent behavior problems and psychophysiological functioning. *Journal of Child Psychology and Psychiatry and Allied Disciplines,* **44**, 1-13.

Burlingham, D. and Freud, A. (1942) *Children in wartime.* London: Allen and Unwin.

Burlingham, D. and Freud, A. (1944) *Infants without families.* London: Allen and Unwin.

Bus, A. G. and Van IJzendoorn, M. H. (1988) Mother-child interactions, attachment, and emergent literacy: A cross-sectional study. *Child Development,* **59**, 1262-1272.

Buss, D. M. and Scheier, M. F. (1976) Self-consciousness, self-awareness, and self-attribution. *Journal of Research in Personality,* **10**, 334-349.

Byng-Hall, J. (1987) *Interview with John Bowlby* (Unedited version). Cited in Van Dijken, 1998, *op. cit.*

Byng-Hall, J. (1990) Attachment theory and family therapy: A clinical view. *Infant Mental Health Journal,* **11**, 228-236.

Byng-Hall, J. (1991) The application of attachment theory to understanding and treatment in family therapy. In C. M. Parks, J. Stevenson-Hinde and P. Marris (Eds.), *Attachment across the life cycle* (199-215). London: Tavistock/Routledge.

Byng-Hall, J. (1995a) Creating a secure family base: Some implications of attachment theory for therapy. *Family Process,* **34(1)**, 45-58.

Byng-Hall, J. (1997) The secure family base. In *Bonding and Attachment, Association for Child Psychology and Psychiatry Occasional Paper,* **14**, 27-30.

Byng-Hall, J. (1995b) *Rewriting family scripts: Improvisations and systems change.* New York: Guilford.

Byng-Hall, J. (1999) Family and couple therapy. Toward greater security. In J. Cassidy, and P.R. Shaver (Eds.), *Handbook of attachment: Theory, research, and clinical applications* (625-645). New York: Guilford Press.

Byng-Hall, J. (2005) *Attachment oriented family therapy.* Talk given to the International Attachment Network, June 3rd, London, England.

Byng-Hall, J. and Stevenson-Hinde, J. (1991) Attachment relationships within a family system. *Infant Mental Health Journal,* **12(3)**, 187-200.

Cairns, K. (2002) *Attachment, trauma and resilience: Therapeutic caring for children.* London: British Association for Adoption and Fostering.

Caldji, C., Diorio, J. and Meaney, M. (2000) Variations in maternal care in infancy regulate the development of stress reactivity. *Biological Psychiatry,* **48**, 1164-1174.

Campbell, F. A., Pungello, E. P., Miller-Johnson, S., Burchinal, M. and Ramey, C. T. (2001) The development of cognitive and academic abilities: Growth curves from an early childhood educational experiment. *Developmental Psychology,* **37**, 231-242.

Campos, J. J. Campos, R. G. and Barrett, K. C. (1989) Emergent themes in the study of emotional development and emotion regulation. *Developmental Psychology,* **25**, 394-402.

Caplan, G. and Bowlby, J. (1948) The aims and methods of child guidance. *Health Education Journal,* **6**, 1-8.

Carlson, C. L., Pelham, W. E., Milich, R. and Hoza, B. (1993) ADHD boys' performance and attributions following success and failure: Drug effects and individual differences. *Cognitive Therapy and Research,* **7**, 269-287.

Carlson, E. A. (1998) A prospective longitudinal study of attachment disorganization/disorientation. *Child Development,* **69**, 1107-1128.

Carlson, E. A. and Sroufe, L. A. (1995) Contribution of attachment theory to developmental psychopathology. In D. Ciccetti and D. J. Cohen (Eds.), *Developmental psychopathology, Volume 1* (581-617). New York: Wiley.

Carlson, V., Cicchetti, D., Barnett, D. and Braunwald, K. (1989) Disorganized/disoriented attachment relationships in maltreated infants. *Developmental Psychology,* **25(4)**, 525-531.

Carlsson, S. G., Fagenberg, H., Horneman, G., Hwang, C. P., Larsson, K., Rodholm, M., Schaller, J., Danielsson, B. and Gundewall, C. (1978) Effects of amount of contact between mother and child on the mother's nursing behaviour. *Developmental Psychobiology,* **11**, 143-150.

Carlsson, S. G., Fagenberg, H., Horneman, G., Hwang, C. P., Larsson, K., Rodholm, M., Schaller, J., Danielsson, B. and Gundewall, C. (1979) Effects of various amounts of contact between mother and child on the mother's nursing behaviour: A follow-up study. *Infant Behaviour and Development,* **2**, 209-214.

Carlsson, S. G., Larsson, K. and Schaller, J. (1980) Early mother-child contact and nursing. Reproduction, Nutrition et Dévelopment, **20**, 881-889.

Carter, C. S. (2003) Developmental consequences of oxytocin. *Physiology and Behavior,* **79**, 383-397.

Cassidy, J. (1988) Child-mother attachment and the self in six-year-olds. *Child Development,* **59,** 121-134.

Cassidy, J. (1994) Emotion regulation: Influences of attachment relationships. In N. Fox (Ed.), Biological and behavioral foundations of emotion regulation, *Monographs of the Society for Research in Child Development,* 59(2/3, **Serial No. 240).**

Cassidy, J. (1999) The nature of the child's ties. In J. Cassidy and P. R. Shaver (Eds.), *Handbook of attachment: Theory, research, and clinical applications* (3-21). New York: Guilford Press.

Cassidy, J. (2003) Continuity and change in the measurement of infant attachment: Comment on Fraley and Spieker (2003). *Developmental Psychology,* **39(3)**, 409-412.

Cassidy, J. and Berlin, L. J. (1994) The insecure/ambivalent pattern of attachment: Theory and research. *Child Development,* **65**, 971-991.

Cassidy, J. and Kobak, R. R. (1988) Avoidance and its relation to other defensive processes. In J. Belsky and T. Nezworski (Eds.), *Clinical implications of attachment* (300-323). Hillsdale, NJ: Lawrence Erlbaum.

Cassidy, J. and Marvin, R. S. with the MacArthur Working Group on Attachment (1992) *Attachment organization in 2½ to 4½ year olds: Coding manual.* Unpublished manuscript, University of Virginia.

Cassidy, J. and Shaver, P. R. (1999) *Handbook of attachment. Theory, research, and clinical applications.* New York: The Guilford Press.

REFERENCES

Cassidy, J., Kirsh, S., Scolton, K. L. and Parke, R. D. (1996) Attachment and representations of peer relationships. *Developmental Psychology,* **32**, 892-904.

Cederblad, M., Hook, B., Irhammer, M., Mercke, A-M. (1999) Mental health in international adoptees as teenagers and young adults. *Journal of Child Psychology and Psychiatry,* **40**, 1239-1248.

Chisholm, K. (1998) A three-year follow-up of attachment and indiscriminate friendliness in children adopted from Romanian orphanages. *Child Development,* **69**, 1092-1106.

Chisholm, K., Carter, M. C., Ames, E. W. and Morison, S. J. (1995) Attachment security and indiscriminately friendly behavior in children adopted from Romanian orphanages. *Developmental Psychopathology,* **7**, 283-294.

Chorpita, B. F. and Barlow, D. H. (1998) The development of anxiety: The role of control in the early environment. *Psychological Bulletin,* **124**, 3-21.

Christensson, K., Cabrera, T, Christensson, E, Uvnas-Moberg, K. and Winberg, J. (1995) Separation distress calls in the human neonate in the absence of maternal body contact. *Acta Paediatrica,* **84(5)**, 468-473.

Christensson, K., Siles, C, Morena, L. Belaustequi, A., de la Fuente, P., Lagercrantz, H., et al. (1992) Temperature, metabolic adaptation and crying in healthy full-term newborns cared for skin-to-skin or in a cot. *Acta Paediatrica,* **82**, 488-493.

Chugani, H. T., Behen, M. E., Muzik, O., Juhasz, C., Nagy, F. and Chugani, D. C. (2001) Local brain functional activity following early deprivation: A study of postinstitutionalized Romanian orphans. *Neuroimage,* **14**, 1290-1301.

Cicchetti, D. and Barnett, D. (1991) Attachment organization in maltreated preschoolers. *Development and Psychopathology,* **3,** 397-411.

Cicchetti, D. and Howes, P. (1991) Developmental psychopathology in the context of the family: Illustrations from the study of child maltreatment. *Canadian Journal of Behavioural Science,* **23**, 257-281.

Cicchetti, D., Ganiban, J. and Barnett, D. (1991) Contributions from the study of high-risk populations to understanding the development of emotion regulation. In K. Dodge and J. Garber (Eds.), *The development of emotion regulation and dysregulation* (15-48). New York: Cambridge University Press.

Cicchetti, D., Rogosch, F. A. and Toth, S. L. (1998) Maternal depressive disorder and contextual risk: Contributions to development of attachment insecurity and behavior problems in toddlerhood. *Development and Psychopathology,* **10**, 283-300.

Cicirelli, V. G. (1995) *Sibling relationships across the lifespan.* New York: Plenum Press.

Cohn, D. A., Cowan, P. A., Cowan, C. P. and Pearson, J. L. (1992) Mothers' and fathers' working models of childhood attachment relationships, parenting styles and child behavior. *Development and Psychopathology,* **4**, 417-431.

Clarke, A. M. and Clarke, A. D. B. (1976) *Early experience: Myth and evidence.* London: Jessica Kingsley.

Clarke, L. and Roberts, C. (October, 2002) *Grandparents' contribution to family life.* Paper presented at workshop sponsored by the Nuffield Foundation, Worcester College, Oxford.

Clarke, L., Ungerer, J., Chadoud, K., Johnson, S. and Stiefel, I. (2002) Attention deficit hyperactivity disorder is associated with attachment insecurity. *Clinical Child Psychology and Psychiatry,* **7(2)**, 179-198.

Clarke-Stewart, K.A. (1988) "The "effects" of infant day care reconsidered" reconsidered: Risks for parents, children, and researchers. *Early Childhood Research Quarterly,* **3**, 293-318.

Cline, F.W. (1992) *Hope for high risk and rage filled children.* Evergreen, CO: Evergreen Center Publications.

Coan, J. A. and Allen, J. J. B. (2004) Frontal EEG asymmetry as a moderator and mediator of emotion. *Biological Psychology,* **6**, 7-49.

Cogill, S. R., Caplan, H. L., Alexandra, H., Robson, K. and Kumar, R. (1986) Impact of maternal postnatal depression on cognitive development of young children. *British Medical Journal,* **292**, 1165-1167.

Cohen, J. (1988) *Statistical power analysis for the behavioral sciences* (2nd ed.). Hillsdale, NJ: Lawrence Erlbaum Associates.

Cohen, P. and Beebe, B. (2002) Video feedback with a depressed mother and her infant: A collaborative individual psychoanalytic and mother-infant treatment. *Journal of Infant, Child and Adolescent Psychotherapy,* **2(3)**, 1-55.

Cohn, D. A. (1990) Child-mother attachment of six-year-olds and social competence at school. *Child Development,* **61**, 152-163.

Cohn, D. A., Silver, D., Cowan, P., Cowan, C. and Pearson, J. (1992) Working models of childhood attachment and couple relationships. *Journal of Family Issues,* **13(4)**, 432-449.

Cohn, J. F. and Campbell, S. B. (2000) Influence of maternal depression on infant affect regulation. In C.A. Nelson (Ed.), *The effects of early adversity on neurobehavioral development. The Minnesota Symposia on Child Psychology, Vol. 31* (103-130). Hillsdale, NJ: Lawrence Erlbaum Associates.

Cohn, J. F., Matias, R., Tronick, E. Z., Connell, D. and Lyons-Ruth, K. (1986) Face-to-face interactions of depressed mothers and their infants. *New Directions for Child Development,* **34**, 31-45.

Colin, V. L. (1996) *Human attachment.* Philadelphia: Temple University Press.

Collins, N. L. and Feeney, B. C. (2000) A safe haven: Support-seeking and caregiving processes in intimate relationships. *Journal of Personality and Social Psychology,* **78**, 1053-1073.

Collins, N. L. and Read, S. J. (1990) Adult attachment working models, and relationship quality in dating couples. *Journal of Personality and Social Psychology,* **58**, 644-663.

Collins, P. F. and Depue, R. A. (1992) A neurobehavioral systems approach to developmental psychopathology: Implications for disorders of affect. *Rochester Symposium on Developmental Psychopathology, Volume 4: Developmental perspectives on depression* (29-101). New York: University of Rochester Press.

Collins, W. A. and Sroufe, L. A. (1999) Capacity for intimate relationships: A developmental construction. In W. Furman, B. B. Brown and C. Feiring (Eds.), *The development of romantic relationships in adolescence* (125-147). New York: Cambridge University Press.

Compas, B. E. (1987) Coping with stress during childhood and adolescence. *Developmental Psychology,* **101(3)**, 393-403.

Conde-Agudelo, A., Diaz-Rossello, J. L. and Belizan, J. M. (2003) Kangaroo mother care to reduce morbidity and mortality in low birthweight infants (Cochrane Review). In: *The Cochrane Library,* Issue 1. Oxford: Update Software.

Constantino, J. and Olesh, H. (1999) Mental representations of attachment in day care providers. *Infant Mental Health Journal,* **20**, 138-147.

Cooper, G., Hoffman, K., Marvin, R. and Powell, B. (1999 and 2000) Secure and limited circles of security. Unpublished material, Center for Clinical Intervention, Spokane, WA and University of Virginia.

Cooper, P. J., Campbell, E. A., Day, A. Kennerley, H. and Bond, A. (1988) Non-psychotic psychiatric disorder after childbirth: A prospective study of prevalence, incidence, course and nature. *British Journal of Psychiatry,* **152**, 799-806.

Corboz-Warnery, A. and Fivaz-Depeursinge, E. (1999) *The primary triangle: A developmental systems view of fathers, mothers, and infants.* New York: Basic Books.

Corcoran, K. and Mallinckrodt, B. (2000) Adult attachment, self-efficacy, perspective taking, and conflict resolution. *Journal of Counselling and Development,* **78**, 473-483.

Costello, E. J. and Angold, A. (1993) Toward a developmental epidemiology of the disruptive behavior disorders. *Development and Psychopathology,* **5**, 91-101

Craig, S., Tyson, J. E., Samson, J. and Lasky, R. E. (1982) The effect of early contact on maternal perception of infant behavior. *Early Human Development,* **6(2)**,197-204.

Craik, K. (1943) *The nature of explanation.* Cambridge: Cambridge University Press.

Creasey, G., Kershaw, K. and Boston, A. (1999) Conflict management with friends and romantic partners: The role of attachment and negative mood regulation expectancies. *Journal of Youth and Adolescence,* **28**, 523-543.

Crick, N. R.and Dodge, K. A. (1994) A review of and reformulation of social-information-processing mechanisms in children's social adjustment. *Psychological Bulletin,* **115**, 74-101.

Criss, M. M., Pettit, G. S., Bates, J. E., Dodge, K. A. and Lapp, A. L. (2002) Family adversity, positive peer relationships, and children's externalizing behavior: A longitudinal perspective on risk and resilience. *Child Development,* **74**, 1220-1237.

Crittenden, P. M. (1985) Maltreated infants: Vulnerability and resilience. *Journal of Child Psychology and Psychiatry,* **26**, 85-96.

Crittenden, P. M. (1987) Non-organic failure-to-thrive: Deprivation or distortion? Infant Mental Health Journal, 8, 51-64.

Crittenden, P. M. (1988) Relationship at risks. In J. Belsky and T. Nezworski (Eds.), *Clinical implications of attachment* (136-174). Hillsdale, NJ: Lawrence Erlbaum Associates.

Crittenden, P. M. (1992) Quality of attachment in the preschool years. *Development and Psychopathology,* **4**, 209-241.

Crittenden, P. M. (1995) Attachment and psychopathology. In S. Goldberg, R. Muir and J. Kerr (Eds.), *Attachment theory: Social, developmental, and clinical perspectives* (367-406). Hillsdale, NJ: Analytic Press.

Crittenden, P. M. (1998) *CARE-Index Manual* (third edition). Miami, FL: Unpublished manuscript available from the author.

Crittenden, P. M. (2000) A dynamic-maturational approach to continuity and change in pattern of attachment. In P. Crittenden, P. M. and Claussen, A. H. (Eds.) (2000), *The organization of attachment relationships: Maturation, culture and context* (343-358). New York: Cambridge University Press.

Crittenden, P. M. (2002) *Modifications and expansions to the Infant Strange Situation.* Unpublished manuscript, Miami, FL.

Crittenden, P. M. and Claussen, A. H. (Eds.) (2000) *The organisation of attachment relationships: Maturation, context and culture.* New York and Cambridge: Cambridge University Press.

Crockenberg, S. B. (1981) Infant irritability, mother responsiveness, and social support influences on the security of mother infant attachment. *Child Development,* **52**, 857-868.

Crowell, J. A. and Feldman, S. S. (1988) Mothers' internal models of relationships and children's behavioral and developmental status: A study of mother-child interaction. *Child Development,* **59**, 1273-1285.

Crowell, J. A. and Treboux, D. (1995) A review of adult attachment measures: Implications for theory and research. *Social Development,* **4**, 294-327.

Crowell, J. A., Fraley, R. C. and Shaver, P. R. (1999). Measures of individual differences in adolescent and adult attachment. In J. Cassidy and P. R. Shaver (Eds.), Handbook of attachment: Theory, research, and clinical applications (434-465). New York: Guilford.

Cummings, E. M. (2003) Toward assessing attachment on an emotional security continuum: Comment on Fraley and Spieker (2003). *Developmental Psychology,* **39(3)**, 405-408.

Dallos, R (2004) Attachment narrative therapy: integrating ideas from narrative and attachment theory in systemic family therapy with eating disorders. *Journal of Family Therapy,* **26**, 40-65.

David, M., Nicolas, J., Roudinesco, J., Robertson, J. and Bowlby, J. (1952) Responses of young children to separation from their mothers: I Observations of children aged 12 to 17 months recently separated from their families and living in an institution. *Courrier de la Centre International de I'Enfance,* **2(2)**, 66-78.

Davidson, R. J. (1993) Cerebral asymmetry and emotion: Conceptual and methodological conundrums. *Cognition and Emotion,* **7**, 115-138.

Davidson, R. J. (1998) Affective style and affective disorders: Perspectives from affective neuroscience. *Cognition and Emotion,* **12(3)**, 307-330.

Davidson, R. J. and Fox, N. A. (1982) Asymmetrical brain activity discriminates between positive and negative affective stimuli in human infants. *Science,* **218**, 1235-1237.

Davidson, R. J. and Fox, N. A. (1988) Cerebral asymmetry and emotion: Development and individual differences. In S. Segalowitz and D. Molfese (Eds.), *Developmental implications of brain lateralization* (191-206). New York: Guilford Press.

Davie, C. (1986) *An investigation into childminding practice in North Staffordshire.* Unpublished report to the DHSS.

Dawson, G. and Ashman, S. (2000) On the origins of a vulnerability to depression: The influence of the early social environment on the development of psychobiological systems related to risk for affective disorder. In C. A. Nelson (Ed.), *The effects of early adversity on neurobehavioral development. The Minnesota Symposia on Child Psychology, Vol. 31* (245-279). Hillsdale, NJ: Lawrence Erlbaum Associates.

Dawson, G., Ashman, S. and Carver, L.J. (2000) The role of early experience in shaping behavioral and brain development and its implications for social policy. *Development and Psychopathology,* **12**, 695-712.

Dawson, G., Ashman, S., Panagiotides, H, Hessl, D., Self, H., Yamada, E. and Embry, L. (2003) Preschool outcomes of children of depressed mothers: Role of maternal behavior, contextual risk, and children's brain activity. *Child Development,* **74(4)**, 1158-1175.

Dawson, G., Frey, K., Panagiotides, H., Hessl, D. and Self, J. (1997b) Infants of depressed mothers exhibit atypical frontal brain activity: A replication and extension of previous findings. *Journal of Child Psychology and Psychiatry,* **38**, 179-186.

Dawson, G., Frey, K., Self, J., Panagiotides, H., Hessl, D., Yamada, E. and Rinaldi, J. (1999) Frontal electrical brain activity in infants of depressed mothers: Relation to variations in infant behavior. *Development and Psychopathology,* **11**, 589-605.

Dawson, G., Klinger, L. and Panagiotides, H. (1997a) Infants of depressed and nondepressed mothers exhibit differences in frontal brain electrical activity during the expression of negative emotions. *Developmental Psychology,* **33**, 650-656.

Dawson, G., Panagiotides, H., Grofer Klinger, L and Hill, D. (1992) The role of frontal lobe functioning in the development of infant self-regulatory behavior. *Brain and Cognition,* **20**, 152-175.

de Chateau, P. and Wiberg, B. (1977a) Long-term effect on mother-infant behavior of extra contact during the first hours postpartum: First observations at 36 hours. *Acta Paediatrica Scandinavia,* **66**, 137-143.

de Chateau, P. and Wiberg, B. (1977b) Long-term effect on mother-infant behavior of extra contact during the first hours postpartum: Follow-up at three months. *Acta Paediatrica Scandinavia,* **66**, 145-151.

de Chateau, P. and Wiberg, B. (1984) Long-term effect on mother-infant behaviour of extra contact during the first hour postpartum. III. Follow-up at one year. *Scandinavian Journal of Social Medicine,* **12(2)**, 91-103.

de Haan, M., Gunnar, M. R., Tout, K., Hart, J. and Stansbury, K. (1998) Familiar and novel contexts yield different associations between cortisol and behavior among 2-year-old children. *Developmental Psychobiology,* **31**, 93-101.

de Kloet, E. R., Rots, N. Y. and Cools, A. R. (1996) Brain-corticosteroid hormone dialogue: Slow and persistent. *Cell Molecular Neurobiology,* **16**, 345-356.

de Mulder, E. K. and Radke-Yarrow, M. (1991) Attachment with affectively ill and well mothers: Concurrent and behavioral correlates. *Development and Psychopathology,* **3**, 227-242.

De Weerth, C., van Hees, Y. and Buitelaar, J. K. (2003) Prenatal maternal cortisol levels and infant behavior during the first 5 months. *Early Human Development,* **74(2)**, 139-151.

De Wolff, M. S. and Van IJzendoorn, M. H. (1997) Sensitivity and attachment: A meta-analysis on parental antecedents of infant attachment. *Child Development,* **68(4)**, 571-591.

DeCasper, A. J. and Fifer, W. P. (1980) Of human bonding: Newborns prefer their mothers' voices. *Science,* **208**, 1174-1176.

DeCasper, A. J. and Spence, M. (1986) Newborns prefer a familiar story over an unfamiliar one. *Infant Behaviour and Development,* **9**, 133-150.

Dennis, W. and Najarian, P. (1957) Infant development under environmental handicap. *Psychological Monographs: General and Applied,* **71**, 1-13.

Dettling, A. C., Gunnar, M. R. and Donzella, B. (1999) Cortisol levels of young children in full-day childcare centers: relations with age and temperament. *Psychoneuroendocrinology,* **24**, 519-536.

Diehl, M., Elnick, A. B., Bourbeau, L. S. and Labouvie-Vief, G. (1998) Adult attachment styles: Their relations to family context and personality. *Journal of Personality and Social Psychology,* **74**, 1656-1669.

Dodge, K.A. (1990) Developmental psychopathology in children of depressed mothers. *Developmental Psychology,* **26**, 3-6.

Downey, G. and Coyne, J.C. (1990) Children of depressed parents: An integrative review. *Psychological Bulletin,* **108**, 50-76.

Dozier, M. (2003) Attachment-based treatment for vulnerable children. *Attachment and Human Development,* **5(3)**, 253-257.
Dozier, M. (2005) Challenges of foster care. *Attachment and Human Development,* **7(1)**, 27-30.
Dozier, M., Chase Stovall, K. and Albus, K.E. (1999) Attachment and psychopathology in adulthood. In J. Cassidy and P. R. Shaver (Eds.), *Handbook of attachment: Theory, research, and clinical applications* (497-519). New York and London: Guilford Press.
Dozier, M., Stovall, K. C., Albus, K. and Bates, B. (2001) Attachment for infants in foster care: The role of the caregiver state of mind. *Child Development,* 72, 1467-1477.
Drew, L. M., Richard, M. H. and Smith, P. K. (1998) Grandparenting and its relationship to parenting. *Clinical Child Psychology and Psychiatry,* **3(3)**, 465-480.
Durbin, E. F. and Bowlby, J. (1939) *Personal aggressiveness and war.* London: Routledge and Kegan Paul.
Klagsbrun, M. and Bowlby, J. (1976) Responses to separation from parents: A clinical test for young children. *British Journal of Projective Psychology and Personality Study,* **21**, 7-21.
Dutton, D.G., Saunders, K., Starzomski, A. J. and Bartholomew, K. (1994) Intimacy-anger and insecure attachment as precursors of abuse in intimate relationships. *Journal of Applied Social Psychology,* 24, 1367-1386.
Duyme, M., Dumaret, A.C., and Tomkiewicz, S. (1999) How can we boost IQs of "dull children"? A late adoption study. *Proceedings of the National Academy of Sciences USA,* **96**, 8790-9794.
Easterbrooks, M. A. and Goldberg, W. A. (1990) Security of toddler-parent attachment: Relation to children's sociopersonality functioning during kindergarten. In M. T. Greenberg, D. Cicchetti and E. M. Cummings (Eds.), *Attachment in the preschool years: Theory, research, and intervention* (221-244). Chicago: University of Chicago Press.
Easterbrooks, M. A. and Lamb, M. E. (1979) The relationship between quality of infant-mother attachment and infant competence initial encounters with peers. *Child Development,* **50**, 380-387.
Edelstein, R. S., Alexander, K. W., Shaver, P. R., Schaaf, J. M., Quas, J. A., Lovas, G.S. and Goodman, G. S. (2004) Parental attachment style and children's reactions to a stressful event. *Attachment and Human Development,* **6**, 31-52.
Egeland, B. and Brunnquell, D. (1979) An at-risk approach to the study of child abuse: Some preliminary findings. *Journal of the American Academy of Child Psychiatry,* **18**, 219-235.
Egeland, B. and Farber, E. A. (1984) Infant-mother attachment: Factors related to its development and changes over time. *Child Development,* **55**, 753-771.
Egeland, B. and Sroufe, L. A. (1981) Developmental sequelae of maltreatment in infancy. In R. Rizley and D. Cicchetti (Eds.), *New directions for child development: Developmental perspectives in child maltreatment, Vol. 11* (77-92). San Francisco, CA: Jossey Bass.
Egeland, B., Jacobvitz, D. and Sroufe, L. A. (1988) Breaking the cycle of abuse: Relationship predictors. *Child Development,* **59(4)**, 1080-1088.
Elgar, F. J., Knight, J, Worrall, G. J. and Sherman, G. (2003) Attachment characteristics and behavioural problems in rural and urban juvenile delinquents. *Child Psychiatry and Human Development,* **34(1)**, 35-48.
Elicker, J., Englund, M. and Sroufe, L. A. (1992) Predicting peer competence and peer relationships in childhood from early parent-child relationships. In R. D. Parke and G. W. Ladd (Eds.), *Family-peer relations: Modes of linkage* (77-106). Hillsdale, NJ: Lawrence Erlbaum.
Emde, R. (1989) The infant's relationship experience: Developmental and affective aspects. In A. Sameroff and R. Emde (Eds.), *Relationship disturbances in early childhood.* (33-51). New York: Basic Books.
Emde, R. N. (1988) The effects of relationships on relationships: A developmental approach to clinical intervention. In R. A. Hinde and J. Stevenson-Hinde (Eds.), *Relationships within families* (354-364). Oxford: Oxford University Press.
Engle, B. T. (1985) Stress is a noun! No, a verb! No, an adjective. In T. Field, P. McCabe and N. Schneiderman (Eds.), *Stress and coping, Volume 1* (3-12). Hillsdale, NJ: Lawrence Erlbaum Associates.
Erickson, M. F. and Farber, E. A. (1983) *Infancy to preschool: Continuity of adaptation in high-risk children.* Paper presented at the meeting of the Society for Research in Child Development, Detroit.
Erickson, M. F., Korfmacher, J. and Egeland, B. (1992) Attachments past and present. Implications for therapeutic intervention with mother-infant dyads. *Development and Psychopathology,* **4**, 495-507.
Erickson, M. F., Sroufe, L. A. and Egeland, B. (1985) The relationship between quality of attachment and behavior problems in preschool in a high-risk sample. In I. Bretherton and E. Waters (Eds.), *Growing points of attachment theory and research: Monographs of the Society for Research in Child Development,* **50** (1-2, Serial No. 209), 147-166.
Essex, M. J., Klein, M. H., Cho, E., and Kalin, N. H. (2002) Maternal stress beginning in infancy may sensitize children to later stress exposure: effects on cortisol and behavior. *Biological Psychiatry,* **52(8)**, 776-784.
Eyer, D. E.(1992) *Mother-infant bonding: A scientific fiction.* New Haven, CT: Yale University Press.
Eysenck, H. J. (1985) *Decline and fall of the Freudian empire.* Harmondsworth: Viking.
Eysenck, H. J. and Wilson, G. D. (1973) *The experimental study of Freudian theories.* London: Methuen.
Fagot, B. I. and Kavanagh, K. (1990) The prediction of antisocial behavior from avoidant attachment classification. *Child Development,* **61**, 864-873.
Fahlberg, V. (2002) *Child's journey through placement.* London: British Association of Adoption and Fostering.
Farrington, D. P. (1986) Stepping stones to adult criminal careers. In Olweus, D., Block, J. and Yarrow, M.R. (Eds.), *Development of anti-social behaviour and prosocial behaviour* (359-384). NewYork: Springer-Verlag.

Farrington, D., Loeber, R., and van Kammen, W. B. (1990) Long-term criminal outcomes of hyperactivity-impulsivity-attention deficit and conduct problems in childhood. In L. Robins and M. Rutter (Eds.), *Straight and devious pathways from childhood to adulthood* (62-81). Cambridge: Cambridge University Press.

Fearnley, S. (1996) *The extra dimension*. Lancashire: Keys Child Care.

Feeney, J. (1999) Adult romantic attachment and couple relationships. In J. Cassidy and P. R. Shaver (Eds.), *Handbook of attachment: Theory, research, and clinical applications* (355-377). New York: Guilford.

Feeney, J. A. and Noller, P. (1990) Attachment style as a predictor of adult romantic relationships. *Journal of Personality and Social Psychology*, **58**, 281-291.

Feeney, J. A. and Noller, P. (1992) Attachment style and romantic love: Relationship dissolution. *Australian Journal of Psychology*, **44**, 69-74.

Feeney, J. and Noller, P. (1996) *Adult attachment*. Thousand Oaks, CA: Sage.

Feeney, J. A., Noller, P. and Callan, V. J. (1994) Attachment style, communication and satisfaction in the early years of marriage. In K. Bartholomew and D. Perlman (Eds.), *Attachment processes in adulthood: Vol. 5. Advances in personal relationships* (269-308). London: Jessica Kingsley.

Fein, G. G. and Fox, N. (1988) Infant day care: A special issue. *Early Childhood Research Quarterly*, **3**, 227-34.

Fenigstein, A., Scheier, M. F. and Buss, A. H. (1975) Public and private self-consciousness: Assessment and theory. *Journal of Consulting and Clinical Psychology*, **43**, 522-527.

Field, T. (1984) Early interactions between infants and their postpartum depressed mothers. *Infant Behavior and Development*, **7**, 527-532.

Field, T. (1988) Infants of depressed mothers show "depressed" behavior even with non-depressed adults. *Child Development*, **59**, 1569-1579.

Field, T. (1992) Infants of depressed mothers. *Development and Psychopathology*, **4**, 49-66.

Field, T. M. (1985) Neonatal perception of people: Maturational and individual differences. In T.M. Field and N.A. Fox (Eds.), *Social perception in infants* (31-52). Norwood, NJ: Ablex.

Field, T. M. (2000) Infants of depressed mothers. In S. L. Johnson and A. M. Hayes (Eds.), *Stress, coping, and depression* (3-22). Mahwah, NJ: Lawrence Erlbaum Associates.

Field, T. M. and Fox, N. A. (Eds.) (1985) *Social perception in infants*. Norwood, NJ: Ablex.

Field, T., Diego, M., Dieter, J., Hernandez-Reif, M., Schanberg, S., Kuhn, C., Yando, R. and Bendell, D. (2004) Prenatal depression effects on the fetus and the newborn. *Infant Behavior and Development*, **27**, 216-229.

Field, T., Fox, N., Pickens, J. and Nawrocki, T. (1995) Relative right frontal EEG activation in 3-6 month-old infants of depressed mothers. *Developmental Psychology*, **31**, 358-363.

Field, T., Lang, C., Martinez, A., Yando, R., Pickens, J. and Bendell, D. (1996) Preschool follow-up of children of dysphoric mothers. *Journal of Clinical Child Psychology*, **25**, 275-279.

Figley, C. R. (1985) *Trauma and its wake: The study and treatment of post-traumatic stress disorder*. New York: Brunner/Mazel.

Finnegan, R. A., Hodges, E. V. E. and Perry, D. G. (1996) Preoccupied and avoidant coping during middle childhood. *Child Development*, **67(4)**, 1318-1328.

Finzi, R., Ram, A., Har-Even, D., Shnit, D. and Weizman, A. (2001) Attachment styles and aggression in physically abused and neglected children. *Journal of Youth and Adolescence*, **30(6)**, 769-786.

Fisher, A. E. (1955) *The effects of differential early treatment on the social and exploratory behavior of puppies*. Doctoral dissertation, Pennsylvania State University, cited in Rajecki et al., 1978, op. cit.

Fisher, L., Ames, E. W., Chisholm, K. and Savoie, L. (1997) Problems reported by parents of Romanian orphans adopted to British Columbia. *International Journal of Behavioral Development*, **20**, 67-82.

Fivaz-Depeursinge, E. (2005) *A method for studying infants' three-way interactions with fathers and mothers: Implications for psychotherapy*. Paper presented at conference organised by University College London, International Attachment Network and Association of Infant Mental Health, entitled *Parent-Infant Research and Psychotherapy*, May 20-21. London: University College.

Fivaz-Depeursinge, E., Frascarolo, F. and Corboz-Warnery, A. (1996). Assessing the triadic alliance between fathers, mothers, and infants at play. In J.P. McHale and P.A. Cowan (Eds.), *Understanding how family-level dynamics affect children's development: Studies of two-parent families. New Directions for Child Development*, **74**, 27-44.

Flinn, M. V. and England, B. G. (1997) Social economics of childhood glucocorticoid stress responses and health. *American Journal of Physical Anthropology*, **102**, 33-53.

Florian, V., Mikulincer, M. and Bucholtz, I. (1995) Effects of adult attachment style on the perception and search for social support. *Journal of Psychology*, **129**, 665-676.

Fogel, A. (1993) *Developing through relationships*. Chicago: University of Chicago Press.

Folkman, S., Lazarus, R. S., Gruen, R. J. and DeLongis, A. (1986a) Appraisal, coping, health status, and psychological symptoms. *Journal of Personality and Social Psychology*, **50(3)**, 571-579.

Folkman, S., Lazarus, R. S., Dunkel-Schetter, C., DeLongis, A. and Gruen, R. J. (1986b) Dynamics of a stressful encounter: Cognitive appraisal, coping and encounter outcomes. *Journal of Personality and Social Psychology*, **50(5)**, 992-1003.

Fonagy, P., Steele, M., Steele, H. and Target, M. (1997) *Reflective-Functioning Manual, Version 4.1, for application to Adult Attachment Interviews*. University College London: Unpulished manual.

Fonagy P., Target, M., Steele, H. and Steele, M. (1998) *Reflective functioning manual for application to adult attachment interviews, Version 5*. University College London: Unpublished manual.

Fonagy, P. (1999) *Attachment theory and psychoanalysis.* New York: Other Press.
Fonagy, P. H., Steele, H. and Steele, M. (1991) Maternal representations of attachment during pregnancy predict the organization of infant-mother attachment at one year of age. *Child Development,* **62,** 891-905.
Fonagy, P., Steele, M., Steele, H., Higgitt, A. and Target, M. (1994) The Emanuel Miller Memorial Lecture, 1992: The theory and practice of resilience. *Journal of Child Psychology and Psychiatry,* **35(2),** 231-257.
Foss, B. M. (Ed.)(1961) *Determinants of infant behaviour, Volume I.* London: Methuen.
Foss, B. M. (Ed.)(1963) *Determinants of infant behaviour, Volume II.* London: Methuen.
Foss, B. M. (Ed.)(1965) *Determinants of infant behaviour, Volume III.* London: Methuen.
Foss, B. M. (Ed.)(1969) *Determinants of infant behaviour, Volume IV.* London: Methuen.
Fox, N. A. (1977) Attachment of kibbutz infants to mother and metapelet. *Child Development,* **48,** 1228-1239.
Fox, N. A. (1991) If it's not left, it's right: Electroencephalogram asymmetry and the development of emotion. *American Psychologist,* **46,** 863-872.
Fox, N. A. (Ed.) (1994) The development of emotion regulation: Behavioral and biological considerations. *Monographs of the Society for Research in Child Development,* **59(2-3, Serial No. 240),** 152-166.
Fox, N. A. and Calkins, S. D. (1993) Pathways to aggression and social withdrawal: Interactions among temperament, attachment, and regulation. In K.J. Rubin and J.B. Asendorpf (Eds.), *Social withdrawal, inhibition, and shyness.* Hillsdale, NJ: Lawrence Erlbaum Associates.
Fox, N. A. and Calkins, S. D. (2003) The development of self-control of emotion: Intrinsic and extrinsic influences. *Motivation and Emotion,* **27(1),** 7-26.
Fox, N. A. and Card, J. A. (1999) Psychophysiological measures in the study of attachment. In J. Cassidy and P. R. Shaver (Eds.), *Handbook of attachment: Theory, research and clinical applications* (226-245). New York: Guilford Press.
Fox, N. A. and Davidson, R .J. (1986) Taste-elicited changes in facial signs of emotion and the asymmetry of brain electrical activity in human newborns. *Neuropsychologia,* **24,** 417-422.
Fox, N. A. and Davidson, R. J. (1988) Patterns of brain electrical activity during the expression of discrete emotions in ten-month-old infants. *Developmental Psychology,* **24,** 230-236.
Fox, N. A., Kimmerly, N. L. and Schafer, W. D. (1991) Attachment to mother/attachment to father: A meta-analysis. *Child Development,* **62,** 210-225.
Fraiberg, S., Adelson, E. and Shapiro, V. (1975) Ghosts in the nursery: a psychoanalytic approach to the problem of impaired infant-mother relationships. *Journal of the American Academy of Child Psychiatry,* **14,** 387-422.
Fraley, R. C. (2002) Attachment stability from infancy to adulthood: Meta-analysis and dynamic modeling of developmental mechanisms. *Personality and Social Psychology Review,* **6,** 123-151.
Fraley, R. C. and Brumbaugh, C. C. (2004) A dynamical systems approach to understanding stability and change in attachment security. In W. S. Rholes and J. A. Simpson (Eds.), *Adult attachment: Theory, research, and clinical implications* (86-132). New York: Guilford Press.
Fraley, R. C. and Brumbaugh, C. C. (2005) *Adult attachment and preemptive defenses: Converging evidence on the role of defensive exclusion at the level of encoding.* Manuscript under review.
Fraley, R. C. and Roberts, B. W. (2005) Patterns of continuity: A dynamic model for conceptualizing the stability of individual differences in psychological constructs across the life course. *Psychological Review,* **112,** 60-74.
Fraley, R. C. and Spieker, S. J. (2003a) Are infant attachment patterns continuously or categorically distributed? A taxometric analysis of Strange Situation behavior. *Developmental Psychology,* **39(3),** 387-404.
Fraley, R. C. and Spieker, S. J. (2003b) What are the differences between dimensional and categorical models of individual differences in attachment? Reply to Cassidy (2003), Cummings (2003), Sroufe (2003), and Waters and Beauchaine (2003). *Developmental Psychology,* **39(3),** 423-429.
Fraley, R. C. and Waller, N. G. (1998) Adult attachment patterns: A test of the typological model. In J. A. Simpson & W. S. Rholes (Eds.), *Attachment theory and close relationships* (77-114). New York: Guilford Press.
Fraley, R. C., Davis, K. E. and Shaver, P. R. (1998) Dismissing-avoidance and the defensive organization of emotion, cognition, and behavior. In J. A. Simpson and W. S. Rholes (Eds.), *Attachment theory and close relationships* (249-279). New York: Guilford Press.
Fraley, R. C., Waller, N. G. and Brennan, K. A. (2000) An item-response theory analysis of self-report measures of adult attachment. *Journal of Personality and Social Psychology,* **78,** 350-365.
Freedman, D. A. (1981) The effect of sensory and other deficits in children on their experience of people. *Journal of the American Psychoanalytic Association,* **29,** 831-867.
Freitag, M. K., Belsky, J., Grossmann, K., Grossmann, K. E. and Scheuerer-Englisch, H. (1996) Continuity in parent-child relationships from infancy to middle childhood and relations with friendship competence. *Child Development,* **67(4),** 1437-1454.
Freud, A. (1946) The psychoanalytic study of infantile feeding disturbances. *Psychoanalytic Study of the Child,* **2,** 119-132.
Frodi, A. and Thompson, R. (1985) Infants' affective response in the Strange Situation: Effects of prematurity and of quality of attachment. *Child Development,* **56,** 1280-1291.
Frodi, A., Bridges, L. and Grolnick, W. (1985) Correlates of mastery-related behaviors: A short-term longitudinal study of infants in their second year. *Child Development,* **56,** 1291-1298.
Garbarino, J, Dubrow, N. Kostelny, K. and Pardo, C. (1992) *Children in danger: Coping with the consequences of community violence.* San Francisco: Jossey-Bass.

Garber, J. and Dodge, K. A. (Eds.) (1991) *The development of emotion regulation and dysregulation.* Cambridge: Cambridge University Press.
Garber, J., Cohen, E., Bacon, P., Egeland, B. and Sroufe, L. A. (1985) *Depression in preschoolers: Resiliency and validity of a behavioral observation measure.* Paper presented at the Society for Research in Child Development, Toronto. [cited in J. Belsky and T. Nezworski 1988, op cit.]
Garmezy, N. and Rutter, M. (Eds.) (1983) *Stress, coping and development in children.* New York: McGraw-Hill.
Garner, L. (1972) Black is bored. *Sunday Times Magazine,* March 18th, 10-16.
Gellner, E. (1985) *The psychoanalytic movement, or the coming of unreason.* London: Paladin.
Genuis, M. L. (1995) Long-term consequences of childhood attachment: Implications for counselling adolescents. *International Journal for the Advancement of Counselling,* **17(4)**, 263-274
George, C. and Solomon, J. (1999) Attachment and caregiving: The caregiving behavioral system. In J. Cassidy and P. R. Shaver (Eds.), *Handbook of attachment: Theory, research, and clinical applications* (649-670). New York: Guilford Press.
George, C., Kaplan, N. and Main, M. (1984/1985/1986/1996) *Adult Attachment Interview.* Unpublished manuscript, Department of Psychology, University of California, Berkeley.
George, C., West, M. and Pettem, O. (1999) The Adult Attachment Projective: Disorganization of adult attachment at the level of representation. In J. Solomon and C. George (Eds.), *Attachment disorganization* (462-507). New York: Guilford Press.
Gerhardt, S. (2004) *Why love matters: How affection shapes a baby's brain.* Hove and New York: Brunner-Routledge.
Gerhardt, S. (2005) *Secure attachments between parents and children aged 0-2.* February 8 2005. Talk given to All Party Parliamentary Group for Children and Families, Portcullis House, London.
Gervai, J. and Lakatos, K. (2004) Comment on "No association of dopamine D4 receptor (DRD4) and -521 C/T promoter polymorphisms with infant attachment disorganization by M. J. Bakermans-Kranenburg and M. H. van IJzendoorn. *Attachment and Human Development,* **6(3)**, 219-222.
Gervai, J., Nemoda, Z., Lakatos, K., Ronai, Z., Toth, I., Ney, K. and Sazvari-Szekely, M. (2005) Transmission disequilibrium tests confirm the link between DRD4 gene polymorphism and infant attachment. *American Journal of Medical Genetics Part B. Neuropsychiatric Genetics,* **132(1)**, 126-130.
Goldberg, S. (1983) Parent-to-infant bonding: Another look. *Child Development,* **54**, 1355-1382.
Goldberg, S. (2000) *Attachment and development.* London: Arnold.
Goldberg, S., Gotowiec, A. and Simmons, R.J. (1995) Infant-mother attachment and behavior problems in healthy and chronically ill preschoolers. *Development and Psychopathology,* **7**, 267-282.
Goldberg, S., Perrotta, M., Minde, K. and Corter, C. (1986) Maternal behavior and attachment in low-birth-weight twins and singletons. *Child Development,* **57(1)**, 34-46.
Goldfarb, W. (1945) Psychological privation in infancy and subsequent adjustment. *American Journal of Orthopsychology,* **15,** 247-255.
Goldfarb, W. (1947) Variations in adolescent adjustment of institutional-reared children, *American Journal of Orthopsychiatry,* **17**, 449-457.
Goldsmith, H. H. and Alansky, J. A. (1987) Maternal and infant predictors of attachment. *Journal of Consulting and Clinical Psychology,* **55**, 805-816.
Goldsmith, H. H. and Harman, C. (1994) Temperament and attachment: Individuals and relationships. *Current Directions in Psychological Science,* **3**, 53-57.
Goldstein J., Freud A. and Solnit A. J. (1973) *Beyond the best interests of the child.* New York: Free Press.
Goldstein J., Freud A. and Solnit A. J. (1979) *Before the best interests of the child.* New York: Free Press.
Goldstein J., Freud A., Solnit A. J. and Goldstein S. (1986) *In the best interests of the child.* New York: Free Press.
Goossens, F. A. and Melhuish, E. C. (1996) On the ecological validity of measuring sensitivity of professional caregivers: The laboratory versus the nursery. *European Journal of Psychology of Education,* **11**, 169-176.
Graham, P. J. and Meadows, C. E. (1967) Psychiatric disorder in the children of West Indian immigrants. *Journal of Child Psychology and Psychiatry,* **8**, 105-106.
Granot, D. and Mayseless, O. (2001) Attachment security and adjustment to school in middle childhood. *International Journal of Behavioral Development,* **25**, 530-541.
Green, J. M. and Murray, D. (1994) The use of the Edinburgh Postnatal Depression Scale in research to explore the relationship between antenatal and postnatal dysphoria. In J. L. Cox and J. M. Holden (Eds.), *Perinatal psychiatry: Use and abuse of the Edinburgh Postnatal Depression Scale* (180-198). London: Gaskell. [cited in Oates, 2002, op cit]
Greenberg, M. T. (1999) Attachment and psychopathology in childhood. In J. Cassidy and P. R. Shaver (Eds.), *Handbook of Attachment: Theory, Research and Clinical Applications* (469-496). New York: Guilford Press.
Greenberg, M. T. and Marvin, R. S. (1982) Reactions of preschool children to an adult stranger: A behavioral systems approach. *Child Development,* **55**, 481-490.
Greenberg, M. T., Cicchetti, D. and Cummings, E.M. (1990) *Attachment in the preschool years: Theory, research, and intervention.* London: The University of Chicago Press.
Greenberg, M. T., Speltz, M. L. and DeKlyen, M. (1993) The role of attachment in the early development of disruptive behavior problems. Special Issue: Toward a Developmental Perspective on Conduct Disorder. *Development and Psychopathology,* **5,** 191-213.
Greenough, W. T., Black, J. E. and Wallace, C. S. (1987) Experience and brain development. *Child Development,* **58(3)**, 539-559.

Gregory, E. (1969, September) Childminding in Paddington. *The Medical Officer, Vol. CXXII,* **10(1)**, 135-139.
Grice, P. (1975) Logic and conversation. In P. Cole and J. L. Moran (Eds.), *Syntax and semantics III: Speech acts* (41-58). New York: Academic Press.
Griffin, D. and Bartholomew, K. (1994) Metaphysics of measurement: The case of adult attachment. In K. Bartholomew and D. Perlman (Eds.), *Advances in personal relationships, Vol. 5: Attachment processes in adulthood* (17-52). London: Jessica Kingsley.
Grosskurth, P. (1986) *Melanie Klein: Her world and her work.* London: Tavistock.
Grossmann, K. E., Grossmann, K. and Zimmermann, P. (1999) A wider view of attachment and exploration. In J. Cassidy and P. R. Shaver (Eds.), *Handbook of attachment. Theory, research, and clinical applications* (760-786) New York: The Guilford Press.
Grossmann, K., Fremmer-Bombik, E. and Rudolph, J. (1988) Maternal attachment representations as related to patterns of infant-mother attachment and maternal care during the first year. In R. A. Hinde and J. Stevenson Hinde (Eds.), *Relationships within families: Mutual influences* (241-262). Oxford: Clarendon.
Grossmann, K., Grossmann, K. E., Spangler, G., Suess, G. and Unzner, L. (1985) Maternal sensitivity and newborn's orientation responses as related to quality of attachment in northern Germany: Growing points of attachment theory and research. *Monographs of the Society for Research in Child Development,* **50(1-2)**, 233-256.
Grossmann, K., Grossmann, K.E., Fremmer-Bombik, E., Kindler, H., Scheuerer-Englisch, H. and Zimmermann, P. (2002) The uniqueness of the child-father attachment relationship: Fathers' sensitive and challenging play as a pivotal variable in a 16-year longitudinal study. *Social Development,* **11(3)**, 307-331.
Grossmann, K.E. and Grossmann, K. (1991) Attachment quality as an organizer of emotional and behavioural responses in a longitudinal perspective. In C.M. Parkes, J. Stevenson-Hinde and P. Marris (Eds.), *Attachment across the life cycle,* 93-114. London: Routledge.
Guldberg, H. (5 October 2004) *The myth of 'infant determinism'.* **On-line essay at:** www.spiked-online.com/Articles/0000000CA71B.htm
Gunnar M. R., Broderson, L., Krueger, K. and Rigatuso, J. (1996) Dampening of adrenocortical responses during infancy: Normative changes and individual differences. *Child Development,* **67**, 877-889.
Gunnar, M. R. (1989) Studies of the human infant's adrenocortical response to potentially stressful events. In M. Lewis and J. Woroby (Eds.), *Infant stress and coping* (3-18). San Francisco: Jossey-Bass, Inc..
Gunnar, M. R. (1998) Quality of early care and buffering of neuroendocrine stress reactions: Potential effects on the developing human brain. *Preventive Medicine,* **27**, 208-211.
Gunnar, M. R. (2000) Early adversity and the development of stress reactivity and regulation. In C. A. Nelson (Ed.), *The effects of early adversity on neurobehavioral development. The Minnesota Symposia on Child Psychology, Volume 31* (163-199). Hillsdale, NJ: Lawrence Erlbaum Associates.
Gunnar, M. R. (2003) *Studying stress in internationally adopted children.* Workshop conducted by Megan Gunnar. Online at: http://www.che.umn.edu/fsos/mtarp/Icarpapers/gunnar.htm
Gunnar, M. R. and Donzella, B. (1999) "Looking for the Rosetta Stone" : An essay on crying, soothing, and stress. In M. Lewis and D. Ramsay, (Eds.), *Soothing and stress* (39-56). Mahwah, NJ: Lawrence Erlbaum Associates.
Gunnar, M. R. and Donzella, B. (2002) Social regulation of the cortisol levels in early human development. *Psychoneuroendocrinology,* **27**, 199-220.
Gunnar, M. R. and Vasquez, D. M. (2001) Low cortisol and a flattening of expected daytime rhythm: Potential indices of risk in human development. *Development and Psychopathology,* **13**, 515-538.
Gunnar, M. R., Kertes, D. A. and the International Adoption Project Team (2003) *Early risk factors and development of internationally adopted children: Can we generalize from the Romanian case?* Presentation for the Society for Research in Child Development. Tampa, FL, April 27, 2003.
Gunnar, M. R., Mangelsdorf, S., Larson, M. C. and Hertsgaard, L. (1989) Attachment, temperament, and adrenocortical activity in infancy: A study of psychoendocrine regulation. *Developmental Psychology,* **25**, 355-363.
Hamilton, C. E. (2000) Continuity and discontinuity of attachment from infancy through adolescence. *Child Development,* **71,** 690-694.
Harlow, H. F. and Zimmerman, R. R. (1959) Affectional responses in the infant monkey. *Science,* **130**, 421-432.
Harlow, H. F., Harlow, M. K., Dodsworth, R. O. and Arling, G. L. (1966) Maternal behavior of rhesus monkeys deprived of mothering and peer associations in infancy. *Proceedings of the American Philosophical Society,* **110**, 58-66.
Harre, R. (1986) *Varieties of realism.* Oxford: Blackwell.
Harris, J. R. (1998) *The nurture assumption: Why children turn out the way they do.* London: Bloomsbury.
Harris, P. L. (1989) *Children and emotion.* Oxford: Blackwell Press.
Harris, T. O., Brown, G. W. and Bifulco, A. (1986) Loss of parent in childhood and adult psychiatric disorder: The Walthamstow Study. 1. The role of lack of adequate parental care. *Psychological Medicine,* **16**, 641-659.
Harris, T. O., Brown, G. W. and Bifulco, A. T. (1990) Depression and situational helplessness/mastery in a sample selected to study childhood parental loss. *Journal of Affective Disorders,* **20**, 27-41.
Harrison, L. and Ungerer, J. (1997) Child care predictors of infant-mother attachment security at age 12 months. *Early Child Development and Care,* **137**, 31-46.
Harrison, L. and Ungerer, J. (2002) Maternal employment and infant-mother attachment security at 12 months postpartum. *Developmental Psychology,* **38**, 758-773.
Hart, A. and Thomas, H. (2000) Controversial attachments: The indirect treatment of fostered and adopted children via Parent Co-Therapy. *Attachment and Human Development,* **2(3)**, 306-327

Hart, J., Gunnar, M. and Cicchetti, D. (1996) Altered neuroendocrine activity in maltreated children related to symptoms of depression. *Development and Psychopathology*, **8**, 201-214.

Hawkins, A. J. and Dollahite, D .C. (Eds.)(1997) *Generative fathering: Beyond deficit perspectives*. Thousand Oaks, CA: Sage.

Hawkins, J. D., Lishner, D. M., Catalano, R. F. and Howard, M. O. (1986) Childhood predictors of adolescent substance abuse: towards an empirically grounded theory. *Journal of Children and Contemporary Society*, **8**, 11-47.

Hay, D. F. and Angold, A. (1993) *Precursors and causes in development and psychopathology*. Chichester: Wiley.

Hazan, C. and Shaver, P. (1987) Romantic love conceptualised as an attachment process. *Journal of Personality and Social Psychology*, **52**, 511-524.

Hazan, C. and Shaver, P. R. (1990) Love and work: An attachment-theoretical perspective. *Journal of Personality and Social Psychology*, **59**, 270-280.

Hazan, C. and Shaver, P. R. (1994) Attachment as an organizational framework for research on close relationships. *Psychological Inquiry*, **5**, 1-22.

Hazen, N. and Durrett, M. (1982) Relationship of security of attachment to exploration and cognitive mapping ability in two-year-olds. *Developmental Psychology*, **18**, 751-759.

Heard, D. (1999) *Attachment and the caregiving system*. Unpublished talk given to the International Attachment Network, London.

Heard, D. and Lake, B. (1996) *The challenge of attachment for caregiving*. London: Routledge.

Heinicke, C. M. and Westheimer, I. (1965) *Brief separations*. New York: International Universities Press.

Heinicke, C. M., Diskin, S. D., Ramsey-Klee, D. and Given, K. (1983) Pre-birth parent characteristics and family development in the first year of life. *Child Development*, **54**, 194-208.

Herschkowitz, N. and Herschkowitz, E. C. (2002) *A good start in life. Understanding your child's brain and behavior from birth to age 6*. New York: Dana Press.

Hertsgaard, L., Gunnar, M., Erickson, M. F. and Nachmias, M. (1995) Adrenocortical responses to the Strange Situation in infants with disorganized/disoriented attachment relationships. *Child Development*, **66**, 1100-1106.

Hertzman, C. (1997) The biological embedding of early experience and its effects on health in adulthood. *Annals of the New York Academy of Sciences*, **896**, 85-95.

Hesse, E. and Main, M. (1999) Second-generation effects of trauma in non-maltreating parents: Previously unexamined risk factor for anxiety. *Psychoanalytic Inquiry*, **19**, 481-540.

Hesse, E. and van IJzendoorn, M. H. (1999) Propensities towards absorption are related to lapses in the monitoring of reasoning or discourse during the Adult Attachment Interview: a preliminary investigation. *Attachment and Human Development*, **1(1)**, 67-91.

Hewlett, B. S. (2004) Fathers in forager, farmer, and pastoral cultures. In M.E. Lamb (Ed.), *The role of the father in child development* (182-195). 4th edition. Hoboken, NJ: Lawrence Erlbaum Associates.

Higgins, E. T., Ruble, D. N. and Hartup, W. W. (1983) *Social cognition and social development: A sociocultural perspective*. Cambrigde: Cambridge University Press.

Hill, J., Fonagy, P., Safier, E. and Sargent, J. (2003) The ecology of attachment in the family. *Family Process*, **42**, 205-221.

Hinde, R. A. (1966) *Animal behaviour. A synthesis of ethology and comparative psychology*. New York: McGraw Hill.

Hinde, R. A. (1972) *Non-verbal communication*. London: Oxford University Press.

Hinde, R. A. (1982a) *Ethology*. Glasgow: Collins.

Hinde, R. A. (1982b) Attachment: Some conceptual and biological issues. In.C. Parkes and J. Stevenson-Hinde (Eds.), *The place of attachment in human behaviour* (60-76). New York: Basic Books.

Hinde, R. A. (1991) When is an evolutionary approach useful? *Child Development*, **62**, 671-675.

Hinshaw, S. P., Lahey, B. B. and Hart, E. L. (1993) Issues of taxonomy and comorbidity in the development of conduct disorder. *Development and Psychopathology*, **5**, 31-49.

Hobfoll, S. E., Ritter, C., Lavin, J., Hulsizer, M. R. and Cameron, R. P. (1995) Depression prevalence and incidence among inner-city pregnant and postpartum women. *Journal of Consulting and Clinical Psychology*, **63(3)**, 445-453.

Hobson, R. P. (2002) *The Cradle of Thought*. London: Macmillan.

Hobson, R. P., Brown, R., Minter, M. and Lee, A. (1997) "Autism" revisited: The case of congenital blindness. In V. Lewis and G. M. Collis (Eds.), *Blindness and psychological development in young children* (99-115). Leicester: British Psychological Society.

Hobson, R. P., Lee, A. and Brown, R. (1999) Autism and congenital blindness. *Journal of Autism and Developmental Disorders*, **29**, 45-56.

Hodges, J. and Tizard, B. (1989) Social and family relationships of ex-institutional adolescents. *Journal of Child Psychology and Psychiatry*, **30**, 77-97.

Hofer, M. A. (1984) Relationships as regulators: a psychobiological perspective on bereavement. *Psychosomatic Medicine*, **46**, 183-197.

Holmes, J. (1993) *John Bowlby and attachment theory*. London: Routledge.

Honig, A. S. (1998) Attachment and relationships: Beyond parenting. Paper presented at the Head Start Quality Network Research Satellite conference (East Lancing MI, 20 August 1998) [*cited in Rolfe 2004, op. cit.*],

Hood, C., Oppe, T. E., Pless, I. B. and Apie, E. (1970) *Children of West Indian immigrants*. London: Institute of Race Relations.

Howe, D. (2003) Attachment disorders: Disinhibited attachment behaviours and secure base distortions with special reference to adopted children. *Attachment and Human Development*, **5(3)**, 265-270.

Howe, D., Brandon, M., Hinings, D. and Schofield, G. (1999) *Attachment theory, child maltreatment and family support: A practice and assessment model*. Basingstoke: Palgrave.

Howes, C. (1999) Attachment and caregiving: The caregiving behavioural system. In J. Cassidy and P. R. Shaver (Eds.), *Handbook of attachment: Theory, research and clinical applications* (649-671) New York: Guilford Press.

Howes, C., Matheson, C. C. and Hamilton, C. E. (1994) Maternal, teacher, and child care history correlates of children's relationships with peers. *Child Development*, **65**, 264-273.

Hoza, B., Pelham, W. E., Milich, R., Pillow, D. and McBride, K. (1993) The self-perceptions and attributions of Attention Deficit Hyperactivity Disordered and nonreferred boys. *Journal of Abnormal Child Psychology*, **21**, 271-286.

Hrdy, S. B. (1999) *Mother nature: A history of mothers, infants, and natural selection*. New York: Pantheon.

Hughes, D. (1997) *Facilitating developmental attachment*. New Jersey: Jason Aronson.

Hughes, D. (1998) *Building the bonds of attachment*. New Jersey: Jason Aronson.

Hughes, D. (2003) Psychological interventions for the spectrum of attachment disorders and intrafamilial trauma. *Attachment and Human Development*, **5(3)**, 271-277.

Hughes, D. (2004) An attachment-based treatment of maltreated children and young people. *Attachment and Human Development*, **6(3)**, 263-278.

Hughes, M., Mayall, B., Moss, P., Perry, J., Petrie, P. and Pinkerton, G. (1980) *Nurseries now*. Harmondsworth: Penguin.

Hunt, J. (2000) The dangers of holding therapy. The Natural Child Project. [Quoting correspondence with Alice Miller]

Hunter, V. (1990) *Interview with John Bowlby*. London: Tavistock Institute library archives; unpublished. Cited in Van Dijken, 1998, *op. cit*.

Huttenlocher, P. R. (1979) Synaptic density in human frontal cortex - developmental changes of aging. *Brain Research*, **163**, 195-205.

Huttenlocher, P. R. and Dabholkar, A. S. (1997) Regional differences in synaptogenesis in human cerebral cortex. *Journal of Comparative Neurology*, **387**, 167-178.

Huttenlocher, P. R. and de Courten, C. (1987) The development of synapses in striate cortex of man. *Human Neurobiology*, **6**, 1-9.

Huttenlocher, P. R., de Courten, C., Garey, L. J. and van der Loos, H. (1982) Synaptogenesis in human visual cortex – evidence for synapse elimination during normal development. *Neuroscience Letters*, **33**, 247-252.

Ingebretson, R. and Solem, P. E. (1997) Attachment, loss and coping in caring for a dementing spouse. In M. L. B. Miesen and G. M. M. Jones (Eds.), *Caregiving in dementia: Research and applications, Volume 2*. London and New York: Routledge.

Inglis, R. (1990) *The children's war: Evacuation 1939-1945*. Glasgow: Fontana/Collins. Cited in Van Dijken, 1998, *op. cit*.

Insel, T. R. (1997) A neurobiological basis of social attachment. *American Journal of Psychiatry*, **154**, 726-735.

Isaacs, S. (1941) *The Cambridge Evacuation Survey: A wartime study in social welfare and education*. London: Methuen.

Isabella, R. A. (1993) Origins of attachment: Maternal interactive behavior across the first year. *Child Development*, **64**, 605-621.

Isabella, R. A. and Belsky, J. (1991) Interactional synchrony and the origins of infant-mother attachment: A replication study. *Child Development*, **62**, 373-384.

Isabella, R. A., Belsky, J. and von Eye, A. (1989) Origins of infant-mother attachment: An examination of interactional synchrony during the infant's first year. *Developmental Psychology*, **25**, 12-21.

Jackson, B. and Jackson, S. (1979) *Childminder. A study in action research*. London: Routledge and Kegan Paul.

Jacobson, J. L. and Wille, D. E. (1986) The influence of attachment pattern on developmental changes in peer interaction from the toddler to the preschool period. *Child Development*, **57**, 338-347.

Jacobson, S. W. and Frye, K. F. (1991) Effect of maternal social support on attachment: Experimental evidence. *Child Development*, **62**, 572-582.

Jacobson, S.W. and Kagan, J. (1979) Interpreting "imitative" responses in early infancy. *Science*, **20**, 215-217.

Jacobvitz, D. and Hazen, N. (1999) Developmental pathways from disorganization to childhood peer relationships. In J. Solomon and C. George (Eds.), *Attachment disorganization* (127-159). New York: Guilford Press.

Jaffe, J., Beebe, B., Feldstein, S., Crown, C. and Jasnow, M. (2001) Rhythms of dialogue in infancy. *Monographs of the Society for Research in Child Development*, **66** (2 Serial No.265), 1-132.

James, B (1994) *Handbook for Treatment of Attachment-Trauma Problems in Children* New York: Lexington Books.

James, W. (1890/1983) *The principles of psychology*. Cambridge, MA: Harvard University Press.

Jenkins, J. M. and Smith, M. A. (1990) Factors protecting children living in disharmonious homes. *Journal of the American Academy of Child and Adolescent Psychiatry*, **29**, 60-69.

Johnson, D. E. (2000) Medical and developmental sequelae of early childhood institutionalization in Easter European adoptees. In C.A. Nelson (Ed.), *The effects of early adversity on neurobehavioural development. The Minnesota Symposia on Child Psychology, Volume 31* (113-162). Mahwah, NJ: Lawrence Erlbaum Associates.

Johnson, M. H. (1999) Cortical plasticity in normal and abnormal cognitive development: Evidence and working hypotheses. *Development and Psychopathology*, **11**, 419-437.

Johnson, M. H. (2001) Functional brain development in humans. *Nature Reviews*, **2**, 475-483.

Johnson, M. H. and Farroni, T. (2003) Perceiving and acting on the eyes: The development and neural basis of eye gaze perception. In Pascalis O. and Slater A. (Eds.), *The development of face processing in infancy and early childhood: Current perspectives* (155-167). New York: Nova Science Publisher.

Jones, N. A., Field, T., Fox, N. A., Lundy, B. and Hart, S. (1998) Newborns of mothers with depressive symptoms are physiologically less developed. *Infant Behavior and Development*, **21**, 537-541.

Juffer, F. (1993) *Verbonden door adoptie. Een experimenteel onderszoek narr hechting en competentie in gezinnen met een adoptiebaby*. [Attached through adoption. An experimental study on attachment and competence in families with an adopted baby]. Amersfoort: Academische uigeverij.

Kagan, J. (1998) *Three seductive ideas*. London: Harvard University Press.

Kagan, J., Snidman, N, Arcus, D. and Reznick, J.S. (1994) *Galen's prophecy: Temperament in human nature*. London: Free Association Books.

Kaplan, N. and Main, M. (1985, April) *Internal representations of attachment at six years as indicated by family drawings and verbal responses to imagined separations*. Paper presented at the meeting of the Society for Research in Child Development, Toronto, Ontario, Canada.

Karen, R. (1994) *Becoming attached: Unfolding the mystery of the infant-mother bond and its impact on later life*. New York: Warner.

Karlsson, H. (1996) Skin to skin care: Heat balance. *Archives of Disease in Childhood*, **75**, F130-F132.

Kay Hall, S. E. and Geher, G. (2003) Behavioral and personality characteristics or children with reactive attachment disorder. *Journal of Psychology: Interdisciplinary and Applied*, **137**, 145-162.

Keck, G. C. and Kupecky, R. (1995) *Adopting the hurt child*. Colorado Springs, CO: Pinon Press.

Keelan, J. P., Dion, K. L. and Dion, K. K. (1994) Attachment style and heterosexual relationships among young adults: A short-term panel study. *Journal of Social and Personal Relationships*, **11(1)**, 201-214.

Kelly, V. (2003) *Theoretical rational for the treatment of disorders of attachment*. Downloadable from http://www.attach.org/theorationale.htm

Kerns, K. A., Keplac, L. and Cole, A. (1996) Peer relationships and preadolescents' perceptions of security in the child-mother relationship. *Developmental Psychology*, **32**, 457-466

Kesner, J., Julian, T. and McKenry, P. (1997) Application of attachment theory to male violence toward female intimates. *Journal of Family Violence*, **12(2)**, 211-228.

Kestenbaum, R., Farber, E. A. and Sroufe, A. (1989) Individual differences in empathy among preschoolers: relation to attachment history. In N. Eisenberg (Ed.), *Empathy and related emotional competence, New Directions for Child Development*, **44**, 51-64.

Kirkpatrick, L. A. and Davis, K. E. (1994) Attachment style, gender, and relationship stability: A longitudinal analysis. *Journal of Personality and Social Psychology*, **66**, 502-512.

Klaus, M. H. and Kennell, J. H. (1976) *Maternal-infant bonding*. St. Louis: Mosby.

Klein, M. (1932/1989) *The psycho-analysis of children*. London: Virago Press.

Knox, J. (2003) Archetype, attachment, analysis: Jungian psychology and the emergent mind. Hove: Brunner-Routledge.

Kobak, R. (1999) The emotional dynamics of disruptions in attachment relationships: Implications for theory, research, and clinical intervention. In J. Cassidy and P. R. Shaver (Eds.), *Handbook of attachment: Theory, research, and clinical applications* (21-43) New York: Guilford Press.

Kobak, R. R. and Hazan, C. (1991) Attachment in marriage: Effects of security and accuracy of working models. *Journal Personality and Social Psychology*, **60**, 861-869.

Kobak, R.R. and Sceery, A. (1988) Attachment in late adolescence: Working models, affect regulation, and representation of self and others. *Child Development*, **59**, 135-146.

Kobak, R.R., Cole, H.E., Ferenz-Gillies, R. and Fleming, W.S. (1993) Attachment and emotion regulation during mother-teen problem solving: A control theory analysis. *Child Development*, **64**, 231-245.

Kochanska, G. (1995) Children's temperament, mothers' discipline, and security of attachment: Multiple pathways to emerging internalization. *Child Development*, **66**, 597-615.

Kochanska, G. (1997) Mutually responsive orientation between mothers and their young children: Implications for early socialization. *Child Development*, **68**, 94-112.

Kochanska, G. (1998) Mother-child relationship, child fearfulness and emerging attachment: A short-term longitudinal study. *Developmental Psychology*, **34(3)**, 480-490.

Kochanska, G. (2001) Emotional development in children with different attachment histories: The first three years. *Child Development*, **72(2)**, 474-490.

Kochanska, G., Coy, K. C. and Murray, K. T. (2001) The development of self-regulation in the first four years of life. *Child Development*, **72**, 1091-1111.

Koniak-Griffin, D., Walker, D. S. and de Traversay, J. (1996) Predictors of depression symptoms in pregnant adolescents. *Journal of Perinatology*, **16**, 69-76.

Kotelchuck, M. (1976) The infant's relationship to the father: Experimental evidence. In M. E. Lamb (Ed.), *The role of the father in child development*. New York: Wiley.

Kozlowska, K. and Hanney, L. (2002) The network perspective: an integration of attachment and family systems theories. *Family Process*, **41**, 285-312.

Kraemer, G. W. (1992) A psychobiological theory of attachment. *Behavioral and Brain Sciences*, **15**, 493-541.

Kunce, L. J. and Shaver, P. R. (1994) An attachment-theoretical approach to caregiving in romantic relationships. In K. Bartholomew and D. Perlman (Eds.), *Advances in personal relationships: Vol. 5. Attachment process in adulthood* (205-237). London: Jessica Kingsley.

Ladnier, R. D. and Massanari, A. E. (2000) Treating ADHD as attachment deficit disorder. In T.M.Levy (Ed.), *Handbook of attachment interventions* (27-65). San Diego: Academic Press.

LaFreniere, P. J. and Sroufe, L. A. (1985) Profiles of peer competence in the preschool: Interrelations between measures influence of social ecology, and relation to attachment history. *Developmental Psychology*, **21**, 56-69.
Laible, D. J., Carlo, G. and Raffaelli, M. (2000) The differential relations of parent and peer attachment to adolescent adjustment. *Journal of Youth and Adolescence*, **29**, 45-59.
Lakatos, K., Nemoda, Z., Toth, L., Ronai, Z., Ney, K., Savari-Szekely, M., et al. (2002) Further evidence for the role of the dopamine D4 receptor (DRD4) gene in attachment disorganization: interaction of the exon III 48-bp repeat and the 521 C/T promoter polymorphisms. *Molecular Psychiatry*, **7**, 27-31.
Lakatos, K., Toth, L., Nemoda, Z., Ney, K., Savari-Szekely, M. and Gervai, J. (2000) Dopamine D4 receptor (DRD4) gene polymorphism is associated with attachment disorganization in infants. *Molecular Psychiatry*, **5**, 633-637.
Lamb, M. E. (1981) *The role of the father in child development*. New York: Wiley.
Lamb, M. E. and Hwang, C. P. (1982) Maternal attachment and mother-neonate bonding: a critical review. In M. E. Lamb and A. L. Brown (Eds.), *Advances in Developmental Psychology, Vol 2* (1-39). Hillsdale, NJ: Lawrence Erlbaum Associates.
Lamb, M. E. and Sherrod, L. R. (Eds.) (1981) *Infant social cognition: Empirical and theoretical considerations*. Hillsdale, NJ: Lawrence Erlbaum Associates.
Lamb, M. E., Pleck, J. H., Charnov, E. L. and Levine, J. A. (1987) A biosocial perspective on paternal behavior and involvement. In J.B. Lancaster, J. Altman, A. Rossi and L.R. Sherrod (Eds.), *Parenting across the lifespan: Biosocial perspectives* (11-42). New York: Academic Press.
Lamb, M. E., Thompson, R. A., Gardner, W., Charnov, E. L. and Connell, J. P. (1985) *Infant-Mother Attachment: The origins and developmental significance of individual differences in Strange Situation behavior*. Hillsdale, NJ: Lawrence Erlbaum Associates.
Lamb, M. E., Thompson, R. A., Gardner, W., Charnov, E. L. and Estes, D. (1984) Security of infantile attachment as assessed in the 'Strange Situation': Its study and biological interpretation. *Behavioral and Brain Sciences*, **7**, 127-47.
Lambermon, M. W. E. (1991) *Video of folder? Korte- en lange-terminijn-effecten van voorlichting over vroegkinderlijke opvoeding*. [Videotaped or written information?] Leiden: DSWO Press.
Lambermon, M. W. E. and Van IJzendoorn, M. H. (1989) Influencing mother-baby interaction through videotaped or written instruction: evaluation of a parent education program. *Early Childhood Research Quarterly*, **4**, 449-459.
Lane, S. K., Donzella, B., Boxer, J. and Gunnar, M. R. (2000) *Cortisol levels in toddlers at full-day childcare: Comparison with home cortisol and temperament*. Paper presented at the International Conference on Infant Studies, Brighton, England.
Langer, E. J. (1983) *The psychology of control*. London: Sage.
Larose, S., Bernier, A., Soucy, N. and Duchesne, S. (1999) Attachment style dimensions, network orientation, and the process of seeking help from college teachers. *Advances in Personal Relationships*, **16**, 225-247.
Larson, M, White, B. P., Cochran, A., Donzella, B. and Gunnar, M. R. (1998) Dampening of cortisol response to handling at 3-months in human infants and its relation to sleep, circadian cortisol activity, and behavioral distress. *Developmental Psychobiology*, **33**, 327-337.
Lay, K., Waters, E., Posada, G. and Ridgeway, D. (1995) Attachment security, affect regulation, and defensive responses to mood induction. In E. Waters, G. Posada and K. Konde-Ikemura (Eds.), *Caregiving, cultural, and cognitive perspectives on secure base behavior and working models: New growing points of attachment theory and research. Monographs of the Society for Research in Child Development*, **60(2-3)**, 179-196.
Lazarus, R. S. and Launier, R (1978) Stress-related transactions between person and environment. In L. A. Pervin and M. Lewis (Eds.), *Perspectives in interactional psychology* (287-327). New York: Plenum Press.
LeDoux, J. E. (1987) Emotion. In V.B. Mountcastle (Ed.), *Handbook of physiology. Section I: The nervous system, Volume 5: Higher functions of the brain* (419-459). Bethesda, MD: American Physiological Society.
LeDoux, J. E. (1992) Emotion and the amygdala. In J.P. Aggleton (Ed.), *The amygdala: Neurobiological aspects of emotion, memory and mental dysfunction* (339-351). New York: Wiley-Liss.
Legendre, A. and Kortinus, M. (1996) *Differences in stress susceptibility among toddlers in day care centers: relationships with frequency of diseases*. International Society for the Study of Behavioural Development, 14th Biennial Meeting, Quebec City. *Reported in Gunnar (1998), op. cit.*.
Lessard, J. C. and Moretti, M. M. (1998) Suicidal ideation in an adolescent clinical sample: Attachment patterns and clinical implications. *Journal of Adolescence*, **21(4)**, 383-395.
Lester, B. M., Hoffman, J. and Brazelton, T. B. (1985) The rhythmic structure of mother-infant interaction in term and preterm infants. *Child Development*, **56**, 15-27.
Levine, S. and Wiener, S. G. (1988) Psychoendocrine aspects of mother-infant relationships in non-human primates. *Psychoendocrinology*, **13**, 143-154.
Lewin, K. (1935) *A dynamic theory of personality*. New York: McGraw-Hill.
Lewis, M. (Ed.)(1987) *Beyond the dyad*. New York: Plenum Press.
Lewis, M. and Brooks-Gunn, J. (1979) *Social cognition and the acquisition of self*. New York: Plenum.
Lewis, M., Feiring, C. and Rosenthal, S. (2000) Attachment over time. *Child Development*, **71**, 707-720.
Lewis, M., Feiring, C., McGuffog, C. and Jaskir, J. (1984) Predicting psychopathology in six-year-olds from early social relations. *Child Development*, **55**, 123-136.
Lieberman, A. F. and Pawl, J. H. (1988) Clinical applications of attachment theory. In J. Belsky and T. Nezworski (Eds.), *Clinical implications of attachment* (327-347). Hillsdale, NJ: Lawrence Erlbaum Associates.
Liedloff, J. (1977) *The Continuum Concept*. New York: Addison-Wesley.

Liedloff, J. (1989) The importance of the in-arms phase. *Mothering*, **50**, 16-19.
Light, K. C., Smith, T. E., Johns, J. M., Brownley, K. A., Hofheimer, J. A. and Amico, J. A. (2000) Oxytocin responsivity in mothers of infants: A preliminary of relationships with blood pressure during laboratory stress and normal ambulatory activity. *Health Psychology*, **19**, 560-567.
Liotti, G. (1992) Disorganized/disoriented attachment in the etiology of the dissociative disorders. *Dissociation*, **5**, 196-204.
Londerville, S. and Main, M. (1981) Security of attachment, compliance, and maternal training methods in the second year of life. *Developmental Psychology*, **17**, 289-299.
Lorenz, K. (1937) The companion in the bird's world. *The Auk*, **54**, 245-273.
Lorenz, K. (1951) *Studies in animal and human behaviour*. Oxford: Clarendon Press.
Love, J. M., Harrison, L., Sagi-Schwartz, A, et al. (2003) Child care quality matters: How conclusions may vary with context. *Child Development*, **74(4)**, 1021-1033.
Lutkenhaus, P., Grossmann, K. E. and Grossmann, K. (1985) Infant-mother attachment at 12 months and style of interaction with a stranger at the age of three years. *Child Development*, **56**, 1538-1572.
Lyons, D., Lopez, J., Yang, C., and Schatzburg, A. (2000) Stress level cortisol treatment impairs inhibitory control of behaviour in monkeys. *Journal of Neuroscience*, **20(20)**, 7816-7821.
Lyons-Ruth, K. and Jacobvitz, D. (1999) Attachment disorganization: Unresolved loss relational violence and lapses in behavioral and attention strategies. In J. Cassidy and P. Shaver (Eds.), *Handbook of attachment: Theory research and clinical applications*, (520-554). New York: Guilford Press.
Lyons-Ruth, K. and Spielman, E. (2004) Disorganized infant attachment strategies and helpless-fearful profiles of parenting: Integrating attachment research with clinical intervention. *Infant Mental Health Journal*, **25(4)**, 318-335.
Lyons-Ruth, K., Alpern, L. and Repacholi, B. (1993) Disorganized infant attachment classification and maternal psychosocial problems as predictors of hostile-aggressive behavior in the preschool classroom. *Child Development*, **64**, 572-585.
Lyons-Ruth, K., Bronfman, E. and Parsons, E. (1999) Maternal frightened, frightening, or atypical behavior and disorganized infant attachment strategies. *Monographs of the Society for Research in Child Development*, **64(3)**, 67-96.
Lyons-Ruth, K., Connell, D. B., Grunebaum, H. and Botein, S. (1990) Infants at social risk: Maternal depression and family support services as mediators in infant development and security of attachment. *Child Development*, **61**, 85-98.
Lyons-Ruth, K., Connell, D. B., Zoll, D. and Stahl, J. (1987) Infants at social risk: Relations among infant maltreatment, maternal behavior, and infant attachment behavior. *Developmental Psychology*, **23**, 223-232.
Lyons-Ruth, K., Repacholi, B., McLeod, S. and Silva, E. (1991) Disorganized attachment behavior in infancy: Short-term stability maternal and infant correlates and risk-related subtypes. *Development and Psychopathology*, **3**, 377-396.
MacArthur, R. H. (1962) Some generalized theorems of natural selection. *Proceedings of the National Academy of Sciences, U.S.A.*, **48**, 1893-1897.
Magid, K. and McKelvey, C. A. (1987) *High risk: Children without a conscience*. New York: Bantam.
Mahler, M., Pine, F. and Bergman, A. (1975) *The psychological birth of the human infant: Symbiosis and individuation*. New York: Basic Books.
Main, M. (1977) Analysis of a peculiar form of reunion behavior seen in some day-care children: Its history and sequelae in children who are home-reared. In R. A. Webb (Ed.), *Social development in childhood: Day-care programs and research* (33-78). Baltimore: John Hopkins University Press.
Main, M. (1983) Exploration play and cognitive functioning related to mother-infant attachment. *Infant Behavior and Development*, **6**, 167-174.
Main, M. (1991) Metacognitive knowledge metacognitive monitoring, and singular (coherent) versus multiple (incoherent) models of attachment. In C. M. Parkes, J. Stevenson-Hinde and P. Marris (Eds.), *Attachment Across the Life Cycle*, (127-159). London: Routledge.
Main, M. (2000) The organized categories of infant, child and adult attachment: Flexible vs. inflexible attention under attachment-related stress. *Journal of the American Psychoanalytic Association*, **48**, 1055-1096.
Main, M. and Hesse, E. (1990) Parents' unresolved traumatic experiences are related to infant disorganized attachment status: Is frightened and/or frightening parental behavior the linking mechanism? In M. T. Greenberg, D. Cicchetti and E. M. Cummings (Eds.), *Attachment in the preschool years* (161-182). Chicago: University Press of Chicago.
Main, M. and Morgan, H. (1996) Disorganization and disorientation in infant strange situation behavior: Phenotypic resemblance to dissociative states. In L. K. Michelson and W. J. Ray (Eds.), *Handbook of dissociation: Theoretical, empirical and clinical perspectives* (107-38). New York: Plenum.
Main, M. and Solomon, J. (1986) Discovery of a new insecure-disorganized / disoriented attachment pattern. In M. Yogman and T. B. Brazelton (Eds.), *Affective development in infancy* (95-124) Norwood NJ: Ablex.
Main, M. and Solomon, J. (1990) Procedures for identifying infants as disorganized/disoriented during the Ainsworth Strange Situation. In M. Greenberg, D. Cicchetti and M. Cummings (Eds.), *Attachment in the preschool years: Theory, research, and intervention* (121-160). Chicago: University of Chicago Press.
Main, M. and Stadtman, J. (1981) Infant response to rejection of physical contact by the mother. *American Academy of Child Psychiatry*, **20**, 292-307.

Main, M. and Weston, D. R. (1981) The quality of toddlers' relationship to mother and father: Related to conflict behavior and the readiness to establish new relationships. *Child Development*, **52**, 932-940.

Main, M., Hesse, E. and Kaplan, N. (2005) Predictability of attachment behavior and representational processes at 1, 6, and 19 years of age: The Berkeley Longitudinal Study. In K.E. Grossmann, K. Grossmann and E. Waters (Eds.), *Attachment from infancy to adulthood: The major longitudinal studies* (245-304). New York and London: Guilford Press.

Main, M., Kaplan, K. and Cassidy, J. (1985) Security in infancy, childhood and adulthood: A move to the level of representation. In I. Bretherton and E. Waters (Eds.), *Growing points of attachment theory and research, Monographs of the society for research in child development*, **50(1-2)**, 66-106.

Maloney, S. (2005) *Be wary of attachment therapy*. Available at Quackwatch website: http://www.quackwatch.org/01QuackeryRelatedTopics/at.html

Marcovitch, S., Goldberg, S., Gold, A., Washington, J., Wasson, C., Krekewich, K. and Handley-Derry, M. (1997) Determinants of behavioural problems in Romanian children adopted in Ontario. *International Journal of Behavioural Development*, **20(1)**, 17-31.

Marrone, M. (1998) *Attachment and interaction*. London: Jessica Kingsley.

Marsh, P., McFarland, F. C., Allen, J. P., McElhaney, K. B. and Land, D. (2003) Attachment, autonomy, and multifinality in adolescent internalizing and risky behavioral symptoms. *Development and Psychopathology*, **15**, 451-467.

Marshall, P. J., Fox, N. A. and the B. E. I. P. Core Group (2004) A comparison of the electroencephalogram between institutionalized and community children in Romania. *Journal of Cognitive Neuroscience*, **16(8)**, 1327-1338.

Marvin, R. S. and Stewart, R. B. (1990) A family systems framework for the study of attachment. In M. Greenberg, D. Cicchetti and E. M. Cummings (Eds.), *Attachment in the preschool years: Theory, research and intervention* (51-86). Chicago: University of Chicago Press.

Marvin, R., Cooper, G., Hoffman, K. and Powell, B. (2002) The circle of security project: Attachment-based intervention with caregiver-preschool child dyads. *Attachment and Human Development*, **4**, 107-124.

Maslin-Cole, C. and Spieker, S. J. (1990) Attachment as basis for independent motivation. In M. T. Greenberg, D. Cicchetti and E. M. Cummings (Eds.), *Attachment in the preschool years: Theory, research, and intervention* (245-272). Chicago, IL: University of Chicago Press.

Matas, L., Arend, R. A. and Sroufe, L. A. (1978) Continuity of adaptation in the second year: The relationship between quality of attachment and later competence. *Child Development*, **49**, 547-556.

Mayall, B. and Petrie, P. (1977) Minder, mother and child. *Studies in Education*, **No. 5**. London: Institute of Education.

Mayall, B. and Petrie, P. (1981) *Under twos in day-care: A study of the service given by childminders and day nurseries to young children and their mothers*. London: Thomas Coram Research Unit.

Mayall, B. and Petrie, P. (1983) *Childminding and day nurseries. What kind of care? Studies in Education, No. 13*. London: Heinemann.

McCrone, E., Carlson, E. and Engler, J. (1993) *Relations of attachment to defensive organization in middle childhood*. Poster presented at the biennial meeting of the Society for Research in Child Development, New Orleans, LA. [cited in Carlson and Sroufe 1995]

McCrone, E., Egeland, B., Kalkoske, M. and Carlson, E. (1994) Relations between early maltreatment and mental representations of relationships assessed with projective storytelling in middle childhood. *Development and Psychopathology*, **6**, 99-120.

McElwain, N. L., Cox, M. J., Burchinal, M. R. and Macfie, J. (2003) Differentiating among insecure mother-infant attachment classifications: A focus on child-friend interaction and exploration during solitary play at 36 months. *Attachment and Human Development*, **5**, 136-164.

McEwen, B. S. and Stellar, E. (1993) Stress and the individual: Mechanisms leading to disease. *Archives of Internal Medicine*, **153**, 2093-2101.

Mead, G. H. (1934) *Mind, self and society*. Chicago: University of Chicago Press.

Mebert, C. J. (1991) Dimensions of subjectivity in parents' ratings of infant temperament. *Child Development*, **62**, 352-361.

Mehler, J., Bertoncini, J., Barriere, M. and Jassik-Gerschenfel, D. (1978) Infant recognition of mother's voice. *Perception*, **7**, 491-497.

Meij, J. Th. H. (1992) *Sociale ondersteuning, gehechtheidskwaliteit en vroegkinderlijke, competentie-ontwikkeling*. [Social support, attachment, and early competence]. Nijmegen, The Netherlands: Catholic University (dissertation).

Meins, E. (1997) *Security of attachment and the social development of cognition*. Hove: Psychology Press.

Meins, E. (1998) The effects of security of attachment and maternal attribution of meaning on children's linguistic acquisitional style. *Infant Behavior and Development*, **21**, 237-252.

Meins, E., Fernyhough, C., Fradley, E. and Tuckey, M. (2001) Rethinking maternal sensitivity: Mothers' comments on infants' mental processes predict security of attachment at 12 months. *Journal of Child Psychology and Psychiatry*, **42(5)**, 637-648.

Meins, E., Fernyhough, C., Russell, J. and Clark-Carter, D. (1998) Security of attachment as a predictor of symbolic and mentalising abilities: A longitudinal study. *Social Development*, **7**, 1-24.

Melges, F. T. and Bowlby, J. (1969) Types of hopelessness in psychopathological process. *Archives of General Psychiatry*, **20**, 690-699.

Melhuish, E. C., Mooney, A., Martin, S. and Lloyd, E. (1990a) Type of childcare at 18 months: 1. Differences in interactional experience. *Journal of Child Psychology and Psychiatry*, **31(6)**, 849-859.

Melhuish, E. C., Mooney, A., Martin, S. and Lloyd, E. (1990b) Type of childcare at 18 months: 2. Relations with cognitive and language development. *Journal of Child Psychology and Psychiatry*, **31(6)**, 861-870.

Meltzoff, A. N. and Moore, M. K. (1977) Imitation of facial and manual gestures by human neonates. *Science*, **198**, 75-78.

Meltzoff, A. N. and Moore, M. K. (1993) Why faces are special to infants - on connecting the attraction of faces and infants' ability for imitation and cross-modal processing. In B. de Boysson-Bardies, S. de Schonen, P. Jusczyk, P. McNeilage and J. Morton (Eds.), *Developmental neurocognition: Speech and face processing in the first year of life* (211-226). Dordrecht: Kluwer.

Mercer, J. (2001) Attachment therapy using deliberate restraint: An object lesson on the identification of unvalidated treatments. *Journal of Child and Adolescent Psychiatric Nursing*, **14(3)**, 105-114.

Mercer, J. (2002) Attachment Therapy: A treatment without empirical support. *The Scientific Review of Mental Health Practice*, **1(2)**, 105-112.

Mercer, J., Sarner, L. and Rosa, L. (2003) *Attachment Therapy on Trial: The Torture and Death of Candace Newmaker*. Westport, CT: Praeger.

Mikulincer, M. and Nachson, O. (1991) Attachment styles and patterns of self-disclosure. *Journal of Personality and Social Psychology*, **61(2)**, 321-331.

Mikulincer, M. and Shaver, P. R. (2003) The attachment behavioral system in adulthood: Activation, psychodynamics, and interpersonal processes. In M. P. Zanna (Ed.), *Advances in Experimental Social Psychology, Volume. 35* (53-152). New York: Academic Press.

Mikulincer, M., Florian, V., Cowan, P. A. and Cowan, C. P. (2002) Attachment security in couple relationships: A systemic model and its implications for family dynamics. Family Process, **41(3)**, 405-434.

Miljkovitch, R., Pierrehumbert, B., Bretherton, I. and Halfon, O. (2004) Associations between parental and child attachment representations. *Attachment and Human Development*, **6(3)**, 305-325.

Minuchin, S. (1974) *Families and family therapy*. Cambridge, MA: Harvard University Press.

Minuchin, S. (1984) *Family kaleidoscope*. Cambridge, MA: Harvard University Press.

Miyake, K., Chen, S. and Campos, J. J. (1985) Infant temperament, mother's mode of interaction, and attachment in Japan: An interim report. In I. Bretherton and E. Waters (Eds.), Growing points of attachment theory and research. *Monographs of the Society for Research in Child Development*, *50* (1-2, Serial No. 209), 276-297.

Moore, T. W. (1964) Children of full-time and part-time mothers. *International Journal of Social Psychiatry*, **Special Congress Issue No. 2**, 1-10.

Morison, S. J., Ames, E. W. and Chisholm, K. (1995) The development of children adopted from Romanian orphanages. *Merril-Palmer Quarterly*, *41*, 411-430.

Murray, L. (1992) The impact of postnatal depression on infant development. *Journal of Child Psychology and Psychiatry*, **33(3)**, 543-561.

Murray, L. and Trevarthen, C. (1985) Emotional regulation of interactions between 2 month-olds and their mothers. In T. Field and N. Fox (Eds.), *Social perception in infants* (177-197). Norwood, NJ: Ablex.

Murray, L., Fiori-Cowley, A., Hooper, R. and Cooper, P. (1996a) The impact of postnatal depression and associated adversity on early mother-infant interactions and later infant outcomes. *Child Development*, *67*, 2512-2526.

Murray, L., Hipwell, A., Hooper, R., Stein, A. and Cooper, P. (1996c) The cognitive development of 5-year-old children of postnatally-depressed mothers. *Journal of Child Psychology and Psychiatry*, **37(8)**, 927-935.

Murray, L., Sinclair, D., Cooper, P., Ducournau, P. and Turner, P. (1999) The socioemotional development of 5-year-old children of postnatally depressed mothers. *Journal of Child Psychology and Psychiatry*, *40*, 1259-1271.

Murray, L., Stanley, C., Hooper, R., King, F. and Fiori-Cowley, A. (1996b) The role of infant factors in postnatal depression and mother-infant interactions. *Developmental Medicine and Child Neurology*, *38*, 109-119.

Nada-Raja, S., McGee, R. and Stanton, W. R. (1992) Perceived attachment to parents and peers and psychological well-being in adolescence. *Journal of Youth and Adolescence*, **21(4)**, 471-485.

Nelson, E. E. and Panksepp, J. (1996) Oxytocin mediates acquisition of maternally associated odor preference in preweanling rat pups. *Behavioral Neuroscience*, **110**, 1-10.

Nelson, E. E. and Panksepp, J. (1998) Brain substrates of infant-mother attachment: Contributions of opioids, oxytocin, and norepinephrine. *Neurosciences and Biobehavioral Reviews*, **22(3)**, 437-452.

Nelson, K. (1989) *Narratives from the crib*. Cambridge: Harvard University Press.

Nelson, K. and Gruendel, J. M. (1981) Generalized event representations: Basic building blocks of cognitive development. In M. E. Lamb and A. L. Brown (Eds.), *Advances in developmental psychology, Volume 1* (131-158). Hillsdale, NJ: Lawrence Erlbaum Associates.

Newton, M. (2003) *Savage girls and wild boys: A history of feral children*. London: Faber and Faber. Information is also available on the web at: www.feralchildren.com.

NICHD Early Child Care Research Network (1997) The effects of infant child care on infant-mother attachment security: Results of the NICHD study of early child care. *Child Development*, **68(5)**, 860-879.

NICHD Early Child Care Research Network (1998) Early child care and self control, compliance, and problem behavior at twenty-four and thirty-six months. *Child Development*, *69*, 1145-1170.

NICHD ECCRN (2001a) Child care and children's peer interaction at 24 and 36 months: The NICHD study of Early Child Care. *Child Development*, **72(5)**, 1478-1500.

NICHD ECCRN (2001b) Child care and family predictors of preschool attachment and stability from infancy. *Developmental Psychology*, *37*, 847-862.

NICHD ECCRN (2001c) Nonmaternal care and family factors in early development: An overview of the NICHD Study of Early Child Care. *Applied Developmental Psychology*, **22**, 457-492.
NICHD ECCRN (2002) Child care structure to process to outcome: Direct and indirect effects of childcare quality on young children's development. *Psychological Science*, **13(3)**, 199-206.
NICHD ECCRN (2003a) Does amount of time spent in child care predict socio-emotional adjustment during the transition to kindergarten? *Child Development*, **74**, 976-1005.
NICHD ECCRN (2003b) Does quality of child care affect child outcomes at age 4 1/2? *Developmental Psychology*, **39**, 451-469.
NICHD ECCRN (2003c) Early child care and mother-child interaction from 36 months through first grade. *Infant Behavior and Development*, **26**, 345-370.
Nichols, M. P. and Schwarz, R. C. (1998) *Family therapy: Concepts and methods*. Boston: Allyn and Bacon.
Oakley, A. (1979) *Becoming a mother*. Bungay, Suffolk: The Chaucer Press.
Oates, M. R. (2002) Adverse effects of maternal antenatal anxiety on children: causal effect or developmental continuum? *British Journal of Psychiatry*, **180**, 478-479.
O'Connor, M., Sigman, M. and Brill, N. (1987) Disorganization of attachment in relation to maternal alcohol consumption. *Journal of Consulting and Clinical Psychology*, **55**, 831-836.
O'Connor, T. G., Heron, J., Golding, J., Beveridge, M. and Glover, V. (2002) Maternal antenatal anxiety and children's behavioural/emotional problems at 4 years. Report from the Avon Longitudinal Study of Parents and Children. *British Journal of Psychiatry*, **180**, 502-508.
O'Connor, T. G., Marvin, R. S., Rutter, M., Olrick, J. T., Britner, P. A. and the English and Romanian Adoptees Study Team (2003) Child-parent attachment following early institutional deprivation. *Development and Psychopathology*, **15**, 19-38.
O'Connor, T. G., Rutter, M. and the English and Romanian Adoptees Study Team (2000) Attachment disorder behavior following early severe deprivation: Extension and longitudinal follow-up. *Journal of the American Academy of Child and Adolescent Psychiatry*, **39**, 703-712.
O'Connor, T.G. and Zeanah, C.H. (2003) Attachment disorders: Assessment strategies and treatment approaches. *Attachment and Human Development*, **5(3)**, 223-244.
Odent, M. (1999) *The scientification of love*. London: Free Association Books.
O'Hara, M. W. and Swain, A. M. (1996) Rates and risk of postpartum depression: A meta-analysis. *International Review of Psychiatry*, **8**, 37-54.
Olson, D.H. (1993) Circumplex model of marital and family system: Assessing family functioning. In F. Walsh (Ed.), *Normal family process* (104-137). New York: Guilford Press.
Olson, S. L., Bates, J. E. and Bayles, K. (1990) Early antecedents of childhood impulsivity: The role of parent-child interaction, cognitive competence, and temperament. *Journal of Abnormal Child Psychology*, **18**, 317-334.
Oppenheim, D., Koren-Karie, N. and Sagi, A. (2001) Mothers' empathic understanding of their preschoolers' internal experience: Relations with early attachment. *International Journal of Behavioral Development*, **25**, 17-27.
Oppenheim, D., Sagi, A. and Lamb, M. E. (1988) Infant-adult attachments on the kibbutz and their relation to socioemotional development 4 years later. *Developmental Psychology*, **24**, 427-433.
Orvaschel, H. (1983) Parental depression and child psychopathology. In S. B. Guze, F. J. Earls and J. E. Barrett (Eds.), *Childhood psychopathology and development* (53-66). New York: Raven Press.
Orvaschel, H., Welsh-Allis, G. and Weijai, Y. (1988) Psychopathology in children of parents with recurrent depression. *Journal of Abnormal Child Psychology*, **16**, 17-28.
Osofsky, J. D. and Eberhart-Wright, A. (1992) Risk and protective factors for parents and infants. In G. J. Suci and S. S. Robertson (Eds.), *Future directions in infant development research* (25-42). New York: Springer-Verlag.
Owen, S. (1988-9) The "unobjectionable" service. A legislative history of childminding. *Children and Society*, **2(4)**, 367-382.
Palkovitz, R. (1997) Reconstructing 'involvement': Expanding conceptualizations of men's caring in contemporary families. In A. J. Hawkins and D. C. Dollahite (Eds.), *Generative fathering: Beyond deficit perspectives* (200-216). Thousand Oaks, CA: Sage
Pancake, V. (1985) *Continuity between mother-infant attachment and ongoing dyadic relationships in preschool*. Paper presented at the biennial meeting of the Society for Research in Child Development, Toronto.
Panksepp, J. (1998) *Affective neuroscience*. Oxford: Oxford University Press.
Papousek, H. and Papousek, M. (1977) Mothering and the cognitive headstart: Psychobiological considerations. In H.R. Schaffer (Ed.) *Studies in mother-infant interaction* (63-88). London: Academic Press.
Papousek, H., Jurgens, U. and Papousek, M. (1992) *Non-verbal vocal communication: Comparative and developmental approaches*. New York: Cambridge University Press.
Papousek, H., Papousek, M. and Bornstein, M. H. (1985) The naturalistic vocal environment of young infants: On the significance of homogeneity and variability in parents' speech. In T. M.Field and N. A. Fox (Eds.), *Social perception in infants* (269-297). Norwood, NJ: Ablex.
Parker, I. (1992) *Discourse dynamics: Critical analysis for social and individual psychology*. London: Routledge.
Parker, S. W., Nelson, C. A. and the Bucharest Early Intervention Project Core Group (2005) The impact of early institutional rearing on the ability to discriminate facial expressions of emotion: An event-related potential study. *Child Development*, **76(1)**, 54-72.
Parkes, C. M. (1995) Edward John Mostyn Bowlby 1907-1990. *Proceedings of the British Academy*, **87**, 247-261.

Pastor, D. L. (1981) The quality of mother-infant attachment and its relationship to toddlers' initial sociability with peers. *Developmental Psychology*, **17**, 326-335.

Paus, T. (2005) Mapping brain maturation and cognitive development during adolescence. *Trends in Cognitive Science*, **9**, 60-68. Online at www2.psych.cornell.edu:16080/cutting/courses/pausadolsce.pdf

Pearson, J., Cohn, D. A., Cowan, P. A. and Cowan, C. P. (1994) Earned and continuous-security in adult attachment: Relation to depressive symptomology and parenting style. *Development and Psychopathology*, **6**, 359-373.

Pederson, D., Gleason, K. E., Moran, G. and Bento, S. (1998) Maternal attachment representations maternal sensitivity, and the infant-mother attachment relationship. *Developmental Psychology*, **34**, 925-933.

Pepler, D. and Rubin, K. (Eds.) (1991) *The Development and Treatment of Childhood Aggression*. Hillsdale, NJ: Lawrence Erlbaum Associates.

Pesonen, A-K. (2004) *Infant temperament in context: Premises of parental perceptions*. Academic dissertation: Faculty of Behavioural Sciences, University of Helsinki. Available on www at http://ethesis.helsinki.fi, March 2005.

Pesonen, A-K., Raikkonen, K., Keltikangas-Jarvinen, L., Strandberg, T. and Jarvenpaa, A-L. (2003a) Perceptions of infant temperament: Does parents' joint attachment matter? *Infant Behavior and Development*, **26**, 167-182.

Pesonen, A-K., Raikkonen, K., Keskivaara, P. and Keltikangas-Jarvinen, L. (2003b) Continuity of difficult temperament: From maternal perceptions to self-ratings over 17 years. *Personality and Individual Differences*, **34**, 19-31.

Petrie, P. (1984) Day care for under 2's at childminders and in day nurseries. *Early Child Development and Care*, **16(3/4)**, 205-216.

Pistole, M. C. (1989) Attachment in adult romantic relationships: Style of conflict resolution and relationship satisfaction. *Journal of Social and Personal Relationships*, **6**, 505-510.

Pistole, M. C. (1993) Attachment relationships: Self-disclosure and trust. *Journal of Mental Health Counselling*, **15**, 94-106.

Posner, M. I. and Rothbart, M. K. (1998) Attention, self regulation and consciousness. *Philosophical Transactions of the Royal Society of London*, **B353**, 1915-1927.

Posner, M. I. and Rothbart, M. K. (2000) Developing mechanisms of self regulation. *Development and Psychopathology*, **12**, 427-441.

Prevatt-Goldstein, B. (2004) *Attachment of mixed parentage children in a racialised society*. Feature address, Separation and Reunion Forum 5th Annual Conference, *Attachment perspectives of people of mixed heritage*, London, November 26th, 2004.

Prince, G. S. (1967) Mental health problems in pre-school West Indian children. *Maternal and Child Care*, **3(26)**, 483-486.

Prince, G. S. (1968) Emotional problems of children reunited with their migrant families in Britain. *Maternal and Child Care*, **4(44)**, 239-242.

Provence, S. and Lipton, R. C. (1962) *Infants in institutions: A comparison of their development with family-reared infants during the first year of life*. New York: International Universities Press.

Pugh, G. (2003) Early childhood services: Evolution or revolution? *Children and Society*, **17**, 184-194.

Radke-Yarrow, M. (1991) Attachment patterns in children of depressed mothers. In C. M. Parkes, J. Stevenson-Hinde and P. Marris (Eds.), *Attachment across the life cycle* (115-126). London: Routledge.

Radke-Yarrow, M., Cummings, E. M., Kuczynski, L. and Chapman, M. (1985) Patterns of attachment in two and three year olds in normal families and families with parental depression. *Child Development*, **56**, 884-893.

Rajecki, D. W, Lamb, M. E. and Obsmascher, P. (1978) Toward a general theory of infantile attachment: a comparative review of aspects of the social bond. *The Behavioral and Brain Sciences*, **3**, 417-464.

Randolph, E. M. (2000) *Manual for the Randolph Attachment Disorder Questionnaire* (RADQ). Evergreen, CO: Attachment Center Press.

Rao, R. and Georgieff, M. K. (2000) Early nutrition and brain development. In C. A. Nelson (Ed.), *The effects of early adversity on neurobehavioural development. The Minnesota Symposia on Child Psychology, Volume 31* (1-30). Mahwah, NJ: Lawrence Erlbaum Associates.

Raval, V., Goldberg, S., Atkinson, L., Benoit, D., Myhal, N., Poulton, L. and Zwiers, M. (2001) Maternal attachment, maternal responsiveness and infant attachment. *Infant Behavior and Development*, **24**, 281-304.

Reite, M. and Capitanio, J. P. (1985) On the nature of social separation and attachment. In M. Reite and T. Field (Eds.), *The psychobiology of attachment and separation* (223-255). New York: Academic Press, 1985.

Renken, B., Egeland, B., Marvinney, D., Mangelsdorf, S. and Sroufe, L. A. (1989) Early childhood antecedents of aggression and passive-withdrawal in early elementary school. *Journal of Personality*, **57**, 257-281.

Repetti, R. L., Taylor, S. E. and Seeman, T. E. (2002) Risky families: Family social environments and the mental and physical health of offspring. *Psychological Bulletin*, **28(2)**, 330-366.

Ressler, E. M., Boothby, N. and Steinbock, D. J. (1988) *Unaccompanied children*. Oxford: Oxford University Press.

Rholes, W. S., Simpson, J. A. and Blakely, B. S. (1995) Adult attachment styles and mothers' relationships with their young children. *Personal Relationships*, **2**, 35-54.

Rice, K.G. (1990) Attachment in adolescence: A narrative and meta-analytic review. *Journal of Youth and Adolescence*, **19(5)**, 511-538.

Richards, M. P. M. (1982) How should we approach the study of fathers? In M. O'Brien and L. McKee (Eds.), *The father figure* (57-71). London: Tavistock.

Richters, J. E. and Zahn-Waxler, C. (1988) The infant day care controversy: Current status and future directions. *Early Childhood Research Quarterly*, **3**, 319-36.

Robertson, J. (1952) *A two-year-old goes to hospital* (Film). Nacton, Suffolk: Concorde Films Council.
Robertson, J. (1953) Some responses of young children to loss of maternal care. *Nursing Times,* **49**, 382-386.
Robertson, J. (1958) *Going to hospital with mother* (Film). Nacton, Suffolk: Concorde Films Council.
Robertson, J. (1962) *Hospitals and children: A parent's eye view*. New York: Gollancz.
Robertson, J. and Bowlby, J. (1952) Responses of young children to separation from their mothers. II. Observations of the sequences of responses of children aged 18-24 months during the course of separation. *Courrier de la Centre International de I'Enfance,* **2(3)**, 131-142.
Robertson, J. and Bowlby, J. (1953) Some responses of young children to loss of maternal care. *Nursing Care,* **49**, 382-386. [Also published in *Courrier de la Centre International de I'Enfance,* **2(2)**, 131-142]
Robertson, J. and Robertson, J. (1967) *Young children in brief separation* (Film): *Kate, 2 years 5 months, in foster care for 27 days*. Nacton, Suffolk: Concorde Films Council.
Robertson, J. and Robertson, J. (1968) *Young children in brief separation* (Film): *Jane, 17 months, in foster care for 10 days*. Nacton, Suffolk: Concorde Films Council.
Robertson, J. and Robertson, J. (1969) *Young children in brief separation* (Film): *John, 17 months, for 9 days in a residential nursery*. Nacton, Suffolk: Concorde Films Council.
Robertson, J. and Robertson, J. (1971) *Young children in brief separation* (Film): *Thomas, 2 years 4 months, in foster care for 10 days*. Nacton, Suffolk: Concorde Films Council.
Robertson, J. and Robertson, J. (1973) *Young children in brief separation* (Film): *Lucy, 21 months, in foster care for 19 days*. Nacton, Suffolk: Concorde Films Council.
Robertson, J. and Robertson, J. (1976) *Young children in brief separation. Guide to the film series*. Barnet: Barnet Press Group.
Robertson, J. and Robertson, J. (1989) *Separation and the very young*. London: Free Association Books.
Rodning, C., Beckwith, L. and Howard, J. (1991) Quality of attachment and home environments in children prenatally exposed to PCP and cocaine. *Development and Psychopathology,* **3**, 351-366.
Roggman, L., Langlois, J., Hubbs-Tait, L. and Rieser-Danner, L. (1994) Infant day care, attachment, and the "file drawer problem". *Child Development,* **65**, 1429-1443.
Rolfe, S. (2004) *Rethinking attachment for early childhood practice: Promoting security, autonomy and resilience in young children*. Crows Nest, NSW: Allen and Unwin.
Rose-Krasnor, L., Rubin, K. H., Booth, C. L. and Coplan, R. (1996) The relation of maternal directiveness and child attachment security to social competence in preschoolers. *International Journal of Behavioural Development,* **19**, 309-335.
Rosenberg, D. M. (1984) *The quality and content of preschool fantasy play: Correlates in concurrent social-personality function and early mother-child attachment relationships*. Unpublished doctoral dissertation, University of Minnesota, Minneapolis. [*cited in Carlson and Sroufe 1995*]
Rosenbluth, D. and Bowlby, J. (1955) The social and psychological background of tuberculous children. *British Medical Journal,* **1**, 946-949.
Rosenbluth, D., Bowlby, J. and Roudinesco, J. (1951) Separation from mother as a traumatic experience, some notes on obtaining a relevant history. *Courrier de la Centre International de I'Enfance,* **1**, 3-18.
Rosenstein, D. S. and Horowitz, H. A. (1996) Adolescent attachment and psychopathology. *Journal of Consulting and Clinical Psychology,* **64**, 244-253.
Ross, L. (1977) The intuitive psychologist and his shortcomings: Distortions in the attribution process. In L. Berkowitz (Ed.), *Advances in Experimental Social Psychology, Volume 10* (174-220). New York: Academic Press.
Rothbart, M. K. and Bates, J. (1998) Temperament. In W. Damon and N. Eisenberg (Eds.), *Handbook of child psychology, Volume 3: Social emotional and personality development* (105-176). New York: Wiley.
Rothbaum, F., Rosen, K., Ujiie, T. and Uchida, N. (2002) Family systems theory, attachment theory, and culture. *Family Process,* **41**, 328-350.
Roy, P., Rutter, M. and Pickles, A. (2000) Institutional care: Risk from family background or pattern of rearing? *Journal of Child Psychology and Psychiatry,* **41**, 139–149.
Rubin, K. H., Hymel, S., Mills, S. L. and Rose-Krasnor, L. (1991) Conceptualizing different developmental pathways to and from social isolation in childhood. In D. Cicchetti and S.L. Toth (Eds.), *Rochester symposium on developmental psychopathology, Volume 2: Internalizing and externalizing expressions of dysfunction* (91-122). Hillsdale, NJ: Lawrence Erlbaum Associates.
Rubin, K. H., LeMare, L. J. and Lollis, S. (1990) Social withdrawal in childhood: developmental pathways to peer rejection. In S. R. Asher and J. D. Coie (Eds.), *Peer Rejection in Childhood* (217-249). Cambridge: Cambridge University Press.
Rutter, M. (1972a) *Maternal deprivation reassessed*. London, Harmondsworth: Penguin.
Rutter, M. (1972b) Maternal deprivation reconsidered. *Journal of Psychosomatic Research,* **16**, 241-250.
Rutter, M. (1979) Protective factors in children's responses to stress and disadvantage. In M. W. Kent and J. E. Rolf (Eds.), *Social competence in children* (49-74). Hanover, NH: University Press of New England.
Rutter, M. (1981) *Maternal deprivation reassessed*. Harmondsworth: Penguin.
Rutter, M. (1982) Temperament: concepts, issues and problems. In R. Porter and G. Collins (Eds.), *Ciba Foundation Symposium 89, Temperamental differences in infants and young children* (1-19). London: Pitman.
Rutter, M. (1987) Temperament, personality and personality disorder. *British Journal of Psychiatry,* **150**, 443-458.

Rutter, M. (1988) The role of cognition in child development and disorder. In S. Chess, A. Thomas and M. E. Hertzig (Eds.), *Annual Progress in Child Psychiatry and Child Development* (77-101). New York: Brunner/Mazel.

Rutter, M. (1990) Psychosocial resilience and protective mechanisms. In J. Rolf, A. S. Masten, D. Cicchetti, K. Neuchterlich and S. Weintraub (Eds.), *Risk and protective factors in the development of psychopathology* (181-215). Cambridge: Cambridge University Press.

Rutter, M. (1995) Clinical implications of attachment concepts: Retrospect and prospect. *Journal of Child Psychology and Psychiatry*, **36(4)**, 549-571.

Rutter, M. (2000) Psychosocial influences: Critiques, findings, and research needs. *Development and Psychopathology*, **12**, 375-405.

Rutter, M. (2002) Nature, nurture, and development: From evangelism through science toward policy and practice. *Child Development*, **73(1)**, 1-21.

Rutter, M. and Giller, H. (1983) *Juvenile delinquency*. New York: Guilford Press.

Rutter, M. and Quinton, D. (1984) Parental psychiatric disorder: effects on children. *Psychological Medicine*, **14**, 853-880.

Rutter, M. and the English and Romanian Adoption Research Team (1998) Developmental catch-up, and deficit, following adoption after severe global early privation. *Journal of Child Psychology and Psychiatry and Allied Disciplines*, **39**, 465-476.

Rutter, M., O'Connor, T. and the ERA Research Team (2004) Are there biological programming effects for psychological development: Findings from a study of Romanian adoptees. *Developmental Psychology*, **40(1)**, 81-94.

Rutter, M., Quinton, D. and Hill, J. (1990) Adult outcomes of institution-reared children: Males and females compared. In L. N. Robins and M. Rutter (Eds.), *Straight and devious pathways from childhood to adulthood* (135-157). Cambridge: Cambridge University Press.

Saarni, C. and Harris, P. L. (Eds.)(1989) *Children's understanding of emotion*. Cambridge: Harvard University Press.

Sagi, A., Koren-Karie, N., Gini, M., Ziv, Y. and Joels, T. (2002) Shedding further light on the effects of various types of quality of child care on infant-mother attachment relationship: The Haifa study of early child care. *Child Development*, **73**, 1166-1186.

Sagi, A., Lamb, M. E., Lewkowicz, K. S., Shoham, R., Dvir, R. and Estes, D. (1985) Security of infant-mother -father, and -metapelet attachment among kibbutz-reared Israeli infants. In I. Bretherton and E. Waters (Eds.), Growing points in attachment theory and research. *Monographs Society for Research on Child Development*, **50(1-2)**, 257-275.

Sagi-Schwartz, A. and Aviezer, O. (2005) Correlates of attachment to multiple caregivers in kibbutz children from birth to emerging adulthood: The Haifa longitudinal study. In K. E. Grossmann, K. Grossmann and E. Waters (Eds.), *Attachment from infancy to adulthood: The major longitudinal studies* (165-197). New York and London: The Guilford Press.

Salter, M. D. (1940) An evaluation of adjustment based upon the concept of security. *University of Toronto Studies Child Development Series*, **Number 18**.

Sameroff, A. J., Seifer, R., Barocas, R., Zax, M. and Greenspan, S. (1987) Intelligence quotient scores of 4-year-old children: Social-environmental risk factors. *Pediatrics*, **79**, 343-350.

Scarr, S. and McCartney, K. (1983) How people make their own environments: A theory of genotype- environment effects. *Child Development*, **54**, 164-170.

Schachner, D. A. and Shaver, P. R. (2002) Attachment style and human mate poaching. *New Review of Social Psychology*, **1**, 122-129.

Schachter, S. and Singer, J. E. (1962) Cognitive, social, and physiological determinants of emotional state. *Psychological Review*, **69**, 379-399.

Schank, R. C. and Abelson, R. P. (1977) *Scripts, plans, goals, and understanding: An inquiry into human knowledge structures*. Hillsdale, NJ: Lawrence Erlbaum Associates.

Scheier, M. F. and Carver, C. S. (1977) Self-focused attention and the experience of emotion: Attraction, repulsion, elation, and depression. *Journal of Personality and Social Psychology*, **35**, 625-636.

Scheier, M. F. and Carver, C. S. (1980) Private and public self-attention, resistance to change, and dissonance reduction. *Journal of Personality and Social Psychology*, **39**, 390-405.

Scheier, M. F. and Carver, C. S. (1988) A model of behavioral self-regulation: Translating intention into action. In L. Berkowitz (Ed.), *Advances in experimental social psychology, Volume 21* (303-346). New York: Academic Press.

Schofield, G. (2002) The significance of the secure base: A psychosocial model of long-term foster care. *Child and Family Social Work*, **7(4)**, 259-272.

Schofield, G. and Beek, M. (2005) Providing a secure base: Parenting children in long-term foster family care. *Attachment and Human Development*, **7(1)**, 3-25.

Schore, A. N. (1994) *Affect regulation and the origin of the self: The neurobiology of emotional development*. Hillsdale, NJ: Lawrence Erlbaum Associates.

Schore, A. N. (1996) The experience-dependent maturation of a regulatory system in the orbital prefrontal cortex and the origin of developmental psychopathology. *Development and Psychopathology*, **8**, 59-87.

Schore, A. N. (1996) The experience-dependent maturation of a regulatory system in the orbital prefrontal cortex and the origin of developmental psychopathology. *Development and Psychopathology*, **8**, 59-87.

Schore, A. N. (1997) Early organization of the nonlinear right brain and the development of a predisposition to psychiatric disorders. *Development and Psychopathology*, **9**, 595-631.

Schore, A. N. (1999) Contributions from the neurobiology of emotional development to models of self-organization. In M.D. Lewis and I. Granic (Eds.), *Emotion, development. and self-organization* (70-99). New York: Cambridge University Press.
Schore, A. N. (2001a) Effects of a secure attachment relationship on right brain development, affect regulation, and infant mental health. *Infant Mental Health Journal*, **22(1-2)**, 7-66.
Schore, A. N. (2001b) Minds in the making: Attachment, the self-organizing brain, and developmentally-oriented psychoanalytic psychotherapy. *British Journal of Psychotherapy*, **17(3)**, 299-328.
Schore, A. N. (2002) The neurobiology of attachment and early personality organization. *Journal of Prenatal and Perinatal Psychology and Health,* **16(3)**, 249-263.
Schuengel, C., Bakermans-Kranenburg, M. and Van IJzendoorn, M. (1999) Frightening maternal behavior linking unresolved loss and disorganized infant attachment. *Journal of Consulting and Clinical Psychology*, **67**, 54-63.
Schwartz, D. B., Granger, D. A., Susman, E. J., Gunnar, M. R. and Laird, B. (1998) Assessing salivary cortisol in studies of child development. *Child Development*, **69**, 1503-1513.
Seay, B. M., Alexander, B. K. and Harlow, H. F. (1964) Maternal behavior of socially deprived monkeys. *Journal of Abnormal and Social Psychology*, **69**, 345-354.
Seligman, M. E. P. (1975) *Helplessness: On depression, development, and death.* San Francisco, CA: W.H. Freeman.
Seligman, M. E. P. and Maier, S.F. (1967) Failure to escape traumatic shock. *Journal of Experimental Psychology*, **74**, 1-9.
Senchak, M. and Leonard, K. E. (1992) Attachment styles and marital adjustment among newly wed couples. *Journal of Social and Personal Relationships*, **9**, 51-64.
Senn, M. J. E. (1977) *Interview with Dr. John Bowlby in London, England, 19 October 1977.* Unpublished: National Library of Medicine, USA. Cited in Van Dijken, 1998, *op cit.*
Shapiro, L. E. and Insel, T. R. (1990) Infant's response to social isolation reflects adult differences in affiliative behavior: A comparative developmental study in Prairie and Montane voles. *Developmental Psychobiology*, **23**, 375-393.
Sharp, D., Hay, D., Pawlby, S., Schmucher, G., Allen, H. and Kumar, R. (1995) The impact of postnatal depression on boys' intellectual development. *Journal of Child Psychology and Psychiatry*, **36**, 1315-1337.
Shaver, P. R. and Fraley, C. (2005) Information at http://psychology.ucdavis.edu/labs/Shaver/measures.htm
Shaver, P. R., Belsky, J. and Brennan, K. A. (2000) Comparing measures of adult attachment: An examination of interview and self-report methods. *Personal Relationships*, **7**, 25-43.
Shaver, P. R. and Mikulincer, M. (2002) Attachment-related psychodynamics. *Attachment and Human Development*, **4(2)**, 133-161.
Shaw, D. S. and Vondra, J. I. (1995) Infant attachment security and maternal predictors of early behavior problems: A longitudinal study of low-income families. *Journal of Abnormal Child Psychology*, **23**, 335-357.
Shaw, D. S., Keenan, K., Vondra, J. I., Delliquadri, E. and Giovanelli, J. (1997) Antecedents of preschool children's internalizing problems: A longitudinal study of low-income families. *Journal of the American Academy of Child and Adolescent Psychiatry*, **36**, 1760-1767.
Shaw, D. S., Owens, E. B., Vondra, J. I., Keenan, K. and Winslow, E. B. (1996) Early risk factors and pathways in the development of early disruptive behavior problems. *Development and Psychopathology*, **8**, 679-699.
Sheperis, C. J., Doggett, R. A. and Hoda, N. E. (2003) The development of an assessment protocol for reactive attachment disorder. *Journal of Mental Health Counseling, 25,* 291-310.
Shi, L. (2003) The association between adult attachment styles and conflict resolution in romantic relationships. *The American Journal of Family Therapy*, **31**, 143-157.
Siegel, D. J. (1999) *The developing mind: How relationships and the brain interact to shape who we are.* New York: Guilford Press.
Simons, R. L., Chao, W., Conger, R.D. and Elder, G. H. (2001) Quality of parenting as mediator of the effect of childhood defiance on adolescent friendship choices and delinquency: A growth curve analysis. *Journal of Marriage and the Family*, **63**, 63-79.
Simpson, J. A. (1990) Influence of attachment styles on romantic relationships. *Journal of Personality and Social Psychology*, **59**, 917-980.
Simpson, J. A. (1999) Attachment theory in modern evolutionary perspective. In J. Cassidy and P. R. Shaver (Eds.), *Handbook of attachment: Theory, research and clinical applications* (115-140). New York and London: Guilford Press.
Simpson, J. A., Rholes, W. S. and Phillips, D. (1996) Conflict in close relationships: An attachment perspective. *Journal of Personality and Social Psychology*, **71**, 899-914.
Simpson, J. A., Rholes, W. S., Campbell, L. and Wilson, C. L. (no date) *Changes in attachment orientation across transition to parenthood.* http://www.psychology.uiowa.edu/events/Simpson/Change.doc
Sluckin, W., Herbert, M. and Sluckin, A. (1983) *Maternal bonding.* Oxford: Basis Blackwell.
Smith, C. A. (1994) Dis-attachment. *Australian and New Zealand Journal of Psychiatry*, **28(4)**, 691-693.
Smith, P. K. and Drew, L. M. (2002) Grandparenthood. In M. H. Bornstein (Ed.), *Handbook of parenting, Volume 3: Being and becoming a parent* (141-172). 2nd edition, Mahwah, New Jersey: Lawrence Erlbaum Associates.
Smuts, A. (1977) *Interview with Dr. John Bowlby on 6 June and 23 July, 1977; and additional written material sent by Dr. Bowlby in September and October, 1979.* London: Tavistock Institute library archives; unpublished. Cited in Van Dijken, 1998, *op cit.*
Solomon, J. and George, C. (1999) *Attachment disorganization.* New York: The Guilford Press.

REFERENCES

Solter, A. (2001) Hold me! The importance of physical contact with infants. *Journal of Prenatal and Perinatal Psychology and Health*, **15(3)**, 193205.

Spangler, G. (1991) The emergence of adrenocortical circadian function in newborns and infants and its relationship to sleep, feeding and maternal adrenocortical activity. *Early Human Development*, **25**, 197-208.

Spangler, G. and Grossmann, K. E. (1993) Biobehavioral organization in securely and insecurely attached infants. *Child Development*, **64**, 1439-1450.

Spangler, G., Schieche, M., Ilg, U., Maier, U. and Ackermann, C. (1994) Maternal sensitivity as an external organizer for biobehavioral regulation in infancy. *Developmental Psychobiology*, **27**, 425-437.

Speltz, M.L. (2002) Description, history, and critique of corrective attachment therapy. *The APSAC Advisor*, **14(3)**, 4-8.

Spemann, H. (1938) *Embryonic development and induction*. New Haven, CT: Yale University Press. [cited in Bruer 2001, op.cit.]

Spieker, S. J. and Booth, C. L. (1988) Maternal antecedents of attachment quality. In J. Belsky and T. Nezworski (Eds.), *Clinical implications of attachment* (95-135). Hillsdale, NJ: Lawrence Erlbaum.

Spitz, R. A. (1945) Hospitalism. An inquiry into the genesis of psychiatric conditions in early childhood. In A. Freud, H. Hartmann and E. Kris (Eds.), *The Psychoanalytic Study of the Child*, **1**, 53-74. New York: International Universities Press.

Spitz, R. A. (1946) Hospitalism: A follow-up report on investigation described in Volume I, 1945. *The Psychoanalytic Study of the Child*, **2**, 113-117. New York: International Universities Press.

Spitz, R. A. (1947) *Grief: A peril in infancy*. Film, Penn State Media Sales (www.mediasales.psu.edu).

Spitz, R. A. and Wolf, K. M. (1946) Anaclitic depression: An inquiry into the genesis of psychiatric conditions in early childhood, II. *The Psychoanalytic Study of the Child, 2* (313-342). New York: International Universities Press.

Sroufe, L. A. (1983) Infant caregiver attachment and patterns of adaptation in preschool: The roots of maladaptation and competence. In M. Perlmutter (Ed.), *Minnesota Symposium on Child Psychology: Vol. 16. Development and policy concerning children with special needs* (41-81). Hillsdale, NJ: Erlbaum.

Sroufe, L. A. (1988) The role of infant-caregiver attachment in development. In J. Belsky and T. Nezworski (Eds.), *Clinical implications of attachment* (18-38). Hillsdale, NJ: Erlbaum.

Sroufe, L. A. (1996) *Emotional development: The organisation of emotional life in the early years*. Cambridge: Cambridge University Press

Sroufe, L. A. and Waters, E. (1977) Attachment as an organizational construct. *Child Development*, **48**, 1184-1199.

Sroufe, L. A., Carlson, E. and Schulman, S. (1993) Individuals in relationships: Development from infancy through adolescence. In D. Funder, R. Parke, C. Tomlinson-Keasey and K. Widaman (Eds.), *Studying lives through time* (315-342). Washington, DC: American Psychological Association.

Sroufe, L. A., Carlson, E., Levy, A. and Egeland, B. (1999) Implications of attachment theory for developmental psychopathology. *Development and Psychopathology*, **11**, 1-13.

Sroufe, L. A., Carlson, E., Levy, A. and Jacobvitz, D. (April, 2001) *Lessons from the study of development*. Poster presented at the Society for Research on Child Development, Minneapolis.

Sroufe, L. A., Erickson, M. F. and Friedrich, W. N. (2002) Attachment theory and 'Attachment Therapy'. *The APSAC Advisor*, **14(4)**, 4-6.

Sroufe, L. A., Fox, N. E. and Pancake, V. R. (1983) Attachment and dependency in developmental perspective. *Child Development*, **54**, 1615-1627.

Sroufe, L. A., Schork, E., Lawroski, N. and Lafreniere, P. (1984) The role of affect in social competence. In C. Izard, J. Kagan and R. Zajonc (Eds.), *Emotional cognition and behavior*. New York: Plenum.

Sroufe, L.A. (1983) Infant-caregiver attachment and patterns of adaptation in preschool: The roots of maladaptation and competence. In M. Perlmutter (Ed.), *Minnesota symposium on child psychology, Volume 16: Development and policy concerning children with special needs* (41-81). Hillsdale, NJ: Erlbaum.

Sroufe, L.A. (2003) Attachment categories as reflections of multiple dimensions: Comment on Fraley and Spieker (2003). *Developmental Psychology*, **39(3)**, 413-416.

Stafford, B., Zeanah, C. H. and Scheeringa, M. (2003) Exploring psychopathology in early childhood: PTSD and attachment disorders in DC: 0-3 and *DSM-IV*. *Infant Mental Health Journal*, 24, 398-409.

Stanley, W. C. and Elliot, O. (1962) Differential human handling as reinforcing events and as treatments influencing later social behavior in basenji puppies. *Psychological Reports*, **10**, 775-788.

Stansbury, K and Harris, M. L. (2000) Individual differences in stress reactions during a peer entry episode: Effects of age, temperament, approach behavior, and self-perceived peer competence. *Journal of Experimental Child Psychology*, **76**, 50-63.

Steele, H. (2003) Holding therapy is not attachment therapy: Editor's introduction to this invited Special Issue. *Attachment and Human Development*, **5(3)**, 219.

Steele, H. and Steele, M. (2005) Understanding and resolving emotional conflict: Findings from the London Parent-Child Project. In K. E. Grossmann, K. Grossmann and E. Waters (Eds.), *Attachment from infancy to adulthood: The major longitudinal studies* (in press). New York: Guilford Press.

Stein, H., Jacobs, N. J., Ferguson, K. S., Allen, J. G. and Fonagy, P. (1998) What do adult attachment scales measure? *Bulletin of the Menninger Clinic*, **62(1)**, 33-82.

Steinberg, L. (2005) Cognitive and affective development in adolescence. *Trends in Cognitive Science*, **9(2)**, 69-74.

Stern, D. N. (1985) *The interpersonal world of the infant: A view from psychoanalysis and developmental psychology*. New York: Basic Books.

Stern, D. N. (2005) *Attachment and intersubjectivity are different systems: A caveat.* Talk given at conference organised by the Association pour le developpment de la recherche sur l'attachement (ADRA), Faculte de Medecine Xavier Bichat, July 6-8, 2005.

Stern, D. N., Beebe, B. Jaffe, J. and Bennett, S. (1977) The infant's stimulus world during social interaction: A study of caregiver behaviours with particular reference to repetition and timing. In H.R. Schaffer (Ed.), *Studies in mother-infant interaction* (177-202). London: Academic Press.

Stockard, C. R. (1921) Developmental rate and structural expression: An experimental study of twins, "double monsters", and single deformities and their interaction among embryonic organs during their origins and development. *American Journal of Anatomy*, **28**, 115-275. [cited in Bruer 2001, op.cit.]

Stovall, K. C. and Dozier, M. (1998) Infants in foster care: An attachment perspective. *Adoption Quarterly*, **2(1)**, 55-87.

Stovall, K. C. and Dozier, M. (2000) The development of attachment in new relationships: Single subject analyses for ten foster infants. *Development and Psychopathology*, **12**, 133-156.

Stroud, C. E. (1967) 100 Mothers: a survey of West Indians in Britain, by Violet Moody and C. Eric Stroud. *Maternal and Child Care*, **3(26)**, 487-91.

Sutton, J., Smith, P. K. and Swettenham, J. (1999) Social cognition and bullying: Social inadequacy or skilled manipulation? *British Journal of Developmental Psychology*, **17**, 435-450.

Svanberg, P. O. (2005) Promoting attachment security in primary intervention using video feed-back: The Sunderland Infant Programme. *Draft paper submitted to Infant Mental Health Journal.*

Svejda, M. J., Campos, J. J. and Emde, R. N. (1980) Mother-infant 'bonding': Failure to generalize. *Child Development*, **51**, 775-779.

Tessier, R., Cristo, M., Velez, S., Girón, M. S.W., Figueroa de Calume, Z., Ruiz-Paláez, J.G., Charpak, Y. and Charpak, N. (1998) Kangaroo mother care and the bonding hypothesis. *Pediatrics*, **102(2)**, Electronic article, no page numbers.

Teti, D. M. (1999) Conceptualizations of disorganization beyond infancy: An integration. In J.Solomon and C.George (Eds.), *Organization and disorganization in attachment: conceptual and methodological considerations* (213-242). New York: Guilford Press.

Teti, D. M. and Ablard, K. E. (1989) Security of attachment and infant-sibling relationships: A laboratory study. *Child Development*, **60**, 1519-1528.

Teti, D. M., Gelfand, D. M., Messinger, D. S. and Isabella, R. (1995) Maternal depression and the quality of early attachment: An examination of infants, preschoolers, and their mothers. *Developmental Psychology*, **31(3)**, 364-376.

Thomas, A. and Chess, S. (1977) *Temperament and development.* Oxford: Brunner/Mazel.

Thomas, N. (2000) Parenting children with attachment disorders. In T.M. Levy (Ed.), Handbook of attachment interventions (67-111). San Diego, CA: Academic Press.

Thompson, R. A. (1986) Temperament, emotionality, and infant social cognition. In J. V. Lerner and R.M Lerner (Eds.), *Temperament and social interaction in infants and children, New Directions for Child Development, No. 31* (35-52). London: Jossey-Bass.

Thompson, R. A. (1988) The effect of infant day care through the prism of attachment theory: A critical appraisal. *Early Childhood Research Quarterly*, **3**, 273-82.

Thompson, R. A. (1990) Emotion and self regulation. In R. A. Thompson (Ed.), Nebraska symposium on motivation: Socioemotional development, 1988 (367-467). Lincoln: University of Nebraska Press.

Thompson, R. A. (1994) Emotion regulation: A theme in search of a definition. *Monographs of the Society for Research in Child Development*, **59(2-3, Serial No. 240)**, 25-52.

Thompson, R. A. (1998) Early sociopersonality development. In N. Eisenberg (Ed.), *Handbook of child psychology, fifth edition, volume 3: Social, emotional and personality development* (25-104). New York: Wiley.

Thompson, R. A. (1999) Early attachment and later development. In J. Cassidy and P. R. Shaver (Eds.), *Handbook of attachment: Theory, research and clinical applications* (265-286). New York: Guilford Press.

Thompson, R. A. and Calkins, S. D. (1996) The double-edged sword: Emotional regulation for children at risk. *Development and Psychopathology*, **8**, 163-182.

Thompson, R. A., Cicchetti, D., Lamb, M. and Malkin, C. (1985) The emotional responses of Down syndrome and normal infants in the Strange Situation: The organization of affective behavior in infants. *Developmental Psychology*, **21**, 828-841.

Thompson, R. A., Flood, M. F. and Lundquist, L. (1995) Emotion regulation: Its relations to attachment and developmental psychopathology. In D. Cicchetti and S. L. Toth (Eds.), *Rochester Symposium on Developmental Psychopathology: Vol. 6. Emotion, cognition and representation.* Rochester, NY: University of Rochester Press.

Tinbergen, N. (1942) An objective study of the innate behaviour of animals. *Bibliotheca biotheorica*, **1**, 39-98.

Tinbergen, N. (1950) The hierarchical organisation of nervous mechanisms underlying instinctive behaviour. *Symposium of the Society for Experimental Biology*, **4**, 305-312.

Tinbergen, N. (1951) *The study of instinct.* London: Oxford University Press.

Tinbergen, N. (1952) Derived activities, their causation, biological significance, origin, and emancipation during evolution. *Quarterly Review of Biology*, **27**, 1-32.

Tinbergen, N. (1953) *Social behaviour in animals.With special reference to vertebrates.* London: Methuen.

Tizard, B. and Hodges, J. (1978) The effect of early institutional rearing on the development of eight-year-old children. *Journal of Child Psychology, Psychiatry and Allied Disciplines*, **19**, 99-118.

Tout, K., de Haan, M., Campbell, E. K. and Gunnar, M. R. (1998) Social behavior correlates of cortisol activity in child care: Gender differences and time of day effects. *Child Development*, **5**, 1247-1262.

Trevarthen, C. (1977) Descriptive analysis of infant communicative behavior. In H.R. Schaffer (Ed.), *Studies in mother-infant interaction* (227-270). London: Academic Press.

Trevarthen, C. (1979) Communication and cooperation in early infancy: a description of primary intersubjectivity. In M. Bullowa (Ed.), *Before speech. The beginning of interpersonal communication* (321-347). Cambridge: Cambridge University Press.

Trevarthen, C. (1989) Development of early social interactions and the affective regulations of brain growth. In C. von Euler, H. Forssberg and H. Lagercrantz (Eds.), *The neurobiology of early infant behavior*. Stockholm: Nobel Institute of Neurophysiology, Karolinska Institiue.

Trevarthen, C. (1990) Growth and education of the hemispheres. In C. Trevarthen (Ed.), *Brain circuits and functions of the mind: Essays in honour of Roger W. Sperry* (334-363). Cambridge: Cambridge University Press.

Trevarthen, C. (1993) The self born in intersubjectivity: The psychology of infant communicating. In U. Neisser (Ed.), *The perceived self: Ecological and interpersonal sources of self-knowledge* (121-173). Cambridge: Cambridge University Press.

Trevarthen, C. (1996) Lateral asymmetries in infancy: Implications for the development of the hemispheres. *Neuroscience and Biobehavioral Reviews*, **20**, 571-586.

Trevarthen, C. and Hubley, P. (1978) Secondary intersubjectivity: confidence, confiding and acts of meaning in the first year. In A. Lock (Ed.), *Action, gesture and symbol* (183-229). London: Academic Press.

Tronick, E. Z. (1989) Emotions and emotional communication in infants. *American Psychologist, 44* (2), 112-119.

Tronick. E. Z., Ricks, M. and Cohn, J. F. (1982) Maternal and infant affective exchange: Patterns of adaptation. In T.Field and A. Fogel (Eds.), *Emotion and early interaction* (83-101). Hillsdale, NJ: Lawrence Erlbaum Associates.

Trowell, J. (2004) Reflections on 'an attachment-based treatment of maltreated children and young people'. *Attachment and Human Development*, **6(3)**, 279-283.

Troy, M. and Sroufe, L. A. (1987) Victimization among preschoolers: Role of attachment relationship history. *Journal of the American Academy of Child and Adolescent Psychiatry*, **26**, 166-172.

True, M. M., Pisani, L. and Oumar, F. (2001) Infant-mother attachment among the Dogon of Mali. *Child Development*, **72**, 1451-1466.

Tustin, F. (1981) *Autistic states in children*. London: Routledge and Kegan Paul.

Tversky, A. and Kahneman, D. (1974) Judgement under uncertainty: Heuristics and biases. *Science*, **185**, 1124-1131.

Urban, J., Carlson, E., Egeland, B. and Sroufe, L. A. (1991) Patterns of individual adaptation across childhood. *Development and Psychopathology*, **3**, 445-460.

Van den Bergh, B. R. H. (1992) Maternal emotions during pregnancy and foetal and neonatal behaviour. In J. G. Nijhuis (Ed.), *Foetal behaviour:Developmental and perinatal aspects*. Oxford: Oxford University Press.

Van den Boom, D. (1988) *Neonatal irritability and the development of attachment: observation and intervention*. Unpublished doctoral dissertation, Leiden University, Leiden (The Netherlands).

Van den Boom, D. (1989) Neonatal irritability and the development of attachment. In G. A. Kohnstamm, J. E. Bates and M. K. Rothbart (Eds.), *Temperament in childhood.*. Chichester: Wiley.

Van den Boom, D. (1991) Preventive intervention and the quality of mother-infant interaction and infant exploration in irritable infants. In W. Koops, H. Soppe, J. L. van der Linden, P. C. M. Molenaar and J. J. F. Schroots (Eds.), *Developmental psychology behind the dykes: An outline of developmental psychological research in the Netherlands* (249-269). Delft: Eburon.

Van den Boom, D. (1994) The influence of temperament and mothering on attachment and exploration: An experimental manipulation of sensitive responsiveness among lower-class mothers and irritable infants. *Child Development*, **65**, 1457-1477.

Van den Boom, D. C. (1995) Do first-year intervention effects endure? Follow-up during toddlerhood of a sample of Dutch irritable infants. *Child Development*, **66**, 1798-1816.

Van Dijken, S. (1998) *John Bowlby: His early life. A biographical journey into the roots of attachment theory*. London and New York: Free Association Books.

van IJzendoorn, M. H. (1995a) Adult attachment representations, parental responsiveness, and infant attachment: A meta-analysis on the predictive validity of the Adult Attachment Interview. *Psychological Bulletin*, **117(3)**, 387-403.

van IJzendoorn, M. H. (1995b) On the way we were: On temperament, attachment, and the transmission gap. A rejoinder to Fox. *Psychological Bulletin*, **117**, 411-415.

van IJzendoorn, M. H. (1995c) Association between adult attachment representations and parent-child attachment, parental responsiveness, and clinical status: A meta-analysis on the predictive validity of the Adult Attachment Interview. *Psychological Bulletin*, **117**, 387-403.

van IJzendoorn, M. H. and De Wolff, M. S. (1997) In search of the absent father-meta-analysis of infant-father attachment: A rejoinder to our discussants. *Child Development*, **68**, 604-609.

van IJzendoorn, M. H., Dijkstra, J. and Bus, A. (1995a) Attachment, intelligence, and language: A meta-analysis. *Social Development*, **4**, 115-128.

van IJzendoorn, M. H., Goldberg, S., Kroonenberg, P. M. and Frenkel, O. J. (1992) The relative effects of maternal and child problems on the quality of attachment: A meta-analysis of attachment in clinical samples. *Child Development*, **63**, 840-858.

van IJzendoorn, M. H., Moran, G., Belsky, J., Pederson, D., Bakermans-Kranenburg, M. J. and Kneppers, K. (2000) The similarity of siblings' attachments to their mother. *Child Development*, **71(4)**, 1086-1098.

van IJzendoorn, M. H., Schuengel, C. and Bakermans-Kranenburg, M. J. (1999) Disorganized attachment in early childhood: Meta-analysis of precursors, concomitants, and sequelae. *Development and Psychopathology*, **11**, 225-249.

van IJzendoorn, M.H., Juffer, F. and Duyvesteyn, M.G.C. (1995b) Breaking the intergenerational cycle of insecure attachment: A review of the effects of attachment-based interventions on maternal sensitivity and infant security. *Journal of Child Psychology and Psychiatry*, **36(2)**, 225-248.

van IJzendoorn, M.H., van der Veer, R. and van Vliet-Visser, S. (1987) Attachment three years later: Relationships between quality of mother-infant attachment and emotional/cognitive development in kindergarten. In L. W. C. Tavecchio and M. H. van IJzendoorn (Eds.), *Attachment in social networks* (185-223). North-Holland: Elsevier Science Publishers.

Vandell, D. L. (2004) Early child care: The known and the unknown. *Merrill-PalmerQuarterly*, **50(3)**, 387-414.

Vandell, D. L., Henderson, V. K. and Wilson, K. S. (1988) A longitudinal study of children with varying quality day care experiences. *Child Development*, **59**, 1286-1292.]

Vaughn, B. E. and Bost, K. K. (1999) Attachment and temperament: Redundant, independent, or interacting influences on interpersonal adaptation and personality development? In J. Cassidy and P. R. Shaver (Eds.), *Handbook of attachment: Theory, research, and clinical applications* (198-225). New York: Guilford Press.

Vaughn, B. E., Egeland, B. R., Sroufe, L. A. and Waters, E. (1979) Individual differences in infant-mother attachment at 12 and 18 months: Stability and change in families under stress. *Child Development*, **50**, 971-975.

Verhulst, F. C. (2000a) Internationally adopted children: The Dutch longitudinal adoption study. *Adoption Quarterly*, **4**, 27-44.

Verhulst, F. C. (2000b) The development of internationally adopted children. In P. Selman (Ed.), *Intercountry adoption: Developments, trends and perspectives* (126-142). London: British Agency for Adoption and Fostering.

Vicary, J. R. and Lerner, J. V. (1986) Parental attributes and adolescent drug use. *Journal of Adolescence*, **9**, 115-122.

Volling, B. L. and Belsky, J. (1992) The contribution of mother-child and father-child relationships to the quality of sibling interaction: A longitudinal study. *Child Development*, **63**, 1209-1222.

von Bertalanffy, L. (1968) *General systems theory*. New York: Braziller.

Vondra, J. I., Shaw, D. S., Swearingen, L., Cohen, M. and Owens, E. B. (2001) Attachment stability and emotional and behavioral regulation from infancy to preschool age. *Development and Psychopathology*, **13**, 13-33.

Ward, M. J. and Carlson, E. A. (1995) Associations among adult attachment representations, maternal sensitivity, and infant-mother attachment in a sample of adolescent mothers. *Child Development*, **66**, 69-79.

Warme, G. E., Bowlby, J., Crowcroft, A. and Rae-Grant, Q. (1980) Current issues in child psychiatry: A dialogue with John Bowlby. *Canadian Journal of Psychiatry*, **25**, 367-376.

Warren, S. L., Huston, L., Egeland, B. and Sroufe, L. A. (1997) Child and adolescent anxiety disorders and early attachment. *Journal of the American Academy of Child and Adolescent Psychiatry*, **36**, 637-644.

Wartner, U. G., Grossmann, K., Fremmer-Bombik, E. and Suess, G. (1994) Attachment patterns at age six in south Germany: Predictability from infancy and implications for preschool behavior. *Child Development*, **65**, 1014-1027.

Wason, P. C. (1960) On the failure to eliminate hypotheses in a conceptual task. *Quarterly Journal of Experimental Psychology*, **12(3)**, 129-140.

Watamura, S. E., Donzella, B., Alwin, J. and Gunnar, M. R. (2003) Morning-to-afternoon increases in cortisol concentrations for infants and toddlers at child care: Age differences and behavioral correlates. *Child Development*, **74**, 1006-1020.

Waters, E. and Beauchaine, T. P. (2003) Are there really patterns of attachment? Comment on Fraley and Spieker (2003). *Developmental Psychology*, **39(3)**, 417-422.

Waters, E., Hamilton, C. E. and Weinfield, N. S. (2000) The stability of attachment security from infancy to adolescence and early adulthood: General introduction. *Child Development*, **71**, 678-683.

Waters, E., Vaughn, B. E. and Egeland, B. R. (1980) Individual differences in infant-mother attachment relationships at age one: Antecedents in neonatal behavior in an urban economically disadvantaged sample. *Child Development*, **51**, 208-216.

Weinfeld, N. S., Sroufe, L. A., Egeland, B. and Carlson, E. A. (1999) The nature of individual differences in infant-caregiver attachment. In J. Cassidy and P. R. Shaver (Eds.), *Handbook of attachment: Theory, research, and clinical applications* (68-88). New York: Guilford Press.

Weinfield, N. S., Whaley, G. J. L. and Egeland, B. (2004) Continuity, discontinuity, and coherence in attachment from infancy to late adolescence: Sequelae of organization and disorganization. *Attachment and Human Development*, **6(1)**, 73-97.

Weiss, J. M, Glazer, H. I. and Pohorecky, L. A. (1976) Coping behavior and neurochemical changes. An alternative explanation for the original "learned helplessness" experiments. In G. Serban and A. Kling (Eds.), *Animal models in human psychobiology* (141-173) New York: Plenum Press.

Weissman, M. M., Paykel, E. S. and Klerman, G. L. (1972) The depressed woman as a mother. *Social Psychiatry*, **23**, 78-84.

Weissman, M., Gammon, G., John, K., Merikangas, K., Warner, V., Prusoff, B. and Sholomskas, D. (1987) Children of depressed parents: increased psychopathology and early onset of major depression. *Archives of General Psychiatry*, **44**, 847-853.

Weisz, J. R., Weiss, B., Han, S. S., Granger, D. A. and Morton, T. L. (1995) Effects of psychotherapy with children and adolescents revisited: A meta-analysis of treatment outcome studies. *Psychological Bulletin*, **117(3)**, 450-468.

Werner, E. E. and Smith, R. S. (1982) *Vulnerable but invincible: A study of resilient children.* New York: McGraw-Hill.

Widom, C.S. (1988) Does violence beget violence? A critical examination of the literature. *Psychological Bulletin*, **106(1)**, 3-28.

Wilson, S.L. (2001) Attachment disorders: Review and current status. *Journal of Psychology*, **135(1)**, 37-51.

Winnicott, C., Shepherd, R. and Davis, M. (Eds.)(1989) *D.W. Winnicott. Psycho-analytic explorations.* London: Karnac.

Wisner, K. L. and Stowe, Z. N. (1997) Psychobiology of postpartum mood disorders. *Seminars in Reproductive Endocrinology*, **15(1)**, 77-89.

World Health Organization (1975) Statistical Classification of Diseases and Related Health Problems. - 9th Revision. Geneva, Switzerland: Author

World Health Organization (1992) Statistical Classification of Diseases and Related Health Problems. - 10th Revision. Geneva, Switzerland: Author

Wright, J. C., Binney, V. and Smith, P. K. (1995) Security of attachment in 8-12 year olds: A revised version of the separation anxiety test, its psychometric properties and clinical interpretations. *Journal of Child Psychology and Psychiatry*, **36**, 757-774.

Young, L. J., Lim, M. M., Gingrich, B. and Insel, T. R. (2001) Cellular mechanisms of social attachment. *Hormones and Behavior*, **40**, 133-138.

Youngblade, L. M. and Belsky, J. (1992) Parent-child antecedents of 5-year-olds' close friendships: A longitudinal analysis. *Developmental Psychology*, **28**, 700-713.

Youngblade, L. M., Park, K. A. and Belsky, J. (1993) Measurement of young children's close friendships: A comparison of two independent systems and their associations with attachment security. *International Journal of Behavioral Development*, **16**, 563-587.

Yudkin, S. and Holme, A. (1963) *Working mothers and their children.* London: Michael Joseph.

Zahn-Waxler, C., McKnew, D. H., Cummings, M., Davenport, Y. B. and Radke-Yarrow, M. (1984) Problem behaviors and peer interactions of young children with a manic depressive parent. *American Journal of Psychiatry*, **141**, 236-240.

Zahn-Waxler, C., Robinson, J. and Emde, R. (1992) The development of empathy in twins. *Developmental Psychology*, **28**, 1038-1047.

Zaslow, R. and Breger, L. (1969) At theory and treatment of autism. In L. Breger (Ed.), *Clinical-cognitive psychology: Models and integration* (246-291). Englewood Cliffs, NJ: Prentice Hall.

Zaslow, R. and Menta, M. (1975) *The psychology of the Z-process: Attachment and activity.* San Jose, CA: San Jose State University Press.

Zeanah, C. H. (1996) Beyond insecurity: A reconceptualization of attachment disorders of infancy. *Journal of Consulting and Clinical Psychology*, **64**, 42-52.

Zeanah, C. H. (2005) *Attachment and foster care.* Talk given at Paris Conference on 'Attachment: Therapeutic applications in infants, children, adolescents and adults. Paris, Faculte de Medecine Xavier Bichat, July 6-8.

Zeanah, C. H. and Fox, N. A. (2004) Temperament and attachment disorders. *Journal of Clinical Child and Adolescent Psychology*, **33**, 32-41.

Zeanah, C. H., Mammen, O. and Lieberman, A. (1993) Disorders of attachment. In C. H. Zeanah (Ed.), *Handbook of infant mental health* (322-349). New York: Guilford Press.

Zeanah, C. H., Benoit, D., Barton, M., Regan, C., Hirshberg, L. M. and Lipsitt, L. P. (1993) Representations of attachment in mothers and their one-year-old infants. *Journal of the American Academy of Child and Adolescent Psychiatry*, **32**, 278-286.

Zeanah, C. H., Benoit, D., Hirshberg, L., Barton, M. L. and Regan, C. (1994) Mothers' representations of their infants are concordant with infant attachment classifications. *Developmental Issues in Psychiatry and Psychology*, **1**, 9-18.

Zeanah, C. H., Nelson, C. A., Fox, N. A., Smyke, A. T., Marshall, P., Parker, S. W. and Koga, S. (2003) Designing research to study the effects of institutionalization on brain and behavioral development: The Bucharest Early Intervention Project. *Development and Psychopathology*, **15**, 885-907.

Zeanah, C. H., Scheeringa, M., Boris, N. W., Heller, S. S., Smyke, A. T. and Trapani, J. (2004) Reactive attachment disorder in maltreated toddlers. *Child Abuse and Neglect*, **28**, 877-888.

Zhang, F. and Labouvie-Vief, G. (2004) Stability and fluctuation in adult attachment style over a 6-year period. *Attachment and Human Development*, **6(4)**, 419-437.

Ziv, Y., Oppenheim, D. and Sagi-Schwartz, A. (2004) Social information processing in middle childhood: Relations to infant-mother attachment. *Attachment and Human Development*, **6(3)**, 327-348.

Appendix 3.1

Measures related to Attachment: An indicative selection

PROJECTIVE MEASURES

Projective measures have more often been used to elicit information about both children's and adults' feelings about separation issues or other attachment-related events.

They involve presenting participants with material and inviting comment, e.g.:
- pictures (usually photos or line drawings) – participants may be asked pre-set questions in relation to each picture
- story stems/verbal scenarios – participants may be asked to comment or to complete the story
- doll play enactments – doll play scenarios are often used in a similar way to story completion, with dolls enacting a story or scene that participants are invited to complete or comment on – sometimes, to avoid aspects, such as sex of doll or ethnicity, which might obstruct imaginative identification, the dolls employed may be figurative rather than realistic (e.g. cones with spheres on top)

Analysis usually involves converting verbal responses into a quantitative scale by employing a formula for identifying and coding different responses

PICTURES

SEPARATION ANXIETY TEST (Hansburg 1972)
Hansburg, H. G. (1972) *Adolescent separation anxiety: A method for the study of adolescent separation problems.* Springfield III: C.C. Thomas.

SEPARATION ANXIETY TEST (Klagsbrun and Bowlby 1976)

Designed for children aged 4-7

Secure children are expected to be more self-reliant in dealing with mild separations

Six cards depicting separation events of varying severity; one set for boys, one for girls:
1) Parents go out for evening, leaving child at home (mild)
2) Mother (father) goes away for weekend, leaving child with aunt/uncle (severe)
3) Child's first day at school; moment of parting from parent (severe)
4) Parents go away for two weeks; prior to departure give child a specially attractive toy (severe)
5) Park scene; parents tell child to run off and play as they want time alone for a while (mild)
6) Father/Mother tucks child up in bed and leaves room (mild)

Scoring involves eight indices:
1) balance of attachment-type and self-reliance in responses forms the Attachment-Self-reliance Index
2) Hostile cf Attachment-related responses
3) Hostile cf Anxious responses
4) Anxious responses as proportion of total responses
5) Avoidant responses
6) Loss of self-esteem
7) Number of bizarre/absurd responses and responses related to death
8) Appropriateness of imagined actions in response to questions

An overall score (ordinal not interval measurement) is derived from these indices.

Klagsbrun, M. and Bowlby, J. (1976) Responses to separation from parents: A clinical test for young children. *British Journal of Projective Psychology and Personality Study,* **21**, 7-27.

SEPARATION ANXIETY TEST (Slough and Greenberg 1990)

Designed for five-year-olds, based on Klagsbrun and Bowlby (1976), but pictures modified to improve the experimental design:
- same parents and boy/girl in each picture
- same situations across boy and girl picture sets
- only mother appears alone (in original set, sex of lone parent was not controlled)
- both aunt and uncle are shown in picture 2
- pictures updated so that people looked more contemporary (then!)
- children were usually depicted in profile or from back so that maximum facial ambiguity was possible

Scoring system cf Klagsbrun and Bowlby but additional measures of attachment style were created to assess
1) ability to express vulnerability (sadness, regret) or need (EMOTIONAL OPENNESS/ATTACHMENT)
2) ability to express self-confidence and feeling OK about separation (SELF-RELIANCE)
3) degree of avoidance in discussing separations (AVOIDANT or AVOIDANT-CONFUSED/ATYPICAL or BIZARRE)

Slough, N. M. and Greenberg, M. T. (1990) Five-year-olds' representations of separation from parents: Responses from the perspective of self and other. *New Directions for Child Development,* **40**, 67-84.

Slough, N. M., Goyette, M. and Greenberg, M. T. (1988) *Scoring indices for the Seattle version of the separation anxiety test.* Unpublished manuscript, University of Washington.

SEPARATION ANXIETY TEST (Wright et al. 1995)

Revised SAT for adolescents.

Wright, J. C., Binney, V. and Smith, P.K. (1995) Security of attachment in 8-12-year-olds: A revised version of the Separation Anxiety test, its psychometric properties and clinical interpretation. *Journal of Child Psychology and Psychiatry,* **36(5)**, 757-774.

ADULT ATTACHMENT PROJECTIVE (George, West and Pettem 1999)

Designed to provide an assessment of attachment in adults which has greater equivalence to assessments in children than AAI, by not relying so heavily on analysis of adult conceptual thought. The AAP enables allocation to one of four main attachment groups (secure, dismissing, preoccupied, unresolved).

Pictures are intended to capture three attachment-related dimensions:
- activation of ABS (pictures are presented in order from lowest to greatest threat/upset)
- availability of a relationship (fear of being alone)
- age

Eight line drawings (first neutral, to establish ability to participate, warm up; seven attachment-related):
1) Neutral/Warm up – Children playing ball
2) Child at window – girl with back to viewer, looks out of window
3) Departure – man and woman face each other with suitcases
4) Bench – youth sits alone on a bench
5) Bed – woman and child face each other at opposite ends of bed, child has arms outstretched
6) Ambulance – woman and child watch person on stretcher being put into ambulance
7) Cemetery – man stands in front of a gravestone
8) Child in corner – side view of child standing in corner with arm stretching out9)

Within the context of an interview setting with questions and open-end probes, interviewers ask participants to make up a story about what is happening in each scene, what might have led up to it, what characters might be thinking and feeling, and what might happen next.

Coding of verbatim transcripts includes assessment of coherency of transcript and nature of personal experience; other scales include measures of self agency (degree to which character is portrayed having an 'internalised secure base' and as having capacity to act), connectedness (degree to which character is portrayed as being in relationship with others) and synchrony (degree to which character is portrayed as in reciprocal, mutually engaging and satisfying relationship); additional scale assesses defensive processes.

The AAP assesses three forms of defensive exclusion:
- Deactivation – marked by devaluing of import of story, minimization, etc.
- Cognitive disconnection – marked by uncertainty, withdrawal, anger, entanglement
- Segregated systems – marked by evidence of failed protection, helplessness, isolation, odd or disturbing material, dissociation (e.g. magical thinking, intrusive thoughts, mental freezing)

George, C., West, M. and Pettem, O. (1999) The Adult Attachment Projective: Disorganisation of adult attachment at the level of representation. In J. Solomon and C. George (Eds.), *Attachment disorganisation* (462-507). New York: Guilford Press.

APPENDIX

STORY STEMS

MSSB: MACARTHUR STORY STEM BATTERY (Bretherton et al. 1990a. 1990b, 1990c)

Designed for assessment of attachment representations in three-year-olds but also used for children up to seven

The story pictures

(1) Warm-up birthday party scene, (2) Exclusion of child from play, (3) Accident caused by disobedience, (4) Scary dog, (5) Parents argue about lost keys, (6) Caught stealing from sweet shop, (7) Fight with friend, (8) Telling tales on a friend, (9) Burglar at night, (10) Dilemma over friend wanting to play although mother has headache

Different research teams have developed their own coding systems

Coding generally consists ratings of narrative content along a large number of dimensions (e.g. affection, sharing, empathy, helping, aggression, reparation, magical thinking, repetition, etc.), ratings of emotional content (engagement, tone, indifference, congruity), the child's engagement with the task (use of dolls, engagement with researcher as well as task, difficulty telling story and story-telling style, non-compliance), narrative quality (coherence, embellishment, quality of resolution etc.), the way the child represents interactions between him- or herself and the characters, mentalising. story content is also subject to detailed analysis

Bretherton, I., Prentiss, C. and Ridgeway, D. (1990a) Family relationships as represented in the story completion task at thirty-seven and fifty-four months of age. *New Directions for Child Development,* **48**, 85-105.

Bretherton, I., Ridgeway, D. and Cassidy, J. (1990b) Assessing internal working models of the attachment relationship: An attachment story completion task for 3-year-olds. In M. Greenberg, D. Cicchetti and E.M. Cummings (Eds.), *Attachment in the preschool years: Theory, research, and intervention* (273-308). Chicago: The University of Chicago Press.

Bretherton, I., Oppenheim, D., Buchsbaum, H., Emde, R.N. and the MacArthur Narrative Group (1990c) *MacArthur Story Stem Battery.* Unpublished manual

DOLL PLAY INTERVIEW (Oppenheim 1990, Oppenheim et al. 1997)

Six story stems

Unlike Cassidy's story stems, the doll play interview attempts to capture only attachment-related events, e.g. separations.

Ratings are made on emotional openness, constructive resolution and emotional tone.

Oppenheim, D. (1990) *Assessing the validity of a doll play interview for measuring attachment in preschoolers.* Unpublished PhD, University of Utah.

Oppenheim, D. (1997) The Attachment Doll-play interview for preschoolers. *International Journal of Behavioural Development,* **20(4)**, 681-697.

Oppenheim, D. and Waters, H. S. (1995) Narrative processes and attachment representations: Issues of development and assessment. *Monographs of the Society of Research in Child Development,* **60**, 197-215.

Oppenheim, D., Emde, R. N. and Warren, S. (1997) Children's narrative representations of mothers: Their development and associations with child and mother adaptation. *Child Development,* **68(1)**, 127-38.

SEPARATION-REUNION STORY COMPLETION TASK (Solomon et al. 1995)

Four story stems, based on two stories

Responses allocated to four content categories: Confident, frightened, casual, busy

Solomon, J. and George, C. (1999) The measurement of attachment security in infancy and childhood. In J. Cassidy and p.R. Shaver (Eds.), *Handbook of attachment: Theory, research, and clinical applications* (287-316). New York: Guilford Press.

Solomon, J. and George, C. (Eds.) (1999) *Attachment disorganisation.* New York: Guilford Press

Solomon, J., George, C. and De Jong, A. (1995) Children classified as controlling at age six: Evidence of disorganized representational strategies and aggression at home and school. *Development and Psychopathology,* **7**, 447-463.

ASCT: ATTACHMENT STORY COMPLETION TEST (Verschueren et al. 1996)

Five story stems

Yields classification into three categories: secure, avoidant, bizarre/ambivalent

Verschueren, K. and Marcoen, A. (1999) Representations of self and socioemotional competence in kindergartners: Differential and combined effects of attachment to mother and to father. *Child Development,* **70**, 183-201.

Verschueren, K., Marcoen, A. and Schoefs, V. (1996) The internal working model of the self, attachment, and competence in five-years-olds. *Child Development,* **67**, 2493-2511.

INTERVIEWS/OBSERVATIONS/SCREENING TESTS

REUNION PROCEDURE (Main and Cassidy 1987, 1988, Cassidy 1986, 1988)

For six-year olds

For the first 20 minutes, child, parent and researcher are together in a toy-filled room at the research centre. Then the parent leaves the child for an hour with the researcher, performing tasks; for the last 15 minutes, the child plays freely. On reunion with parent, no instructions are given. Ratings (nine-point scales relating to child's initiation of a warm, intimate relationship with parent and of avoidance) and classifications are made of child's behaviour during 3-5 minutes of reunion (four categories: secure, insecure/avoidant, insecure/ambivalent, insecure/controlling – also finer distinctions within these four categories).

Cassidy, J. (1986) *Attachment and the self at age six.* Unpublished doctoral dissertation: University of Virginia.

Cassidy, J. (1988) Child-mother attachment and the self in six-year-olds. *Child Development,* **59,** 121-34.

Main, M. and Cassidy, J. (1987) *Reunion-based classifications of child-parent attachment organisation at six-years of age.* Unpublished scoring manual, University of California, Berkeley.

Main, M. and Cassidy, J. (1988) Categories of response to reunion with the parent at age six: Predictable from infant attachment classifications and stable over a one-month period. *Developmental Psychology,* **24,** 415-426.

ATTACHMENT INTERVIEW (Bartholomew and Horowitz 1991)

Conducted with undergraduate students

Semi-structured interview (c 1 hour) about past and current close friendships and romantic relationships; also asks about loneliness, shyness, trust of others, impressions of other people's evaluations of them, hopes for changes in social lives.

Interviews are audiotaped and the four prototype descriptions (secure, preoccupied, avoidant fearful, avoidant dismissive) are rated on 9-point rating scales. Ratings across raters are averaged and the highest scoring prototype is selected as the most salient attachment style.

Bartholomew, K. and Horowitz, L. M. (1991) Attachment style among young adults: A test of a four category model. *Journal of Personality and Social Psychology,* **61(2)**, 226-244.

PRESCHOOL ASSESSMENT OF ATTACHMENT (Crittenden 1992)

Designed for use with children aged 21 months and over

Identifies children as:

- Type A Defended
  A1-2 Inhibited; A3 Over-bright affect and role-reversal; A4 Compulsively compliant.

- Type B Secure
  B1-2 Reserved; B3 Comfortable; B4 Reactive
- Type C Coercive
  C1 Threatening; C2 Disarming; C3 Aggressive; C4 Helpless

- A/C Defended/Coercive
- IO Insecure Other
- AD Anxious Depressed

Crittenden, p.M. (1992) Quality of attachment in the preschool years. *Development and Psychopathology,* **4,** 209-241.

MCAST: THE MANCHESTER CHILD ATTACHMENT STORY TASK

(Green, Stanley, Smith and Goldwyn 1999)

Designed for children aged 5-8

Should be used as part of full assessment

Aims, like the AAI, to "surprise the unconscious" by asking unexpected questions as children are engaged in imaginative doll play about early attachment relationships. Unlike most other doll play interviews, child is asked to imagine self in situation rather than other person.

Vignettes include: having breakfast *(control)*, nightmare, hurt knee, achievement, illness, friends fighting, shopping, family trip *(intended as debrief vignette)*.

Children are encouraged to use doll play to act out vignettes, the topic of which is introduced by the researcher who then asks the child, "What happens next in the story?"

Coding is along the lines both of MacArthur Story Stems and of AAI and takes into account the quality of the child's engagement (involvement, mood, turn-taking), categorisation of narrative components, play content, interpersonal strategy (Attachment security), mentalising and coherency of discourse.

It produces the three basic Attachment categories as well as an estimate of level of Disorganisation.

Green, J., Stanley, C., Smith, V. and Goldwyn, R. (1999) The identification of representations of attachment in 5-8 years old children: Validation of a Child Attachment Interview. Paper presented at the European Science Foundation Workshop, *Attachment Disorganisation and Psychopathology in Development,* 9 September, Leiden, The Netherlands.

Green, J., Stanley, C., Smith, V. and Goldwyn, R. (1999) A new method of evaluating attachment representations in young school-age children: The Manchester Child Attachment Story Task. *Attachment and Human Development,* **2(1)**, 48-70.

Green, J., Stanley, C., Smith, V. and Goldwyn, R. (1999) The Manchester Child Attachment Story Task: relationship with parental AAI, SAT and child behaviour. *Attachment and Human Development,* **2(1)**, 71-84.

CHILD ATTACHMENT INTERVIEW

(Target and Schmuel, not published, University College London, UK)

For 6-12 year olds

Structured interview with 18 questions similar to AAI though modified for children, e.g. tell me the story of the people in your family, tell me three words to describe what it's like to be with your Mum/Dad, what happens when your Mum/Dad gets upset with you, what happens when your Mum/Dad is ill, can you tell me about a time when you were upset and wanted help, what happens when you are ill, what happens when you hurt yourself, has anyone close to you ever died, has an animal ever died; children are also asked about separation experiences, experiences of non-family care, whether parents argue and what kind of Mum/Dad they would like to have. Each question is accompanied by prompts.

The interview is rated along similar dimensions to AAI and produces similar classificatory information.

CHILD ATTACHMENT INTERVIEW (Zimmerman and Scheuerer-Englisch 2000, unpublished, University of Regensburg)

For 8-12 year olds

Children are interviewed about their current relationship with their parents and about their attachment strategies. Videotapes of interviews are rated on:
- Attachment representation – five-point rating for each parent on emotional availability and support when child feels distressed (ranges from rejection to comfort)
- Attachment behaviour strategies – five-point rating on reported attachment behaviour when feeling distressed (ranges from avoidance to proximity-seeking)
- Emotional distress induced by parents – yes/no – report of harsh discipline, long-lasting conflicts in family, effects of parents' negative emotions on children
- Coherency – number of answers that avoid topic, are contradictory, incoherent, do not answer the question, disorganised

REFLECTIVE-SELF FUNCTION SCALE/REFLECTIVE FUNCTIONING SCALE

(Fonagy, Steele, Steele and Target 1997)

Based on the notion that individuals vary in their capacity to 'mentalize' (conceptualise the covert intentions, feelings, beliefs, desires, etc. of others, or understand that others have minds of their own; this capacity to mentalize is also thought to relate to individuals' capacity to reflect upon their own experience and the role that they play in determining outcomes, i.e. their sense of personal agency).

The earlier reflective-self functioning was replaced by the concept of reflective functioning since the scale relates both to interpersonal functioning and self-reflective functioning.

The scale evolved from Main's theories about metacognitive monitoring and involves ratings of:
- awareness of mental states (inc. difficulty of being sure about others' mental states, making allowances for others' potentially complex motivations and for other points of view, potential role played by own mis/interpretations/impact on others/possibility that others may misperceive oneself)
- recognising developmental aspects of mental states (differences due to alternative historical perspectives, immaturity, etc.)
- mental states in relation to the viewer (assumed knowledge of other, emotional attunement, realising that other is separate from self)
- ways in which reflective functioning can be restricted or inaccurate (e.g. refusal to think about mental states, bizarre/inappropriate accounts, distortions inc. under- or over-elaboration)

Reflective functioning capacity is rated on a scale from -1 (anti-reflective) through a range of increasingly effective reflective-functioning to 9 (full or exceptional) reflective functioning. Different parts of the Adult Attachment Interview are rated first, then an aggregated score is obtained for the whole interview.

Fonagy, P., Steele, M., Steele, H. and Target, M. (1997) *Reflective-functioning manual, Version 41*.

An alternative way of coding information from the AAI

AAQ: ADOLESCENT ATTACHMENT QUESTIONNAIRE (West et al. 1998)

Three scales of three statements, each of which is rated on a Likert-like scale:
- Availability – confidence in availability and responsiveness attachment figure

- Goal-Corrected Partnership – extent to which adolescent considers and is empathetic to needs and feelings of attachment figure
- Angry Distress – amount of anger in adolescent–parent relationship.

Developed and validated in a large normative sample (n = 691) and a sample of 133 adolescents in psychiatric treatment. Initial testing indicates high convergent validity between AAQ and AAI.

West, M., Rose, M. S., Spreng, S, Sheldon-Keller, A. and Adam, K. (1998) Adolescent Attachment Questionnaire: A brief assessment of attachment in adolescence. *Journal of Adolescence,* **27(5)**, 661-673.

IPPR: INVENTORY OF PARENT AND PEER ATTACHMENT

(Armsden and Greenberg 1987)

Not directly comparable with other assessments of attachment style and questionable whether it really taps the construct of attachment or simply hypothesised correlates of attachment.

Three subscales measuring adolescents' perceived attachment to parents:
- Parental trust
- Parental communication
- Parental alienation

Each rated on 3-point Likert-like scale ranging from 0 (doesn't apply) to 2 (definitely applies)

Armsden, G. C. and Greenberg, M. T. (1987) The inventory of parent and peer attachment: Individual differences and their relationship to psychological well-being in adolescence. *Journal of Youth and Adolescence,* **16**, 427-454.

Q-SORT MEASURES

ATTACHMENT Q-SORT/Q-SET (Waters 1987)

Designed for use in any setting where 1-5 year olds are interacting with carers

Ideally requires two observation sessions, c1.5-2 hours each; two observers to enable reliability checks on independent observations

Observations and sort can be done by mother rather than by researchers (with appropriate support and training) but need to be aware of possible differences between mothers' perspective and researchers'

Need to ensure that child and mother are well and not tired, hungry, etc. when being observed

Observers might bring materials designed to encourage mother-child interaction but objective is to observe typical interaction; observers instructed to behave as if on a social visit so interact as normally might with child and mother; not typical observational methodology as observers are free to ask questions to elicit relevant information too

The Q-Set contains 90 items describing negative and positive aspects of mother-child interactions, e.g.

'Interrupts activity that is likely to be dangerous'

Sorting can be done in a number of ways. The most common method is to make nine piles.

All 90 items could hypothetically be placed in centre (neither very characteristic of mother-child interaction nor very uncharacteristic of mother-child interaction) but the task of the researcher is to allocate each statement to a position relevant to the degree to which it is either a very good or a very poor description of the interactions observed.

Sorted items can be compared with Criterion sorts (distributions of cards which produce hypothetical scores indicating maximum scores expected for on dimensions, for example, of attachment and dependency).

Waters, E. (1987) Attachment Behavior Q-set (Revision 3.0) Unpublished instrument, State University of New York at Stony Brook, Department of Psychology *Was available on internet.*

Waters, E. (1995) The Attachment Q-Set (Version 3.0). In E. Waters, B. E. Vaughn, G. Posada and K. Kondo-Ikemura (Eds.), Caregiving, cultural, and cognitive perspectives on secure-base behavior and working models. New growing points of attachment theory and research. *Monographs of the Society for Research in Child Development,* **60 (2-3, Serial No. 244**), 234-246.

Waters, E. (1997) The AQS Advisor. http:www.psy.sunysb.edu/ewaters/AQS/htm

More details can be found at the following websites:

Pederson, D. R., Moran, G. and Bento, S. (1999) *Maternal behaviour Q-sort Manual, Version 3.1*

http://www.ssc.uwo.ca/psychology/pedmor/pedermor.html

Waters, E. *Assessing secure base behaviour and attachment security using the Q-Sort Method*

http://www.psychology.sunysb.edu/attachment/measures/content/aqs_method.html

SELF-REPORT QUESTIONNAIRES

Self-report questionnaires focused on attitudes to close relationships are either designed only for people in relationships or require that respondents imagine a hypothetical ideal relationship – this needs to be borne in mind when interpreting results: the extent to which the self-report is a reflection of state (quality of current relationship) as opposed to a more general trait (attachment-related behaviour and attitudes) seems important to consider.

Training is not a requisite for use of self-report questionnaires. However, the psychometric properties of the scales need to be examined carefully and there are serious questions about whether scales are sensitive to lifespan attachment style or current state of mind with regard to attachment.

The following are a selection of measures developed to assess attachment-related dimensions.

INVENTORY OF PARENT AND PEER ATTACHMENT (Armsden and Greenberg 1987)

For adolescents

Attachment-relevant subscales: alienation, communication, trust

Armsden, G. C. and Greenberg, M. T. (1987) The Inventory of Parent and Peer Attachment: Individual differences and their relationship to psychological well-being in adolescence. *Journal of Youth and Adolescence,* **16**, 427-454.

PARENTAL ATTACHMENT QUESTIONNAIRE (Kenny 1990)

For adolescents and young adults

55 items, each rated on five-point scale re how much they describe relationship between person and parent; covers dimensions such as perceived parental availability, understanding, acceptance, respect for autonomy, interest in interaction with parents, affect towards parents, help-seeking behaviour under stress, satisfaction with help obtained from parents.

Questionnaire has three subscales:
- Affective quality of attachment
- Parental fostering of autonomy
- Parental role in providing emotional support

Kenny, M. (1990) College seniors' perceptions of parental attachments: The value and stability of family ties. *Journal of College Student Development,* **31**, 39-46.

ADULT ATTACHMENT QUESTIONNAIRE (Hazan and Shaver 1987)

Single item, forced choice between three prototypical descriptions (Chapter Three has more information)

Revised version involves rating clauses taken from descriptions

Hazan, C. and Shaver, P. R. (1987) Romantic love conceptualised as an attachment process. *Journal of Personality and Social Psychology,* **52**, 511-524.

RECIPROCAL ATTACHMENT QUESTIONNAIRE (West and Sheldon 1988)

Scales for assessing four dimensions of pathological attachment in adults: compulsive self-reliance, compulsive care giving, compulsive care seeking, angry withdrawal

Also tested as 43-item scale with each item rated according to its accuracy in describing relationship with most important attachment figure (West et al. 1987)

West, M. and Sheldon, A. E. R. (1988) Classification of pathological attachment patterns in adults. *Journal of Personality Disorders,* **212**, 153-159.

West, M. and Sheldon-Keller, A. (1992) The assessment of dimensions relevant to adult reciprocal attachment. *Canadian Journal of Psychiatry,* **37**, 600-606.

West, M., Sheldon, A. and Reiffer, L. (1987) *Patterns of relating: An adult attachment perspective.* New York: Guilford Press.

ADULT ATTACHMENT SCALE (Simpson 1990)

13 items, each rated on a 7-point scale – regarding feelings toward romantic partners 'in general'

Attachment-relevant subscales: anxiety, avoidance, security

Simpson, J. A. (1990). Influence of attachment styles on romantic relationships. *Journal of Personality and Social Psychology*, **59(5)**, 971-980.

REVISED ADULT ATTACHMENT SCALE (Collins and Read 1990)

18 items, each rated on 5-point scale – how well they describe feelings about romantic relationships

Attachment-relevant subscales: anxiety, comfort with closeness, comfort depending on others

Collins, N. L. and Read, S. J. (1990) Adult Attachment, working models, and relationship quality in dating couples. *Journal of Personality and Social Psychology*, **58**, 644-663.

ATTACHMENT STYLES INVENTORY (Sperling and Berman 1991)

Based on Hazan and Shaver prototypes; respondents are required to rate prototypes four times in relation to relationship with (1) mother, (2) father, (3) friends, (4) sexual partners.

Can therefore be used to rate range of different types of relationship.

Responses allocated to one of four attachment styles: avoidant (low anger, low dependence), dependent (low anger, high dependence), resistant/ambivalent (high anger, high dependence), hostile (high anger, low dependence).

Sperling, M. B. and Berman, W. H. (1991) An attachment classification of desperate love. *Journal of Personality Assessment*, **56(1)**, 45-55.

RELATIONSHIPS QUESTIONNAIRE (Bartholomew and Horowitz 1991)

Based on Bartholomew's (1990) four-category framework.

Each of four prototype descriptions is rated on 7-point scale regarding 'general relationship style'.

Can be use to rate self or other, and to rate relationships in general or specific relationships.

Bartholomew, K. (1990) Avoidance of intimacy: An attachment perspective. *Journal of Social and Personal Relationships*, **7**, 147-178.

Bartholomew, K. and Horowitz, L. M. (1991) Attachment styles among young adults: A test of a four-category model. *Journal of Personality and Social Psychology*, **61**, 226-244.

FEAR OF INTIMACY SCALE (Descutner and Thelen 1991)

35 items, five-point rating scales for each item

Items relate to fear of proximity, self-disclosure, dependency; scale requires respondents to imagine they are in a close dating relationship and to respond as if in that relationship, also to reflect on past relationships.

Descutner, C. J. and Thelen, M. H. (1991) Development and validation of a Fear-of-Intimacy Scale. *Journal of Consulting and Clinical Psychology,* **3(2)**, 218-225.

ATTACHMENT STYLE QUESTIONNAIRE (Feeney, Noller and Hanrahan 1994)

40 items, each rated on six-point scale in relation to self and others

Attachment-relevant subscales: confidence (in self and others), discomfort with closeness, need for approval, preoccupation with relationships and relationships as secondary.

Feeney, J. A., Noller, P. and Hanrahan, M. (1994) Assessing adult attachment. In M. B. Sperling and W. H. Berman (Eds.), *Attachment in adults: Clinical and developmental perspectives* (128-152). New York: Guildford Publications.

WHOTO QUESTIONNAIRE (Hazan and Zeifman 1994)

12-items

Attachment-relevant subscales: attachment functions (proximity seeking, safe haven, secure base and separation protest) in relationship, overall attachment to partner.

Hazan, C. and Zeifman, D. (1994) Sex and the psychological tether. *Advances in Personal Relationships,* **5**, 151-177.

CAREGIVING QUESTIONNAIRE (Kunce and Shaver 1994)

32 items

Designed to assess four caregiving dimensions: 'proximity versus distance', 'sensitivity versus insensitivity, cooperation versus control and compulsive caregiving.

Kunce, L. J. and Shaver, P. R. (1994) An attachment-theoretical approach to caregiving in romantic relationships. In K. Bartholomew and D. Perlman (Eds.), *Advances in Personal Relationships,* Vol. 5 (205-237). London: Jessica Kingsley Publishers.

MEASURE OF ATTACHMENT QUALITIES (Carver 1994, 1997)

Based on factor analysis of items from Simpson 1990 and Collins and Read 1990

Thirteen items in four Attachment-relevant subscales:
1. Avoidance (5 items: 3 avoidant, 2 non-avoidant)
    e.g. I get uncomfortable when someone wants me to be very close
2. Ambivalence-Worry (3 items: 2 worry, 1 non-worry)
    e.g. I often worry my partner will not want to stay with me
3. Ambivalence-Merger (3 items about desire to merge with partner)
    e.g. My desire to merge with people sometimes scares people away
4. Security
    e.g. It feels relaxing and good to be close to someone

Respondents rate on a 4-point scale where 1=strongly disagree and 4=strongly agree

Carver, C. S. (1994) Personality and adult attachment. Unpublished manuscript, University of Miami, Coral Gables, FL.

Carver, C. S. (1997) Adult attachment and personality: Converging evidence and a new measure. *Personality and Social Psychology Bulletin,* **23**, 865-883.

RELATIONSHIP SCALES QUESTIONNAIRE (Griffin and Bartholomew 1994)

30 items, each rated on 5-point scale for feelings about close relationships overall.

Attachment-relevant subscales: dismissiveness, fearfulness, preoccupation, security

Griffin, D. and Bartholomew, K. (1994) Metaphysics of measurement: The case of adult attachment. In K. Bartholomew and D. Perlman (Eds.), *Advances in personal relationships, Vol. 5: Attachment processes in adulthood* (17-52). London: Jessica Kingsley

WAS: WAGNER ATTACHMENT SCALE (Wagner and Vaux 1994)

Attachment-relevant subscales: model of self, model of others

Wagner, L. and Vaux, A. (1994) *The Wagner Attachment Scale (WAS): Reliability and validity of a self-report measure of adult attachment.* Paper presented at the annual meeting of the Midwestern Psychological Association, Chicago.

RECIPROCAL ATTACHMENT QUESTIONNAIRE (West and Sheldon-Keller 1994)

From 300 items derived from clinical experience and from clinical literature, a 43-item questionnaire with five dimensional scales, each with three items:
- **proximity-seeking**, e.g. I feel lost if I'm upset and my attachment figure isn't around
- **separation protest**, e.g. I feel abandoned when my attachment figure is away for a few days
- **feared loss of partner**, e.g. I'm afraid that I will lose my attachment figure's love
- **availability of partner**, e.g. I worry that my attachment figure will let me down
- **use of partner as a secure base**, e.g. I talk things over with my attachment figure

and four pattern scales, each with seven items:
- **compulsive caregiving**, e.g. I put my attachment figure's needs before my own
- **compulsive care-seeking**, e.g. I often feel too dependent on my attachment figure
- **compulsive self-reliance**, e.g. I feel it is best not to depend on my attachment figure
- **angry withdrawal**, e.g. My attachment figure only seems to notice me when I am angry

Respondents are required to identify an attachment figure (defined as a peer rather than a member of the family of origin, someone they plan to continue sharing life with, someone to whom they are very close and with whom they can share problems and most private feelings, someone they can depend on for comfort and turn to to be held).

West, M. and Sheldon-Keller, A. (1992) The assessment of dimensions relevant to adult reciprocal attachment. *Canadian Journal of Psychiatry,* **37**, 600-606.

West, M. L. and Sheldon-Keller, A. E. (1994) *Patterns of relating: An adult attachment perspective.* New York: Guilford Press

In their 1994 book West and Sheldon-Keller also describe an interview format – the Reciprocal Attachment Interview, that they consider less prone to social desirability bias but lengthy to administer and score – within this interview, line drawings of attachment related events are used to elicit feelings about attachment (e.g. child in bed, stretching out arms to female adult seated at the end of the bed).

West and Sheldon-Keller also describe a self-report questionnaire designed to elicit information specifically about avoidance (The Avoidant Questionnaire for adults) which consists of four dimensions, each with six items:
- Maintains distance in relationships, e.g. I don't let anyone get close to me
- High priority on self-sufficiency, e.g. I take great pride in not needing anyone
- Attachment relationship is a threat, e.g. Being close to someone makes me think of suffocation
- Desire for close affectional bonds, e.g. I long for someone to share my feelings with

DIMENSIONS OF ADULT ATTACHMENT (Brennan and Shaver 1995)

Seven 10-item attachment scales: Attachment-relevant subscales: ambivalence, anxious clinging to partners, jealousy/fear of abandonment, frustration with partners, proximity-seeking, self-reliance, trust.

Brennan, K. A. and Shaver, P. R. (1995) Dimensions of adult attachment, affect regulation, and romantic relationship functioning. *Personality and Social Psychology Bulletin,* **21**, 267-283.

EXPERIENCES IN CLOSE RELATIONSHIPS (ECR) QUESTIONNAIRE (Brennan et al. 1998)

36-item self-report attachment measure derived from a factor analysis of most of 14 existing self-report measures of adult romantic attachment.

Attachment-relevant subscales: avoidance (nine items relating to discomfort with closeness and nine relating to discomfort with depending on others) and anxiety (nine items relating to fear of rejection and nine to abandonment).

Brennan, K. A., Clark, C. L. and Shaver, P. R. (1998) Self report measurement of adult attachment: An integrative overview. In J. A. Simpson and W. S. Rholes (Eds.), *Attachment theory and close relationships* (46-76). New York and London: Guilford Press.

EXPERIENCES IN CLOSE RELATIONSHIPS REVISED (ECR-R) (Fraley, Waller, and Brennan 2000)

Like the ECR, the ECR-R is a 36-item self-report questionnaire that yields scores on similar subscales to the ECR. A self-scoring version of the ECR-R is available on-line at www.yourPersonality.net.

Fraley, R. C., Waller, N. G. and Brennan, K. A. (2000) An item-response theory analysis of self-report measures of adult attachment. *Journal of Personality and Social Psychology,* **78**, 350-365.

STANDARD VISITING PROCEDURE (SVP)

The Standard Visiting Procedure (SVP) (Miesen 1992, 1998) was developed on the basis of observations of dementia patients during visits and on wards as well as on the Strange Situation procedure.

The elderly person is introduced to a room specially constructed to look like an old-fashioned living room. The Standard Visiting Procedure lasts about fifteen minutes and consists of five stages:

1) elderly person is with a stranger (interviewer)
2) a family member unexpectedly arrives for a visit
3) the family member suddenly leaves
4) the elderly person is left with the stranger
5) the family member returns

The presence of attachment-related behaviours (e.g. touching, turning toward the other person, crying, touching self, turning to stranger, looking toward, calling to, or running after the visitor). Coding also takes account of the extent to which the elderly person refers to close relatives who are no longer alive.

Miesen, B. (1990) *Gehechtheid en dementie. ouders in de beleving van dementerende ouderen (Attachment and dementia. How demented elderly persons experience their parents)*. Almere: Versluys.

Miesen, B. M. L. (1992) Attachment theory and dementia. In G. Jones and B. M. L. Miesen (Eds.), *Caregiving in dementia: Research and applications, Volume 2* (38-56). London: Routledge.

Miesen, B. (1993) Alzheimer's disease, the phenomenon of parent-fixation and Bowlby's attachment theory. *International Journal of Geriatric Psychiatry,* **8(2)**, 147-153.

Miesen, B. M. L. (1998) Attachment behavior in dementia: Parent orientation and parent fixation (POPFiD) theory. In G. H. Pollock and S. I. Greenspan (Eds.), *The course of life, Volume VII, Completing the journey*. Madison, Connecticut: International Universities Press.

Appendix 3.2

A   The original Strange Situation classifications
B   The Adult Attachment Interview
C   Information about training

A   Ainsworth's descriptions of patterns of attachment in the Strange Situation procedure

(Based on the Baltimore sample of 106 white, middle-class children drawn from four separate studies: Ainsworth et al. 1978)

Group A
Conspicuous avoidance of proximity to or interaction with the mother in the reunion episodes. Either the baby ignores his mother on her return, greeting her casually if at all, or, if there is approach and/or a less casual greeting, the baby tends to mingle his welcome with avoidance responses, turning away, moving past. Little or no tendency to seek proximity to or interaction or contact with the mother, even in the reunion episodes. If picked up, little or no tendency to cling or to resist being released. On the other hand, little or no tendency toward active resistance to contact or interaction with the mother, except for probable squirming to get down if indeed the baby is picked up. Tendency to treat the stranger much as the mother is treated, although perhaps with less avoidance. Either the baby is not distressed during separation, or the distress seems to be due to being left alone rather than to his mother's absence. For most, distress does not occur when the stranger is present, and any distress upon being left alone tends to be alleviated when the stranger returns.

Subgroup A1
Conspicuous avoidance of the mother in the reunion episodes, which is likely to consist of ignoring her altogether, although there may be some pointed looking away, turning away, or moving away. If there is a greeting when the mother enters, it tends to be a mere look or smile. Either the baby does not approach his mother upon reunion, or the approach is 'abortive' with the baby going past his mother, or it tends to occur only after much coaxing. If picked up, the baby shows little or no contact-maintaining behaviour. He tends not to cuddle in; he looks away; and he may squirm to get down.

Subgroup A2
The baby shows a mixed response to his mother on reunion, with some tendency to greet and to approach, intermingled with a marked tendency to turn to, or move away from her, move past her, avert the gaze from her, or ignore her. Thus there may be moderate proximity seeking, combined with strong proximity avoiding. If he is picked up, the baby may cling momentarily; if he is put down, he may protest or resist momentarily; but there is also a tendency to squirm to be put down, to turn the face away when being held, and other signs of mixed feelings.

Group B

The baby wants either proximity and contact with his mother or interaction with her, and he actively seeks it, especially in the reunion episodes. If he achieves contact, he seeks to maintain it, and either resists release or at least protests if he is put down. The baby responds to his mother's return in the reunion episodes with more than a casual greeting – either with a smile or a cry or a tendency to approach. Little or no tendency to resist contact or interaction with his mother. Little or no tendency to avoid mother in the reunion episodes. He may or may not be friendly with the stranger, but he is clearly more interested in interaction and/or contact with his mother than with the stranger. He may or may not be distressed during the separation episodes, but if he is distressed this is clearly related to his mother's absence and not merely to being alone. He may be somewhat comforted by the stranger, but it is clear that he wants his mother.

Subgroup B1

The baby greets his mother, smiling upon her return, and shows strong initiative in interaction with her across a distance, although he does not especially seek proximity to or physical contact with her.

If picked up, he does not especially seek to maintain contact. He may mingle some avoiding behaviour (turning away or looking away) with interactive behaviour, but he shows little or no resistant behaviour and, in general, seems not to have feelings as mixed as an A2 baby. He is likely to show little or no distress in the separation episodes.

Subgroup B2

The baby greets his mother upon reunion, tends to approach her, and seems to want contact with her, but to a lesser extent than a B3 baby. Some B2 babies seek proximity in the pre-separation episodes, but not again until episode 8, and then perhaps only after some delay. The B2 baby may show some proximity avoiding, especially in episode 5, but this gives way to proximity seeking in episode 8, thus distinguishing him from the A2 baby. Although he accepts contact if he is picked up, he does not cling especially, and does not conspicuously resist release. On the other hand, he shows little or no resistance to contact or interaction, and in general shows less sign of mixed feelings than A2 babies. He tends to show little distress during the separation episodes. He resembles a B1 infant, except that he is more likely to seek proximity to his mother.

Subgroup B3

The baby actively seeks physical contact with his mother, and when he gains it he is conspicuous for attempting to maintain it, actively resisting her attempts to release him. Most B3 babies show their strongest proximity-seeking and contact-maintaining behaviour in episode 8, but some do so in episode 5 and are so distressed in the second separation episode that they cannot mobilize active proximity-seeking and resort to signalling. Occasionally, a baby who seems especially secure in his relationship with his mother will be content with mere interaction with and proximity to her, without seeking to be held. At the same time, the B3 baby may be distinguished from other groups and subgroups by the fact that he shows little or no sign of either avoiding or resisting proximity to or contact or interaction with his mother. He may or may not be distressed in the separation episodes, but if he shows little distress, he is clearly more active in seeking contact and in resisting release than B1 and B2 babies. Although his attachment behaviour is heightened in the reunion episodes, he does not seem wholly preoccupied with his mother in the pre-separation episodes.

Subgroup B4
The baby wants contact, especially in the reunion episodes, and seeks it by approaching, clinging, resisting release; he is, however, somewhat less active and competent in these behaviours than most B3 babies, especially in episode 8. He seems wholly preoccupied with his mother throughout the Strange Situation. He gives the impression of feeling anxious throughout, with much crying. In the second separation, particularly, he seems entirely distressed. He may show other signs of disturbance, such as inappropriate, stereotyped, repetitive gestures or motions. He may show some resistance to his mother, and indeed he may avoid her by drawing back from her or averting his face when held by her. Because he also shows strong contact-seeking behaviour, the impression is of some ambivalence, although not as much as is shown by Group C infants.

Group C
The baby displays conspicuous contact- and interaction-resisting behaviour, perhaps especially in Episode 8. He also shows moderate-to-strong seeking of proximity and contact and seeking to maintain contact once gained, so that he gives the impression of being ambivalent to his mother. He shows little or no tendency to ignore his mother in the reunion episodes, or to turn or move away from her, or to avert his gaze. He may display generally "maladaptive" behaviour in the Strange Situation. Either he tends to be more angry than infants in other groups, or he may be conspicuously passive.

Subgroup C1
Proximity seeking and contact maintaining are strong in the reunion episodes, and are also more likely to occur in the pre-separation episodes, than in the case of Group B infants. Resistant behaviour is particularly conspicuous. The mixture of seeking and yet resisting contact and interaction has an unmistakably angry quality and indeed an angry tone may characterise behaviour even in the pre-separation episodes. Angry, resistant behaviour is likely to be shown toward the stranger as well as toward the mother. The baby is very likely to be extremely distressed during the separation episodes.

Subgroup C2
Perhaps the most conspicuous characteristic of C2 infants is their passivity. Their exploratory behaviour is limited throughout the Strange Situation, and their interactive behaviours are relatively lacking in active initiative. Nevertheless, in the reunion episodes they obviously want proximity to and contact with their mothers, even though they tend to use signalling behaviour rather than active approach, and protest against being put down rather than actively resist release. Resistant behaviour tends to be strong, particularly in Episode 8, but in general the C2 baby is not as conspicuously angry as the C1 baby.

Examples of classification of strange situation behaviours

	BEHAVIOUR TO MOTHER ON REUNION				CRYING		
	Proximity-seeking	Contact-maintaining	Proximity-avoiding	Contact-resisting	Pre-separation	Separation	Reunion
A1	Low	Low	High	Low	Low	Low or High	Low
A2	Moderate to High	Low	High	Low to Moderate	Low	Low or High	Low
B1	Low to Moderate	Low	Low	Low	Low	Low	Low
B2	Low to Moderate	Low to Moderate	Low to Moderate	Low	Low	Low to Moderate	Low
B3	High	High	Low	Low	Low	Moderate to High	Low
B4	High	High	Low	Low	Low	High	Low to Moderate
C1	High	High	Low	High	Low to Moderate	High	Moderate to High
C2	Low to Moderate	Low to Moderate	Low	High	Low to Moderate	High	Moderate to High

A1/A2 Avoidance is the same or greater on second reunion
B1 Positive greeting to mother on reunion and distance interaction
B2 Avoidance increases on second reunion; may show proximity-seeking in pre-separation episodes
B3 Proximity-seeking or contact-maintaining vary directly with separation distress; recovery from distress before two minutes and then quick return to play is typical
B4 Proximity-seeking and attention to mother throughout
C1 Difficult to comfort on reunion; strong resistance of contact with stranger during separation; often angry toward mother on reunion
C2 Exploratory behaviour is weak throughout; difficult to comfort on reunion

B   The Adult Attachment Interview (AAI)

The AAI interview contains 20 questions (though fewer in some versions), and each question has a number of related 'probe' questions and there are instructions to interviewers at certain points to enable them to keep the interview on track.

The introduction suggested in the interview protocol is as follows:

I'm going to be interviewing you about your childhood experiences, and how those experiences may have affected your adult personality. So I'd like to ask you about your early relationship with your family, and what you think about the way it might have affected you. We'll focus mainly on your childhood, but later we'll get on to your adolescence and then to what's going on right now.

This interview often takes about an hour, but it could be anywhere between 45 minutes and an hour-and-a-half.

The questions are as follows:

1. Could you start by helping me to get oriented to your early family situation, where you lived, and so on? If you could tell me where you were born, whether you moved around much, what your family did at various times for a living?
   The interviewer is instructed to keep the answer to this question to two or three minutes and to make it clear that all that is needed is a list of who is who in the family, so that the interviewer has this basic demographic information to set the scene.
   If it seems likely that interviewees were not raised by biological or adoptive parents, the opening question may simply be "Who would you say raised you?"
   Prompts include questions about grandparents and amount of contact with these and questions about other people living in the house (brothers, sisters, other people)

2. I'd like you to try to describe your relationships with your parents as a young child. If you could start from as far back as you can remember.
   The interviewer is asked to encourage respondents to try to remember as far back as possible, around age five or earlier. They are told to reassure participants that it is natural to find this difficult, and to wait patiently in silence while participants try to respond.

3. Now I'd like you to choose five adjectives or words that reflect your relationship with your mother starting from as far back as you can remember in early childhood -- as early as you can, but say, age five to 12 is fine. I know this may take a bit of time, so go ahead and think for a minute... then I'd like to ask you why you chose them. I'll write each one down as you give them to me.
   It is important that the interviewer speaks the words 'relationship with your mother' clearly so that interviewees realise that they are not simply being asked for a description of their mother. The interviewer is instructed to wait patiently for responses and to make it clear that it is not uncommon for participants to find this exercise difficult. Once the five words have been elicited, the interviewer asks, in relation to each description, whether any memories or incidents come to mind in respect of that word. Further probes are suggested in relation to interviewees' response to these requests

4. Question three is repeated with respect to the interviewee's childhood relationship with their father.

5. Now I wonder if you could tell me, to which parent did you feel the closest, and why? Why isn't there this feeling with the other parent?
   Even if the answer to this question may have already emerged earlier in the interview, the interviewer might acknowledge this but still ask the interviewee about it.

6   When you were upset as a child, what would you do?
    This is considered a critical question. Respondents are left to interpret 'upset' in their own way first, then probes are used to ask about emotional upset, being hurt physically, any episodes of illness, and whether ever parents held the interviewee at these times.
7   What is the first time you remember being separated from your parents? How did you respond? Do you remember how they responded? Are there any other separations that stand out in your mind?
8   Did you ever feel rejected as a young child? Of course, looking back on it now, you may realise it wasn't really rejection, but what I'm trying to ask about here is whether you remember ever having *felt* rejected in childhood.
    Probe questions include, "How old were you when you first felt this way, and what did you do? Why do you think your parent did those things -- do you think he/she realised he/she was rejecting you? Did you ever feel pushed away or ignored? Were you ever frightened or worried as a child?
9   Were your parents ever threatening with you in any way – maybe for discipline, or even jokingly?
    Interviewers are advised to be aware that some communities may have customs that are considered abusive in other communities and that these may need to be specifically probed for. Experiences of abuse are also probed for at this point, "Some people have memories of threats or some kind of behaviour that was abusive – Did anything like this ever happen to you, or in your family? How old were you at the time? How often did it happen? Do you feel this experience affects you now as an adult? Does it influence your approach to your own child? Did you have any such experiences involving people outside your family? Specific instructions are given here to interviewers in order that neither elicitation of information nor respect for the interviewee's welfare are compromised.
10 In general, how do you think these experiences with your parents have affected your adult personality?
    Probes include questions about whether the interviewee may have felt any aspect of their early experiences were a set-back in their development/held your development back/had a negative effect on the way you turned out?
11 Why do you think your parents behaved as they did during your childhood?
12 Were there any other adults with whom you were close as a child, or any other adults who were especially important to you?
13 Did you experience the loss of a parent or other close loved one while you were a young child – for example, a sibling, or a close family member?
    Prompts relate to timing, circumstances, response and feelings at the time, later and now
13a Did you lose any other important persons during your childhood? *(Same prompts)*
13b Have you lost other close persons, in adult years? *(Same prompts)*
14 Other than any difficult experiences you've already described, have you had any other experiences which you would regard as potentially traumatic?
    This question was added after the original 1996 interview protocol – not all interviewers will ask it.
15 Now I'd like to ask you a few more questions about your relationship with your parents. Were there many changes in your relationship with your parents (or remaining parent) after childhood? We'll get to the present in a moment, but right now I mean changes occurring roughly between your childhood and your adulthood?
16 What is your relationship with your parents (or remaining parent) like for you now as an adult? Here I am asking about your current relationship.
    Probes relate to amount of contact, sources of satisfaction/dissatisfaction

17 I'd like to move now to a different sort of question – it's not about your relationship with your parents, instead it's about an aspect of your current relationship with (specific child of interest to the researcher/all children). How do you respond now, in terms of feelings, when you separate from your child/children? (Prompt: Do you ever feel worried about your child?)
For individuals without children, this question is posed hypothetically

Now I'd like you to imagine that you have a one-year-old child, and I wonder how you think you might respond, in terms of feelings, if you had to separate from this child? Do you think you would ever feel worried about this child?

18 If you had three wishes for your child 20 years from now, what would they be? I'm thinking partly of the kind of future you would like to see for your child. I'll give you a minute or two to think about this one.
Similar question posed hypothetically to interviewees without children.

19 Is there any particular thing which you feel you learned above all from your own childhood experiences? I'm thinking here of something you feel you might have gained from the kind of childhood you had.
This question is intended to help to integrate difficult feelings and to bring the interview down to a light close.

20 We've been focusing a lot on the past in this interview, but I'd like to end up looking quite a way into the future. We've just talked about what you think you may have learned from your own childhood experiences. I'd like to end by asking you what would you hope your child (or your imagined child) might have learned from his/her experiences of being parented by you?
At this point, the interviewer talks about practicalities of future contact, etc.

C Information about training

SS TRAINING

To find out where training is taking place, it is generally necessary to contact one of the qualified trainers in the US, e.g. Professor L. Alan Sroufe who is based at The Institute of Child Development, University of Minnesota, 51 East River Road, Minneapolis, MN 55455 (email srouf001@tc.umn.ac) or Professor Mary Main who is based at the University of California at Berkeley – there is no public email address but details of how to contact her are available on http://psychology.berkeley.edu/directories/faculty_l-r.html

Patricia Crittenden at the Family Relations Institute (see below) also offers training in the Strange Situation procedure.

AAI TRAINING
Institute for the Adult Attachment Interview

The Adult Attachment Interview training institutes are an intensive 10-day training course in the analysis of the Adult Attachment Interview – perhaps the most important clinical and research tool to emerge from the field of attachment. The institute is designed for researchers and professionals intending to use the AAI in their research and professional activities. The focus of the institute is on the application of the AAI coding system developed by Mary Main, Ruth Goldwyn and Erik Hesse to AAI interview transcripts and transcript fragments. This is a demanding workshop, meeting from 9:00 am to 4:00 pm Monday to Friday over 10 days. There will be a transcript to code most evenings and on the middle weekend. The 2-week full-time course culminates in participants being eligible to take the AAI Reliability Test, administered by Drs. Mary Main and Erik Hesse at the University of California at Berkeley, leading to qualification as a 'Trained AAI Rater'.

David and Deanne Pederson, are accredited AAI trainers. For further information, email: pederson@uwo.ca or fax care of: Dr. David R. Pederson, Department of Psychology, 1-519-661-3961.
http://www.ssc.uwo.ca/psychology/faculty/pedmor/pedermor.html

There is also a Nordic AAI Institute where two-week training courses are run at the University of Göteborg in Sweden. For further information, contact:

Tord Ivarsson, MD	Anders Broberg Ph D
Consult. Child- & Adolesc. Psychiatrist	Professor of clinical psychology
Queen Silvia children's hospital	Göteborg University
Tel. + 46 31 343 68 24	Tel. + 46 31 773 1703
E-mail: tord.ivarsson@vgregion.se	E-mail: Anders.Broberg@psy.gu.se

Family Relations Institute
http://www.patcrittenden.com/local.php

Courses run by Patricia Crittenden
Training Courses: 2005-2006

The training courses to be listed are open to researchers, clinicians, and students from other communities and institutions. Inquiries should be directed to the organiser.

In most cases, the courses are taught in English and the written teaching materials are in English; videotapes of children are in many languages. In all cases, the videotapes/interviews used for the reliability test are in the participants' native language. Fluency in speaking English is not required, but participants must understand spoken English reasonably well and be able to read English fluently.

When taught in Italy, the course is given entirely in Italian. The manuals are also in Italian.

In Russia, the Infant Strange Situation and Preschool Assessment of Attachment courses will be given in translation for Russian speakers. The Adult Attachment Interview course, however, requires competence in written and spoken English (comprehension of spoken English is sufficient; the ability to speak English is not required).

Training Courses on the Adult Attachment Interview

The training involves 18 days of full-time effort coding transcripts; the days are usually arranged in 2 or 3 segments, separated by about 3-4 months' time. The first 6 days cover most of the Ainsworth-based patterns that form the basis for the Main and Goldwyn system. The second 6 days cover most of the atypical patterns in the dynamic-maturational approach. The third 6 days cover the A/C and AC combinations and the modifiers of patterns, e.g., lack of resolution of trauma and loss, depression, and re-organisation. Course participants read, code, and classify two transcripts each day for discussion the following day. The routine, therefore, is 4 hours of training per day followed by independent reading and classifying of the next day's transcripts. Each transcript takes 2-3 hours to prepare. Consequently, participants should be entirely free of other obligations during the training. Between each segment of training, a set of practice transcripts is made available to course participants.

Following the training, a set of transcripts is given to each participant for classification; these transcripts constitute a reliability test. As with all courses offered by Dr. Crittenden, participants are given a written and signed statement of their percent agreement with the standard. This reliability can be reported in research articles. Evidence of reliability should be requested if the participant will code data for another researcher.

To inquire about the course in general, interested parties can contact Dr. Crittenden directly at <pmcrittenden@worldnet.att.net>

Dr. Crittenden does not handle registration or fee payment.

Requests to run a new course can be directed to Dr. Crittenden.

Appendix 5.1

AINSWORTH'S (1969) MATERNAL SENSITIVITY SCALES

FOUR SUBSCALES: SENSITIVITY VS. INSENSITIVITY
COOPERATION VS. INTERFERENCE
ACCEPTANCE VS. REJECTION
ACCESSIBILITY VS. IGNORING AND NEGLECTING

SENSITIVITY VS. INSENSITIVITY

9 Highly sensitive
- exquisitely attuned to the baby's signals and responds to them promptly and appropriately
- able to see things from the baby's point of view
- perceptions of baby's signals and communications not distorted by own needs and defences
- "reads" baby's signals and communications skilfully
- knows the meaning of even subtle, minimal and understated cues
- nearly always (though not invariably) gives baby what he indicates that he wants
- tactfully acknowledges infants requests and offers acceptable alternative if necessary
- has "well-rounded" interactions with the baby (i.e. transactions are smoothly completed, both baby and mother are satisfied)
- mother's responses are temporally contingent upon baby's cues.

7 Sensitive
- interprets baby's communications accurately
- responds to communications promptly and appropriately but with less sensitivity than higher rated mothers may be less attuned to baby's more subtle behaviors
- perhaps because less skilful in dividing attention between baby and competing demands, may sometimes miss cues
- baby's clear and definite signals are neither missed nor misinterpreted
- empathizes with baby and sees things from his point of view
- her perceptions of baby's behavior not distorted
- responses not as consistently prompt or as finely appropriate (perhaps because perception less sensitive than higher rated mothers)
- interventions and interactions never seriously out of tune with baby's tempo, state and communications (though may occasionally be little mismatches).

5 Inconsistently sensitive
- mother can be quite sensitive on occasion, though is insensitive to baby's communications at some times
- apparent lacunae in regard to sensitive dealings with baby

- sensitive at some times or in respect to some aspects of baby's experience, but not others
- awareness of baby may be intermittent, often fairly keen but sometimes impervious
- perception of baby's behaviour may be distorted (one or two aspects) though accurate in other important aspects
- may be prompt and appropriate in response to communications at times and in most respects, but either inappropriate or slow at other times and in other respects
- on whole, more frequently sensitive than insensitive
- striking feature: mother can be very sensitive on so many occasions but very insensitive on others

3 Insensitive
- mother frequently fails to respond to baby's communications appropriately and/or promptly although on some occasions shows capacity for sensitivity
- insensitivity seems linked to inability to see things from baby's point of view
- may be too frequently preoccupied with other things and therefore inaccessible to signals and communications
- may misperceive signals and interpret them inaccurately because of own wishes/defences
- may know well enough what baby is communicating but be disinclined to give him what he wants (because it is inconvenient/not in the mood for it/determined not to "spoil" him)
- may delay an otherwise appropriate response to such an extent that it is no longer contingent on baby's signal/no longer appropriate to baby's state or mood
- fragmented/incomplete/perfunctory/half-hearted/impatient responses (e.g. may respond with seeming appropriateness but break off before baby is satisfied)
- despite such clear evidence of insensitivity, not as consistently or pervasively insensitive as lower rated mothers with even lower ratings
- if baby is very distressed/compelling or baby's needs mesh with mothers can modify her own behavior and goals and show some sensitivity of response

1 Highly insensitive
- seems geared almost exclusively to her own wishes, moods, and activity
- interventions and initiations of interaction are prompted or shaped largely by signals within mother
- if mother's interactions mesh with baby's signals, often no more than coincidence
- sometimes mother responds appropriately if baby's signals are intense/prolonged/repeated enough
- delay in response is in itself insensitive
- mother routinely ignores or distorts the meaning of baby's behaviour
- mother's response to baby's signal is inappropriate/fragmented/incomplete

COOPERATION VS. INTERFERENCE SCALE

9 Conspicuously cooperative
- baby viewed as separate, active, autonomous person whose wishes and activities are valid in own right
- respects baby's autonomy and avoids confrontations

- shows foresight in planning ahead to minimise need for interference and direct control (e.g. arranges physical environment or own timing of household routines)
- avoids interrupting baby's ongoing activity
- when needs to intervene, engages baby's cooperation by mood-setting/inviting/diverting
- picks up on cues and capitalizes on baby's spontaneity, to help present what she wants as something that is also congenial to baby
- inevitably instructs baby to some extent/attempts to elicit particular behaviors, but these mildly controlling interactions both constitute a small proportion of total interaction and are appropriate enough to baby's mood and activity-in-progress to be considered co-determined
- only in rare emergency situations interferes with the baby abruptly or with physical force
- structures freedom-to-explore situations so that gives some, though rare, distal commands
- co-determining does not imply either over-permissiveness or a "laissez-faire" attitude

7 Cooperative
- does not have as conspicuous a respect for her baby's autonomy and ongoing activity as higher rated mothers
- is cooperative and non-interfering on the whole
- shows less foresight than higher rated mothers in arranging physical environment and routine
- more occasions when feels it necessary to interrupt/exert control
- may give more verbal commands or prohibitions than higher rated mothers but she tries to avoid too much interference
- rarely, if ever, intervenes in direct, abrupt, physical ways
- seeks baby's cooperation in routines and in shifts of activity by mood-setting, etc. (as 9 rated)
- may be somewhat less skilful than higher rated mothers in capitalizing on spontaneity to achieve optimum cooperation
- balance is in favor of spontaneity in play and in exchanges of vocalization, may be somewhat more frequently instructive or "eliciting" than higher rated mothers

5 Mildly interfering
- not so much an interfering or controlling person but more inconsiderate of baby's wishes and activities
- interrupts and interferes more frequently than higher rated mothers

3 Interfering
- interference tends to be mild rather than being direct, abrupt, and physically forceful
- tends to issue more verbal commands and prohibitions to control baby across a distance than higher rated mothers
- tends to rely more on instructive eliciting modes of play and interaction than higher rated mothers
- is less spontaneous than higher rated mothers
- most conspicuous difference from higher rated mothers is in regard to routine-interventions and shifts of activity
- pays much less attention to mood-setting and other techniques
- tends to be matter fact

- apparently disregards possibility that her intervention may interrupt baby's activity-in-progress/clash with baby's present mood
- substantially more interfering than higher rated mothers either in frequency or in quality of interference or both
- displays more physical interference or restraint or much more frequently interferes mildly than higher rated mothers
- spends greater proportion of time interfering than higher rated mothers

Note

Mothers with a "3" rating usually have some kind of rationale for actions which is perceivable to the observer (even though it may seem undesirable) and interference is not obviously arbitrary. They may be somewhat obsessed with desire to undertake a specific routine at this time (e.g. being a "training" kind of mother, determined to shape the baby to her way of doing things). Unlike a "1" rated mother who is more frequently arbitrary and who seems to interfere for no reason at all, there is some reason for a "3" mother's interference.

1 Highly interfering
- shows no respect for baby as a separate, active, and autonomous person
- seems to assume that the baby is hers and that she has a perfect right to do whatever she wishes
- imposes her will on baby/shapes baby to her standards
- following her own whims without regard to baby's moods, wishes, or activities
- arbitrariness of interference is striking
- much (though not all) interference is "for no apparent reason"
- some interference by these mothers is conspicuously direct, physical or forceful
- some mothers interrupt/restrain very conspicuously more than others
- seem to be "at" the baby most of the time (instructing, training, eliciting, directing, controlling)
- tend to combine both types of interference, even though she may emphasize one type more than the other
- conspicuous for showing extreme lack of respect for the baby's autonomy
- break into what baby is doing with complete disregard for need to explain to others or even to justify to themselves reasons for interrupting

ACCEPTANCE VS. REJECTION

9 Highly accepting
- very accepting of baby and his behaviour, even of behaviours that other mothers find hurtful or irritating
- values fact that baby has will of own, even if it opposes hers
- pleased to observe baby's interest in other people and in exploring environment, even if occasionally baby ignores her overtures
- respects baby's anger
- is occasionally (though rarely) irritated or frustrated by baby's behaviour but only in passing
- never occurs to mother that baby should ever be target of her anger
- both loves and respects baby as an individual
- accepts responsibility of caring for baby and never chafes against ties that may restrict her from spending more time on her own interests

7 Accepting
- still very positive and accepting, with irritation and resentment comparatively infrequent
- not quite as respecting of baby and baby's autonomy as higher rated mothers·
- not as much obvious acceptance of fact that baby is often interested in other people and things as higher rated mothers
- not as accepting of baby's anger as higher rated mothers
- generally patient with baby and patience seems to involve a genuine acceptance of his demands and inefficiencies rather than over-compliant, long-suffering pseudo-patience
- seems to suppress/repress relatively little of negative feelings because she has relatively few
- generally accepts the limitations to her own autonomy imposed by responsibilities for baby

5 Ambivalent
- chiefly positive in feelings toward baby, and on occasion evidently enjoys him; nevertheless resentment or hurt may break through in inappropriate ways
- sometimes takes some of baby's behaviour (anger/frustration/assertion of will) as deep-seated hostility, opposition or rejection of mother and retaliates by rejecting baby
- may be somewhat impatient and irritable with baby at times, rejecting when baby is not compliant or endearing enough
- enough positive interaction to preclude lower rating
- may point out either frequently or inaccurately that baby rejects her, because he either seems to prefer someone else or will not come to her readily
- dwelling on behaviour that she interprets as rejection seems to imply undercurrent of rejection of baby
- mother may tease when baby is upset, angry or otherwise difficult, which aggravates the difficulty

For a rating of '5', the expressions of negative feeling must not be predominant over positive mutually enjoyable interaction, whatever the assessment of underlying dynamics. If they are, a lower rating should be given.

3 Substantially rejecting
- negative responses, veiled or open, are frequent enough to outweigh expressions of positive feelings towards baby – although neither as openly or strongly rejecting as lower rated mothers
- rejects baby by (a) by putting baby away from her when he does not do what she wants or by deliberately ignoring baby as retaliation (not just insensitivity but clear rejection), (b) by dwelling in conversation on baby's bad points and the difficulties caused by baby to exclusion of good points, (c) by saying uncomplimentary, critical or nasty things about baby (even if in a 'jokey' way), (d) by veiled irritation designed to conceal long-suffering pseudo-compliance to baby's demands (perfunctory, not satisfying compliances) which occasionally becomes overt in impatient, rejecting behaviour, (e) marked impatience, (f) sadistic undercurrent which is largely concealed but comes out in little ways.

Mother who shows hurt, retaliatory behaviour more frequently or more strongly than the '5' or '4' mothers might be coded '3'.

1 Highly rejecting
- mother is clearly rejecting of baby and her rejecting, angry, resentful feelings frequently overwhelm her positive feelings – this may be manifested in any one or a combination of different ways
- may openly voice attitude of rejection, saying she is sorry she ever had baby
- may somewhat less openly voice rejection by implying that baby is great nuisance and that he interferes substantially in her life and with what she would like to be able to do
- she may complain about baby even more specifically, pointing out baby's defects and shortcomings
- even though she may refrain from voicing her rejection, she may manifest it by a constant opposition to baby's wishes, by a generally pervasive atmosphere of irritation and scolding, by jerking baby about with ill-concealed anger, and by joining battle with baby whenever her power seems to be challenged
- may be positive aspects in relationship which suggest potential for enjoyment but these are rare and isolated in their manifestations

Difficulties have been encountered in rating highly defended mothers who seem bland or emotionally detached, and who give no evidence of positive acceptance as defined by ratings of '9' or '7', nor of the hostile components or feelings or behaviour as specified by the other scale points. These women are better rated '5' despite the fact that they do not manifest the negative feelings specified at that scale point.

The intermediate points, '4' and '6', can also be used, depending upon the tendency for either negative or positive feelings to break through the generally emotionless facade. A seemingly 'matter of fact' emotionless mother can also be rated '3' if there is enough veiled rejection in evidence.

ACCESSIBILITY VS. IGNORING AND NEGLECTING

9 Highly accessible
- arranges things so that she can be accessible to baby and baby to her
- keeps baby close enough so that she can be aware of baby's states, signals and activities
- very alert to baby's whereabouts and activities
- even when baby is asleep, has a selective filter tuned in to any sounds baby might make
- capable of distributing her attention between baby and other people and things
- rarely so preoccupied that she is unaware of baby and unresponsive to what baby is doing
- rarely, if ever, ignores any active approach or demand of baby's, even though she may not do what baby seems to want her to do
- does not even pretend to ignore baby but, rather, acknowledges baby's presence and demands/overtures in some way
- rarely, if ever, enters a room without giving baby some acknowledgement that she is aware of baby

7 Usually accessible
- usually accessible psychologically

- there may be brief periods when other demands/activities prevent her from being aware of baby and what baby is doing, but most usually her attention is 'tuned in' to baby
- not as smooth about dividing her attention between competing demands as are higher rated mothers, but rather tends to alternate; nevertheless can fairly easily switch her attention to baby
- may sometimes be preoccupied enough with her own activities, including activities concerned with baby's care, that she fails to acknowledge baby, perhaps going in and out of the room without seeming to see baby's interest in her presence
- for most part, however, she acknowledges baby when she enters a room, especially if they have been apart for more than a few moments

Mothers may be given this rating also if they habitually ignore the baby under a particular set of circumstances, for example, ignoring any crying when baby is put down for a sleep, and yet they are highly accessible at most other times.

5 Inconsistently accessible
- inconsistent in accessibility to baby
- fairly long periods of close attention alternate with periods of seeming obliviousness to baby when mother is occupied with other things in spite of baby's presence and perhaps also in spite of baby's attempts to attract her attention
- some mothers' inaccessibility may be quite unpredictable because of tendency to become easily preoccupied with their own activities and thoughts
- other mothers may regularly and routinely plan periods of non-availability, e.g. in time set aside for housework – during these planned and unplanned times, mother may ignore baby when she enters a room, even after a considerable absence, because she is occupied with other things
- may become so caught up in a conversation, activity, or thought that she seemingly forgets about baby and ignores what baby is doing, responding neither to baby's bids for attention nor to dangerous or naughty behaviour which would usually elicit an intervention
- nevertheless, on whole, more frequently accessible than inaccessible
- when accessible, can be highly responsive to baby

3 Often inaccessible, ignoring, or neglecting
- occasionally responds to baby's behaviour and to implicit signals, but is more often inaccessible than accessible
- may be too preoccupied with own thoughts/activities to notice baby
- may notice and correctly interpret signals but fail to acknowledge them
- typically enters and leaves room without acknowledging baby or baby's signals, whether signals are conspicuous, subtle or muted
- although frequently ignores baby, is not entirely oblivious
- if baby signals strongly or persistently enough, mother may respond – therefore is not rated as low as '1'

If the baby is undemanding and does not signal much or strongly, mother's accessibility must be judged in accordance with extent to which she does acknowledge baby, whether or not in response to bids. The mother with this rating, to an even greater extent than mothers given '1' rating, tends to give baby attention according to her own agenda rather than in accordance with baby's needs, although she may give intense attention on the occasions when she decides to.

1 Highly inaccessible, ignoring or neglecting
- mother is so preoccupied with her own thoughts and activities for most of the time that she simply does not notice baby
- enters room without even looking, let alone acknowledging, baby
- doesn't return baby's smiles
- when baby is elsewhere mother seems to forget baby's existence
- baby's sounds do not seem to filter through to mother
- may talk to baby but it seems that the imagined baby is more real than the actual baby who may be crying upstairs, rocking, playing, or even actively demanding mother's attention
- mother only responds to baby when she deliberately turns her attention to do something to or for baby, making a project of it
- in fact, mother rarely responds to baby in sense of giving care and social attention contingent upon baby's behaviour; rather, is often so completely unaware of baby's signals that her interventions are characteristically at her own whim and convenience

Appendix 5.2

- **The CARE-Index (Crittenden)**
- **The Empathic Understanding Procedure (Oppenheim et al.)**
- **Emotional Availability Scales (Biringen)**
  - Self-Assessment (for parents of children under two)
  - Self-Assessment (for parents of children older than two)

The CARE-Index (Crittenden)

The CARE-Index is a simple and versatile attachment measure. It assesses mother-infant interaction from birth to about two years of age based on a short, videotaped play interaction of 3-5 minutes. Once the coder is trained, coding of an interaction takes about 15-20 minutes.

The measure assesses mothers on three scales: sensitivity, covert and overt hostility, and unresponsiveness. There are also four scales for infants: cooperativeness, compulsive compliance, difficultness, and passivity. The scales:
1. correlate highly with the Strange Situation attachment patterns
2. differentiate between abuse, neglect, abuse-and-neglect, marginal maltreatment, adequacy
3. can be used during intervention
4. can be used to assess the effectiveness of intervention.

Information derived from the CARE-Index can be used as quasi-continuous or categorical data. The procedure is easily applied to 'live' observations though observations alone are not reliable and videos are needed in order to obtain reliable data. The method is held to be effective in the same way that other guided observations or interviews are and can be useful as a tool for sharpening observation and a means of conveying accurate information about what the dyad did and why it should be interpreted in a particular manner.

Training Courses
(1) 5-day course, taught from videotapes – focus is on adult and infant behavior (non-verbal behaviour, interpersonal strategies, developmental processes). The course includes a preliminary reliability test based on a standardised set of American mother-infant dyads. At the conclusion of the course, participants generate a set of videotapes that reflect their intended applications and culture(s). These tapes are used to create a course-specific reliability test.
(2) 4-day course on toddlers (15-30 months): patterns include a wider array of compulsive patterns and coercive patterns (both aggressive and passive) as well as combinations.
Participants receive a written and signed statement of their per cent agreement with the standard. This reliability can be reported in research articles though evidence of reliability needs to be requested if the participant is to code data for another researcher.

In addition, courses are offered from time to time for people who wish to become trainers. There are also advanced clinical seminars offered to international groups of experienced coders. These are held in central Italy and on the coast of Nova Scotia, Canada.

Info at http://www.patcrittenden.com/m_care.php

EMPATHIC UNDERSTANDING PROCEDURE

(EU: Oppenheim, Koren-Karie and Sagi 2001)

N.B. This has recently been re-named as a measure of Parental Insightfulness (Oppenheim 2005, personal communication) – for more information about courses, email David Oppenheim at oppenhei@psy.haifa.ac.il or Nina Koven-Karie at nkoren@psy.haifa.ac.il

Explanation given by authors (on website of University of Haifa): "According to Attachment Theory, mothers' sensitivity to their infants' signals is critical for the development of a secure mother-infant attachment. A sensitive mother reads infants' signals correctly and responds to them appropriately, and she is able to do so by seeing things from the infant's point of view (Ainsworth et al. 1978), a capacity that we refer to as Empathic Understanding. The mother's capacity for Empathic Understanding of the inner world of the child is manifested in the mother's understanding of the motives underlying the child's behaviour within a balanced, coherent, and accepting frame."

Mothers view three video-taped segments of their interactions with their infants. They are then asked, in relation to each segment, questions about their understanding of the child's thoughts, feelings and motives. They are asked to support their statements with examples from the segments and from everyday life.

Interviews are transcribed verbatim and coded on 10-point scales (e.g. insight into child's motives, balanced description of child, maintenance of focus on child) which serves as basis of EUP classification.

EMPATHIC UNDERSTANDING PROCEDURE CLASSIFICATION
(EU; Oppenheim, Koren-Karie and Sagi 2001)

EMPATHICALLY UNDERSTANDING	NON-EMPATHIC/ONE-SIDED (OS)
Insight into the motives underlying the child's behaviour Balanced description of child Openness in viewing video segments Coherence of speech	Non-balanced, all-positive or all-negative description of child Pre-set conception of child which is imposed on video segments Incoherent speech
NON-EMPATHIC/DISENGAGED (DE)	**NON-EMPATHIC/MIXED (MX)**
Lack of emotional involvement Limited and flat responses Irritation with the interview's themes	Lack of a consistent style, mix of styles

Oppenheim, D., Koren-Karie, N. and Sagi, A. (2001) Mothers' empathic understanding of their preschoolers' internal experience: Relations with early attachment. *International Journal of Behavioral Development,* **25**, 17-27.

Emotional Availability Scales

(EAS: Biringen 2004)

There are several versions of these, for parents of under-twos and parents of older children. They can be used either for self-assessment or for assessment of parents by others. Only the self-assessment forms are discussed here and, for copyright reasons, only illustrative items are included. Use of the EAS requires training.

It is emphasised that parents vary in the extent to which they are emotional available, that the extent to which they are emotionally available will depend to some degree on their relationship history, and that high scores can be obtained with practice using certain strategies of interaction with babies and older children.

Both the Emotional Availability Self-Assessment Scales (for parents with children under two) and the Emotional Availability Self-Assessment Scales (for parents with children of two and over, consist of 28 and 27 items, respectively, in relation to each of which parents are required to rate, on a scale from one to five, where '1' = 'Almost never', '3' = 'Sometimes' and '5' = 'Almost always'.

The items on the scale for parents of younger children reflect the degree to which the parent sees the infant as a social being, how autonomous the infant is, how much the parent and infant communicate and how effectively, the degree of enjoyment in the relationship, the infant's temperament, how the infant usually responds on being left and re-met, how much the parent worries about the baby and how they respond to the baby's behaviour.

The scale for parents of children under two contains items such as:
- *My baby is upset whenever I leave the room and seems to play mostly near me*
- *My baby doesn't seem to notice when I come back into the room*
- *My baby is lots of fun to be around*
- *My baby is very independent and mostly likes to play on his/her own*
- *My baby is 'cranky' most of the time*
- *I feel my baby tries to communicate with me*

The items on the scale for parents of older children are similar to those on the scale for younger children but also reflect the extent to which the parent sees the child as socially able and communicative, and also contain reference to the parent's own ability to separate from the child and to be at ease in the child's company

The scale for parents of children of two and over contains items such as:
- *My child seems happy when with other children*
- *My child doesn't talk to me much about what goes on at preschool/school*
- *I feel I don't have a lot of control, and my child is the one with control around here*
- *I don't feel like I know this child*
- *When things go wrong, I get bent out of shape easily*
- *It's difficult for me to separate from my child for school, sleepovers, or play dates*

All scales are available through Zeynep Biringen's website as well as in her book.
Biringen, Z. (2004) *Raising a secure child: Creating an emotional connection between you and your child*. New York: Perigree.
http://www.emotionalavailability.com

Appendix 7.1

Diagnostic criteria for Reactive Attachment Disorder

DSM-IV, AMERICAN PSYCHIATRIC ASSOCIATION, 1994

Criterion A

Markedly disturbed and developmentally inappropriate social relatedness in most contexts, beginning before age 5, as evidenced by either A1 or A2:

A1 Persistent failure to initiate or respond in a developmentally appropriate fashion to most social interactions, as manifest by excessively inhibited, hypervigilant, or highly ambivalent and contradictory responses (e. g., the child may respond to caregivers with a mixture of approach, avoidance, and resistance to comforting or may exhibit frozen watchfulness).

A2 Diffuse attachments as manifested by indiscriminate sociability with relative failure to exhibit appropriate selective attachments (e. g. excessive familiarity with relative strangers or lack of selectivity in choice of attachment figures).

Criterion B

The disturbance in Criterion A is not accounted for solely by developmental delays (as in mental retardation) and is not a symptom of pervasive developmental disorder.

Criterion C

Pathogenic care as evidenced by at least one of the following:
- Persistent disregard of the child's basic emotional needs for comfort, stimulation, and affection.
- Persistent disregard of the child's basic physical needs.
- Repeated changes of primary caregiver that prevent formation of stable attachments frequent changes in foster care.

Criterion D

There is a presumption that the care in criterion C is responsible for the disturbed behavior in Criterion A (e.g. the disturbances in Criterion A began following the pathogenic care in Criterion C).

Specify Type:

Inhibited Type: if Criterion A1 predominates in the clinical presentation
Disinhibited Type: if Criterion A2 predominates in the clinical presentation

ICD-10 CRITERIA FOR ATTACHMENT DISORDERS: REACTIVE ATTACHMENT DISORDER

[Note: From the ICD-10 Classification of Mental and Behavior Disorders; Clinical Descriptions and Diagnostic Guidelines (pp. 279-282), by the World Health Organization, 1992, Geneva, Switzerland: Author. Copyright 1994 by the World Health Organization.]

Inhibited Attachment Disorder

A Onset before age of 5 years.
B Strongly contradictory or ambivalent social responses that extend across social situations (but which may show variability from relationship to relationship).
C Emotional disturbance as shown by misery, lack of emotional responsiveness, withdrawal reactions, aggressive responses to one's own or another's distress, and/or fearful hypervigilance.
D Evidence of capacity for social reciprocity and responsiveness as shown by elements of normal social relatedness in interactions with appropriately responsive, non-deviant adults.

Disinhibited Attachment Disorder

A Diffuse attachments as a persistent feature during the first five years of life (but not necessarily persisting into middle childhood). Diagnosis requires a relative failure to show selective social attachments manifested by:

  A normal tendency to seek comfort from others when distressed.

  An abnormal or relative lack of selectivity in the person from whom comfort is sought.

B Poorly modulated social interactions with unfamiliar persons. Diagnosis requires at least one of the following: generally clinging behavior in infancy or attention seeking and indiscriminately friendly behavior in early or middle childhood.

C Lack of situation-specificity in the aforementioned features. Diagnosis requires that the first two features are manifest across the range of social contexts experienced by the child.

Appendix 7.2

Attachment Disorder Checklist

Information available on the web, 2005

A professional assessment is necessary to determine whether or not a child has an attachment disorder. At the Center we use several tests as part of a comprehensive assessment to determine what attachment issues are causing problems and what will be the most effective treatment plan. We work very closely with the parents to develop a plan to help remediate attachment problems. This checklist can help you identify areas of potential problem. This checklist is not meant to substitute for a professional assessment and treatment plan.

For copyright reasons, only selected examples from the full list of 32 items are reproduced

ITEM NUMBER	
2	My child often does not make eye contact when adults want to make eye contract with my child.
3	My child is overly friendly with strangers.
5	My child argues for long periods of time, often about ridiculous things.
7	My child acts amazingly innocent, or pretends that things aren't that bad when caught doing something wrong.
9	My child deliberately breaks or ruins things.
13	My child steals, or shows up with things that belong to others with unusual or suspicious reasons for how my child got these things.
14	My child demands things, instead of asking for them.
17	My child 'shakes off' pain when hurt, refusing to let anyone provide comfort.
18	My child likes to sneak things without permission, even though my child could have had these things if my child had asked.
20	My child is very bossy with other children and adults.
21	My child hoards or sneaks food, or has other unusual eating habits (eats paper, raw flour, package mixes, baker's chocolate, etc.).
22	My child can't keep friends for more than a week.
24	My child chatters non-stop, asks repeated questions about things that make no sense, mutters, or is hard to understand when talking.
25	My child is accident-prone (gets hurt a lot), or complains a lot about every little ache and pain (needs constant band aids).

Attachment Disorder Checklist continued

ITEM NUMBER	
26	My child teases, hurts, or is cruel to animals.
27	My child doesn't do as well in school as my child could with even a little more effort.
28	My child has set fires, or is preoccupied with fire.
30	My child was abused/neglected during the first year of life, or had several changes of primary caretaker during the first several years of life.
31	My child was in an orphanage for more than the first year of life.
32	My child was adopted after the age of eighteen months.

If you find that more than a few items (more than five or so) have been circled, your child may be experiencing difficulties that require professional assistance. If, in addition to several items being marked, any of the last three items is checked, your child may be experiencing attachment related problems.

Arthur Becker-Weidman

Author index

A
A.A.R.P. (American Association for Retired Persons) *365*
Abelson, R. P. 51, *389*
Aber, J. L. *365*
Ablard, K. E. 106, *392*
Abrams, K.Y. 177, *365*
Ackerman, B. P. 168, *365*
Ackermann, C. *391*
Adelson, E. *376*
Ainsworth, M. D. S. 10, 17, 26, 29–34, 36, 49, 53, 56, 58–64, 66–68, 71, 73–75, 77, 81, 82, 102, 128, 132, 133, 137, 138, 139, 140, 141, 160, 166, 175, 178, 183, 194, 228, 239, 244, 255, 257, 259, 282, 283, 297, 314, 323, 325, 329, 337, 341, 342, 343, 346, 348, 349, 350, 353, 356, *365*, *384*, *412*, *419*, *421*, *430*
Aitken, K. J. 143, *365*
Akister, J. 298, *365*
Alansky, J. A. 133, *377*
Albus, K. E. *374*
Alexander, B. K. *374*, *390*
Alexander, K. W. *374*
Alexandra, H. *371*
Allen, J. 369, *390*
Allen, J. G. *387*
Allen, J. J. B. 237, *371*
Allen, J. P. 113,118,139,*365*, *384*
Alpern, L. 100, *383*
Alwin, J. *394*
American Psychiatric Association *365*, *432*
Ames, E. W. 202, 203, 204, 205, 210, 212, *365*, *366*, *371*, *375*, *385*
Amico, J. A. *383*
Anderson, G. C. 242, 328, *366*
Angold, A. 117, 228, *372*, *379*
Anisfeld, E. 240, 241, 244, 279, *366*
Anthony, E. J. 17, 169, *366*
Apie, E. *380*
Applegate, J. L. 148, *366*
Archer, J. 41, *366*
Arcus, D. *381*
Areias, M. E.238, *366*
Arend, R. 100, 102, *366*
Arend, R. A. *384*
Arling, G. L. *378*
Armsden, G. C. 113, 120, *366*, *404*, *406*
Ashman, S. 228, 232, 233, 234, 235, *366*, *373*

Atkinson, L. 140, *366*, *387*
Aviezer, O. 256, *366*, *389*

B
B. E. I. P. Core Group *384*
Bacon, P. 377, *386*
Bakermans-Kranenburg, M. J. 117, 179, 241, 244, 271, 279, 281, 282, 283, 284, 354, *366*, *368*, *377*, *390*, *394*
Ballard, C. G. 238, *366*
Bank, S. P. 192, *366*
Bar-Haim, Y. 117, *366*
Barker, P. 298, *366*
Barkley, R. A. 171, *366*
Barlow, D. H. 172, *371*
Barnard, K. E. 279, *366*
Barnes, J. 238, *366*
Barnett, B. 279, *366*
Barnett, D. 168, 176, *366*, *370*, *371*
Barocas, R. *389*
Baron-Cohen, S. 162, 317, *366*
Barrett, H. 28, 208, 217, 218, 238, 280, *367*
Barrett, K. C. 148, *367*, 370
Barriere, M. *384*
Barros, H. *366*
Bartholomew, K. 56, 75, 83, 84, 120, 121, 268, *367*, *374*, *375*, *378*, *382*, *401*, *407*, *408*, *409*
Bartlett, F. C. 20, *367*
Barton, M. *395*
Barton, M. L. *395*
Bates, B. *374*
Bates, J. 129, *388*
Bates, J. E. 99, 106, 130, 139, 148, 285, *367*, *372*, *386*, *393*
Bateson, P. 225, *367*
Bayles, K. 99, 106, *367*, *386*
Beauchaine, T. P. 59, 62, 74, *376*, *394*
Beck A. 170, *367*
Beckwith, L. 139, 280, *367*, *388*
Beebe, B. 156, 354, *367*, *371*, *380*, *392*
Beek, M. 311, *389*
Behen, M. E. *371*
Belaustequi, A. *371*
Belizan, J. M. *372*
Bell, S. 67, *365*

Belsky, J. 11, 100, 102, 104, 107, 108, 114, 118, 131, 132, 133, 135, 139, 144, 145, 173, 174, 175, 189, 219, 220, 221, 222, 255, 262, 268, 271, 273, 315, 316, 325, 326, *367*, *368*, *369*, *370*, *372*, *376*, *377*, *380*, *383*, *390*, *391*, *394*, *395*
Ben-Aaron, M. *368*
Bendell, D. *375*
Bennett, S. *392*
Benoit, D. 182, 184, *368*, *387*, *395*
Bento, S. *387*, *405*
Bergman, A. *383*
Berlin, L. J. 108, 112, 192, *368*, *370*
Bernier, A. *382*
Berson, Y. *366*
Bertenthal, B. I. 148, *368*
Bertoncini, J. *384*
Bettelheim, B. 161, *368*
Beveridge, M. *386*
Bifulco, A. T. *378*
Biller, H.H. 189, *368*
Binney, V. *395*, 392
Biringen, Z. 11, 55, 139, 193, *368*, *429*, *430*, *431*
Black, J. E. 240, *377*
Blakely, B. S. *388*
Blatz, W. E. 30, *368*
Blehar, M. C. *365*
Blignault, I. *366*
Block, J. 148, *368*, *374*
Block, J. H. 148, *368*
Bokhorst, C. L. 132, *368*
Bond, A. *372*
Booth, C. L. 71, 102, 167, 168, *366*, *368*, *388*, *391*
Boothby, N. *387*
Boris, N.W. 272, *368*, *395*
Bornstein, M. H.225, *368*, *387*, *391*
Bost, K. K. 127, 129, *394*
Boston, A. 31, *366*, *372*, *386*
Botein, S. 100, *383*
Bourbeau, L. S.*373*
Bowlby, J. See Bibliography 360-364
Boxer, J. *382*
Bradley, R. H. 169, *368*
Brandon, M. *380*
Bråten, S. 143, *368*
Braunwald, K. *370*
Brazelton, T. B. 145, 284, *369*, *382*, *383*
Breger, L. 275, *395*

Brennan, K. A. 85, 120, 121, 122, 126, *369, 376, 389, 390*, 410
Bretherton, I. 51, 302, *367, 369, 374, 384, 385, 389*, 399
Bridges, L. *376*
Bridges, L. J. 171, 189, 255, *369*
Brill, N. *386*
Britner, P. A. *386*
Broderson, L. *378*
Bronfenbrenner, U. 302, 329, *369*
Bronfman, E. *383*
Brook, J. S. 67, 118, *369*, 405
Brooks-Gunn, J. 148, *382*
Brown, A. L. *382, 388*
Brown, B. B. *372*
Brown, G. W. 230, *369, 378*
Brown, R. *379*
Brownley, K. A. *383*
Bruer, J.T.225, 226, 227, 228, 237, 238, *366, 369, 391, 392*
Brumbaugh, C. C. 345, 349, *376*
Brunnquell, D. 100, 260, *374*
Bryant, B. 216, *369*
Bucharest Early Intervention Project, *387, 395*
Bucholtz, I. *375*
Buhrmeister, D. 117, *369*
Buist, A. 238, *369*
Buitelaar, J. K. 251, 252, 254, *369, 373*
Burchinal, M. *370*
Burchinal, M. R. *384*
Burgess, K. B. 106, *369*
Burleson, B. R. *366*
Burlingham, D. 25, 192, *369*
Bus, A. G. 147, *370, 394*
Buss, A. H. *375*
Buss, D. M. 171, *370*
Byng-Hall, J. 18, 187, 188, 297, 298, 300, 301, 355, *370*

C

Cabrera, T. *371*
Cairns, K. 192, 311, *370*
Caldji, C. 253, *370*
Calkins, S. D. 129, *376, 392*
Callan, V. J. *375*
Cameron, R. P. *379*
Campbell, E. A. *372*
Campbell, E. K. *393*
Campbell, F. A. 221, *370*
Campbell, L. *390*
Campbell, S. B. 229, *368, 371*
Campos, J. J. 99, 148, *367, 370, 385, 392*
Campos, R. G. *370*
Capitanio, J. P. 148, 149, *387*
Caplan, G. *370*
Caplan, H. L. *371*
Card, J. A. 129, *376*
Carlo, G. *382*
Carlson, C. L. 171, *370*
Carlson, E. *384, 391, 393*

Carlson, E. A. 98, 99, 100, 103, 107,112, 182, *370, 394*
Carlson, V. 106, 176, 178, *370*
Carlsson, S. G. 243, *370*
Carter, C. S. 248, *370*
Carter, M. 204, 205, *365*
Carter, M. C. *371*
Carver, C. S. 110, 114, *389, 408*, 409
Carver, L. J. 373
Casey, P. H. *368*
Casper, V. *366*
Cassidy, J. 11, 74, 99, 102, 108, 110, 111, 112, 126, 192, 206, 210, 267, 287, 324, *365, 367, 368, 369, 370, 371, 372, 374, 375, 376, 377, 378, 380, 381, 383, 384, 390, 392, 394*, 399, 400, 401
Catalano, R. F. *379*
Cederblad, M. 202, *371*
Chadoud, K. *371*
Chao, W. *390*
Chapman, M. *387*
Charnov, E. L. *382*
Charpak, N. *392*
Charpak, Y. *392*
Chase Stovall, K. *374*
Chen, S. 99, *385*
Chess, S. 129, 254, *389, 392*
Chisholm, K. 202, 203, 204, 209, 210, *366, 371, 375, 385*
Cho, E. *374*
Chorpita, B. F. 172, *371*
Christensson, E. *371*
Christensson, K. 243, *371*
Chugani, D. C. *371*
Chugani, H. T. 209, 212, 213, 214, 215, *371*
Cicchetti, D. 99, 117, 148, 176, 229, *369, 370, 371, 374, 377, 379, 383, 384, 388, 389, 392*, 399
Cicirelli, V. G. 192, *371*
Clark, C. L. *369, 385*, 410
Clark-Carter, D. *385*
Clarke, A. D. B. 202, *371*
Clarke, A. M. 202, *371*
Clarke, L. 108, 124, *371*
Clarke-Stewart, K. A. 220, *371*
Claussen, A. H. 11, 108, 178, *372*
Cline, F. W. 305, *371*
Coan, J. A. 237, *371*
Cochran, A. *382*
Cogill, S. R. 229, *371*
Cohen, D. J. *370*
Cohen, E. *377*
Cohen, J. 140, 280, *371*
Cohen, M. *394*
Cohen, P. 354, *371*
Cohen, R. S. *363*
Cohen, S. E. *367*
Cohler, B. J. 363

Cohn, D. A. 107, 121, 147, *371, 387*
Cohn, J. F. 229, *368, 371, 393*
Cole, A. *381*
Cole, H.E. *381*
Cole, P. 378
Colin, V. L. 11, *371*
Collins, G. *388*
Collins, N. L. 120, 121, 122, *371, 407, 408*
Collins, P. F. 148, *368*
Collins, W. A. 114, *368, 372*
Compas, B. E. 169, *372*
Conde-Agudelo, A. 245, *372*
Conger, R.D. *390*
Connell, D. *371*
Connell, D. B. 100, *383*
Connell, J. P. *369, 382*
Constantino, J. 192, *372*
Coolbear, J. *366*
Cools, A. R. *373*
Cooper, G. 291, *372, 384, 385*
Cooper, P. *385*
Cooper, P. J. 228, *372*
Coplan, R. *388*
Corboz-Warnery, A. 143, *372, 375*
Corcoran, K 122, *372*
Corter, C. *377*
Costello, E. J 117, *372*
Cowan, C. *371*
Cowan, C. P. *371, 385, 387*
Cowan, P. *371*
Cowan, P. A. *371, 375, 385, 387*
Cox, M. J. *377, 384*
Coy, K. C. *381*
Coyne, J.C. 228, *373*
Craig, S. 243, *372*
Craik, K. 51, *372*
Creasey, G. 122, *372*
Crick, N. R. 171, *372*
Criss, M. M. 117, *372*
Cristo, M. *392*
Crittenden, P. M. 11, 60, 71, 72, 73, 87, 94, 100, 106, 108, 139, 178, 210, 295, 316, 345, 346, 348, 359, *372*, 401, 418, 419, 420, 429
Crnic, K. *368*
Crockenberg, S. B. 132, *372*
Crowcroft, A. *394*
Crowell, J. A. 87, 147, *372*
Crown, C. *367, 380*
Cullen, P. C. *366*
Cummings, E. M. 62, 74, *372, 374, 377, 383, 384, 387, 395*
Cunningham, N. *366*

D

Dabholkar, A. S. 227, *380*
Dallos, R. 298, *372*
Danielsson, B. *370*
Davenport, Y. B. *395*
David, M. *373*
Davidson, R. J. 231, *373, 376*

Davie, C. 217, *373*
Davis, K. E. *376, 381*
Davis, M. *395*
Davis, R. *366*
Dawson, G. 228, 229, 232, 233, 234, 235, 236, 237, *366, 373*
Day, A. 216, 219, *372, 383, 387*
Dean, C. *366*
DeCasper, A. J. 48, *373*
de Chateau, P. 242, *373*
de Courten, C. *380*
de Haan, M. *373, 393*
de Kloet, E. R. 221, *373*
DeKlyen, M. *377*
de la Fuente, P. *371*
Delia J. G. *366*
Delliquadri, E. *390*
DeLongis, A. *375*
de Medina, P. G. *369*
de Mulder, E. K. 229, *373*
Dennis, W. 214, *373*
Depue, R. A. 148, *371*
de Traversay, J. *381*
Dettling, A. C. 221, *373*
De Weerth, C. 252, *373*
De Wolff, M. S. 140, 141, *373, 394*
Diaz-Rossello, J. L. *372*
Diego, M. *375, 382, 392*
Diehl, M. *373*
Dieter, J. *375*
Dijkstra, J. *394*
Dion, K. K. *381*
Dion, K. L. *381*
Diorio, J. *370*
Diskin, S. D. *379*
Dodge, K. A. 148, 171, 228, *367, 371, 372, 373, 377*
Dodsworth, R. O. *378*
Doggett, R. A. *390*
Dollahite, D. C. 189, *379, 386*
Donzella, B. 221, 222, *373, 378, 382, 394*
Downey, G. 228, *373*
Dozier, M. 126, 192, 268, 269, 270, 310, *374, 392*
Draper, P. *368*
Drew, L. M. 124, *374, 391*
Dubrow, N. *376*
Duchesne, S. *382*
Ducournau, P. *385*
Dumaret, A. C. *374*
Dunkel-Schetter, C. *375*
Durbin, E. F. *374*
Durkin, S. *369*
Durrett, M. 99, 104, *379*
Dutton, D.G. 123, *374*
Duyme, M. 202, *374*
Duyvesteyn, M.G.C. *394*
Dvir, R. 99, *389*

E

Easterbrooks, M. A. 99, 102, *374*
Eberhart-Wright, A. *386*
Edelstein, R. S. 147, *374*

Egeland, B. 100, 139, 167, 168, 192, 239, 260, *374, 377, 384, 387, 391, 393, 394*
Egeland, B. R. *394*
Elder, G. H. *390*
Elgar, F. J. 118, *374*
Elicker, J. 106, 107, *374*
Elliot, O. 44, *391*
Elnick, A. B. *373*
Embry, L. *373*
Emde, R. N. 188, *368, 374, 392, 395, 394, 395*
England, B. G. 30, 172, 204, *370, 375, 382, 389, 390*
Engle, B. T. 168, *374*
Engler, J. *384*
Englund, M. *374*
ERA Research Team *389*, 435
Erickson, M. F. 100, 101, 102, 103, 106, 118, 262, 281, *374, 379, 391*
Eshel, Y. *368*
Essex, M. J. 252, 253, *374*
Estes, D. 99, 100, *382, 389*
Eyer, D. E. 242, *374*
Eysenck, H. J. 327, 328, *374*

F

Fagenberg, H. *370*
Fagot, B. I. 112, *374*
Fahlberg, V. 311, *374*
Farber, E. A. 100, 102, 139, 239, *374, 381*
Farrington, D. P. 202, *374, 375*
Farroni, T. 155, 156, *381*
Fearnley, S. 305, *375*
Fearon, R. M. P. 262, *367, 368*
Feeney, B. C. 122, *371*
Feeney, J. A. 84, 120, 121, 126, *375*, 408
Fein, G. G. 220, *375*
Feiring, C. *372, 382, 383*
Feldman, S. S. 147, *372*
Feldstein, S. *367, 380*
Fenigstein, A. 110, *375*
Ferenz-Gillies, R. *381*
Ferguson, K. S. *392*
Fernyhough, C. *384, 385*
Field, T. M. 48, 148, 149, 229, 230, 232, 241, 242, *374, 375, 381, 385, 387, 393*
Fifer, W. P. 48, *373*
Figley, C. R. 169, *375*
Figueiredo, E. *366*
Figueroa de Calume, Z. *392*
Finch, S. *369*
Finnegan, R. A. 111, *375*
Finzi, R. 112, *375*
Fiori-Cowley, A. *385*
Fischer, K. W. 148, *368*
Fisher, A. E. 44, *375*
Fisher, L. 204, *375*
Fivaz-Depeursinge, E. 48, 75, 143, 353, *372, 375*

Fleming, W. S. *381*
Flinn, M. V. 172, *375*
Flood, M. F. *392*
Florian, V. 120, *375, 385*
Fogel, A. 148, *375, 393*
Folkman, S. 169, *375*
Fonagy P. H. 10, 11, 34, 36, 163, 164, 165, 169, 182, 335, 354, *368, 375, 376, 379, 392, 403*
Foss, B. M. 34, *365, 376*
Fox, N. A. 100, 129, 148, 189, 190, 231, 255, 273, *369, 370, 373, 376, 381, 384, 385, 387, 391, 393, 395*
Fox, N. 220, *375*
Fox, N. E. *391*
Fradley, E. *384*
Fraiberg, S. 347, *376*
Fraley, R. C. 73, 74, 81, 84, 85, 87, 122, 345, 348, 349, *370, 372, 376, 390, 391, 394*, 410
Frankel, K. A. 99, *367*
Frascarolo, F. *375*
Freedman, D. A. 156, *376*
Freeland, C. A. B. *367*
Freitag, M. K. 107, 189, *376*
Fremmer-Bombik, E. *378, 394*
Frenkel, O. J. *394*
Freud, A. 20, 25, 27, 34, 36, 46, 109, 189, 192, 288, 315, 327, *369, 376, 377, 391*
Freude-Lagevardi, A. 238, *366*
Frey, K. *373*
Friedrich, W. N. *391*
Frith, U. *366*
Frodi, A 99, 108, 131, *376*
Frye, K. F. 280, 281, *380*

G

Gammon, G. *395*
Ganiban, J. *371*
Garbarino, J. 169, *376*
Garber, J. 148, 267, *371, 377*
Gardner, W. 99, 100, *382*
Garduque, L . 100, *368*
Garey, L. J. *380*
Garmezy, N. 169, *377*
Garner, L. 216, *377*
Geher, G. 274, *381*
Gelfand, D. M. *392*
Gellner, E. 22, *377*
Genuis, M. L. 117, *377*
George, C. 11, 56, 75, 76, 259, 324, *377, 380, 391, 392*, 398, 400
Georgieff, M. K. 216, *387*
Gerhardt, S. 11, 109, 151, 152, 172, 193, 199, 203, 224, 254, 271, 276, 277, 278, 296, 297, 351, *377*
Gervai, J. 179, *377, 382*
Giller, H. 202, *389*
Gilstrap, B. *368*
Gingrich, B. *395*

Gini, M. *389*
Giovanelli, J. *390*
Girón, M. S. W. *392*
Given, K. *379*
Glazer, H. I. *395*
Gleason, K. E. *387*
Glover, V. 23, *386*
Gold, A. *384*
Goldberg, S. 11, 69, 70, 99, 102, 108, 139, 141, 242, *368, 372, 374, 377, 384, 387, 394*
Goldfarb, W. 210, 214, *377*
Golding, J. *386*
Goldsmith, H. H. 127, 133, *377*
Goldstein J. 24, 48, *377, 387*
Goldstein S. 24, 48, *377, 387*
Goodman, G. S. *374*
Goossens, F. A. 99, 192, *377*
Gotowiec, A. *377*
Gove, F. L. 100, *366*
Graham, P. J. 217, *377*
Granger, D. A. *390, 395*
Granot, D. 107, 108, *377*
Green, J. M. 251, *377*, 401, 402
Greenberg, M. T. 11, 106, 113, 120, 195, 206, 268, 270, 272, 274, *366, 374, 377, 383, 384*, 392, 394, 404, 406
Greenough, W. T. 226, 227, *369, 377*
Greenspan, S. *389*, 411
Gregory, E. 217, *378*
Grice, P. 77, 78, 80, *378*
Griffin, D. *378*, 409
Griffin, R. *366*
Grofer Klinger, L. *373*
Grolnick, W. S. 171, *369, 376*
Grosskurth, P. 23, *378*
Grossmann, K. 107, 259, 260, *378*
Grossmann, K. E. 107, 179, 259, 260, *378, 391*
Gruen, R. J. *375*
Gruendel, J. M. 51, *385*
Grunebaum, H. 100, *383*
Guger, S. *366*
Guldberg, H. 276, 349, *378*
Gundewall, C. *370*
Gunnar, M. R. 148, 150, 171, 202, 209, 211, 212, 213, 221, 222, *369, 373, 378, 379, 382, 390, 393, 394*

H

Halfon, O. *385*
Hamilton, C. E. 256, 258, 259, *367, 378, 380, 394*
Han, S. S. *395*
Handley-Derry, M. *384*
Hanney, L. 298, *381*
Har-Even, D. *375*
Harlow, H. F. 43, 45, 46, *378, 390*
Harlow, M. K. 43, *378*
Harman, C. 127, *377*
Harre, R. 299, 300, *378*

Harris, J. R. 117, 118, *378*
Harris, M. *369*
Harris, M. L. 222, *391*
Harris, P. L. 148, *378, 389*
Harris, T. O. 230, 271, *369, 378*
Harrison, L. 222, *378, 379, 383*
Hart, A. 311, *378*
Hart, E. L. *379*
Hart, J. 172, *373, 379*
Hart, S. *381*
Hartup, W. W. *379*
Hawkins, A. J. 189,, *379, 386*
Hawkins, J. *365*
Hawkins, J. D. *379*
Hay, D. F. 228, *367, 379, 390*
Hazan, C. 81, 82, 84, 119, 121, 122, 126, 350, *379, 381*, 406, 407, 408
Hazen, N. 104, 108, *379, 380*
Heard, D. 11, 321, *379*
Heinicke, C. M. 138, 182, 201, *379*
Heller, S. S. *368, 395*
Henderson, V. K. *394*
Herbert, M. *390*
Hernandez-Reif, M. *375*
Heron, J. *386*
Herrling, S. *365*
Herschkowitz, E. C. 250, *379*
Herschkowitz, N. 250, *379*
Hertsgaard, L. 179, *378, 379*
Hertzman, C. 172, *379*
Hesse, E. 168, 176, 268, *379, 383, 384*, 418, 419
Hessl, D. *373*
Hewlett, B. S. 317, *379*
Higgins, E. T. 329, *379*
Higgitt, A. *376*
Hill, D. *366, 373, 377, 379, 382, 389, 395*
Hill, J. 298, 300
Hinde, R. A. 37, 39, 41, 43, 45, 135, 175, 355, *365, 370, 374, 378, 379, 383, 387*
Hinings, D. *380*
Hinshaw, S. P. 117, *379*
Hipwell, A. *385*
Hirshberg, L. *395*
Hirshberg, L. M. *395*
Hobfoll, S. E. 228, *379*
Hobson, R. P. 141, 156, 157, *369, 379*
Hoda, N. E. *390*
Hodges, E. V. E. *375, 379, 393*
Hodges, J. 202, 215, *374*
Hofer, M. A. 238, 245, 296, *379*
Hoffman, J. *382*
Hoffman, K. *372, 384*
Hofheimer, J. A. *383*
Holme, A. 216, *395*
Holmes, J. 11, 17, 18, 19, 20, 21, 22, 26, *379*
Holmes, S. *366*
Honig, A. S. 192, *380*
Hood, C. 216, *380*

Hook, B. *371*
Hooper, R. *385*
Horneman, G. *370*
Horowitz, H. A. 118, *388*
Horowitz, L. M. 56, 75, 83, 84, 118, 120, 121, 268, *367*, 401, 407
Howard, J. *388*
Howard, M. O. *379*
Howe, D. 11, 307, 311, *380*
Howes, C. 102, 192, 222, *380*
Howes, P. 117, *366*
Hoza, B. 171, *370, 380*
Hrdy, S. B. 189, *380*
Hrncir, E. 100, *368*
Hubbs-Tait, L *388*
Hubley, P. 142, 143, *393*
Hughes, D. 308, 309, 310, *380*
Hughes, M. *380*
Huizink, A. C. *369*
Hulsizer, M. R. *379*
Hunt, J. 303, *380*
Hunter, V. 19, *380*
Huston, L. *394*
Huttenlocher, P. R. 227, *380*
Hwang, C. P. 99, 242, *370, 382*
Hymel, S. *388*

I

Ilg, U. *391*
Ingebretson, R. 124, *380*
Inglis, R. 25, *380*
Insel, T. R. 246, 248, *380, 390, 395*
International Adoption Project Team *378*, 440
Irhammer, M. *371*
Isaacs, S. 25, *380*
Isabella, R. A. 100, 139, 141, 144, 145, *380, 392*
Izard, C. *365, 391*

J

Jackson, B. 216, 217, 218, *380*
Jackson, S. 216, 217, 218, *380*
Jacobs, N. J. *392*
Jacobson, J. L. 103, *380*
Jacobson, S. W. 48, 280, 281, *380*
Jacobvitz, D. 106, 108, 176, *374, 380, 383, 391*
Jaffe, J. 146, 156, *367, 380, 392*
James, W. 148, *380*
James, B. 303, *380*
Jarvenpaa, A-L. *387*
Jaskir, J. *383*
Jasnow, J. *367*
Jasnow, M. *380*
Jassik-Gerschenfel, D. *384*
Jenkins, J. M. 192, *380*
Joels, T. *366, 389*
Johns, J. M. *365, 383*
Johnson, D. E. 203, 214, *380*
Johnson, M. H. 148, 155, 156, 352, *380*

Johnson, M. L. *361*
Johnson, S. *371*
Johnson, S. L. *375*
Jones, N. A. 230, *380, 381*, 411
Juffer, F. 280, *366, 381, 394*
Juhasz, C. *371*
Julian, T. 37, *381*
Jurgens, U. *386*

K

Kagan, J. 48, 97, 98, 117, 127, 128, 129, 148, 194, 196, 254, 285, 349, *380, 381, 391*
Kahn, M. D. 192, *366*
Kahneman, D. 57, *393*
Kalin, N. H. *374*
Kalkoske, M. *384*
Kaplan, K. 56, 75, 99, 101, 259, 377, *381, 384*
Karen, R. 11, 194, 239, *381*
Karlsson, H. 243, *381*
Kavanagh, K. 112, *374*
Kay Hall, S. E. 274, *381*
Keck, G. C. 305, *381*
Keelan, J. P. *381*
Keenan, K. *390*
Kelleher, K. J. *368*
Kelly, V. 305, *365, 381*
Keltikangas-Jarvinen, L. *387*
Kennell, J. H. 238, 242, *381*
Kennerley, H. *373*
Keplac, L. *381*
Kerns, K. A. 107, *381*
Kershaw, K. *372*
Kertes, D. A. *378*
Keskivaara, P. *387*
Kesner, J. 122, *381*
Kestenbaum, R. 103, *381*
Kidwell, S. L. *366*
Kilmer, S. L. *365*
Kimmerly, N. L. *376*
Kindler, H. *378*
King, F. *385*
Kirkpatrick, L. A. *381*
Kirsh, S. *371*
Klagsbrun, M. *374, 396, 397*
Klaus, M. H. 238, 242, *381*
Klein, M. 23, 327, *378, 381*
Klein, M. H. *374*
Klerman, G. L. *395*
Klinger, L. *373*
Kneppers, K. *394*
Knight, J. *374*
Knox, J. 11, *381*
Kobak, R. R. 108, 111, 114, 115, 116, 120, 262, 349, *370, 381*, 433
Kochanska, G. 132, 148, *381*
Koga, S. *395*
Kogos, J. *365*
Koniak-Griffin, D. 228, *381*
Koren-Karie, N *386, 389*, 430
Korfmacher, J. *374*
Kortinus, M. 222, *382*

Kostelny, K. *376*
Kotelchuck, M. 75, *381*
Kozlowska, K. 298, *381*
Kozlowski, B. *369*
Kraemer, G. W. *381*
Krekewich, K. *384*
Kroonenberg, P. M. 99, *394*
Krueger, K. *378*
Kuczynski, L *387*
Kuhn, C. *375*
Kumar, R. *366, 371, 390*
Kunce, L. J. 122, 316, *382*, 408
Kupecky, R. 305, *381*
Kuperminc, G. P. *365*

L

Labouvie-Vief, G. 262, *373, 395*
Lachmann, F. *367*
Ladnier, R. D. 108, *382*
Lafreniere, P. J. *391*
Lagercrantz, H. *371, 393*
Lahey, B. B. *379*
Laible, D. J. 117, *382*
Laird, B. *390*
Lakatos, K. 179, *377, 382*
Lake, B. 11, 321, *379*
Lamb, M.E. 99, 100, 126, 129, 148, 168, 189, 194, 242, *368, 374, 379, 381, 382, 385, 386, 387, 389, 392*
Lambermon, M. W. E. 280, *382*
Land, D. L. 113, *365, 384*
Land, D. J. 360
Lane, S. K. 222, *382*
Lang, C. *375*
Langer, E. J. 170, *382*
Langlois, J. *388*
Lapp, A. L. *372*
Larose, S. 120, *382*
Larrieu, J. A. *368*
Larson, M. 221, *378, 382*
Larson, M. C. *373*
Larsson, K. *370*
Lasky, R. E. *372*
Launier, R. 169, *382*
Lavin, J. *379*
Lawroski, N. *391*
Lawson, J. *366*
Lay, K. 65, 100, *382*
Lazarus, R. S. 169, *375, 382*
Leadbeater, B. J. *365*
LeDoux, J. E. *382*
Lee, A. *369, 379*
Legendre, A. 222, *382*
LeMare, L. J. *388*
Leonard, K. E. 122, *390*
Lerner, J. V. 118, *392, 394*
Leslie, A. *366*
Lessard, J. C. 117, *382*
Lester, B. M. 146, *382*
Leung, K. H. *366*
Levine, J. A. *382*
Levine, S. 221, *382*
Levy, A. *382, 391, 392*

Lewin, K. 148, 329, *382*
Lewis, M. 106, 112, 148, 189, 256, 257, 258, *369, 378, 382, 390*
Lewis, V. *379*
Lewkowicz, K. S. 99, *389*
Lieberman, A. *395*
Lieberman, A. F. 274, *383*
Liedloff, J. 241, *383*
Light, K. C. 246, *383*
Lim, M. M. *395*
Liotti, G. 176, *383*
Lipsitt, L. P. *395*
Lipton, R. C. 214, *387*
Lishner, D. M. *379*
Lloyd, E. *385*
Loeber, R. *375*
Lollis, S. *388*
Londerville, S. 99, 102, *383*
Lopez, J. *383*
Lorenz, K. 39, 40, 41, 42, 43, 225, *383*
Lounsbury, M. L. *367*
Lovas, G. S. *374*
Love, J. M. 222, 276, *379, 383*
Lundquist, L. *392*
Lundy, B. *381*
Lutkenhaus, P. 99, 104, *383*
Lyons, D. 100, 106, 112, 176, 177, 253, 280, *371, 383*
Lyons-Ruth, K 100, 106, 112, 176, 177, 280, *371, 383*

M

MacArthur, R. H. 174, *370, 383, 394*, 402
MacArthur Working Group on Attachment, *370*
Macfie, J. *384*
Magid, K. 303, *383*
Magyary, D. *366*
Mahler, M. 153, *383*
Maier, S.F. 170, *390*
Maier, U. *386*
Main, M. 33, 56, 60, 67, 71, 72, 73, 75, 82, 84, 93, 94, 99, 101, 102, 108, 111, 121, 164, 168, 175, 176, 178, 181, 189, 210, 211, 239, 255, 256, 257, 259, 260, 329, 348, *369, 377, 379, 381, 383, 384, 395*, 401, 403, 418, 419
Malkin, C. *392*
Mallinckrodt, B. 122, *372*
Maloney, S. 302, 303, *384*
Mammen, O. *395*
Mangelsdorf, S. *378, 387*
Marcovitch, S 209, 210, *384*
Marrone, M. 271, *384*
Marsh, P. 118, *384*
Marshall, P. *369, 395*
Marshall, P. J. 214, 215, 216, *384*
Martin, S. *368, 385*
Martinez, A. *375*

AUTHOR INDEX

Marvin, R. S. 31, 33, 206, 211, 290, 291, 292, 297, 300, 301, 354, 365, 370, 372, 377, 384, 386
Marvinney, D. 387
Maslin, C. 99, 108, 367, 384
Maslin-Cole, C. 108, 384
Massanari, A. E. 108, 382
Matas, L. 100, 101, 102, 384
Matheson, C. C. 380
Matias, R. 371
Mayall, B. 216, 218, 380, 384
Mayseless, O. 107, 108, 377
McBride, K. 380
McCartney, K. 130, 389
McCrone, E. 107, 384
McElhaney, D. B 365
McElhaney, K. B. 384
McElwain, N. L. 103, 384
McEwen, B. S. 171, 384
McFarland, F. C. 384
McGee, R. 385
McGuffog, C. 383
McKelvey, C. A. 303, 383
McKenry, P. 381
McKnew, D. H. 395
McLeod, S. 383
Mead, G. H. 20, 49, 148, 329, 384
Meadows, C. E. 217, 377
Meaney, M. 370
Mebert, C. J. 129, 384
Mehler, J. 48, 384
Meij, J. Th. H. 280, 384
Meins, E. 164, 165, 166, 167, 354, 384, 385
Melges, F. T. 385
Melhuish, E. C. 192, 216, 377, 385
Meltzoff, A. N. 48, 385
Menta, M. 275, 395
Mercer, J. 275, 302, 303, 304, 306, 385
Mercke, A-M. 371
Merikangas, K. 395
Messinger, D. S. 392
Mikulincer, M. 120, 121, 122, 375, 385, 390
Milich, R. 370, 380
Miljkovitch, R. 189, 385
Miller-Johnson, S. 370
Mills, S. L. 388
Minde, K. 99, 377
Minter, M. 379
Minuchin, S. 298, 301, 385
Mitchell, S. K. 366
Miyake, K. 99, 103, 133, 139, 385
Mohan, R. N. 366
Mooney, A. 385
Moore, C. 365
Moore, C. W. 365
Moore, G. 368
Moore, M. K. 48, 385
Moore, T. W. 216, 385
Moran, G. 378, 387, 394, 405
Morena, L. 371

Moretti, M. M. 117, 382
Morgan, H. 176, 180, 383
Morison, S. J. 204, 371, 385
Morse, C. A. 369
Morton, T. L. 385, 395
Moss, P. 380
Mulder, E. J. 229, 369, 373
Mulholland, K. A. 302, 369
Mundfrom, D. J. 368
Murray, D. 251, 377
Murray, K. T. 381
Murray, L. 141, 229, 230, 353, 385
Muzik, O. 371
Myhal, N. 387

N

Nachmias, M. 379
Nachson, O. 120, 121, 122, 385
Nada-Raja, S. 117, 385
Nagy, F. 371
Najarian, P. 214, 373
Nawrocki, T. 375
Nelson, C. A. 371, 373, 378, 380, 385, 387, 395
Nelson, E. E. 246, 247, 248, 385
Nelson, K. 51, 148, 385
Nemoda, Z. 377, 382
Newton, D. 369
Newton, M. 57, 380
Ney, K. 377, 382
Nezworski, T. 11, 367, 370, 372, 377, 383, 391
Niccols, A. 366
NICHD Early Child Care Research Network 72, 220, 221, 347, 349, 385, 386
Nichols, M. P. 301, 386
Nicolas, J. 373
Noller, P. 84, 120, 126, 375, 408
Nozyce, M. 366

O

O'Beirne-Kelly, H. 365
O'Connor, M. 106, 386
O'Connor, T. G. 204, 205, 206, 208, 250, 251, 252, 273, 303, 305, 381, 384
O'Hara, M. W. 228, 386
Oakley, A. 241, 386
Oates, M. R. 251, 377, 386
Obsmascher, P. 387
Odent, M. 238, 386
Olesh, H. 192, 372
Olrick, J. T. 386
Olson, D.H. 102, 298, 299, 386
Olson, S. L. 102, 386
Oppe, T. E. 380
Oppenheim, D. 99, 139, 189, 190, 255, 386, 395, 394, 395, 429, 430
Orvaschel, H. 228, 229, 386
Osofsky, J. D. 367, 369, 386
Oumar, F. 393
Owen, S. 217, 386

Owens, E. B. 390, 394

P

Paglia, A. 366
Palkovitz, R. 189, 386
Panagiotides, H. 366, 373
Pancake, V. R. 100, 107, 386, 391
Panksepp, J. 246, 247, 248, 296, 385, 386
Papousek, H. 141, 148, 386, 387
Papousek, M. 141, 148, 386, 387
Pardo, C. 376
Park, K. A. 395, 396
Parke, R. D. 371, 374, 391
Parker, G. 366
Parker, I. 299, 386
Parker, K. C. H. 182, 184, 366, 368
Parker, S. W. 215, 216, 386, 395
Parkes, C. M. 20, 365, 378, 379, 383, 387
Parsons, E. 383
Pasco Fearon, R. M. 368
Pastor, D. L. 100, 101, 103, 387
Paus, T. 227, 387
Pawl, J. H. 274, 383
Pawlby, S. 390
Paykel, E. S. 395
Payne, A. 366
Pearson, J. 147, 269, 371, 387
Pearson, J. L. 371
Pederson, D. 183, 387, 394, 405, 419
Pelham, W. E. 370, 380
Pepler, D. 387
Perrotta, M. 377
Perry, D. G. 375
Perry, J. 380
Pesonen, A-K. 129, 387
Petrie, P. 216, 218, 380, 384, 387
Pettem, O. 377, 398
Pettit, G. S. 367, 372
Philliber, S. 365
Phillips, D. 390
Pickens, J. 375
Pickles, A. 388
Pierrehumbert, B. 385
Pillow, D. 380
Pine, F. 383
Pinkerton, G. 380
Pisani, L. 393
Pistole, M. C. 121, 122, 387
Pleck, J. H. 382
Pless, I. B. 380
Pohorecky, L. A. 395
Pope, S. K. 368
Posada, G. 365, 382, 405
Posner, M. I 148, 387
Poulton, L. 366, 387
Powell, B. 372, 384
Prevatt-Goldstein, B. 48, 387
Prince, G. S. 216, 217, 387
Provence, S. 214, 387
Prusoff, B. 395
Pugh, G. 216, 387

Pungello, E. P. *370*

Q
Quas, J. A. *374*
Quinton, D. 202, 229, *389*

R
Radke-Yarrow, M. 71, 72, 73, 229, 348, *373, 387, 395*
Rae-Grant, Q. *394*
Raffaelli, M. *382*
Raikkonen, K. *387*
Rajecki, D. W. 10, 44, 335, *375, 387*
Ram, A. *375*
Ramey, C. T. *370*
Ramsey-Klee, D .*379*
Randolph, E. M. 271, 274, 275, *387*
Rao, R. 216, *387*
Raval, V. 183, *387*
Read, S. J. 120, 121, *371, 407, 408*
Regan, C. *395*
Reibstein, J. 298, *365*
Reite, M. 148, 149, *387*
Renken, B. 112, *387*
Repacholi, B. 100, *383*
Repetti, R. L. 171, *387*
Ressler, E. M. 169, *387*
Reznick, J. S. *381*
Rholes, W. S. 147, *369, 376, 388, 390,* 410
Rice, K.G. 114, *388*
Richard, M. H. 18, *374*
Richards, M. P. M. 99, 189, *388*
Richters, J. E. 220, *388*
Ricks, M. *393*
Ridge, B. *367*
Ridgeway, D. *382*, 399
Rieser-Danner, L. *388*
Rigatuso, J. *378*
Rinaldi, J. *373*
Ritter, C. *379*
Roberts, B. W. 349, *376*
Roberts, C. 124, *371*
Robertson, J. 26, 27, 30, 31, 57, 208, *373, 386, 388*
Robinson, J. *395*
Robinson, J. L. *368*
Robson, K. *371*
Rodholm, M. *370*
Rodning, C. 176, *388*
Roggman, L. 220, *388*
Rogosch, F. A. *371*
Rolfe, S. 11, 55, 192, 193, 194, 380, *388*
Romanian Adoptees Study Team, *386*
Romanian Adoption Research Team, *389*
Ronai, Z. *377, 382*
Rosa, L. *385*
Rose-Krasnor, L. 103, *368, 388*

Rosen, K. 99, *388*
Rosenberg, D. M. 100, 103, *388*
Rosenberg, K. *368*
Rosenbluth, D. 31, *388*
Rosenstein, D. S. 118, *388*
Rosenthal, S. *382*
Ross, L. 57, *388*
Rothbart, M. K 129, 133, 148, *367, 387, 388, 393*
Rothbaum, F. 298, *388*
Rots, N. Y. *373*
Roudinesco, J. *373, 388*
Rovine, M. J. 100, 131, 132, 273, *367, 368*
Roy, P. 202, *388*
Rubin, K. H. 133, 171, 268, *368, 369, 376, 387, 388*
Ruble, D. N. *379*
Rudolph, J. *378*
Ruiz-Paláez, J. G. *392*
Russell, J. *385*
Rutter, M. 118, 126, 129, 151, 159, 169, 201, 202, 204, 205, 206, 208, 223, 229, 351, *367, 375, 377, 386, 388, 389*

S
Saarni, C. 148, *389*
Safier, E. *379*
Sagi, A. 99, 190, 221, 256, *366, 383, 386, 389, 395*, 430
Sagi-Schwartz, A. 256, *383, 389, 395*
Salter, M. D. 30, *389*
Sameroff, A. J. 169, *374, 389*
Samson, J. *372*
Sargent, J.. *379*
Sarner, L. *385*
Saunders, K. *374*
Savari-Szekely, M. *382*
Savoie, L. *375*
Sazvari-Szekely, M. *377*
Scarr, S. 130, *389*
Sceery, A. 120, *381*
Schaaf, J. M. *374*
Schachner, D. A. 122, *389*
Schachter, S. 170, *389*
Schafer, W. D. *376*
Schaller, J. *370*
Schanberg, S. *375*
Schank, R. C. 51, *389*
Schatzburg, A. *383*
Scheeringa, M. S. *368, 391, 395*
Scheier, M. F. 110, 114, 171, *370, 375, 389*
Scheuerer-Englisch, H. *376, 378, 402*
Schieche, M. *391*
Schmucher, G. *390*
Schoff, K. *365*
Schofield, G. 311, *380, 389*

Schore, A. N. 11, 109, 148, 151, 152, 153, 154, 155, 156, 157, 158, 159, 160, 172, 199, 203, 224, 254, 278, 352, 353, *389*
Schork, E. *391*
Schuengel, C. 177, *366, 368, 390, 394*
Schulman, S. *391*
Schwartz, D. B 221, 256, *383, 389, 390, 395*
Schwarz, R. C. 301, *386*
Scolton, K. L. *371*
Seay, B. M. 46, *390*
Seeman, T. E. *387*
Seifer, R. *389*
Self, H. *373*
Self, J. *373*
Seligman, M. E. P. 170, 203, *390*
Senchak, M. 122, *390*
Senn, M. J. E. 21, *390*
Shapiro, L. E. 246, *390*
Shapiro, V. *376*
Sharp, D. 229, *390*
Shaver, P. R. 11, 81, 82, 84, 87, 119, 120, 121, 122, 126, 316, 350, *365, 367, 368, 369, 370, 372, 374, 375, 376, 377, 378, 379, 380, 381, 382, 383, 385, 389, 390, 392, 394, 395,* 406, 407, 408, 410
Shaw, D. S. 106, 112, 167, 295, *390, 394*
Sheperis, C. J. 274, *390*
Shepherd, R. *395*
Sherman, G. *374*
Sherrod, L. R. 148, *382*
Shi, L. 120, 121, *390*
Shnit, D. *375*
Shoham, R. 99, *389*
Sholomskas, D. *395*
Siegel, D. J. 133, *390*
Sigman, M. *386*
Siles, C. *371*
Silva, E. *383*
Silver, D. *371*
Simmons, R. J. *377*
Simons, R. L. 113, *390*
Simpson, J. A 122, 325, *369, 376, 388, 390,* 407, 408, 410
Sinclair, D. *385*
Singer, J. E. 170, *389*
Siteraneos, G. *366*
Sluckin, A. 242, 243, *390*
Sluckin, W. 242, 243, *390*
Smith, C. A. 108, *374, 383, 390, 391, 392*
Smith, M. A. 192, *380*
Smith, P. K. 124, *391, 397*
Smith, R. S. 169, *395*
Smith, T. E. *383*
Smith, V. 401, 402
Smuts, A. 21, *391*
Smyke, A. T *395*
Snidman, N. *381*

AUTHOR INDEX

Solem, P. E. 124, *380*
Solnit, A. J. *377*
Solomon, J. 11, 72, 175, 176, 178, 324, *377, 380, 383, 384, 391, 392*, 398, 400
Solter, A. 201, *391*
Soucy, N. *382*
Spangler, G. 99, 133, 139, 179, 221, *378, 391*
Speltz, M. L. 303, *377, 391*
Spemann, H. 225, *391*
Spence, M. 48, *373*
Spieker, S. J. 70, 71, 72, 73, 74, 108, 167, 168, *366, 370, 372, 376, 384, 391, 394*
Spielman, E. 177, *383*
Spitz, R. A. 26, 201, 203, *391*
Spritz, B. *368*
Sroufe, L. A. 69, 71, 74, 86, 97, 98, 100, 102, 103, 104, 105, 107, 108, 113, 114, 148, 149, 151, 167, 168, 195, 200, 239, 255, 262, 267, 303, 349, *366, 369, 370, 372, 374, 376, 377, 381, 382, 384, 387, 388, 391, 393, 394*, 418
Stadtman, J. 99, 239, *384*
Stafford, B. 274, *391*
Stahl, J. 100, *383*
Stanley, C. *385*, 401, 402
Stanley, W. C. 44, *391*
Stansbury, K. 222, *373, 391*
Stanton, W. R. *385*
Starzomski, A. J. *374*
Stayton, D. *365*
Steele, H. 179, 274, 303, 304, *375, 376, 391, 392,* 403
Steele, M. 179, *375, 376, 391, 392,* 403
Stein, A. *385*
Stein, H. 87, *392*
Steinberg, L. 227, *392*
Steinberg, L. D. 220, *362, 363*
Steinbock, D. J. *387*
Stellar, E. 171, *384*
Stern, D. N. 51, 141, 145, 146, 148, 151, 294, 353, *392*
Stevenson, J. *369*
Stevenson-Hinde, J. 355, *365, 370, 374, 378, 379, 383, 387*
Stewart, R. B. 220, 297, 300, 301, *371, 384,* 436
Stiefel, I. *371*
Stockard, C. R. 225, *392*
Stovall, K. C. 192, 310, *374, 392,* 436
Stowe, Z. N. 230, *395*
Strandberg, T. *387*
Stroud, C. E. 216, 217, 218, *392*
Suess, G. 99, *378, 394*
Sumner, G. *366*
Susman, E. J. *390*
Sutton, J. 171, *392*
Svanberg, P. O. 354, *392*

Svejda, M. J. 243, *392*
Swain, A. M. 228, *386*
Swearingen, L. *394*
Swettenham, J. *392*

T
Tager-Flusberg, H. *366*
Target, M. *375, 376,* 402, 403
Taylor, D. G. 100, *368*
Taylor, S. E. *387*
Tessier, R. 243, 244, 245, *392*
Teti, D. M. 106, 229, *392*
Thomas, A. 129, 254, *384, 388, 389, 392,* 396
Thomas, H. 311, *374, 378*
Thomas, N. 306, *387, 392*
Thompson, R. A. 100, 107, 110, 118, 126, 129, 131, 148, 149, 150, 151, 220, 228, *369, 376, 382, 392*
Tinbergen, N. 39, 40, 41, 43, *392, 393*
Tizard, B. 202, 214, 218, *379, 393*
Tobey, A. E. 369
Tomkiewicz, S. *374*
Toth, I. *377*
Toth, L. *382*
Toth, S. L. *369, 371, 388, 392*
Tout, K. 221, *373, 393*
Trapani, J. *395*
Treboux, D. 87, *372*
Trevarthen, C. 48, 141, 142, 143, 144, 146, 148, 163, 353, *365, 385, 393*
Tronick, E. Z. 145, 148, *371, 393*
Trowell, J. 309, 356, *393*
Troy, M. 108, *393*
True, M. M. 177, 341, *393*
Tuckey, M. *384*
Turner, P. *385*
Tustin, F. 160, 161, 162, *393*
Tversky, A 57, *393*
Tyson, J. E. *372*

U
Uchida, N. *388*
Ujiie, T. 99, *388*
Ungerer, J. 222, *371, 378, 379*
Unzner, L. 99, *378*
Urban, J. 100, 107, *393*
Uvnas-Moberg, K. *371*

V
Van den Bergh, B. R. H. 102, 221, 222, *394*
Van den Boom, D. C. 250, 280, 284, 285, 287, *393*
van der Loos, H. *380*
van der Veer, R *394*
Van Dijken, S 17, 18, 19, 21, 22, 25, *370, 380, 390, 391, 393*
van Hees, Y. *373*

van IJzendoorn, M. 106, 117, 118, 126, 140, 141, 147, 175, 176, 179, 182, 183, 186, 189, 192, 268, 271, 279, 330, *366, 368, 377, 379, 393, 394*
van Kammen, W. B. *375*
van Vliet-Visser, S. *394*
Vandell, D. L. *394*
Vasquez, D. M. 171, *378*
Vaughn, B. E. 100, 118, 127, 129, 262, *365, 394,* 405
Velez, S. *392*
Verhulst, F. C. 202, *394*
Vicary, J. R 118, *394*
Visser, G. H. *369, 394*
Volling, B. L 189, *394*
von Bertalanffy, L. 298, *394*
Vondra, J. I 133, 167, 262, 295, *390, 394*
von Eye, A. *380*

W
Walker, A. *368*
Walker, D. S. *381*
Wall, S. *365*
Wallace, C. S. *377*
Waller, N. G. 84, 85, *376,* 410
Ward, M. J. 182, *394*
Warme, G. E. *394*
Warner, V *381, 395*
Warren, S. L. 126, *394,* 400
Wartner, U. G. 99, 103, *394*
Washington, J .232, *365, 384, 391,* 397
Wason, P. C. 57, *394*
Wasson, C. *384*
Watamura, S. E. 221, *394*
Waters, E. 59, 62, 67, 69, 71, 74, 86, 100, 148, 149, 167, 200, 256, 257, 258, 259, *365, 367, 369, 374, 376, 382, 384, 385, 389, 391, 392, 394, 395,* 404, 405
Weijai, Y. *386*
Weinfeld, N. S. *394*
Weinfield, N. S. 100, 114, 141, 256, 260, 261, 262, *394*
Weiss, B. *395*
Weiss, J. M. 170, *394*
Weissberg, R. P. *365*
Weissman, M. 228, *395*
Weissman, M. M. 229, *395*
Weisz, J. R. *395*
Weizman, A. *375*
Welsh-Allis, G. *386*
Werner, E. E. 169, *395*
West, M. 217, 218, *377, 380, 387, 392, 393,* 403, 404, 406, 409, 410
Westheimer, I. 138, 201, *379*
Weston, D. R. 71, 99, 102, 189, 255, *384*
Whaley, G. J. L. *394*
Wheelwright, S. *366*

White, B. P. *382*
Whiteman, M. *369*
Whiteside, L. *368*
Wiberg, B. 242, *373*
Widom, C.S. 277, *395*
Wiener, S. G. 221, *382*
Wilkinson, C. W. *366*
Wille, D. E. 103, *380*
Wilson, C. L. *390*
Wilson, G. D. 327, *374*
Wilson H. H. 360
Wilson, K. S. *394*
Wilson, S. L. 303, *395*
Winberg, J. *371*
Winnicott, C. 25, 287, *395*
Winslow, E. B. *390*
Wisner, K. L. 230, *395*
Wittig, B. 33, 56, 58, 74, *365*
Wolf, K. M. 201, *391*
World Health Organization, 29, 30, 35, 199, 201, 341, 351, *395*, 433
Worrall, G. J. *374*
Wright, J. C 108, *386*, *395*, 397, 437

Y
Yaari, G. *368*
Yamada, E. *366*, *373*
Yando, R. *375*
Yang, C. *383*
Young, L. J. 246, *395*
Youngblade, L. M. 102, 107, 255, *395*
Youngstrom, E. *365*
Yudkin, S. 216, *395*

Z
Zahn-Waxler, C. 148, 220, 229, *388*, *395*
Zaslow, R. 275, *395*
Zax, M. *389*
Zeanah, C. H. 182, 202, 214, 271, 272, 273, 303, 305, 338, *368*, *386*, *391*, *395*
Zhang, F. 262, *395*
Zimmerman, R. R. 46, *378*
Ziv, Y. 107, 108, *366*, *389*, *395*
Zoll, D. 100, *383*
Zwiers, M. *387*

Subject index

Abuse, 12, 44–45, 52, 176, 271, 277
Adolescence, 113–121
Adolescent Attachment Interview, 403–404
Adoption, 202–216, 351
Adult Attachment, 56, 75–87
- Adult Attachment Interview (AAI), 56, 75–81, 347–348, *Appendix 3.2*
- AAI classifications, 77–81
- Adult Attachment Projective, 398
- Attachment Interview, 401
- self-report measures, 81–85, 119, 405–410
Aggression, 37, 52, 103, 107
Ainsworth, Mary, *see also Strange Situation*, 10
- Ganda study, 31–3, 67
- Baltimore study, 33–4, 68
- PhD with Blatz, 30
- work in London, 31
Animal studies, 38–9, 41–6
Ambivalent attachment, *see also Attachment insecurity*, 94–5, 121, 122–3, 195–6, 197, 267
Anxiety, Anxious attachment, *see also Attachment insecurity*, 84–7, 120–3
Assessment, *see also Measurement, Strange Situation, Adult Attachment, Appendix 3.1*
Attachment,
- activation of attachment behaviour system, 69–70
- as organiser, 147–9
- assessment, *see also Strange Situation*, 30, 32–3, 45, 55–87
- attachment behaviours, 31–33, 55
- attachment disorders, 270–275, *Appendix 7.1, Appendix 7.2*
Attachment Q-Sort/Q-Set, 404–405
- attachment relationships *see also*, 55, 130
- correlates in late adolescence, 120–121
- disorganisation, 71–2, 93–4, 106, 175–179, 196, 346–347

- 'earned' security, 86, 269
- function of attachment, 46–7
- insecure attachment, *see also Strange Situation classifications*, 55, 100–118, 121–121, 271, 359
- operational definition (lack of), 63
- phases in development, 47–51
- predictiveness *see stability,*
- reactive attachment disorder, *see attachment disorders,*
- secure attachment, *see also Strange Situation classifications*, 30, 32–3, 53–4, 55, 92–96, 100–118, 120, 121, 134, 197, 345, 358
- stability, 96–8, 118, 134–5, 255–264, 347–348, 359
Attachment Parenting, 241, 355, 356
Attachment Theory (AT),
- alternative theories, 10
- constructivist form of AT, 10, 198, 264
- controversial status, 12, 35, 340, 342
- determinist form of AT, 10, 30, 198, 264
- evaluation of, 313–339
- evolution of, 36–54, 341, 357–358
- major theoretical claims, 13, 53–54
- misinterpretation of AT, 11, 302–306, 352–353
- policy implications, 337–339
Assertiveness, 103
Attention processes/disorders, 108–9, 114–115, 215
Attributional processes, 170–171
Attunement, *see also Misattunement,* 142–146
Autism, 156–7, 160–4, 216
- pseudo-autism, quasi-autism, 208, 217
Autonomy, 166
Avoidance, 68–70, 78–79, 81–5, 92–5, 195, 197, 345

Baby carrying, *see also Kangaroo care,* 238–241
Baby massage, 242
Behaviourism, 20, 36

Behaviour control systems, 41, 313–326
Behaviour problems, 104–6, 111–2, 253, 267–268
Bereavement, 18–19, 24, 27–8, 124, 287
Biological sex, *see also gender roles,* 126–127
Blindness, 156–7
Boarding school, 18–19, 21
Brain development, 151, 212–216, 224, 226–228, 278–279, 351
Bullying, 108

CARE-Index, *Appendix 5.2*
Caregiving, 37
- compulsive caregiving, 84
Child Attachment Interview, 371–372
Circle of Security Project, 289–293
Clinical populations, 117, 125, 268–271
Cognitive development, 49–51, 108
Compliancy, 102
Conditioning, 43–5
Conflict resolution, 101–2, 103
Continuum concept, 241
Coping, *see Stress,*
Couple relationships, 121–122
Critical period, 24, 42, 204, 222–228, 353
Crittenden classifications, 74
Cultural variations, 194–195
'cupboard love', 46

Dating, *see also Romantic relationships,* 114
Day care, 192–222, 349–350
Delinquency, 22–24, 29–30, 202, 216
Depression, 215, 228–238, 271
Differential susceptibility hypothesis, 132–133, 268, 271
Disobedience, 102
Disorganisation, *see Attachment disorganisation,*
Dismissing attachment style, *see also Avoidance,* 78–9
Diversity, 86, 135, 195, 345, 359
Domestic violence, 122–123

Early experience, 25–28, 37, 197–198, 223–263

Early intervention, *see also Therapy*, 238, 244-245, 280-287
Effect size, 140-141, 241, 280
Electro-encephalogram (EEG), 230-238
Embarrassment, 157-8
Emotional arousal, 131-132
Emotionally disturbed children, 20-22, 23, 24-25, 29
Emotional self-regulation, *see Self Regulation*,
Empathy, 103
Empiricism, 20
Environmental reactivity, *see Resilience*,
Ethology, 36-43
- four 'whys' of ethology, 40
Evacuees, 25
Evolutionary theory, 37, 40
Experience-dependent development, 226-228
Experience-expectant development, 226-228
Experimental approach, 39, 56-57
Exploration, 92-96, 103, 108
Eye contact, eye gaze, 155-6, 275, 305

False self, 287-288
Family scripts, 187-8
Family therapy, 297-302, 354-355
Fathers, 19, 26, 34-5, 49, 157, 189, 238, 354, 358
Fear, 103
Feeding/Food, 36, 40
Feminists, 11, 35
Fixed action patterns, 39-40
Fostering, 27
Friendships, 107, 117

Gender roles, 19, 35
Generational boundary dissolution, 113-114
Grandparents, 123-4, 192
Grice's maxims, 77

Holding therapy, 304-306
Homelessness, 29-30
Hospitals, 26, 27
Hostility, 103
Hypothesis-testing, 38

Idealisation, 113
Independence, *see also Autonomy*, 113
Imprinting, 41-3
Impulsiveness, *see Self control*,
Institutional care, *see also Therapeutic foster care*, 29-30, 201-216
Instinct, 37-8, 40-1
Intelligence, 126
Interactive synchrony, 144-5
Intersubjectivity, 142-144

Intergenerational transmission, 9, 180-188, 276-277
Internal working models, 50-4, 91, 135, 157
Inventory of Parent and Peer Attachment, 406
Irritable babies, 284
Kangaroo care, 243-245
Key workers, 27, 143
Lausanne Trilogue Play Paradigm, 41-43
Learning theory, *see Behaviourism*,
Limbic circuits/structures, 153-60, 213
Longitudinal studies, *see Attachment stability*,
Looked after children, *see also Institutional care*, 306-310
Lorenz, Konrad, 41-3, 225

Mahler, Margaret, 153
Maltreatment, *see Abuse*,
Manchester Child Attachment Story Task (MCAST), 401-402
Mania, *see Over-sociability*,
Mating, 174
Measurement, 58-87, 344-346, 348, 350
- operational definitions, 58-9, 61-2
- reliability, 59-60
- validity, 60-61, 126
Mentalising, 162-167, 346
Mental health, 267-271, 342
Misattunement, 177-8, 229
Monotropy, 49-50, 188-191
Mothers,
- acceptance, 138
- employment, 35
- helpfulness, 147
- influence on child's personality, 53, 275, 357, 358
- maternal mind-mindedness, *see Mentalising*,
- maternal sensitivity, 33-4, 138-141, 346, Appendix 5.1
- mother-infant bond, 21, 29, 36, 49, 138
- rejection, 138
- surrogacy, 46
Mourning, *see Bereavement*,
Multiple models, 53

Nannies,
- Nanna Friend, 18
- Minnie, nursemaid, 18
Negative stereotyping, 86-7
Newborns, 48
NEWPIN, 294-295
Nurture groups, 293

Observational approaches, 39, 56-7
Oxford Parent Infant Programme (OXPIP), 295-297
Oxytocin, 245-48
Orphans, *see Institutional care, Adoption,*
Over-sociability, 208, 24-31

Parents,
- blame, 9, 193, 275-278, 276
- coping strategies, 168-9, 177, 292
- frightening behaviour, 177
- influence, *see also Mothers, Fathers*, 54, 91, 106-7, 132, 177, 289, 356-358
- malpractice, 288-289
- Parental Insightfulness Scale, 430-431
- quality of care, 55, 137-195, 249
- need for multiple strategies, 12, 151
- need for support, 10, 337-339
- reparation, 291, 338
- uncertainty, 9, 12, 35, 358
Passivity, 103
Peer pressure, 113
Perceptual ability, 126
PIPPIN, 293-294
Play, 103-4
Popularity, *see Social skills*,
Positron emission tomography, 211, 212
Postnatal depression, *see Depression*,
Poverty, 168
Prejudice, stereotyping, 63, 82, 88
Prenatal stress, 250-254
Preoccupied attachment, *see also Adult attachment*, 79-80, 268
Preschool Assessment of Attachment, 370
Preschoolers, 100-106
Problem-solving, 101-2, 115-116
Projective tests/measures, 396 *et seq*
Protest-despair-detachment, 27-8
Psychoanalysis, 22-3, 34-5, 36
Psychobiological regulation, 147-151, 157-160
Psychopathology, *see also Behaviour problems*, 53, 267-271
Psychosocial adjustment, *see also Behaviour problems*, 114, 125-6
Punishment, *see Conditioning*,

Q-Sort Measures, *see Attachment Q-Sort*,

Rebirthing, 303-304
Reflective function, 164-5, 403
Relationships Questionnaire, 57, 82
Reliability, *see Measurement*,

SUBJECT INDEX

Reparation, 124–5
Representations of family, 100–101
Resilience, 118, 169, 174–5
Resolution, lack of, 348
Reward, *see also Conditioning*, 154–155
Right hemisphere asymmetry, *see Brain development*,
Risk-taking, 118–119
Riviere, Joan, 22
Robertsons,
– studies of separation, 26
– films, 26–27
Role reversal, *see also Generational boundary dissolution*, 114
Romanian orphans, *see Institutional care, Adoption*,
Romantic relationships, *see also dating*, 125

Sanitoria, TB, 27
Secure base, *see also Attachment security*, 30
Self awareness, *see Sense of self*,
Self consciousness, *see Sense of self, Temperament*,
Self confidence, Self efficacy, 103, 114
Self control *see self regulation*,
Self esteem, 103, 114
Self regulation, 101–4, 109–111, 132–33, 157–160
Sense of self, 109–110
Sensitive period, 50, 225–6, 237
Separation,
– anxiety, separation anxiety, 34, 50
– early separation , 22, 24–31, 199–222
– effects of separation, 24–31, 45–7, 199–222
– films on separation, 26–7
– responses to separation, 27–8
Separation Anxiety test, 397
Separation–Reunion Procedure/ Reunion Procedure, 400–401, 399–400
– classification system, 207
Set goals, 41
Skin-to-skin contact, *see also Baby carrying*, 43, 238–245
'Social brain', *see Brain development*,
Social class, 34–5
Social deprivation, *see also Separation*, 57
Social isolation, *see Separation*,
Social skills, 103, 107, 108, 134
Specific linkage hypothesis, 111–2
Stability, *see Attachment stability*,
Standard Visiting Procedure, 410–411
Stealing, 21–2, 23, 24
Stop-distance procedure, 117

Story Stem tests, 399 *et seq*
– Attachment Story Completion Test, 400
– Doll Play Interview, 399–400
– Macarthur Story Stem Battery, 399
– Separation–Reunion Story Completion Task, 400
Strange Situation procedure, 33, 56, 58–60, 62–72, 341
– classifications, 67–75, 78–9, *Appendix 3.2*
– limitations, 72–76, 348
– predictiveness, *see also Attachment stability*, 106–7
– sensitisation effects, 132
Stress, *see also Prenatal stress* , 249, 352
– associated with institutionalisation, 211–212
– associated with day care, 221–222
– coping and coping mechanisms, 104, 108, 111, 168–174
– chronicity, 167–8, 171
– cortisol and immune system responses, 171–2, 251–254
– HPA axis involvement, 170–171
– SAM involvement, 171
Sunderland Infant Programme (SIP), 295
Symbiosis, 153–4

Tavistock seminars, 34
Temperament, *see also Irritable babies*, 107, 127–34, 267
– irritability, 230
– temperament hypothesis, 128
Theory of Mnd, *see Mentalising*,
Theory-testing, 327–339
– testability, 327–330
– fertility, 327, 331
– generalisability, 327, 331–333
– explanatory power, 327, 333–336
Therapy, 279–311
– 'Attachment Therapy', 302–306, 344, 355–356
– Bowlby's five principles, 288
– need for regulation, 311–312
– parent co-therapy (*PCT*), 311
– 'therapeutic foster care', 306
Tinbergen, Niko, 39–41
Touch, *see also Baby carrying, Skin–to–skin contact*, 305
Training,
– Strange Situation Procedure, 412
– Adult Attachment Interview, 416–420
Triadic interactions, 143
Trauma, *see also Bereavement*, 287

Unresolved attachment, *see also Adult Attachment*, 78, 80

Validity, *see Measurement*,
Victimisation, *see Bullying*,
Video-based observations, 293–295, 353, 354
Vulnerability, *see Resilience*,

Working models, 10
World Health Organization, Monograph, 29
Classification of diseases, 268, 428